The Good

Katie Wood is a name many travellers are familiar with. As a well established travel writer and journalist, she has tackled everything from backpacking in Europe, in her bestseller *Europe by Train*, to the deluxe world of country house hotels and continent-hopping in *The Round the World Air Guide*. With eighteen successful guidebooks to her name, and a string of freelance commissions, from the *Guardian* and *Scotsman* to the *Observer* and *Traveller* magazine, she is well qualified to comment on all aspects of the travel industry. She also regularly broadcasts on travel for the BBC and ITV.

The perfect marriage of minds, from this series' point of view, has resulted from her marriage to Syd House. Syd is a graduate of ecological sciences and has considerable experience of practical management in conservation. Working as a Forest District Manager for the Forestry Commission, he is responsible for the management and conservation of a large part of Scotland, from Fife to the Angus glens. He has travelled the world in his own right, before combining his skills with those of his wife and looking at the impact of tourism on the environment. Together they bring you the definitive work on 'green travel', examined from both the tourist and the environmental points of view.

Syd and Katie are both graduates of Edinburgh University and share a Scottish background. Katie was born in Edinburgh. After graduation she worked in journalism, and following an eighteen-month spell backpacking in Europe, her first travel guide was published in 1983. A Fellowship from the Royal Geographical Society, several travel consultancies and fifty-seven countries later she is still writing and travelling full-time. Syd, originally from Gourock, travelled the world before returning to Scotland, where he became immersed in conservation matters and resumed managerial work within the Forestry Commission. He too is a Fellow of the Royal Geographical Society.

The couple married in 1984. They have two young sons, Andrew and Euan, live in Perth, Scotland, and lead a lifestyle punctuated with foreign travel, midnight writing, and an active involvement in conservation matters. They have recently completed consultancy work for, among others, the English Tourist Board, working on a policy document on green tourism.

By the same author

Europe by Train
The Round the World Air Guide
European City Breaks
The Best of British Country House Hotels
Holiday Ireland
Holiday Scotland
The Cheap Sleep Guide to Europe
The 100 Greatest Holidays in the World*
The 1992 Business Travel Guide*
The Good Tourist*
The Good Tourist in France*

*Also available from Mandarin Paperbacks

The Good Tourist in the UK

**KATIE WOOD
& SYD HOUSE**

Mandarin

A Mandarin Paperback
THE GOOD TOURIST IN THE UK

First published in Great Britain 1992
by Mandarin Paperbacks
Michelin House, 81 Fulham Road, London SW3 6RB

Mandarin is an imprint of the Octopus Publishing Group,
a division of Reed International Books Limited

Copyright © 1992 by Katie Wood and Syd House
The authors have asserted their moral rights.

A CIP catalogue record for this title
is available from the British Library
ISBN 0 7493 0811 7

Typeset by Falcon Typographic Art Ltd,
Edinburgh
Printed and bound in Great Britain
by Cox & Wyman Ltd, Reading, Berks

This book is sold subject to the condition
that it shall not, by way of trade or otherwise,
be lent, resold, hired out, or otherwise circulated
without the publisher's prior consent in any form
of binding or cover other than that in which
it is published and without a similar condition
including this condition being imposed
on the subsequent purchaser.

The Good Tourist Series

This book is aimed at the educated, probably well travelled, but most importantly environmentally-aware person. The person who loves travel but doesn't want to spoil what he or she sets out to see. It is quite different from any other guide you are likely to have seen. It is not written for the extremist Green fringe. We don't advocate everyone cycles everywhere, eats vegan and sleeps in communes. It's a soft but effective green message you'll get from this guide, and indeed any book in the *Good Tourist* series. But it works and is practical.

This series aims to show you how to visit a country in a way that gives you the most pleasure and also does the least harm (and often does actual good) for the region you are holidaying in. So, for example, we recommend you to try alternative routes rather than the crowded, well-documented ones; suggest you stay in a family-run B&B, rather than check in to the sanitised chain-hotel down the road; and we encourage you to meet the locals, giving practical suggestions on where to do this, and to learn about the impact that tourism has (and therefore the impact YOU will have) in that region. It's amazing to think that no other guidebook in the bookshop will actually tell you, the tourist, things like how many other tourists go to that area; how much money you and other visitors bring to the region in the form of tourism, and where tourism is having a detrimental impact on the environment or society, and what you can do to help.

There is a new breed of tourist; keen to learn as much as possible about where they're travelling, not just have run-of-the-mill info regurgitated in a bland style. We give you the sort of info only the locals will tell you. **Because we've asked the locals:** we've asked them to tell us where the best places to go, stay and eat are; we've asked them how tourists can be more sensitive in their area; we've asked for their opinions. Everyone from the local Ecological Group to the regional tourist councils have been canvassed and have had their say where tourists should go, and what they should know about their region. Not exactly earth shattering stuff, you might think. But, believe it or not, it's not been done before, and you'll soon see the difference it makes. Now you really can experience a genuine slice of local culture, not one put on for the tourist hordes.

Our contributors and researchers all know and have travelled extensively in (and in 99 per cent of cases, actually lived in) the regions on which they comment. Syd House and I have laid our thoughts on tourism out in the guide which launched this series – *The Good Tourist – a worldwide guide for the green traveller* (Mandarin Paperbacks £5.99). We believe that whilst immense problems are created by mass tourism and its associated developments, there are ways in which tourism can be developed which bring benefits not only to tourists, but also to the host countries and the natural environment. We hope through this series to encourage the tourist to be aware of the issues, and by following the practical guidelines found in the books, to enjoy being what until recently has been called a contradiction in terms – a 'good tourist'.

Katie Wood

Contents

Acknowledgements ix
Maps xi
Introduction 1
Highlights of Britain 1 Natural History 3
Geography 7 Climate 10 Industry 11 History 13
The Real Britain 18 The Tourist Industry 23
How Green is Britain? 30 Sightseeing 36
Communications 38 The Art of Being a Good
Tourist 41 Red Tape 44 Budgeting 46 When
to Go 47 Where are the Positive Holidays? 48
General Holidays 48 Adventure/Activity
Holidays 51 Holidays Afloat 53 In the Saddle 54
Skiing 55 Multi-Activity 56 Special Interest 58
Wildlife/Ecological Holidays 59 Volunteer
Conservation Holidays 60 Travelling There
Independently 63 Accommodation 65 Checklist for
the Good Tourist 68 Further Information 69

Scotland
1 The Highlands and Islands   77
2 Tayside and Grampian   120
3 Edinburgh, the Lothians and Fife 148
4 Glasgow, Central and Ayrshire   177
5 Borders and South-West Scotland   205

England
6 Northumbria   237
7 Cumbria   263
8 The North-West   294
9 Yorkshire and Humberside   329
10 The East Midlands   357
11 The Heart of England   391
12 East Anglia   437
13 Thames and Chilterns   462

14	London	503
15	The South-East	533
16	The West Country	570

Wales

| 17 | Wales | 615 |

Northern Ireland

| 18 | Northern Ireland | 661 |

Acknowledgements

Our thanks are owed to the following people:

Editorial Assistant
Donald Greig
Following an honours degree at Stirling University, Donald Greig is now an established freelance travel writer, editing, up-dating and writing for a number of publishers. He has worked on many of Katie Wood's book projects, including *The Good Tourist – a worldwide guide for the green traveller*.

Researchers
Claire Foottit – Introduction.
A graduate of geographical and landscape studies, Claire Foottit has particular knowledge of the issues facing the land and has a particular interest in the impact of tourism. She now works as a freelance travel writer.

Douglas Willis – The Highlands & Islands.
Fellow of the Royal Geographical Society, Douglas Willis is a head geography teacher and has lived and worked in the Highlands all his life. He has contributed to a variety of magazines and journals on geographical and environmental themes, and is also author of two recent books on the Scottish countryside.

James McCarthy – Tayside & Grampian; Borders & South-West Scotland.
Newly retired deputy director of the Nature Conservancy Council for Scotland, James McCarthy lives and works in Scotland, and has particular knowledge of its countryside and the issues that face it.

Frank Howie – Edinburgh, Fife & Lothians; Glasgow, Central & Ayrshire.
Lecturer in tourism and with a degree in land use and ecology, Frank Howie is one of Scotland's leading voices on green tourism, living and working in the area on which he writes.

Gary Mason – Northern Ireland; Thames & Chilterns.
Lecturer in tourism and travel adviser to BBC Radio 5, Gary Mason is currently reading for an MA in the Social Anthropology of Tourism in London. He lives in the Thames & Chilterns area.

Pat Yale – Wales; Northumberland; Yorkshire and Humberside.
Travel writer (author, *The Budget Travel Guide*) and tourism lecturer, Pat Yale has travelled extensively and is actively involved in the sustainable tourism movement in the UK. She undertook a large-scale research trip for her chapters and is continuing to work freelance for other titles in the *Good Tourist* series.

Heather Lewis – East Midlands; Heart of England; North-West.
After working in Africa for a spell and travelling widely, Heather Lewis has now been based in England for many years. She has thoroughly explored the regions on which she writes, particularly their lesser-known corners which she scrutinises with the eyes of a writer, active conservationist and qualified artist.

Peter Mason – East Anglia; The West Country (with **Donald Greig**).
Author of *Tourism: Environment & Development Perspectives* (WWF), Peter Mason is a lecturer in tourism and a leading figure in green tourism, and writes here on the areas he has lived in and knows well.

Amanda Cotton, Donald Greig – London; S-E England.
Following her degree in the Social Anthropology of Tourism, Amanda Cotton is working with Tourism Concern, and writes on her native part of Britain.

Kathleen Greig, Colin Greig – Cumbria.
Kathleen and Colin Greig have been avid travellers for much of their lives. They originally met in Canada, having both arrived from their native countries: Kathleen from Scotland and Colin from Australia. In the course of their work they have lived in many countries around the world, from remote glens in the north of Scotland to high-rise apartments in Hong Kong and wooden cabins in the jungle of Malaysia. Having moved house over 25 times in as many years, they are now settled in rural North-East Fife, from where they are once again discovering Britain.

1. Scotland

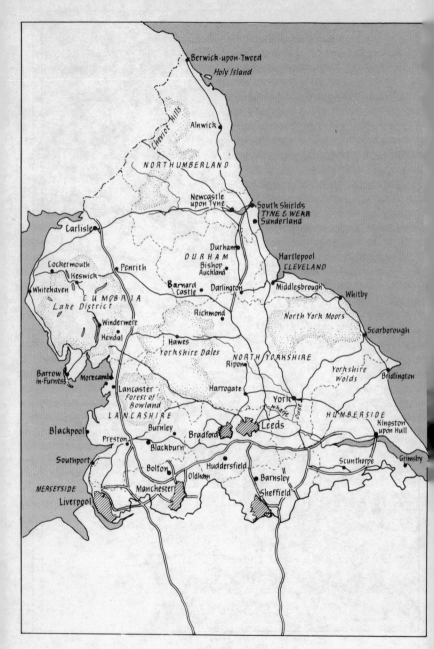

2. Northern England

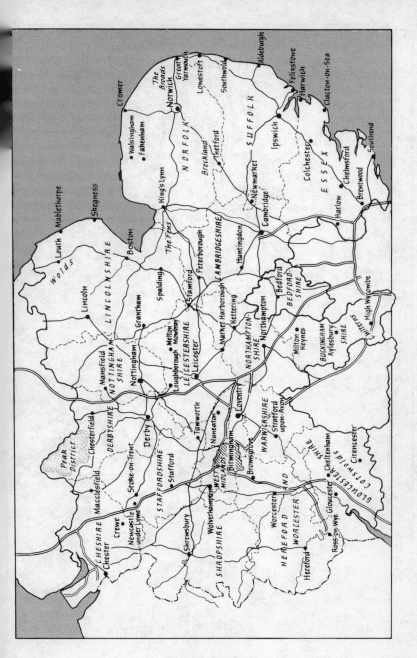

3. Central England

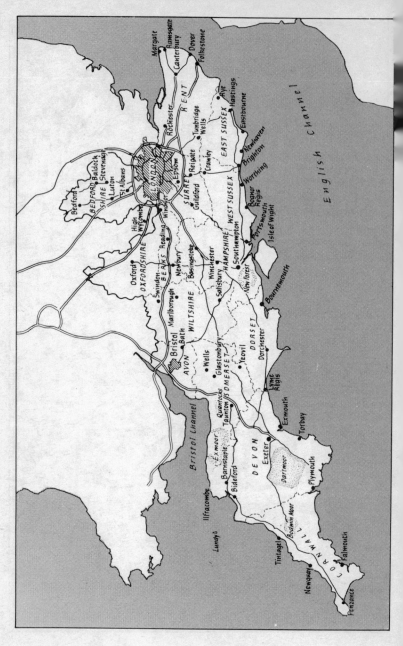

4. Southern England

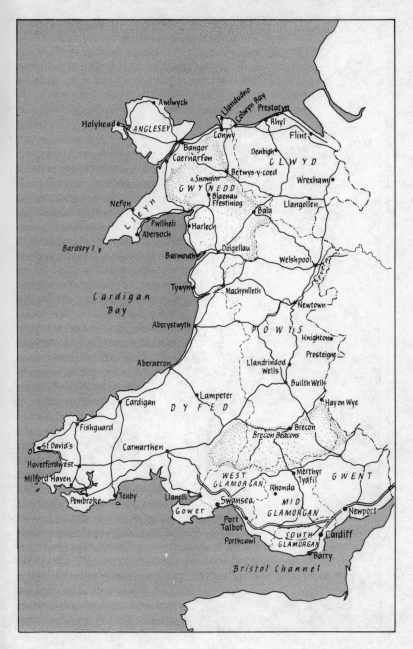

5. Wales

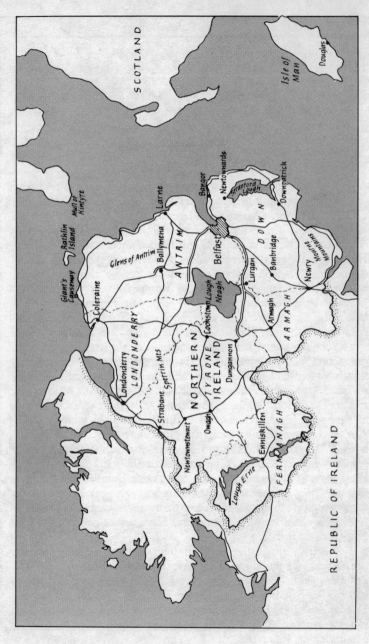

6. Northern Ireland

Introduction

Highlights of Britain

A land of scenic beauty and contrasts, Britain is steeped in tradition with a rich cultural inheritance. Many visitors express surprise and delight at the marked regional differences which occur within these small islands, where the countryside changes significantly over comparatively short distances. The rugged moors of the Scottish Highlands, the gentle, green valleys of Wales and the rolling plains of southern England, not to mention the craggy cliffs and sandy beaches of the longest coastline in Europe, reflect the range of physical characteristics which give so much variety to Britain's landscape. These differences are echoed in the strongly independent cultures of England, Wales, Scotland and Northern Ireland.

The countryside of Britain today stands as a testimonial to man's interaction with the environment through the centuries. Britain was first inhabited in Neolithic times, and the landscape and buildings reveal the colourful history of invasions and settlement which gave rise to the British nation. Nowhere is this more apparent than in the magnificent architectural heritage: Neolithic temples, Iron Age settlements, Roman artifacts, Norman castles, Tudor manor houses, Georgian crescents and Romanesque cathedrals are just a few of Britain's treasures. The architectural fabric is woven by the island's history. But, despite the remarkable number of buildings that have been preserved, much of what is attractive in Britain is still commonplace. Rural villages retain their quaint charm and market towns the character of a bygone era. Nostalgia can be indulged at every turn in Britain.

The British are justly proud of their heritage and, as well as preserving their buildings, they have wonderful museums and art galleries to visit. The Natural History Museum, the Victoria & Albert and the Tate Gallery in London, are examples. But it's not just in London that good interpretive museums exist – every town has one in some form or another. The local museum like the local library is a hallmark of British life.

2 The Good Tourist in the UK

London is world famous as a centre of culture, as well as business. Here you can see many of the displays of pomp and circumstance which have come to be associated with British tradition, such as the changing of the guard at Buckingham Palace. Britain is unusual in that it still has a monarchy that plays an active role in British public life, although it no longer has any real powers. Many people are fervently patriotic and support 'Queen and Country'. The Royal Family symbolises a tradition of hereditary sovereignty; some would say a living tradition, though others find it outmoded. But the significance of the Royal Family through history should not be underestimated, and it makes it all the more intriguing when exploring castles and museums to see the influence of the monarchy and the aristocracy upon Britain's heritage. Even today, this strong thread of monarchic tradition persists in annual events like Royal Ascot and the garden parties which the Queen hosts at Buckingham Palace, where formality is rigidly observed. Despite a tendency towards adverse media coverage in recent years, the majority of British people hold the Royal Family in high esteem and affection.

With so many reasons for going there, where do you start in deciding which part of Britain to visit? Any attempt to 'do' all of Britain in one go will result only in a frenetic blur of unsatisfying and shallow impressions. Instead, choose a theme for your trip: an activity holiday, in a mountainous area or along a stretch of canal, for example. Or base your trip on one town or city, exploring it and the surrounding region. It's easy to see why **London**, with its monuments, shops and entertainment is so popular. But there are many other cities and towns in Britain which, rewarding and fascinating in themselves, also make useful bases for exploring some of the most interesting areas of the country. **Winchester**, for centuries the capital of England, possesses one of the longest cathedrals in Europe, in which almost every style of English architecture is represented, and the city is a fine location for exploring the south coast and the South Downs. **Bath**, with its Georgian crescents and Roman baths, is an ideal touring centre for the south-west of England, where you can sample Somerset cider in attractive coastal resorts and Devon teas in thatched cottages and farmhouses. **Stratford**, birthplace of William Shakespeare and home to the Shakespeare Theatre Company and the Shakespeare Theatre, is within access of the university town of Oxford, Warwick Castle and the Vale of Evesham. **Cardiff**, capital city of Wales, a university town, important port and economic and cultural centre, is not far from the Brecon Beacons. **Chester**, with its canals and waterways, medieval shops, two miles of city walls and the largest Roman amphitheatre in Britain, is within easy access of the coast and mountains of north Wales. **Liverpool** has one of the largest harbours in the world, is home of the Beatles (and there are plenty of reminders), possesses an impressive maritime museum and art galleries and is close to the Wirral and within access of the north-east. The secret capital of the north of England, **York**, is famous for its Minster, the largest medieval church in Britain, and 'The Shambles', while the North York Moors are nearby. **Edinburgh**, Scotland's capital city, has a fine selection of museums and art galleries and is famous for its castle, where the military tattoo is performed at the international festival each year. It is an ideal centre for exploring the Scottish borders and the Highlands. **Glasgow** possesses a long association with shipbuilding on the Clyde and was 'cultural city of Europe' in 1990. It is a good base for exploring the west coast, passing through Loch Lomond and Glencoe. **Inverness**, capital of the Highlands, is ideal for touring the north and west of Scotland and the Hebridean islands. **Belfast**, capital of Northern Ireland, is easily accessible by ferry from the Scottish mainland, and is central to touring many unspoilt areas of Northern Ireland. With the compactness of Britain, it is possible to choose a number of locations as touring bases, so browse through literature and select your own itinerary.

Finally, with all the opportunities for touring and sightseeing, it is easy to overlook the fact that the key to understanding Britain and appreciating it fully is to make some effort to get to know the British people themselves. National characteristics are most pronounced, with differences in traditions and variations in language between England, Scotland, Wales and Northern Ireland, and even within each country there are still subtle regional differences. Variety is something which Britain possesses in abundance. The kind of visitor who will gain most out of a holiday here is someone who extends their interest in the country's culture and history to the inhabitants who have made it the way it is.

Natural History

Britain is internationally recognised as the most important breeding ground in Europe for migratory birds and also for a range of sub-species which developed in isolation from mainland Europe after the Ice Age. It has a diverse range of flora and fauna, with 1750 species of flowering plants, grasses and ferns. Although less varied than Europe, due to its island status, it is possible to see a wide range of habitats within a small area.

The present pattern of vegetation and its associated variety of ecosystems developed due to the climatic changes which occurred after the last advance of the Quaternary ice, and have since been modified by man. Indeed there is very little truly natural undisturbed habitat in Britain due to man's presence and action. Over much of the country woodland was the climax vegetation following the Ice Age. Since 5500 BC, Britain's climate has gradually become wetter, whilst it was at this time that the rising sea level separated Britain from mainland Europe. By 500 BC the climate became cooler, similar to the sub-Atlantic climate of today. Since the retreat of the ice, man has also had an impact on the general vegetation pattern. Forests were cleared for cultivation and many animals dependent on the forest were eradicated or reduced. Woodland clearance was particularly rapid during Norman times, a trend that has only recently been reversed to some extent by the plantation forestry of the 20th century. New grassland ecosystems evolved with man's management of the land for domestic animals, creating semi-natural habitats. Indeed virtually all the beautiful landscapes for which the British countryside is justly famous have been produced as a direct result of man's management.

Man's impact on the land has been accelerated since the 1939–45 war by the development of intensive farming techniques and land development. As a result many habitats have been severely reduced. For example, since 1950 England has lost one third of its heaths and upland grasslands, half its ancient woodlands, four fifths of its chalk and limestone grasslands, over 95 per cent of its lowland herb-rich grasslands, together with large areas of lowland marshes. In parallel, there has been a species decline as plants and animals have had their habitat destroyed or reduced. Dragonflies and butterflies are examples of this loss, and many of their species have either disappeared or been drastically reduced due to agricultural intensification and aerial pollution. Birds, on the other hand, are more resilient, but even so, there has been a decline in thirty-six breeding species over the last thirty-five years. Barn owls and lapwings, once comparatively common, are typical of this decline.

Despite this, Britain still has vast tracts of wilderness where it is possible to see red deer and feral goats in the mountains of Scotland, roe deer in woodland glades, and if you're lucky, a golden eagle soaring overhead. Ospreys, thanks to protective measures, are nesting at Boat of Garten in Inverness-shire and various other sites, where it is possible to go and see the osprey sitting on its nest. Around the coast of Britain, seals are still a common sight. Where agriculture is less intensive, wildflowers are in abundance, and on set-aside land in England, which was formerly intensively farmed, fields of poppies may now be seen.

Britain's countryside captures a mixture of elements, from the windswept heather moors of the uplands to the peaceful solitude of a woodland stream. Due to its variety and distribution, it is not possible to cover the range of flora and fauna in great depth, but the principal habitats may be broadly divided into the following areas:

The **Coastal Land** of Britain has a wide range of habitats. Seabirds such as puffins and guillemots have nests precariously perched on cliff faces. Salt marshes, off-shore mudflats and estuaries are a haven for a multitude of water fowl. Machair grassland is associated with dune systems in windy coastal areas of Scotland. Sandy beaches show the treasures from the sea.

Woodlands cover 10 per cent of Britain, but 80 per cent of this is conifer. There are a few remaining examples of ancient broadleaved woodland in the New Forest with its associated rich ground flora, and scattered remnants of the Caledonian Pine forest in Rothiemurchus and Glen Affric in Scotland. The lowlands have examples of mature oak and beech woods, while conifer plantations characterise recent upland forestry. Broadleaved woodlands provide a more diverse habitat which can support a wider range of species, whereas conifer plantations are species-poor although they have resulted in increased populations of pine marten and crested tit. The Forestry Commission is responsible for the public forests, and their policy is to encourage multipurpose forestry to incorporate sound silvicultural management with good conservation practice and recreational opportunities for all members of society.

The **uplands** are located in the north-west of Britain and are similar to the altitudinal vegetation in Scandinavia. Many areas within the potential tree limit have been altered to a secondary vegetation of molinia grasslands, heather and bracken due to grazing by sheep and cattle. The moorland is home to the red grouse, merlin, ring ousel and hen harrier. In particularly high areas examples of tundra-like alpine vegetation occur, such as the spring gentian. On the highest land one also finds the ptarmigan and mountain hare.

The **peatlands** mainly occur in the upland areas of Dartmoor, the Peak District, the North Pennines, North York Moors, upland Wales and north Scotland. On the west coast of Scotland the peat is cut as a fuel source. In recent years large areas of peat have been commercially mined for horticultural use. The bogland mires are characterised by cotton grass, orchid and insectivorous plants and the aromatic bog myrtle. Peat land was formerly widespread in the lowlands, such as the fenland of Cambridgeshire and Lincolnshire, but these have been drained and converted into farmland.

The **lowland grassland heaths** are mostly concentrated in southern England, and this has been a habitat which has taken a particular battering from changes in agriculture. The smoothsnake and sand lizard have come under threat due to having much of their habitat destroyed. There has been a decline in populations of the Common Frog and Toad and certain species, such as bats, have had their feeding areas reduced. The most important wild mammal in these areas is the rabbit whose grazing prevents the growth of colonising shrub and tree species.

Rivers, streams and lakes are abundant in Britain. The open waters are home to a range of fish, such as salmon and trout, pike and carp. The waters range between the oligotrophic waters, nutrient poor, of the lochs of northern Scotland, and the eutrophic waters, nutrient rich, of the south. Water pollution has been caused by industrial waste and agricultural run-off which have impaired fish stocks and suffocated any form of life through algae blooms. However, many rivers, such as the Clyde and the Thames, are less polluted now than fifteen years ago, and water quality control has corresponded to measures that have been taken to combat pollution.

Manmade, or artificial, ecosystems have been developed over the centuries, creating a semi-natural habitat which has become important in its own right. Examples of these are the biologically rich ecosystems which developed on the chalk grasslands due to grazing, and the Norfolk Broads which were created by medieval peat diggings. The Norfolk Broads, although artificial in origin, developed their own natural characteristics and are one of the most important wetland complexes in the country. They are particularly rich in peatland invertebrates. Nevertheless, the popularity of the Broads as a recreation area has destroyed habitat and disturbed wildlife communities. As a result, areas have been zoned off from tourists.

The pressure on wildlife has become a national concern, with conservation bodies, both public and private, battling to protect Britain's natural heritage. There has been a surge in public awareness and interest in the countryside. The reason for this is probably two-fold. Britain's population is now predominantly urban, but the British still retain a romantic notion about the countryside and deep concern for wildlife. Also there has been an increase in the number and membership of organisations which actively work in conservation; for example the World Wide Fund for Nature has doubled in size in the last three years. Certain species of bird, mammal and plant are protected by legislation under the Wildlife and Countryside Act 1981. There are a range of land use designations, such as nature reserves and sites of special scientific interest, which are aimed at protecting some of the most important habitats. These are described in the section 'How green is Britain?' on page 30.

Geography

Britain covers a total land area of 95,000 square miles (246,000 sq. km.) with some 1200 square miles (3,100 sq. km.) of inland waters. Comprising a series of islands and often referred to as 'the British Isles', Britain is flanked on the west coast by the Atlantic Ocean and separated from Scandinavia by the North Sea in the east. The Irish Sea divides Ireland from mainland Britain, and the English Channel, one of the busiest shipping routes in the world, separates England from mainland Europe and, immediately, France. The mainland is divided between Scotland in the north, Wales in the west, and England. Northern Ireland occupies the north-east corner of the island of Ireland, with the rest comprising the Republic of Ireland, or Eire.

Situated off mainland Britain are the island groups of Shetland and Orkney, to the north of Scotland; a chain of islands, the Inner and Outer Hebrides, off its west coast, together with the islands of Arran, Islay, Jura, Colonsay and Mull. Anglesey lies off the north coast of Wales. The Isle of Man lies off the west coast of England and the Isle of Wight off the southern English coast. The Channel Islands, although geographically closer to France, have politically been part of Britain for hundreds of years. Mainland Britain stretches from Cape Wrath in the north of Scotland, to Land's End in Cornwall, south-west England, a distance of 600 miles (965 km). At its broadest point, the mainland is 300 miles (483 km) wide.

Britain's land mass is derived from a complex and ancient geological history, which has weathered to form the diverse range of scenery which we see today. The chief visual contrasts are between highland and lowland, with the topography reflecting the underlying geological structure. A line from the River Exe in south-west England to the River Tees in north-east England may be taken as the division between highland and lowland Britain. In general, the highlands are formed from older, more weather-resistant rocks, some dating back to pre-Cambrian times over 570 million years ago. The main mountain and hill ranges were formed by a series of earth movements: the Caledonian uplift formed the predominant mountain mass in Scotland; the Pennines, Malvern and Mendip hills were formed during the Hercynian uplift. The Alpine uplift, which also formed the Swiss Alps, folded and stressed the rocks, forming weaknesses in the strata where volcanic intrusions subsequently occurred. Edinburgh Castle is built on top of one of these igneous intrusions. The lowlands are predominantly derived from sediments of sandstones, limestones, clays and chalks which were deposited in lakes during more recent geological times. The most recent phenomenon in geological history was the Ice Age, when Britain was covered by an ice cap which extended south as far as the Bristol Channel and Thames Valley. Much of the scenery which we see today is due to the sculpting and depositing of rocks during this time. Equal in diversity to Britain's landforms is the coastline, which, at 7000 miles (11,260 km), is the longest of any country in Europe. Its features range from salt marshes and sand dunes to long beaches of sand, pebbles or boulders, spectacular cliffs and fjord-like inlets.

The north of Britain features areas of rugged wilderness in the Highlands of Scotland. Mountains rise dramatically beside inland lochs, and large areas of land are covered by blanket bogs, such as in the Flow Country of the far north of Scotland. The Cairngorm mountains form a plateau in the north-east of Scotland, contrasting with the spectacular rockfaces of Glencoe which lie further west. To the south lie the southern uplands which are more undulating. The two upland areas are divided by the Central Basin which incorporates the Glasgow and Edinburgh conurbations, where the majority of the Scottish population is located. Scotland is famous for its salmon rivers, namely the Dee and Don, the Tay and Tweed. Other major rivers are the Clyde, with its past history of shipbuilding, and the Forth.

The English countryside is predominantly agricultural, with fertile plains and gently rolling hills. The Cheviot hills form a link with the southern uplands of Scotland. To the west are the Cumbrian hills and the Lake District, where Scafell Pike, England's highest peak at 3162 ft (964 m.), is situated. The Pennines, 'the backbone of England' run in a north–south line as far as Birmingham in the Midlands. The English Midlands, in the centre of England, are essentially a plain. Located in the east are the lowland areas of the fens. To the south lie the Thames Basin and the Hampshire Basin. They are separated by the North and South Downs, chalk ridges which culminate in the famed white cliffs of Dover. The English scarplands also give a distinctive feature to the landscape. Characterised by gentle inclines and steep escarpments, they are found from the Yorkshire coast to Dorset and Devon. In the south-west the main upland features are Exmoor and Dartmoor. The Cheddar Gorge, an example of limestone topography, is also situated in this area. The English rivers have always been important for communications and commerce, from the Middle Ages to the present day. London, for example, is situated on the Thames, and Liverpool on the Mersey. Other major rivers are the Tyne, Tees, Severn, Avon, Trent, Ouse and Humber.

The Welsh landscape is extremely varied. Famous for its beaches and bays, mountains and green valleys, the countryside of Wales is generally softer and less dramatic than in Scotland, although still rugged in many parts. The Cambrian mountains in the north are dominated by Yr Wyddfa, the highest peak of Snowdonia at 3560 ft. (1085 m.). Rising from the foothills of the English counties of Shropshire and Herefordshire are the Brecon Beacons and the Black Mountains of South Wales. The Vale of Glamorgan is the main lowland region. Cardigan Bay occupies much of the west coast, while the north features many seaside resorts. The principal rivers are the Wye, Severn, Dee and Towy, which meander through gentle valleys.

Northern Ireland also boasts a diversity of scenery. Divided between the highland areas of the Sperrin and Mourne mountains and the high moorland plateau of Antrim, the lowlands are to the south and include the glens and drumlin country of County Down. The Bann, the main river, flows from the large inland lake of Lough Neagh.

The population of Britain is 57 million, with a density of 590 to the square mile (228 per sq. km.), although half of the population lives in the sixty largest towns. The metropolitan area of London has a population of about ten million, followed by Birmingham, the second largest city, with one million. The majority of the population lives in England, which has a population of 46 million. In comparison, Scotland has a population of 5.1 million, with a much lower population density. Edinburgh has a population of 460,000 and Glasgow 750,000. The population of Wales is 2.8 million, with 300,000 living in Cardiff, whilst the population of Northern Ireland is 1.5 million. Since World War II there has been a steady increase in urbanisation. Many rural areas have a diminishing population, leaving large tracts of unpopulated areas, as can be seen in the highlands of Scotland, although interestingly there has been a reversal of this decline in recent years. English is spoken throughout Britain, but Welsh is spoken by one quarter of the Welsh population and Gaelic is localised on the west coast of Scotland and the Hebrides, with 88,000 speakers. The surge in national identity and culture has been encouraged through language, with both Welsh and Gaelic having their own radio and TV programmes. Signs are bilingual in Wales and in some parts of Scotland. Business is conducted in Welsh in many parts of Wales.

For administrative purposes Britain is divided into 45 counties in England, 7 counties in Wales, 6 counties in Northern Ireland and 12 regions in Scotland. Government is centralised in London (Westminister), but many domestic matters in Scotland, Wales and Northern Ireland are the responsibility of separate government departments which are located in each country and come under the jurisdiction of the respective Secretaries of State.

Climate

The weather has long been a popular topic of conversation among the British thanks to its unpredictable nature. However, in general, Britain has a temperate, oceanic climate with mild winters and cool summers. Seasonal variations throughout the year are limited. The mean temperature rarely rises above 26°C (75°F) in the summer months or below freezing during the winter. The mean temperature of the winter months is 4°C (38°F).

With most of the country lying a few feet above sea level, and the highest mountain, Ben Nevis, lying at 4000 ft (1220 m.), temperature variations are primarily due to latitude, with slight differences between the north and south of Britain, and between east and west. The mean annual temperature in southern England is around 11°C (57°F), while in the far north of Scotland it is 7°C (45°F). The west coast is milder and wetter, due to the Atlantic influence and the Gulf Stream: palm trees grow in sheltered coastal locations from the south-west of England to the highlands of Scotland. South-westerly winds prevail across the country. The rain-bearing westerly winds cause air to rise against the hill ranges of the west coast, leaving a rainshadow on the east coast. There is a significant rainfall variation between the west and east coasts of the country. For example, Fort William on the west coast of Scotland has an annual rainfall of 82 inches (208 cm.), while Edinburgh on the east coast has 28 inches (71 cm.).

Rainfall is distributed mostly during the winter months, between

October and January, with the months March–June having least. Winters, although mild, are punctuated with gales and rain, with snow common on the high ground in Scotland at this time. Due to the high humidity, over 90 per cent in winter, fog is common over large areas of lowland. Ground frosts can occur at any time between October and June.

The variety and inclemency of British weather makes it essential for the visitor to have adequate warm and waterproof clothing. Weather forecasts are given regularly on national and local radio and TV stations, but while a useful guide they are not always reliable, so the secret is to be prepared for 'rain or shine'. A waterproof jacket and umbrella can be needed at any time of year, and in the winter a heavy coat is recommended.

Industry

During the mid-19th century, Britain was the leading industrial nation accounting for half the world's industrial output. Regarded as the 'workshop of the world', it was a major exporter of manufactured goods. In 1900 Britain produced 18 per cent of the world's industrial output; in 1937, 13 per cent, and today only 7 per cent. This decline has been caused by the ending of the Empire, a source of cheap raw materials; stiff post-World War II competition from the other major industrialised nations – the USA, Japan, West Germany and France – and a lack of ability to update industry with the latest technology. Recent years have seen something of a renaissance in the entrepreneurial spirit of the British, with a greater willingness to compete for a share of world trade, and today the country ranks fifth in the world trade league.

Manufacturing is still important to the British economy, with the aerospace, chemical and pharmaceutical industries playing a significant part as export earners. Recently there has been much foreign investment into Britain, notably from Japan, as in the motor industry, which is poised to retain its position as a major competitor in the European market place. Britain's other main manufacturing industries are mechanical engineering, textiles, electrical engineering and computers. In an effort to remain viable, many industries underwent a stringent programme of rationalisation during the Thatcher years. In coal mining, between 1985 and 1989 half the pits were closed and the workforce halved, but remarkably output remained constant. British Steel had losses of £1.8bn in 1980, but recorded profits of £600m in 1989.

A sense of change has surrounded the north of England, the Midlands, southern Wales and central Scotland, former areas of heavy manufacturing. Unemployment is well above the national average in these parts, and government policy has been to try and breathe life back by encouraging businesses to locate in Development Areas and Enterprise zones by offering loans and fiscal incentives in an effort to create employment.

In the financial services sector, the City of London has maintained its leading role as an international centre for many of the world's financial institutions. Edinburgh too is growing in importance as a financial centre.

Natural resources also have a significant impact on the economy. Traditionally coal was the main source of fuel for the power stations, but in order to reduce the pollution caused by the release of sulphur dioxide, which causes acid rain, and due to concern about future sources of fuel for energy, Britain has invested heavily in nuclear power stations. It is one of the leading nations in Europe using nuclear power for peaceful purposes, and nuclear fuels are a growing export earner.

Oil started flowing from the North Sea in 1975, and indeed by the mid-1980s Britain was the world's fifth largest producer, making the country self-sufficient. The revenue from oil has made a considerable contribution to the balance of payments. Production peaked in 1985, but the industry has reserves to last into the next century. Oil-related employment has been centred on Aberdeen and the Grampian region in north-east Scotland. Gas is another energy source which has been developed in the North Sea, with benefits to the British consumer.

Agriculturally, Britain is highly productive despite the small land area. Remarkably, only one fifth of the land is used for the cultivation of crops, an indication of the intensive farming that has taken place since World War II. This has not been without its problems, as many water sources have been polluted by nitrates being washed off the land. Only 10 per cent of Britain is covered by forest which supplies 12 per cent of the country's needs, and timber is one of Britain's largest imports. The fishing industry has been hit by declining fish stocks and operates under a quota system, although there has been a rapid growth in fish farming over the last decade.

Tourism ranks as one of the major growth industries, and is being encouraged as it is an important earner of foreign exchange and creates employment throughout the country. In 1983, 12.5 million visitors came to Britain, with a revenue estimated at £3000 million.

In 1989, 17.2 million visitors came, earning £6.8 billion, 4 per cent of the GNP.

History

Britain's history portrays a colourful tapestry of events woven over the centuries into a rich cultural heritage. The diversity of history is intricately depicted in the fabric of its buildings; in literature and the arts; in customs and in the language. A knowledge of the main events which have influenced this island's history will give a greater appreciation of the wealth of culture for which Britain is world famous.

Britain's history dates from the **Stone Age** which commenced somewhere around 60,000 BC. During the Middle Stone Age, incomers from the north and west of Europe brought with them the Neolithic farming culture. Archaeological evidence may be seen throughout Britain, from Skara Brae in Orkney to Stonehenge near Salisbury. It is now known that Stonehenge, a solar temple, was built by the Beaker people between the 15th and 19th centuries BC.

The **Bronze Age** followed around 1600 BC, when the Wessex culture gave rise to a trade in gold and tin. The Urnfield culture, in 1400 BC, introduced the growing of wheat and barley which spread from England into Scotland and Ireland. The first Celts arrived in 600 BC. The **Iron Age**, dating from 500 BC, heralded a new influx of Celts from northern France, the Brythons.

In 55 BC the **Romans** under Julius Caesar first attempted to gain control over Britain, but it was not until AD 45, after a successful invasion, that the south-east of England became a Roman province. With their powerful legions, the Romans went on to infiltrate Scotland as far as Inverness. The Antonine Wall was built across Scotland between the Forth and the Clyde, but the natives, known as the Picts, constantly harried the invaders, and the Romans retreated south as far as Yorkshire. In 122 Hadrian's Wall was built across the north of England, from the Tyne to the Solway, to protect Roman territory from the northern invaders. Remnants can be seen today, a worthy testimonial to the outstanding engineering skills of the Romans. In the south of England examples of Roman villas and baths may be seen. Towns with names ending in 'ester' originate from Roman times, as in Chichester, Dorchester, Gloucester. London (Londinium) also dates from this era.

The Romans finally withdrew in AD 410 to protect their homeland from invasion. They took their culture with them and Britain lapsed back into the **Dark Ages**. Invaders from northern European tribes, such as the Angles and Saxons, gradually exerted more influence, eventually giving their name to the country, England, and to the Anglo-Saxon period. The Picts and Celts were relegated to Scotland and Wales, whilst the Anglo-Saxons founded seven kingdoms in England: Kent, Sussex, East Anglia, Wessex, Mercia and Northumbria. Blond-haired and blue-eyed, they brought with them new techniques for timber construction and assimilated the Roman masonry techniques.

The 6th century heralded the arrival of **Christianity** which was to play a fiery part in the centuries that followed. Introduced by the monk Augustine, who was sent from Rome in 596, Christianity gradually took hold in England. St Patrick, patron saint of Ireland, had converted the Irish almost single-handedly much earlier in 432. Exquisite examples of book illumination date from the 8th century, such as the Lindisfarne Gospels and the Irish Book of Kells. The coming of Christianity to Scotland owed much to the efforts of St Ninian and St Columba, the latter being Irish and forming a strong bond with the Celtic Church of his native land.

The beginning of the 9th century marked the start of almost a century of **Viking** raids and invasions; the Viking tradition is still remembered annually in the Up Helly Aa celebrations in Shetland. By this time, England was dominated by the kingdom of Wessex, with King Alfred the Great able to confine the Viking invasion to the north-east of England. By the time of Edward the Confessor in 1042, England was the most highly organised state in Europe.

The **Battle of Hastings** in 1066 marked the beginning of a series of wars between England and France. King Harold was killed, shot through the eye during the battle, and Duke William of Normandy (William the Conqueror) became William I of England. The battle is famously recorded in the Bayeux Tapestry. Thus began the **Norman** era, when the Norman feudal system was imposed upon the country and Anglo-Saxon landowners were replaced by Norman barons. French and Latin became the languages of the ruling classes and Anglo-Saxon the language of the uneducated. There are many examples of Norman architecture in England, including village churches, and eminent cathedrals such as Durham and Lincoln. Inheritance and dynastic marriage gave England jurisdiction over most of France during the 12th century, but King John lost Normandy and in 1215 was compelled by his barons to sign the **Magna Carta**, a charter of rights which has been the foundation stone of British life and government ever since; the country still has no written constitution.

In the 13th and 14th centuries England turned its attention to trying to incorporate Wales and Scotland into its powers. In 1295 King Edward I defeated the Welsh and promised them a Welsh prince as a ruler, one who had been born in Wales and spoke no English or French. He brought forward his baby son, also called Edward, who had been born a few days earlier at Carnaervon Castle; ever since then the eldest son of the king of England has been called the Prince of Wales and England and Wales have formed one kingdom. In Scotland, Edward I was invited to adjudicate over the succession to the Scottish throne. The temptation to meddle in Scottish affairs proved too much, precipitating an English invasion and subsequent conquest. After the succession of Edward II, the Scots, rallied and led by Robert the Bruce, defeated Edward at the **Battle of Bannockburn**, near Stirling, in 1314 and chased him out of Scotland. The Scots regained their independence, although rivalry continued between the two countries long afterwards.

Henry VIII made a significant step in Britain's history when, in 1527, he sought annulment of his marriage to Catherine of Aragon. The Catholic Church refused to recognise his divorce, so he broke links with Rome to found the Church of England and began the **dissolution of the monasteries** and the **Reformation**. It was the start of another stormy period for Christianity. Henry was succeeded by Edward VI who supported the reformed church, but when Mary I, who married Philip of Spain, came to the throne in 1553, she restored Catholicism and persecuted the Protestants. Elizabeth I, the red-headed spinster Queen, succeeded in 1558; the reformed church was re-established and there was an economic upsurge. The ground was laid for the beginnings of the **British Empire** with Drake and Raleigh's expeditions to the West Indies and North America. A privateering war was fought against Spain and climaxed with the destruction of the **Spanish Armada** in 1588. This was the 'Golden Age' of English literature, culminating in the plays of William Shakespeare. Hampton Court and Longleat House are examples of Elizabethan architecture, which show an Italian influence. Scotland had its own kingdom at this time, ruled by Mary Queen of Scots, who was executed under the command of Elizabeth I. However, it was Mary's son, James VI of Scotland and I of England, who unified the two countries.

Charles I came to the throne in 1625 and precipitated England's sole venture into republicanism. Pitting his wishes against the will of Parliament, a bloody civil war ensued between his supporters, the Cavaliers, and the Roundheads, who supported Parliament and were led by Oliver Cromwell. The Royalists were defeated and Charles I was beheaded, paving the way for the constitutional supremacy of Parliament. Cromwell became Lord Protector over a republic, but amid much relief the monarchy was restored in 1660 when Charles II was invited back to be king. His successor, James II, supported the Catholic cause, which created a crisis, culminating in his being deposed in 1688, and banished abroad in favour of his daughter, Mary, and her husband, William of Orange, the Dutch king and a strong supporter of the Protestant cause. The whole episode signalled a significant development in the role of Parliament and the accountability of the Monarchy. Under Queen Anne, the Parliaments of England and Scotland united under the **Act of Union** in 1707, further strengthening the central role of Parliament over the whole country, and increasing the concept of Great Britain as a political entity.

All was not yet peace, however, for when George I succeeded to the throne in 1714, within a year he was plagued by the **Jacobean uprisings**, during which the Scottish clans rose to the defence of the deposed Stuarts, descendants of James II. George II finally quelled the Scottish uprisings at the **Battle of Culloden** in 1745, where the romantic and enigmatic figure of Bonnie Prince Charlie, the 'Young Pretender', was defeated. In other spheres, under George III's reign Britain's colonial expansion continued but suffered a reverse when she lost her American colonies in the **American War of Independence**. However, during the **Napoleonic Wars**, when Britain's rivalry with France continued, Britain emerged victorious, with Nelson winning the **Battle of Trafalgar** (1805) and Wellington the **Battle of Waterloo** (1815). The architecture of the period shows a swing to the neo-classical, often known simply as 'Georgian'. Fine examples may be seen in the crescents of Bath and Edinburgh. There was a flourishing of the decorative arts, such as Chippendale furniture and the ceramics of Josiah Wedgewood, which even extended outside to the English Landscape Garden style. It was the age of the great portrait painters such as Reynolds and Gainsborough in England and Raeburn in Scotland. The style and appeal of English country life, to which many still aspire today, was captured in the paintings of Stubbs and Morland.

Queen Victoria, the longest-reigning monarch, came to the throne in 1837. It was the time of the **Industrial Revolution** and the expansion of the **British Empire**, which covered a fifth of the world during the Victorian period. It was also a time of great prosperity, and interest in the decorative arts continued unrivalled, with a Gothic Revival being seen in the work of Nash, as visible in London's Regent Street. Crystal Palace, a building of cast iron and glass, was built by Paxton in London's Hyde Park for the Great Exhibition of 1851, which laid the foundations for the development of modern architecture. The 19th century was also a period of great urban growth and demographic expansion within Britain.

In 1901 Edward VII came to the throne, at the start of a period of considerable change. Britain had been involved in the **Boer War** and under George V was soon heavily involved in the **First World War** (1914–18), when Britain and her allies fought against Germany. A civil war in Ireland was resolved by the establishment of the **Irish Free State** in 1922, forming today's boundaries, with the province of Ulster remaining under the jurisdiction of Great Britain as Northern Ireland.

After the rapid expansion under the Victorian era, the 1920s and 1930s suffered a great depression, although the Empire was flourishing and developed to become the **British Commonwealth of Nations**. The strain and drain of the war had swept away the old order in Europe; Britain's national morale was shattered and the flower of a generation had perished in the mud of Flanders. In 1936 Edward VIII abdicated in favour of his brother, George VI, who inherited the throne as the threat of Hitler began to loom large. An unprovoked German attack on Poland in 1939 started the **Second World War**.

Since peace returned in 1945, Britain has been struggling to maintain her economic standing, fighting to retain a foothold in a competitive world market. It was largely this aspect of affairs which led the Conservative government of Edward Heath to take Britain into the **European Economic Community** (the so-called Common Market) in 1973. The question of Britain's links with Europe has always been an uneasy one and the debate now hotted up, culminating, after a Labour victory in the 1974 election, in a national referendum (uniquely for Britain) in 1975, which voted in favour of remaining within the EEC. Britain has now orientated herself towards Europe, particularly with the signing of the **Single European Act** in 1986, which will open up the single market in 1992. However, the country is a strong supporter within the EEC of keeping an open trade policy with the outside world.

Nationalism has grown in Wales and Scotland, but whilst the referendum in the two countries in 1976 showed considerable support for the establishment of semi-independent national assemblies, it was not enough to overcome the stringent qualifications placed on the vote. Devolution remains an issue in both Welsh and Scottish politics.

After a series of strikes and industrial unrest the Conservatives were re-elected in 1979 and **Margaret Thatcher** became the first woman prime minister in Britain, serving until the end of 1990. With a strict monetary policy, there has been a constant battle to keep inflation under control, and policy has been dominated by the principles of non-intervention, privatisation and tight controls on public spending. Since 1969 all this has been played out against the background of religious, social and political disturbances in Northern Ireland, known as 'the troubles'. The British army still has a permanent presence there and the question of a satisfactory resolution to a centuries-old problem remains the outstanding thorn in the side of domestic British politics and harmony. Despite it all, however, and despite her size, Britain has retained a high profile in international affairs.

The Real Britain

English genteelness – afternoon cricket and cucumber sandwiches; kilted, canny, whisky-swilling, haggis-eating Scots; Welsh choirs and hardworking miners; Irish gaiety, Guinness and traditional jigs. Many such observations have been made about the British character, but how true are they? And what are the British really like? How does the real Britain differ from the glossy tourist brochures enticing you to explore these small islands?

Being an island people has certainly had an effect upon the development of the British character. Situated on the fringe of Europe, historically Britain has not been influenced directly by mainstream European events, and as a result, the British have retained an individual character. Its importance as a major country in world affairs, its history of colonial conquest and its military supremacy in two World Wars has given the British a strong sense of patriotism and an independence of spirit which is still cultivated.

Despite this patriotism towards Great Britain as a whole, and a tendency to jump to the defence of any adverse criticism of the country, each nation within Britain exhibits fierce national pride and its own patriotic fervour. There is marked difference between the English, the Scots and the Welsh. A Scot will feel righteously insulted if he is called English! With England's dominance politically, the Scots, Welsh and Irish often feel hard done by, and cling to their nationalism. There has been a strong upsurge in nationalism over the last decade, particularly with people becoming more interested in their roots and placing a greater value on their cultural inheritance. With closer association with the Common Market and free trade within the EEC commencing in 1992, the Scottish National Party, which represents a minority of Scots, is keen for Scotland to have independent representation in the European Assembly.

The visitor will probably come across the British class system, which is confusing in that it is not strictly related to wealth or education. Many argue that the class system has broken down and, certainly, in recent years the edges have become considerably blurred. For example 'working class' tends to equate with 'lower class', yet many professional people are 'working' in every sense of the word. There has been greater vertical integration of the classes since World War II, a process accelerated in the last ten years following Thatcherite government policies, espousing popular capitalism and encouraging a large share-and home-owning group within the traditional working class. The push to rediscover entrepreneurial talents in all sections of society has seen a move towards a more American-influenced social structure, yet much of the traditional class system remains. It is an inheritance from the days of the landowners, tradesmen and labourers, who used to form the three major socio-economic groups, with the landowners traditionally making up the 'upper class', the tradesmen the 'middle class', and the labourers the 'working class'. Today there are endless refinements, with groups being pigeonholed into different classes, although the divide is often indistinct.

The nuances are difficult for an outsider to grasp, but essentially, the division into classes is roughly as follows: the hereditary aristocracy, with its titled earls, dukes and lords, who can sit in the House of Lords, together with families which in the past have accrued enough wealth for their commercial origins to be waived, find themselves labelled 'upper class'. Interestingly, money is not necessarily of importance, with many families having lost their former wealth, but still being considered 'upper class'. The 'middle class' is subdivided between the upper and lower middle class. Traditionally the 'upper middle class' was characterised by professional people, who lived in large houses and whose children attended fee-paying schools. By reputation conservative, the 'lower middle class' was represented by office workers and shop assistants, who lived in smaller houses and flats. They equated with the European *petit bourgeoisie*. The 'working class' were largely made up of manual workers who traditionally lived in low-rent housing. Their children attended State schools, and fewer went on to higher education. Nowadays these classifications are less rigid – for example, many people who might otherwise fall into the 'working class' category now own their homes.

There are also the different racial groups who do not necessarily fit into the traditional class pattern. Immigrants arriving from the colonies in the 1950s often filled the most menial jobs. Unfortunately this has created friction with the working classes in times of unemployment. Racial tension does exist in inner cities, normally provoked by unemployment and poverty. Britain is now a multi-cultural society and, although the process has been slow, the advantages in terms of a diverse and varied community are becoming obvious. The contributions of the West Indian, Indian, Pakistani and Chinese communities are wide and varied, ranging from providing cheap and good quality alternatives to 'traditional' British cooking in the many ethnic restaurants, through to the entrepreneurial skills of businessmen who exhibit much of the traditional drive of immigrants to new countries, intent on improving their lot.

Accent is by custom another measure for determining class category. It was George Bernard Shaw who once said, 'It is impossible for an Englishman to open his mouth without making some other Englishman despise him.' As a general rule, the Queen's English has been equated with the pronunciation of English as spoken in the south of England by the educated classes. Regional accents were for many years looked down upon as being 'inferior' because they identified the speaker as being provincial and uneducated, rather than using the received pronunciation taught in the more expensive public schools. Thankfully attitudes have relaxed enormously in recent years and there is a positive drive to encourage a varied use of the English language, including regional dialects and local words. Nevertheless, there is also a tendency towards standardisation and homogenisation as a result of the influence of the media – TV, radio, the press – which tend to dilute local differences.

There is also a regional discrepancy over social attitudes. For example, the southern counties of England with their close proximity to London tend to be wealthier, and have a reputation for arrogance and materialism which is less prevalent in other areas of Britain. Although regional differences are less marked than they used to be due to improved communications, a growing TV culture, and a more mobile workforce, many of the traditional regional customs are becoming thinner on the ground. For example, in the Highlands of Scotland, local barn dances with local musicians playing traditional dance music, are being superseded to some degree by the demands of the young for disco music.

Although having an essentially religious inheritance, the British are not keen church goers, and church attendances are declining. On mainland Britain, religious tolerance is high, with the Anglican Church of England, Presbyterian Church of Scotland, and Roman Catholic Church happy to co-exist with other religions, such as Muslim, Hindu, Buddhist and Jewish. The role of the Church has, to some degree, become limited to carrying out weddings and funerals, and celebrating major festivals such as Christmas and Easter. However, in Northern Ireland the religious divide is still strong between Protestants and Catholics, even amongst educated people, thereby fuelling the continuing troubles.

Britain has a comparatively lower standard of living than her immediate European neighbours and the United States, but wealth is, in general, more evenly distributed, despite the growing divide between the rich and poor. Two thirds of the 23 million households are owner-occupied. Two thirds of the households possess a car and one fifth have two cars or more. The eating habits of many have changed from the traditional large home-cooked family meals to take-aways or ready-prepared supermarket meals. The weekly shopping is usually done at one of the major supermarkets. Drinking habits too have changed, with fewer people drinking beer, and more wine being consumed. Surprisingly, the British are amongst the world's keenest drinkers of champagne! The British reputation for unimaginative, stodgy food with over-cooked vegetables is no longer valid. Exotic cookery demonstrations on television and a desire to eat more healthily have had some influence on choice of food. Restaurants offer a wide variety of choices to suit most tastes and pockets.

Informal socialising takes place in the home or in pubs and winebars. Cinema entertainment is staging a revival, although the arts in general are poorly attended, inadequately subsidised and dependent on foreign visitors. In the north of England the working men's clubs are still popular, providing cabaret and entertainment. Weekends away in country cottages are the privilege of the wealthy, creating frustrated outbursts from local residents who cannot afford the inflated prices that holiday cottages impose on local properties. In Wales there have been arson attacks on these second homes.

The British do have a strong affiliation with the countryside, despite 80 per cent of the population being town dwellers. Villages in the commuter belts surrounding the major conurbations have often suffered from a large influx of commuters, many of whom do not participate in the community; this can create resentment and, once again, their inability to pay higher prices prevents local people from buying in their own community.

A love of sport is fairly universal among the British. Many people actively participate in some sport or other and there are also plenty of armchair enthusiasts. Football (soccer) has a strong following across the board and rugby is guaranteed to instil national pride at the annual Internationals. Traditional sports featuring on the national calendar include the Oxford v. Cambridge boat race, Royal Ascot, the Derby, the Grand National, Wimbledon, Cowes week and the Henley Regatta. Golf, cricket, tennis, squash, hockey, athletics and basketball are popular activities. There is also a growth in outdoor pursuits, such as sailing, windsurfing, cycling, riding, hill-walking and skiing. Traditional rural pursuits like fox-hunting, fishing (especially) and shooting are still popular, although there is a strong anti-fox-hunting lobby.

In many respects the British are a home-loving people. Favourite pastimes are home improvements and gardening. TV and videos provide ready home entertainment and, as a result, many people stay at home. Pets – cats and dogs – are also popular and it has been said that the British show more affection to their animals than to their children. Noticeable reserve, a 'stiff upper lip' and a lack of visible emotion are national characteristics which even the British themselves would generally confess to.

This has given rise to the notion that they are unfriendly and do not warm quickly to strangers. This is arguable and indeed it is difficult to make a generalisation. Whilst this may be the case in some instances, there will be as many to refute the argument. But on the whole, if not giving an over-enthusiastic welcome to strangers, the British are polite and hospitable and can be extremely friendly once they have got over their inherent shyness and suspicion of foreigners. Although the Scots have a reputation for meanness, the Highlanders are renowned for their hospitality and the Glaswegians for their friendliness. Again this gives rise to the regional differences within Britain. Devon is still famous for delicious cream teas, Somerset still makes scrumpy cider, Yorkshire pudding is still eaten in Yorkshire and haggis and neaps are still eaten in Scotland, although porridge and haggis are far from the staple diet of the Scots today!

As with other parts of the world, Britain has its 20th-century problems – unemployment, crime, discrimination against racial minorities in the inner cities, together with industrial and rural decline. It is easy to form a rosy-tinted image of Britain, with its glorious heritage and quaint insular customs, but the British are continually evolving, assimilating ideas from other cultures and adapting to the socio-economic forces of today.

The Tourist Industry

The leisure or tourist industry is one of the great economic growth areas of the post-World War II western world. Increase in car ownership, air travel, a higher standard of living, and more leisure time have all added to this phenomenon. While previously a luxury only affordable by the wealthy, travel is now within the reach of everyone and is a vast and growing industry. Recent trends suggest that tourism will undoubtedly be the most important economic activity in the world by the turn of the century.

The pattern of holidays has changed in Britain since the 1950s. Then, virtually all Britons took their annual holidays, usually a fortnight in July or August, within the United Kingdom, by the seaside in a resort or holiday centre. The only holiday-makers going abroad were the wealthy or a few intrepid travellers. The pattern has considerably altered. The rise of the package holiday market and the lure of guaranteed Mediterranean sunshine had, by the 1960s and 1970s, attracted millions of Britons away from the traditional seaside resort. Recent years have seen a further decline in the status of many of these venerable attractions. Such names as Brighton, Bridlington, Scarborough, Whitley Bay and Rothesay all seemed to pale into a vision of dull, grey July days, compared to the brash excitement of the Costa Brava, Majorca and the Greek islands. Who wanted to go to Morecambe when you could have Majorca and the sun for the same price?

Growth of travel by Britons going overseas has increased phenomenally over the last thirty years, to the extent that 20 million Britons now make 30 million foreign trips or thereabouts every year. This is all part of the great travel and tourism boom worldwide. Domestically tourism in Britain has benefited considerably with over 17 million foreign visitors visiting in 1989, representing an average annual increase of nearly 4 per cent since 1984. Britain now ranks fifth in the world tourist league of international earners behind the United States of America, France, Spain and Italy.

Domestic tourism (meaning British tourists holidaying in the United Kingdom) is still extremely important. In fact, British tourists make something like five times as many holiday trips as foreign visitors although the spending per trip by foreigners is, not surprisingly, considerably higher. Inevitably the structure and type of domestic holidays have altered. Britons tend to take more short breaks at destinations reasonably close to home – the typical weekend break being to a resort or country house hotel. The holiday market has recognised this trend and has responded accordingly, by providing more of these places. Even the so-called unfashionable seaside resorts have staged a comeback, altering their image and improving the quality of services and attractions. Indeed, Blackpool Pleasure Beach is consistently the top United Kingdom tourist attraction, with over six million visitors a year.

In 1989, 17.3 million people visited Britain. Of these, 3.5 million came from North America, 10.7 million from Western Europe and 3.2 million from the rest of the world. Interestingly there is a general trend towards more independent travel as opposed to inclusive holiday packages. Independent visits totalled 5.3 million, while inclusive holidays only two million. There has been a marked increase in business travel with a record 4.4 million business visits in 1989. The traditional months of July and August still remain the peak period with half of the domestic holidays taking place at this time, coinciding with the school summer holidays. However, only a quarter of day visits take place at this time. There is evidence to suggest that there is a greater spread over the holiday season, with May, June, September and October growing in importance for short holidays.

So, what attracts visitors to Britain? Traditionally the weather is certainly not held up as a major attraction, but the relatively mild climate allows a considerable range of outdoor activities. Apart from visiting friends and relations, it is Britain's rich historical, cultural and natural heritage that forms the main attraction. Tourists have become more discerning in their requirements. They are demanding higher quality, and are more interested in their environment. Special-interest holidays are increasingly popular with the visitor wanting to know more about the people and history of an area. Part of Britain's attraction as a tourist destination is probably due to the quality of the holiday offered together with the choice of heritage attractions. Visits to historic houses, cities and towns, rural beauty spots and museums rate highly as reasons for choosing Britain as a place to visit.

Heritage tourism is a major feature, with historical sites amongst the top attractions. Westminster Abbey, St Paul's Cathedral, York Minster, Stapely Water Gardens, the British Museum, the National Gallery and Albert Dock in Liverpool boasted visitor numbers of between 1 and 6.5 million in 1989. In the last decade, visits to heritage attractions have increased by almost a quarter, and there has been a marked increase in visitors to historic towns. Consequently there has been a 25 per cent increase in the number of historic buildings open to the public during the last decade and a 34 per cent increase in museums. Occasional murmurs of discontent are sometimes heard about parts of Britain being turned into open-air museums of spurious 'heritage', hosting events such as 'Medieval Banquets', but by and large the interest has been positive in helping to protect, conserve and enhance many features. Many old buildings and country houses have found new uses as hotels or visitor centres, when they would otherwise have disappeared.

Most visitors stay on average about ten days. While those from North America and Western Europe average ten days or less, visitors from further afield have a tendency to stay longer. Air travel forms the most popular mode of coming to Britain, accounting for two thirds of passenger traffic, while one third arrive by sea. London is the main gateway for international travel, and visitors to Britain spend more than 50 per cent of their time in the capital. The regional pattern of overseas tourism varies greatly. For example, 89.3 per cent of tourists visit England, 8.3 per cent Scotland, 3.7 per cent Wales and 0.4 per cent Northern Ireland. Within England, regional differentiations are extreme: London accounts for 56.9 per cent of visitors, the south-east accounts for 10.8 per cent, but only 1.8 per cent visit Northumbria. Within this pattern there are also variations on the regional preference by individual countries. The majority of Americans spend 75 per cent of their time in London, while only just over 10 per cent visit Scotland.

Tourism in Britain is booming and set to continue to grow. It generates a high economic return, both from the domestic market and overseas revenue. It also makes a healthy contribution to the balance of payments, although, interestingly, Britons spend considerably more abroad as tourists than foreign visitors spend in Britain. In 1989 (last collected figures) the value of tourism to Britain was £24.4 billion, representing over 4 per cent of the total GDP. It comes as a surprise to many to find that tourism is the single largest employer in Britain, with 1.4 million working in directly-related sectors, 6 per cent of all employees in employment. Spending by overseas visitors accounts for £6.9 billion a year, with over half of this being spent on business trips. The largest spenders are the Americans, French, (West) Germans and those from the Middle East. An American on average spends about £487 per visit. The domestic expenditure on tourism was £10.9 billion, while day trippers spent £3 billion. Payments by overseas residents to British carriers accounted for £1.6 billion. As an export earner, it ranks fourth in importance after non-electrical machinery, chemicals and transport equipment, but it comes third in the growth rate. Between 1971 and 1989, the revenue earned from tourism grew by a remarkable 1,299 per cent. Current forecasts in growth estimate that there will be 23 million overseas visitors in 1995, bringing in a revenue of £12 billion, which will grow to 28 million overseas visitors by 2000 with a revenue of £20 billion.

As tourism plays such a vital role in the economy, it is heavily marketed both in Britain and abroad. The British Tourist Authority promotes Britain as a holiday destination overseas, and has offices in twenty-seven countries. Internally, there is a hierarchy of organisations promoting tourism. At the national level, the English Tourist Board, the Scottish Tourist Board and the Welsh Tourist Board target the domestic market, whilst the Northern Ireland Tourist Board promotes Northern Ireland overseas as well as to the domestic market. At regional level, there are twelve regional tourist boards in England, thirty-two Area Tourist Boards in Scotland and three regional Tourism Councils in Wales. They are specifically responsible for promoting their region. At the local level, there are local tourist offices and tourist information centres located in individual towns and cities. These are supported by the local authorities and give detailed local information about places of interest, transport, eating out and entertainment.

The tourist information centres also provide detailed lists of accommodation, ranging from five-star hotels to camp sites. Britain has a wide range of accommodation types which are classified by the standard of facilities on offer. Large hotels tend to be owned by the large chains, such as Trust House Forte, but there are a number of smaller hotels and guest houses which are normally run by the proprietor. At the cheaper end of the scale, farmhouse and bed and breakfast accommodation are available and there is a growing increase in budget hotels. For longer holidays, self-catering accommodation is most popular and caravanning still ranks highest with 22 per cent of people on holiday staying in caravans. Holiday camps, such as Butlins in the 1960s, used to be considered rather down-market, but have now been upgraded, and are growing in popularity. Center Parcs, which has created a sub-tropical paradise in Sherwood Forest has proved to be a highly successful attraction and, as a result, a similar development has been located at Elveden Forest near Newmarket.

A comprehensive network of information exists for the visitor to

Britain. With the increase in tourism, marketing is being targeted at distributing visitors more evenly throughout the year, by promoting spring and autumn breaks, for example, and attracting visitors away from the areas of overcrowding.

Inevitably, the rapid growth of tourism has had a significant impact on the economy, on the environment, and on the local populations. While it has provided jobs throughout the country; attracted new investment into areas of decline; put a value on heritage areas, buildings and landscapes, thereby encouraging their conservation, there has also been a detrimental side to this rapid growth. In more sensitive landscapes, such as the Lake District, damage has been caused by excessive visitor pressure. Footpaths are eroding due to excess use. Popular rural villages, such as Broadway in the Cotswolds, have been swamped, tourists outnumbering local people many times over; traffic congestion has been accentuated in historical towns like Oxford and Bath, making life unpleasant for locals and tourists alike. In some places the failure to come to grips with the rapid increase in visitors, together with their associated vehicles, has resulted in tourism damaging the very attraction which those people have come to see. The rather haphazard way in which much tourism development has taken place has led inadvertently to tourism becoming a victim of its own success.

In common with many countries, the end of the 1980s and the early 1990s saw an upsurge in Britain in concern for the environment. Green issues became a firm fixture on the political agenda. Belatedly, some would say, the Government has taken an increased interest. Tourism and its associated infrastructure has not been immune to criticism. The Department of Employment, which is responsible for tourism, has stated, 'The Government attaches great importance to the environmental impact of tourism. Our view, however, is that a balance must be maintained between preserving or conserving those aspects of the environment which we all care about, whilst acknowledging that sensitive and imaginative developments can do much to enhance the enjoyment of our surroundings . . . We believe that with the correct management of resources and infrastructure tourism can and does have a beneficial effect on the environment.' This increasing concern for tourism and its impact on the environment was the subject of a special task force which was set up by the Government to review the situation in England in 1990. A similar report has now been completed for Scotland.

The task force comprised eighteen experts from the tourist industry, environment and conservation groups, heritage organisations, national government and local authorities. They set out to look at the impact of tourism on the environment, and to seek a harmonious balance between tourists, local residents and the environment. They looked at visitor management in historic towns, at popular tourist and heritage sites and in the countryside. They have made important recommendations concerning the future development of the tourist industry in England.

The report states, 'Whilst tourism is almost universally welcomed for the benefits and opportunities it creates, there is also a growing recognition of the need to see tourism in its environmental context – to acknowledge that tourism and the environment are interdependent and to look for ways to reinforce the positive relationship between the two.' In order to look at this relationship, they considered the interaction between the tourist, the host population and the destination.

To avoid the negative cycle that can result from poor management of visitors and the resource, the report recommends tourism management strategies which can be undertaken without depleting the resource, cheating the visitor or exploiting the local population. In essence, sustainable tourism. To implement such practices, the report lists the following guiding principles:

- The environment has an intrinsic value which outweighs its worth as a tourism asset. Its enjoyment by future generations and its long term survival must not be prejudiced by short term considerations.
- Tourism should be recognised as a positive activity with the potential to benefit the community and the place as well as the visitor.
- The relationship between tourism and the environment must be managed so that the environment is sustainable in the long term. Tourism must not be allowed to damage the resource, prejudice its future enjoyment or bring unacceptable impacts.
- Tourism activities and developments should respect the scale, nature and character of the place in which they are sited.
- In any location, harmony must be sought between the needs of the visitor, the place and the host community.
- In a dynamic world some change is inevitable and change can often be beneficial. Adaptation to change, however, should not be at the expense of any of these principles.
- The tourism industry, local authorities and environmental agencies all have a duty to respect the above principles and to work together to achieve their practical realisation.

The report has correctly identified the importance of good management practice as being critical to implementing these principles.

Undoubtedly there is a need for greater co-ordination of tourism strategies and policies and between the Government, the tourist industry and the local population and tourists. It recommends that structure and local plans should be the vehicle for implementing policy, having liaised closely with all the bodies who will be affected by the policy, and that informal plans and strategies should be used for implementing plans and solving management issues.

There are already several initiatives in place to promote such an approach. For example, in the Lake District the Cumbrian Tourist Authority is actively promoting five areas outside the main area of congestion, the idea being to encourage tourists to these sites to reduce the pressure on the Lake District. In Windsor, where 20 per cent of visitors arrive by coach, a large coach park has been built, which is signposted out of town, and avoids creating congestion in the centre. Some historic buildings, such as Chartwell in Kent, have introduced a timed ticketing system, where a fixed number of tickets are sold for 15-minute intervals, which prevents overcrowding, enables the visitor to appreciate the tour, and prevents damage to artifacts due to excessive visitor pressure. At Warwick Castle information on conservation is given to visitors, helping them to appreciate the resource and to identify with the work that is being done. In the North Pennines, which is an Area of Outstanding Natural Beauty, a Tourism Development Action Programme has been introduced to encourage tourism development in a sensitive manner, involving the local community in its inception. The English Tourist Board has published two practical management guides to help to disseminate information. One is for tour operators in National Parks, and the other is a *Green Tourism Manual* for use by both tour operators and developers.

These initiatives all bode well for the future of tourism in Britain. But is it enough, and are the measures sufficient? More information is needed about the visitor and the resource; techniques on visitor management will need to be refined and all the bodies involved in tourism – local authorities, developers, tour operators – will need to have a joint approach to achieve a balance between tourism and the environment. Government needs to lay down a comprehensive strategy for sustainable tourism, with penalties for those who breach it, reinforcing the recommendations given in the task force report. And finally, all the initiatives put forward will require substantial funding by the tourist industry.

There is some cynicism within the environmental lobby that, while the work of the task force has been laudable, it is not clear how much teeth the report's recommendations will have in dealing with contentious cases where the pressure for tourism development based on economic grounds is strong. As ever, the answers are easy to talk about, but difficult to implement. Nevertheless, there does appear to have been an important recognition on the part of the Government and the tourist industry that it must manage the whole range of tourism activities in a manner which does not destroy the very things that make them an attraction. In reality it has proved enormously difficult to give real values to the features which attracted people in the first place. The tourist industry does not contribute directly to a Highland landscape, or clean beaches, or maintaining rights of way; yet these are the very features that people come to see. Some initiatives have been taken, such as declaring some districts as Environmentally Sensitive Areas (ESAs), where farmers are encouraged through subsidies to farm in a way which conserves and enhances the landscape and its natural features. Certainly there is more room for other such initiatives and for solutions which seek to promote tourism which is socially acceptable, economically viable and environmentally sustainable.

How Green is Britain?

Britain has been dubbed 'the dirty man of Europe', but this singles out only one of the current 'green' issues – pollution. It does not portray a clear picture of the public concern for conservation held in Britain where over one million people have an active interest in wildlife, nor does it illustrate the amount that has been achieved by the conservation movement since World War II. In fact, the planning policies which have arisen from the Town and Country Planning Acts since the war have done a great deal to prevent development in areas of sensitivity by regulating it through planning controls. Green belts are to be found around the edges of larger towns and cities, and these have prevented much of the development sprawl that has occurred in other parts of the world.

The principal 'green issues' with which Britain is concerned today are: environmental protection and conservation of natural heritage; combating pollution, particularly atmospheric pollution (acid rain) and the pollution of water sources; recycling to maximise the use of resources; the protection and conservation of the built environment; the sustainable use of natural resources; and, on a global level, the contribution which Britain can make to alleviate the use of CFCs to combat the greenhouse effect.

The environment and green issues now feature highly on the political agenda, but this has not always been the case. Much of it is due to the increasing public concern for the environment which occurred during the 1970s and early 1980s, to the efficient lobbying by environmental organisations and to the increasing influence upon British legislation deriving from the European Community in Brussels. The Wildlife and Countryside Act 1981 amended all former UK legislation to conform to EEC standards. It strengthened the law to protect wild birds, animals, plants and endangered species. It created powers to establish Marine Nature Reserves and it revised the measures to safeguard Sites of Special Scientific Interest.

The beginnings of the nature conservation movement in Britain stem from the end of the 18th century. The Royal Society for the Prevention of Cruelty to Animals was behind the Bird Protection Act in 1869, and a local society established a bird reserve at Breydon Water as early as 1888. In 1889, the Royal Society for the Protection of Birds (RSPB) was set up and in 1895 the National Trust was formed. These two bodies are still widely supported today and rate among the most powerful non-governmental organisations. The Society for Preservation of Flora and Fauna, now the Flora and Fauna Preservation Society, was established in 1903. Charles Rothschild founded a Society for the Promotion of Nature Reserves in 1912 and by 1915 it had listed 251 areas of national importance for wildlife, of which 52 were recommended as nature reserves. The long-standing interest of the Victorians in natural history and science led to the formation of numerous amateur and scientific societies, such as The Royal Society and the British Ecological Society.

The Government officially gave recognition to the importance of nature conservation in Britain after World War II. The Society for the Promotion of Nature Reserves called a conference in 1941 to consider the establishment of nature reserves as part of post-war rural policy. They proposed that nature reserves should be used as wildlife sanctuaries, for research and education and for the enjoyment of the public. Their report coincided with the National Parks Committee report.

The Government's response was to form the Nature Conservancy, given statutory powers and duties by the National Parks and Access to the Countryside Act of 1949. Its remit was 'to provide scientific advice on the conservation and control of the natural flora and fauna of Great Britain; to establish, maintain and manage nature reserves in Great Britain, including maintenance of physical features of scientific interest; and to organise and develop the research and scientific services related thereto.' It was able to protect areas of important natural and semi-natural habitat through the establishment of national nature reserves, which were bought through an acquisition programme. By 1973 there were 135 national nature reserves covering 278,328 acres (112,723 hectares). This land-use designation was complemented by a network of Sites of Special Scientific Interest, SSSIs, where management agreements were made with owners, and compensation given if it prevented them from developing their land. In 1973 the organisation was reconstituted as the Nature Conservancy Council, with its research responsibilities being transferred to the Natural Environment Research Council under the Institute of Terrestrial Ecology. The first Marine Nature Reserve was recently established on Lundy island, although the Marine Conservation Society also has a number of voluntary reserves.

The Department of Environment is the government body with overall responsibility for land use policy, and has been responsible for funding the Nature Conservancy Council since 1973. The other department which had responsibility for the countryside and which had the same status as the Nature Conservancy Council, was the Countryside Commission which had a socio-economic role as opposed to a purely scientific one. The Commission was responsible for 'promoting conservation and enhancement of natural beauty and scenic amenity'. It also had responsibility for giving advice and administering grants to voluntary bodies and individuals for conservation improvements such as tree planting. It was responsible for England and Wales, but in Scotland the separate Countryside Commission for Scotland played a similar role. Also incorporated under the umbrella of the Department of Environment is responsibility for government policy on water and sewage, undertaken by the Water Authorities in England and Wales and by the River Purification Boards in Scotland.

There have been numerous recent changes and reviews in the organistion of the government bodies dealing with the British countryside. Since 1990 the role of the Countryside Commission and the Nature Conservancy Council combined to some degree. The Environmental Protection Act 1990 split the Nature Conservancy Council into three country agencies. In England, the Countryside Commission and Nature Conservancy Council have maintained their individual role, although the Nature Conservancy Council has changed its name to English Nature, but the two organisations were amalgamated in Wales to form the Countryside Council for

Wales in 1990. The Countryside Commission for Scotland and the Scottish Nature Conservancy Council will be merged in 1992 to form Scottish Natural Heritage. Meantime, a separate scientific committee, the Joint Nature Conservation Committee, was formed in 1991 which oversees all national and international aspects of nature conservation in Britain. This rationalisation will inevitably take time to work through, but many people see the unification as beneficial in the long term – a marriage of two natural partners who should never have been separated.

However, other government departments also have a significant influence on land use, such as the Ministry of Agriculture, Fisheries and Food. Government policy on agriculture determines land use of over 80 per cent of Britain. Since the Agriculture Act of 1947, government policy has been to produce food as cheaply and efficiently as possible. With the price support mechanisms of the Common Agricultural Policy, there is an unlimited market for the food produced. The success of the agricultural industry in meeting its remit, through the intensification of agricultural practices, has had a devastating effect upon the natural environment. Land owners who consider themselves conservationists at heart have taken a battering from the conservation lobby.

In forestry too there also came a time when foresters and conservationists could not see eye to eye and doggedly opposed each other, as commercial forestry became primarily coniferous, and the scale of afforestation in the uplands became a matter for public debate. However, the government body responsible for forestry, the Forestry Commission, has changed its emphasis from purely commercial forestry to multi-purpose forestry, giving a greater emphasis to management for wildlife, conservation and recreation. The Forestry Commission has successfully pioneered the way by example, and the forests of today are being managed to create habitat diversity as well as to produce a commercial crop of timber. The Forestry Commission has forty-two Forest Nature Reserves.

The lack of integrated resource management, as advocated by the World Conservation Strategy, has inevitably led to conflicting interests. As responsibility for the environment does not rest solely with the Department of Environment, there has been conflict between development and conservation due to the territorial and segmented approach of various government departments. Conservation equated with being anti-development, and individual interests clashed with broader interests. People struggling to make a living in rural areas found themselves faced with the ideals of urban man. This created resentment in rural parts where it was felt that the community and landscape were being preserved in aspic for the summer visitors. Fortunately, conservation has moved on since then. There have recently been developments in environmental economics, as put forward by Professor David Pearce in his *Blueprint for a green economy* which has tried to put an economic tag on the value of a natural resource. As a result, some initiatives have been taken, as in the forestry industry, to adopt a strategic planning appraisal approach to land use, to incorporate different land uses for the benefit of all. There is now greater communication between conservationists and others involved in land use and a greater recognition of the value of our nature resources.

Many areas have been protected by legislation and land-use designation and there are as many, if not more, non-statutory designations which have been put forward by wildlife trusts. There are ten National Parks in England and Wales which cover 10 per cent of the two countries. They are situated in the uplands and have their own planning and development controls which apply within the park area. The Peak District National Park and Snowdonia National Park are examples. In these areas, buildings must conform to the character of the area, and certain farming practices are restricted, so that the character of the landscape is retained. The Parks provide ranger services, environmental education and interpretation services for visitors, while managing the land to protect the landscape and wildlife, and also providing for public recreation. In certain areas, the Parks are so popular that honeypots have been created, with overcrowding and damage to the resource, so it has been necessary to zone off areas of greatest sensitivity and to encourage visitor movement to other areas.

In Scotland there are no National Parks, but the former Countryside Commission for Scotland designated forty National Scenic Areas within Scotland, which are conserved through planning measures and management agreements. In 1990 they produced a discussion document for the conservation and management of the mountain areas of Scotland. The Countryside Commission for Scotland recommended the establishment of four National Parks in the country. However, it is unlikely that the Government will make a decision before Scottish Natural Heritage is formed, and Scottish Natural Heritage are currently considering the formation of Natural Heritage Areas along the same lines.

In agriculture, the decision to encourage farmers to diversify into other areas, and to release land from agricultural production, has resulted in a plethora of different incentives. Land can be set aside from agricultural production with wildflower meadows being accepted as an alternative. Certain areas have been designated Environmentally Sensitive Areas, and these can qualify for various grants to enable farmers to practise farming in an environmentally sensitive way. Stone dykes can be reinstated, as can hedgerows. Grants are available for new tourism and leisure enterprises, and farm buildings can be adapted for other uses such as tea rooms, holiday cottages and workshops.

Other initiatives have been taken by the respective Countryside Commissions. In England and Wales, Heritage Coasts have been designated in areas of specific beauty or vulnerability. Long-distance footpaths have been created, and there have been a number of community schemes, particularly on the urban fringe, such as Community Forests. Local planning authorities have been encouraged to incorporate local conservation strategies in their work. Urban fringe projects, urban conservation, local nature reserves and the management of country parks are just some of the areas with which they are involved. Recycling initiatives for paper, glass, aluminium and plastic have been started in towns and cities throughout Britain. With 80 per cent of Britain's population living in towns, it is encouraging to see the degree of community involvement and enthusiasm for these schemes.

Pollution is a problem which has not been tackled until recently. Water sources have been polluted due to fertiliser run-off into streams; rivers have been polluted due to industries releasing untreated waste, and raw sewage is still pumped out to sea. Large industries using coal as a power source release huge amounts of sulphur into the atmosphere, which has caused acid rain in Scandinavia. Despite the recent shift in government policy to try and ensure that the 'polluter pays', power stations have done little to rectify their emissions. Car exhaust emissions came under legislation in 1991, and they are now tested to approved standards. Encouraging people to use unleaded petrol has also been advocated by the Government.

Britain's beaches have a poor reputation for cleanliness, and many fail to come up to EEC standards on water quality. The Marine Conservation Society is demanding legislation to protect bathers on Britain's polluted beaches. In 1990, 103 of the 446 designated British bathing waters failed basic sewage pollution standards. The Government has launched a £3 billion clean-up initiative. Beaches which have a high standard of water quality and services are given a Blue Flag Award by the Foundation for Environmental Education in Europe. Britain currently ranks sixth from the bottom of the European league.

Apart from the immense developments for conservation which have been instigated by the various government departments, mention must be made of the powerful and committed non-governmental organisations concerned with the conservation of our natural resources. Their persistent dedication and professional approach to lobbying has been a significant factor in raising the profile of conservation in Britain. They range from the overall pressure groups such as Greenpeace and Friends of the Earth, which take a general view over a number of issues, to a significant number of organisations which specialise in specific areas. The Royal Society for Nature Conservation has over 250 area groups which are serviced by the society but run by local trusts. They have about 1400 reserves. The Royal Society for the Protection of Birds has created a powerful lobby for bird protection, and is now a major landowner in Britain with 118 reserves covering 187,000 acres (75,735 hectares). They have a huge membership which stands at 850,000 of which 117,000 are junior members. This highlights the significant increase in their membership, which was 6000 in 1946. The National Trust manages land and houses which have been bequeathed to the nation, and they too have had a significant increase in membership. The World Wide Fund for Nature (UK) initiates and funds conservation programmes within the UK. The Council for the Protection of Rural England, the Ramblers Association, the Council for Environmental Conservation, the Wildfowl Trust, the Historic Houses Association, the British Trust for Ornithology, the Mammal Society, the Woodland Trust, the Scottish Wildlife Trust, the British Trust for Conservation Volunteers are just a selection of the many organisations which are helping to conserve the natural and built environment.

In politics, the Green Party was established in 1985, but its vote is too fickle and evenly spread to give parliamentary representation. The main political parties have since adopted greater recognition of green principles in their manifestos, although rhetoric on the part of politicians of all persuasions has yet to be translated fully into action on a grand scale.

Sightseeing

As Britain's popularity as a tourist destination increases, it becomes more and more difficult to avoid the hordes of other visitors travelling around the country and visiting its attractions. Yet, with some planning, a little imagination and originality, you can still enjoy Britain at its best, without the crowds.

In summer and winter, London is still the most popular tourist destination, with 60 per cent of international visitors visiting the capital during their stay in Britain. So it is vital that you choose the timing of any trip to London very carefully. Arrive at the wrong time, and you could end up with the impression that every hotel bed in the city is already booked, except naturally the most expensive; not to mention all the theatre entertainment. It is best to avoid the peak holiday periods of July and August, and also holiday periods such as Easter, Christmas and Bank Holidays. The London Tourist Board provides useful information which will help determine your plans. If possible, visit heritage attractions out of season, but if you must visit during the busy summer months, try visiting major attractions on weekdays or go early to beat the masses.

If you do visit Britain during the summer, be prepared for congested holiday traffic, more expensive accommodation and overcrowding at the popular tourist attractions, such as Buckingham Palace, as well as in popular historical towns, such as Oxford and Bath. The majority of holidays are taken in the south of England, so if you want to avoid congestion, try heading north. While 78 per cent of overseas tourists visit London and the south-east, only 2 per cent visit Northumberland; and Scotland, Wales and Northern Ireland have plenty to offer too.

With the diversity of Britain's built and natural heritage there is no need to follow the crowds, and you will be well rewarded if you travel slightly off the beaten track. Typical 'English villages' can be found throughout England, and the undiscovered ones are preferable to ones like Broadway in the Cotswolds, where visitors outnumber local residents during the summer months. One of the aims of this guide is to encourage visitors to try and pick the areas which are not given a high profile.

At the level of individual towns and tourist attractions, Britain's most problematic honeypots tend to be in London itself, or within easy reach of London. So be prepared to jostle with countless others if you visit any of London's better known attractions, such as Westminster Abbey and St Paul's Cathedral, during the high season, or any of the following: Bath, Oxford, Cambridge, York, Windsor Castle or Hampton Court. Other honeypot areas are in National Parks, where, for example, places like the Lake District have become victims of their own popularity, with consequent problems of overcrowding. It is worth finding out where these areas are, as they can sometimes be difficult to enjoy due to the sheer volume of visitors.

Communications

A comprehensive rail, road and air transport network makes travelling within the British Isles relatively straightforward. Information is readily accessible, and it remains for visitors to select the mode or modes of transport which best suit their holiday requirements. Cars can be hired to give increased independence; rail passes may be obtained for those who do not want to drive; or a combination, such as flying and driving, may provide the best option. For the good tourist, of course, our advice would be to use public transport wherever possible, and if driving is the preferred method, to explore motorail options where practicable. Lead-free petrol is readily available in all but the most remote parts of Britain, and this is to be actively encouraged.

The **rail network** provides a fast and comfortable service between all the country's main cities and towns. Run by British Rail, the prices when compared with European countries are relatively expensive, but there are plenty of special offers available, and it is well worth finding out about them from the main railway stations. Mostly they have special conditions, such as only being available on off-peak services, but the cost savings are considerable.

For those coming from abroad, Britrail passes or Travel passes should be purchased in the home country prior to arrival in Britain. These offer unlimited rail miles, sometimes in combination with ferries and buses. Within Britain there are a number of special railcards for families, students, young persons, senior citizens and those in the armed forces. 'All-over Rover' tickets may be purchased for those who want to travel throughout Britain, or alternatively the Rail Rover ticket can be bought by those who wish to travel in specific regions. On certain routes, such as London to Edinburgh, it is possible to buy an Apex ticket, one week prior to travelling. Saver tickets are more economical than return tickets, but again, certain rules apply to travel times. An ordinary return fare is no cheaper than two single fares, but a day return fare is cheaper. During high season, there are a variety of excursion fares. For example it is possible to do a 'Grand Highland Circular' tour by train and bus from Inverness to Fort William, Mallaig, Armadale, Kyle and back to Inverness. Details of different types of fares and excursions are available from British Rail, and are also published in the magazine *Scene*.

Between the major cities, British Rail operates its Inter-City service, which has faster trains. In the summer of 1991, British

Rail introduced the 225 service, which offers a speedier service on the principle direct routes. Other routes are less fast, often with fairly antiquated rolling stock, but these are gradually being improved. On the major routes, first- and second-class rail travel is available, first-class generally being about 33 per cent more expensive. There is a notable difference between the comfort offered, but in the main, first-class tends to be used by business executives. Pay phones, a restaurant car, buffet and bar are available on the main routes, and timetables usually give an indication of the services offered on each journey. The food is variable, sometimes excellent and at other times notoriously bad. A sleeper service, both first- and second-class, is available between certain cities, namely Aberdeen, Inverness and Edinburgh to Euston, and Fort William and Edinburgh to Bristol. This is an ideal way to travel if you don't want to have to sit in a train all day, as long as you don't mind missing the scenery! It is also possible to take your car on these routes. The motorail service saves a day's car journey which would probably have been spent on one of the motorways – an option to be carefully reviewed for its environmental considerations, not to mention the frustration of delays as a result of the heavy volume of traffic and never-ending roadworks.

In all cases, and especially when travelling on a special ticket, it is well worthwhile booking in advance. Many trains become uncomfortably full at certain times, and reserving a seat will make a considerable difference to the comfort of the journey.

Travelling by **air** is an alternative to rail and car, and comes into its own where rail or car journeys exceed four hours. Britain's main gateway airports are Heathrow and Gatwick in London, and Glasgow and Manchester, which receive many international flights. Other regional airports, of which there are over thirty, offer internal flights within Britain, and many have increasing traffic links with Europe. There are several domestic airlines operating in Britain. British Midland and British Airways offer a service between Heathrow, Glasgow, Edinburgh, Manchester, Birmingham and Belfast. There are a range of other airlines, such as Dan Air, Air UK, Manx Airlines and Loganair. The travel time between London and Edinburgh is one hour fifteen minutes, although you have to take into consideration the time on the ground checking in and recovering baggage. A light snack and drinks are offered on most services, and there is generally a good bus link between the airports and their home cities. Ticket prices vary a great deal. Again it is worth investigating special offers, which are available at off-peak times. Apex fares, super-saver returns and standby tickets can give up to 50 per cent discount off the standard fares. Information on flights is readily available from the airports and flight companies.

There are several options available if travelling by **road**: coach, bus or car, and taxi if in a town. The road network is well developed, but due to the increased amount of traffic, congestion is a major problem, especially during holiday periods. Traffic congestion is principally concentrated in the south-east of England, centring on London. The M25 which circles London is continuously overcrowded, as are the motorways which link onto it. Road maintenance can also cause severe delays, so it's worth finding out where this is taking place. Tune in to local radio stations or telephone the AA or RAC before embarking on your journey. The road network may be divided into three types of road: the motorways, which are the principal routes linking different parts of Britain, have two or three lanes going in each direction and have a speed limit of 70 m.p.h (113 km.p.h); dual carriageways, as their name implies, have two lanes of traffic each way; and trunk roads, which have a lane of traffic in each direction and are graded between A and C, with A being the more direct route and of a higher quality. The AA (Automobile Association) has a route planning service, and can also advise on which routes to avoid. In the case of an accident or breakdown the AA also provides a call-out service, and will arrange for the car to be transported to a garage or, if a relay member, to your destination.

In Britain you drive on the left hand side of the road, and distances are measured in miles. It is compulsory to wear a seat belt if sitting in the front of the car and, according to new legislation, in the back, if seatbelts are fitted; children must be strapped in and sit in the back seat and penalties are given for breaking the speed limit. Penalties are particularly severe for drinking-and-driving.

Travelling by car obviously gives a great deal of independence for exploring less well-known places, but using trains, buses and bikes can also achieve this. Scenic routes and places of historical interest are signposted off motorways and main roads. Petrol is expensive. One litre of unleaded petrol on average costs 50 pence. If you are planning a long journey but need the flexibility of a hired car, it can be cheaper to travel the long distances by train or plane, then hire a car at your destination. Discounts on car hire are given to passengers by British Rail and also by some of the flight companies, such as British Airways. The price of car hire varies, but a Ford Escort will cost in the region of £170 for a week with unlimited mileage, with a sliding scale price charge if hiring for a longer period. The same car if hired for one month would cost £22 per day.

The express buses or coaches link 2000 towns and cities. They offer a competitive service to British Rail, often costing a great deal less. In more remote areas they can be the only form of public transport available. Over the last decade, inter-city coach travel has become more sophisticated, with travellers receiving a similar service to flying: on a long journey a light snack is offered and a video will sometimes be played.

Local buses are frequently available in towns, and a limited service is normally offered in rural areas. Information is given by the local information offices, or at the bus stations. *On the Move* is a useful magazine which gives information on travelling by bus in Britain, and is available from newsagents.

Being an island, travelling by water is another means of transport. Britain has good ferry links with Europe, Ireland and the outer islands. Most ferries take cars, but there are also some passenger-only ferries. On the longer routes, ferries get booked well in advance, especially during peak holiday periods, so it is best to make an advance reservation through a travel agent. The Channel Tunnel opens in 1993, creating a rail link with France, which will provide an alternative to travelling by ferry or plane. Within Britain there is also a well-developed canal network, and the waterways provide a peaceful, if slow, means of travelling through the countryside.

The Art of Being a Good Tourist

The art of being a good tourist may be divided into two stages: the initial planning stage, including the choice of holiday, accommodation and means of transport; and, secondly, the code of conduct once at your destination. There are no hard and fast rules about being a good tourist in Britain, but a little thought about the reasons why you are travelling to a specific destination and how you behave when you arrive can make a difference to your own appreciation of your holiday and to your reception in the area of your choice. Have you considered the impact you make on your holiday destination as a tourist, or how perceptions of tourists may be influenced by your behaviour?

A great deal of the fun of going on holiday can be derived at the planning stage. Local libraries and tourist board literature can give you plenty of ideas of places to visit and what to see when you are there. The timing of your visit can definitely make a difference to your enjoyment. During the peak holiday season of July and August, many areas, such as beach resorts, National Parks and the main heritage attractions, become overcrowded, spoiling the visitor experience and exerting pressure on local resources; so if you have the choice, visit at a different time of year, or visit some of the less well-known places.

The majority of visitors to Britain arrive by plane, and most Britons holidaying in the country prefer to travel independently in their own cars. For the visitor from abroad, hiring a car can provide a high degree of freedom; however, cars are about the least environmentally-friendly choice of transport on offer, even if most are now converted to lead-free petrol. Congestion on major routes, especially in the south-east of England, is a serious problem, making for stressful journeys that can take twice as long as anticipated, particularly over Bank Holiday periods. So it is well worth considering other transport options. Train and coach services are comfortable and reliable and link the main cities throughout Britain. Internal flights offer another option. If you still want the independence of travelling by car, what about travelling the long distances by public transport, and hiring a car at the other end, or taking your car on motorail for long journeys? Alternatively, why not consider going on a walking, cycling or sailing holiday, where you not only get plenty of fresh air and physical activity, but – as long as you choose your destination carefully – have less impact on the environment as well?

There are plenty of choices of holiday accommodation and these can provide you with the opportunity of meeting the locals and paying money to boost the local economy, which is often fragile in rural areas and heavily dependent on the income derived from tourism. At the upper end of the scale, many **country house hotels** are located in former stately homes, which have been restored for tourism purposes. **Small hotels** and **guest houses**, which are run by the proprietor, and **bed and breakfast (B&B)** accommodation where local people take you into their homes, are preferable to staying in a large chain hotel, and you are more assured of a personal welcome and a genuine interest in your welfare. **Self-catering** accommodation too, where people let houses, cottages and chalets, can help you to fit harmoniously into the local community while benefiting its economy. **Caravanning and camping**, on the other hand, provide little income to the local community if you bring all your provisions with you, and caravans especially make for traffic congestion on roads, causing irritation to local people. If you do not want to stay on a large, self-contained site, the Caravan Club supplies to its members a list of sites which accept no more than five caravans. These 'certificated locations' are often in farmers' fields and are a good source of supplementary income to the farmer, without being an eyesore. When staying on a farm in this manner, or as a B&B guest, ask if any of their produce is for sale.

If you are going on a self-catering holiday, or travelling with a caravan, try to shop locally, instead of doing a mega-shop at your home supermarket, and if you are shopping for souvenirs, try and buy local arts and crafts rather than something made in Taiwan. It all helps the local economy and also helps tourists integrate into the community. Sport is another area where you can soon become assimmilated into the local community. Similar interests can quickly dispel any mistrust, and friendships can easily be made. If you have a particular sporting interest, such as sailing, check out local regattas with your tourist office.

A degree of sensitivity and a consideration for other people's welfare is essentially all that is required of a tourist's **behaviour**. If staying in the countryside, remember that the local people are often up working at the crack of dawn, and do not appreciate the revelry of late-night parties. Many people go to the country and to the seaside for peace and quiet, and noise can seriously impede their enjoyment. Ghettoblasters on the beach or in a quiet country setting destroy the tranquillity of the countryside for other people.

The British are generally courteous to visitors although the manner of greeting people varies considerably. If passing someone in the countryside, most people will say 'Good morning' or 'Hello'. In the towns and cities there is rarely any dialogue between strangers. All people in Britain speak English, but to their chagrin, do not have the multilingual fluency of their European neighbours; so it is useful to have a reasonable command of the English language.

The British are liberal in their dress, with an attitude of 'each to their own'. In smart restaurants and hotels, the appropriate dress is expected, but for example, if going out to the theatre the choice of dress is optional. In places of worship, there are no strict rules on dress, as in some other countries; nevertheless, shorts and T-shirts should be avoided. Photography too, although rarely forbidden, can upset people who have come to worship. The photography of people is very much up to the discretion of the photographer, but a good rule is 'if in doubt, ask'. Payment is optional and again depends on the situation; however, street performers deserve a few pennies in the hat.

In the major cities of Britain, such as London and Edinburgh, begging is now more common than it was. Britain does have a social security system, but policy changes in the last few years have seen a dramatic rise in the homeless. Although many beggars are genuine, there are also some who make false appeals to your sympathy, displaying signs of 'homeless, hungry and suffering from

AIDS', who can be people out to make a quick buck. Should you wish to give more than your loose change, consider giving a donation to one of the many charities for the homeless.

Women are able to travel around Britain with a high degree of freedom from harassment. In the cities, certain rough areas should be avoided late at night, but on the whole it is as safe as anywhere else for the single woman travelling alone. In London there is a late-night taxi service run for women, and there are also some holidays which cater specifically for the woman traveller, as well as hostels like the YWCA.

When staying in the countryside, try to practise the **country code**. Avoid dropping litter, close gates, keep to footpaths, and avoid making fires, particularly in areas such as forests which have a high fire risk; a careless match can wreak havoc on tree plantations, which are often in remote areas and take years to grow. However enticing it might be to pick wild flowers, and collect shells, remember that we have a diminishing wilderness.

Red Tape

Visitors to Britain must produce a valid national passport or, in the case of EC nationals, an identity card, with which to establish their identity and nationality. Visitors from the EC, USA, Japan, most of South America and many Commonwealth countries need nothing else. Visas are required by nationals of Bangladesh, Ghana, India, Nigeria, Pakistan, Sri Lanka, Albania, Bulgaria, Czechoslovakia, Hungary, Poland, Romania, Turkey, Russia, Argentina, Haiti and Cuba. All African citizens require a visa except Cote d'Ivoire, Niger and South Africa. All Asian citizens require a visa except Bahrain, Israel, Japan, Kuwait, Korea, Qatar and the United Arab Emirates, and these can be obtained from British embassies, high commissions or consulates. If in doubt about your visa requirements, check before arriving in Britain.

There is no restriction on the amount of currency or travellers' cheques being brought in and out of Britain. The UK has a decimal currency system where £1 (one pound sterling) = 100 pence. Notes are issued to the value of £50, £20, £10 and £5. Coins are £1, 50p, 20p, 10p, 5p, 2p and 1p. Scotland, the Channel Islands and the Isle of Man also have some different notes and coins, but their monetary system is the same although only Scottish money is interchangeable. Travellers' cheques are widely accepted, as are the major credit cards such as American Express, Visa/Barclaycard,

Mastercard/Access and Diners Club. Sterling travellers' cheques are preferable. Eurocheques, although perhaps less useful than in other EC countries, are also widely accepted in the hotels, restaurants and stores of the major cities. For the best exchange rates use the high street banks, which offer a better rate of exchange than hotels and *bureaux de change*.

It is advisable to travel with a comprehensive health insurance, but the National Health Service provides free first aid/emergency treatment to all visitors. Thereafter, charges are made, unless the visitor's country has a reciprocal health care agreement with the UK. All EC countries are covered, and other nationals should check with their country prior to leaving. Alternatively, full details are available from the Department of Health. No special immunisations are required for entry into Britain. In the case of an emergency, the number to dial for an ambulance is 999. Many of the larger towns have 24-hour chemists.

The main public holidays are: January 1, January 2 (Scotland only), March 17 (Northern Ireland only), late March/early April: Good Friday, Easter Monday (except Scotland), first Monday in May, last Monday in May, 12 July (Northern Ireland only), first Monday in August (Scotland only), last Monday in August (except Scotland), December 25 and December 26. If Christmas Day, Boxing Day or New Year's Day falls at the weekend, the next weekday is taken as a public holiday.

On these days, banks, shops and almost everything else will be closed. In addition, there are many local holidays, details of which are available from the local tourist boards and information centres. Most towns have a tourist information centre, identified by a small '*i*', which is an excellent source of local information. Many are linked into a national computer network, which can provide you with details for the next area you are visiting.

In addition to this local network there are the national tourist boards. These can be contacted at the following addresses:

British Tourist Authority: Thames Tower, Black's Road, London W6 9EL (Tel 081 846 9000).

English Tourist Board: Thames Tower, Black's Road, London W6 9EL (Tel 081 846 9000).

Scottish Tourist Board: 23 Ravelston Terrace, Edinburgh EH4 3EU (Tel 031 332 2433) or 17 Cockspur Street, London SW1Y 5BL (Tel 071 930 8661).

Wales Tourist Board: Brunel House, 2 Fitzalan Road, Cardiff, CF2 1UY (Tel 0222 499909) or The Wales Bureau, The British

Travel Centre, 12 Lower Regent Street, London SW1 4PQ (Tel 071 409 0969).

Northern Ireland Tourist Board: River House, 48 High Street, Belfast, BT1 2DS (Tel 0232 231221/246609) or 11 Berkeley Street, London WIX 5AD (Tel 071 493 0601).

Budgeting

For visitors to Britain, the cost of a holiday is comparable with France and North America.

An average 2-star hotel will cost about £30 per double room, with an additional £3–£8 for breakfast. In the cities the cost of a 2-star room rises to anywhere between £45 and £65. It is possible to dine out well in Britain without breaking the bank. In the larger cities, such as London and Birmingham, there's a greater choice of restaurants, so it is still possible to have a reasonable 3-course meal for £15 (add another £10 for wine and coffee with the meal), without having to venture out to the more expensive restaurants. However, stopping for morning coffee or afternoon tea can soon make a hole in your purse. A Devon tea, with fresh scones, cream and jam will see little change out of £5.

Taxis charge 60p for picking you up, and have a scale of charges thereafter – 90p for the first 400 yards, 10p per additional 200 yards, 10p per extra passenger, 10p for extra luggage and so on. Roughly, a mile journey would cost about £2.50. If travelling in town, buses are very reasonable, costing on average about 50p per ride. It is difficult to generalise about rail fares, as their pricing mechanism is closely tied in with their marketing system, so there is no scale charge per kilometre as on the Continent. If travelling around Britain, a travel pass or All-over Rover ticket is the best option, but still expensive, working out at £320 for a 15-day pass. If coming from abroad, the cheapest option is to buy a Brit Rail pass before you leave. Pick up a copy of British Rail's *Scene* magazine which will give you all the different budget options. On the whole, coach travel still works out cheaper than travelling by rail, even with the special option tickets available from British Rail. Petrol averages about 50p a litre for unleaded, but there is no charge for travelling on Britain's motorways. Car hire costs about £170 a week for a Ford Escort with unlimited mileage. If hiring a car, it will probably work out cheaper to travel long distances by train or plane, and hire a car at the other end. It is possible to hire cars from most main-line stations, and some flight companies have arrangements with car hire firms for reduced hire charges for their passengers.

Entry charges to museums and monuments vary between, on average, £3–£5, although many are free, and some have one day a week when the entry fee is reduced.

All in all, a budget of about £60 per person per day will guarantee a reasonably comfortable existence, staying in clean, safe accommodation, doing a bit of sightseeing, and eating out twice a day in not-too-basic restaurants. But add another £25 or so for days spent in cities, or if you are travelling alone, with no one to share the cost of the bedroom.

When to Go

Travelling out of season in Britain can have many advantages. Fewer crowds at the favourite tourist attractions, such as the Tower of London; cheaper accommodation, with special offers for short breaks, such as two nights for the price of one; less traffic on the roads and fewer people in the popular touring areas, such as the Lake District. The golden hills of autumn in the Highlands of Scotland, with stags roaring during the rut, or the fresh green of spring in the valleys of Wales can be more breathtaking than the scenery of high summer. Even in winter months, there can be clear, sunny days, but the days are short, with only six hours of good daylight in the far north during mid-winter.

British destinations in general are less congested outside the high tourist season of spring and summer and consequently do not suffer from the inflationary prices that equate with the high season. Details of special offers and short breaks can be obtained from the tourist authority. It is also worthwhile checking with them what attractions are open and whether they are open for a restricted time period, as many places close down completely during the winter – the downside to travelling out of season. Another aspect to consider is the weather. Although British weather is unpredictable at the best of times, statistically there is more rain during the winter months. However, winter temperatures rarely extend much below freezing and average 4°C in winter. On the other hand, the off-peak months of the tourist season, during the spring and autumn, can yield bright spring days or Indian summers.

There is a general tendency to encourage more people to visit Britain during spring and autumn, and many towns have taken to organising arts programmes and short festivals during this time. For example, in Edinburgh, apart from the international festival in August, there is an annual folk festival in March, a spring jazz festival, and a 'spring fling' which is a mini-festival of sorts, and offers a selection of workshops in dance, drama and practical art. Details are available from regional and local tourist information centres.

Where are the Positive Holidays?

How do you recognise a good, or in green travel terms, a 'positive' holiday package, when there is such a variety of holidays to choose from? Initially, you can obtain a great deal of information from the holiday brochure. Things to look out for are: information about the cultural and ecological background of the holiday region; guidelines on appropriate, tactful behaviour at the destinations; mention of any contribution which the company makes to conservation bodies; and text and photographs which avoid clichés and stereotypes. Does the brochure talk about the good and bad and make an honest attempt to reflect reality? Do they use resources responsibly, printing on recycled paper perhaps?

Apart from the brochure, you should analyse the tour operator itself. Is it small in scale, and therefore more likely to be low-impact? Do they use locally-owned facilities? Do they accurately reflect the character of the region in what they offer? – its natural, cultural and historical riches? What impact does the tour operator have on the region? Are they socially and environmentally responsible? Do they give you the opportunity to get to know members of the local community? Is the accommodation on offer in keeping with the character of the homes of the local inhabitants? And is public transport used to get you around? Considering all these options will give you a flavour of the type of company running the tours and can help you to decide which one to choose.

The following section contains recommended national tour operators and organisations. For local operators specialising in small-scale tours to their own region, look under the *Good Alternatives* section of the appropriate regional chapter.

General Holidays

The majority of overseas visitors who come to Britain prefer to travel independently, accounting for 30 per cent of foreign tourists, as compared with the 12 per cent who come on an inclusive package holiday. However, although about one third of Britons head abroad to the sun for their main holiday, there has been a great increase in the number of people taking short holidays within Britain. Holiday resorts and holiday camps still retain their popularity, and the last few years have seen enormous improvements in the quality of holiday offered.

The advantages of choosing a package are that you know exactly what is included in the price and what is not, and you can budget accordingly. Also, you can rest assured that everything is arranged for you, so that you can concentrate on enjoying your holiday without any of the administrative hassles. When choosing a tour operator, check to see if they or their holidays are recommended by the tourist boards, and whether they are members of the **Association of Independent Tour Operators (AITO)** (PO Box 180, Isleworth, Middlesex, TW7 7EA. Tel 081 569 8092). A further plus point is deserved if they are supporters of **Green Flag International**. The Green Flag Scheme aims to encourage tour operators to work in partnership with conservation.

If you go to a travel agent, there is a wealth of literature to choose from on a variety of package holidays, ranging from touring holidays by coach to self-drive, rail or air, with accommodation included in the package. Many hotels offer bargain deals – short breaks, two nights for the price of one, no single-room supplement, seven nights for the price of six, children under 16 for less than half price, and mid-week reductions – with attractive travel options by rail, coach and air.

Self-catering accommodation, inclusive of travel to the site, is not typical, as most people prefer to make their own arrangements when caravanning, camping or staying in a chalet or cottage. There are, however, a few companies which offer self-catering packages, one of which is **Warner** (bookable through a travel agent only) which offers a selection of self-catering and chalet family holidays in holiday centres and holiday villages in England and Wales, with the option of special rail and coach fares. Voted the English holiday and travel company of the year in 1990, a week's holiday staying in a chalet, sleeping six, at the Chesil Beach Holiday Village in Weymouth costs about £300. If travelling from London to Weymouth by train, the additional return fare would be about £15, or about £10 by coach. Many of the holiday centres and holiday villages are located in or near traditional seaside resorts, which still offer the usual amenities – a leisure centre, swimming pools, theatres, cinemas, amusement arcades, sea and river trips and miniature railways, together with a variety of festival/carnival events and a sandy beach. When choosing a holiday resort see if they have received a 'rose' or 'thistle' award, a tourist board classification for excellence, and look out for beaches which have a **Blue Flag Award**, as this sign of high standards means not only that the seawater is of an acceptable quality, but is also indicative of a responsible attitude towards the environment.

Another option is to take a touring holiday by **coach or mini-bus**, or to take a **self-drive** tour, where all accommodation is arranged for you. There are a number of companies offering this type of package. **Wallace Arnold Tours Ltd** (107 Hope Street, Glasgow, G2 6LL. Tel 041 221 8921) offer a selection of coach holidays throughout Britain, ranging from a five-day mid-week break to a ten days centred holiday or a nine days touring holiday. With pick-up points in Northern Ireland and Scotland, prices are extremely reasonable. For example, a seven day spring break in Torquay costs about £150, fully inclusive, and also incorporates an excursion programme. At the upper end of the market, **Farm and Country Tours in Great Britain Ltd** (4 West Stanhope Place, Edinburgh, EH12 5HQ. Tel 031 337 7722) offer a 14-day tour around Britain in a luxury coach, costing around £1160 per person. The company also offers a self-drive touring holiday in rural Britain, where you can take your own car or hire one, and a personalised itinerary, route plan and bed and breakfast accommodation will be arranged for you. A week's car hire and bed and breakfast will cost on average about £510 for a couple.

Hotel packages are predominantly connected with the large hotel groups and often include rail and air travel options at a reduced rate. Some, such as **Stakis** and **Trust House Forte**, operate their own schemes. The hotels are of a high standard, and given a start rating of one to five which compares with the tourist board classifications for accommodation standards. Travel agents can provide plenty of literature on this type of holiday, with publications such as *Superbreak*, *Goldenrail*, *Rainbow* and *Embassy Breaks*. British Airways offer their own special breaks programme under *Leisure Traveller* (bookable through travel agents). Featuring short breaks in Britain and Ireland, staying in 2-5 star hotels, a three night stay, flying from Heathrow to Shetland, staying in a 3-star hotel, would cost about £350. There are certain conditions attached, such as the break must include a Saturday night, and there can be restrictions on times of travel. However it is possible to opt for a fly-drive package only; take an optional excursion; or have a reduction for children under eleven.

Packages inclusive of air travel are not restricted to British Airways alone. Hotel groups have linked up with other flight companies, such as Dan Air, Air UK and Manx Airlines. Similarly hotel groups have joined with British Rail and Inter-City to offer inclusive rail packages. One example is **Goldenrail** London breaks (bookable through travel agents). A week's holiday in a 3-star hotel would cost about £220 for the hotel and, if travelling from Glasgow, about £100 by rail and about £120 by plane.

There are also a number of '**home-stay** schemes', whose classifications range from 'standard' to 'up-market'. Some of the organisations running these schemes are: **Visit Britain** (The Old Brickyard, Rye, East Sussex, TN31 7EE. Tel 0797 224 871); **Country Homes and Castles** (118 Cromwell Road, London, SW7 4ET. Tel 071 370 4445) and **Families in Britain** (Martins Cottage, Martins Lane, Birdham, Chichester, West Sussex, PO20 7AU. Tel 0243 51222).

Adventure/Activity Holidays

Britain's diversity of natural resources offers a range of opportunities for the outdoor enthusiast, from long-distance walking, mountaineering, skiing, cycling and riding to water-based activities such as sailing, canoeing and windsurfing. Interest in these activities has developed enormously with the general trend towards health and fitness. The other growth area is in activities which relate to a special hobby or interest – from study tours to lace-making, painting and steam engines.

Walking

A favourite outdoor activity is walking, and there is a network of footpaths throughout Britain, from the traditional rights of way through the countryside to the long-distance footpaths such as the West Highland Way, and many of these routes have been developed or upgraded in recent years. Hill-walking has long been a popular pastime, and in Scotland many rise to the challenge of walking 'munroes', which are peaks over 3000 ft. (900 m.). The **Ordnance Survey** (Maybush, Romsey Road, Southampton, SO9 4DH. Tel 0703 792000) provides detailed maps of the whole country at a scale of 1:50,000, known as the 'Landranger' maps. These give details of footpaths, as well as contours, and are ideal for short and long-distance walking for the experienced walker. As the highest peak in Britain is only just over 4000 ft. (1200 m.), many people do not anticipate adverse conditions in the hills, and each year there are mountain-rescue call-outs for people who have got into difficulties through being inadequately prepared. The weather can change very quickly, so suitable clothing and footwear, a map and a compass should be taken. It is not often appreciated that Arctic conditions can be simulated in the Cairngorms during the winter.

In Scotland, there is a regular weather report on Radio Scotland for hill-walkers at the weekends. The **Ramblers' Association** (1–5 Wandsworth Road, London, SW8 2XX. Tel 071 582 6878) aims to protect rights of way and campaigns for access to open countryside and an increased awareness of the environment. It has details of a programme of walks throughout Britain. Guided walks at a local level are often arranged by rangers in National Parks and Nature Reserves. For example, the **Scottish Wildlife Trust** (25 Johnstone Terrace, Edinburgh, EH1 2NY. Tel 031 226 4602) has guided walks on some of its larger reserves.

There are a number of specialised walking holidays, which range from short walks to long-distance treks. One of these is **C n' Do Scotland Ltd** (Howlands Cottage, Sauchieburn, Stirling, FK7 9PZ. Tel 0786 812355) which has a programme of walking holidays throughout Scotland. All holidays are accompanied by an experienced guide, and groups are limited so that parties blend into their surroundings and ample opportunities are provided for appreciating the countryside, its flora and fauna. All transport is provided to and from the base at Stirling and holidays range from wilderness backpacking treks, camping out or staying in bothies and carrying your own equipment, to serviced holidays on the long-distance routes, where you only need to carry a light pack. Summer and winter walking programmes are available, and the company gives comprehensive information on what equipment you need to bring. As members of British Rail's 'Ticketline', they are also able to offer rail-inclusive holidays. **Ossian Guides** (Sanna, Newtonmore, Inverness-shire, PH20 1DT. Tel 05403 402) offer a variety of walking options, from back-packing wilderness treks to comfortable hotel-based walking holidays. They provide transport from airports and railway stations, and a week's walking holiday costs about £250.

English Wanderer (13 Wellington Court, Spencers Wood, Reading RG7 1BN. Tel 0734 882515) offer weekend to week-long walking holidays with guides, in various attractive locations in England, Wales and Scotland. The company is a member of BAHA and prices start at around £75 for a weekend break, or £200 for one of the longer holidays, inclusive of accommodation, meals and transport. For walks with a theme, try **Instep Linear Walking Holidays**, (35 Cokeham Road, Lancing, Sussex BN15 5AF. Tel 0903 766475), many of whose walks follow canals. Other itineraries include the South Downs Way and Wainwright's Coast-to-Coast walk. Weekend breaks (including accommodation and tuition) start at about £60, while a fortnight's holiday will cost £300 or more.

A combination of walking and mountaineering holidays is provided by specialist centres, such as **Glenmore Lodge Training Centre** (NSTC, Aviemore, Inverness-shire, PH22 1QN. Tel 0479 86256), which has established itself as one of the leading outdoor centres in Europe for summer and winter activities, or specialist companies like **Mountain Craft** (Glenfinnan, Fort William, PH37 4LT. Tel 039 783 213) who are members of the Association of Mountaineering Instructors in Britain, and offer accommodation, equipment and instruction by qualified experts in mountain craft, rock climbing, winter mountaineering and snow and ice climbing, as well as arranging guided hill-walking and back-packing packages. **Leada Adventure Holidays** (A45, Red Scar, Preston, Lancashire, PRI 5NB. Tel 0772 705679.) offer trekking holidays based in the Lake District, Yorkshire Dales, and North Wales, and include long-distance treks.

Holidays Afloat

Taking to the water, there are a number of different types of holiday available: from ocean sailing to cruising along the many miles of British waterway, or participating in a range of water sports from windsurfing, dinghy sailing, water skiing and canoeing to deep sea diving. Many **Outdoor Centres** offer a diversity of watersports, often linked with other outdoor activities. Some, such as **Loch Insh Watersports Centre** (Insh Hall, Kincraig, Inverness-shire, PH21 1NU. Tel 05404 272) offer full board or self-catering packages for windsurfing, sailing and canoeing, with prices ranging from around £40 to £230. Ocean sailing holidays could involve chartering your own yacht through companies which have met with the standards of the Yacht Charter Association, such as **Alba Yacht Services Ltd** (Dunstaffnage Yacht Haven, Oban, Argyll, PA37 1PX. Tel 0631 65630) which provide fully-equipped yachts with prices starting at about £660 per week for a six-berth vessel. Alternatively you could opt for a skippered charter, with full sailing instruction if required. **Sinbad Charters** (Ardenkyle House, Kilcreggan, G84 0HP. Tel 0436 84 2247) offers RYA certified courses with informal tuition around the west coast of Scotland costing about £125 per person per week. Young people wishing to go to sea on board a 70-foot ketch belonging to the finest sailing fleet in the British Isles should contact the **Ocean Youth Club** (The Bus Station, South Street, Gosport, Hants PO12 1EP. Tel 0705 528421/2). The Club's holidays include tuition, last from a weekend to one week or longer, and take place around the United Kingdom and Northern Ireland coasts, costing about £30 a day, inclusive. For those interested in combining interests, such as folk music, art, local history or birdwatching, with sailing, **Lorne Leader** (Ardfern, by Lochgilphead, Argyll, PA31 8QN. Tel 08525 212) offer special-interest cruises in a traditional sailing vessel around the Hebrides. Six or 12-day all-inclusive cruises cost about £250 per person per week.

If you prefer the tranquillity of meandering along inland waters to the high seas, there are plenty of companies offering barge holidays in traditional longboats. **Blakes Holidays Ltd** (Wroxham, Norwich, Norfolk, NR12 8DH. Tel 0603 7829) provide a choice of holidays on Britain's waterways, cruising up rivers such as the Avon and the Thames, or exploring canals. Prices start from around £55 per person per week. If you decide to go on a barge holiday, take your bike with you, as it's possible to ride along the tow paths. **Willow Wren Cruising Holidays** (Room GB, PO Box 2, Rugby, Warwickshire, CV21 1TD. Tel 0788 69153) offer hotel boat cruises along the rivers and canals of England and Wales. These all-inclusive holidays last from three to seven days and hold special appeal for wildlife enthusiasts.

In the Saddle

Mountain-bikes, with all their gears, have revolutionised cycling holidays, but it is particularly important for those choosing a mountain-biking holiday to check that the holiday company's itinerary does not include areas where these bikes cause environmental problems such as erosion. A number of companies offer a cycling package where all the equipment and accommodation is provided and your luggage transferred to your next stop.

Green Bicycle Company (Cairnleith, North Forr, Crieff, Perthshire, PH7 3RT. Tel 0764 2080) offers weekends and weeks which start at £35 per night and include a bike, detailed circular routes, instructions and daily luggage transfer to quality hotels and bed and breakfast accommodation. **Puffin Cycle Tours** (Miltonburn, Aviemore, Inverness-shire, PH22 1RD. Tel 0479 810214) offer unaccompanied or guided tours along quiet roads and tracks in the Scottish Highlands. Prices for a four night, guided, all-inclusive trip, start at around £115. **Bicycle Beano** (59 Birch Hill Road, Clehonger, Hereford HR2 9RF. Tel 0981 251087 or 0432 278226) describes its bicycle holidays in mid-Wales, the Pembrokeshire Coast, Shropshire and Herefordshire as 'non-macho'. Meals are wholefood vegetarian and accommodation ranges from camping and hostels to local inns and a former priory. Prices are around £200 a week. The **Cyclists Touring Club (CTC)** (69 Meadrow, Godalming, Surrey GU7 3HS. Tel 0483 417217) can give further information on cycle tours in Britain.

An alternative 'in the saddle' holiday, is to go horse-riding, and these holidays range from advanced riding instruction to pony trekking and long distance trail riding. The **British Horse Society** (British Equestrian Centre, Kenilworth, Warwickshire, CV8 2LR. Tel 0203 696697) can provide details of recognised riding establishments throughout Britain. The **Scottish Trekking and Riding Association** (Arlarach, Ardfern, by Lochgilphead, Argyll. Tel 085 25 270) has details of about fifty riding centres throughout Scotland which have been inspected and approved and which have undertaken to observe the Association's code of conduct and high standards. One of these is the **Castle Riding Centre** (Brenfield, Ardrishaig, Argyll. Tel 0546 3274) which has an exciting trail ride of 130 miles (200 km) through mountains and glens, with beach gallops and swimming. Activity packages with accommodation cost about £155 per week, and reductions are available for agents, groups and unaccompanied children.

Young people wishing to go on a riding holiday, perhaps for the first time, might consider one of two organisations: **Euroyouth** (301 Westborough Road, Westcliff, Southend-on-Sea, Essex SS0 9PT. Tel 0702 341434) offers two-week courses at BHS or ABRS approved centres, during which accommodation is with local families; while **PGL Young Adventure** (Alton Court, Penyard Lane, Ross-on-Wye, Herefordshire HR9 5NR. Tel 0989 764211) run riding and pony trekking holidays for 8- to 18-year-olds in various hill country areas.

Skiing

Skiing is an increasingly popular outdoor activity, although it takes place only in Scotland – at Cairngorm, Glenshee, Glencoe and Aonach Mor. It is now one of the most popular winter activities, having seen a huge increase in numbers over the last twenty years. Weekend skiing can be horrendously overcrowded in Scottish resorts and can result in queuing for lifts for up to an hour and severe congestion on the slopes.

At the beginning and end of the ski season, limited snow cover prevents skiing to the bottom of lifts, and it is not unusual to see people taking to heather or grass skiing, which has a drastic impact on the environment. Due to the high elevation of the skiing areas and the short growing season, the groundcover is not able to recover fully before the next season's onslaught, so the natural growth cycle is severely, if not completely, retarded. As a result, conflict between conservationists and skiers has often been bitter.

Developers see skiing as providing much-needed jobs during winter months and meeting a very real public demand for a larger skiing area. Conservationists, on the other hand, do not want to see a sensitive and valuable ecosystem completely destroyed. Compromise, to some degree, has been the result, with areas being developed to conform with environmental conditions and development being restricted to areas outside the most valuable habitats. If possible, choose cross-country skiing, rather than the downhill variety, as it is far less damaging to the environment.

There are a variety of companies offering ski packages for the Scottish slopes. The **Glenshee Chairlift Company** (Cairnwell, Braemar, Aberdeenshire, AB3 5XU. Tel 033 97 41320) offers significant mid-week ski packages which include ski hire, ski instruction and a lift pass for around £75. **Glenbeag Mountain Lodges** (Spittal of Glenshee, Blairgowrie, Perthshire. Tel 033 97 41320) offers self-catering accommodation, ski instruction, hire and uplift for about £90 for five days. Companies such as **Activity Travel Ltd** (19 Castle Street, Edinburgh, EH2 3AF. Tel 031 225 9457) offer weekend packages from about £75 for half-board.

Cross-country skiing is available in the Cairngorms, but ski mountaineering is the domain of independent enthusiasts. An alternative choice is to head for a 'dry' ski slope where you can prepare for 'the real thing'. Dry ski slopes are often closer to home and are also less environmentally damaging. **Calshot Activities Centre** (Calshot Spit, Fawley, Southampton, SO4 1BR. Tel 0703 892077) has the largest dry ski slope in Britain. Recognised by the **Ski Club of Great Britain** (118 Eaton Square, London SW1H 9AF. Tel 071 245 1033), it offers weekend and evening courses for all standards under qualified instructors. A weekend package, inclusive of equipment, instruction and full board costs about £90.

Multi-Activity

Many centres offer a full range of multi-activity sporting holidays, with opportunities for riding, biking, mountain sports, air sports and water sports under qualified instruction. The **Outward Bound Trust** (Chestnut Field, Regent Place, Rugby, CV21 2PJ. Tel 0788 60423/4/5) was one of the original organisations to offer multi-activity holidays, and owes much of its success to an original and simple format which aims to provide healthy, adventurous, stimulating and challenging courses. Its centres are spread throughout Britain, covering most types of outdoor activity. They are established experts in the art of conserving the environment whilst putting it to the best possible use. Prices vary throughout the year and start at about £300.

There are Outdoor Centres situated throughout Britain which have facilities for families and children and give qualified instruction. They provide a range of accommodation and can be located in idyllic surroundings. For example, **Bearsports Outdoor Centre** (Windy Gyle, Belford, Northumberland, NE70 7QE. Tel 0668 213289), open all year round, is a founder member of BAHA, is RYA and BCU approved and can cost as little as £50 per person for a 2-night weekend, inclusive of full board and activities. **Raasay Outdoor Centre** (Raasay House, Isle of Raasay, Off Isle of Skye, Ross-shire IV40 8PB. Tel 047862 266) is situated on a beautiful Hebridean island and provides courses in canoeing, climbing, abseiling, windsurfing, sailing and archery. All equipment is provided together with expert tuition. Special skills and challenge courses can be arranged for individual groups and full board accommodation is provided in historic Raasay House. **Outface Adventures** (PO Box 14, Monmouth, Gwent, Wales, NP5 4YW. Tel 0600 83482) run a similar enterprise. Based in a 17th-century farmhouse hotel on the edge of the Wye Valley, they offer a range of outdoor pursuits with qualified instruction. Prices vary, but a weekend break costs about £250, all inclusive, while a week's course costs about £390. The **Youth Hostels Association** (Trevelyan House, 8 St Stephens's Hill, St Albans, Herts, AL1 2DY. Tel 0727 55215) has developed 'Great Escape' holidays, offering a choice of being led by an experienced leader, or picking a 'Go As You Please' package. Activities include the usual range of outdoor recreations and hostels offer anything from supervised holidays for 12- to 15-year-olds to weekend breaks which are suitable for the over-50s. Packages are affordable and start at around £50, covering overnight accommodation, mainly in Youth Hostels, full board, transport to cover the itinerary, and specialist instruction and guides. At the Activity Centres of Llangollen and Edale you can try your hand at mountain-biking, sailing, canoeing, abseiling and pony trekking, under instruction, for around £70.

Other activity holidays are specifically targeted towards children. An example is **PGL Adventure Holidays** (Alton Court, 100 Penyard Lane, Ross-on-Wye, Herefordshire, HR9 5NR. Tel 0989 764211) which provides activity holidays for unaccompanied children aged 6–18, as well as for families and groups. They have twenty residential centres in England and arrange escorted travel from twenty-three pick-up points throughout Britain. All equipment and instruction is provided. Prices start from around £75 per person for a 2-night weekend, which is inclusive of full-board, activities and instruction.

Special Interest

Special interest holidays are growing in number and diversity. Study Tours have gained in popularity and cover a wide range of subjects in the arts, historical and natural heritage, often in association with universities and colleges. **Saga Holidays Ltd** (Folkstone, Kent, CT20 1BR.) offer a cultural programme for the over-60s. A week's study course on Welsh heritage costs around £225. For those interested in farming and the countryside **Farm and Country Tours** (see page 50 for address) offers 14-day coach tours of Britain and will also provide individual itineraries and cater for special-interest groups by arrangement.

There are a variety of holidays on offer for those who wish to concentrate on their spiritual side. The **Western Buddhist Order** (London Buddhist Centre, 51 Roman Road, Bethnal Green, London E2 OHU. Tel 081 981 1225) offers a number of retreats throughout the year in Norfolk, Wales and Shropshire. The retreats are single sex and, in terms of personal development and raising awareness of self and others, have proved to be highly successful and expertly instructed. The costs of a retreat vary, some based on a fixed fee and others on a nightly rate, and can start from as little as £10 per night.

The wide range of outdoor activity and special interest holidays available in Britain makes it impossible to list here all the companies offering a quality package. In the *Good Alternatives* section of each regional chapter, you will find a selection of small, low-impact tour operators who arrange activity holidays in their home area. In addition, the tourist boards, both national and regional, have comprehensive literature on different activities. Once you have decided on an activity and the area you want to visit, it is then a case of investigating the qualities of the package being offered and checking them out to see that they meet with the approval of organisations such as the RYA for sailing and BAHU for outdoor activities.

Wildlife/Ecological Holidays

Birdwatching, studying flora and fauna, wildlife photography and general interest wildlife holidays are just some of the range of wildlife and ecological holidays that are available, offering opportunities for the dedicated specialist and the enthusiastic amateur.

Birdwatching is one of the most popular pursuits, and there are a number of holidays specialising in this, using the services of an expert ornithologist. **Barn Owl Travel** (27 Seaview Road, Gillingham, Kent, ME7 4NL. Tel 0634 56759) are specialists in the birds of the British Isles. Holidays are arranged for individuals and for groups of up to eight. Trips range from weekends in the Kent countryside to boat trips on the river Medway. **Birdwatching Cruises** (Manor Farm, Chaigley, Clitheroe, Lancashire BB7 3LS. Tel 025 486 591) offer cruises around the Scottish islands. Run by the manager of the Nature Conservancy Council Rhum Sea Eagle Project, tours offer clients the opportunity to view the wealth of wild life on the western islands of Scotland. The **Wildfowl and Wetlands Trust** (Slimbridge, Gloucester, GL2 7BT. Tel 0453 890503) has seven centres throughout Britain, focusing on wetlands and wetland wildlife.

General Wildlife holidays are offered by a variety of companies giving the opportunity to explore on foot or view from a boat. **Erskine Expeditions** (16 Braid Farm Road, Edinburgh, EH10 6LF.) offers cruises to St Kilda and the other Scottish islands, and gives the opportunity to disembark and to view the wildlife with an experienced leader. Prices start from £800. **Photo-stalking** (Dornoch Lodge, Glen Lyon, Aberfeldy, PH15 2NH. Tel 0887 235) arranges trips primarily for wildlife photographers, although anyone is welcome. It provides opportunities to photograph eagles, falcon, ptarmigan, grouse, badgers and deer. **Beach Villas Wildlife Holidays** (8 Market Passage, Cambridge, CB2 3QR. Tel 0223 353222) offer guided holidays in East Anglia from around £120. Members of the RSPB business supporter scheme and of Green Flag International, they make donations for every holiday taken to local and international conservation groups.

HF Holidays Ltd (Imperial House, Edgware Road, Colindale, London NW9 5AL. Tel 081 905 9556) offer a wide range of outdoor pursuits including wildlife and bird-watching. Accommodation is generally in the company's own properties located in beautiful regions of Britain. Holiday activities are based around an observance of the provisions of the country code and experienced guides are often included as part of the trip. Prices start from £200 for one week's holiday.

There are many opportunities for **wildlife study** with courses offering the study of flora and fauna in field centres or at sea. **Sealife Cruises** (Quinish, Dervaig, Isle of Mull, PA75 6QT. Tel

06884 223) operate in conjunction with the Whale and Dolphin Conservation Society, and undertake observation and survey work in the sea around Mull. Full board and accommodation are provided in 19th-century Quinish House, or alternatively camping is available. The trips aim to study the migratory patterns and existence of indigenous pools of killer, minke and pilot whales and are recommended for enthusiasts only. Prices for full board start at about £460 per person for a 4-day package. The **Dyfed Wildlife Trust** (7 Market Street, Haverfordwest, Dyfed, SA61 1NF. Tel 0437 765462) arranges courses and accommodation on nearby Skogholm island. Special courses include the island's ecology, wildlife art and photography, and are taken by experienced and qualified leaders. Skogholm is internationally famous for its sea-birds, such as guillemots, razorbills, fulmars and puffins, and was the site of Britain's first bird observatory. Prices commence at £155 per week, fully inclusive, although additional supplements are required for some of the courses.

Volunteer/Conservation Holidays

There are a variety of types of conservation holidays for volunteers who are keen to help preserve Britain's natural and built environment, ranging from looking after animals to repairing footpaths and joining archaeological digs. Unless you know exactly what you want to do, and which conservation organisations are responsible for your chosen activity, there are two associations which help to put people in touch with suitable projects. The first of these is the **National Council for Voluntary Organisations** (26 Bedford Square, London WC1B 3HU. Tel 071 636 4066) which aims to act as a central agency for the promotion of voluntary services throughout Britain. Whilst the Council cannot find work for individuals, for 95p it will send a comprehensive list of addresses of local and regional offices with which it is in contact. Volunteers may then contact their local or regional organisation which will provide them with information on local volunteer requirements. The second is the **Volunteer Centre UK** (29 Lower King's Road, Berkhamstead, Hertfordshire HP4 2AB. Tel 044 277 3311) which is an independent charity and reviews aspects of volunteer involvement in Britain. For prospective volunteers, the Centre has an information bank and produces regular publications.

The **British Trust for Conservation Volunteers (BTCV)** (38 St Mary's Street, Wallingford, Oxfordshire, OX10 OEU. Tel 0491 39766) is Britain's largest organisation co-ordinating volunteers in a variety of conservation projects ranging from making and repairing footpaths, to woodland management, drystone dyking and pond and coastal work. It has an extensive network of 540 community groups and is affiliated with 875 schools. Its 'Natural Break' programme in Britain runs throughout the year, with most breaks lasting a week. Volunteers must be members of BTCV and holiday prices vary from £15–£30 inclusive of food and accommodation. Volunteers work for eight hours a day, with at least one day off a week, and are supervised by a trained leader who provides instruction where necessary. The Scottish branch of BTCV is **Scottish Conservation Projects** (Balallan House, 24 Allan Park, Stirling, FK8 2QG. Tel 0786 79697) which offers 70 'Action Breaks' throughout the year, normally of 10 days' duration. Costs are from £20 inclusive.

Cathedral Camps (Crow Hill, High Birstwith, Harrogate, North Yorks, HG3 2LG. Tel 0423 771850) provides volunteer holidays for those interested in restoring and maintaining some of Britain's heritage cathedrals, abbeys and churches. Over 20 camps are held each year and work varies from routine cleaning to stonework restoration under the eye of experienced craftsmen. Camps last for a week and take place between July and September, costing about £30 inclusive of food and accommodation. Volunteers work a 36-hour week and first timers need a letter of recommendation. Volunteers must be aged 16–30.

The **National Trust Acorn Projects** (Volunteer Unit, PO Box 12, Westbury, Wiltshire, BA13. Tel 0373 826826) arranges over 200 projects a year from March to October at many of the Trust's 300 properties in England, Wales and Northern Ireland. Projects include footpath restoration and erosion control, and last for one week, costing from £29 inclusive. The equivalent projects in Scotland are the **National Trust for Scotland Thistle Camps** (5, Charlotte Square, Edinburgh, EH2 4DU. Tel 031 226 5922). Over 20 conservation camps are held each year, and projects include bothy construction, croft work and habitat management. Details are available in January and early booking is advisable, especially for island projects. The **National Trust for Scotland** (see page 70 for address) also organises work parties to such places as St Kilda, where conservation work is combined with learning about the history and wildlife of the area.

The **Royal Society for the Protection of Birds (RSPB)** (The Lodge, Sandy, Bedfordshire. Tel 0767 80551) has an extensive volunteer network, in addition to its campaigns and educational programmes. Voluntary work includes national research and survey projects, recording birdlife in Britain throughout the year and acting as wardens on specific projects. A small fee is charged for accommodation and board and volunteers on holiday projects normally work for one week or more.

Earthwatch Europe (Belsyre Court, 57 Woodstock Road, Oxford, OX2 6HU. Tel 0865 311600) is one of the largest private funders of field research in the world, and lays special emphasis on environmental research. As well as overseas projects, Earthwatch has research projects in Britain. Volunteers share the expense of mobilising and executing research projects they join, and costs start at £500.

If you fancy your hand looking after unusual animals, the **Monkey Sanctuary** (Murrayton, Looe, Cornwall, PL13 1NZ. Tel 05036 2532) offers the opportunity of assisting with the successful breeding and preservation of monkeys. Volunteers are involved in all aspects of running the sanctuary, from food preparation and cleaning to spending time with the monkeys in their enclosures. Full board and accommodation is provided throughout the year and volunteers are expected to work for two weeks or more.

Working on the waterways of Britain and restoring canals to their former glory, are projects co-ordinated by the **Waterway Recovery Group** (Canal Camps, 24A Avenue Road, Witham, Essex, CM8 2DT). Volunteers are allocated to local trusts and societies involved in restoration projects on canals throughout Britain. Work may include dredging, bricklaying and excavation work, and full instruction is given. Accommodation is basic and full board costs about £20 per week.

Working on the railways of Britain, the **Ffestiniog Railway Company** (Harbour Station, Porthmadog, Gwynedd LL49 9NF. Tel 0766 2340) maintains a 150-year-old narrow gauge railway between Porthmadog and Blaenau Ffestiniog, and relies upon volunteers and enthusiasts to keep the line open. Volunteers must organise their own accommodation; projects, from line work and locomotive maintenance to staffing the shops, last a week.

If you are interested in working on the land, **Working Weekends on Organic Farms** (19 Bradford Road, Lewes, Sussex, BN7 1RB. Tel 0273 476286) puts volunteers in touch with organic farmers who need labour to replace the chemicals and herbicides used in conventional food production. Affectionately known as WWOOFFERS, the volunteers have free bed and board in return for working in the fields.

There are a number of organisations which specialise in providing holidays for underprivileged children, and which require volunteers for driving, catering and supervising activities. There are too many to list here, but an example is the **Birmingham Young Volunteers**

Adventure Camps (3rd Floor, 24 Albert Street, Birmingham B4 7UD. Tel 021 643 8297). Holidays are provided in England and Wales for underprivileged children, and volunteers are needed for 24-hour care of the children. The camps take place for one week only between July and September, with meals and accommodation provided, together with travel costs from Birmingham to the destination. Other similar organisations are **Flysheet Camps Scotland** (Finniegill Children's Farm, Dumfries-shire. Tel 05766 211) and **Liverpool Children's Holiday Organisation** (Room L8, Wellington Road School, Wellington Road, Liverpool L8 4TY. Tel 051 727 7330)

Travelling Independently

Britain is a favourite destination for the independent traveller: only about 12 per cent of people travelling to Britain come on an inclusive package tour. Much to the agents' chagrin, the wide range of travel and accommodation options makes it easy to make independent arrangements in Britain. Of course, independent travellers have to use a bit more initiative than those opting for an inclusive holiday, especially if on the kind of free-wheeling holiday which requires accommodation and travel to be arranged as you go along. But with a bit of forward planning, there is not much that can go wrong. Where it is most possible to come unstuck is in arriving late at a destination, with no accommodation booked. The great concentration of holidays is during July and August, and this makes it a particularly risky business at that time of year. In cities it is usually possible to find something, but at a price. Avoid having to fall back on this kind of enforced luxury by booking ahead.

The book-ahead principle also applies to any sustainable tourism programmes which interest you, especially where these are restricted to small groups only. The tourist boards (see under *Red Tape*, page 44) can provide you with a great deal of free information on accommodation and different types of special interest holidays, and the tourist information centres offer a booking service for accommodation, as well as additional more localised information. The booking service varies with each individual tourist information centre. If booking ahead, some need four days' notice, whilst others can book direct. In addition to the free literature, the tourist boards publish their own guides on a range of subjects from where to stay to holidays afloat. There are numerous guides for sale on 'Where to stay in Britain', but you're as well sticking to the tourist board publications in so far as you know what you're getting, thanks to their comprehensive classification scheme for accommodation (see *Accommodation* on page 65 for further details). The guides are reasonably priced, averaging about £5, and some are free.

There are a variety of travel options available for travelling within Britain, details of which are given under the *Communications* section of this book on page 38.

Accommodation Options

For those going it alone, the accommodation options increase according to how out-of-season one goes. In most regions, there is little point in going to the local tourist information centre in search of accommodation to let during July and August, as the chances are that it will already be booked. There is a general preference towards **self-catering** holidays, either chalets, cottages, or caravans, and as a result these tend to get booked up early for the peak season; so it is best to book these types of accommodation direct with the owner during January or February.

For overnight stays on touring holidays, a range of options is available: those travelling alone, with no one to share the cost of a room, could find accommodation in a **youth hostel**. Britain has three different grades of hostel which offer dormitory accommodation, sharing with between 7 and 15 others. A grade 2 hostel charges £4.20 for a night's accommodation, with an additional £2.90 for dinner and £2.20 for breakfast. It is a prerequisite to be a member of the Youth Hostels Association, which costs £5 a year if you're over 18, and to have a sleeping bag. It is possible to hire a sleeping bag for 60p a week. The Youth Hostels Association (Trevelyan House, St Stephen's Hill, St Albans, Herts ALI 2DY. Tel 0727 55215) provides a guide incorporating details of the hostels of Britain for £1.95.

Bed and Breakfasts offer another alternative for overnight stops, and are a convivial way of meeting British people in their own homes and getting an authentic insight into everyday lives. They are predominantly located in rural areas and cost about £15 per person per night. Some also provide an evening meal, the cost of which varies, but can be from £10 upwards. Don't be caught out by people offering 'supper' in Scotland, where 'tea' refers to an evening meal, and supper is a snack before you go to bed! The tourist board guides are a useful reference source for bed and breakfast accommodation, which you can then book direct. Alternatively the local tourist information centre can make booking arrangements for you. This also applies to **guest**

house and hotel accommodation, where prices range from about £30 upwards, depending on facilities and quality. Graded listings are given in the tourist board guides.

Another alternative is **camping or caravanning**. For a family of four with a caravan/tent and car, an overnight stop in a 4-star site costs £5. When choosing a caravan park look out for one that has been inspected by the British Graded Holiday Parks Scheme, and for the ones which have received a 'Rose Award' in England and a 'Thistle Award' in Scotland. The English and Scottish tourist boards each produce a publication on camping and caravan parks, which is a useful source of reference. During the busy summer months, the most popular sites get booked up early, so you need to book ahead. Tourist information centres do not offer a booking facility for caravans, so it's necessary to book direct.

Accommodation

The tourist organisations in Britain (English Tourist Board, Scottish Tourist Board, Wales Tourist Board and Northeen Ireland Tourist Board) have a comprehensive grading and classification scheme for a range of accommodation types, from bed and breakfast, guest houses and hotels through to self-catering and caravanning options. Each establishment has been individually inspected by the tourist board. As a result, you can be assured of a certain standard if you choose accommodation participating in this scheme.

In England, Scotland and Wales, the tourist boards operate a crown rating scheme, which reflects the range of facilities available. The crowns are given on a scale of one to five, with five crowns as the maximum. In addition to this is the grading scheme which reflects the quality of the accommodation provided. This ranks from 'approved', which is accommodation of an acceptable standard, to 'commended' which reflects good quality, and 'highly commended' which is given for very high quality. So a highly commended, two crown establishment will be of a higher quality than a commended four crown establishment, although it would not offer so many facilities and services. The scheme is applied to hotels, guest houses, bed and breakfasts, farmhouses, inns and hostels, and in Scotland is also used for self-catering accommodation.

In England and Wales, two different schemes, with the same principles, apply for self-catering accommodation. Instead of using a crown system, in Wales a 'dragon' system is used, and in England a 'key' system. Again, these indicate the facilities offered, not the quality of accommodation provided, and the more keys or dragons there are, the greater the number of facilities provided.

Caravan and camping parks also fall into a similar classification system under the British Graded Holiday Parks Scheme. A 'tick' is given for different facilities, once again ranging from one to five. In addition to this, Scotland operates a 'Thistle emblem of excellence' award for luxury caravans, and England the 'Rose award for excellence'.

Northern Ireland operates its own classification scheme, which applies to hotel and guest house accommodation. Hotels are graded, A*, A, B*, B & C, with A* being the most upmarket, and C offering simple, but acceptable accommodation. Guest houses are graded A and B with A providing better facilities.

The tourist boards can advise on accommodation requirements and offer a booking service. They also provide an enormous amount of free literature, as well as a range of publications and guides, such as *Scotland: Bed and Breakfast 1991* and *Caravan Holiday Homes Parks – 1991 Holidays in England*, which are updated each year and usually cost £5 or less.

The preference for different types of accommodation will very much depend on the individual. **Bed and Breakfast** (B & B) is a great tradition in Britain, providing simple but often excellent service and hospitality. Many B&Bs are in private homes, others in pubs and farmhouses. The owners have a personal interest in their guests, and can be an excellent source of local information. Most rooms do not have private facilities and most provide only breakfast, although some will provide dinner as well. The traditional British cooked breakfast of eggs, bacon, sausage, tomato and fried bread, is nearly always offered, as well as cereals, fruit juice and toast and marmalade. It is not necessary to book ahead, although this is sometimes advisable during the peak summer holiday season, when local tourist information centres can help you. Prices vary throughout the country, and normally average about £15 a night, although out of season it is sometimes possible to find accommodation for £10 or less. Be prepared to pay in cash, as many B&Bs do not accept payment by credit card or cheque. Another form of cheap accommodation is staying in **Youth Hostels**. There are over 370 throughout Britain, which provide basic, dormitory style accommodation for travellers of all ages. Family rooms are sometimes available, but need to be booked in advance. Hostels provide an excellent opportunity to meet fellow travellers, and are the original examples of community living and tourist integration. Most hostels are affiliated to the Youth

Hostels Association, of which you need to be a member. Thereafter, self-catering accommodation is about £3 a night.

Guest Houses are normally slightly larger than B&Bs, and offer private facilities and an evening meal. Whilst B&Bs can be found in any area, there is a tendency for guest houses to be located in towns and the larger holiday resorts. In the countryside, **Farmhouse** accommodation has become popular, with many farmers diversifying into tourism to provide additional income. Accommodation varies from B&B to self-catering units in renovated farm buildings. These often represent good value for money when staying in rural areas, and are popular with children.

Offering a compromise between bed and breakfasts and the more expensive hotels are the **family run hotels**, which offer a degree of privacy and comfort whilst providing fewer facilities than a more expensive hotel. These are usually small, with a limited number of guests, and the proprietors take a personal interest in your welfare. If you prefer a more prestigious establishment, there are a number of expensive **country house hotels**, which are usually historic buildings and are often located in traditional parkland surroundings.

Self-catering accommodation gives an enormous choice, from renting a chalet, cottage, apartment or house to taking a self-catering unit at one of the universities. Prices will vary according to size and location, but a typical price for a week's holiday in June in accommodation sleeping six would be in the region of £250. Another self-catering alternative is to go **caravanning and camping**. The British graded holiday parks scheme, and the rose and thistle awards, make it easier to determine the quality of the park you are visiting. Within this scheme too, **village holiday parks** are sometimes included, offering self-catering accommodation in apartments and cottages, whilst being linked to a holiday park.

The traditional **holiday resort** offers a mixture of accommodation, depending on the type of resort. For example, at the top end of the range are resorts like Gleneagles which are fiendishly expensive, whilst at the other end of the scale are resorts such as Woolacombe Bay Holiday Village, which can cost as little as £150 a week for a family of four. Holiday resorts vary a great deal in what they have to offer. Some, like many of the seaside resorts, are action-packed, offering non-stop entertainment and involvement, whilst others are more secluded and offer an atmosphere of peace and quiet.

If you are keen to join a family for a holiday, and take part in their daily activities, you can opt for a **home stay**. A company specialising in home stays is Country Homes and Castles (see address on page

51), which arranges accommodation with host families. Essentially you are a 'paying guest' and the aim is for visitors to be completely involved in the British way of life. Prices vary depending on the type of accommodation provided, from £90 for a weekend in the Lake District to £200 a week staying in a listed Georgian building.

In the rest of this guide, low-impact, traditional, family-run establishments have been recommended, with price brackets for accommodation and eating out breaking down as follows: *First Class*: over £50 per double room or meal for two, (starter, main course, dessert); *Middle Range*: £25–£50; and *Economy*: under £25.

Checklist for the Good Tourist

1. Have I learned enough about my destination to be able to properly appreciate it and understand the issues facing this area when I arrive?
2. Can I go out of season to avoid further tourist congestion?
3. Can I use local tour operators, local transport and stay with local people?
4. If going with a tour operator, check the company:
   - Works with the local community and ensures their operations are as environmentally friendly and socially acceptable as possible;
   - contributes to local initiatives to keep the destination in good condition;
   - creates local employment;
   - uses local guides and locally owned accommodation and transport;
   - integrates tourists with locals and teaches you, prior to departure, about the destination.
5. When there, consume local produce; use public transport.
6. Remove all excess packaging before packing your case, and take biodegradable sunscreens and toiletries.
7. Buy souvenirs that are locally made and reflect the indigenous culture. Avoid all produce made from endangered species. Help conserve the native fauna and flora.
8. Be sensitive to the local customs regarding photography and tipping.

All these and many more positive ideas on how to be a Good Tourist and get more fun out of your holiday are found in *The Good Tourist – a worldwide guide for the green traveller* (Mandarin Paperbacks £5.99)

Further Information

General Environmental Issues

Friends of the Earth (26–28 Underwood Street, London NI 7JQ. Tel 071 490 1555). A pressure group which campaigns on a variety of environmental issues.

Greenpeace (30–31 Islington Green, London NI 8XE. Tel 071 354 5100). An international, independent, environmental pressure group.

Environment Council (80 York Way, London, NI 9AG. Tel 071 278 4736). A national coalition which facilitates co-operation between organisations concerned with the environment, focusing attention on environmental issues; makes authoritative representations to Government.

Fauna and Flora Preservation Society (79–83 North Street, Brighton, NBI IZA. Tel 0273 820445). Aims to ensure the conservation of endangered species of wild animals and plants worldwide.

Royal Society for Nature Conservation (RSNC) (The Green, Nettleham, Lincoln, LN2 2NR. Tel 0522 752326). Aims to promote the conservation of nature and to protect endangered plants and animals throughout the UK.

Wildlife Protection

Royal Society for the Protection of Birds (RSPB) (The Lodge, Sandy, Bedfordshire. Tel 0767 80551). A conservation body which aims to protect and conserve wild birds, and to acquire and manage land for birds and other wildlife.

Scottish Wildlife Trust (25 Johnstone Terrace, Edinburgh, EH1 2NY, Tel 031 226 4602). Aims to take appropriate measures to conserve and protect the flora and fauna of Scotland.

Wildfowl and Wetlands Trust (Slimbridge, Gloucester, GL2 7BT. Tel 0453 890503). Conserves and studies wetland environments.

Dyfed Wildlife Trust (7 Market Street, Haverfordwest, Dyfed, SA61 1NF. Tel 0437 765462). Cares for wildlife through the acquisition of nature reserves of different habitats.

Whale and Dolphin Conservation Society (20 West Lea Road, Bath, Avon, BA1 3RL. Tel 0225 334511). Aims to increase and maintain public awareness of whales and dolphins; provides opportunities to join whale watching tours.

World Wide Fund for Nature United Kingdom (WWF-UK)

(Panda House, Weyside Park, Godalming, Surrey, GU7 IXR. Tel 0483 426444). Aims to conserve nature and natural resources, especially endangered species and threatened habitats.

Marine Conservation Society (9 Gloucester Road, Ross-on-Wye, Herefordshire, HR9 5BU. Tel 0989 66017). Campaigns on marine conservation issues and assists with the establishment of Marine Conservation Areas.

Heritage Conservation

National Trust (26 Queen Anne's Gate, London SWIH 9AS. Tel 071 222 9251). Aims to preserve places of historic interest and natural beauty in England, Wales and Northern Ireland; opens houses and gardens to the public.

National Trust for Scotland (5, Charlotte Square, Edinburgh, EH2 4DU. Tel 031 226 5922).

Council for the Protection of Rural England (CPRE) (Warwick House, 25–27 Buckingham Palace Road, London SEI OPP. Tel 071 976 6433). Promotes the improvement and protection of rural England.

Council for the Protection of Rural Wales (Ty Gwyn, 31 High Street, Welshpool, Powys, SY21 7JP. Tel 0938 552525).

Association for the Protection of Rural Scotland (14A Napier Road, Edinburgh, EH10 5AY. Tel 031 229 1081).

Historic Houses Association (HHA) (38 Ebury Street, London, SWIW OLU. Tel 071 730 9419). Aims to establish an environment where private owners can maintain Britain's historic country houses for the benefit of the nation.

British Archaeological Association (Admont, Dancers End, Tring, Herts, HP23 6JY). Promotes the study of archaeology and the preservation of national antiquities.

British Trust for Conservation Volunteers (Room GT, 36 St Mary's Street, Wallingford, Oxon OX10 0ED. Tel 0491 39766).

Scottish Conservation Projects (Balallan House, 24 Allan Park, Stirling FK8 2QG. Tel 0786 79697).

Government

Department of Employment (Caxton House, Tothill Street, London, SWIH 9NF. Tel 071 273 6969). Ministry responsible for tourism.

Department of Environment (DoE) (2 Marsham Street, London SWIP 3EB. Tel 071 276 3000). Ministry with overall responsibility for environmental protection, water, countryside affairs, sport and recreation, conservation, historic buildings and ancient monuments.

Ministry of Agriculture, Fisheries and Food (MAFF) (Whitehall Place, London SWIA 2HH. Tel 071 270 3000). Responsible for administering Government policy for agriculture, horticulture and fishing in England.

Department of Agriculture and Fisheries for Scotland (DAFS) (Pentland House, 47 Robb's Loan, Edinburgh EH14 ITW. Tel 031 556 8400). Promotes the agriculture and fishing industry in Scotland.

Department of Agriculture for Northern Ireland (DANI) (Dundonald House, Room 657A, Upper Newtownards Road, Belfast, BT4 3SB. Tel 0232 650111). Develops the agricultural, fishing and forestry industries in Northern Ireland.

Forestry Commission (231 Corstorphine Road, Edinburgh EH12 7AT. Tel 031 334 0303). The national forest authority for Great Britain.

English Nature (Northminster House, Peterborough, Cambs PEI IUA. Tel 0733 4035). Responsible for nature conservation in England.

Nature Conservancy Council for Scotland (12 Hope Terrace, Edinburgh EH9 2AS. Tel 031 447 4784). Responsible for nature conservation in Scotland.

Countryside Commission (John Dower House, Crescent Place, Cheltenham, Glos. GL50 3RA. Tel 0242 521381). Responsible for landscape conservation and countryside recreation in England.

Countryside Commission for Scotland (Battleby, Redgorton, Perth, PHI 3EW. Tel 0738 27921). Responsible for landscape conservation and countryside recreation in Scotland.

Countryside Council for Wales (43 The Parade, Roath, Cardiff. Tel 0222 485111) Responsible for nature and landscape conservation and countryside recreation in Wales.

English Heritage (Fortress Houses, 23 Saville Row, London WIX 2HE. Tel 071 734 6010). The Historic Buildings and Monuments Commission for England, responsible for conservation of the historic environment.

Historic Buildings and Monuments (20 Brandon Street, Edinburgh, EH3 5RA. Tel 031 244 3101). Maintains and manages historic sites in Scotland.

Tourism Network

British Tourist Authority (Thames Tower, Black's Road, London W6 9EL. Tel 081 846 9000).

English Tourist Board (Thames Tower, Black's Road, London W6 9EL. Tel 081 846 9000). Provides information on tourist attractions, accommodation, and addresses of regional and local tourist offices within England.

Scottish Tourist Board (23 Ravelston Terrace, Edinburgh EH4 3EU. Tel 031 332 2433. Or 19 Cockspur Street, London SW1Y 5BL. Tel 071 930 8661). Provides information on tourist attractions, accommodation, and addresses of regional and local tourist offices in Scotland.

Wales Tourist Board (Brunel House, 2 Fitzalan Road, Cardiff, CF2 1UY. Tel 0222 499909. Or The Wales Bureau, The British Travel Centre, 12 Lower Regent Street, London SWI 4PQ. Tel 071 409 0969). Provides information on tourist attractions, accommodation and local tourist offices in Wales.

Northern Ireland Tourist Board (River House, 48 High Street, Belfast, BTI 2DS. Tel 0232 231221/246609. Or 11 Berkeley Street, London WIX 5AD. Tel 071 493 0601). Provides information on tourism and accommodation in Northern Ireland.

London Tourist Board (26 Grosvenor Gardens, Victoria, London, SWIW ODU. Tel 071 730 3488). Provides information and an accommodation booking service for London.

Special Interests

Ramblers Association (1–5 Wandsworth Road, London SW8 2XX. Tel 071 582 6878). Aims to protect rights of way and campaigns for access to open countryside and an increased awareness of the countryside.

Cyclists Touring Club (CTC) (69 Meadrow, Godalming, Surrey GU7 3HS. Tel 0483 417217).

British Horse Society (British Equestrian Centre, Kenilworth, Warwickshire, CV8 2LR. Tel 0203 696697).

Scottish Trekking and Riding Association (Arlarach, Ardfern, by Lochgilphead, Argyll. Tel 085 25 270).

Ski Club of Great Britain (118 Eaton Square, London SWIH 9AF. Tel 071 245 1033).

Royal Yachting Association (RYA House, Romsey Road, Eastleigh, Hampshire, FO5 4YA. Tel 0703 629 962).

Sports Council (16 Upper Woburn Place, London WCIH OQP. Tel 071 388 1277). The government body for the promotion of sport in England.

Sports Council of Wales (National Sports Centre for Wales, Sophia Gardens, Cathedral Road, Cardiff, CFI 95N. Tel 0222

397571). The government body for the promotion of sport in Wales.

Scottish Sports Council (Caledonia House, South Gyle, Edinburgh, EH12 9DQ. Tel 031 317 7200). The government body for the promotion of sport in Scotland.

British Mountaineering Council (Crawford House, Precinct Centre, Booth Street East, Manchester, M13 9RZ. Tel 061 273 5835).

National Council for Voluntary Organisations (26 Bedford Square, London WC1B 3HU. Tel 071 636 4066).

Volunteer Centre UK (29 Lower King's Road, Berkhamstead, Hertfordshire HP4 2AB. Tel 044 277 3311).

Inland Waterways Amenity Advisory Council (1 Queen Anne's Gate, London SW1 9BT. Tel 071 222 4939).

Earthwatch Europe (Belsyre Court, 57 Woodstock Road, Oxford, OX2 6HU. Tel 0865 311600).

Waterway Recovery Group (Canal Camps, 24A Avenue Road, Witham, Essex, CM8 2DT)

These national associations are supplemented by numerous regionally based groups, many of which specialise in issues of local interest. Contacting them, preferably in advance of your trip, is a good way of discovering more about the local community and its priorities; their addresses are listed in the *Useful Local Contacts* section of each chapter.

SCOTLAND

1 The Highlands and Islands

This is a region whose very name is an expression of its character; a land of rugged mountains and ancient rocks etched by deep glens, and dotted with countless lochs and offshore islands. To the west lie the islands of the Hebrides where the Atlantic breakers spend themselves along a coastline of rocky peninsula and windy promontories. Eastwards, the strong Highland landscape softens into a more mellow lowland fringe where a patchwork of farmland and forest overlooks the sheltered waters of the firths.

Removed from the populous settlements of the south, yet accessible by road, sea and air, peace and quiet are still an integral part of the character here. The region is diverse and rich in its cultural background. In the west, its Celtic roots are still firmly expressed in the Gaelic language and wealth of distinctive place names, while the far north retains its own Norse overlay from Viking days. Music and tradition are firmly intertwined and richly expressed, and everywhere there is a strong sense of the past. The military might of days gone by is seen in impressive castles and fortifications, and more lowly ways are recalled in the excavated Stone Age settlements of the north.

Wildlife abounds. Eagles soar over moorland hills with their herds of browsing deer. Red squirrels and capercaillies share the ancient Caledonian pine forest of Strathspey, and salmon leap at rushing waterfalls. Reindeer, introduced from Lapland, lend an Arctic touch to the Cairngorm Mountains. Perversely, the Highlands' best known wildlife attraction is also the most elusive, although this is no deterrent to visitors who, ever hopeful, continue to scan the murky waters of deep Loch Ness for a sighting of its legendary 'monster'.

In this land for all seasons, summer and winter can have equal attraction, offering the visitor a variety of pursuits, such as angling, hill walking, watching wildlife or just quietly enjoying a forest walk or pleasant picnic. And of course there are also the active attractions of skiing and winter sports. Islands have their own special charm, which is why so many visitors are drawn 'over the sea to Skye'.

A visit to a distillery will show how, with the aid of local barley, the pure rushing water of the hill streams is transformed into *uisge beatha*, better known as malt whisky, the Highlander's 'water of life'. Other traditional island crafts, like Hebridean tweed and Shetland hand knitting, are now internationally famous. Skills continue to evolve in this region, and seeking out the less familiar products of the Scottish craft industries can provide the holidaymaker with an interesting pastime.

Lack of development in the past has left the Highlands and Islands with a wealth of unspoiled attractions. As a result, many areas have been designated nature reserves or classed as Sites of Special Scientific Interest (SSSI), thus helping to ensure their unblemished survival. The Highlands and Islands are one of the few large natural wild places remaining in Europe, a fact illustrated each year by the influx of Continental visitors.

With the increased role of tourism in the local economy, there has come a heightened awareness of the value of environment as a visitor attraction, and therefore as a money earner also. Increasingly, the area is seeking to interpret its historic past and its present wealth of natural beauty in a growing number of museums and visitor centres. Perhaps nowhere else in Britain is there a region with such a diversity of form and shape, which is why tourism is currently classed as one of the area's growth industries.

History

All history is rooted in the past, but in the Highlands and Islands the roots go deeper than in most other places. At Skara Brae in Orkney a complete Stone Age village can be seen. This dramatically reappeared in the middle of last century when its covering shroud of sand was whipped away in a storm. The strange and compelling stone circles of the Northern and Western Isles raise more questions than they answer; the shadowy folk who erected them have left few clues as to their purpose.

Shetland – the Romans' 'Ultima Thule' – is renowned for its brochs, strange stone-built forts which once dominated the landscape. But who did their builders fear so much that they were moved to erect such enduring defences? As yet that remains one of Scotland's unsolved historical mysteries. The Picts, too, are a real enigma. Their marvellously inscribed and sculpted stones may be seen in the eastern Highlands, but the life and times of the skilled craftsmen who shaped them remain unclear. In recent times the value of the Pictish stones as art forms as well as historical remains has been increasingly recognised.

Before the Battle of Culloden in 1746, when an English army defeated the Jacobites, the clan system dominated the Highlands. Afterwards, clan tartans were forbidden for many years. Each clan was an extended family, occupying a large tract of land and headed by a paternalistic clan chief. The chiefs were all-powerful and could at any time summon their clansmen to do battle with their neighbours. Their castles survive here and there as memorials to those unsettled times and as a lasting tribute to the workmen who built them. On a day of clear skies and summer sun, it is easy to see why Eilean Donan Castle on Loch Duich in Wester Ross, and Urquhart Castle on the shores of Loch Ness, are such major attractions.

The impressive stone ramparts of Fort George overlook the Moray Firth. This is the finest 18th-century military fortification in the whole of Europe. Built by the government as a base for soldiers, and as a threat to Highlanders who supported the Jacobite rebellion, it can still be visited today. History and romance are linked in the story of Bonnie Prince Charlie whose attempt to regain the crown was lost at Culloden, the last great battle fought on British soil.

The 19th century is tainted by memories of the Highland Clearances, when people were dismissed from their homes and land to make way for sheep. Passions still run strong among Highland folk on the subject of these mass evictions. The displaced families became the crofters, whose tiny croft houses and land holdings line the west coast and pepper the islands. Others were forced to move away, which is why so many Canadians, Americans, Australians and New Zealanders cherish such strong Scottish roots.

In two world wars, the great anchorage of Scapa Flow in Orkney was a major naval base. At the end of the first war, in 1918, incredulous islanders living around the firth could only blink in disbelief as the surrendered German Grand Fleet was deliberately sunk in the greatest scuttling operation of all time.

In the post-war years the Highland region settled back into its routines of crofting, farming, forestry and fishing. In the 1960s the Highlands and Islands Development Board (now Highlands and Islands Enterprise) was brought into being, charged with attempting to develop the region's economy and stemming its population flow. Large-scale industry in the area has never really succeeded, resulting in the closure of the pulp mill at Fort William and the aluminium smelter on the Cromarty Firth. But the eastern firths are now dominated by the towering rigs being prepared for the North Sea oil industry – a development which some observers have described as the Highlands' new industrial revolution. That the region still lies largely untouched by industrial development is, however, a major bonus for its tourist appeal.

Geography

Though usually regarded as one region, the Highlands and Islands are made up of several distinctive parts. The long form of Loch Ness marks the line of the Great Glen, a massive geological fault which almost splits the mainland into two. To the south lies the mountain massif of the Cairngorms, its north-facing corries overseeing the valley of the fast-flowing Spey and the dark green pine forests which are the last remnant of the wildwood of Caledon.

To the west are the mountains of the Western Highlands, their rugged faces scoured and sculpted by ancient glaciers. The hard metamorphic rocks such as schist and gneiss which underlie this area are amongst the oldest in the world. Soils are often poor or peaty, and of limited value for farming. Beyond the fretted mainland edge lie Skye and Mull and all the scatter of the Inner Hebrides, and beyond that again the long chain of the Western Isles, from Lewis down to Barra.

To the east and north are the more prosperous peninsulas of the Black Isle and Easter Ross; fertile farmland areas which enjoy the benefits of their low-lying situation as well as a spectacular backcloth in the outline of the western hills. Northwards again the countryside opens via Sutherland's eastern flank to the plain of Caithness and the mainland's end at John O' Groats, with a distant beckoning glimpse of Orkney across the Pentland Firth.

Orcadians call visitors who cross the intervening firth 'ferry loupers'. The ferry journey from Caithness passes Britain's most spectacular sea stack, the towering Old Man of Hoy. Orkney's low green isles contrast markedly with the dark-faced moorlands of Shetland, a fascinating group of islands which can claim to be as close to Bergen in Norway as to Aberdeen, and which lie at the same latitude as the southern tip of Greenland.

People have long looked to the land for their support in this limiting environment. Crofting continues to dominate the western and northern rim, providing a grudging return from a difficult landscape. The uplands are the domain of deer and grouse which provide plenty of sport for the well-to-do, but only the grazing of native blackface and Cheviot sheep can provide any kind of farming income from the rough moorland pastures. In the eastern Highlands and along the valley straths where the land is better, farming is much more intensive, especially on the mixed and arable farmlands around the Inner Moray Firth. In recent times, the income from farming salmon in a multitude of western sea lochs has overtaken that from any other form of farmed livestock in the Highlands and Islands.

Forestry has come to dominate the use of much of the upland area, with the exotic Sitka spruce being the dominant species in many plantations. This is due to a combination of a faster growth rate than that of other conifers such as the native Scots pine, and the inevitable economic factor which dominates planting policy. Nevertheless, there is a renewed interest in conserving the remnants of the native pinewoods on Speyside and in Glen Affric in Inverness-shire.

Taken over all, the Highlands and Islands must rank as one of the most sparsely populated areas of Western Europe. The legacy of rural depopulation in the past is to be seen in countless ruined cottages. A scarcity of resources has led to a low level of economic development, and Inverness alone can claim any real size as an urban centre. Towns, villages and population generally tend to be focused on the lowland fringes, especially on the east side.

With such a low population density and no perception of pressure on the land, the idea of National Parks found little favour in Scotland when they were being designated in England and Wales after the Second World War. Consequently there are as yet no Scottish National Parks (although the idea is much in the air again), but areas like the mountain massifs of the Cairngorms and Beinn Eighe in Wester Ross have long been National Nature Reserves. The Nature Conservancy Council for Scotland has been responsible for identifying areas worthy of statutory conservation, but in recent times the Royal Society for the Protection of Birds and the Scottish Wildlife Trust have acquired a wide variety of nature reserves. Some are quite small, but others, like the RSPB's Abernethy Forest reserve, represent significant areas of high ecological and landscape interest and are becoming visitor attractions in their own right. Here are to be seen golden eagles and peregrine falcons, some of the last important populations of these magnificent birds of prey in Europe. Birds like the osprey and the colourful Slavonian grebe are a major attraction, but for some birdwatchers the distinctive but tiny Scottish crested tit is the star turn. In miniature glory and sheer attraction, however, it is easily matched by the rare Scots primrose which grows in Orkney and along the north mainland coast: nowhere else in the rest of the world can you find the perfect pink blooms of *Primula scotica*, the real flower of Scotland.

Climate

There is a common perception of the climate of northern Scotland which is far removed from reality. It is not true that the area lives out the winter under an unrelenting blanket of snow. Areas like the Cairngorms do usually maintain a white winter covering to delight the skiers, but the North Atlantic Drift which begins its life in the Gulf of Mexico keeps the west coast comparatively mild and free of frost. Average winter temperatures for the north-west are consequently in excess of those for Norfolk! The higher areas of the west are wetter and cloudier; for example Fort William has one of the highest UK rainfall figures at almost 2000 millimetres (78.8 inches) per year. By contrast, the Eastern Highlands enjoy comparatively dry and sunny conditions (Nairn has a low average of under 600 millimetres (23.6 inches) rainfall per year, and around five hours sunshine per day in June/July). But it is worth remembering that in the west, May and June are often the best months, with average sunshine up to six hours daily.

Attractions

Spectacular scenery, a comparatively unspoiled landscape and the sensation of being far removed from the noise and pressures of late 20th-century living: these are the major attractions of this vast and varied region. For those whose pleasure is of a more passive type, uncrowded roads ensure that there are usually plenty of opportunities to drive at a leisurely pace and admire the passing scene, or to stop at will and take in your surroundings.

Island hopping has a pleasure all of its own, and there is an undeniable feeling of adventure in stepping on to a little pier as all the necessities of island living, from groceries to gas cylinders, are carried ashore. Of course, you must allow yourself a day or two to get a true feel of island ways, but there are day trips and shorter excursions to enjoy the scenery and wildlife of island places. Sea anglers can boast legitimately of 'the one that got away', for giant skate and cod and even porbeagle sharks are often reeled ashore.

Wildlife is becoming one of the region's major attractions, and a number of companies and individuals now offer wildlife and exploration holidays, staying in locations as diverse as hotels, a Victorian Highland lodge, and even a lighthouse.

The Highland rural economy depends heavily on income from the sporting estates which occupy vast areas. Indeed, small communities and hotels in the further reaches often depend on the employment and business which is generated by field sports. Red deer are stalked on the uplands, moorland grouse shooting begins on 12 August. The fast-flowing rivers are renowned for their salmon fishing, though many anglers are content to fish for brown trout on the more peaceful lochs. Fishing permits are widely available for visitors.

Rivers and lochs provide a different sort of attraction for an increasing number of canoeists. In such a vast expanse of upland, hill walking is a widespread and popular activity, while the more dedicated can pit their wits against more demanding high peaks and rock faces. Walkers should however, bear in mind that disturbance of deer and grouse during the shooting season is highly unpopular. Many estates put up signs warning walkers to avoid certain areas.

Towns like Lerwick in Shetland, Kirkwall in Orkney, Wick in Caithness, Tain in Easter Ross, and Cromarty in the Black Isle all have a strong sense of the past now matched by a pride in showing it to visitors. Stornoway in Lewis, Ullapool in Wester Ross and Oban in Argyll function as ferry ports, but provide their own interest for those staying there or passing through. By contrast, Aviemore unashamedly presents itself as an all-year family holiday resort with a wide range of accommodation and attractions for all ages.

Winter skiing is firmly based on Aviemore, but there are other centres too, such as the recent development at Aonach Mor near Fort William. Viewing the Cairngorms and Monadhliath Mountains from a hot-air balloon is a more recent attraction of Speyside, but a sighting of the nesting ospreys from a powerful telescope near Loch Garten has been a major summer attraction for three decades.

Watching wildlife and visiting historical remains provide a varied interest for visitors of all ages and states of fitness. Museums vary greatly in character, from the commanding presence of Fort George near Inverness, with its reconstructed 18th-century barrack room (not to mention an occasional flowering of purple marsh orchids under the drawbridge), to the simplicity of Highland cottage furnishings of a century ago at the Highland Folk Museum at Kingussie on Speyside.

Cuisine

Mention the Highlands, and whisky immediately comes to mind. The main concentration of distilleries, each with its own malt whisky, lies off the valley of the Spey, and there is a whisky trail to help visitors seek out their delights. As a result of malt whiskies, names like Glenmorangie and Glenfiddich have changed from mere local place names to household words around the world, but a scatter of lesser-known stills produce equally palatable products throughout the area.

The use of whisky in cooking has become widespread in recent times, and is often seen in 'Taste of Scotland' menus offered by hotels and restaurants. Drambuie, an internationally-known Scottish liqueur, was originally perfected on the Isle of Skye, and has strong connections with Bonnie Prince Charlie whose ghost, it is said, haunts the Highlands to this day. Cranachan is an unusual but delicious dessert made by toasting pinhead oatmeal, then mixing it with whisked cream and sometimes Drambuie.

Much of the shellfish caught and gathered in the Highlands and Islands is exported to grace more southerly tables, but enough is retained to make this one of the finest elements of Highland fare today. Salmon, both wild and farmed, is widely featured on menus in a wide variety of forms. Venison, sometimes from the hill, but often from one of the deer farms, likewise is one of the culinary attractions of the region.

Cheesemaking has been a long-standing tradition of the area. Fortunately, it has not been allowed to die and some fine local cheeses are available. Crowdie is a soft cheese which is delicious when spread on an oatcake. Orkney markets its own cheddar in smoked and unsmoked form, and a small company at Tain produces Caboc, a most distinctive soft cheese rolled in oatmeal.

Level of Tourism

Over the past thirty years, tourism in the Highlands and Islands has steadily grown into a multi-million pound industry. Between 3 and 4 million visitors per year generate around £450m of the region's economy, with some 20,000 people employed in tourism and recreation. Although many visitors do avail themselves of fast communications from the south to enjoy a weekend break in the Highlands, visitors generally stay for a week or more, and prefer to tour by car and experience the different areas which make up this diverse region. Traditionally, most visitors come from further south in Britain, but the Unites States market is also important, while in recent times, large numbers of Dutch, Germans and other Continental visitors have been encouraged to visit through publicity campaigns abroad.

As with northern tourist areas everywhere, summer is naturally the main visitor season. Also, the long days are an attraction in the far north, and around midsummer, Shetland boasts its own 'midnight sun' experience. July and August are the peak months, but an increasing number of visitors are finding that the earlier and later months are quieter and have their own appeal. Winter tourism is largely skiing-orientated, with the focus firmly on Aviemore and the Cairngorms. The Viking Fire Festival of Up Helly Aa is a striking attraction of Shetland in January, while Hogmanay in the Highlands has become a popular way to celebrate the New Year.

Travel to the islands, especially with a car, is constrained by ferry sailings and cost, but once there the opportunities are enormous. In the more out-of-the-way parts of Lewis and Harris, for example, you can easily feel that you are the only visitor around, though the ferries to Stornoway or Tarbert are usually well filled with touring vehicles.

On the whole, visitor impact is low, though there are exceptions. Tourist honeypots in the extreme forms known elsewhere are rare. Settlements like Ullapool in Wester Ross and Oban in Argyll have come to know both the benefits of mass summer tourism and the effects of the sheer pressure of so many people and cars. Fortunately, the grandeur of the surrounding hills and sea lochs does help to counteract any feeling of suffocation amid the summer evening crowds who congregate around the piers to watch the fishermen at their boats and the varied disgorgings of the ferries arriving from the islands.

Aviemore is thronged with visitors these days, as it has been for the past two decades, and its face shows a few wrinkles here and there. Its high-rise hotel block may be nothing compared with the towering monstrosities of the Costas, but it still jars in this Highland valley setting. With improvements to the A9 road, Aviemore has certainly reaped the benefit of increased accessibility from the south, and is packed with day-trippers from the Central Belt during the skiing season.

Though some tourist trails and routes have been developed and signposted around the Highlands, nowhere is there a great feeling of roads being clogged by visitor traffic. Main routes, especially the A9 leading into and out of Inverness, and some of the West Coast routes can, however, be very busy at the peak of the tourist season and require special care. A spate of accidents in recent years caused by Continental motorists driving on the wrong side of the road has prompted local police to issue reminder stickers to foreign motorists.

Inverness acts as the hub of the Highlands, with routes converging on it – or radiating out from it, depending on your perspective. At the height of the tourist season the town is an interesting mix of cosmopolitan bustle and conventional Highland tradition. Despite it being the busiest settlement by far, the visitor should experience no real difficulty in negotiating the old streets of the Highland capital.

In recent times, the construction of road bridges over the Inverness and Cromarty Firths has made the north much more accessible, and the Dornoch Bridge will complete the crossings of the firths with a fast modern route. On the other hand, there are many narrow roads where frustrations can build up as inconsiderate motorists fail to allow following vehicles to pass, or block a vital passing place with a parked car while viewing the scenery or taking a photograph.

Some environmental damage to fragile areas is inevitable, given that walkers will tend to take the same paths in mountain areas and that families will congregate on the same restricted area of sandy beach. The scarring effect on mountains is seen to a limited degree in Wester Ross, and more markedly in the Cairngorms, where pressure from the skiing industry has also left an impress on the face of the northern corries which can be seen from some miles away. A few beaches in Wester Ross and West Sutherland have suffered sand blow-outs as the fragile seaside turf has succumbed to visitor pressure, making remedial and conservation work necessary.

As in mountain areas throughout Europe, there are many second homes in the region which lie empty for most of the year. In the circumstances, the resentment of local people unable to obtain reasonably priced housing is understandable.

Some nature reserves offer visitor centre facilities which help avoid problems of disturbance to wildlife, though species like loch-nesting black- and red-throated divers are vulnerable to nest disturbance from anglers and thoughtless photographers, either unaware or unheeding of the fact that it is illegal to disturb these, and equally photogenic birds of prey, at their nests. One of the major conflicts of interest in the Highlands in recent years has been the proposal to extend skiing activities from their present focus at Corrie Cas and Corrie na Ciste on the northern flank of the Cairngorms into an unspoiled area known as Lurcher's Gully. After much heated debate, the proposal was turned down at Government level. In fact, the Cairngorms may be set to join far flung St Kilda off the Western Isles as Britain's second World Heritage Site. Accommodating tourism and recreation in environmentally sensitive areas will inevitably present a problem if thought is not given to a well-conceived management and conservation strategy. Given that so many areas within this region fit that description, this should present the planners of tourist development with a challenge for the future.

Good Alternatives

The various area tourist offices can supply a range of information on the many types of activity which make this region so attractive to the visitor.

Meeting People

Much of the area is taken up by farming, crofting or estate land. **Farm visitor centres** are becoming increasingly popular, featuring everything from red deer to milking sheep. **Farm holidays** have recently been launched – contact M. Burnett, Farm Holiday Bureau (Tel 086288 262). **Crofting holidays**, during which visitors stay with the family on a working croft, help with the hay or peat cutting, or just unwind, are an opportunity to enjoy real Highland living. There's even a chance to learn some Gaelic, too. For more information and bookings, contact Hi-Line, Dingwall, Ross-shire (Tel 0349 63434). These holidays make a significant contribution to the local economy without causing disruption either to it or to the traditional way of life.

The workings of a real Highland estate are on view at Rothiemurchus on Speyside, where a safari tour gives an in-depth look at the management of this attractive valley and mountain estate. Contact Rothiemurchus Estate Visitor Centre, by Aviemore, Inverness-shire (Tel 0479 810858). **Summer agricultural shows**, such as the Black Isle Show, provide plenty of interest in other aspects of the Highland environment, as well as an opportunity to mix with local people.

A useful leaflet, *Farm Connection*, available from tourist offices, gives details of the above and many other land-based holiday activities.

Discovering Places

There are now many varied small-scale, and often privately-run, enterprises which use the Highland environment in a sympathetic way. The small numbers involved avoid the problems of mass tourism and the honeypot situations all too obvious elsewhere. As such, they are important elements of the sustainable tourism philosophy which planning authorities and tourist organisations would like to foster in this little-spoiled region.

Special interest holidays on offer vary from shooting the rapids in a canoe near Fort William, to relaxing with an easel and paints on the Isle of Mull. And, of course, skiing is a speciality of the high mountains. The Cairngorms are most developed, but the more recently developed centre at Aonach Mor in Lochaber offers less congested sport.

To help you choose from the huge variety of special interest holidays, a comprehensive brochure is available from tourist offices, or from Highland Direct, Station Road, Dingwall, Ross-shire (Tel 0349 65000).

Enjoying the wild Highlands is made easier in organised adventure holidays based at such locations as a guest house in the far north-west of Sutherland or the spectacular setting of Rubha Reidh lighthouse on the rugged coastline of Wester Ross.

There are several field centres where local wildlife can be studied, from the Isle of Skye in the west to Aigus near Beauly in the eastern Highlands, where specialists are on hand to help guests explore and learn about the rocks, plant and bird life. From their base high in the hills above Loch Ness, **On the Wild Side** offers week-long study holidays based on self-catering chalet accommodation. For details contact Terry Nutkins (Tel 07697 281).

Shetland and the Isle of Bute on the Firth of Clyde have well-organised natural history tours looking at birds, archaeological sites, gardens and other island attractions. Brochures are available from **Scotsell Limited**, Suite 2D, Churchill Way, Bishopbriggs, Glasgow G64 2RH (Tel 041 772 5920).

Communications

How to Get There

AIR: **British Airways** operate flights from Glasgow and Inverness Airports to the Western Isles. Orkney and Shetland are served from Aberdeen Airport. **Loganair** fly from Glasgow to the Western Isles and also operate inter-island flights in both Western and Northern Isles. **Dan Air** fly direct daily connections between London (Heathrow) and Inverness.

RAIL: **InterCity** services operate from London to Glasgow and Inverness (Tel 0463 238924), where there is a Motorail terminal.

FERRY: Connections to Lerwick in Shetland (taking fourteen hours) operate from Aberdeen, with some sailings via Orkney. The short sea crossing is from Scrabster in Caithness to Stromness. Contact **P&O Ferries**, Jamieson's Quay, Aberdeen (Tel 0224 572615). The **Orkney**

Islands Shipping Company Ltd, 4 Ayre Road, Kirkwall (Tel 0856 2044) runs several 'ro-ro' and passenger ferries.

COACH: Regular express coach services connect the area with the rest of Scotland and the south.

When You're There

RAIL: The area is served well by local lines. The **West Highland Line** from Fort William to Mallaig, and the **Kyle Line** from Inverness to Kyle of Lochalsh, are two of the most scenic train journeys in Europe. From Inverness, the North Line serves Wick and Thurso.

BUS: A number of companies operate bus services throughout the area. Small post buses provide access to more remote areas and are an excellent way of getting to know small communities. For details of these and local minibus trips, it is best to consult local tourist offices. Alternatively, **Highland Scottish Omnibuses** can be contacted at Inverness Bus Station (Tel 0463 233371).

BOAT: For services within Shetland, contact **Shetland Islands Council** in Lerwick (Tel 0595 2024). Main Western Isle services are operated by **Caledonian MacBrayne**, The Ferry Terminal, Gourock, Renfrewshire (Tel 0475 33755). The **British Waterways Board**, Clachnaharry, Inverness offers summer cruising on the Caledonian Canal and Loch Ness. There are also many small operators providing pleasure trips and island links. Details can be obtained from area tourist offices.

CYCLING: Bicycle hire has not been a strong component of tourism in the area, but is now becoming more common. Remember that steep hills are a feature of the Highland landscape, and that the growing number of mountain-bikes is causing some stress on fragile mountain paths.

WALKING AND RIDING: Enjoying the mountain scenery from the back of a sure-footed Highland pony is the attraction at many pony trekking establishments scattered throughout the region. Walking into the hills with a guide is another option that is becoming increasingly popular. Argyll and Glencoe are only two of a number of locations where this type of holiday is available.

By far the best way to plan any form of travel in the Highlands and Islands is to use 'Getting Around the Highlands and Islands', published annually by FHG Publications and the Highlands and Islands Development Board, and available from tourist offices. A Travelpass allows unlimited travel by rail and ferry for seven or fourteen days. For details contact the Highlands and Islands booking and information service – Hi-Line, Dingwall (Tel 0349 63434).

Useful Local Contacts

The **Forestry Commission** encourages public use of forests and provides many fine walks and accompanying leaflets. Contact 21 Church Street, Inverness (Tel 0463 232811).

The **Scottish Wildlife Trust** maintains a wide range of nature reserves around the Highlands and Islands, while **The Royal Society for the Protection of Birds** is responsible for many fine reserves throughout the north and west.

The **Nature Conservancy Council for Scotland** oversees the many large National Nature Reserves in this ecologically rich region. Their office at 17 Rubislaw Terrace, Aberdeen is responsible for the Northern Isles and Speyside. The office at 9 Culduthel Road, Aberdeen covers the remaining areas of the Highlands and Islands. The **National Trust for Scotland** also cares for large tracts of West Highland scenery.

Geographical Breakdown of Region

Inverness

Patterns of travel throughout the Highlands and Islands are largely determined by routeways. Inverness (pop. 43,000), at the mouth of the River Ness, is the regional centre and heart of the communications network. The red sandstone castle dates only from Victorian times, but is impressively situated above the fast-flowing river, whose banks are a popular attraction for evening walks below the floodlit castle.

This is the most convenient base for visiting other parts of the area. The shops reflect the town's importance as a service and tourist centre, offering a wide variety of Highland craftwork. The museum is well worth a visit for its bright displays on local geology, history and wildlife, plus a splendid collection of locally produced antique silver. **Eden Court Theatre**, where good productions and an impressive restaurant make for an enjoyable night-time venue, is in an attractive riverside setting.

The **Tourist Office** in Church Street (Tel 0463 234353), is a rich source of information, and can supply a vast range of leaflets with suggestions for visits to more unusual and less crowded places.

Inner Moray Firth

With the Kessock Bridge now providing a more direct route for tourists following the A9 to the north, the old road along the Beauly Firth to the west of the town has become much quieter. This allows a less stressed opportunity to view the scenery with its wonderful combination of firth and surrounding hills. In summer, large flocks of Canada geese gather along the shore, and common seals bask on the mudflats.

At **Drumchardine**, the firthside former church is now home to Highland Aromatics where soaps are given Highland fragrances from heather and other local plants. Nearby **Moniack Castle** has a winery, which makes a range of Scottish wines from local plants and fruits. After crossing the old Lovat Bridge, a turn to the left follows the route up **Strathglass**, passing the hydroelectric dams in their spectacular gorge settings at **Kilmorack** and **Aigas**. At the latter, visitors may see the fish lift in operation, allowing the salmon upstream to spawn.

At nearby **Cluanie** there is one of the best-known deer farms in the Highlands. A worksheet is available for children, and there are also less common livestock breeds. A tea-room and a bookshop specialising in Scottish and natural history titles are popular recent additions to the farm centre.

Although the village of **Cannich** has an end-of-the-road feel to it, a road strikes off to Drumnadrochit on Loch Ness. Beyond lies lonely **Glen Affric** cutting deeply into the hills. Although more tourists have been discovering the attractions of this unspoiled backwater, the area retains its peaceful character. The Forestry Commission has fenced off a large part of the lochside and now, safe from sheep and browsing deer, regeneration of the old Caledonian pines is under way in this forest nature reserve. A useful leaflet grades the walks in the area, from easy through to strenuous. They start from the car parks, traversing some of the finest valley scenery in the whole of the Highlands, with a chance of seeing deer and eagle, or perhaps the rare crested tit among the pines.

Beauly, built around its square, is the site of a ruined medieval priory. Nearby **Muir of Ord** has its golf course laid out on gravels washed out of a glacier at the end of the Ice Age. Here the hardy black Highland cattle used to be rested by the drovers who had walked (and swum) them over from Skye and the West Coast. Today, the **Black Isle Show** is one of the region's major attractions. Held on the first Thursday in August, it shows off the best in local farm livestock, while also providing many opportunities for learning about the Highland environment in general.

From Muir of Ord, a road turns off to the peninsula of the **Black Isle** (which may be reached more directly via the Kessock Bridge from Inverness). The name may refer to the once black appearance of the interior before large-scale tree planting. Today, it is a fertile green place of farming, forestry and fishing, with an increasing number of commuters travelling to work in Inverness.

The fishing village of **Avoch** is notable for its name (pronounced Auch) – a trap for the unwary. **Fortrose** is built around its ruined 13th-century cathedral and re-enacts its ancient St Boniface Fair on the second Thursday of July.

Nearby **Chanonry Point**, with its neat white lighthouse, is noted as one of the best remaining sites in Britain for seeing bottle-nosed dolphins. A recent proposal to create a new sewage outlet for Inverness nearby has met with strong local opposition from those who fear for the safety of this last viable inshore population.

Rosemarkie has an award-winning museum with a range of inscribed Pictish stones and rubbings. Its beach has become something of a honeypot in recent times, testing the village's capacity to accommodate the many cars which throng there on fine summer days. **Cromarty** is noted as birth-place of Hugh Miller, one of the fathers of modern geology, whose thatched cottage is a museum in this well-preserved old Scottish burgh.

With the building of the Kessock and Cromarty Firth bridges, the Black Isle has become much more accessible to the large numbers of day visitors from Inverness. Despite this, it is an area of surprisingly unchanged character, with a wealth of wildlife such as the plentiful buzzards. The Black Isle and its surrounding area offer the visitor a chance to enjoy beautiful countryside at a refreshingly unhurried pace.

The **Tourist Office** in Church Street (Tel 0463 234353) is a good source of information and can supply a vast range of leaflets with suggestions for visits to more unusual and less crowded places.

Accommodation

First Class

Bunchrew House Hotel, Bunchrew, near Inverness IV3 6TA (Tel 0463 234917). 17th-century country house on the shores of the Beauly Firth, set in its own grounds. Salmon and sea trout fishing are available on the estate.

Dunain Park Hotel, Inverness IV3 6JN (Tel 0463 230512). Georgian house set in delightful gardens just outside Inverness. Traditional comfort and cuisine, as well as an indoor heated swimming pool and sauna.

Craigmonie Hotel, 9 Annfield Road, Inverness IV2 3HX (Tel 0463 231649). 19th-century town house hotel close to the centre of Inverness. Family owned and offering excellent cuisine.

Middle Range

Palace Hotel, Ness Walk, Inverness IV3 5NE (Tel 0463 223243). Pleasant hotel near the river and opposite the castle, recently restored.

Moray Park Hotel, 1 Island Bank Road, Inverness IV2 4SX (Tel 0463 233528). Privately owned hotel close to the town centre and overlooking the River Ness.

Glendruidh House, Old Edinburgh Road, Inverness IV1 2AA (Tel 0463 226499). Charming small country house set in its own gardens and overlooking the Moray Firth, Inverness and the Black Isle.

Economy

Ballifeary House Hotel, 10 Ballifeary Road, Inverness IV3 5PJ (Tel 0463 235572). No-smoking hotel situated in its own grounds in a quiet residential area of Inverness, ten minutes from the centre of town.

Ardmuir House Hotel, 16 Ness Bank, Inverness IV2 4SF (Tel 0463 231151). Family run hotel on the banks of the Ness close to the town centre and offering warm hospitality.

Moyness Hotel, 6 Bruce Gardens, Inverness IV3 5EN (Tel 0463 233836). Family run hotel in a quiet area of Inverness, convenient for town and Eden Court Theatre, with sporting facilities close by.

Eating Out

First Class

Culloden House Hotel, near Inverness (Tel 0463 790461). Magnificent Georgian mansion built around a Jacobean castle, where Bonnie Prince Charlie based himself before the Battle of Culloden. Excellent Scottish cuisine in a wonderful dining-room.

Le Chardon, Church Street, Cromarty (Tel 03817 471). French cuisine from Scottish produce, including vegetarian dishes.

Middle Range

Moniack Castle Restaurant, Kirkhill (Tel 046383 336). Traditional stone-built restaurant serving good Scottish food and, of course, Moniack wines.

Nico's Bistro, Glen Mhor Hotel, 9–12 Ness Road, Inverness (Tel

0463 234308). Scottish and international cuisine, snacks, light lunches and more substantial meals, in this popular local bistro.

Economy

Castle Restaurant, Castle Street, Inverness (Tel 0463 230925). Good value meals throughout the day, including breakfast.

Haydens, 37 Queensgate, Inverness (Tel 0463 236969). Licensed restaurant and coffee shop serving food all day.

Speyside

South-east from Inverness, the busy A9 crosses upland country. The valley itself however, has plenty of interest, and can be discovered at a rather less hectic pace by following the signposted route of the old road and calling in at the now bypassed villages.

Carrbridge retains only a remnant of the ancient stone bridge which gave it its name. On the outskirts of the village, Landmark provides an excellent audio-visual presentation of the area's wildlife and historic past. There is also a **Forest Heritage Centre**, woodland trail, and an opportunity to learn about the ancient Caledonian pines which once covered the Highlands.

Boat of Garten can be reached by steam train from Aviemore, and is best known for **Loch Garten Nature Reserve**, where ospreys nest under the watchful eye of the Royal Society for the Protection of Birds. Although Speyside is a number one tourist attraction, sympathetic conservation measures mean that these magnificent fish hawks are not disturbed. While the car park and visitor hide may be thronged in summer, the surrounding lochside area manages to retain an air of peace, in which the resinous scents of the pinewood and the calls of crossbill and crested tit are a rich part of the atmosphere of this precious relic of the Highland wildwood.

Aviemore has a stir and tourist bustle to it that is best avoided if the true atmosphere of Speyside is to be appreciated. Nevertheless, it does provide a useful base for getting to know the surrounding area. Being an all-year resort, there is no shortage of things going on. The **Tourist Office** on the main road is open all year (Tel 0479 810363).

Nearby, pine-fringed **Loch Morlich** and **Loch an Eilean** in their attractive mountain settings have tended to suffer from their accessibility, with eroded paths and exposed tree roots. The all-year chairlift up **Cairngorm** allows access to the high plateau with its ptarmigan and alpine flowers. Unfortunately, the scarring effect of development and skiing pressure are obvious from some miles away in this, the Highlands' greatest tourist and recreation pressure point.

Near Kincraig, **Loch Insh** provides an alternative way to view the lochside sandpipers and surrounding scenery: from a canoe hired from the lochside water sports centre which also houses a log-built cafe. The **Highland Wildlife Park** shows Highland wildlife as it used to be, including bears and wolves. (The last wolf in Britain was exterminated in Speyside in the 18th century). From its elevated site, the Park also has superb views over the mountains and valley where a wealth of wildfowl congregate at the RSPB's **Insh Marshes Nature Reserve**.

Kingussie has been released from traffic congestion by its bypass. The **Highland Folk Museum** gives an appreciation of Speyside and Highland life as it was in days gone by in its reconstructed croft buildings and rich collection of home furnishings. Also freed from the noise of traffic by the bypass is **Newtonmore**, Kingussie's rival in the Highland sport of shinty.

An alternative to returning to Inverness is to take the A938 from Carrbridge. Close to Dulnain Bridge is the **Heather Centre** at Skye of Curr, where a vast assemblage of cultivated heathers is complemented by a visitor centre showing the varied uses of Scotland's symbolic plant. There is also a tea-room with home baking.

Grantown-on-Spey is noted as a centre for fishing, birdwatching, hillwalking, or merely relaxing in a quiet environment. It is also well located for following the **Whisky Trail** around the classic Speyside distilleries. This is well signposted and featured in information from the **Tourist Office**, High Street, open all year (Tel 0479 2773).

Nairn is a traditional seaside resort with sandy beaches and an abundance of accommodation. There is a keen local awareness of history and culture here, which can be appreciated in the town's Heritage Trail. It is also a convenient place from which to explore the **Culbin Forest**, once the Culbin Sands, which were known as 'Britain's Desert' until massive afforestation commenced in the 1920s.

The B9006, avoiding the traffic on the main A96 coast road, passes through **Culloden Moor**, scene of the defeat of the clans in the battle of 1746. **Leanach Cottage** (National Trust for Scotland) tells the story of this classic Scottish battle.

Accommodation

In terms of price category, there are few 'Good Tourist' hotels in this area which could by price be rated as First Class. There are, however, a good number of Middle-Range establishments which provide a very high standard of comfort and service and which, in almost all respects save the tariff at the end of the day (which nobody will complain about), can offer visitors a First-Class experience but at lower prices.

Middle Range

Dalrachney Lodge Hotel, Carrbridge PH23 3AT (Tel 047 984 252). Former hunting lodge now operating as a relaxed country house hotel in delightful and extensive grounds on the banks of the Dulnain River.

Craigard Hotel, Kinchurdy Road, Boat of Garten PH24 3BP (Tel 047983 206). Traditional family run country house hotel overlooking a golf course and the Cairngorms.

Red MacGregor Hotel, Grampian Road, Aviemore PH22 1RH (Tel 0479 810256). Attractive old-world hotel in the centre of Aviemore which is now benefiting from a five-year refurbishment scheme. Indoor leisure centre available.

Columba House Hotel, Manse Road, Kingussie PH21 1JF (Tel 0540 661402). Small, family run hotel in an elegant 19th-century manse, offering traditional home comforts and lovely secluded gardens (croquet, putting and tennis available).

Ravenscourt House Hotel, Seafield Avenue, Grantown-on-Spey PH26 3JG (Tel 0479 2286). Privately owned and run hotel in a former manse; lots of watercolours, oil paintings and comfy chairs. Situated in a quiet area close to the town centre and offering a particularly pleasant conservatory-style restaurant serving good Scottish cuisine.

Economy

Ard-Na-Coille Guest House, Station Road, Carrbridge PH23 3AN (Tel 0479 84239) Friendly hotel in its own grounds on the banks of the Dunlain River.

Corrour House Hotel, Inverdruie, Aviemore PH22 1QH (Tel 0479 810220). Family run country house hotel with views of the Rothiemurchus and Cairngorm mountains.

The Ardlarig, Woodlands Terrace, Grantown-on-Spey PH26 3JU

(Tel 0479 3245). No-smoking bed and breakfast in a Victorian family home in its own gardens.

Eating Out

First Class

The Cross, High Street, Kingussie (Tel 0540 661166). The Cross is what Scottish restaurants are all about: fine Scottish cuisine served in elegant surroundings and complemented by well-chosen wines.

Middle Range

The Old Bridge Inn, Dalfaber Road, Aviemore (Tel 0479 811137). Popular with the locals, good Scottish fare in a distinctive building by the river.

The Winking Owl, Main Road, Aviemore (Tel 0479 810646). Friendly restaurant in a converted farm cottage known for its Scottish food.

Economy

Ecclefechan Bistro, Main Street, Carrbridge (Tel 047 984 374). Imaginative range of Scottish food at a variety of prices. If you're looking for a cheap meal, come earlier in the day as prices are more 'Middle Range' in the evening.

Wester Ross and Skye

Wester Ross, with its rugged mountains, sheltered sea lochs and countless small islands, has long exerted a powerful attraction. Even so, the tourist impact has been comparatively slight and the area retains a strong wilderness quality.

The route north and west via Dingwall offers a painless traverse of spectacular countryside. **Dingwall** was until 1975 the small county town of Ross and Cromarty, but has now become an unhurried shopping and service centre with an interesting small museum of local history.

Strathpeffer looks like no other Highland village, which is hardly surprising, since it was modelled on Baden-Baden in Germany. The Victorians flocked here to take the waters at the North of Scotland's only health spa. Visitors can still taste the sulphurous springs, and an attempt is being made to revive the importance of the village as a spa. The centre can be very busy on a fine summer's day, but there is a quiet walk to the top of nearby Knockfarrell Hill with its Iron Age fort and a superb viewpoint.

Rogie Falls mark the change from eastern lowland to western upland. There is an information board and walk to the suspension bridge, from which salmon can be seen leaping into the turmoil of peat-stained water. On a fine summer's day, the car park can be thronged with vehicles, but use of wooden duckboards has avoided damage to the ground. Early and late season visitors may glimpse a few Icelandic whooper swans mirrored on nearby **Loch Garve**. On the moorland slopes around **Loch Glascarnoch** (a hydroelectricity reservoir) red deer often graze the moors, but their camouflage coats mean that they can be difficult to spot.

Closer to Ullapool, **Corrieshalloch Gorge** is a dramatic defile spanned by a suspension bridge. Sympathetic felling of trees opposite the car park has improved the site. Hydroelectric schemes have reduced the gorge's water flow (just like Niagara Falls!), but the sight is still impressive. Hydroelectricity is arguably the Highlands' greatest renewable resource. It does not pollute the water and its environmental impact has been fairly low.

The eastern slopes of Loch Broom have produced exotic conifers for the Forestry Commission for many decades, but living relics of much older plantings can be seen in the giant Wellingtonias at the **Lael Forest Garden**. A leaflet provides a guide to this long-established arboretum, which is maintained by the Forestry Commission and complemented by a nearby signposted forest walk offering good views across the strath. Evening visitors have been known to spot a pine marten near the car park.

Ullapool (its name refers to some almost-forgotten Viking) is the most popular centre for exploring this north-western edge. A rough path up the hill above the village (stout shoes are essential) gives the best impression of the settlement's grid-iron pattern – the legacy of its tidy-minded founders, the British Fishery Society, in 1788. Uilapool remains an important mackerel fishing base, frequented by Scottish and East European fleets. It is also the ferry port for Stornoway in Lewis.

Active pursuits on offer are pony trekking and offshore sea angling. While Ullapool suffers from the honeypot syndrome at the height of summer, with endless lines of cars crowding the sea front, the tourist impact on the surrounding landscape remains surprisingly low. Climbers and hillwalkers can choose from a wide selection of routes into the hills, though Beinn Dearg and Stac Pollaidh have particular appeal. The lower slopes of Stac Pollaidh beside the roadside car park, however, have all too obviously suffered the concentrated pressure of too many boots. In the interests of conservation, the less direct route should be considered.

'Bird cruises' offered by local small boat operators are excellent opportunities for seeing the abundant offshore seal and seabird populations which frequent the Summer Isles, an unspoiled cluster of small islands often outlined in memorable West Coast sunsets.

There is plenty of scope around Ullapool for leaving the bustle of the village and sampling the real Highlands in one of the many activities on offer, or simply in relaxing by the shores of a loch. The village **Tourist Office** at the Ferry Terminal (open Easter to September, Tel 0854 2135) can provide an abundance of information on the area and 'book a bed ahead' for you in advance of your travelling.

About eight miles (12 km.) north of Ullapool, the single-track road to **Achiltibuie** passes the broad expanse of Achnahaird beach – one of the finest and cleanest in the north – to Achiltibuie's straggling crofting township, where the land now plays a declining role in the local way of life. You can watch the smoking of local salmon and venison at the village smokehouse.

Lochinver is the location of Highland Stoneware, a pottery known world-wide for its designs based on local landscape themes from seashore to black-faced sheep. Achmelvich Bay can be reached by the B869 north of Lochinver. Conservation measures have been taken to save its attractive but vulnerable beach from tourist pressure. Information on the local environment is available locally from the Countryside Ranger (Tel. 05714 315).

The B832 south from Ullapool passes through wild goat territory and follows the shores of Little Loch Broom towards Gairloch. (The road is an example of one of the 'destitution roads' built to provide employment during the potato famine last century). The landscape beyond is attractive though not entirely unspoiled – its native forest cover has long been effaced, and grazing sheep and deer ensure that it does not return. Nevertheless, it has a true wilderness character. **Inverewe Garden**, run by the National Trust for Scotland, is a totally unexpected green oasis with palm trees and a variety of exotic shrubs. Its success is due to the mild winter influence of the North Atlantic Drift and to screening from the wind, (and not to any sub-tropical micro-climate, as many people claim!). There is a restaurant and shop attached.

Gairloch has a nine-hole golf course of character and botanical interest with seaward views, and a fine sandy beach. Its award-winning **Heritage Museum** (open Easter to October) helps interpret the area's history and wildlife.

The countryside south from Gairloch is often reckoned to be one the finest scenic areas in Scotland. Pine-fringed Loch Maree is its centrepiece, with tree-covered islets and surrounding mountain massifs. Visitors can enjoy loch fishing using one of the boats for hire with a chance of seeing a black-throated diver on the water or a planing eagle overhead.

Beyond the southernmost end of the loch, the A832 branches off at Kinlochewe for the Torridon area. **Beinn Eighe National Nature Reserve** takes its name from the imposing mountain mass to the right before Glen Torridon opens up to its sea loch beyond. Information on the area's environmental attractions may be obtained from **Aultroy Visitor Centre** and **Torridon Countryside Centre** (open June–Sept), the latter housing a deer museum.

South-west Ross can be reached either by continuing via the A896 and Plockton, or from Inverness, using the A887 via Glen Moriston and Glen Shiel to Loch Duich. The latter route passes beneath the dramatic **Five Sisters of Kintail**, part of the strong scenic interest of an area where development has been carefully guided by the National Trust for Scotland. From here you may walk to the **Falls of Glomach**, one of Britain's most dramatic waterfalls.

Loch Duich may provide a glimpse of an otter or two. The detour westwards to Glenelg via the minor road from Shiel Bridge is not a journey for the faint-hearted, but there is a car park near the top to allow the car engine to cool and to admire the stunning view to the head of the loch below, and across to the hills of Kintail. The reward for the detour is a view of the remarkably preserved **Iron Age brochs of Glenelg**, and for the more adventuresome, the shore path to Sandaig where Gavin Maxwell (of *Ring of Bright Water* fame) once delighted to watch his otters play. An alternative to returning to Shiel Bridge is to take the small car ferry (summer only) from Glenelg across to Skye on a route which is much less frequented by tourists than the main crossing point from Kyle of Lochalsh.

Kyle of Lochalsh is a good base for a day trip to **Skye**, though remember that ferry queues can be frustratingly long. The island easily repays a longer stay. Its romantic associations with Bonnie Prince Charlie have guaranteed it a steady stream of tourists. However, its attractions go far beyond the historical side, and the island can offer much more to the good tourist.

The ferry crossing point at **Kyleakin** is a hive of summer tourist activity. The A850 gives a first taste of the spectacular combination of sea and mountain which characterises the scenery of Skye. A unique attraction which may be reached by a detour off this road is the **Kylerhea Otter Haven**. This offers an opportunity to glimpse the world of the wild otter from a hide set among stunning scenery in a Forest Nature Reserve. Details are available at all the local tourist information centres.

From Breakish, the A851 continues into the **Sleat Peninsula**, passing Isleornsay and ruined Knock Castle. Armadale Castle is home to the **Clan Donald Centre** which provides an audio-visual display and summer programme of guided walks.

From Easter to September, **tourist information** may be obtained at Broadford (Tel 04712 361). The A881 skirts the attractive Red Hills and takes a detour around Loch Slapin to the village of **Elgol**, giving an unhurried opportunity to appreciate some of Skye's finest scenery, including **The Cuillins**, a mecca for rock climbers. The A850 continues among sea lochs such as Loch Ainort. Sconser is the crossing point for **Raasay**, an island noted for its rich botanical interest. Past Sligacahan the road follows the valley of the Varrgill River to **Portree**, the island's main and busiest settlement. At the height of the summer tourist season, the bustle of Portree contrasts sharply with the peace and quiet which can be found in so many parts of the island. The **Tourist Office** is open all year (Tel 0478 2137).

Following the A855 northwards allows a complete circuit of the **Trotternish Peninsula** and an opportunity to enjoy volcanic scenery unmatched anywhere else in the country. On the east side, **The Old Man of Storr** is the best known of Skye's bizarre volcanic outcrops. **Uig** looks out on Loch Snizort and is the ferry connection for Tarbert in Harris and Lochmaddy in North Uist.

The A850 follows the windings of the coastline past Loch Snizort Beag and Loch Greshornish to **Dunvegan** where the castle is the seat of the MacLeods of Skye. Crofting townships line the shores of Loch Dunvegan on the edge of the **Duirinish Peninsula**, Skye's western extremity. It was here and in other parts of Skye that the oppressed crofters defied the might of the law in the Crofters' War of the 1880s.

Northwards from Kyle of Lochalsh, the A890 passes Strome Ferry (a bridge has replaced the ferry over Loch Carron). An unusual attraction is the **West Highland Dairy Sheep Farm** (strange as it may seem, milking of sheep was a tradition of the Highlands in days gone by).

The lochside village of **Plockton** is built in a line along a raised beach and has a slightly exotic air created by its palm trees (actually Australian cordylines) and abundance of garden hydrangaeas. Nearby **Craig Highland Farm** is a centre for rare breeds of livestock.

Although Wester Ross and Skye are the most visited parts of the Highlands and Islands, mass tourism cannot be said to have created widespread problems. At the height of the summer season, however, some roads and villages are subject to congestion, and pressure points do exist in what is a fragile environment. The proposed bridge to Skye has been greeted with enthusiasm by much of the island community, but others feel that it will mean the end of the island's special character.

Fortunately, there is a growing awareness on the part of the local authority, Highland Regional Council, that the area is vulnerable and that development must be carefully managed. The scenery is the area's greatest resource for tourism, but, as local people are quick to point out, the natural landscape is highly susceptible to thoughtlessly-inflicted damage and, even were it not, beauty in itself cannot sustain the community at large.

In a region suffering from low employment opportunity, development and conservation sometimes come into conflict. Recent proposals to create a National Park in Wester Ross have not met with universal enthusiasm. Many local people have expressed fears that economic development might be restricted by such a designation. The debate continues.

Accommodation

Middle Range

The Ceilidh Place, West Argyle Street, Ullapool IV26 2TY (Tel 0854 2103). Pleasant accommodation overlooking Loch Broom, and good food, including vegetarian dishes, served in the restaurant.

Gairloch Hotel, Gairloch IV12 2BL (Tel 0445 2001). Impressive hotel overlooking the sea and with a wonderful mountain backdrop. Tennis, windsurfing, golf, angling and a host of other activities organised.

Loch Maree Hotel, Talladale, Loch Maree, By Achnasheen IV22 2HN (Tel 044584 288). Classic Highland hotel where Queen Victoria once stayed; beautiful position on the edge of the loch.

Kintail Lodge Hotel, Glenshiel, by Kyle of Lochalsh IV40 8HL (Tel 059981 275). Excellent value accommodation in a former shooting lodge on the shores of Loch Duich at the foot of the Five Sisters of Kintail.

Cuillin Hills Hotel, Portree, Isle of Skye IV51 9LU (Tel 0478 2003). Charming country house hotel just outside Portree, set in extensive grounds with fabulous views over the bay to the Cuillins.

Economy

Timaru House Hotel, Strathpeffer IV14 9DH (Tel 0997 21251). Comfortable accommodation in one of the village's most eye-catching Victorian houses.

Raasay Outdoor Centre, Isle of Raasay IV40 (Tel 047862 266). Budget accommodation in a marvellous location overlooking the Sound.

Viewfield House Hotel, Portree, Isle of Skye IV51 9EU (Tel 0478 2217). Bed and breakfast in a quiet situation just outside the town.

Eating Out

First Class

The Lochalsh Hotel, Kyle of Lochalsh (Tel 0599 4202). Popular restaurant (booking advised) in this impressive Highland hotel, making excellent use of Scottish produce.

Isle of Raasay Hotel, Isle of Raasay (Tel 047862 222). Intimate hotel with a good restaurant serving Scottish cuisine and offering wonderful views.

Middle Range

Frigate Restaurant, Shore Street, Ullapool (Tel 0854 2488). Friendly restaurant offering local seafood.

Three Chimneys Restaurant, Colbost, near Dunvegan, Isle of Skye (Tel 047081 258). An old crofter's cottage turned into a good seafood restaurant in a very atmospheric setting.

Economy

The Old Inn, Gairloch (Tel 0445 2006). Charming old coaching inn serving wholesome Scottish fare.

The Steading Restaurant, Achtercairn, Gairloch (Tel 0445 2449). Restaurant/cafe located in converted farm buildings adjacent to the Gairloch Heritage Museum.

The Western Isles

The Western Isles (or Outer Hebrides) lie at Europe's outermost edge. Throughout the many islands, there is an almost limitless variety of scenes and attractions. From loch-studded Lewis in the north to the sandy green fringes of the southern isles of Barra and South Uist, each place has its own character. And each is bound by ties of culture and language, for the Gaelic tongue is still strong here. The island environment is one of continual surprise, from the primrose-rich pastures of May to the breathtaking sunsets of summer evenings.

Though air links to the mainland exist for those in a hurry, island-going has its greatest appeal when travelling by ferry. **Lewis** is most easily explored from **Stornoway** (pop. 6,100), the island capital, using the connection across The Minch from Ullapool. Stornoway is dominated by the Victorian **Lews Castle** and its surrounding woodlands, which have an out-of-place look in such a windswept environment, but form a rare island habitat for woodland birds.

The A857 leads north to the **Butt of Lewis** with its tall lighthouse and legendary wind gusts. On a calm day, the seas around the Butt are a naturalist's paradise, with fulmar petrels hanging on the cliff updraught and gannets (or solan geese) gliding over the wave tops. The men of Ness still go annually to remote Sulisgeir to harvest the young solans, though you are unlikely to find one of the 'gugas' on an island menu, for they are prized local delicacies!

The closely-packed crofting townships of north Lewis, with such odd names as Fivepenny Borve, tell their own tale of the overcrowding which forced so many Lewismen to seek a living abroad last century. The A858 follows the west side and takes the visitor to the preserved island blackhouse in the crofting township of **Arnol**. To step through the low door of the thatched cottage is to step back into the past, for this is the way Lewis people lived for centuries. There is an excellent guidebook available.

At **Callanish** there is one of the most impressive stone circles in the country. Surrounded by towering stone monoliths, the visitor can sense that feeling of the past and wonder at the folk who raised them up and at their purpose in doing so. The nearby tea-room has been converted from a blackhouse, and you can contemplate the interior of the thatch while buttering your scones.

Southwards from Stornoway, the A859 passes through crofting land and bleak moors where peat is cut as a winter fuel. The road passes close to Loch Seaforth, the most fjord-like sea loch in the Western Isles, then in among the hills of South Harris to **Tarbert**, the ferry connection with Uig in Skye. On the way to South Harris from Tarbert, be prepared for the shock of suddenly leaving the enclosing moorland hills and coming upon the sweep of golden sands and flanking machair at Luskentyre by the Sound of

Taransay. **Leverburgh** provides a convenient stopping place at the south end of the island. South Harris has its land's end at **Rodel**, noted for its attractive old church.

There is an alternative return to Tarbert via the narrow and winding road up the east. Few inhabited places can be more rugged than this island fringe where croft houses lose themselves among grey rock outcrops in one of the most unusual landscapes to be found anywhere in the British Isles.

The more southerly islands of **North Uist**, **Benbecula** and **South Uist** are in reality one group joined by causeways and bridges. **Barra** maintains its insularity, but has just been linked by causeway to the island of Vatersay. The east side is mostly higher, but the Atlantic west is a delightful expanse of sand and coastal turf.

Less intensive crofting methods here have preserved much of the plant and wildlife interest. The RSPB maintains its **Balranald Nature Reserve** close to Loch Druidibeg in South Uist. Greylag geese nest locally and corncrakes still hang on precariously, having been displaced by more intensive farming ways on the mainland. The ecological value of these southern islands of the Outer Hebrides has been confirmed in their recent designation as Environmentally Sensitive Areas.

Tourism is as yet at a low level of development in the Western Isles, which gives the area an unspoiled attraction hard to match in any other part of Europe at the present time. The aim of Bord Turasachd Nan Eilean, the Western Isles Tourist Board, is to foster the type of sustainable tourism which helps retain people in local communities while maintaining an awareness of the need for environmental protection.

Accommodation and Eating Out

Middle Range

Dark Island Hotel, Liniclate, Isle of Benbecula PA88 5PJ (Tel 0870 2283). Modern hotel in a pleasant position offering comfortable accommodation. Scottish cuisine is served.

Ardvourlie Castle, Isle of Harris PA85 3AB (Tel 0859 2307). Tastefully restored Victorian hunting lodge in the mountains of North Harris on the shore of Loch Seaforth. In the dining-room, fine Scottish cuisine is served.

Baile-Na-Cille, Timsgarry, Isle of Lewis PA86 9JD (Tel 085175 242). Small, family run hotel offering peace and quiet in a secluded area on Lewis. Particularly good position for outdoor pursuits, including natural history. 'Good fresh nosh' is served!

Economy

Hebridean Guest House, Bayhead, Stornoway, Isle of Lewis PA87 2DZ (Tel 0851 2268). Pleasant guest house close to the town centre and car ferry.

Minchview House, Tarbert, Isle of Harris PA85 3DB (Tel 0859 2140). Well-situated bed and breakfast with views of the Isle of Skye. Guided walks available.

Craigard Hotel, Castlebay, Isle of Barra PA80 5XD (Tel 08714 200). Small hotel overlooking the bay and offering wholesome Scottish fare.

Orkney and Shetland

There is a magic about offshore Scotland that finds full expression in these Northern Isles.

Orkney is a scatter of soft green isles made productive by generations of farmers. Yet much of the natural interest remains, with uncommon bird species like the hen harrier nesting on the moors. The RSPB has a number of Orkney nature reserves; details may be obtained from the Society's Orkney Officer at Smyril, Stenness (Tel 0856 850176). Along the coasts, high cliffs alternate with low sandy beaches, where you can watch teeming seabird cities or simply relax amidst an unhurried island scene.

Mainland, the largest island, is rich in prehistoric sites. **Skara Brae** gives a rare glimpse of the Stone Age past, and the eerie black interior of the **Maeshowe** burial chamber evokes the atmosphere of ancient days. Mainland lochs, such as Stenness and Harray, are renowned for their brown trout. In summer, visitors can share in the social round of the agricultural shows and mingle with island folk.

Kirkwall is the main town, easily accessible from the surrounding area. The town's shops stock a range of distinctive island products, including Orkney silver, patterned with local Norse and wildlife designs, and the addictive Orkney fudge. The Highland Park Distillery invites visitors to watch the production of its distinctive island malt whisky. The historical interest of Tankerness House Museum is matched by the impressive red sandstone St Magnus Cathedral, a lasting reminder of the Viking presence. The **Tourist Office** in Broad Street is open all year (Tel 0856 2856). A wide range of suggestions for holiday activities, accommodation and eating places is available.

Stromness has narrow flagstone streets and alleyways (look for the

Khyber Pass!). The ships of the Hudson Bay Company watered at the town's well last century on their way to the Arctic. The **Tourist Office** at the ferry terminal is open April to October (Tel 0856 850716).

The South Isles (reached by small ferry from Stromness) are dominated by **Hoy**, the highest of Orkney's islands. The atmospheric old township of Rackwick seems to belong to a time far removed from the present. The North Sea Oil terminal on Flotta has brought prosperity without too much environmental impact. South Ronaldsay is linked to Mainland by the Churchill Barriers, built in World War II to bar German U-Boats from the naval anchorage of Scapa Flow. The best known wartime relic is the ornately-decorated Italian Chapel on the island of Burray, created by Italian prisoners of war from a lowly Nissen hut.

The North Isles have personalities all of their own, from low-lying North Ronaldsay with its solar-powered bird observatory, to the moorland mass of Rousay with its prehistoric remains. A round trip by sea or air from Kirkwall can give a flavour of the islands, but a short stay is a more soothing tonic for the pressures of modern living.

Shetland is distinctly different. Plunging cliffs thronged with nesting seabirds overlook seas fished by generations of crofter-fishermen. The tammie norrie (puffin) has become something of a symbol for these islands. The past is brought to life in literally dozens of different sites, from the Norse remains at **Jarlshof** in South Mainland to the **Broch of Mousa**, best preserved of all Scotland's enigmatic broch towers. At a more down to earth level there is the Croft House Museum at Dunrossness with its working water mill.

'Crofts and crafts' sums up much of Shetland's interest. Hand knitting with Fair Isle patterns is the most famous craft (the finest Shetland shawls can be passed through a wedding ring). Whiteness is a good centre. Shetland silver with its ancient Celtic and Norse motifs is a speciality of Weisdale.

Lerwick, the main town, is a surprisingly busy hive of island commerce, but remembers its past in the Shetland Museum. **Tourist Information** is at the Market Cross (Tel 0595 3434).

The North Isles of **Yell**, **Unst** and **Fetlar** are valued by visitors for their unspoiled character and rich wildlife interest. Fetlar's most famous birds are the snowy owls which first put in an appearance in the 1970s. **Fair Isle** is harder to get to, but worth it for its spectacular cliffs and rare migrant birds.

As in Orkney, visitor pressure in Shetland is as yet low, though improved communications have rendered the islands less remote. The visitor can therefore enjoy an environment that is little stressed by tourist impact and where wildlife and wild places are a valued part of the island scene, and increasingly of the island economy. Sustainable tourism is viewed as a key feature of the islands' economic development.

Environmental threats may seem far removed, but there is a massive oil terminal at Sullom Voe. Oil spillages have presented occasional problems, but a greater concern has been the breeding disasters at the huge seabird colonies; conservationists have pointed to overfishing of the sand eel stocks as one possible cause.

Orkney and Shetland tourist organisations are able to supply comprehensive information on a wide variety of accommodation and specialist interests. Contact the **Orkney Tourist Board**, 6 Broad Street, Kirkwall, Orkney (Tel 0856 2856); or **Shetland Tourist Organisation**, Information Centre, Market Cross, Lerwick, Shetland (Tel 0595 3434).

Accommodation and Eating Out

Middle Range

Ayre Hotel, Ayre Road, Kirkwall, Orkney KW15 1QX (Tel 0856 3001). Family owned hotel overlooking the harbour and close to the town centre.

West End Hotel, Main Street, Kirkwall, Orkney KW15 1BU (Tel 0856 2368). Early 19th-century hotel tastefully renovated and situated in the town centre.

Queens Hotel, Commercial Street, Lerwick ZE1 (Tel 0595 2826). Traditional small hotel on the edge of the sea with wonderful views of Bressay.

Fair Isle Bird Observatory Lodge, Fair Isle, Shetland ZE2 9JU (Tel 03512 258). Pleasant accommodation, ideal for bird-lovers.

Economy

Stoneyquoy, Lyness, Hoy, Orkney KW16 3NY (Tel 0856 79 234). Lovely stone-built croft farmhouse offering good value bed and breakfast.

Kierfield House, Sandwick, Orkney KW16 3JE (Tel 0856 84 503). Mid-19th-century dower house set in its own gardens.

Pinewood Guest House, Upper Toft, Aywick, East Yell, Shetland

ZE2 9AX (Tel 0957 2077). Delightful modernised crofthouse set in pleasant gardens and with good views.

Knysna Guest House, 6 Burgh Road, Lerwick, Shetland ZE1 0LB (Tel 0595 4865). Friendly and personally run guest house close to the town centre.

Loch Ness and Lochaber

There's much more to **Loch Ness** than the myth of its monster (on which the tourist trade so heavily depends). The long loch occupies the deep trench of the Great Glen Fault which shattered the land 400 million years ago. Thomas Telford used this natural pass to build his celebrated **Caledonian Canal**, which still links Scotland's east and west coasts. The lochside road has many stopping places from which the scenery and wildlife may be viewed, but be warned, this is one of the most popular trails in the Highlands, and the lay-bys are filled to overflowing on summer days with hopeful 'Nessie' spotters.

A more peaceful alternative is to take to the water in a cabin cruiser and explore the quieter corners of the loch. Boats are available for hire from Caley Cruisers at Canal Road, Inverness (Tel 0463 236328).

Drumnadrochit has the Loch Ness Monster Exhibition Centre which attempts to probe the mystery of the elusive Nessie. With an estimated 250,000 visitors per year, this is by far the most popular tourist site in the whole of the Highlands and Islands. Two miles (3 km.) south of the village, ruined **Urquhart Castle** forms one of the classic viewpoints of the Highlands. Its 'shortbread-tin lid' status makes it one of the busiest places in the Highlands with over 100,000 visitors per year.

Invermoriston is the turn-off for Kintail and South-west Ross. **Fort Augustus**, at the south-west extremity of the loch, takes its name from the fortification built by General Wade in the 18th century during the Jacobite unrest, when the government attempted to repress support for Bonnie Prince Charlie. The remains of the fort are incorporated into the Benedictine Abbey. The Great Glen Heritage Exhibition (open May to October) interprets the history of the area. **Inchnacardoch Forest Walks**, just to the south-west of the town, allow a quiet insight into the area's natural history. The **Tourist Office** (Tel 0320 6367) in the village car park is open May to September and can provide further information on local natural attractions.

The A82 route south follows the line of **Loch Oich** and Loch Lochy into Lochaber, where the landscape is dominated by Ben Nevis (4403 feet; 1343 m.), the highest mountain in the British Isles. Its reputation draws all too many visitors to tackle the widening track which ascends the steep slopes. The area's human and natural history is the subject of displays in the local West Highland Museum.

Fort William (pop. 11,000) provides a base for exploring the surrounding area. The town is dominated by its mountain backcloth and offers a wide range of activities based on hill and loch. Past Inverlochy, on the A82 is the imposing Spean Bridge Commando Memorial, which depicts commandos looking across the wilderness area in which they trained during the Second World War. The nearby **Parallel Roads of Glen Roy** mark successive falls in water level of an Ice Age loch.

The A830 west from the town passes long Loch Eil and the site of the raising of the Jacobite standard in 1745 at **Glenfinnan**. The National Trust Visitor Centre brings to life the heady days of Prince Charles Edward Stuart's ill-fated campaign to regain the British throne. The view down Glen Shiel with its long, ribbon loch enclosed by steep mountains must rank as one of the most magnificent landscapes in the Highlands. From **Arisaig** it is possible to cruise round the islands of **Eigg**, **Muck** and **Rhum**, otherwise known as the Small Isles. At the end of the road, **Mallaig** is a fishing port, terminus for the West Highland Line, and ferry link for the Small Isles and Ardvasar in Skye. The **Tourist Office** is open from May to September (Tel 0687 2170).

The A82 south of Fort William crosses over the Ballachulish Bridge and leads on through **Glencoe**, a deep pass of many moods. The name of the glen became infamous in Highland history after the massacre of February 1692, when forty members of the Clan MacDonald perished at the hands of the Campbells, who had been enjoying their hospitality for some time before. The memory of the episode gives an added atmosphere to a visit to this deep glen. The outstanding landscape of Glencoe is in the hands of the National Trust for Scotland. The Glencoe Visitor Centre gives an introduction to the scenery and wildlife attractions, which include wildcat and golden eagle. Glencoe is also noted for its challenging climbs and as a winter skiing centre. This tends to be a well-frequented tourist route exploiting the area's historic past and, perhaps inevitably, the erosion of footpaths is becoming a cause for concern. However, the wildness of the scenery is such that tourists present no real threat as yet to an area that is as impressive in its landscape as it is rich in wildlife interest.

Accommodation

First Class

Inverlochy Castle Hotel, Torlundy, by Fort William PH33 68N (Tel 0397 702177). Privately owned and run Baronial mansion set in delightful grounds.

Middle Range

Lochview Guest House, Heathercroft, off Argyll Terrace, Fort William PH33 6RE (Tel 0397 703149). Comfortable accommodation in a quiet location with panoramic views over Loch Linnhe and the Ardgour Hills.

Inchnacardoch Lodge Hotel, Loch Ness, by Fort Augustus PH32 4BL (Tel 0320 6258). Country house hotel offering traditional comfort and cuisine and with fine views of Loch Ness.

Economy

Benleva Hotel, Drumnadrochit IV3 6UH (Tel 04562 288). Family run guest house in an attractive area offering home cooking.

Marine Hotel, Mallaig PH41 (Tel 0687 2217). Family run hotel in the centre of the village.

Eating Out

First Class

The Moorings Hotel, Banavie, Fort William (Tel 0397 772797). Popular restaurant of a local hotel making excellent use of fresh produce in a Jacobean-style dining-room.

Middle Range

Crannog Seafood Restaurant, The Pier, Fort William (Tel 0397 5589). Converted fisher store at the Town Pier, run by fishermen and offering an extensive range of fish dishes.

Glen Nevis Restaurant, Fort William (Tel 0397 5459). Fresh local produce served in a striking setting at the foot of Ben Nevis.

Economy

Lovat Arms Hotel, Fort Augustus (Tel 0320 6206). Victorian hotel set in its own grounds with a good bar and restaurant.

Glenmoriston Arms, Invermoriston (Tel 0320 51206). Former coaching inn now offering good value bar lunches (more expensive for dinner), and traditional Scottish cuisine.

Easter Ross, Sutherland and Caithness

Following the A9 route across the Cromarty Firth Bridge into Easter Ross, there is usually a good chance of seeing common seals basking on the mudflats. The firth is known today for its towering oil rigs undergoing repair, although its former importance as a fleet base is marked by a **Naval Trail**, which can be followed using the tourist leaflet and firthside indicator boards.

Many visitors prefer to leave the busy A9 and follow the A836 scenic route northwards over **Struie Hill**, avoiding a detour round by Tain. The high-level viewpoint overlooks the Dornoch Firth and a magnificent sweep of hill, forest and water.

A stop at the old Easter Ross town of **Tain** is well worth the longer run. Medieval pilgrims once flocked here to the shrine of St Duthus. Beyond the town stretches the Morrich More, a wild stretch of sandy coastal heath with strong ecological interest, where controversy recently raged over the decision to site a North Sea pipeline assembly yard.

Bonar Bridge, the small crossing-point settlement near the head of the firth, will soon be bypassed by the Dornoch Bridge. A short distance off the A9 lies the old Sutherland county town of **Dornoch**, internationally known for its classic links golf course, but showing little evidence of tourist pressure. **Tourist Information** is at the Square (Tel 0862 810400).

Dunrobin Castle at the side of the firth is a fairy-tale building which is the seat of the Dukes of Sutherland. The enormous statue which overlooks the small town of Golspie from the hill above is of a former duke. In the fishing village of **Helmsdale** is Timespan Heritage Centre. The nearby **Strath of Kildonan** attracts gold panners each summer to try their luck in the burn.

Don't be put off by the flatness of Caithness; the landscape is full of interest for the discerning visitor and tourist traffic is light. The northwards road passes croft land and a string of coastal villages. North of Dunbeath, **Laidhay Croft Museum** is a well-preserved thatched Caithness croft in a vernacular style which has all but vanished from the area. The **Grey Cairns of Camster**, one of Caithness's best known prehistoric sites, lie six miles (9.5km) north of the village of Lybster.

Wick (pop. 8800) had its heyday in the 19th-century herring trade, recalled in its Heritage Museum. **Tourist Information** is at Whitechapel Road (Tel 0955 2596.)

The hinterland is perhaps best viewed from the railway which loops through the desolate Flow Country, where the visitor may sense a real feeling of wilderness. In an area of limited economic opportunity, forestry became an important new land use in the 1980s, with vast areas of peat bog ploughed to accommodate conifer plantations. However, the area is also rated extremely highly in conservation terms, with scarce species like black-throated diver and greenshank nesting among the bogs and wet peat flows. Fortunately, it has been agreed at government level that large tracts should be left unplanted, though conservationists would argue that a great deal of damage has already been done.

Thurso (pop. 9700), Scotland's most northerly mainland town, has a memorial to Robert Dick, a celebrated amateur botanist of the Victorian age. The Heritage Museum (open June–September) interprets Caithness life in the past. To the east are Holborn and Dunnet Heads with their red sandstone cliffs; the surrounding area offers much more of interest than the well-trodden tourist trail to John O'Groats.

To the west, along the A836 at **Dounreay**, the dome of the power station is a reminder of both the importance of the nuclear plant to local employment, and the current controversy over whether the area should be used as a nuclear waste repository.

The crofting townships of the north coast were laid out by people cleared off the land to make way for sheep. At **Bettyhill**, there is a remarkable example of sand-blow, while the surrounding lime-rich rocks support Alpine plants such as the uncommon mountain dryas, which normally do not occur at sea level. This area is well known for its botanical interest, and particularly for the exquisite *Primula scotica* which blooms along the wild northern shore. The village **Tourist Office** is open from May to September (Tel 06412 342).

The nearby **Strathnaver Museum** has reminders of the Highland Clearances early last century when people were forcibly moved from the inland strath to make way for the Cheviot sheep. This was perhaps the most notorious of the evictions, and local feelings still run high on the subject. A quiet road runs up Strathnaver and allows a visit to **Rosal**, one of the cleared settlements or clachans, where an information board interprets the layout and history of the site.

Close to the attractive, long inlet of the Kyle of Tongue, lies **Tongue** village, an ideal centre for hill-walking, pony trekking and birdwatching in an unspoiled area. Beyond the Kyle is **Durness** with its huge limestone **Cave of Smoo**, the result of rock solution over countless thousands of years.

Tourist levels along this northern coast are still very low, as most visitors to the Highlands prefer to follow the more popular West Coast routes. As a result, there is a low density of road traffic. This enables the visitor to enjoy one of the lesser-known, but decidedly interesting parts of the north.

Accommodation

First Class

Dornoch Castle Hotel, Castle Street, Dornoch IV25 3SD (Tel 0862 810216). Formerly the Bishop's Palace and now a traditional hotel with a reputation for excellent food opposite the cathedral.

Middle Range

Pentland Hotel, Thurso (Tel 0847 63202). Accommodation and good food in the centre of town.

Lundies Guest House, Tongue (Tel 084755 256). Traditional sandstone building with good views of the mountains and sea.

Economy

Trevose Guest House, Dornoch (Tel 0862 810269). Friendly welcome (with a touch of Gaelic) in a red sandstone guest house.

Bilbster House, near Wick (Tel 0955 82212). Historic 18th-century farmhouse offering bed, breakfast and dinner in a rural setting five miles west of Wick.

Eating Out

Middle Range

Foulis Ferry Restaurant, Evanton (Tel 0349 830535). Imaginative food combined with good views at an old ferry crossing.

Farr Bay Inn, Bettyhill (Tel 06412 230). 200-year-old inn in a peaceful setting on the edge of the village serving good food (vegetarians catered for).

Economy

Bunillidh Restaurant, Helmsdale (Tel 04312 457). Local restaurant serving fresh seafood, next door to the Heritage Centre.

Argyll and the Isles

Oban is a natural centre for the tourist who wishes to get to know this most southerly province of the Highlands and Islands. It is an area of diverse geography and a land of islands and peninsulas each with its own personality. As a result, it has not felt a heavy tourist impact. Mull and Iona are perhaps best known, but places like the outer islands and the Cowal Peninsula have their own distinctive charm. The milder conditions of the western seaboard encourage the growth of exotic plants, making the numerous gardens a special attraction.

Oban is the centre for ferry connections. Services are operated by Caledonian MacBrayne to the islands of Mull, Coll and Colonsay and to Iona. Full details of all sailings, including local excursions from Oban Pier, may be obtained all year round from the **Tourist Information Office** in Argyll Square (Tel 0631 63122) or directly from Caledonian MacBrayne, Ferry Terminal, Railway Pier (Tel 0631 62285).

Though undeniably Scottish in its setting of hill and firth, Oban has a slightly classical air about it, thanks to the amphitheatre-like pillars of McCaig's Tower, an unfinished Victorian 'folly' which dominates this busy port and regional centre.

The narrow isle of **Lismore** provides a convenient day excursion. Its pleasant greenness is due to the underlying limestone rock which sweetens the soil. **Mull** is the most popular of the Hebridean Islands, offering a diversity of scenery that ranges from wooded slopes to plunging cliffs. The car ferry from Oban arrives at Craignure Pier. From here the main road goes north through Salen and past **Aros Castle**, the 14th-century seat of the Lords of the Isles. **Tobermory**, the delight of the photographer, with the pastel shades of its seafront houses reflecting in the water, is the island's only town. Its sheltering bay is best known as the resting place of a gold-laden galleon from the Spanish Armada. Nearby **Aros Park** offers pleasant winding walks among azaleas and rhododendrons, at their best in early summer.

Calgary gave its name to the Canadian Prairie town, but today is popular with geologists interested in the local rock formations. The granites of the peninsula of the **Ross of Mull** are another attraction in an island which also boasts many volcanic landforms. **Fionnphort** at the west end of the island provides a short sea crossing to **Iona** with its restored abbey and memories of St Columba, who introduced Christianity to Scotland.

The more isolated island of **Colonsay** to the south is reached directly by ferry down the Firth of Lorne from Oban. It is far enough off the tourist track to offer a holiday with guaranteed peace. The gardens at Kiloran represent one of the area's lush botanical attractions. By contrast, **Coll** is approached through the narrow Sound of Mull. This is one of the finest boat trips in Scotland, offering a relaxing way to enjoy the scenery, the spectacular rock formations and abundant wildlife. Coll is a stopping place on the way to **Tiree**, flattest and most fertile of the Inner Hebrides. The sandy bays with their encircling beaches and Atlantic swell have made Tiree one of the country's most popular wind surfing centres. However, the island has a remarkably unspoiled and tranquil feel to it, and of particular attraction are the whitewashed thatched cottages with their double walls. These represent some of the best remaining examples of Hebridean vernacular architecture, and their future has been assured by a local group known as the Friends of the Thatched Houses. The island is also noted for its rich wildlife interest and its remarkably high sunshine record.

North of Oban on the A828 is **Barcaldine** on the southern shore of Loch Creran. Here the Sea Life Centre allows an unusual opportunity to glimpse the underwater world that is normally hidden from view beneath the waves. Directly opposite Lismore lies **Port Appin** which provides a short crossing to the island.

Mid-Argyll is bisected by **Loch Awe**, a long glaciated ribbon loch. The A85 from Oban heads through the narrow Pass of Brander, past **Ben Cruachan** with its hydroelectric underground pumped storage scheme. This is a unique Highland tourist attraction, and there is a reception centre for tours. **Inveraray** on Loch Fyne is noted for its striking 18th-century castle, seat of the Clan Campbell. The **Tourist Information Centre** in the village is open from April to September (Tel 0499 2063). Nearby **Crarae Gardens** rank amongst the finest in Scotland, with their bamboo and rhododendron thickets set among impressive scenery.

Inveraray is a useful touring centre. The A83 heads north-east from the town along Loch Fyne to join the A815 into the less frequented **Cowal Peninsula**, which the local tourist guide describes as 'Scotland's best kept secret'. The B839 leads to Lochgoilhead, which has an unusual attraction in its Sheep Show. Between April and October, visitors can see many different sheep breeds and learn about shearing and sheepdog working. Close by Loch Eck on the A815 is the famed **Younger Botanic Garden**, one of the great showpieces of Scottish botany. Its plantings of giant redwoods and rhododendrons date back to last century, giving the garden a mature look in a superb setting.

Dunoon (pop. 10,200) is the regional centre. Its 13th-century ruined castle is a reminder of less peaceful times, but in this age Dunoon is an excellent centre for enjoying the unhurried countryside of Cowal. Its most colourful attraction is the Cowal Highland Gathering, held at the end of August, when pipe bands compete in an unrivalled spectacle. The **Tourist Office** (Tel 0568 52056), located on the pier, is open all year round and can provide information on the varied attractions of the nearby **Argyll Forest Park**, with its wealth of woodland and wildlife interest and superb forest walks.

From Inveraray, the A83 goes south-westwards into **Kintyre**, Scotland's longest peninsula. **Tarbert** is a traditional west coast fishing village where sea angling has become a modern attraction. Southwards from the village by way of the A83, Tayinloan is the crossing-point for the island of **Gigha** which is noted for its varied collection of exotic shrubs at Achamore House. **Campbeltown**, the peninsula's main settlement, is a pleasant town best known to the outside world for the quality of its malt whisky. **Southend**, as its name implies, is at the peninsula's extremity. From the Mull of Kintyre, it is only a short distance across to Northern Ireland.

The island of **Islay** is accessible by car ferry from Kennacraig, near Tarbert. Details of sailings may be obtained from Caledonian MacBrayne, Ferry Terminal, Kennacraig (Tel 088973 253). This is a lovely island which deserves to be better known. The distinctive 'Islay Malts' from the island distilleries appeal to whisky drinkers the world over. It is also a noted area for wildlife, including some quite rare species such as the Greenland whitefronted geese which arrive in the autumn. Controversy recently surrounded the extraction of distillery peat from their traditional feeding grounds, but the matter has been resolved. The neighbouring Isle of **Jura** can be approached across the Sound of Islay from Port Askaig. It too is noted for its distillery, and the visitor who makes the effort to reach the island will be rewarded with a feeling of complete detachment from life on the mainland.

Bute and Arran complete the island picture. Because of its comparative accessibility, **Bute** has traditionally been a holiday island for Glasgow and the populous Strathclyde Region. From Wemyss Bay on the Firth of Clyde, a ferry operates to **Rothesay**, a popular family resort with plentiful accommodation and eating places, and a good centre for exploring the island's extensive road system.

By contrast, the island of **Arran** has a wilder feel to it, especially in its inner upland areas. Caledonian MacBrayne operate the ferry service from Ardrossan on the Ayrshire coast (Tel 0294 63470). The high point of **Goat Fell** dominates the island scene, and the circular main road links a chain of attractive small villages of surprisingly varied character. Arran is an ideal holiday island for those who either seek hill paths, wildlife treasures and geological formations, or who simply want to relax in a setting of peace and charm.

Accommodation

First Class

Skipness Castle, Tarbert, Loch Fyne (Tel 08806 207). Delightful country house in a rural setting overlooking the Arran Hills and Kilbrannan Sound. Fishing and walking offered.

Middle Range

Lerags House, near Oban (Tel 0631 63381). Accommodation and superb home cooking overlooking Loch Feochan roughly four miles (6 km.) south of Oban.

Ballegreggan House, Campbeltown (Tel 0586 52062). Comfortable accommodation in an attractive countryside setting.

Economy

Lorne View, Ardconnel Road, Oban (Tel 0631 65500). Situated in a quiet street overlooking Oban Bay.

Ardmory House Hotel, Rothesay (Tel 0700 2346). Set in a large garden with panoramic views over the town and Loch Striven.

Eating Out

First Class

Crinan Hotel, Crinan, Lochgilphead (Tel 054 683 261). Excellent seafood restaurant in the lovely village of Crinan, with magnificent views of Loch Crinan and the islands.

Beverley's Restaurant, Ardfillayne Hotel, Bullwood Road, Dunoon (Tel 0369 2267). The best fresh Scottish produce (with a few French touches) in a lovely country house above Dunoon.

Middle Range

The Anchorage Restaurant, Quayside, Harbour Street, Tarbert (Tel 0880 820881). Fresh seafood, virtually straight from the sea, on Tarbert quayside.

Kilchoman House Restaurant, by Bruichladich, Isle of Islay (Tel

049685 382). Popular restaurant in a local manse run by two residents. Real traditional Scottish hospitality, cuisine and surroundings.

Economy

Esplanade Restaurant, Oban (Tel 0631 66594). Good Scottish fare in a waterfront setting.

Sea Life Centre Restaurant, Barcaldine (Tel 063 172 386). Seafood and home baking.

2 Tayside and Grampian

Tayside and Grampian encompass two adjoining but separate local authority regions. It is not surprising therefore that marked contrasts distinguish the character of each, not only in landscape and architecture, but also in people and culture. This offers the visitor variety and interest. There could hardly be a greater difference beween the bleak expanse of peat bog on Rannoch Moor in West Perthshire and the rich settled farmland of Strathmore, or the dramatic cliff coastline of Buchan and the heather moorland of Glenlivet. With the exception of the sea lochs and islands of the west coast, every other major Scottish landscape is represented, from high mountain to estuary. This is primarily an east coast region, distinguished by a hard-working Protestant culture, and characterised by tidy farms and solid burghs.

Before the Industrial Revolution this was the most populated part of Scotland, due to good farmland and easy lowland access; indications of human habitation go back to 7000 BC. It is pre-eminently the country of the feared Picts, described by the Romans as the 'Painted People', who left mysterious signposts to their culture in the form of hill forts and standing stones. Norman influence helped to create the great ecclesiastical centres of Dunkeld and Elgin, which in turn developed the many small burghs of the region and its pattern of agriculture. The population now is just over one million, although about half of this is absorbed by the cities of Dundee and Aberdeen, whose fortunes are linked in the past to their seafaring traditions and positions as European and Empire ports. The appearance and economy of the countryside ranges from the large landed estates of Perthshire and Upper Speyside, with their dependence on extensive hill sheep farming and sporting use for grouse shooting and deer stalking, to the well-established mixed lowland farms of Strathmore and the Mearns, including the smallholdings of soft fruitgrowers in the Carse of Gowrie. Parts of north Aberdeenshire and Buchan still have a relict crofting system and the area has retained the strongest rural culture which is unique in Scotland (so too is the wide and popular use of the local dialect!) The yeoman farmers of this district could hardly be more different from the retired southern incomers of Crieff, or indeed the millworkers of Dundee. What they have in common is ready access to a region of great natural and cultural diversity, where the discriminating visitor can find a genuine Scottish tradition and environment.

History

Evidence of human occupation in eastern Scotland dates man's presence to the 4th millenium. Recent archaeological surveys of numerous hut circles and funerary relicts in north-east Perthshire have revealed that the Neolithic population was higher here than anywhere else in the country. A Bronze Age culture developed on the east coast between 1800 and 1500 BC, resulting in the clearance of the more lightly wooded areas and the introduction of grain and domestic stock. The Picts, with a Celtic language and culture, have left little evidence of their existence, other than the many stone monuments scattered throughout the region. A Pictish kingdom probably emerged in the 3rd century AD with its centre in Strathmore, and successfully harried the Romans who rarely ventured north of the Forth after AD 200. Substantial hill forts, notably in Angus and Aberdeenshire (the most complete is on the summit of Tap O' North, west of Strathbogie in Aberdeenshire) bear witness to their military organisation. These warlike people also united with the Scots from the west against the Viking invaders, but were absorbed into the kingdom of the Scots with the enthronement of Kenneth McAlpine in 843.

Despite their tenuous hold on this part of Scotland (there is no evidence that they succeeded in crossing the Spey), the Romans have left their mark in the string of forts in Strathearn and Glenalmond. Smaller marching camps stretch from here north-eastwards across Strathmore to near Stonehaven, and then northwards again to Keith. The next major influence was that of the Vikings, primarily Danes, who landed on the Moray coast, and in the 12th century raided Aberdeen. At the same time there was warfare between Celts and Angles from the south.

Despite this, Christianity in the Celtic tradition had made considerable headway, though orthodox Christianity was consolidated by the Normans from the 11th century onwards, particularly during the reign of David I who established the triad of castle, church and burgh which was to dominate the social, economic and defensive settlement environment. Good examples of this urban pattern can be seen in the narrow 'wynds' of Montrose, Elgin and Inverurie, while Arbroath, Dunkeld and Elgin were pre-eminent ecclesiastical centres, and important civilising influences on their hinterlands. At the same time as the founding of the Royal Burghs and small market towns, large-scale agriculture developed around the latter, often using the better-drained soils of the raised coastal beaches.

The Wars of Scottish Independence ravaged the countryside of the north-east in the late 13th and early 14th centuries, while those which followed were often characterised by mutually destructive power struggles between Protestants and Catholics. Mary Queen of Scots journeyed through this country, only to be imprisoned in 1567 in Loch Leven Castle, from where she made her dramatic escape. After the Union of the Crowns in 1603, there was a short period of peace, but in the mid-17th century the north-east was the scene of much conflict between the Protestant Covenanters and the Catholic supporters of the House of Stuart. Bonnie Prince Charlie's route to and from England in the rebellion of 1745 took him through Atholl in Perthshire, and the Black Watch, a famous Highland regiment raised at Aberfeldy, was used to maintain the subsequent peace. In the years that followed, many of the roads and fine bridges which still stand today, were built by the English General Wade and his lieutenants. The century saw much progress in agriculture, and innovators such as Sir Archibald Grant of Monymusk in Donside pioneered new crops and rotations, while the Dukes of Atholl established the first major conifer plantings. Other 18th- and early 19th-century landlords were responsible for the planned towns and villages which are typical of this region, such as Fochabers, Tomintoul, Ballater and Burghead.

The 19th century saw further development of agriculture and industry, particularly fishing for herring from the ports of the north-east and whaling from Dundee, which at this time also established a thriving jute trade. It was this that was largely responsible for taking Dundee's population from 26,000 in 1800 to 160,000 in 1900, albeit often under desperate social and economic conditions. In Speyside, whisky distilling changed from a local pastime into a regular industry, while Deeside began to attract tourists as a result of the Royal family holidaying at Balmoral. Many of the skills involved in both whisky distilling and the tourism industry have now been adapted to the modern needs of high technology. In addition, oil exploration and production have become central to the area's economy and, despite recent fluctuations, have brought a high level of prosperity to the North-east (but have not supplanted the area's traditional farming base).

Geography

The topography of Tayside and Grampian is greatly influenced by the regions' river systems. The Tay, with the largest catchment of any river in Britain, rises in the Breadalbane Mountains of west Perthshire and flows eastwards via Perth and Dundee to the North Sea. The Spey, with it's source high in the Cairngorms, carves its way through whisky country (where there are more distilleries than anywhere in the world) north to the Moray Firth. The Dee and the Don, both of which rise on the eastern flanks of the same massif, end their journeys in the granite city of Aberdeen. These rivers cut through varied geology in their courses, from hard quartzite granites in the upper reaches of the Dee and Spey, which form the vast barren tundra of the Cairngorms, dominating the eastern frontier of Grampian Region, to the rich sedimentary sandstone of the Carse of Gowrie and Strathmore. The crystalline rocks of the higher mountains contrast with the softer volcanic lavas of lower hill ranges such as the Sidlaws and the Ochils (noticeable along the shores of the Tay between Dundee and Perth). One of the dominant structural features of the region is the Highland Boundary Fault, running south-west from Stonehaven and separating the central plain of Scotland from the Highlands. The waterfall of the Reekie Linn on the River Isla near the Perthshire–Angus border is a spectacular manifestation of this feature.

The cresent of uplands on the western margins of the region gives way to fertile lowlands along the lower reaches of the river systems and raised beaches behind the coast. Scenic glens and passes abound, such as those at Dunkeld, Killiecrankie and Glen Clova. The middle Dee and the Avon are also here, the latter being a tributary of the River Spey and claimed to be the most perfect glen in Scotland. There is a great undulating shelf of land stretching northwards from the Dee to the Moray Firth, reputed to be, with 10,000 farms, the largest continuous agricultural area in Britain. South of the Dee, the Howe of Mearns is another important agricultural area, straddling Kincardine and North Angus and celebrated in Lewis Grassic Gibbon's evocative descriptions of this stern country, *A Scots Quair*.

The North Sea coast is cold and exposed, but offers great variety: from the extensive sand dune systems north of Aberdeen to dramatic sculptured sea cliffs south of Stonehaven and Peterhead. Post-glacial deposits have produced wide estuaries such as the Tay and Ythan in Gordon District, while the turbulent Spey – probably the most active major river in Britain – ends in substantial coastal shingle banks.

Most of the important towns are situated on the coast at the river mouths. In the past they developed trade links with France, the Low Countries and the Baltic, and this is reflected in the distinctive Continental architecture in their older areas. Inland the Grampian Mountain range formed a considerable historic barrier to communications between the north and south of the region, which until relatively recent times was traversed only by drove roads. One consequence was the development of small towns and burghs on the periphery of the mountain mass, such as the settlements of Alyth, Forfar, Kirriemuir, Brechin and Edzell at the foot of the Angus Glens, all on routes which lead to the more fertile agricultural lowlands.

Climate

This is one of the drier areas of Scotland, particularly in the lowlands east of the main Grampian massif. Rainfall drops to as low as 24 inches (610 mm) on the coast at Arbroath. The region has one of the best sunshine records in Scotland, with some 1500 hours per annum. Areas such as Strathmore and Moray are protected from the wettest weather by the Highlands to the north and west. In Perthshire however, at the west end of Loch Tay annual average rainfall is about 60 inches (1524 mm) and visitors are likely to encounter a summer midge problem! August is often a rainier month than others, but the northern summer does have the compensation of long daylight hours, so that it is still possible to read out of doors up to 11 p.m.

The temperature range is largely conditioned by altitude and proximity to the coast. At Braemar, well inland, the average January temperature is no more than 1°C (35°F) and in 1982 reached a record low of minus 27.2°C (minus 40°F). Conversely, these inland areas can reach relatively high summer temperatures; for example, the mean daily maximum for Crieff in July is 19.5°C (67°F). Such areas also have the advantage of avoiding the summer sea mist ('haar') which is a common feature of the North Sea coast. A word of caution to intending hillwalkers: even in the height of summer, the high land of this region can be subject to rapid changes in weather, and hypothermia in June is not unknown on the mountain tops.

Attractions

The most obvious attraction of this region is its sheer diversity, embracing as it does many of the characteristic faces of both Highland and Lowland Scotland: from the open sweep of high heather moorland with old birch and pine woodland, to rich coastal farmland and thriving, attractive towns and villages. Here too are some of the most famous salmon rivers in Scotland, flowing into wide firths and estuaries renowned for their bird life. The hill scenery of Perthshire with its famed lochs is extremely picturesque, and for many visitors presents a less bleak and intimidating aspect than the more remote landscapes of the north-west. With the exception of the relatively limited environs of Dundee and Aberdeen, there is a complete absence of urban sprawl, and because many of the small towns and villages have developed over long periods of time, they often have considerable charm and character.

This region also has an unusual density of historical and cultural features, from prehistoric remains and ecclesiastical settlements to the architectural and social interest of 18th- and 19th-century townships. There is an almost embarrassing wealth of riches in the number of fortified houses, castles and mansions, many of which have interiors and collections of outstanding value, reflecting much of Scotland's story in a remarkably small compass. At a more humble level, the enquiring visitor will also find a rich heritage of folklore, story and indigenous music; this is the home of great fiddle composers and musicians such as Neil Gow and Scott Skinner, and is a real stronghold of popular Scottish country dance and music. In the rural districts of the north-east in particular, there is a lasting tradition of ballads and music-making which has been maintained to the present day.

Most of the attractions of this region are readily accessible and do not involve long-distance travel between points of interest. Apart from the higher mountains, most of the outdoors does not require special equipment or expertise for its enjoyment. Within the towns, there are an increasing number of facilities interpreting local social and industrial history. This is especially true of the famous Whisky Trail which is supported by many distilleries offering free tours and well-presented exhibits. Perhaps the outstanding attraction of this region is the proximity of such interests to a landscape and wildlife which is largely varied and unspoiled. It is perfectly possible to spend a morning visiting a great castle and viewing its contents, and an afternoon trekking over local moors and glens – every day for a fortnight if that's what you want!

Cuisine

Tayside and Grampian are home to some of Scotland's most renowned dishes. Salmon (fresh or smoked and often from the Tay) features strongly throughout the region, as does a wide range of fish: trout, sea fish and shell fish are all firm favourites. In addition Arbroath is known for its 'smokies': fresh haddock, dry-salted and smoked in pairs.

This is also real game country, and there are few pastimes more pleasurable to the Scottish gentleman than stalking the woods in search of deer, grouse and pheasant. All are traditional Scots delicacies which will be offered time and again.

Possibly the region's most famous indigenous culinary export is Aberdeen Angus beef, best served as a traditional Sunday roast with the minimum of trimmings. For something lighter, Forfar 'bridies' are a round of pastry folded over a filling of meat (sometimes with potato and vegetables also), something akin to a Cornish pasty.

To round off, what better than any one of a large variety of Angus-grown raspberries, topped with cream from a nearby dairy. Alternatively, or for afternoon tea, Tayberries (like a large raspberry crossed with a bramble) are equally as tasty, while Dundee cake is rich and dark, and filled with fruit and nuts.

And then there's whisky; or, in the words of Compton Mackenzie, 'Whisky Galore'. Distilleries on the Malt Whisky Trail (the only one in the world) are: Cardhu, Glenfarclas, Glenfiddich, Glen Grant, the Glenlivet, Strathisla, Tamdhu, and Tamnavulin. Speyside produces some of the most famous malts in the world, and visitors are offered a unique insight into malting, mashing, fermentation and distilling.

Level of Tourism

This region has been in the forefront of Scottish tourism for well over a century, largely due to Queen Victoria's patronage and the descriptions given by 19th-century writers. Small Victorian resorts such as Pitlochry have a particular charm based on the fashionable baronial architecture of the time, combined with a reassuring solidity which has allowed them to take a measured approach to modern tourism. Their success depends upon meeting the needs of generations of tourists, who are seeking the scenery and atmosphere of 'Traditional

Scotland'. Areas which are less known for tourism are now marketing their attributes more aggressively.

The Angus coast and traditional holiday resorts such as Monifeith and Arbroath are well served by public transport, notably railways. Increasing car ownership has allowed visitors to exercise a much wider choice of destination, and coastal resorts have seen a relative decline in their fortunes. Against this however, de-trunking of the old coastal route between Dundee and Aberdeen and replacement by the upgraded inland route for faster traffic, has encouraged leisure motorists to take the quieter coastal option. Now areas such as Angus are developing inland information centres (a 25 per cent increase in 1989) to promote a better spread of visitors. At the same time, over a third of local establishments have improved their accommodation standards.

By contrast, Perthshire has a very well-developed tourist infrastructure and, it is claimed, the largest tourist sector (relative to other economic activities) in the country. But even here there are particular areas, such as the Carse of Gowrie, which reap little benefit from tourism, as visitors head for the better known country to the north. There are notable exceptions to the general lack of interpretive services, including the very enterprising 'Locus' project in Aberfeldy (see *Good Alternatives* page 129). The district does promote personal contact between visitors and locals however, through organisations such as its ranger service. Eighty-five per cent of visitors arrive by car, and there is still relatively little integration of public transport facilities. Perthshire is keen to promote activity holidays as a recognised growth area, and the tourist board is currently establishing a consortium of operators, with some ninety-eight different establishments presently involved.

Activity holidays are also specifically identified for the first time in the most recent Grampian Region Tourist brochure. The local tourist boards are increasingly aware that such holidays depend on the maintenance of natural resources as a primary visitor attraction and have recently raised objections to forestry proposals in a scenic area in Deeside. The same tourist authority is keen to promote more general public access and to encourage more positive provisions by estates. Grampian publishes very practical guides to all its towns (colour-coded by district) including local walking routes. There are few obvious attractions specifically for children, with the notable exception of 'Storybook Glen' in Aberdeen, and a lack of wet-weather facilities. There is also a demand for more self-catering accommodation, which would encourage family visitors. Possibly because of the Royal connections of this district, there is a higher than average (25–30 per cent) proportion of international visitors.

Aberdeen is very aware of its image and is currently conducting a campaign on the theme of 'Clean and Green Aberdeen' (the city's award-winning parks testify to its long-standing concern to maintain its reputation in this respect). It is also known for its annual international festivals, which cover everything from music and football to roses.

In the districts north of Aberdeen, there is a growing awareness of the need to promote environmentally acceptable tourism policies. 'Green Gordon' for example, has involved several of the community councils as active bodies, largely because this area is neglected by many visitors, despite its attractions. For example, Donside and Gordon have a treasury of gardens, castles and many important Pictish relics, which the district is promoting through its archeological trails, improved signposting of sites, and walking routes like the West Gordon Way. Alternative tourist routes take in the high country between Aberdeen and Culloden via Alford, Tomintoul and Grantown on Spey.

In summary, although there are traditional tourist areas which can become relatively crowded in peak season, the general level of tourism over this whole area is still relatively modest by any standards, and there is little evidence that present visitation is causing serious problems. (A local exception might be the wear and tear on the footpath up Ben Lawers in Perthshire.) Tourism is still firmly based on the natural attractions of scenery, and small towns which have maintained much of their vernacular charm. It is possible to travel the length and breadth of the whole region along scenic routes through rural landscapes of high quality without encountering any despoilation or large scale development. In a number of areas there is an untapped capacity and increasing awareness of the potential of tourism to generate economic benefits and employment, notably in farming communities now facing a severe downturn in the agricultural economy.

Good Alternatives

Meeting People

There are a number of opportunities for making contact with both local residents and other like-minded visitors in this region. **The Findhorn Community** in Morayshire welcomes longer-stay visitors who are genuinely interested in the Community's life and activities, which includes a wide range of arts and crafts, not to mention conservation projects. At **Corgarff**, south of Cock Bridge on the A939 to Tomintoul, the tiny hill community (the school has only 8 pupils) has organised a rural exhibition in the village hall and offers home-baked teas in a homely kitchen. This provides an opportunity to meet the local residents who create the local crafts and who are happy to discuss their life and work with visitors. Another dimension is added by the nearby herb garden at **Old Semeil**, and the impressive **Corgarff Castle** where the keeper gives an excellent picture of the life of the redcoat soldiers stationed there after the 1745 rebellion.

The **Locus Project** in Aberfeldy, assisted by the local authority, the Scottish Development Agency and others, is especially interesting in that it is an initiative taken by local residents to combine conservation of the area's very considerable natural assets with a visitor service to co-ordinate tourist facilities through quality marketing and information. Based in an old church building in the Aberfeldy Town Square and with a full-time project officer, this enterprise focuses on interpretation of the landscape and its working community through a series of loop trails (by car or foot) in the surrounding area. At the same time it links facilities and themes, from farms to craft workshops, where visitors are welcomed. Further information is available from Locus Project, Locus Breadalbane Ltd, The Square, Aberfeldy, Perthshire PH15 2DD (Tel 0887 29442).

On a less ambitious and more informal basis, a similar initiative has been taken by a number of businesses in central Angus in the Kirriemuir area. At Kingoldrum, the old manse is now used as a quality knitwear outlet ('Just-Tina'), providing some ten local people with (self-)employment as out-knitters. In addition, the owner, in response to visitor requests to explore the local area, has developed a small-scale cycle hire enterprise. This and other local businesses have worked together to improve their collective effectiveness, particularly through co-operative marketing and informing visitors of activities such as regular craft demonstrations organised at Peel Farm Coffee and Craft Shop at Lintrathen, just off the B954 (Tel 05756 205). The nearby caravan site of Nether Craig (Tel 05756 204) is on the same road near Alyth on an attractive site and is well run.

Co-operative marketing and co-ordinated visitor provision is also a feature of a number of local enterprises based in Tomintoul and nearby **Glenlivet**. Both benefit from the active involvement of the very large Crown Estate there, which promotes integrated public access in conjunction with farming, forestry, distilling and visitor accommodation. There is a countryside ranger service and outdoor activities, including adventure holidays (which provide a good opportunity to meet knowledgeable local residents) are available, based at the Glenavon Hotel, Tomintoul (Tel 08074 218).

Discovering Places

This region is ideally suited to walking, both for serious hill trampers and more casual pedestrians, and the Grampian Regional Council publication *Hillwalking in the Grampian Highlands*, regularly updated and available from information centres, is well worth purchasing. Grampian has three long-distance paths: the **Speyside Way**, **West Gordon Way** and the **Buchan Walkway**, which utilises a disused railway line. The Speyside Way has transport facilities (see *Communications*) and a ranger service, together with frequent information points. With its whale-back hills and long slopes, the region is also especially suitable for the increasingly popular cross-country skiing, often well into the spring at higher altitudes. A recommended centre is **Knockshannoch Lodge**, Glenisla, by Alyth, Perthshire PH11 8PE (Tel 057582 238/207), where marked ski trails are available for both day visitors and course residents. For those who want to discover places from a completely different angle, **gliding** is possible in Deeside (Deeside Gliding Club, Aboyne Airfield Dinnet, Aberdeenshire AB3 5LB, Tel 03398 85339) and from Dallachy Airfield near Fochabers (Tel 0343 820568). Also on offer is paragliding over the mountains organised by Scottish Paragliders, 4 Candacraig Square, Strathdon, Aberdeenshire AB3 8XT (Tel 09756 51207).

More suitable for motorists, but also possible by cycle, the **Fishing Heritage Trail** extends along the length of the East and North coasts from Dundee to Buckie and includes the history of fishing, vessels, and even fish identification. Split into sections, each of which can be comfortably covered in a day or two, the trail also directs visitors to some of the more remote fishing hamlets on this North Sea coast. Another theme is the **Victorian Heritage** of Deeside and Kincardine, which is well described in an illustrated trail leaflet available from information centres. This takes in not only the popular sights, but also some of those less well known, such as **Fasque House**, near Fettercairn, home of William Gladstone. The same district also has enormous interest for the naturalist, with no less than six National Nature Reserves open to the public, from the wilderness of the **Cairngorms** (the largest nature reserve in Europe) to the coastal dunes and cliffs of **St Cyrus**. In between are the **Muir of Dinnet** (see *Geographical Breakdown of the Region*), and the old pinewoods of **Glen Tanar** which are served by a ranger and small visitor centre.

This series of sites, from the mountain tops through the river valleys to the sea, is a classic transect through the landscape of the region and introduces the visitor to many of its important natural habitats. The **Scottish Field Studies Association** (Kindrogan Field Centre, Enochdhu, Blairgowrie, Perthshire PH10 7PG, Tel 025081 286) runs a wide range of residential courses for natural history enthusiasts from its base in one of Perthshire's most attractive glens. For those with a general interest in the Scottish countryside and its recreation opportunities, a visit to the **Countryside Commission for Scotland's Information Centre** (off the A9 a few miles north of Perth at Battleby, Redgorton, Tel 0738 27921) is recommended, not only for the literature available but also for the outside display of 'countryside furniture' in an attractive old estate setting.

Communications

How to Get There

AIR: **Aberdeen Airport** (Tel 0224 722331) is the principal airport of the region. As well as receiving domestic flights from around the UK, it also receives flights from Amsterdam, Bergen, Copenhagen, Paris and Stavanger. Flights from Esbjerg, Aberdeen and Manchester also go to **Dundee Airport** (Tel 0382 643242).

RAIL: Main British Rail stations are at **Aberdeen** (Tel 0224 594222); **Dundee** (Tel 0382 28046), and **Perth** (Tel 0738 37117). There are regular connections both to and from the area with the rest of Scotland and the UK.

COACH: **Caledonian Express/Stagecoach** run a comprehensive system of buses connecting main towns with each other and with the rest of the country. Services usually cost considerably less than the equivalent rail journey. They can be contacted in Perth (Tel 0738 33481) and Aberdeen (Tel 0224 580275).

When You're There

RAIL: With the inauguration of railways, the Highlands became accessible to tourists. The Royal Deeside Line was built in 1853 and closed exactly a century later. Nowadays this network has been reduced to the main through route to Inverness from Perth and the coastal route via Dundee and Aberdeen. In addition, smaller, local routes connect main cities with outlying towns. **Pitlochry Travel Association**, 22 Atholl Road, Pitlochry (Tel 0796 2215/2751) offers reduced rail travel to Perthshire.

BUS: **Bluebird Northern Buses** run several times daily between

Aberdeen and Braemar and there is a summer service to Grantown-on-Spey, Glenshee and Tomintoul. Up-to-the-minute information is available from the depot at Guild Street, Aberdeen (Tel 0224 591387). Alternatively, there is the **Heather Hopper and Speyside Rambler** network which has recently been developed as a summer (24 June to 14 September) service linking Deeside, Speyside, Pitlochry and Elgin, including a very useful link-up with points along the long-distance footpath, the Speyside Way. Timetables are available from Tourist Information Centres and Grampian Regional Council Public Transport Unit, Woodhill House, Westburn Road, Aberdeen (Tel 0224 682222).

Tayside Regional Council are to be commended for their individual guides to public transport around all the main centres, which include both timetables and places of interest in the vicinity. These are available from Tayside Regional Council Transport Unit, Parker Street, Dundee DD1 5RW.

If time is not critical, it is often possible to reach many of the smaller settlements using the **Postbus** system. There are some twenty routes in the region including, for example, the very scenic drive from Pitlochry to Rannoch Station, and from Ballater to Linn of Dee. A complete timetable is produced by the Post Office Public Relations Unit, 102 West Port, Edinburgh. EH3 9HS.

CAR: There was no development of Roman roads in this region, but considerable use was made of coastal waters. From medieval times onwards, there was regular communication between the flat and fertile lowlands, such as Moray and Strathmore, using the more passable Angus glens to shorten the long-distance route via Aberdeen. These glen routeways, such as the Tolmount, Monega Pass, or Capel Mounth, were also used by armies, whisky smugglers and cattle rustlers, as well as by more law-abiding folk. In the 17th and 18th centuries for example, drovers followed such famous routes as the Lairig Ghru into Speyside. After the 1745 rebellion, General Wade's roads changed the whole picture of communications, opening up new trade routes and incidentally reducing such activities as whisky smuggling. His most important contributions were the roads from Dunkeld to Inverness via the high Pass of Drummochter, and the Stirling to Inverness route via Crieff and Aberfeldy. Nowadays, for those in a hurry, the main A9 provides a rapid route from the south via Kinross and Perth and on to Blair Atholl, complemented by the main route to Aberdeen via Dundee, Forfar and Brechin. Both roads are dual carriageway for much of their length. An alternative is to take any of the many slower scenic routes, which often take in attractive towns and villages and are usually free of heavy traffic. Those like the Ballater to Tomintoul Road are spectacular high moorland routes which call for careful driving, and a wary eye on the weather. Even in the height of summer many minor rural roads are virtually free of traffic, but by the same token, they are not replete with formal picnic sites!

CYCLING AND WALKING: Although the region offers numerous walking routes, including long-distance paths such as the serviced **Speyside Way** from Spey Bay to Tomintoul, there are no officially designated cycle routes as such. Grampian Tourist Board has published details of a cycle route from Stonehaven to Forres, however, mainly via the north-east coast, but also venturing inland to Inverurie and Fyvie. At an average of thirty miles per day, it would take eight days to cycle. Another scenic route is the B9102, which follows the west bank of the Spey from Grantown to the Moray Coast and offers a varied and quiet cycleway through whisky country. In the south-east of the region, the Angus Glens provide many opportunities, and the route from Edzell to Banchory on Deeside follows a traditional hill route. The popular Deeside road can be avoided by taking the B9119 from Ballater to Aberdeen via Midmar and Lumphanan.

For mountain-bikers, **The Green Bicycle Company** ('Cairnleith, North Forr, Crieff PH7 3RT. Tel 0764 2080) offers excellent mountain-biking holidays around Crieff, The Trossachs and Strathearn in Tayside and Central regions.

Useful Local Contacts

Groups concerned with the local environment range from the long-established **Scottish Wildlife Trust**, with branches and affiliated local groups covering Dundee and Angus, Aberdeen and Kincardine, and Perth Districts respectively, to much newer associations such as the **Urban Wildlife Groups** which have developed in the main towns – eg, **Aberdeen Urban Studies Centre** (61 Skene Square, Aberdeen AB2 4UN. Tel 0224 640864) and the **Dundee Urban Wildlife Group**, Barrack Street Museum, Barrack Street, Dundee (Tel 0382 23141).

Dundee also boasts a **Cycle Action Group** concerned with improving facilities for cycling in the district. Groups who aim to improve the amenity of the countryside primarily through native tree and shrub planting include the **Scottish Community Woods Campaign** (3 Kenmure Street, Aberfeldy PH12 2AW. Tel 0887 20392) and the **Loch Garry Tree Group** (Berbice, The Terrace, Blair Atholl, PH18 5SZ. Tel 079 681435). The **North East Mountain Trust** (Top Flat, 288 Hardgate, Aberdeen AB1 6AD. Tel 0224 581077) campaigns for the conservation of Scotland's mountains, particularly the Cairngorms. For those concerned with the whole question of land use and conservation there is the **Rural Development Discussion Group** (Haughend, Finzean, Aberdeenshire AB3 3PP. Tel 033 045264).

The **Findhorn Foundation** (The Park, Findhorn, Forres, Morayshire. Tel 0309 30311) established in 1962, now has an international reputation (it is perhaps better known abroad than in Britain) for innovative thinking and action, based on community living with an ecological and spiritual bias. As well as its respected organic vegetable gardening and tree planting programmes, it supports artistic and cultural ventures of a wide variety. Visitors are encouraged to join its afternoon guided tours which take in the impressive Universal Hall, a multi-purpose auditorium, art gallery and recording studio.

Most of the main voluntary conservation organisations in Scotland are co-ordinated through the **Scottish Countryside and Wildlife Link** which has its headquarters in Perth (Box 64, Tel 0738 3084).

Geographical Breakdown of Region

Tayside

Dundee is an attractively situated city near the mouth of the Tay with an ancient history. As an important port, it always looked outwards to the world beyond and maintained strong associations with India in the days of Empire, and with both the Arctic and Antarctic in its heyday as the premier whaling base in Britain. One of its main attractions is the **Royal Research Ship** *Discovery*, located in Victoria Dock, which provides an imaginative reconstruction of life at sea during its period of Antarctic exploration (open from 31 March to 7 October, Tel 0382 201175). The Whaling theme is continued in the **Barrack Street Museum** (open daily except Sunday) which concentrates on natural history and contains the impressive skeleton of the great whale which beached near Dundee in the late 19th century.

Although the townscape of the city has been affected by unsympathetic modern developments, there are a large number of attractive parks, several of which were established by the wealthy jute barons when this was the dominant industry. **Camperdown Park** on the north-west boundary of the city is the largest and contains a display of Scottish wildlife past and present (golden eagle, badgers, wolf, brown bear), as well as supporting a varied programme of summer events. **Dundee Tourist Board** at City Square, Dundee, DO1 3BA (Tel 0382 27723), is also the main Information Office.

The **Angus** hinterland of Dundee stretches from a relatively unspoilt coast to the very attractive glens north of the smaller country towns of Forfar, Kirriemuir and Brechin. This quiet farming country, renowned for its concentrations of Pictish relicts is worth taking time to explore. At the eastern end of the fertile vale of Strathmore, with its fields of raspberries, is the recently renovated National Trust for Scotland **House of Dun** (open from 13 April to 21 October), some four miles (6.4 km.) north of Montrose on the A935. This Palladian house was designed by William Adam and built in 1730. In addition to the fine original furniture and plasterwork, the courtyard buildings now house the last hand loom linen weavers in Scotland. Of much greater antiquity is **Glamis Castle** off the A94, fifteen miles (24 km.) east of Blairgowrie. Open from 13 April to 15 October daily from noon onwards, it is an imposing building in the typical Scots baronial style and is popularly famous as the childhood home of Queen Elizabeth, the Queen Mother.

Arbroath on the Angus coast is not only known for its excellent smoked haddock ('smokies') but is also an important point on the **Fishing Heritage Trail**, which links the fishing settlements throughout the length of the east and north coasts. The **Signal Tower Museum** (open daily except Sundays) in the town has this as one of its main themes. **Arbroath Abbey**, although ruined, is still an impressive memorial to local early Norman influence and is something of a place of pilgrimage for Scottish patriots, as the scene of the historic signing of the Declaration of Independence in 1320. The **Angus Tourist Board** and **Information Office** has its headquarters at Market Place, Arbroath DD11 1HR (Tel 0241 72609/76680).

For those with natural history interests, there are two National Nature Reserves which illustrate the contrasts of this district. The sand dunes and coastal cliffs at **St Cyrus** provide a dramatic overview of the estuary of the North Esk, and are located just over the border in Kincardine, five miles (8 km.) north of Montrose off the A92. Apart from its natural interest (especially dune and cliff flora) it is one of the few working salmon fishing stations remaining on this coast. The visitor centre (Tel 067483 736) is open from Tuesday to Sunday. This could hardly be more different from **Caenlochan**, occupying the high plateau at the head of the Angus Glens, with its ice-carved corries and Arctic-alpine flowers. It is most easily reached from the head of Glen Doll via the old drove route known as Jock's Road, but should not be attempted by inexperienced walkers. There is an attractive car park and picnic area at the head of the glen maintained by the Forestry Commission which serves both day trippers seeking mountain air and long-distance walkers attempting any one of the three long-distance rights of way which converge on the glen.

Accommodation

First Class

Swallow Hotel, Kingsway West, Invergowrie, Dundee DD2 5JT (Tel 0382 641122). A modern hotel, Scottish Tourist Board commended, with good leisure facilities and set in its own grounds on the outskirts of Dundee.

Old Mansion House Hotel, Auchterhouse, near Dundee DD5 0QN (Tel 082 626366/7). 16th-century baronial house set in extensive grounds and renowned for its cuisine.

Middle Range

Beach House Hotel, 22 Esplanade, Broughty Ferry, Dundee DD5 2EQ (Tel 0382 76614). Small, friendly hotel with good views of the Fife coast, four miles (6 km.) from the city centre.

Idvies House Hotel, Letham, by Forfar DD8 2QJ (Tel 030781 787-9). Privately run Victorian country house hotel set in delightful grounds and offering traditional Scottish cuisine.

Economy

Kingsley Guest House, 29-31 Marketgate, Arbroath DD11 1AU (Tel 0241 73933). Family run guest house in the town centre but close to the harbour and beach. A games room is available as well as organised trips to the surrounding area free of charge.

Northern Hotel, 2 Clerk Street, Brechin DD9 6AE (Tel 03562 2156). Former coaching inn (a listed building) in the town centre close to all amenities.

Eating Out

First Class

Angus Steak Bar, 101 Marketgate, Dundee (Tel 0382 26874). Excellent steak house serving prime Scottish beef and a good selection of red wines, located in the Angus Thistle Hotel.

Meadowbank Inn, Montrose Road, Arbroath (Tel 0241 75755). Traditional and nouvelle Scottish cuisine served in the Carriage Room restaurant. Good use made of fresh, local produce, including home-made bread.

Middle Range

Mains Castle, Caird Park, Dundee (Tel 0382 456797). You may think the prices here are more suited to a First Class restaurant, but what you're paying for is not only a traditional Scottish Jacobean banquet, but the entertainment and dancing as well.

But 'n' Ben, Auchmithie, near Arbroath (Tel 0241 77223). Seafood, steaks and home-made food, all totally Scottish, served in an atmosphere equally as traditional.

Economy

Raffles, 18 Perth Road, Dundee (Tel 0382 26344). Scottish, international and some vegetarian dishes served, overlooking the River Tay.

Byre Restaurant, near Arbroath (Tel 02416 245). Arbroath 'smokies' and 'cloutie dumpling' are just two of the traditional Scottish dishes served in this converted byre on a local dairy farm. Situated on the Dundee to Brechin road, near Arbroath, it's probably best to ring for directions first.

Perth and Kinross

The city of **Perth** has the particular attraction of the River Tay flowing through the centre of the town, with the city greens of the **North** and **South Inches** on its banks providing a considerable amenity for visitors. The city itself offers a variety of attractions, from the **Lower City Mills** (Lower West Mill Street. Tel 0738 30872), where Scotland's largest working power water-wheel has been restored, to the **Caithness Glass Factory** (Tel 0738 37373) on the northern outskirts of the town off the main A9. The production process can be seen on weekdays, but the visitor centre is also open on

Saturdays. On the opposite boundary of the city, off the Dundee Road (A85), the National Trust property at **Branklyn Gardens** is a mecca for alpine plant enthusiasts (open daily 1 March–31 October Tel 0738 25535). A quite different experience is provided by **Balhousie Castle** in Hay Street which houses the Museum of the Black Watch, the famous Royal Highland regiment of Tayside, with its distinctive dark green tartan. **Scone Palace** (open daily from 13 April to mid-October) off the A93, two miles (3.2 km.) north-east of Perth, has important historic associations with the coronations of the Scottish kings. Today it houses collections of fine furniture and china and offers attractive estate grounds. Perth **Tourist Information** is at 45 High Street PH1 5JJ (Tel 0738 38353). This is also the location of the Perthshire Tourist Board.

In the extreme south-east corner of the district, **Loch Leven** is not only a National Nature Reserve, but also provides the island setting for the atmospheric **Loch Leven Castle**, where Mary Queen of Scots was imprisoned and from where she made her dramatic escape. It is accessible by ferry from the Kirkgate Park and is open from 1 April to 30 September.

Crieff is an excellent centre for exploring west Perthshire. In the town itself, The **Weavers House and Highland Tryst Museum** in Burrel Street (Tel 0764 5202) is an award-winning centre which encourages interaction with visitors. The **Tourist Information Centre** is located at the Town Hall, High Street (Tel 0764 2578). More specialised and on the history and manufacture of tartan (including a dye plant garden) is the **Scottish Tartans Museum** (Tel 0764 7079) at nearby **Comrie**, which is an attractive Perthshire village in its own right.

Just over two miles (3.2 km.) south-east of Crieff, on the B8062 lies the collegiate chapel (dated 1507) of **Innerpeffray**, together with the 19th-century schoolhouse and the oldest (1691) surviving free library in the country. One mile (1.6 km.) west of Crieff on the A85, the **Glenturret Distillery** (open Monday–Saturday, March–December. Tel 0764 2424) is Scotland's oldest, and provides an award-winning audio-visual presentation and exhibition.

Travelling north from Perth (preferably on the quieter old A9 road) visitors should not bypass the historic town of **Dunkeld** (**Tourist Information Centre** at The Cross, Tel 03502 688). This charming town in a fine situation on the banks of the Tay boasts an ancient **Cathedral** and an outstanding assemblage of vernacular houses (Dunkeld 'Little Houses') restored by the National Trust. There is a **Town Trail** and many beautiful woodland walks (such as **The Hermitage**) in a locality famous for fine trees, including some of the earliest conifer plantings in Scotland. Two miles (3.2 km.) north-east of the town off the A923 is the Scottish Wildlife Trust Reserve of **Loch of the Lowes**, where breeding ospreys can be viewed in season from the hide.

Like Dunkeld, the Victorian spa town of **Pitlochry** (where every hotel takes on the appearance of a Scots baronial castle!) has benefited greatly from the diversion of through traffic on to the new A9 and is a convenient centre for touring north Perthshire. The **Information Centre** is at 22 Atholl Road (Tel 0796 2215/2751). A long-standing tourist attraction is the Hydroelectric Power Station (open daily 2 April–28 October) with its **Fish Ladder**, where migrating salmon can be seen battling their way upstream.

Six miles (9.7 km.) north-west of Pitlochry off the A9, **Blair Castle** (open daily 1 April–26 October), with its white turrets, represents a classic image of a Highland seat, and contains notable collections of furniture, pictures and Jacobite relicts, along with one of the most impressive displays of personal arms in the country. The extensive grounds have a variety of visitor facilities.

To the west of Pitlochry lies the very scenic loch area of west Perthshire, including **Loch Tummel** and **Loch Rannoch**, on the famed *Road to the Isles*. **Aberfeldy (Information Centre** at 8 Dunkeld Street. Tel 0887 20276) is an attractive centre from which to explore this ideal walking country, from the renowned gorge woodland of the **Birks of Aberfeldy** (well signposted from the centre of the town), to the **Black Wood of Rannoch**, one of the finest examples of old Caledonian Scots pinewood on the shores of Loch Rannoch, where there are some magnificent specimens of ancient 'granny' trees. Forest walks of different levels are well marked from the Forestry Commission car park at **Carie**, some three miles (6.4 km.) west of Kinloch Rannoch on the south shore of the loch. In fact the Commission has created the Tummel Forest Park in the area where visitors are encouraged to enjoy the forest through walking, cycling and sight-seeing. The locally-available guide details the various activities and attractions of the park. Overlooking Loch Tay is **Ben Lawers** (3984 ft., 1215 m.), Perthshire's highest mountain about seventeen miles (27 km.) west of Aberfeldy. The National Trust Visitor Centre (open 13 April–30 September. Tel 05672 397) is off the A827 and is the starting point for short and longer mountain trails which display the ecology and specialised flora of this National Nature Reserve. In Aberfeldy itself, it is worth paying a visit to the traditional watermill in Mill Street (open

20 March to 30 October excluding Wednesdays. Tel 0887 20803), an award-winning restoration which incorporates an audio-visual presentation.

Accommodation

First Class

Murrayshall Country House Hotel, Scone, by Perth PH2 7PH (Tel 0738 51171). Country house set in 300 acres (121.5 hectares) and noted for its award-winning restaurant and selection of sporting facilities.

Kinloch House Hotel, Kirkton of Glenisla, By Blairgowrie PH13 9AS (Tel 025084 237). Friendly, medium-sized hotel, built in 1840 and overlooking the Sidlaw Hills.

Kinnaird House, Kinnaird Estate, Dalguise, By Dunkeld PH8 0LB (Tel 079682 440). Grade 'B' listed building on its own estate overlooking the Tay north of Dunkeld. Traditional service and comfort combined with up-to-date sporting facilities.

Middle Range

Salutation Hotel, 34 South Street, Perth PH2 8PH (Tel 0738 30066). Historic hotel in the centre of town, established in 1699 and once the headquarters of Bonnie Prince Charlie.

Cultoquhey House Hotel, By Crieff PH7 3NE (Tel 0764 3253). A true Scottish country house capturing perfectly the spirit of Scotland. Four-poster beds in some rooms, fine views, traditional cuisine and log fires.

Guinach House, By the Birks, Aberfeldy PH15 2ET (Tel 0887 20251). Turn-of-the-century private country house with a large garden. Comfortable, good cooking and close to the Birks of Aberfeldy.

Economy

Knockendarroch House Hotel, Higher Oakfield, Pitlochry PH16 5HT (Tel 0796 3473). Middle range/economy hotel in an impressive Victorian house. Family owned and run and lovingly looked after.

Alpine Guest House, 7 Strathview Terrace, Perth PH2 7HY (Tel 0738 37687). Personally-run, no-smoking guest house close to the town centre.

The Firs, St Andrews Crescent, Blair Atholl PH18 5TA (Tel 079681 256). Family-run bed and breakfast close to the town centre.

Eating Out

First Class

17/21st Lancers, 8–10 North Port, Perth (Tel 0738 441427). 18th-century Georgian town house, now a restaurant serving Indian and traditional Scottish cuisine.

Number Thirty-Three Seafood Restaurant, 33 George Street, Perth (Tel 0738 33771). Wide selection of seafood dishes for both light and main meals.

Middle Range

Windlestrae, The Muirs, Kinross (Tel 0577 63217). Intimate restaurant making good use of fresh local produce.

The Four Seasons, St Fillans (Tel 076485 333). Fresh fish dishes and light snacks in this terraced restaurant with good views.

Economy

Tappit Hen, 7 Atholl Street, Dunkeld (Tel 03502 472). Delightful coffee shop offering the best of Scottish baking and home-cooked food.

The Devil's Cauldron, Comrie (Tel 0764 70352). Attractive lounge bar and restaurant serving wholesome local produce in a 200-year-old building.

Grampian

The Grampian Region looks to **Aberdeen** as its principal city, now a busy oil centre and port, but also a historic town distinguished by its characteristic sparkling granite buildings and outstanding parks and gardens. The **University** precincts provide interesting contrasts between **King's College** in Old Aberdeen, established in the 15th century by Papal decree and built from sandstone, and **Marischal College**, founded a century later for Protestant education and built with a shining granite Gothic façade. The latter houses the award-winning **Museum of Human History** (open Monday–Friday, and Sunday afternoons) with its remarkable collection of artefacts. Opposite the college is the **Tourist Information Centre** (St Nicholas House, Broad Street. Tel 0224 632727).

A more contemporary presentation of the history of 3000 years ago is presented in **'Jonah's Journey'** (Rosemount Place, open Monday–Friday, 10am–4pm), an activity-based museum for all ages which has received a number of commendations. The other museum which should not be missed (given its particular associations with the city's seafaring heritage) is the **Maritime Museum** in Provost Ross House (Shiprow, open Monday–Saturday). **Duthie Park and Winter Gardens** (off Polmuir Road) are open throughout the year and, in addition to housing a wide range of exotic plants, offer an aquarium and restaurant.

Deeside

West of Aberdeen, **Deeside** is justly acclaimed for its scenic attractions, allied to its Royal associations. Its landscape, dotted with battlemented keeps and castles, and characterised by sweeps of heather moorland interspersed with birch and pine forest, is as distinctive as any in Scotland. Framed by the southern Cairngorm massif and the landscape of *Dark Lochnagar* this is the setting for the Scottish Wildlife Trust's **Loch Muick and Lochnagar Wildlife Reserve**, which adjoins the Royal Estate of Balmoral. It can be reached by following the B796 South Deeside Road westwards from Ballater for just under one mile (1.5 km.) to the signposted junction for Glen Muick and the Trust's Visitor Centre, from where red deer can usually be seen. Not far from here, at Dinnet near Aboyne, the **Muir of Dinnet National Nature Reserve** has a wealth of wildlife habitats, including glacial lochs and the spectacular ice-carved kettle hole known as the **Burn O' Vat** reached by an easy walk from the visitor centre and tea room.

Tourist Information Centres on Deeside can be found at Station Square, Ballater (Tel 03397 55306) and Ballater Road Car Park, Aboyne (Tel 03398 86060). Kincardine and Deeside Tourist Board has its main office at 45 Station Road, Banchory (Tel 03302 2066).

Gordon

Of the numerous Castles of Mar, **Craigievar** (four miles – 6.5 km. – south of Alford on the A980) is perhaps the finest example in the country of the Scots baronial style, with as many crow-stepped gables and turrets as the most avid romantic could wish for. The castle itself is open 28 April to 30 September, but the grounds are open all year. Further south the 16th-century restored **Corgarff Castle** is set in magnificent open hill country and has a special atmosphere linked to its bloody history. It lies to the south of the A939 approximately one mile (1.5 km.) west of the junction with the B973 and is open 1 April to 30 September.

A somewhat newer visitor attraction is the recommended **Leyhead Sheep Dairy** near Lumphanan off the A980, where guided tours introduce visitors to the arts of ewe milking and cheesemaking (any afternoon except Wednesdays, suitable for the disabled). The historic ecclesiastical settlement of **Monymusk** on the B993 between Alford and Kenmay has a variety of interests, including an **arts centre** with crafts and music, and a **museum** of local pioneering agricultural development. Nearby is **Monymusk Walled Garden** which can trace its history to the 18th century and, at present, is undergoing restoration. To the north of Monymusk, the massif of **Bennachie** stands out in isolation from the surrounding fertile farmland of Donside, and as a result, its many well-signposted walks from a number of car parks on its lower boundary provide outstanding views.

In this district of Gordon, north of Aberdeen, there is a wealth of historic houses and castles, the latter excellently promoted in an illustrated leaflet produced by the local tourist board. **Haddo House**, near Ellon is a Palladian mansion designed by William Adam in a prosperous estate setting. It provides a marked contrast to the obviously defensive architecture of many of the older fortified habitations such as **Fyvie Castle**, which has been magnificently restored, with collections of fine paintings and armour. Situated on the A947 north-west of Aberdeen between Turriff and Banff, it is open from 28 April to 30 September. The local **Information Centre** is at Fyvie Castle car park (Tel 06516 597).

The coastline of Grampian is still relatively unspoiled, and a fine example of a sand dune system with abundant birdlife can be seen near Newburgh at the **Sands of Forvie National Nature Reserve**. The **interpretative centre** at Little Collieston Croft introduces the area's wildlife (open May to September daily). A change in coastal scenery is provided by the dramatic cliffs and chasms of the **Bullers of Buchan** off the A975 south of Peterhead, which is also an important seabird nesting locality. To the north of the town, **Rattray Head** is a wild lunar landscape of dunes.

Accommodation

First Class

Ardoe House Hotel, South Deeside Road, Blairs, By Aberdeen AB1 5YP (Tel 0224 867355). Baronial-style country house with fine views of the Dee Valley.

Invery House, near Banchory AB3 3NU (Tel 03302 4782). Country house hotel on the River Feugh just outside the attractive town of Banchory. Golfing and fishing both available.

Pittodrie House Hotel, Chapel of Garioch, By Inverurie AB5 9HS (Tel 04676 444). Magnificent family owned country house set on a 3000-acre (1215 hectares) estate and serving fine cuisine.

Middle Range

Atholl Hotel, Kings Gate, Aberdeen AB9 2YN (Tel 0224 323505). Traditional Aberdeen granite town house situated in the west end. Good food and service.

Burnett Arms Hotel, 25 High Street, Banchory AB3 3TD (Tel 03302 4944). Former 18th-century coaching inn on the main street, no frills but respectable and with a good reputation.

Kildrummy Castle Hotel, Kildrummy, By Alford AB3 8RA (Tel 09755 71288). Impressive country mansion, tastefully furnished and decorated and set in delightful gardens.

Economy

Brentwood Villa Guest House, 560 King Street, Aberdeen AB2 1SR (Tel 0224 491113). Friendly guest house close to the city centre. Free transport from the station by arrangement.

Gairnshiel Lodge, Glengairn, Ballater AB3 5RD (Tel 03397 55582). Victorian hunting lodge with wonderful views. Log fires, home baking and especially suitable for walkers and birdwatchers.

New Leslie Farmhouse, Leslie, By Insch AB5 6PE (Tel 0464 20508). Traditional farmhouse in beautiful countryside. No smoking and exclusively vegetarian.

Eating Out

First Class

Braemar Lodge, Glenshee Road, Braemar (Tel 03397 41627). Traditional Scottish fare offered in a former Victorian shooting lodge. Reservations strongly advised.

Banchory Lodge Hotel, near Banchory (Tel 03302 2625). Historic country house serving fine Scottish cuisine in delightful surroundings. Reservations advisable.

Middle Range

Betty Burkes, 45 Langstane Place, Aberdeen (Tel 0224 210359). Good home-made food in a busy restaurant full of local atmosphere.

Lairhillock Inn and Restaurant, Netherby, Stonehaven (Tel 0569 30001). Excellent quality and value food, especially good for Sunday lunch.

Economy

Jaws, 5 West North Street, Aberdeen (Tel 0224 645676). Aberdeen's only wholefood, vegetarian cafe. Very popular.

Wild Boar Gallery and Restaurant, 19 Belmont Street (Tel 0224 624216). Atmospheric, candle-lit restaurant displaying original art and serving good, cheap food.

Banff & Buchan

Peterhead Harbour and Fishmarket, one of the busiest in the country, selling up to 14,000 boxes of fish each day, is well worth a visit if you're an early riser (from 7.30 on weekdays and 8.00 on Saturdays). In Golf Road, there is the 400-year-old Uigie Salmon Fish House where salmon smoking can be seen on weekdays. Peterhead **Tourist Information** is at 54 Broad Street (Tel 0779 71904).

Inland from the town on the A950 at **Mintlaw**, the **Aden Country Park** has a wide variety of quality visitor facilities, ranging from an Agricultural Heritage Centre, wildlife exhibits, ranger services and restaurant, as well as events organised throughout the summer season. It is especially suitable for children and has facilities for the disabled. Mintlaw **Information Centre** is in the Farm Square (Tel 0771 23037). For something quite different, **Maund Mart** (due west of Mintlaw) offers one of the largest weekly livestock markets in Britain on a Tuesday or Wednesday morning. Also on the north-east agricultural scene are the **New Pitsligo Peat Cuttings**, off the Strichen Road.

Moray

The district of Moray incorporates one of Scotland's sunniest stretches of coast (with an annual average of around 1200 hours of sunshine) and follows the valley of the Spey to near its source high in the Cairngorms. The main town of **Elgin** is noted for a fine Norman **Cathedral** which is complemented by the 13th-century Benedictine Monastery at **Pluscarden Abbey** (six miles – 9.6 km. – south-west of Elgin off the B9010), where a religous community is actively engaged in fine restoration work. The Abbey is open to visitors 'at all reasonable times'. The main **Information Centre** is at 17 High Street, Elgin (Tel 0343 542666/543388).

The district is also noted for its Pictish relicts, and the unique stones known as the **Burghead Bulls**, probably dating from 6–7 century AD), can be seen in Burghead Library. The nearby **fort** is three times as large as any in Scotland and was once the centre of the Pictish kingdom in Moray. **Sueno's Stone**, on the Findhorn Road (B9011) just outside Forres, is a superb 1000-year-old intricately carved monument, accessible at all times. At the seaward end of the **Speyside Way** (the walking route following this famous river as far as Tomintoul), **Tugnet Ice House** at Spey Bay has been restored to present the fascinating history of the river and its timber and fishing industries (open June to September. Tel 0309 73701).

Accommodation

First Class

Waterside Inn, Fraserburgh Road, Peterhead AB4 7BN (Tel 0779 71121). Modern hotel offering every comfort. Good range of leisure facilities and an award-winning restaurant.

Mansion House Hotel, The Haugh, Elgin IV30 1AW (Tel 0343 548811). The best of the old combined with the most efficient of the new, in a 19th-century mansion house with a peaceful riverside setting.

Middle Range

County Hotel, 32 High Street, Banff AB4 1AE (Tel 02612 5353). Elegant Georgian house overlooking Banff bay. Good value accommodation and cuisine.

Minmore House Hotel, Glenlivet, Bellinadalloch AB3 9DB (Tel 08073 378). One-time home of the original Glenlivet distilling family, situated in its own grounds overlooking the River Livet, and specialising in fine Scottish cuisine.

Economy

Carmelite House Private Hotel, Low Street, Banff AB4 1AY (Tel 02612 2152). Bed and breakfast (and evening meal) in a family run Georgian townhouse. Situated in the town centre and close to the golf course.

Archiestown Hotel, The Square, Archiestown, Aberlour IV34 7QX (Tel 03406 218). Family run hotel in a quiet rural village, well situated for a number of good walks along the River Spey.

Eating Out

First Class

Old Monastery, Drybridge, near Buckie (Tel 0542 32660). Atmospheric restaurant in a converted chapel (the bar is in the cloisters) with good views and serving nouvelle Scottish cuisine. Lunches are cheaper than dinners and reservations are advised for both.

The Highland Haven, Shore Street, Macduff (Tel 0261 32408). Popular restaurant in a local hotel serving Scottish cuisine. Local fish is a speciality.

Middle Range

Clouseau's Wine Bar, 48a High Street, Elgin (Tel 0343 49737). Very popular wine bar serving a wide range of dishes, but with an emphasis on Scottish produce. Comprehensive wine and beer selection.

Buster's Bistro, 39 High Street, Forres (Tel 0309 75541). Cheerful restaurant making good (and often imaginative) use of local produce. Some vegetarian dishes.

Economy

Crown and Anchor Inn, Findhorn, Forres (Tel 0309 30243). Early 18th-century coaching inn offering traditional Scottish hospitality and home-cooked food. Huge selection of whiskies, around 100 foreign beers and seven cask ales.

Hawthorne, Fordyce, near Portsoy (Tel 0261 43003). Good value innovative cooking using local produce.

3 Edinburgh, the Lothians and Fife

Scotland's capital city, Edinburgh, exerts a powerful influence throughout the region, though this may well be more an assumption made by visitors than a fact noticed by locals. Edinburgh enjoys a similar influence throughout Scotland, though from a Highland or West Coast perspective the city sometimes seems frustratingly distant and is often regarded as no more than an extension of England, rather than as the true capital of Scotland.

'West endy and east windy'; 'fur coats and no knickers'; 'more public schools than public toilets'; 'posh ('Morningside') accents'; 'stuck-up and unfriendly': the list of criticisms is endless, yet in surveys of the quality of life in British cities Edinburgh continually ranks highly. Perhaps it is fitting that a capital city should be perceived in such a variety of contradictions. And if, like other Scots, Edinburghers are said to be 'dour', then perhaps what the casual observer is dwelling on is the occasional outburst of Calvinism which they sometimes inflict upon themselves to temper the natural high spirits that come from living in such a beautiful place.

The spectacular skyline is world famous; the city boasts the best-preserved neo-classical town planning developments in the country. Yet not so long ago Edinburgh had some of the worst slums in Europe, just off the famous Royal Mile. It is a medical centre of world standing – famous doctors and scientists are household names – yet in some of its peripheral housing estates, products of well-meaning but sadly misguided planning in the 1960s, the levels of AIDS and HIV infection are the highest in Britain. Environmentally, Edinburgh is rapidly changing from a dark place of smoke-blackened buildings (the 'Auld Reekie' of yesteryear) to a city of mellow, golden sandstone, yet until 1977 it pumped raw sewage into the River Forth. Musselburgh, ten miles (16 km.) down the coast, still cannot eat the mussels that gave it its name, and warning signs extend a further twenty miles (32 km.) to Dunbar. And the good citizens, along with the rest of the Scots, have one of the most unhealthy diets – a passion for cakes and biscuits and fatty foods.

Whatever the contradictions of the capital city, whatever its political and cultural influences, the rest of the region has its own characteristics and a marked natural diversity. Lothian is made up of four districts: the City of Edinburgh itself and East, West and 'Mid-Lothian'. In the east, rich farmland rolls down to the North Sea coastline, presenting a striking contrast to the more industrial landscapes of the west, while Midlothian, as the name implies sits comfortably in the middle, drawing on the characters of each. Two fine ranges of hills occupy the southern fringes of Lothian. The Pentlands, rising to 1500 ft. (457.5 m.) and providing a striking backdrop to Edinburgh, were christened the 'Hills of Home' by Robert Louis Stevenson. This is good sheep raising country to the farmers and a natural playground for the citizens of Edinburgh. Further east lie the Moorfoot Hills and the Lammermuirs, similarly given over to upland agriculture and, to a lesser extent, recreation.

To the north, across the waters of the Firth of Forth, lies Fife. Proudly independent of the southern heartland, boasting the title 'The Kingdom of Fife', this once isolated peninsula is indeed a distinctive area, though it too shows an east–west contrast in character. West Fife is a predominantly industrial area, though its early wealth in coal is now depleted, while East Fife (and the north east in particular) is a gentle landscape of rolling farmland with a fringe of beaches and fishing villages.

This region occupies much of the eastern half of the Central Lowlands, the comparatively low-lying land between the Highlands and the Southern Uplands. Some 75 per cent of the population of Scotland live in this area, though rambling in the Pentland Hills or walking down a country lane in East Lothian there is little hint of this.

Visitors from the south will enter the region along good roads passing through and between the Pentland, Moorfoot and Lammermuir Hills. These follow the course of old routes used by early invaders and settlers of the region. The Votadini were one such early people, referred to by Ptolemy in AD 160 as inhabiting a settlement with the Celtic name, Dunedin. This was an important defensive site at that time and 'Edinburgh' is an Anglicised version of the name. Anglian settlements, such as the one unearthed in Dunbar in 1989, are evidence of the fact that the region was once part of the ancient kingdom of Northumbria. At that time Edinburgh was not the capital city of Scotland; that lay further north, over the Forth at Dunfermline, away from the troublesome peoples in the south.

History

Cairnpapple Hill near Bathgate in West Lothian is an ancient site spanning the Stone Age and the Bronze Age, although there is little evidence of the Roman presence in the region.

Ancient Caledonia, as the Romans called it, was a forbidding place. Julius Agricola in AD 80–83 marked a frontier between the lands of the unconquerable northern tribes and occupied Roman Britain along a line from the Firth of Forth to the Firth of Clyde. Half a century later the Antonine Wall was built along this line, although it was abandoned after forty years. Thirty-six miles (58 km.) long, stretching from Old Kilpatrick in Strathclyde Region to the site of present day Falkirk in Central Region, it is best seen today at Rough Castle near Bonnybridge by Falkirk, where there were Roman headquarters and barracks. At Cramond in Edinburgh, by the shore of the River Forth, there are remains of a Roman fort. Otherwise there is little evidence of the centuries between the Iron and Dark Ages.

In the 7th century the Firth of Forth marked the southern boundary of the lands of Picts, or Painted People, who occupied most of Northern and Eastern Scotland.

Christianity arrived in Scotland with St Ninian in AD 397. It reached as far as the southern boundaries of Pictland and early cave shrines have been found on the Fife coast. Two hundred years later, around 563, St Columba crossed from Ireland. The Celtic Christian Church progressively converted ancient 'Alba' to what was to become a united Christian Scotland. Other invaders of Scotland at this time were the Norsemen, though again there is little evidence to testify to their presence. In the 12th century King Malcolm III (better known as Canmore, or Bighead) built Edinburgh Castle, or at least the beginnings of the castle we recognise today: it was merely a hunting lodge amidst the wooded country surrounding the castle rock. His court was in Dunfermline, over the Forth in Fife. His queen, Margaret (later St Margaret) built the chapel which is still present within the castle walls. Their son David I built the Abbey of Holy Rood a mile from the Castle at the foot of today's Royal Mile below the ancient (and extinct) volcano that is Arthur's Seat. Both Holyrood and Arthur's Seat are important features of present day Edinburgh.

By this time, Edinburgh was an important town and well worthy of attack and conquest by the Old Enemy, England. The Battle of Bannockburn in 1314 saw King Robert the Bruce send English forces packing and released the castle from almost twenty years of English occupation; to avoid further risk of occupation he demolished it, sparing only St Margaret's Chapel! In 1389 he did, however, give Edinburgh the status of Royal Burgh it retains today.

The rest of the century saw the reconstruction and enlargement of Edinburgh Castle by both Scottish and English occupiers, the latter who were covetous of it as a base for control of the rich lands of the Lothians. By the late 14th century, house building was permitted within the castle walls – it was never exclusively a Royal residence – and the medieval walled town was beginning to take shape.

The 'Auld Alliance' between Scotland and France flourished briefly in the 15th and early 16th centuries. Mary Queen of Scots, today famed throughout the country on tins of shortbread and historic sites alike, was a product of this. The daughter of James V, of the famous Stuart family, she returned from France to Scotland in 1565. Despite her fame and contradictory to the unashamed way her name is exploited in the tourist image of Scotland, she spent much of her life in exile in England as a victim of political and religious forces and the prisoner of her cousin, Queen Elizabeth I. Mary's son James, became King James VI of Scotland and I of England, the first king of a united kingdom of Scotland and England.

By the 16th century, Edinburgh was the capital of Scotland. The 'Old Town' had acquired the architecture and character visible today, and was reasonably secure with the Flodden Wall, parts of which can still be seen, as at the Vennel by the Grassmarket. The ensuing years saw continuing strife between Scotland and England, notably with the Glencoe massacre of 1692 and the Jacobite rebellion of 1745–46. The Jacobites occupied Edinburgh briefly.

The formal union between Scotland and England occurred in 1707. While such events as the Highland clearances remain as examples of the darker side of this union, the 18th century in Edinburgh marked the dawn of a Golden Age. The Georgian New Town was begun in 1752, to the design of James Craig. The medieval Old Town saw the departure of first the upper, then the middle classes to the orderly, gridiron planned, spacious streets of the New Town to the north. The streets of that New Town retain their elegance today. Princes Street is one of the world's most beautiful thoroughfares, with shops on the north side, and gardens and a spectacular view of the castle and its crag to the south. George Street links the financial heart of the city, Charlotte Square, with the less imposing St Andrew Square in the east. Queen Street maintains a rigid formality of design, while its private gardens symbolise the division of Edinburgh society that the New Town instigated.

The medieval Old Town had evolved 'organically' over the centuries. Buildings went up with little or no overall plan and sanitation amounted to the famous cry of 'Gardyloo' (from the French, *gardez l'eau* or 'mind the water') as household unmentionables were thrown into the street to await eventual removal. But for all its overcrowding and lack of health standards, the Old Town populace of all classes shared the same patch. The only physical hierarchy was within the high tenement flats – the rich at the bottom and the poor at the top!

The city became known as 'The Athens of the North' in the 18th century. No longer a political centre, but the cultural/intellectual focus of the 'Scottish Enlightenment', it was home to David Hume the philosopher, then in the 19th century to literary figures such as Sir Walter Scott and Robert Louis Stevenson. Medical pioneers Lister (antiseptics) and Simpson (chloroform) both lived here, as well as characters such as Burke and Hare who also served medicine in their own, highly dubious manner as grave robbers.

Radical change in the region was not confined to the capital. The orderly farmlands of East Lothian and East Fife are largely a product of the 18th- and 19th-century improvers who pursued the then current ideals of order and efficiency. In West Lothian and the west of Fife, oil shale and coal mining were rapidly developing to supply the growing city and the expanding British Empire.

Present day Edinburgh continues the historical pattern set by the union with England: political emasculation and (comparative) cultural and financial strength, with the New Town, a financial centre second only to that of London. The city still awaits a measure of political power as the home of the Scottish Assembly, or 'full' power as capital of a once-again independent Scotland, albeit as a small country within the European Community. Both aspirations manifest themselves on the streets of the capital in marches and posters. The physical home is ready and waiting on Calton Hill, its corridors still echoing with the dashed hopes of the referendum for a Scottish Assembly held in 1979, when an insufficient majority of the Scottish people (33 per cent) voted for a measure of independence.

Geography

Historical, cultural and economic developments are inseparably tied to the fundamental ecological resources of soil, topography and climate. East Lothian's agricultural heritage of grain crops is largely due to the inherent fertility of its rich, red soils and its dry climate. In West Lothian, wetter conditions and heavier soils encouraged smaller farms, grassland and dairying, while coal and oil shale industries further modified the character of the landscape. Much of West Lothian is upland acid moorland rising to the Pentland Hills themselves. Midlothian is comparatively low lying – the Midlothian basin, a glacial plain framed by hills.

The underlying geology of the Lothians is inescapable. Little wonder that the science of geology saw its beginnings in Edinburgh – pioneers such as Hutton were undoubtedly inspired by the clear evidence of the violent volcanic past. Edinburgh itself is dominated by ancient volcanoes. The castle sits atop an ancient volcanic plug scraped by the glaciers of the Ice Age into the distinctive crag and tail features. Arthur's Seat overlooks much of the city, an 823 foot (251 m.) miniature mountain forming a wonderful wild park near the city centre. This is, indeed, a city of hills, as any cyclist will testify, but they give a rich character. Edinburgh Zoo sits on the slopes of Corstorphine Hill, its exotic wildlife complemented by the wild fox and badger beyond its fences. The city's two observatories occupy other hills: Calton Hill and Blackford Hill. Further afield in East Lothian, North Berwick Law rises out of the farmland, while offshore is the Bass Rock, painted white by countless generations of resident gannets.

The human geography of latter-day Edinburgh and the region was examined and interpreted in the early years of the century by the pioneer geographer, sociologist and planner, Patrick Geddes. Taking Edinburgh as a case study, he emphasised the interdependence of cities and their regions, and of the regions within the world. Geographical features and resource limitations led to the strategic importance of Edinburgh Castle site and, equally forcibly, to construction of the New Town to the north. This necessitated considerable land engineering to drain the Nor'Loch (now Princes Street Gardens) and to construct the Mound, the man-made hill rising from Princes Street to the Old Town.

Across the Forth Estuary lies Fife, a peninsula isolated from the rest of the country by the Ochil Hills to the west and water on three sides. This comparative isolation was broken only by the building of the rail bridges across the Tay and Forth estuaries in the late 19th century, and the road bridges in the 20th century. The coal mining industries have shrunk to a tiny fraction of their former glory, throwing entire communities into despair, though new industry and service jobs are being created. Much of the earlier industrial landscapes of west Fife have been reclaimed after years of dereliction.

Rivalling the Pentlands of Lothian are the Lomond Hills of Fife. Also volcanic in origin, they are today moorland and rough grazing. Like the Pentlands, they are a Regional Park and respect traditional land uses, while also providing recreation areas.

Further east lies the rich farmland of the Howe of Fife next to the East Neuk, where there are volcanic remains such as Largo Law. King James VI called Fife 'A beggar's mantle fringed with gold' on account of the important coastal harbours and ports. Trade with the Baltic and the Mediterranean was the origin of the ancient burghs such as Leven, St Monance, Crail, Pittenweem and Anstruther. Fishing has long since replaced it, but even that is in decline. In its place, tourism has become an important source of employment for these attractive harbour towns, sheltered beaches and rocky headlands. On the east coast St Andrews is famous for its golf connections, its university and its fine architecture and beaches.

Like the great majority of Scottish landscapes, what is seen in Lothian and Fife is the end result of long habitation by man. Sometimes improving, but often mismanaging the land through deliberate forest clearance and subsequent soil impoverishment, much of the area would have been wooded – Scots pine and birch on the Pentlands and other hills, with oak woods on the lower, richer soils. Today's landscape retains only traces of that sylvan past.

The modern region is characterised by the activities of the service sector of the economy – including finance and tourism – and by the hi-tech electronics industries. The traditional or 'smoke stack' industries are largely gone or going, though brewing, still a 'heavy' industry, remains. Each year Edinburgh produces millions of pints of 'Heavy' (similar to English 'Bitter' though superior to it). Remnants of the formerly dominant mining and shale industries can be found in the form of the 'bings' or tips of spent shale of West Lothian, or of coal in West Fife, today forming, sadly to some, the basis of interesting tourist attractions.

Climate

It is often pointed out that Edinburgh is as far north as Moscow. Like the rest of Britain however, the climate is greatly moderated by the proximity of the sea. While Edinburgh's climate was frequently and famously cursed by one of her native sons, Robert Louis Stevenson, the region is in fact one of the driest in Scotland. The east of Scotland

Edinburgh, the Lothians and Fife

generally lies within a pronounced rain-shadow, with most of the Atlantic's rainfilled clouds depositing their contents over the west of the country. Annual rainfall in Edinburgh is around 710 mm (28 inches), and Dunbar in East Lothian claims the highest sunshine records in Scotland. But the infamous east winds do exist and can show themselves both as cool breezes tempering warm summer days, and as carriers of the chilling, damp blanket of 'haar' or North Sea mist that so much oppressed Stevenson. Rainfall is distributed fairly evenly throughout the year, though March averages out as the driest month with around 38 mm (1.5 inches) and August as the wettest with around 80mm (3.1 inches). As elsewhere in the country, temperatures are influenced by altitude and moderated by the proximity of the sea: August averages 14°C (56°F) and January 4°C (40°F). These are, of course, averages and a long spell of summer days in the mid-20s (70°F) is not unknown. Snow lies on the ground for around twenty mornings in an average winter and early spring. Generally, the east of the region – East Fife and East Lothian – has a few annual centimetres less rain and the west a few more. Humidity is only very rarely a factor reducing comfort.

Attractions

Edinburgh is undoubtedly the principal destination in the region for most tourists; unfortunate in some ways, since the city's wealth of interest tends to distract from the quieter charms of the rest of the region. The city offers the range of attractions to be expected from a capital, but goes beyond that in its sheer physical beauty, blending the works of man and nature. In few parts of the city is the visitor out of sight of formal parkland and gardens, or apparently wild countryside within the city boundary. The view from Princes Street is an excellent example: on one side, one of the world's fine shopping streets, while on the other Princes Street Gardens, complete with flower beds, putting greens, pigeons and band stands, the whole nestling snugly at the base of the Castle Rock. Climb to the top of the Scott Monument within the gardens, and the hills and coastlines of Lothian are clearly visible, while beyond lies Fife and, on a clear day, the mountains of the lower Highlands.

Princes Street lies, in effect, between the two Edinburghs of the New Town and Old Town. The Georgian New Town occupies a gently sloping ridge to the north. The names of the streets are a celebration of the 'marriage' between Scotland and England, though this is rarely mentioned today: Princes Street, George Street, Hanover Street and so on. Its grid-plan symmetry and formality contrast markedly with the Old Town up on the 'tail' of Castle Rock. The Old Town was not planned, it simply evolved over the centuries free from the restrictions of such later concerns as health and sanitation, traffic circulation and congestion. Health hazards are long gone but traffic congestion is still a problem, and attempts to exclude private cars from some areas are still met with hostility by local traders.

While the New Town is now largely the province of financial institutions and other offices, the Old Town remains a living community where local shops co-exist with all the paraphernalia of modern tourism. A great deal of rehabilitation and general improvement work has taken place in the Old Town and elsewhere in recent years and this continues today. After decades of decay since the 1960s, streets formerly run-down are coming back into life and business.

Around the Old Town the many literary, artistic, scientific, medical, political and other personalities associated with Edinburgh are commemorated in statues, plaques and place names.

The Edinburgh countryside is extensive, extending from the shoreline of the Forth Estuary to the slopes of the Pentland Hills and including many fine parks and open ground. The Edinburgh green belt is formally recognised and protected from inappropriate development, though periodic battles over its sanctity are not unknown between developers and town planners.

Beyond the city, East Lothian is noted for its fine agricultural countryside as well as its beaches and sand dunes. This is a rich, man-made landscape generally in good heart, though few of the population are now employed in agriculture. Attractive villages, once serving the needs of agriculture as market towns and workers' communities, are now highly desirable residential and commuter areas, though the air is still that of working, rural homesteads, now benefiting from the spin-off wealth from the city.

To the west, a different landscape gives West Lothian a harder look. With few exceptions the villages and towns seem more utilitarian. Modern housing, steadily 'infilling' the spaces within these settlements, is typical of today's 'anywhere architecture' that knows no frontiers. Linlithgow, a historic town in the district, is famed as the birthplace of Mary Queen of Scots, and has a fine ruined palace. The world famous Forth Bridge, whose 100th anniversary was celebrated in 1990, links West Lothian with Fife.

Midlothian has both 19th-century housing estates and some gems of rural architecture. Fine, small-scale landscapes can be found behind the hedgerows and high walls of former estates, which are now maintained for public enjoyment, as well as for farming or private pleasure. Many are close to relics of former industry, which have also found new life through tourism. Miles of winding country lanes belie the compactness of the district.

The ancient, independent Pictish state of Fife is long gone, but a certain independence remains, summed up in the locals' persistent reference to 'The Kingdom'. Redevelopment of the former industrial landscape characterises much of west Fife, an acclaimed symbol being Lochore Meadows, near Lochgelly. Only recently a despoiled remnant of the coal mining industry, determined and skilful reconstruction has created a fine country park. West Fife is not all reconstruction however: Culross retains its original 16th-century character in its architectural styles, while Dunfermline celebrates its rich history as the one-time capital of Scotland. In the east, the beautiful university town of St Andrews is the home of golf, and nearby are the East Neuk fishing villages.

Cuisine

The porridge and haggis stereotypes of Scotland still tend to be better known than the realities of Scottish regional cuisine. The best of Scottish fare is often associated with French cuisine, reflecting the 'Auld Alliance' between the two countries. Unfortunately Scottish cuisine also tends to be associated by many with up-market restaurants, and most visitors (and Scots) settle for a conventional 'European' diet, though favouring an excess of sugar and fats, or American fast-food. With a long coastline and much upland agriculture, sea food, meat and game are deservedly well known. The Scottish breakfast is a substantial affair, including porridge (with salt or sugar), and kippers. In Edinburgh, food of most nations can be enjoyed from a wide range of restaurants, and even vegetarian haggis is available. Famous Edinburgh 'sweeties' include Edinburgh Rock, available in boxes of six flavours, and hard mints known as pan drops.

Level of Tourism

During 1990 an organisation emerged in Edinburgh dedicated to fostering a new approach to the city's tourism industry: Edinburgh Marketing aims to co-ordinate – and inspire – a partnership between the public and private sectors to further develop tourism. This is to be achieved by promoting the city not only as a cultural/historic and Festival centre, but also as a business and conference tourism destination, and by extending the traditional tourism season to incorporate more of the year through short breaks and special interest holidays. The task is not without its problems however, for there is already a feeling that the city has passed the point where tourist numbers begin to threaten the quality of the experience initially sought. In addition, city-centre locals are complaining about the closure of shops catering to local requirements in order to make way for tourist-oriented facilities, and the difficulty of parking their cars. They joke (?) about abandoning Edinburgh to the tourists for the summer. The tourism industry says the answer lies in 'spreading the load', and therefore the benefits, of tourism in both time and place; that is, by extending the season and developing more attractions to draw crowds away from the honeypots.

There is every reason to maintain the heart of the city, notably the Old Town, as a living, working community. Simultaneously however, Edinburgh's business people and residents must accept that many of the facilities they enjoy would be insupportable without the very considerable financial input from tourism. A solution which advocates tourism without tourists is simply not attainable.

Serious thought is being given to improving the 'tourism product' of Edinburgh. Even such holy grails as the castle and the annual military tattoo are not exempt. It has long been recognised that visitor facilities in the castle are less than satisfactory, and many question both the audio and visual impact of erecting the seating for the tattoo on the castle esplanade. It has been suggested that the tattoo could take place on a permanent site, possibly down in Princes Street Gardens, with the castle and its rock as the stupendous backdrop. At the same time however, it is arguable whether anywhere else in the city could recreate the gripping atmosphere of the castle esplanade.

Despite serious competition from Glasgow in recent years, Edinburgh will retain its appeal as the Scottish capital, and as the gateway to Scotland for incoming tourists. Time spent in the city however, might also be shared with trips to the 'second capital' only an hour away. If anything, Edinburgh should welcome the attention Glasgow has successfully fought for: it has at least forced the capital to shake off the complacency generated by years of continued success.

With such a wealth of attractions available in Edinburgh, it is all too easy to overlook the rest of the region. The history and geography of the area's quiet villages and attractive towns offer some of the pleasures of the capital without the peak season crowds, and there is every reason to take an hour or so by train to reach the outer limits of the region.

Good Alternatives

Meeting People

Edinburgh's pubs can be excellent places for meeting local people. This is a city of two universities and many colleges, however, and many pubs are little more than honeypots for non-resident students. If looking for a traditional 'local' (in terms of both pub and residents), try some of the bars away from the university area.

During the summer Princes Street Gardens are a popular gathering point, although frequented as much by tourists as locals.

Bed and Breakfast and Guest House accommodation brings the visitor into the homes of local people. Reasonable prices and high standards are set by the local tourist authority for registration, and generally offer comfort and homeliness rather than facilities such as en-suite bathrooms.

Discovering Places

Edinburgh extends far beyond the Princes Street/city centre area, and exploration of its neighbourhoods gives an alternative insight into local life.

Leith was until recently a seedy, run-down (but rich in community spirit) part of the city. The Port of Leith has regained much of its early vitality and character through a successful public–private 'Development Initiative', pushed hard by the Scottish Development Agency. Some would say that too much of the previous character has given way to 'Yuppiedom', but there is plenty for all tastes – wine bars and pubs of character, and recently improved attractions such as the Scottish Woollen Mill. In addition there are the actively working docks, although as yet few concessions to visitors have been made.

Gorgie-Dalry is a busy, 'ordinary' Edinburgh neighbourhood, just a ten minute bus ride from Princes Street. Nineteenth-century tenements with street-level shops form the townscape. The Heart of Midlothian or 'Hearts', football ground is here, a Mecca for many; so is the city's only City Farm.

Morningside is generally associated with the 'Miss Jean Brodie' accent said to be spoken by the residents. Allegedly, 'Sex is what Morningside people put coal in . . .' ('Sacks')! Today it is a busy, 'desirable' residential area with good local shops.

Stockbridge is on the northern fringe of the New Town. Still considered a trendy area, it is busy with a wide range of small, essential and interesting shops, notably selling antiques and bric-à-brac. A number of pubs here are ideal for meeting the locals.

Communications

How to Get There

AIR: **Edinburgh Airport** (Tel 031 333 1000) is situated at Turnhouse, less than ten miles (16 km.) west of the city centre. In addition to receiving flights from throughout the UK, there are regular connections to and from Europe. From the airport, a regular bus service is available into town.

RAIL: Edinburgh is easily reached by rail from throughout the UK. **Waverley** (Tel 031 556 2451) is the main British Rail station, situated at the east end of Princes Street. InterCity trains are fast and frequent and the introduction of the InterCity 225 in summer 1991, serving Edinburgh and the east coast, brought the city within four hours of London.

COACH: Both **National/Caledonian Express** and **Scottish City Link** coaches connect Edinburgh with the rest of the country. St Andrew's Bus Station (Tel 031 556 8464) is situated at the east end of George Street, next to St Andrew's Square.

When You're There

RAIL: Although Edinburgh has two stations (Waverley at the east end and Haymarket at the west end of Princes Street), train travel is not really suited (or necessary) to cross-town journeys. Both stations however, provide convenient starting points for trips out of town, going in any direction. There are regular services to Fife (and beyond), Glasgow and down the east coast.

BUS: Deregulation of the city's buses has led to an increase in the range of private operators offering services around town. **Lothian Regional Transport** run one of the most comprehensive networks and details of routes and times are available from 14 Queen Street (Tel 031 226 5087).

CAR: Driving in Edinburgh is not really recommended or, indeed, necessary. The city experiences the same rush hour problems and congestion as most capital cities and, even at other times, can be very busy. Parking is always a problem, despite two multi-storey car parks: one at the east end in the St James Centre and one at the west on Castle Terrace. During the festival in particular and the summer months in general, visitors are best advised not to drive unless absolutely necessary.

From Edinburgh however, there are good roads to outlying areas. Motorway connections to both Fife (across the Forth Road Bridge) and Glasgow are fast and efficient, although it has to be said that both can be prone to delays due to road works. There is no motorway down the east coast of Scotland and roads, although (or because they are) scenic, can become very congested (especially during the summer).

CYCLING: In a city with so many hills, cycling is not always the most relaxing way of getting around. There is however, a developing network of cycle paths which make use of disused railway lines and the tow-path of the Union Canal, which once ran from Edinburgh to Falkirk and then on to Glasgow. Details are available from **Tourist Information** and bicycles can be hired from **Central Cycle Hire** (Tel 031 228 6333) at Tollcross, or **Edinburgh Bicycle Cooperative Ltd** (Tel 031 228 1368) at Bruntsfield.

East Lothian is wonderful cycling country and the East Lothian Tourist Board produces an excellent leaflet, *Cycling in East Lothian* which highlights routes and points of interest.

WALKING: Edinburgh is a compact and highly 'walkable' city for anyone reasonably fit. It may be hilly, but the topography greatly adds to the variety. A circular tour of the city centre area, including the Royal Mile and some of the Old Town, Princes Street and some of the New Town, can be a leisurely day, allowing lots of time for browsing in shops and taking in sights. At the same time though, a whole week could be spent simply exploring the Old Town.

The **Patrick Geddes Trail** runs the length of the Royal Mile and gives a behind-the-scenes view of some of Edinburgh's most famous sights. Walks along the **Water of Leith** are another alternative and, apart from one or two sections, it is possible to walk from the Port of Leith to Balerno near the slopes of the Pentland Hills (which are excellent walking country in their own right). Also in the city, **Arthur's Seat** offers an energetic but safe scramble to the top, from where there are magnificent views of Edinburgh and the surrounding countryside. Details of walks are available from the city **Planning Department** (Tel 031 225 2424).

Useful Local Contacts

A very large number of Scottish environmental, community, political and other voluntary bodies have their headquarters in Edinburgh. In fact, it is one of the historic realities of the capital that voluntary bodies, notably those concerned with the man-made environment, have played a major part in making Edinburgh what it is today. They have successfully countered undesirable urban road proposals, fought against demolition plans, and generally been a gadfly to the sometimes insensitive forces of both the public and private sectors. The **Cockburn Association** (Tel 031 557 8686) is an example of the old-established and prestigious societies campaigning on a wide range of civic issues. **SPOKES** (Tel 031 313 2114), the Lothian Cycle Campaign, has achieved a great deal in a decade or so, helping urban/commuter cycling in particular gain acceptance as a viable alternative, with increasingly good routes throughout the city. **Edinburgh Greenbelt Initiative** (Tel 031 652 1114) protects this component of the city's 'green lung' from inappropriate development. The **Scottish Wildlife Trust** (Tel 031 226 4602) campaigns for nature conservation and manages its own nature reserves throughout Scotland. They have a visitor centre in Queen's Park. **Friends of the Earth Scotland** (Tel 031 554 9977) headquarters are also in the city.

Geographical Breakdown of Region

Edinburgh

Edinburgh Castle (Tel 031 244 3101), in one form or another, has occupied the natural defensive site of Castle Rock for thirteen centuries. The present structure dates largely from the 14th to 16th centuries. **St Margaret's Chapel** is the oldest existing building, dating from the 12th century. The Scottish **Crown Jewels** are housed in the castle and the **Esplanade** offers a fine view over the city and countryside beyond. The castle is open all year round.

Patrick Geddes' **Outlook Tower**, a short distance down the Royal Mile, is now a privately run visitor centre; the **Camera Obscura** on its roof offers fascinating views of city and countryside. Across the road is the **Scotch Whisky Heritage Centre**, a modern heritage centre using moving seats and a multi-lingual taped commentary to give the visitor a quick tour around creatively lit scenes from the history of whisky. A more traditional visitor attraction is **Gladstone's Land**, a genuine early 17th-century building with period furnishings and decor. **Lady Stair's House** is a museum dedicated to three literary Scots: Robert Burns, Sir Walter Scott and Robert Louis Stevenson.

Brodie's Close is the former residence of William Brodie, an 18th-century respected citizen by day and thief by night, who inspired Stevenson's *Dr Jekyll and Mr Hyde*. **St Giles Cathedral** – the High Kirk of St Giles – is an impressive 14th-century building, also housing the Thistle Chapel with its beautiful wood carvings. Near the entrance is a heart-shaped pattern of cobblestones, the **Heart of Midlothian**.

Behind is **Parliament House**, where the Scottish parliament sat until the union with England in 1707. The medieval **Mercat Cross** is in Parliament Square. Further down is the **Tron Church**, a traditional Hogmanay (New Year's Eve) gathering place.

Beyond the intersection with North Bridge is the **Museum of Childhood**, with displays of children's toys through the ages. Across the road is the 15th-century **John Knox's House** named after the religious reformer, and at number 105, **Still's Gallery** of photography.

St Mary's Street just off the Royal Mile, was saved in the 1980s from a development proposal and is now a conservation area. It is also the sort of area Patrick Geddes was interested in and is worth noting for its traditional Scots Baronial architecture. Down the street and into the Cowgate is **Bannerman's Bar**, an interesting pub with stone floors and church pews. **Canongate Tolbooth** once marked the boundary between Edinburgh and the Canongate, now part of Edinburgh. It houses a museum, **The People's Story**, which has fascinating displays of recent Edinburgh social history. In the cemetery of **Canongate Church** Adam Smith, the 18th-century economist is buried. **Huntly House** opposite contains a fascinating collection of local history. Beside it is the **Scottish Stone and Brass Rubbing Centre**, where rare pieces can be 'rubbed' by anyone. Marking the end of the Royal Mile is the 16th-century **Palace of Holyrood House**, the official residence of the Royal Family in Scotland. The ruined, 12th-century **Holyrood Abbey** is adjacent. Behind is **Holyrood Park**, a manicured park which contrasts dramatically with the rugged **Arthur's Seat** and **Salisbury Crags** looming above. Patrick Geddes considered this close interplay of 'green' and built environment an ideal in the design of truly civilised cities.

The South Side district is a short walk from the Royal Mile. On George IV Bridge is the **National Library of Scotland** (Tel 031 226 4531). Opposite, Victoria Street branches off, a distinctive curved street with an intriguing variety of antique and curio shops. This leads down to the **Grassmarket**, complete with pubs, antique shops and a dramatic view up to the Castle. Leaving the Grassmarket by Candlemaker Row leads to the statue of **Greyfriars Bobby**, the dog who guarded his master's grave for fourteen years in the 19th century. The dog received the honour of being buried in **Greyfriars Churchyard**. Greyfriar's Bobby is also a popular pub, just next door to the churchyard, which serves food until late. The **Royal Museum of Scotland** is in Chambers Street. It is an imposing Victorian building and houses the finest collection of seemingly every object imaginable in the country. Edinburgh

University's impressive **Old College** is nearby and houses the **Talbot Rice Gallery**.

Princes Street has one of the most impressive settings of any street in the world. While the few distinctive buildings are now overpowered by modern chain stores, the south side of the wide street is entirely free of buildings. There, **Princes Street Gardens** offers unobstructed views of Castle Rock. The 'Gothic sky rocket' of the **Scott Monument**, recently stone-cleaned, pierces the panorama. Built in 1840 in memory of Sir Walter Scott and 200 ft (61 m.) tall, its 287 just-climbable steps lead to a spectacular view. Near its base is the **National Gallery of Scotland** which includes in its permanent collection a notable display of Turner watercolours. Adjacent is the **Royal Scottish Academy**, housing temporary exhibitions. Beyond the east end of Princes Street is **Calton Hill**, the site of **Nelson's Monument** and the **Playfair Observatory**. Below the hill is the **St James Centre** shopping complex, for many years criticised for the visual impact of its great bulk on the city.

North of Princes Street is the Georgian **New Town**. A number of self-guided trail brochures are available from Tourist Information. One of the New Town's finest components is **Charlotte Square**, including the **Georgian House**, furnished by its owners the National Trust for Scotland as it would have been in the late 18th century. It provides a fascinating contrast with life in the Trust's 16th-century Gladstone's Land in the Royal Mile.

Close to the city centre, the **National Portrait Gallery** displays portraits of famous Scottish figures from early kings and queens to the 20th century. The **Museum of Antiquities** displays life in Scotland from the Stone Age to modern times. They are housed together in an impressive building in Queen Street. Other galleries include the **Printmakers' Workshop** at 23 Union Street and the **Scottish National Gallery of Modern Art** in Belford Road.

Nearby is **Dean Village**, an interesting cluster of different architectural styles overlooking the Water of Leith. The **Royal Botanic Gardens**, among the finest in the country, have what is arguably the largest collection of rhododendrons in the world. They are located north of the New Town at Inverleith Row. Out by Holyrood Park is the **Royal Commonwealth Pool** (Tel 031 667 7211), a well-appointed swimming pool with a series of water slides. Further south is the **Royal Observatory** on Blackford Hill, an important astronomical observatory with a good visitor centre. Three miles (4.8 km.) east of the city is **Craigmillar Castle** (Tel 031 661 4445), associated with Mary Queen of Scots.

Around Edinburgh

This is one of the few regions of Scotland without nationally acknowledged landscape designations – neither National Scenic Areas nor (proposed) National Parks. Here, the natural beauty and interest is on a smaller and more intimate scale. Good walks exist throughout the hills of the region. **Hillend Country Park** with its long artificial ski slope (Tel 031 445 4433) lies just on Edinburgh's southern boundary on the northern slopes of the Pentlands, now the **Pentland Hills Regional Park**. Like all regional parks it maintains and supports traditional land uses of the hills – upland agriculture and forestry – while integrating recreation and tourism through interpretation services and walks. Though only reaching 1500 ft. (457 m.) at the summit they form a superb backdrop to the city.

Edinburgh Zoo, famous for its penguins, is west of the city centre on Corstorphine Road. It is built on an attractive hilltop site and, when first opened, was innovative in its attempts to avoid the animals-behind-bars approach. **Beaches** are within easy reach at **Silverknowes**, near the city village of Cramond to the north, or at **Portobello** to the east.

Accommodation

First Class

The Howard Hotel, 32–36 Great King Street, Edinburgh EH3 6QH (Tel 031 557 3500). Arguably Edinburgh's most prestigious town house hotel, reopened in 1989 after comprehensive refurbishment. Intimate and luxurious in every way, offering traditional comfort and service.

Royal Terrace Hotel, 18 Royal Terrace, Edinburgh EH7 5AQ (Tel 031 557 3222). Elegant town house hotel situated at the east end just five minutes from Princes Street. Opulent surroundings and a delightful terraced garden at the back. The Royal also has a leisure club.

The Balmoral Hotel, Princes Street, Edinburgh EH2 2EQ (Tel 031 556 2414). Previously the North British, the Balmoral has been transformed into a top-of-the-range traditional hotel following a £23 million refurbishment. Public rooms recreate the atmosphere of times gone by and bedrooms are based on the original design themes of the hotel. Situated at the east end of Princes Street next to Waverley Station.

The Caledonian, Princes Street, Edinburgh EH1 2AB (Tel 031 225

2433). At the west end of Princes Street, the Caledonian is still one of Edinburgh's most respected establishments. Indeed, to many, the hotel will always be the city's grand old lady. Traditional, luxurious and offering good views of the castle.

Middle Range

George Hotel, George Street, Edinburgh EH2 2PB (Tel 031 225 1251). The George was established in 1950 and consists of three terraced Georgian houses, two minutes from Princes Street. Strictly speaking, it falls somewhere between First Class and Middle Range, with high prices but lacking the extra polish displayed by the above establishments. Nevertheless, comfortable in every way.

Roxburghe Hotel, 38 Charlotte Square, Edinburgh EH2 4HG (Tel 031 225 3921). The only hotel situated in Edinburgh's beautiful Charlotte Square, right next to Princes Street. High standards of comfort and service.

Christopher North House Hotel, 6 Gloucester Place, Edinburgh EH3 6EF (Tel 031 225 2720). Welcoming, family run Georgian hotel situated in the New Town close to the popular Stockbridge area and ten minutes from Princes Street. The public bar downstairs is a friendly place and popular with the locals.

Ellersly House Hotel, Ellersly Road, Murrayfield, Edinburgh EH12 6HZ (Tel 031 337 6888). Delightful Edwardian town house situated in two acres of ground, yet just fifteen minutes from the city centre. Also close to the international rugby ground.

Economy

Halycon Hotel, 8 Royal Terrace, Edinburgh EH7 5AB (Tel 031 556 1033). Town house hotel on one of Edinburgh's most beautiful terraces, five minutes from Princes Street.

Osbourne Hotel, 53–59 York Place, Edinburgh EH1 3JD (Tel 031 556 5746). Good value hotel at the east end of town in a listed Georgian building.

Ellwyn Hotel, 37–39 Moira Terrace, Edinburgh EH7 6TD (Tel 031 669 1033). Small, friendly hotel in a quiet residential area, one mile (1.6 km.) from the city centre and on the main bus route.

Victoria Hotel, 3–5 Forth Street, Edinburgh EH1 3JX (Tel 031 556 1616). No frills but comfy and convenient, situated at the east end two minutes from Princes Street.

Campus accommodation is available at the University of Edinburgh (Tel 031 667 1971); Herriot Watt University (Tel 031 449 5111), and Queen Margaret College (Tel. 031 317 3000). The **Scottish Youth**

Hostels Association has two Grade 1 hostels at 7 Bruntsfield Crescent (Tel 031 447 2994) and 18 Eglinton Crescent (Tel 031 337 1120). The latter is open from May to November only.

Eating Out

First Class

Martin's, 70 Rose Street North Lane (Tel 031 225 3106). Arguably one of the best restaurants in Edinburgh serving Scottish food. Intimate and personally run, it can be difficult to find, situated on a back lane off Rose Street between Frederick and Castle streets.

Prestonfield House, Priestfield Road (Tel 031 668 3346). 17th-century country house virtually within town. Scottish cuisine, good Sunday lunches.

Cafe Royal Oyster Bar, 17a West Register Street (Tel 031 556 4124). Fish dishes are a speciality in this atmospheric old-world Victorian bar, complete with stained-glass windows. Tucked away on a side street between St Andrew's Square and Princes Street.

Middle Range

Howtowdie, 25a Stafford Street (Tel 031 225 6291). Elegant restaurant offering good Scottish cuisine with a few French touches.

The Witchery, 352 Castle Hill, Royal Mile (Tel 031 225 5613). 'The most haunted restaurant in town' right next door to Edinburgh Castle, serving Scottish cuisine.

Kelly's Restaurant, 46 West Richmond Street (Tel 031 668 3847). Warm and welcoming Scottish restaurant in a converted bakehouse south of Princes Street.

Economy

Keeper's Restaurant, 13B Dundas Street (Tel 031 556 5707). Game and poultry dishes are a speciality in this Georgian basement restaurant. Top end of the economy range, but excellent value for money.

Henderson's Salad Bar, Hanover Street (Tel 031 225 2131). One of Edinburgh's original vegetarian restaurants serving a wide range of dishes. Even popular with omnivores!

Cornerstone Restaurant, St John's Church, Princes Street (Tel 031 229 7565). Atmospheric wholefood restaurant serving light meals and snacks in the converted basement of a church at the west end of Princes Street.

Entertainments

At the west end of town, **Lothian Road** is basically a traffic artery running from Tollcross to Princes Street. It is also however, the site of Edinburgh's theatres and a number of cinemas. The **King's Theatre** (Tel 031 229 1201) and **Royal Lyceum Theatre** are both here, usually showing mainstream plays and musicals. On the same side of the road is the **Usher Hall** (Tel 031 228 1155), home of the Scottish National Orchestra and Edinburgh's main venue for classical concerts, and opposite is the **Filmhouse** (Tel 031 228 2688), where more off-beat (or less mainstream) films are screened. At the other end of town, down the hill at the east end of Princes Street, the **Playhouse** (Tel 031 557 2590) hosts more contemporary concerts, comedians and (usually) touring productions of London's West End musicals.

For something slightly more unusual, the **Traverse Theatre** (Tel 031 226 2633) in the Grassmarket shows new Scottish plays and foreign translations. Down in Stockbridge, the **Theatre Workshop** (Tel 031 226 5425) is a small venue which hosts new productions and experimental or innovative work.

The **Edinburgh Festival** has grown dramatically since its humble beginnings in 1947 to become the largest arts festival in the world. It usually begins on the second Sunday in August and runs for three weeks. It now has six parts. The Official Festival (Tel 031 226 4001) attracts world-class international music, drama and dance. The **Edinburgh Military Tattoo** (Tel 031 225 1188) is a highlight for many local people, since some claim they feel excluded from the 'highbrow' official festival. It is a martial and musical extravaganza drawing tens of thousands of visitors every year. For many others **The Fringe** (Tel 031 226 5259) is *the* festival. Over 500 companies of every nationality and of every standard from superb to 'not bad' occupy every available performance space.

Every two years, next in 1993, the **Book Festival** (Tel 031 225 1915) attracts literary figures to speak amidst displays of new books. The **Film Festival** (Tel 031 228 2688) is a year older than the Official Festival and the oldest of its kind in the world. It is a highly respected showcase for British premières. The **Jazz Festival** (Tel 031 557 1642) is one of Europe's biggest.

Useful addresses

Edinburgh Tourist Centre, 3 Princes Street EH2 2QP (Tel 031 557 1700).

Edinburgh Marketing Advance Reservations Department, 3 Princes Street EH2 2QP (Tel 031 557 2727).
Tourist Information Centre, Edinburgh Airport EH12 9DN (Tel 031 333 2167).
Scottish Tourist Board Headquarters, 23 Ravelston Terrace EH4 3EU (Tel 031 332 2433).
Edinburgh Environment Centre, Cochran Terrace EH7 4QP (Tel 031 557 2135).
Post Office: Central, 2–4 Waterloo Place EH1 1AA (Tel 031 550 8243).
Police: Headquarters, Fettes Avenue EH4 1RB (Tel 031 311 3131).
Hospital: Royal Infirmary, 1 Lauriston Place EH3 9YW (Tel 031 229 2477).

The Lothians

East Lothian

Dunbar, North Berwick, Yellowcraig, Gullane and **Aberlady** are all attractive villages or small towns with distinctive architecture and beaches and a pleasant coastal atmosphere. Dunbar is the birthplace of John Muir, who inspired the now international National Park movement. Oddly enough, the land of his birth still has no National Parks, but Dunbar has a small museum in the house in which he was born, and the nearby **John Muir Country Park**'s 'wild, rocky shore' gives a flavour of the inspiration that led him to campaign so successfully for the world's wild places. The **Bass Rock**, literally a huge, sheer sided lump of rock off North Berwick, is a spectacular bird sanctuary with gannets and huge nesting colonies of kittiwakes, puffins, fulmars and guillemots. It is reached by regular boats from North Berwick (Tel 0620 2838). Also close to North Berwick is **Tantallon Castle**, a dramatic ruin with fine views out to the Bass Rock. **Haddington** is a market town with attractive, conserved Georgian buildings in its centre. **Dirleton** is claimed by some to be the most attractive village in Scotland, retaining its medieval form with two village greens and interesting buildings, including a beautiful ruined 13th-century castle. **Preston Mill and Phantassie Doocot** is a working water-mill near East Linton. The **Museum of Flight** at East Fortune has over thirty historic aircraft. The **Scottish Mining Museum** at Prestongrange, near Prestonpans, gives an excellent and enjoyable insight into the conditions faced by generations of coal miners, using the original buildings and machinery, now stark symbols of the death of Britain's 'smoke stack' industries.

A network of quiet rural roads, ideal for the cyclist, crisscross the East Lothian countryside. The wealth of interesting villages can be explored following trail guides which cover *Historic Towns, Villages and By-Ways* and *The Coastline*. These, and further information, are available from **East Lothian Tourist Board**, Brunton Hall, Musselburgh EH21 6AF (Tel 031 665 3711).

Midlothian

Midlothian offers **Vogrie Estate Country Park**: 250 acres (101 hectares) with a good network of gentle walking and nature trails. There is also an orienteering course and a 'rustic' adventure playground, barbecue and picnic areas and a plant nursery with a walled garden. **Vogrie House** itself contains the park Interpretive Centre, with details of the park's history. **Dalkeith Palace Estate** (entered from the town of Dalkeith) also offers (for an admission fee) guided nature walks and an adventure playground within a woodland setting.

The **Scottish Mining Museum** has a site at Lady Victoria Colliery at **Newtongrange** (run by the same organisation as the East Lothian site). The visitor centre has a souvenir shop and restaurant, and the village of Newtongrange is an interesting example of how traditional miners' cottages (which are not a museum display!) are being adapted to modern needs. **Rosslyn Glen** is an attractive country park through which the River Esk meanders. Fifteenth-century **Rosslyn Chapel**, renowned for its wonderful intricately-carved stonework, and **Rosslyn Castle** itself, both lie within the park. **Edinburgh Butterfly and Insect World** is a novel experience (on the A7 between Edinburgh and Dalkeith). The visitor can walk amongst exotic butterflies and other insects from around the world, thriving on hot climate plants, all within protective glass houses. The **Edinburgh Canal Centre** (Tel 031 333 1320) at Ratho offers cruising canal boat restaurants and self-hire boats on the Union Canal.

Further information is available from **Midlothian Tourism** (Tel 031 440 2210) at 7 Station Road, Roslin EH25 9PF.

West Lothian

Hopetoun House is a fine stately home near **South Queensferry**, itself a historic town, noted for its position on the coast between the **Forth Road and Rail Bridges**. **Linlithgow** is an attractive town with a boating lake by the ruins of the **Royal Palace**, the birthplace of Mary Queen of Scots. A particularly pleasant stretch of the **Union**

Canal is nearby, with boat hire and launching facilities. **Beecraigs Country Park** offers peaceful walks and nature trails, while for something more contemporary, **Bo'ness Heritage Trust** (62 Union Street, Bo'ness. Tel 0506 825855) can advise on the industrial heritage of the district.

Livingston New Town is, perhaps unexpectedly, home to **Livingston Mill Farm**, which is part of the **Almond Valley Heritage Centre**. Visitors can stroll around an area displaying country life from a century ago. Farm animals and millwheels tell the rural story and there is also insight into the high technology of the past: **James 'Paraffin' Young** developed the area's shale oil industry and is the forefather of oil barons throughout the world today. Further information about the area in general is available from **Forth Valley Tourist Board**, Burgh Halls, The Cross, Linlithgow EH49 7AH (Tel 0506 844600).

Accommodation

First Class

Greywalls Hotel, Muirfield, Gullane, East Lothian EH31 2EG (Tel 0620 842144). Edwardian house designed by Edward Lutyens, set in beautiful gardens. Overlooking Muirfield Golf Course, the Forth and the Lammermuir Hills.

Borthwick Castle, North Middleton, Gorebridge, Midlothian EH23 4QY (Tel 0875 20514). Borthwick Castle, just south of Dalkeith, is the largest complete twin-towered keep in Scotland and is over 500 years old. The whole place is simply filled with history, notably concerning the time spent here by Queen Mary and Bothwell. Today the castle is a luxury country house hotel with only ten bedrooms and a dining-room in the stone-vaulted great hall.

Houston House, Uphall, West Lothian EH52 6JS (Tel 0506 853831). Sixteenth-century fortified towerhouse in a secluded parkland setting. Mary Queen of Scots' advocate once lived here. Traditional country house luxury and style with four-poster beds in many of the bedrooms.

Middle Range

Tweeddale Arms Hotel, Gifford, East Lothian EH41 4QU (Tel 062081 240). Converted 17th-century inn tastefully modernised in keeping with the general atmosphere of Gifford, a charming conservation village. Well situated for exploring either the Lothians or the south of Scotland.

Dalhousie Castle Hotel, Bonnyrigg, Midlothian EH19 3JB (Tel 0875 72380). Historic country house hotel dating from the 13th century and still, incredibly, under the ownership of the same family. Richly decorated and offering limited leisure facilities, at the upper end of the Middle Range price category.

Economy

Ballencrieff Farm, Longniddry, East Lothian EH32 OPJ (Tel 08757 362). Mrs Playfair runs an excellent bed and breakfast establishment in her lovely Georgian farmhouse, situated on an arable farm close to the beach and golf course.

Dalhousie Mains Farmhouse, Eskbank, Dalkeith, Midlothian EH22 3LZ (Tel 031 663 5182). Charming bed and breakfast with extensive gardens in a peaceful countryside location just seven miles outside Edinburgh.

Eating Out

First Class

Open Arms Hotel, Dirleton, East Lothian (Tel 062085 241). Although a quality hotel, the Open Arms is renowned for its restaurant. Dating from 1685, it has been run by the same family for the past forty years, has a pleasant location with views of the castle, and serves excellent Scottish cuisine.

Howgate Inn, Howgate, Midlothian (Tel 0968 74244). One-time haunt of some of Scotland's most famous literary figures, including Sir Walter Scott and Allan Ramsay. Fine Scottish cuisine served, and eaten outside when the weather's warm.

Middle Range

Champany Inn, Linlithgow, West Lothian (Tel 0506 834532). Popular whitewashed farmhouse just outside Linlithgow serving Scottish fare (steaks are a speciality) and expensive wines.

Waterside Inn, Nungate, Haddington East Lothian (Tel 0620 825674). Excellent value restaurant offering steaks and seafood in a waterside setting.

Economy

Hawes Inn, South Queensferry, West Lothian (Tel 031 331 1990). Quality bar meals served in this historic 16th-century inn. Sir Walter Scott used to come here and it is featured in Robert Louis Stevenson's *Kidnapped*. During the summer meals can be taken outside, from where there are good views of the Forth Bridges and Fife.

The Foresters, 107 Main Street, Pathhead, Midlothian (Tel 0875 320273). Family run restaurant in an original coaching inn serving good, wholesome pub meals.

Fife

Crossing the Firth of Forth by train brings you to Fife by means of the magnificent **Forth Bridge**. For the best views of this Victorian ironwork monument, drive or walk across the Forth Road Bridge which runs parallel to it. Better still, view the bridge by twilight, when the floodlighting installed for the bridge's 100th anniversary in 1990 creates a marvellous picture. Between Lothian and Fife lies the island of **Inchcolm** with the 12th-century **St Colm's Abbey**. A large colony of grey seals often basks here. The island is inhabited only by a warden, and boats cross regularly from South Queensferry.

The village of **Culross** (pronounced 'Cooross') has changed little in 300 years. This gem of traditional architecture was one of the first rescue enterprises carried out by the National Trust for Scotland and is now in the heart of a district where the closure of the mining industries has robbed many other villages of their purpose and spirit. Culross retains much of its original 16th-century architecture and character, stemming from a prosperous past based on salt and coal and trading links with Scandinavia, the Netherlands and Germany. The neighbouring village of **Valleyfield**, a somewhat run-down mining settlement, provides a stark contrast. An interesting example of the work of the famous landscape gardener, Sir Humphrey Repton, is currently being restored. Five miles (8 km.) east is the town of **Dunfermline**. Once the capital of Scotland, it now has picturesque ruins of the Abbey. **Pittencrieff Glen** is an extensive public park and formal garden. The town was the birthplace of **Andrew Carnegie** who made his fortune in the USA and returned a share of it to the town in the form of Carnegie Hall, Carnegie Library and the Glen; his house is now a small museum (Tel 0383 724302).

Lomond Hills Regional Park lies some way to the north. It offers countryside recreation amid moorland and hill farming.

Heading east and hugging the coast on the 'Fife National Tourist Route', **Aberdour** is a small holiday resort with an attractive beach. Slightly inland, **Lochore Meadows** near Lochgelly are an example of something worthwhile arising from the despair of dying industry. Boating, picnic and barbecue areas and walks surround the poignant skeleton of the winding gear that once lowered miners to the coal seams. Back on the coast, **Kirkcaldy** is a popular shopping town once famed for its linoleum manufacturing. The economist Adam Smith was born here in 1723. Nearby are the villages of **East and West Wemyss** (pronounced 'Weems') and **Dysart**, the latter with houses restored by the National Trust for Scotland. **Falkland** village is noted for its beautiful 15th-century Palace. Further east lies the **East Neuk** of Fife with attractive fishing villages, now popular as holiday resorts. Houses here are built in the East Coast style: red pantiles on the roofs and 'crow stepped' gables and wind and sea-spray-cleaned sandstone walls or neatly whitewashed 'harling'. **Elie** is a favourite local resort with a mile (1.6 km.) of sandy beach. **Pittenweem** features many houses beautifully restored by the National Trust for Scotland. Along the road, or using a pleasant seashore path, is **Anstruther**, which features the excellent **Scottish Fisheries Museum**. The **Tourism Department** and **East Neuk Ltd** (Tel 0333 312203/4) are at Murray Library, Shore Street, Anstruther, Fife KY10 3EA. **East Neuk Outdoors** (Tel 0333 311929) in Anstruther offers a range of activity holidays. The most easterly of the East Neuk villages is **Crail** which has a beautiful harbour and quaint, narrow streets. **Cambo Country Park**, a farm park with rare farm animals, is nearby.

A trip inland from the coast brings you into the rich Fife countryside and the market town of **Cupar**. The Scottish Deer Centre is three miles (4.8 km.) west of Cupar with red deer, exhibitions and children's activity areas. Visitors are invited to feed and touch the native Scottish red deer being raised there. While a very enjoyable experience for children, adults can contemplate the reality of the red deer in Scotland – it is a beautiful symbol of the country but is also over-populous and an exploitable food resource. **Hill of Tarvit**, a fine Edwardian mansion, is nearby, as are the picturesque village of **Ceres** and the **Fife Folk Museum**.

The **Howe of Fife** is crossed by many pleasant back roads which eventually reach **St Andrews**, the home of golf and the **Royal and Ancient Golf Club**; the **British Golf Museum** traces the history of golf over 500 years. This is a very attractive town with many fine buildings belonging to **St Andrews University**, which is the oldest in Scotland, dating from 1412. The ruins of **St Andrews Cathedral** and **St Andrews Castle** have a dramatic setting by a rocky part of the seashore. The recently opened **St Andrews Sea Life Centre** and the **East Sands Leisure Centre** (Tel 0334 76506), as well as nearby **Craigtoun Park**, a fifty acre (20 hectare) site with a range of interests, complement St Andrews' traditional attractions. **Tentsmuir Forest** is

Edinburgh, the Lothians and Fife 175

an attractive area for picnics with wildlife interest and a fine beach managed by the Forestry Commission. It is north of St Andrews, off the back road from Leuchars to Tayport.

St Andrews and North-East Fife Tourist Board (Tel 0334 72021) is at 2 Queens Gardens, St Andrews KY16 9TE, and **St Andrews Tourist Information Centre** (Tel 0334 72021) is at 78 South Street, St Andrews KY16 9JX.

Accommodation

First Class

St Andrews Old Course Hotel, Old Station Road, St Andrews KY16 9SP (Tel 0334 74371). Luxury hotel overlooking the famous 17th Road Hole offering two good restaurants and a range of leisure facilities.

Fernie Castle Hotel, Letham, near Cupar KY7 7RU (Tel 033781 381). Historic 16th-century country house now run as a small hotel. Traditional service and hospitality, and highly-rated cuisine. Some bedrooms have four-posters. Situated just outside Cupar and within half an hour of St Andrews.

Rufflets Country House Hotel, Strathkinness Low Road, St Andrews KY16 9TX (Tel 0334 72594). Charming hotel which has been owned and run by the same family for over almost forty years. Set in award-winning gardens and situated just outside St Andrews.

Middle Range

Sandford Hill Hotel, near Wormit, Newport-on-Tay DD6 8RG (Tel 0382 541802). Picturesque country house hotel set in delightful gardens and built around three sides of an attractive courtyard.

The Golf Hotel, Bank Street, Elie KY9 1EF (Tel 0333 330209). Traditional Scottish Baronial style mansion, personally run and offering true comfort in the pleasant coastal village of Elie, ten miles (16 km.) from St Andrews.

Crusoe Hotel, 2 Main Street, Lower Largo KY8 6BT (Tel 0333 320759). Pleasantly situated hotel on the harbour of the small village of Lower Largo, birthplace of Alexander Selkirk's Robinson Crusoe. The Crusoe is benefiting from a new development project which highlights the Robinson Crusoe theme. Bedrooms are appropriately named ('Island Oasis', 'Sailor's Rest') and there is a signpost marking the direction of the 7500 miles (12,067 km.) from Lower Largo to the island of Juan Fernandez, where Alexander Selkirk was marooned.

Economy

Smuggler's Inn, High Street, Anstruther KY10 3DQ (Tel 0333 310506). Atmospheric inn overlooking the harbour. Warm, cosy and friendly.

Redlands Country Lodge, By Ladybank KY7 7SH (Tel 0337 31091). Log cabin bedrooms in the beautiful grounds of an old lodge. Excellent value, with golf, shooting and a range of outdoor activities available as well.

Hawkcraig House, Hawkcraig Point, Aberdour KY3 0TZ (Tel 0383 860335). Situated on the waterfront with splendid views across the bay to Inchcolm Abbey, Hawkcraig has two bedrooms offering incredible value (with dinner also). The owner has acquired an excellent reputation and booking in advance is necessary. No smoking.

Eating Out

First Class

The Peat Inn, Peat Inn (Tel 033484 206). The restaurant of this pleasant 18th-century inn is recognised as one of the finest in Scotland, if not Britain. The best of Scottish produce is served in delightful surroundings, just six miles from St Andrews.

Ostlers Close, Bonnygate, Cupar (Tel 0334 55574). Charming, intimate restaurant situated up an alley off Cupar's main street. Run by a husband and wife team (he cooks, she looks after the dining-room). Scottish cuisine and local produce.

Middle Range

The Cellar, 24 East Green, Anstruther (Tel 0333 310378). Fresh fish is a speciality at this respected restaurant, situated right next to where the catch is brought in twice a day.

The Grange Inn, Grange Road, St Andrews (Tel 0334 72670). Game, seafood and home-cooked meals, all in a lovely setting on a hill overlooking St Andrews.

Economy

Brambles, 5 College Street, St Andrews (Tel 0334 72970). Very popular cafe/restaurant serving light meals and coffees.

The Merchant's House, 49 South Street, St Andrews (Tel 0334 72595). Coffee shop and licensed restaurant with 16th-century painted ceilings, vaults and a conservatory-style area at the rear.

4 Glasgow, Central and Ayrshire

Glasgow is Scotland's second city. It is also the country's largest in terms of population, with 696,600 people. For a century Glasgow was known as the 'Second City of the Empire' on account of its industrial might, though this has declined since the 1940s. Its fortunes have been revived in recent years, through determined efforts by the District Council in partnership with the Scottish Development Agency and private companies. These efforts have been directed at regenerating areas and communities, subsequently replacing the industrial past with a heady cocktail of culture and commerce. Now Glasgow is arguably on course to become the first city of the 'post-industrial' era.

As the name implies, Central Region is the heartland of Scotland: the boundary between Highland and Lowland, drawing on the landscape, character and heritage of both. The region contains Stirling, one of the most important towns in Scottish history; Loch Lomond, whose 'bonny banks' are world renowned, and the hills and lochs of the Trossachs, a microcosm of the Highlands. Ayrshire is a region of great diversity famous for its beaches, resorts, castles and golf courses and, most notably, for its strong associations with Scotland's national poet, Robert Burns. The Clyde Valley is a cradle of industry, while to the north the gentler, lowland character gives way to the mountains and lochs of the Highlands.

Such variety in landscape and history within a short distance of Glasgow and just over an hour from Edinburgh, gives the region enormous appeal. Yet, away from the honeypots, the better known destinations, the traveller can find many peaceful, virtually unknown spots.

History

Glasgow

Glasgow's origins lie in the 4th century, when St Ninian carried out missionary work among the ancient Britons of Strathclyde and consecrated a plot of ground, later the site of Glasgow Cathedral. The city's patron saint, St Mungo, established a monastery here in the early 7th century. The name Glasgow may originate from two Celtic words: 'glas' for church and 'gow' from Mungo's name. Alternatively, 'Gles Ghu', meaning 'green place' was the name of the early settlement that grew around the monastery. It was here that routes from all parts of Scotland converged, close to the lowest fording point of the River Clyde. There may also have been a small fishing village by the river and these two sites became the growth points for the future city.

Glasgow was largely bypassed by the struggles that marked much of Scotland's early history (even the cathedral was largely unscathed by the Reformation) and was allowed to develop progressively. By the late 17th century the city's great trading and industrial saga had begun. The Act of Union of 1707 opened access to England's colonies, notably North America and the Caribbean, and gave the 'tobacco lords' the profits needed to build Glasgow's fine architecture. With the American War of Independence and the loss of trade however, Glasgow then developed its weaving industry, exporting cotton products to Europe. In the 19th century, the River Clyde as it is seen today was 'created', when the river bed was lowered by almost thirty feet (9 m.) to permit the passage of steam ships. This was the beginning of the development of the dockyards, which for years were synonymous with industrial Glasgow. At the same time the city was expanding rapidly to accommodate the workforce migrating from all over Scotland and Ireland. The middle years of the 20th century saw the decline of Glasgow, as the old 'smoke stack' industries died and housing stock deteriorated. This gave rise to an outward migration of the population to New Towns which had been constructed to give new hope to the displaced. Only in the last few years have the fortunes of the city been revived and now Glasgow seems set to carve out a new and vigorous future.

The Clyde Valley

Although the Clyde Valley boasts artefacts such as the Bronze Age cairns on Tinto Hill and the excavated Roman bath-house in Strathclyde Country Park, the district is more famous for its recent history than for that of ancient times. The Clyde Valley is a cradle of industry of international importance. Its development was strongly influenced by the River Clyde itself, which not only created the river valley that formed a route for earlier peoples, but also powered the embryonic Industrial Revolution. In 1785 David Dale realised the potential of this great river when he came as a tourist to the spectacular Falls of Clyde. Near this strategic point he installed the water wheels that were to harness the water and drive the looms of the cotton industry he began here. At this site he established the village of New Lanark and offered work to Highlanders displaced from their land by the notorious Clearances. Although his cotton mill complex became one of the biggest in the world, the village is largely remembered because of Dale's son-in-law, Robert Owen, who introduced social reforms for the workers. These covered education and hours of work and leisure, and were far ahead of their time.

Another great figure hailing from the Clyde Valley is David Livingston, who was born in the village of Blantyre in 1813. He worked in the cotton mills by day and studied by night, eventually becoming a doctor, then explorer and missionary along the Nile and Zambesi rivers.

The history of the Clyde Valley is taken up in the market town of Biggar, the birthplace of the great Victorian prime minister, Gladstone. Four small museums explore different themes: associations with the Scottish patriot William Wallace, said to have evaded English troops here in 1297; past life-styles in the Clyde Valley; the Covenanters and religious persecution – the 'Killing Times'; and the Victorian heritage, displayed in a reconstruction of an indoor street.

Central

Central Region also displays an industrial face, notably in the east where it meets West Lothian. Heading west from Edinburgh along the Forth Valley, by road or rail, the petrochemical plant at Grangemouth presents, in the right weather conditions, an awesome spectacle.

Stirling is steeped in history. It was for a long time a natural crossing point between the Highlands and central Scotland, where passing trade and armies could be controlled from the heights commanded by the castle. The Scottish royal court sat in Stirling and the town was Scotland's capital for over 500 years; only the lack of a deep water port caused the move to Edinburgh around 1600. William Wallace defeated the English here, closely followed by Robert the Bruce's famous victory at Bannockburn in 1314, which secured the independence of the country for 400 years. Much of Stirling's (and therefore Scotland's) history is recalled throughout the summer in enactments performed on the Old Town's Broad Street.

Further north around Loch Lomond and the Trossachs the principal popular historic associations centre on Rob Roy. A member of the Macgregor clan, which had been ruthlessly suppressed by

Government forces, he acquired the reputation of a Scottish Robin Hood for his role as both a patriot and successful cattle thief. He symbolises for many the values of a way of life swept away by the rapid absorption of early 18th century Scotland into the rest of Britain.

Ayrshire

The Ayrshire valleys to the south of the region can trace the presence of Stone Age hunters, Bronze and Iron Age farmers, Roman soldiers, and Vikings, each commemorated by cairns and other memorials. The most profound mark on the land came in the 18th century when the agricultural revolution increased the size of fields and farms, introduced new farming methods and removed much of the ancient woodland cover. The Industrial Revolution also had great effect, with towns and villages growing in size as a result of the successful export of locally manufactured goods.

The Ayrshire coast and islands' most celebrated historical connection is with the Vikings. At the Battle of Largs in 1263 the Scots repelled the attacking Norsemen, celebrating the only Viking defeat on mainland Scotland.

Ayrshire and Burns Country in the south and along the Firth of Clyde coast share much of the prehistory of the region. In later days, the Ayrshire Kennedys of the 16th century brought a certain notoriety to the area. They yielded power from their many castles which were scattered through the district, and were known locally as the Kings of Carrick – the land which stretches south from Alloway to Finnarts Bay. As well as being the scene of bloody inter-clan battles, Carrick was also the home of Robert the Bruce and for many years thereafter a smugglers' coast.

It is with Robert Burns, Scotland's national bard, that this district is principally associated. Born in the village of Alloway (now a suburb of Ayr) on 25 January 1759, Burns spent his early years here, before moving to Mount Oliphant in 1766. The cottage he was born in had been built by his father two years previously, and still stands today, a place of homage for Burns admirers throughout the world. At Mount Oliphant his father became a tenant farmer and the young Burns wrote his first poem in his fifteenth year while working on the family farm. In 1784 his father died and Robert became head of the family. They moved to Mossgiel, another farm, and lived there for six years. It was while here that Burns won fame, when the 'Kilmarnock Edition' of his works was published in 1786. He died at the early age of thirty-seven, leaving behind over six hundred poems and songs, as well as an 'Immortal Memory', celebrated annually throughout the world on his birthday.

Quite what Burns thought of the historical changes that were taking place in his country at that time can only be surmised from the allusions in his poems and songs. He cared deeply for the common man, which perhaps explains his popularity in Russia. A strong republican streak runs through some of his work, although he also praised the Jacobite cause (this may have been little more than a hankering after a Scotland fast disappearing). He doubted the motives of many of his countrymen who supported Scotland's Union with England – 'Such a parcel o' rogues in the nation' – and he lamented the loss of nationhood. But he saw certain economic benefits and, after a hard early life working the poor soil of the family farm, perhaps would have applauded the changes in the Ayrshire landscape about to take place: reclamation and enclosure of land, laying out the rich farmlands, introducing dairy herds, and planting the shelter belts of woodland that are now such an integral part of the area.

Geography

The coastal plain on either side of the Firth of Forth to the east of Stirling is the site of many ancient routes. To the north lie the hills of the great Highland Boundary Fault (running from Helensburgh to Stonehaven), penetrated in places by rivers and their valleys, in turn being used as important routes. Callander on the River Teith thus controlled access to the Trossachs, hence its name 'Gateway to the Trossachs', while Strathallan provided the through route to Perth and the north, permitting Stirling the title 'Gateway to the Highlands'.

Further west is the watershed of the rivers Clyde and Forth. Flowing from the south-east is the Clyde itself in the fertile Clyde Valley. Beyond is Glasgow lying in a basin surrounded by low hills, which partly explains its long early history as a comparatively small settlement, linked by valley routes to other areas.

To the south is Ayrshire, with a distinctly different character from the heavily populated and industrialised area so close to its northern boundary. The two areas developed together: as Glasgow's population grew, Ayrshire developed its dairy industry to supply the demand. On the Clyde coast is a low-lying coastal strip, narrow in the north around Largs, then widening to give a broad, low hinterland to other coastal towns and resorts from Ardrossan to Ayr. Inland, the coastal strip gives way to rolling hills and moorlands rising to around 2000 ft

(610m). Sheep grazing and commercial conifer plantations dominate the scene.

North of Glasgow and within a short distance are Loch Lomond and the Trossachs, beautiful and internationally known areas, where small towns cater to heavy tourist demand. The dramatic change in landscape is due to the great Highland Boundary Fault. To the south are the Menteith Hills giving way to the flatlands of the Carse of Stirling; to the north are the southern Grampians, a country of high mountains, steep-sided glens and countless lochs. Ben Lomond lies in the west looking down over Loch Lomond while Ben Vorlich lies on the eastern boundary of the region. The high country in between occupies almost half of the Central Region. Such diverse topography gives rise to marked variations in climate, natural habitat and wildlife.

The high country to the north was at one time covered by forest – Scots Pine at the highest levels and oak forest on the lower slopes. As elsewhere in Scotland however, much of this was cleared by man over a long period of time, notably from the 18th century onwards. Remnants of the ancient Caledonian forest of pine linger on near Crianlarich, while coppiced oaks are still in evidence around the Trossachs and Loch Lomond. Vegetation cover is generally rough grass and heather. This supports sheep grazing but is also the habitat of red deer. In addition red grouse are encouraged in the area by controlled burning of the heather. There are sizeable areas where forest is returning, although now largely for commercial use. Increasingly these are established and managed with more regard for amenity than in the past, as in Queen Elizabeth Forest Park. The high tops are least affected by man, and ptarmigan and golden eagle are present. The lochs of the Highlands are clean and cold and valued as a water supply for the great populations to the south; Loch Katrine is a well known example.

The lowlands are characterised by three areas. Flanders Moss, west of Stirling, is the largest raised valley bog in Britain, with associated insects and plants. The extensive mud flats of the Forth estuary provide feeding grounds for wading birds and over-wintering wildfowl and the Lake of Menteith ('Scotland's only lake') has reed-bordered inlets attractive to several species of wildfowl.

Climate

The climate of the region is generally mild and damp, although the areas around Ayr and Troon have the lowest rainfall in the west of

Scotland. There is in fact a marked variation in rainfall in the region, indicated by the fact that Loch Lomond receives more than twice that of Stirling, little more than twenty miles (32 km.) to the east. More specifically, Glasgow has a total annual rainfall of around 1120 mm (44 inches). Typical of the western side of the country, most rain falls between October and March: the June low is 65 mm. (2.5 inches) and the January high 135 mm. (5.3 inches). Temperatures throughout the year range from an average low of 4°C (40°F) in January to an average high of around 15°C (59°F) in July. While there are the odd 'muggy' days, oppressive humidity is rare.

Attractions

The region's great diversity and its ready accessibility from Scotland's main population centres make this a highly popular tourist destination.

In Central Region the main attractions are the Trossachs, the 'bonny banks' of Loch Lomond, and historic Stirling, while along the Clyde coast visitors flock to traditional seaside resorts and the contrasting fjord-like sea lochs. The Clyde Valley attracts primarily domestic tourists, although increasing numbers of overseas visitors are drawn to the area's industrial history and heritage, notably to the Heritage Site of New Lanark. The beaches of the Ayrshire coast have drawn visitors from Glasgow, and further afield, for generations.

The golf connections of Ayr are world renowned (there are over thirty quality courses here, including two of world class) and are outweighed only by the area's associations with Robert Burns. Many towns, villages and quiet country corners are immortalised in Burns' poems and songs, and the good roads and lanes of this agricultural area enable them to be readily enjoyed.

Glasgow offers the contrasting pleasures of a great Victorian industrial heritage and a modern, cosmopolitan and determinedly cultured city.

Cuisine

The traditional Scottish tea-room has its origins in Glasgow. The coffee houses of the 18th and 19th centuries were exclusively male domains, but in 1884 Mrs Cochrane set up a very successful tea-shop in Argyll Street, followed by others throughout the city. A scone, traditionally cooked on a griddle and eaten with butter or jam, makes a pleasant accompaniment to a pot of afternoon tea. Another Glaswegian, William Lang, pioneered the snack bar around 1880.

Level of Tourism

The early history of mass tourism is illustrated in the popularity of resorts such as Largs or Millport on the island of Great Cumbrae. Generations of Glaswegians went 'doon the watter' from the turn of the century to the 1960s, when attention turned to the availability of cheap flights to the Spanish Costas. Glasgow itself has embraced tourism in a big way in an incredibly short time. Beginning in the mid-1980s with a smiling yellow cartoon face that adorned coats and cars alike, the 'Glasgow's Miles Better' campaign proclaimed the city to a startled world. 'New Glasgow' had arrived. The momentum of the renaissance was further fuelled by the Garden Festival in 1988 and by the naming of Glasgow as European City of Culture in 1990. Meanwhile, behind the scenes, an equally impressive restoration of much of the fabric of the city was going on, backed by massive investment. Although there is undeniably some tension between traditional, working-class Glasgow and the new city of wine-bars and waterside studio flats, tourism interest in the city is certainly escalating – numbers in 1990 were over 300 per cent higher than in the previous year.

Stirling's Tourism Development Unit encourages tourism in its District through tapping the enormous reserve of historical associations of the town itself and focusing on the 'Royal Stirling' theme. There also appears to be an overall strategy into which individual initiatives will fit, rather than an *ad hoc* approach to further tourism development. The history of Stirling is to a great extent the history of Scotland, and it is surprising that this rich heritage has only recently received increased attention; indeed it is surprising that Stirling itself has not been a much greater tourist destination.

In the Highland area, several locations – such as the Trossachs and Loch Lomond – can be exceedingly busy in high season. The pattern was established in the early 1800s by William Wordsworth and others, who came to seek the picturesque idyll as described by Sir Walter Scott. (In his novels, Scott had populated the country with gallant knights and fair damsels.) The ease of access from Glasgow and other major centres in the Central Belt adds to the situation. Villages and towns such as Aberfoyle and Callander can be stretched to capacity in the height of the season, though somehow the restaurants and cafes seem to cope.

The situation is reaching a point where new tactics are necessary. No matter how urbane the 'New Glasgow' has become, it is surely no bad thing to encourage Glaswegians and others to enjoy Scotland's natural heritage. Loch Lomond is at present a Regional Park. Although this status permits an overall strategy for recreation, tourism and traditional land uses, it is funded largely by local authorities and the money available is inadequate to handle the national and international interest in the area. Loch Lomond is proposed as one of four National Parks in Scotland (there are none at present) and if accepted, this approach is likely to establish appropriate management which can integrate conservation with controlled public access and enjoyment.

Tourism in Ayrshire is centred mainly on the areas associated with golf and with Robert Burns, as well as on the traditional resorts. These activities and those who take part seem to thrive on a crowd level that would see the hillwalker packing his rucksack for remoter parts. Fortunately here there is still room for everyone's choice, and a growing awareness of limits to growth on the part of the tourism authorities should avoid a worsening situation.

Good Alternatives

Meeting People

Meeting the locals in Glasgow is not a problem. Renowned for their friendliness towards outsiders, Glaswegians are a jovial bunch who enjoy conversation and company. Take time to explore the city's lively pub scene or wander around the public gardens and the chances are you'll soon end up exchanging stories with the locals. Alternatively, stroll down the Barras market and get to grips with the 'real' Glasgow. The people and the place are the salt of the earth.

In terms of structured projects aimed at introducing visitors to Glasgow people, the city seems to fall slightly short of the mark. Although there are a number of groups working to integrate further the different communities of Glasgow, the city lacks a definite Meet the Locals programme which could cater primarily for tourists. Details of community projects taking place throughout the city are available from the **Scottish Office of the Association of Community Technical Aid Associations**, 58 Fox Street, Glasgow G1 4AU. It should be noted however, that many of these projects might be of little interest to the short-term visitor.

A final suggestion is simply to visit Glasgow in May, at the time of the Mayfest celebrations. Now regarded as one of the country's most significant Arts Festivals, Mayfest offers the opportunity to enjoy Glasgow at a time when the city is especially receptive to visitors.

Discovering Places

The 'New Glasgow' has captured the limelight. The warehouses and offices of the old merchant city have been transformed from grimy grey to golden sandstone, revealing the architectural beauty of the city's Victorian and Charles Rennie Mackintosh buildings. The Burrell Collection, the Scottish Exhibition and Conference Centre, the new shopping developments of St Enoch's Square and Prince's Square, floodlighting of the magnificent City Chambers, the School of Art, the Mitchell Library, the Clyde bridges and other dynamic innovations have put Glasgow firmly on the world stage. All are worth visiting for their own sake and as examples of how a city can create a new image for itself. The experiment has all but eclipsed the Glasgow of hard men and hard times.

But the 'Old Glasgow' lingers on. Indeed, some say it is even fighting back against an image from which it feels excluded. The Gorbals once epitomised the old city: appalling housing in dank, dark tenements and multiple deprivation amongst the people. Yet the area captured the essence of working-class Glasgow, in its perseverance in adversity and strong community spirit. The Gorbals are near the centre of Glasgow and two heritage trails explore the area. Guide books are available from the **District Council** (Tel 041 227 5701). Following the wholesale redevelopment of the area after World War II, many original features were removed for ever (rightly so), although clues to the myth and misery of the teeming closes do remain. Similarly, traditional tenements on Dumbarton Road permit a glimpse of the fact that working-class Glasgow continues to flourish alongside the new city, while the Hutchesontown high rise flats indicate that well-meaning plans to replace squalid slums with functionally efficient dwelling units are not guaranteed to create utopia.

Walkways and cycleways are being steadily extended and form an ideal way to explore the contradictions and contrasts of the two Glasgows. The Kelvin Walkway runs from Kelvingrove to Dawsholm Park, and is being extended to meet the West Highland Way to the north and the Clyde Walkway in the city centre to the south. Six miles (10.5km.) of the Loch Lomond Walkway/Cycleway is within Glasgow along a former railway line. And, despite being Scotland's largest city, some 24 per cent of Glasgow area is official 'countryside', including arable land at Summerston and Robroyston, the Forth and Clyde Canal, a section of the Roman Antonine Wall, and Sites of Special

Scientific Importance – Bishop Loch, Kittoch Valley, Possil Marsh and Waulkmill Glen.

While the inquiring tourist can, with time and determination, discern the true nature of a city or region, a helping hand is often welcome. 'Heritage industry' is a current, rather scathing reference to the rapid growth in visitor attractions throughout the country, based on aspects of heritage. Here there is a wide range of attractions and visitors can choose from small, often enthusiast-run local museums with genuine artefacts, relying heavily on the face-to-face communication skills of the curator, to large, modern centres offering an 'experience' largely reliant on audio-visual and other sophisticated technology. Both have their place, but the essential ingredient is 'authenticity', the key to good interpretation of the natural or man-made environment. Such centres give a genuine insight into the *genius loci* or spirit of place, and guidance on how to enjoy the essence of good tourism.

A number of centres are available around the region. In the Loch Lomond and Trossachs area the Forestry Commission's Queen Elizabeth Forest Park centre is a fairly simple but effective interpretive display which stirs the visitor's imagination and encourages exploration of the surrounding forests. The Rob Roy Centre in Callander is more hi-tech, using tableaux and 'talking heads' to tell its story. A smaller attraction is the Tenement House in Glasgow, a humble flat, unembellished and frozen in time as it was when the last resident died. Summerlee Heritage Park in Coatbridge is a functional, noisy and hands-on celebration of the industrial past with a working, electric tramway and various steam engines.

Long-distance walks have their critics, but they are another means of offering the visitor a gently-assisted insight into the back country. The West Highland Way runs through this region, from almost the centre of Glasgow, by Loch Lomond, to Fort William in the West Highlands. This route is self-guided, though a Ranger Service is on hand if desired. Contact Central Regional Council, Planning Department (West Highland Way), Viewforth, Stirling FK7 ZET (Tel 0786 73111, ext. 390). A number of companies offer guided walks through other parts of the region, some with particular themes such as natural history.

Communications

How to Get There

AIR: The whole region is readily accessible from nearby Glasgow and the Central Belt where the great bulk of Scotland's population live and most incoming tourists arrive. The recent introduction of an 'Open Skies' policy resulted in **Glasgow International Airport** (Tel 041 887 1111) being permitted to receive transatlantic flights. There are over 100 shuttle services each week to London. The airport is eight miles (12.8 km.) west of the city centre via the M8 (Renfrew) motorway and there are regular bus connections into town.

RAIL: The main **British Rail** stations in Glasgow are Queen Street linking to Edinburgh, the east and the north, and Central providing services to London and the south. Railways (Tel 041 204 2844) provide a comprehensive service around Glasgow, the Clyde Valley and Ayr but the country to the north much less so. Only the southern tip of Loch Lomond can be reached by rail, at Balloch, and the northern stretch from Tarbet to Ardlui. The Trossachs have no rail connections.

CAR and COACH: Good **roads** are present to and within the region. Glasgow is the main nodal point of the Scottish transport system. The M8 motorway runs through the city – much regretted by some – providing access to Edinburgh and the east of the country. The M8 links with the M74/A74 route to Carlisle and the south and with the M73 to Stirling and the north. Express **coach** services connect Glasgow with the rest of the UK (Tel 041 332 9191).

When You're There

RAIL AND BUS: There is a high level of **public transport** provision in Glasgow and a relatively low level of private car ownership – 173 cars per thousand people compared to an average 324 for Britain as a whole. Glasgow can also boast the only Scottish **Underground system**, the 'Clockwork Orange' (Tel 041 226 4826). **Bus** services (Tel 041 226 4826) serve the city, operated by the Strathclyde Passenger Transport Executive and the Scottish Bus Group Companies.

CAR: The A82 trunk road follows the west shore of Loch Lomond and in the main tourist season can suffer from congestion. It is used by commercial and other traffic intent simply on reaching their destination and with little particular interest in the scenery, but naturally the car-borne tourists prefer to drive slowly, admiring the magnificent views. The two do not mix well. The road on the east side of the loch is a secondary ('B') road only and ends at Balmaha, with only a minor road continuing northwards. The Clyde Valley Tourist Route is well signposted throughout the valley area.

BOAT: **Ferries** ply the waters of the Clyde coast. Details are available from the ubiquitous **Caledonian MacBrayne** (The Ferry Terminal, Gourock PA19 1QP. Tel 0475 33755).

For a voyage of pure pleasure, the world's last seagoing paddle steamer, the PS *Waverley* is available (Waverley Terminal, Anderston Quay, Glasgow, G3 8HA. Tel 041 221 8152).

CYCLING AND WALKING: A walkway/cycleway connects the Scottish Exhibition and Conference Centre in Glasgow with Loch Lomond. Though not marked as such, most Forestry Commission and Regional Water Authority roads (which are closed to motor traffic) can be cycled. **Bicycles** can be hired from Dales Bicycles Ltd, 150 Dobbies Lane, Glasgow (Tel 041 332 2705); Tourist Information Centre at Callander (Tel 0877 30342); Trossachs Cycle Hire at Aberfoyle (Tel 08772 614), and Stewart Wilson Cycles of Stirling (Tel 0786 65292).

Useful Local Contacts

Glasgow Environmental Education Urban Projects Group (GEE-UP) aims to promote interest in practical environmental education and projects (Education Department, Glasgow Division, 129 Bath Street, Glasgow G2 2SY. Tel 041 227 2639). **Glasgow Urban Wildlife Group** promotes and studies wildlife conservation within the city boundaries (Mugdock Country Park, Craigend Visitor Centre, Craigallian Road, Milngavie, Glasgow G62 8EL. Tel 041 956 6100). **Glasgow for People** campaigns for public transport and opposes the type of massive road-building that created Glasgow's urban motorways (42 Sauchiehall Street, Glasgow G2 3JD. Tel 041 445 2466). **Glasgow Cycling Campaign** is at 53 Cochrane Street.

The **Clyde Calders Urban Fringe Management Project** (25a Motherwell Business Centre, 132 Coursington Road, Motherwell. Tel 0698 63138/9) is a co-operative venture between five local authorities and three central government bodies. Set up in 1983 it seeks to improve the environment and the potential for recreation, and encourage community involvement in areas of dereliction around the towns of the Clyde Valley. In the Loch Lomond area, visitors might also contact **Friends of Loch Lomond**, Ravenswood, Arrochar, Dumbartonshire G83 7AA (Tel 030 12 240), a local group concerned with conserving the Loch and surrounding area.

Geographical Breakdown of Region

Glasgow

Glasgow's main attractions are scattered throughout the city, but are accessible by underground and bus, if walking is not possible. There are also coach tours with guides (Tel 041 942 6453). Queen Street railway station is by **George Square**, the centre of Glasgow. A great civic square, it contains statues of literary and political figures and the impressive architecture of the **City Chambers** built in Italian Renaissance style in the late-19th century. The original Glasgow began a mile (1.6 km.) or so east at the **Cathedral**, a Gothic building which is actually the fourth church on the site since St Mungo's in the 7th century. The saint's tomb is in the crypt. Nearby is the **Necropolis**, a burial ground with elegant tombstones on a sloping site, offering fine views of the cathedral and the city. Here too is **Provand's Lordship** dating from 1471 and, along with the Cathedral, the only remaining building of medieval Glasgow. The **High Street** runs south-west from the cathedral, and is now sadly rather shabby in places. This is the axis of the medieval town with **Glasgow Cross** at the southern end. The Saltmarket leads down to a crossing of the River Clyde adjacent to **Glasgow Green** and the **People's Palace** (Tel 041 554 0223), both dear to the heart of working-class Glasgow. The Palace is a museum of social history. Visible from its entrance, like a mirage of the Doge's Palace in Venice, is **Templeton's Carpet Factory**, an 18th-century extravaganza, today housing offices. **Argyle Street** runs west from near Glasgow Cross.

Major shopping areas are in the central area of the city and include **Buchanan Street**, with the recently opened **Princes Square**, an enclosed complex for specialist shopping, and **St Enoch Centre**, another enclosed complex at 55 St Enoch Square. Locals refer to it as the 'big greenhouse'. Off Sauchiehall Street at 167 Renfrew Street is **Glasgow School of Art**, designed by and famed for its associations with architect and designer Charles Rennie Mackintosh. The **Tenement House** at 145 Buccleuch Street is maintained by the National Trust for Scotland as it was in the Victorian era. **Sauchiehall Street** is partially pedestrianised and a busy shopping area. **The Willow Tea-room** is a pleasant refreshment stop designed in Charles Rennie Mackintosh style. The street runs west for two miles (3.2 km.) to **Kelvingrove Park** and **Kelvingrove Art Gallery and Museum**, ten minutes by bus from the city centre. The **Museum of Transport** (Tel 041 357 3929) is nearby. **Glasgow University** and the **Hunterian Museum and Art Gallery** are on the northern fringe of the park.

Accommodation

First Class

The White House Hotel, 11–13 Cliveden Crescent, Glasgow G12 0PA (Tel 041 339 9375). Arguably the best hotel in Glasgow, the

White House is small and has the air of a country house hotel, yet is set in the city's elegant West End.

One Devonshire Gardens, 1 Devonshire Gardens, Great Western Road, Glasgow G12 OUX (Tel 041 339 2001). Small, exclusive hotel close to the city centre.

Gleddoch House, Langbank, Renfrewshire PA14 6YE (Tel 0475 54711). Country house built by Sir James Lithgow, the great Scottish shipbuilder, in 1927, situated just thirty minutes' drive from the centre of Glasgow. Traditional comfort and cuisine.

Middle Range

Babbity Bowster, 16–18 Blackfriars Street, Glasgow G1 1PJ (Tel 041 552 5055). Comfortable rooms above a pub which in its time has been a merchant's house and a fruit and vegetable market.

Albion Hotel, 405–407 North Woodside Road, Glasgow G20 6NN (Tel 041 339 8620). Bed and breakfast in a small, privately run hotel in the heart of Glasgow's West End.

Boswell Hotel, 27 Mansionhouse Road, Glasgow G41 3DN (Tel 041 632 9812). Twelve rooms with bed and breakfast in an old Victorian house south of the city centre.

Sherbrooke Castle Hotel, 11 Sherbrooke Avenue, Glasgow G41 4PG (Tel 041 427 4227). Bed and breakfast in an impressive red-stone castle in the Pollockshields area.

Economy

The Town House, 4 Hughenden Terrace, Glasgow G12 9XR (Tel 041 357 0862). Bed and breakfast and evening meal in this delightful late Victorian townhouse in the Kelvinside area. Excellent value.

Kirklee Hotel, 11 Kensington Gate, Glasgow G12 9LG (Tel 041 334 5555/339 3828). Scottish Tourist Board 'Commended' bed and breakfast on a West End terrace in one of Glasgow's attractive conservation areas.

Adamson Hotel, 4 Crookston Drive, Glasgow G52 3LY (Tel 041 882 3047). Situated on the west side of town, not far off the main West Paisley Road, a pleasant family run bed and breakfast.

Campus accommodation is available at the University of Glasgow (Tel 041 330 5385); University of Strathclyde (Tel 041 552 4400, ext. 3560), and Jordanhill College (Tel 041 950 3320). The **Scottish Youth Hostels Association** has a hostel at 11 Woodlands Terrace (Tel 041 332 3004), and there is a **caravan park** with caravans to let at Balloch (Tel 0389 59475).

Self-drive motor caravans can be hired from Jim Nearly Self-Drive, 15 Fairley Street, Glasgow G51 2SN (Tel 041 427 7244), and Cabervans, Cloch Road, Gourock PA19 1BA (Tel 0475 38775).

Eating Out

First Class

Rogano, 11 Exchange Place (Tel 041 248 4055). Art deco interior, exceptional food (especially the fish) and a good wine list.

The Buttery, 652 Argyle Street (Tel 041 221 8188). Scottish nouvelle cuisine in a Victorian hunting lodge atmosphere.

The Ubiquitous Chip, 12 Ashton Lane (Tel 041 334 5007). Scottish specialities prepared by one of Glasgow's most inventive chefs.

Middle Range

Cafe Gandolfi, 64 Albion Street (Tel 041 552 6813). Continental ambience, excellent smoked salmon, and some vegetarian dishes.

Balbir's Vegetarian Ashoka, 141 Elderslie Street (Tel 041 248 4407). Vegetarian curry house where everything is served in generous portions.

Willow Tea-Room, 217 Sauchiehall Street (Tel 041 332 0521). The original tea-room, now restored to Charles Rennie Mackintosh's design. Open for breakfast, light lunches and afternoon tea.

Economy

Cafe JJ, 180 Dumbarton Road (Tel 041 357 1881). Popular underground cafe in the West End serving vegetarian dishes and home baking.

The Third Eye Centre, 350 Sauchielhall Street (Tel 041 332 7521). Wholefood menu offered at the back of this popular gallery.

Cul de Sac, 44–46 Ashton Lane (Tel 041 334 4749). Snacks and light meals in the university area, occasionally accompanied by live accordion music.

Entertainments

Glasgow's recent and much-vaunted rebirth as a cosmopolitan and vibrant city has to an extent been carried on the shoulders of its already established artistic wealth. The **King's Theatre** (Tel 041 552 5961) in Bath Street attracts top international acts. The **Theatre Royal** (Tel 041 331 1234) is the principle theatre regularly hosting Scottish Opera and Scottish Ballet. Classical concerts are offered at the **Pavilion Theatre** (Tel 041 332 1846) in Renfield Street. Other popular venues are the **Citizen's Theatre** (Tel 041 429 0022/8177) in Gorbals Street, the **Mitchell Theatre** (Tel 041 552 3748) in Granville Street, and the **Tron Theatre** (Tel 041 552 3748) in Parnie Street.

Useful Addresses

Greater Glasgow Tourist Board and Convention Bureau, Tourist Information Centre, 35 St Vincent Place, Glasgow G1 2ER (Tel 041 204 4400).

Scottish Tourist Guides Association, 3 Myrtle Avenue, Lenzie, G66 4HW (Tel 041 776 1052).

Post Office: George Square, Glasgow G2 1AA (Tel 041 248 2882).

Hospital: Royal Infirmary, Castle Street, Glasgow (Tel 041 552 3535).

Central

Stirling

All roads once led to Stirling when it was Scotland's capital. At that time it was the lowest bridging point on the River Forth, surrounded by hostile marshes and hills. Due to drainage and bridge building however, it was robbed of that advantage and has been brought within easy distance from Edinburgh and Glasgow. **Stirling Castle** and the **Old Town** occupy a crag with a commanding view over the lowland plain and the edge of the Highlands to the north. The castle was a favourite royal residence, later used as a barracks after the Union of the Crowns and the departure of the royals for London, and fine buildings still remain – the Renaissance palace of James IV, the Chapel Royal of 1594 and an impressive 16th-century Hall. The Old Town contains a number of restored buildings on Broad Street, such as **Argyll Lodging**, dating from 1632 and now a youth hostel. Further down the hill is the Victorian part of the town, and then the modern commercial centre. During the summer this area is filled with street-theatre artists, recalling Stirling's history through plays and traditional musical entertainments.

A mile (1.6 km.) or so north east of the town is the **Wallace Monument**, commemorating William Wallace who defeated the English at Stirling Bridge in 1297. This is a mid-19th century tower, 220 ft. (67 m.) high, perched on Abbey Crag. Bannockburn was another important battle for Scotland's independence, fought and won in 1314 by Robert the Bruce, and today it is the focus of the **Bannockburn Memorial and Information Centre** two miles

(3.2 km.) south on the A80. Stirling University campus contains the **MacRobert Arts Centre** (Tel 0786 61081) with film, theatre, opera and an art gallery. Ten miles (16 km.) or so north-west of the town is **Blair Drummond Safari Park** (Tel 0786 84156).

Accommodation

First Class

Heritage Hotel, 16 Allan Park, Stirling FK8 2QG (Tel 0786 73660). Small hotel in an elegant Georgian town house dating to around 1820, good restaurant.

Park Lodge Hotel, 32 Park Terrace, Stirling FK8 2JS (Tel 0786 74862). Part Victorian, part Georgian mansion with beautiful gardens at the top of the town, overlooking the park and Castle.

Middle Range

Castle Hotel, Castle Wynd, Stirling FK8 1EG (Tel 0786 72290/ 75621). Privately owned hotel offering bed and breakfast in a 15th-century building at the entrance to Stirling Castle.

Blairlogie House Hotel, Blairlogie, Stirling FK9 5QE (Tel 0259 61441). Small country house with seven rooms, set in eleven acres (4.5 hectares) of private gardens ten minutes outside Stirling.

Economy

Garfield Hotel, 12 Victoria Square, Stirling FK8 2QU (Tel 0786 73730). Family run hotel close to the golf course and within five minutes walk of the town centre.

Forth Guest House, 23 Forth Place, Riverside, Stirling FK8 1UD (Tel 0786 71020). Small terraced guest house, close to the station and town centre.

Campus accommodation is available in the beautiful grounds of Stirling University FK9 4LA (Tel 0786 73171, ext. 2039/2033). Also here is the **Stirling Management Centre** (Tel. 0786 51666) offering luxury Middle Range accommodation.

Eating Out

First Class

Cromlix House, Kinbuck, Dunblane (Tel 0786 822125). Lunch, afternoon teas and dinner available in the charming restaurant of this country house hotel just north of Stirling.

Airth Castle Hotel, Airth, by Falkirk (Tel 0324 83411). Superb

14th-century castle now converted to a country house hotel and offering a fine restaurant serving Scottish nouvelle cuisine. Twenty minutes from Stirling.

Middle Range

Littlejohn's, Port Street, Stirling (Tel 0786 63222). Excellent value steaks, fish dishes and hamburgers in a lively town centre restaurant.

The Topps Farm, Fintry Road, Denny (Tel 0324 822471). New farmhouse and working sheep and cashmere goat farm roughly twenty minutes from Stirling, serving the best of traditional Scottish fare.

Economy

The Settle Inn, 91 St Mary's Wynd, Stirling (Tel 0786 74609). Wholesome 'pub grub' in Stirling's oldest ale house, built in 1733.

The Birds and the Bees, Easter Cornton Road, Causewayhead, Stirling (Tel 0786 73663). Snacks and an à la carte menu offered in this award-winning converted farm steading five minutes from the town centre (towards the university).

Trails

A number of trails in the region are recommended by the Tourist Board and trail guides are available. Although intended for car users they could be cycled or walked, taking detours indicated.

The HIGHLAND GATEWAY TRAIL can begin at **Callander**, a popular visitor destination situated north-west of Stirling on the A84 and the 'Tannochbrae' of television's *Dr Finlay's Casebook*. **The Rob Roy Visitor Centre** is in Ancaster Square and combines the functions of **Tourist Information** office and shop with a modern-style interpretive centre on the main theme of Rob Roy.

Leaving Callander the trail cuts through the **Pass of Lenny** above the town then on towards the high country of **Breadalbane**. The very name, *Braghaid Albin* in Gaelic, means 'the high land of Scotland' suggesting a land that captures the country's romantic ideal: mountains, glens, lochs, clan history and mystical legends. The trail leads through **Strathyre** and detours to the village of **Balquhidder**, where Rob Roy is buried in the churchyard. It passes **Lochearnhead**, an affluent, residential village and watersports centre, then climbs onto the Glen Ogle road, giving spectacular views to what seems an impenetrable mountain wall ahead. The road to the east descends through the village of **Killin** on the **Falls of Dochart**. The trail goes west, through

Glen Dochart to **Crianlarich** then through Strathfillan to **Tyndrum**. For villages with such a spectacular setting, overlooked by high peaks, they are rather disappointing in themselves. Crianlarich has no image of note, while Tyndrum is simply strung out along the road. Although a good watering hole, it ought to be far more.

The **Mill Trail** explores the country east of Stirling in the smallest (former) county of Scotland, Clackmannanshire. The county's history of weaving and woollen processing goes back to the 16th century and the tradition is perpetuated in wool shops and small interpretive centres. The **Hillfoots** are small towns and villages along the A91 following the foothills of the **Ochil Hills**, a pleasant range with many easy hill and glen walks. **Tillicoultry** has the **Clock Mill Heritage Centre** with a small audio-visual display and traditional looms. At **Dollar, Castle Campbell** is situated in a very picturesque setting.

The **Trossachs Trail** is a circular tour around this vignette of the Highlands. Bustling tourist towns sit amid a splendid landscape of hills and lochs, all on a smaller scale than the mountains further north, yet offering great pleasure to sightseers and walkers alike. The translation of Trossachs is, loosely, 'bristly', and this is well deserved. The trail could begin at **Callander**. The A821 road leads west alongside **Loch Vennacher**, then **Loch Achray**. Further west is **Loch Katrine**, the classic Trossachs loch, on which a sailing trip is available on the *Sir Walter Scott*. The clean waters are piped to Glasgow and somehow the ninety-year-old steamboat does not look out of place. Turning back to the A821 the road leads down through **Achray Forest**. The **Queen Elizabeth Forest Park Centre** (Tel 08772 258), formerly the David Marshall Lodge, is a pleasant visitor centre run by the Forestry Commission, set in attractive grounds and within forest laced by almost 200 miles (322 km.) of forest trail offering great views of the surrounding countryside. This is the sort of country that gives an inkling of how much beauty a sensitive approach to afforestation could bring to many other bare parts of upland Scotland. Native Scottish oaks and birches mix with alien conifers – European larches and American spruces – many planted by the Forestry Commission in the 1940s. Further on down a winding road is **Aberfoyle**, a popular tourist town strongly associated with Rob Roy. From here the A81 leads east, passing the **Lake of Menteith**. A ruined 13th-century priory is on an island reached by ferry in the summer months. A few miles south, across the River Forth, here a mere stream meandering through Flander's Moss, is **Kippen**, a pleasant village whose main claim to fame was the 'world's largest vine' which produced 2000 bunches of grapes a year until it was removed in 1964. Stirling is a few miles further east.

The Highland country of the Trossachs has been renowned since at least 1810, when William Wordsworth's *The Lady of the Lake* became a best seller. He set the work in the Trossachs and tourists came in increasing numbers to find the locations he described.

The **Clyde Coast and Sealochs Trail** explores the Firth of Clyde coastline and the fjord-like sea lochs of this part of the West Highlands. **Dumbarton** on the A84 from Glasgow was once the capital of the Ancient Briton's kingdom of Strathclyde; **Castle Rock** has been fortified since Roman times. It is now a whisky distilling centre. Dumbarton's more recent shipbuilding heritage can be traced in the **Denny Ship Model Experiment Tank** museum. The A814 follows the north shore of the Clyde westward to **Helensburgh**. Above the promenade and parks of this traditional resort is Charles Rennie Mackintosh's **Hill House**. Helensburgh lies at the south-west end of the Highland Boundary Fault and to the north the hills begin to rise. The road follows the eastern shore of **Gareloch**, where pleasure craft share the waters with Britain's nuclear deterrent, the Polaris fleet, based at **Faslane**. A detour can be made at the head of the loch down onto the **Rosneath** peninsula, where pleasant villages such as **Rhu** are situated, as well as **Coulport** on the west shore, where further facilities of the nuclear fleet are found. The A814 continues northwards to the narrow, upper reaches of **Loch Long**, another sea loch with fjord-like characteristics. At the head is **Arrochar** set against a backdrop of **Beinn Ime** ('The Cobbler') in the 'Arrochar Alps', a spectacular group of mountains with an important place in the history of Scottish mountaineering. Only two miles (3.2 km.) to the east is **Tarbet**, meaning in Gaelic 'place of portage', on the shores of Loch Lomond. In 1263 Vikings sailed up Loch Long, before dragging their boats across this short isthmus and relaunching them onto Loch Lomond, where they plundered the lochside settlements.

Loch Lomond

Britain's largest freshwater lake, Loch Lomond is about 25 miles (40 km.) on the A811 from Stirling. From Glasgow it is an even shorter distance by road or by train, helping to explain the area's popularity. The loch is also one of Britain's most beautiful lakes and takes in a magnificent range of scenery from its wide southern waters, where gentle grass and heather-clad slopes contrast with its tree-covered islands, to the high bens and 'Munros', hills higher than 3000 feet (915 m.), such as Ben Lomond itself, looming over the narrow northern reaches. Loch Lomond merits its status as a National Scenic Area and as a Regional Park, and is currently proposed as one of Scotland's first four national parks. The **Park Authority** can be contacted at The Old Station, Balloch Road, Balloch G83 8SS (Tel 0389 53311).

The range in scenery in the Loch Lomond area is reflected in the level of tourism development: facilities for the many overseas and domestic tourists are primarily found in the villages in the south. The north, though accessible by the A82 on the west shore, is hikers' country. The south is the widest end of the loch and here are almost all of the thirty islands. Five of the islands are within the **Loch Lomond National Nature Reserve**, along with part of the south-east shore on account of the fine oak woodlands, winter wildfowl concentrations and an unusual fish, the powan, or freshwater herring, which is of very limited distribution in Britain. The B837 runs a short way up the east shore of the loch, as far as **Balmaha**. This spot is popular for boating and fishing and the **West Highland Way** meets the shore here. Surfaced road continues a further few miles to **Rowardennan**, while a popular trail – in places needing protection from hard use – continues to the summit of **Ben Lomond**, Scotland's most southerly Munro. It is also possible to cycle right from the heart of Glasgow to the south end of the loch using the Glasgow–Loch Lomond Cycleway, a distance of 21 miles (33.8 km.).

It has to be said that there are proposals for hydroelectric development at **Craigroyston**. The Friends of Loch Lomond Society argue that this would result in the wholesale destruction of the wild natural beauty which characterises the eastern shore of the loch north of Rowardennan. The society questions the acceptability of the environmental impact and the strategic need for the proposed scheme. Sadly, even the 'clean power' of hydroelectricity does not come without a catch.

Balloch is a popular resort at the south end of the loch. Balloch Castle stands in **Balloch Castle Country Park**. The cruiser, *Countess Fiona* operates on the loch (Tel 041 248 2699) leaving from Balloch, and boats can be hired from several companies in the area. The Loch Lomond Park Authority at Balloch are able to advise on the area while Countryside Ranger Services operate throughout Loch Lomond, Stirling and the Trossachs.

Accommodation & Eating Out

First Class

Roman Camp Hotel, Callander FK17 8BG (Tel 0877 30003). Country house dating from 1625, set in its own grounds beside the River Teith. Fourteen rooms and a fine restuaurant.

Cameron House Hotel, Loch Lomond, Alexandria G83 8QZ (Tel 0389 55565). Luxury country house hotel on its own 108-acre (44 hectares) estate right on the banks of Loch Lomond.

Middle Range

Leny House, Leny Estate, Kilmahog, Callander FK17 8HA (Tel 0877 31078). A magnificent 15th-century turreted country home offering bed and breakfast and situated within its own grounds.

Inverard Hotel, Loch Ard Road, Aberfoyle FK8 3TD (Tel 08772 229). Large country house high above the town with magnificent views over the River Forth and hills beyond.

Economy

Invervey Hotel, Tyndrum, by Crianlarich FK20 8RY (Tel 08384 219). Family run hotel in a beautiful location on the West Highland Way.

Tullichewan Hotel, Balloch Road, Balloch G83 8SW (Tel 0389 52052). Privately run hotel offering bed and breakfast and complete with a crèche play area.

Forth Valley

East of Stirling in the Forth Valley, **Bo'ness**, **Grangemouth** and **Falkirk** are small towns, firmly based on industry past and present. Grangemouth is a major petrochemicals centre and, along with the other towns, offers industrial heritage-based tourist attractions. Steam trains operate out of Bo'ness run by enthusiasts of the **Scottish Railway Preservation Society** (Tel 0506 822298). Indeed Bo'ness may become a future success story in tourism-based regeneration. Its image has long been one of a declining mining town, earning itself the title 'Black Bo'ness', but it now seeks to create an image of itself in its heyday at the forefront of the industrial revolution.

Falkirk has become a good shopping centre in recent years, although at present its industrial past exists as a grim legacy rather than as a 'heritage capital' on which to build. Yet its heritage is authentic: the great Carron Ironworks, now closed, began in 1760 with the manufacture of 'Carronades' (small, naval cannons) for Nelson's fleet. Falkirk also has the best remains of the Roman **Antonine Wall**, nearby at Bonnybridge.

Clyde Valley

Blantyre is a few miles south-east of Glasgow. It was the birthplace in 1813 of David Livingston, doctor, missionary and explorer. The **David Livingston Centre** (Tel 0698 823140) tells how he worked his way from humble origins through medical school, then journeyed through Africa. **Chatelherault Country Park** (pronounced 'shatlero') is on the Clyde Valley Tourist Route, near Hamilton, south-east of Glasgow. The Park centres on the recently restored 17th-century Adam hunting lodge, completed in 1744. An interpretive centre gives an account of the life and times of the estate, from the aristocracy to the miner and gardener at the bottom of the pile. Whatever the iniquities of the estate system, it offers some valuable lessons in integrated land management. Attitudes to nature in the 18th century can also be deduced; even the River Clyde was forced to conform to the ideals of formality. The beautiful surrounding parklands can be enjoyed by all in these more democratic times. The impressive **Duke's Bridge** spans the River Avon that runs through the park. Further south on the A72 is **New Lanark**, designated a World Heritage Site on account of its importance as a cradle of industry and a pioneering experiment in social reform. The visitor centre gives an excellent insight into the careful restoration of this important site and into Robert Owen's utopian vision for industrial society. Perhaps inevitably for the times, this was no democratic vision, rather one man's view of how life should be led – temperate, healthy and God-fearing – and we can only speculate about how the workers felt about it. Nearby is **The Falls of Clyde**, a tourist 'must' since the 18th century, and now part of a Scottish Wildlife Trust Reserve. There is a visitor centre at New Lanark.

Biggar has a number of visitor attractions giving an insight into life in the district, including a reconstructed Victorian street at **Gladstone Court Museum**; a 17th-century farmhouse at **Greenhill**

Covenanters' House; a more general local history museum at **Moat Park Heritage Centre**; and **Biggar Gasworks**, built in 1839 and the oldest rural gasworks in Britain.

Leadhills and **Wanlockhead** are Scotland's highest villages with long associations with lead mining. Early industrialism is commemorated at Wanlockhead where lead mining was long practised. A mine, smelt mill and miners' cottages can still be seen. Nearby at Leadhills, another early example of social concern is Britain's oldest subscription library, established in 1741. An underground experience is available in the now disused mines (Tel 0659 74387).

Ayrshire Coast and Islands

Leaving Glasgow and following the northern shore of the Clyde estuary, the heritage of shipbuilding is inescapable (even today, when old industrial areas such as Clydeside are in decline and wait with bated breath for the as yet uncharted 'post-industrial age'). Tourism is one of the pillars of this scenario and, like Glasgow, **Greenock**, now an unemployment blackspot, is preparing for its future. Further still, **Gourock** is a popular yachting centre and resort, offering fine views over the Firth of Clyde. Continuing 'doon the watter', **Largs** is the most popular Clyde resort. Traditional resorts have hit hard times since the population turned to 'Sun, Sand and Sex' on the Spanish Costas, but Largs continues to thrive, now benefiting from the 'greying' of the population by converting former holiday accommodation into retirement homes. **Kelburn Country Centre**, an estate offering walks, gardens, shops and a farming museum, is a few miles south on the A78.

A short ferry trip from Largs is **Great Cumbrae** island and its resort **Millport**. A further 'island hop' away is **Bute**. The island's principal resort is Rothesay, the ultimate destination of the traditional Glaswegian journey down the Clyde. The Isle of **Arran** is reached by ferry from **Ardrossan**. In Arran's 200 square miles (518 sq.km.), mountains, glens, lochs, castles and standing stones account for its title 'Scotland in miniature'. **Goat Fell** at 2866 ft. (874 m.) offers a significant challenge to climbers, and red deer are common on the hills. The **Marine Biological Station and Museum** has an excellent aquarium. Geologically, the island is half highland and half lowland, lying astride the Highland Boundary Fault.

Irvine was a small village, now better known as one of Scotland's New Towns; a purpose-built community planned as a growth point for new industry and aimed at easing the population pressures of the old industrial areas. The town boasts the **Magnum Centre**, one of Europe's most successful sports and leisure centres.

Ayrshire and Burns country

The **Royal Troon Golf Course** (Tel 0292 311555) is probably the best known attraction of **Troon**, but the sandy beach is pleasant with fine views over to Arran. **Prestwick** is probably best known for its transatlantic airport – surprisingly Scotland's only one until 1990 – but was also the scene of the first-ever British Open Golf Championship in 1860. **Girvan**, further down the coast, is a similar coastal resort. On the way is the magnificent **Culzean Castle**, designed by Robert Adam in 1777 and now run by the National Trust for Scotland. The surrounding country park is well managed with a variety of interests. Visible from much of this coastal route is **Ailsa Craig**, the 1114 ft. (340 m.) high granite plug of an ancient volcano 10 miles (16 km.) offshore. With its vertical cliffs this is a spectacular bird reserve and was once the source of the granite for the best curling stones. The awe-inspiring cliffs can best be appreciated from a boat and trips are available from Girvan and Ayr, notably on the paddle steamer *Waverley* (Tel 041 221 8152). **Ayr** is the most popular resort on the west coast of Scotland and still enjoys strong associations with Robert Burns. These include the **Auld Kirk** of 1654 where Burns was baptised, just off the High Street; the **Auld Brig**, and the **Tam O' Shanter Museum**. For this reason alone the town deserves exploration.

The Burns Heritage Trail starts from where the poet was born in 1759 in the village of **Alloway**, now on the southern fringes of Ayr. The cottage he was born in is maintained in the style of that period. Also in Alloway is the **Land O' Burns** visitor centre, set in attractive gardens, and the **Burns Monument**. **Alloway Kirk** and the **Brig o' Doon** are nearby, both featuring in his poem 'Tam O' Shanter', a tongue-in-cheek tale of the supernatural and the evils of drink, the latter being a favourite indulgence of the Bard himself. Many places associated with him are in this vicinity, though to pay final respects at his grave it is necessary to travel on to the **Burns Mausoleum** in St Michael's Churchyard, Dumfries.

Accommodation

First Class

Pickwick Hotel, 19 Racecourse Road, Ayr KA7 2TD (Tel 0292 26011). Family run country house hotel in an impressive mansion just a few minutes from the beach.

Chestnuts Hotel, 52 Racecourse Road, Ayr KA7 2UZ (Tel 0292 264393). Family owned and run hotel in a Georgian villa with a good restaurant.

Middle Range

Caledonian Hotel, Dalblair Road, Ayr KA7 1UG (Tel 0292 269331). Modern hotel near the town centre, complete with leisure centre and indoor swimming pool.

Belleisle House Hotel, Belleisle Park, Doonfoot Road, Ayr KA7 4DU (Tel 0292 42331). Once the property of the Magistrates of Ayr, eighteen bedrooms and two dining-rooms, one decorated in imitation of Marie Antoinette's music room, and the other after her bedroom.

Economy

Arrandale Hotel, 2–4 Cassillis Street, Ayr KA7 1DW (Tel 0292 289959). Scottish Tourist Board 'Commended' bed and breakfast, family run and offering a friendly welcome.

Craggallan Guest House, 8 Queens Terrace, Ayr KA7 1DU (Tel 0292 264998). Homely bed and breakfast, family run and offering six rooms.

Eating Out

First Class

Burns Byre Restaurant, Mount Oliphant Farm, Alloway (Tel 0292 43644). Traditional and nouvelle Scottish cuisine in a converted farm byre just south of Ayr.

Old Racecourse Hotel, 2 Victoria Park, Ayr (Tel 0292 262873). Straightforward Scottish cooking at its best, including afternoon teas, just over one mile (1.6 km.) from the town centre and close to the beach.

Middle Range

Fouter's Bistro, 24 Academy Street, Ayr (Tel 0292 261391). Inventive French cuisine using Scottish produce.

Stables, Queen's Court, 41 Sandgate, Ayr (Tel 0292 283704). Light lunches and fuller dinners in a converted 18th-century courtyard.

Economy

The Hunny Pot, 37 Beresford Terrace, Ayr (Tel 0292 263239). Popular coffee shop and health food restaurant in the town centre.

Tudor Restaurant, 8 Beresford Terrace, Ayr (Tel 0292 261404). Traditional Scottish fare, including excellent high teas with cakes and scones. Children's menu.

5 Borders and South-West Scotland

The border country between Scotland and England, extending from the North Sea to the Irish Sea, encompasses as great a variety of landscapes as anywhere in Britain, ranging from the rugged mountain scenery of western Galloway to some of the richest lowland agricultural country in the Berwickshire merse. The area includes the local authority regions of the Borders in the east, and Dumfries and Galloway in the west, and in this guide, Galloway is used as shorthand to include Dumfries. There are few large towns in the area, evidence of manufacturing is minimal, and the predominant industries are farming and forestry, with fertile arable land in the east and green stock rearing area in the west and uplands. The first impression to the visitor is one of neat and tidy towns and villages set in a countryside of enormous diversity, with a coastline which includes everything from high, rocky cliffs to great sweeps of marshland, mudflats and sand dunes. On the whole this is gentle country, although its turbulent past is reflected in the many castles and fortified houses which are scattered throughout the whole borderland. Compared to Highland Scotland, the region seems less wild and more settled.

For the most part, the southern uplands are characteristically rounded and green and more welcoming in appearance than the inhospitable mountains of the north. Nevertheless conditions can vary markedly between the exposed and extreme climate of the central Moffat hills and the sheltered mildness of the Solway coast. In the lowlands meanwhile, east Berwickshire has relatively long hours of sunshine. A low population density gives rise to a feeling of uncrowded space, and yet distances between towns and villages are not great.

It is this combination which has made more accessible coastal areas such as Galloway popular retirement places. The indigenous population finds its roots in an ancient stock of Celtic immigrants who formed the original British tribes over 8000 years ago, mainly in the west. This has been overlain by subsequent invasions of Angles and Saxons from the east, and Vikings from the north – a mixture that is reflected in place names which include traces of Gaelic (Galloway was one of the last places to retain Gaelic-speaking communities in south Scotland), Norse, Lowland Scots, and even French from the early Norman settlements.

Notwithstanding these disparate influences, a distinctive rural culture exists (especially evident in the towns of the eastern Borders), based on a strong sense of community. The industry of the region is firmly rooted in its natural resources: wool from local sheep goes to the Borders' tweed mills (thus continuing an industry whose origins are in medieval times), while in the west, lush pasturelands form the basis of food processing and dairy products. The Berwickshire coast supports important local fishing communities, and throughout the uplands and moorlands afforestation, greatly expanded in recent times, contrasts with the mixed woodlands of large estates. Tourism has become increasingly important but does not dominate the local economy, nor have large resort developments taken over areas of natural beauty.

History

Early hunters and food gatherers from before 4000 BC, and subsequent Neolithic farmers – mainly from Western Europe and Ireland – have left evidence of their settlements in the hill forts of the Borders and the rock carvings and chambered tombs of Galloway. The Roman invasion of the first century left its mark in such important sites as Trimontiun near Melrose and the Roman road of Dere Street. Due to the resistance of local British tribes, and Pictish attacks from the north, the Romans departed in the 4th century. Even before this, immigrants had established small Christian communities in the region, but the arrival of St Ninian at Whithorn in Wigtownshire in AD 398 marked a significant point in early Christian foundation, almost two centuries before the landing of St Columba. During this time there were continuing waves of invaders, including Angles and Saxons from north Europe, especially in the 6th and 7th centuries, while the Norse invasion extinguished the Picts as a separate ethnic group.

Two key events occurred between AD 800 and 1100: the Viking forest clearances and the increasing infuence of the Anglo-Norman culture from the south. Celtic Christianity survived in Galloway until the 12th century, but elsewhere was supplanted by orthodox Catholicism. With the Anglo-Normans came the foundation of the great abbeys and monasteries in the 11th century, which among other things did much to establish the subsequent wool trade and they were also associated with the building of Norman castles and the development of a quasi-feudal system, which was more English than Scottish.

In the period between the 12th and 15th centuries, because of developments along the key routes of Nithsdale, Annandale and Tweed, the Border region gained considerable economic and strategic importance. Indeed, Border towns such as Peebles, Selkirk, Kelso and Jedburgh are amongst the oldest in Scotland. At the same time, and continuing into the 16th century, there was almost constant warfare. The wars of Scottish independence in the 13th and 14th centuries led to widespread and repeated devastation in the Borders by English armies, culminating in the disastrous Battle of Flodden in 1513 and the death of James IV and most of the Scottish aristocracy.

As elsewhere in Scotland, the Reformation (mainly in the 16th century) had an important bearing, bringing further unrest and continued invasions from the south. Parallel to these national events was the notorious centuries-long warfare between powerful landed families and their followers on both sides of the border, which led to the area being known as the 'Debatable Lands'. Permanent settlement and development was therefore confined to a few fortified enclaves. This turbulence had barely subsided when the 'Killing Times' broke out in the mid-17th century, with the struggle of the Covenanters against Episcopalianism. Today the Border hillsides are marked by Covenanters' graves.

From that time onwards, settled conditions and improved communications allowed for the consolidation of towns and the development of modern farming during the period of the Agricultural Revolution. This was the time when the 'Improving Landlords' established great houses and estates, particularly in the lowlands of the east and often from industrial wealth generated elsewhere. By the mid-19th century important cattle markets, based largely on the Irish cattle trade, had become a focus in the main towns of Dumfries and Galloway. Whole towns and villages were planned to serve the needs of local industry, which included fishing and farming. During the Industrial Revolution there was substantial expansion of the woollen trade, using good water supplies for both washing and power. The success of the industry in more modern times has fluctuated, but with quality products gaining in importance in the post-war period, it appears to be undergoing something of a revival; over one fifth of the working population in the Borders is now employed in textiles. Fishing has declined, as has upland sheep farming, and been largely replaced by industrial forestry. Tourism however, based on both the unspoiled natural landscape and historic interest, is expanding.

Geography

All of the region lies south of the great Southern Upland fault which separates central Scotland from the uplands to the south. Other significant boundaries are the Solway Firth in the west and the lower River Tweed in the east, both marking roughly the Scotland/England border. The geology of the area is predominantly Ordovician slate and shale, but with substantial outcrops of granite in Galloway and red sandstone in Berwickshire and Dumfries. It is this harder rock which produces the rugged 'Highland' scenery of west Galloway. The dominant features of the landscape are the uplands, stretching from the southern flanks of the Lammermuirs in the east to the hills and moors of Wigtownshire in the west. The Tweed rises in the centre of the uplands and cuts a swath from west to east, separating the hills from the Cheviots which straddle the border with England to the south. There are only a few subsidiary river valley systems – such as the Annan, Nith and Dee – which provide north–south routes through the main southern upland massif. The coastal plain on the north shore of the Solway Firth is an important agricultural zone in Dumfries and Galloway, and complements the lowlands around the mouth of the Tweed known as the Merse.

The combination of climate, geology and land-form has produced a considerable diversity of natural habitats and wildlife. The region is still notable for its sweeps of green hill and rolling heather moorland, which are the haunt of golden eagle, hen harrier, peregrine, curlew and other typical hill birds. (Cairnsmore of Fleet National Nature Reserve and the National Trust for Scotland's property on the Moffat Hills are both good examples.) Native broadleaf woodland has almost completely disappeared, although good examples can still be seen at Abbey St Bathans, Glen Trool, and the Fleet Valley, where bluebells and other spring flowers are spectacular.

An oustanding feature is the variety of coastal landscape, most of which is undeveloped and provides a refuge for an abundance of flora and fauna. The southerly aspect and mild climate of the Galloway coast allows many flower and insect species to survive at the northern limits of their British range. There is a wealth of plant habitats between the rocky islands and headlands, as well as expanses of saltmarsh around the Cree and Nith estuaries, and sand dune systems along the whole of the Solway shore. Associated with this are some of the most important bird populations in Britain, notably over-wintering wildfowl and waders, which can be found roosting along the sheltered mudflats of the inner Solway and feeding on nearby saltmarshes and farmland. This area is of international value for species such as the barnacle goose, for which Caerlaverock National Nature Reserve near Dumfries was originally established. By contrast, in the late spring and early summer breeding season, St Abbs Head Reserve on the high cliffs of the Berwickshire coast provides the spectacular sight of thousands of guillemots and razorbills.

Wetlands are scarce in the eastern Borders, but Galloway has a number of peatlands. The Silver Flowe near Newton Stewart is outstanding as an example of wet bog, with its variety of sphagnum species and water-filled hollows. The Loch Ken and River Dee marshes between New Galloway and Castle Douglas are notable for wetland birds and secretive otters. In the east the River Tweed itself is locally renowned as a premier salmon river, but is also an ecologically important system in its own right, supporting many natural habitats.

Throughout the region, deer (especially roe) are plentiful, while red deer are commonly seen in the Galloway hills. Rather more unusual are the herds of wild goats on the Moffat Hills and in Galloway Forest Park. Five National Scenic Areas have been designated at Upper Tweeddale, Eildon Hills, Nith Estuary, East Stewartry Coast and Fleet Valley.

Climate

The climate of the region varies considerably over its wide east–west range and altitudinal differences. While some of the highest annual average rainfall levels in Scotland have been recorded at Loch Dee in west Galloway (2197 mm at an altitude of 244 metres or 86.5 inches at 800 feet), conversely the coastal areas of Berwickshire and its hinterland have among the longest periods of sunshine per year (an average of 1523 hours) and relatively low rainfall (550 mm at an altitude of 23 metres or 21.6 inches at 75 feet). At the same time however, the Solway Coast does enjoy comparatively high levels of summer sunshine, and even boasts the record for the highest air temperature ever recorded in Scotland: 32.8°C (90°F) at Dumfries in 1908!

The Rhinns of Galloway, in the path of the Gulf Stream, experience some of the highest winter temperatures in Scotland (as is evident from the range of sub-tropical plants which are able to grow out of doors at Logan Gardens). Temperature variation is least in west

Galloway, and most in the Moffat Hills, roughly central between east and west coasts. During the winter months this area can be subject to very low temperatures, frequently recording a mean daily minimum in January of below zero. This is most obvious along the Beattock Summit road where there is an average of thirty-eight days of snow lying on the ground. It is notable however, that this is only half the number experienced by the more northerly high road at Drummochter Pass in Inverness-shire.

Attractions

The outstanding attractions of this region are its unspoiled and thriving pastoral countryside, combined with the range of historic towns and villages. A successful agricultural industry gives a sense of purpose to the landscape, maintaining its fabric and displaying few signs of the rural dereliction often found further north. It is tranquil without being desolate, and in both town and country there is a self-respect which takes pride in tidiness and order. There is also a genuine indigenous culture which retains its local character and taste, without giving way completely to the whims of large numbers of tourists: visitors will not normally be exhorted to buy tartan dolls or mini Loch Ness monsters!

Most towns have programmes of festivals and events throughout the summer season at least. Some of the most notable are the historic Common Ridings celebrated by each town, when geographical boundaries are marked on horseback and festivities take place around the countryside. The Borders are also pre-eminent in rugby football, and regular matches testify to the fierce loyalties to town teams such as Kelso and Hawick.

In contrast to other remote areas in Scotland, there are many alternative roads to disperse traffic and motoring can be a pleasurable experience. For cyclists, the lack of traffic away from north–south routes is particularly attractive. For walkers there is an almost infinite variety of paths from coast to mountain, incuding remote hill tracks and more accessible strolls around villages. The Southern Upland Way is the only coast to coast long distance route in Scotland, extending for 212 miles (341 km.). Naturalists are especially favoured in an area with such ecological diversity, particularly birdwatchers.

Historians will find equal interest, especially following the recent discovery of early Christian settlements at Whithorn. With the possible exception of Aberdeenshire, the region is also probably richer in castles and stately homes than any other in Scotland. Those with an interest in Scots literature will find many strong associations with the romantic novels of Sir Walter Scott, or the high-adventure tales of John Buchan. There is great untapped potential in these literary and cultural resources, including the Border ballads and history of the reivers. For visitors seeking a quality holiday experience away from the often unwelcome modern trappings of tourism, this region can be a rewarding discovery.

Cuisine

Cuisine from Dumfries and Galloway and the Borders is not as distinct as that found in other parts of Scotland. There are however, one or two specialities which should not be missed. On the savoury side, salmon from the Tweed is popular as either a starter or main course, while Border lamb and Galloway beef are firm favourites for a Sunday roast. The area produces vast quantities of potatoes which are liable to be served at every possible occasion in every manner imaginable.

Barley is a common crop, and is used to make Scotch broth soup which is often served in pubs and guest houses, as well as being transported further north for malt whisky.

Galloway cheddar is a medium cheese particularly popular in its home area, or if you prefer something sweet, Selkirk bannock is a fruit loaf usually spread with butter and enjoyed at afternoon tea. Moffat toffee is a rich sweet that does nothing for the teeth but is nevertheless addictive, while Berwick cockles, not as popular now as they used to be, are stripey green and white mints from the east coast.

Level of Tourism

One of the charms of the region is that while tourism is becoming increasingly significant to the local economy, it remains relatively unobtrusive and evenly spread. There are few, if any, tourist developments catering for the mass market, although the area is clearly gaining in popularity (visitor numbers to the Borders' 40 main attractions rose 12 per cent between 1989 and 1990). There are few existing facilities suffering from over-use, although some locations readily accessible by car (such as the Grey Mare's Tail waterfall) are showing signs of erosion. Many who have discovered the area's attractions make repeat visits, notably from the north of England, from where 40 per cent of all visitors originate. Many others view the area simply as a through-route to Edinburgh and the north (which accounts for the relatively low proportion of overseas visitors), often only stopping for a single night or breaking their journey for a few hours at such favoured points as Moffat, which in high season can seem almost crowded. The tourist boards are anxious to attract both younger and older people without children, who are able to holiday outside the main period and therefore extend the season. Unlike the Highlands, both the Borders and Galloway lack the promotion of a distinctive image, despite a wealth of visitor attractions and their accessibility from the north of England. Various schemes have been suggested for larger-scale developments, but as yet none have materialised. Certainly the local authorities are keen to encourage visitors to stay longer and would look favourably upon appropriate and sensitively designed projects which could contribute to the local economy. A scheme such as Aberfeldy's Locus Project in Tayside (page 129), or a well-structured system of home-stays with local residents might well be a good starting point.

In Galloway the majority of tourism is concentrated on the coast, although the region would welcome more development inland, around the attractive Glenkens area for instance. Most visitors come to Galloway to enjoy the environment rather than sophisticated facilities, and local residents welcome the economic benefits which contribute to the maintenance of amenities and services used by the community at large. With the relative ease of access from the south and an apparent trend back towards holidaying in Britain, pressure will undoubtedly increase to expand tourist development here. This has already happened on Loch Ken, where conflicts between water-skiers, fishermen, birdwatchers and others have been resolved through an integrated management plan.

It is clear that preservation of the environment is central to the continuation of a firm tourist base, and local authorities would welcome national and even regional park designations which would highlight the area's outdoor attractions. In both Galloway and the Borders there is a recognised need to improve and expand existing facilities, specifically aimed at catering for short-break activity holidays, rather than promoting new, non-indigenous large-scale attractions. There is scope for marketing and making better use of the Southern Upland Way for example, not to mention loch shores, river environs and the coast itself. Extensive tracts of conifer forest, mainly owned by the Forestry Commission, also offer opportunities for screened development in conjunction with the recreation potential of the forest land. The possibilities are various, although progress must depend on careful planning.

Two special-interest pursuits already of significance to the local economy are shooting and fishing, both of which attract thousands of visitors each year. These activities help to maintain employment both directly and indirectly, notably through ancillary services such as fishing tackle supplies and gun repairs. Hotels in some towns (and many country house establishments) specialise in this type of holiday, as well as offering successful golfing packages. Other special interest breaks have yet to be fully developed, and accommodation services need to be integrated with organised activities such as painting and natural history.

Good Alternatives

Meeting People

Guest houses and bed and breakfast accommodation are widely available throughout the region. Generally of a high quality, they provide excellent value for money, although there is still an unusually high proportion of establishments with limited amenities (for example, no en-suite bathrooms). Bed and breakfast proprietors often constitute the first point of real contact with local residents, and as such can be important sources of information. The Borders now has its own **Farm Holiday Bureau** (contact Borders Tourist Information, Municipal Buildings, High St, Selkirk TD7 4JX. Tel 0750 21886), a member-owned co-operative which offers visitors insight into farming, the dominant activity of the region. There is still potential for more farm tourism however, which goes beyond the traditional B&B type experience and furthers understanding of the local area. Such holidays can also be the start of lasting friendships between hosts and guests, and can thus encourage visitors to return to the same area in future years.

A new innovation is low-cost bunkhouse accommodation for walkers, such as that along the Southern Upland Way or at the Gordon Arms Hotel in the Yarrow Valley. In addition there is an increasing number of establishments which combine accommodation with special interest activities such as walking, birdwatching and, in at least one case, guided weekend breaks. Caravanning is popular, although some of the larger static caravan sites are inadequately designed and screened. Also available are registered linked caravan parks, run with an advertised system of grading and accommodation. Touring caravans appear to have declined in recent years.

Youth Hostels provide an excellent means of meeting people, both locals and non-residents alike. There are no less than ten hostels in the area, run by the Youth Hostels Association, and which are often less crowded than their equivalents elsewhere in Scotland. At the same time though, there is a demand for more hostel accommodation in more crowded areas. Self-catering is becoming increasingly popular for longer-stay holidays, and there is a wide range of self-catering properties available. Although it tends to be fully booked during the summer, it runs far below capacity throughout the rest of the year.

The famous Common Riding tradition of the Border towns is associated with historic pageantry, and visitors are welcome to attend, although the origins and organisation of events remain strongly local. Nevertheless, Common Ridings offer a good opportunity to mingle with local communities.

Discovering Places

Apart from long-established museums, there are a number of small scale visitor centres based on either the natural resources or history of the region, usually offering interpretation to adults and children alike. The **Wildfowl Trust Centre** at Caerlaverock and the Forestry Commission's **Deer Museum** at Clatterinshaws near New Galloway are relatively well known and highlight aspects of natural history. Newer ventures include **Skyreburn Aquarium** near Gatehouse-of-Fleet and **Luce Bay Shore Centre** at Monreith in Wigtownshire. There are now a number of **farms** open to the public, ranging from a typical hill farm such as **Palgowan** in Glen Trool to the **Galloway Farm Heritage Centre** near New Galloway. An excellent example of interpretation is provided free at **Legerwood Farm** between Lauder and Earlston, which is also where the first self-guided farm trail in the Borders was established.

Other contact with farming and the land is provided by a number of large estates open to the public. These vary from a simple woodland walk to linked interpretive exhibitions, such as those at **The Hirsel** and **Abbey St Bathans**. Several of these estates also have the added attraction of historic houses and special provisions for children, such as at **Bowhill** and **Drumlanrig**. In a similar vein are the various forest centres like those at **Gatehouse-of-Fleet**, **Newton Stewart** and **Jedburgh**, which offer the chance to learn about woodland wildlife and habitats. Near Lauder there is also **Wooplaw Community Woodland**, occasionally used for music and poetry recitals or as a dance venue, while the **Eskdalemuir Centre** focuses on deer management. A mention should be made at this point of the many facilities provided by the Forestry Commission, from campsites and visitor centres to walks and summer events.

Interpretive provisions such as these provide an introduction to three of the region's most important resources: the sea and coast; farmland, and forest.

Angling is another important activity, whether sea fishing from the coastal ports or salmon fishing on the Tweed. Much less expensive is trout fishing, for which permits must be obtained (contact Tourist Information). Whether novice or old hand, a number of good angling guides are available. The **Tweed Foundation** (Dock Road, Tweedmouth, Berwick-upon-Tweed) has been established to conserve the river and its environs not just for fishing, but for its many other leisure and natural history interests as well. Its telephone service, 'Tweed-Line', offers up-to-date information on river levels, prospects and last-minute lets.

Communications

How to Get There

RAIL: The tragedy of the closure of the Edinburgh–Carlisle rail route linking Border towns, and likewise the Dumfries–Stranraer route prior to that, has left the area with a skeleton system which virtually bypasses this part of Scotland. Apart from Dumfries and Stranraer, the only other towns served by rail are Berwick-upon-Tweed and Sanquar. British Rail information is available from Dumfries station (Tel 0387 64105).

COACH: There are bus services linking Carlisle to the main centres, although connections for smaller towns are infrequent. From Edinburgh there are also services down through the Borders, some going by Penicuik and Peebles and others by Dalkeith.

When You're There

BUS: Large areas of upland Galloway are without any form of regular public transport, although Dumfries itself is unusual in having a regular 'town-link' mini-bus service which calls at points around the town centre, railway station and shops. Bus services are listed in a leaflet obtainable from the Department of Roads and Transportation at Dumfries and Galloway District Council. Alternatively, contact **Western Scottish and Citylink Bus Service** in Dumfries (Tel 0387 53496).

Similarly, a *Borders Travel Guide* is published by the same department of the Borders Regional Council, which also produces a free leaflet on bus transport for access to the Southern Upland

Way. Useful detailed information on all transport to this route is given in the *Southern Upland Wayfarer*, a free guide. In addition there is the Harrier Scenic Bus network which provides access to popular locations not covered by other public services, including scenic circular routes around Moffat and a new service connecting Eyemouth and St Abbs to the main Border towns. Reduced-price tickets are available on the Waverley Wanderer and Border Reiver services. There are a few postbus services in more isolated areas, but these tend to be slow because of deliveries. For full information on Borders bus services, contact **Lowland Scottish Bus Service** in Hawick (Tel 0450 72784).

CAR: Due to the predominant lie of the land there are few north–south routes through the uplands. The A1 and A77 follow east and west coast routes via Berwick and Stranraer respectively, while the A74 (Beatock), A68 (Jedburgh), A7 (Galashiels) and A76 (Sanquar) are the main central routes. The A74 takes much of the heavy through-traffic and has a reputation for being dangerous. The A1 can also be congested. Fortunately the A75 between Carlisle and Stranraer bypasses many small towns which suffer from convoys of heavy container lorries going to and from the Irish ferry, but Dumfries with its crossing of the River Nith remains a serious bottleneck. Elsewhere in the region traffic is light and even in the height of the tourist season minor roads can be a pleasure to drive on (in the Borders there are 18.5 miles (29.8 km.) of road per 1000 people, higher than in most regions of Scotland).

Leaflets carrying information on a number of well signposted tourist trails for motorists are available from Information Centres, and include the **Solway Coast Heritage Trail, Galloway Tourist Route to Ayr** and **Borders Tourist Route to Edinburgh**. Other routes which are not signposted can also be followed by leaflets. All cover stopping points of interest. In addition there are guidebooklets giving details of circular walks for motorists.

CYCLING: There are special provisions for cycling in the area (Dumfries and Galloway is the only region in Scotland to have appointed a full-time Rights of Way Officer). Galloway has magnificent cycling country (the world's first pedal cycle was built in Thornhill around 1840), notably along the coastal routes around the Machars of Wigtown and Rhinns of Galloway. The tourist authority has commissioned a feasibility study to promote the area's potential for this activity, and one company, **North Riding Cycles** (John Stead, 4 Blair Terrace, Portpatrick. Tel 077681 568) is already specialising in cycle tours and holidays. By contrast the Borders have a number of cycling centres, two of which use mountain-bikes: at Peebles and Bowhill. **Scottish Border Trails** (Drummore, Venlaw High Road, Peebles. Tel 0721 20336) offers a comprehensive service including itineraries and accommodation. Also worth contacting are **Coldstream Cycles** (The Lees Stables, Coldstream. Tel 0890 2709), and **Tweed Valley Hotel** in Walkerburn (Tel 089687 220), which offer activity and special interest holidays, including cycling.

It has to be said that one of the deterrents to visitors who wish to bring their own bikes is the truncated rail service throughout the region. Unless you have a car, reaching anywhere between Edinburgh and the English border can prove a major problem, especially if you're carrying a bike at the same time. Fortunately there are a growing number of cycle-hire firms in the main towns.

Tourist Centres in both the Borders and Galloway produce free leaflets on cycling in their areas, including the addresses of hire and holiday companies.

WALKING: The region offers many excellent guided walks, in particular the long-distance **Southern Upland Way**. Detailed mapguides are available for this walk and also cover recommended accommodation, including campsites and bothies along the route. This is not a walk to be undertaken lightly however, as there are several long exposed sections and, on certain stretches, considerable isolated distances. Short sections can be walked more easily at either end of the way. In addition there are a number of companies who provide guides to this and other walks, and equally as importantly, transport to the remoter areas. In Dumfries and Galloway visitors might contact **Craigshiels Walking Guides** (Douglas Allison, The Old Farmhouse, 58 Nunholm Road, Dumfries. Tel 0387 61818); **Quinta Galloway Walking Holidays** (Gerry Douglas, Anchordale, Colvend, Dalbeattie. Tel 0387 78240); **Walk the Scottish Way** (Stewart Wilson, Wauchope Lodge, Moffat. Tel 0683 20183), or **Carsphairn Heritage Group** (Smitton, Dalry, Galloway. Tel 06446 206), while in the Borders **Scottish Border Trails** (address under *Cycling* above) offers guided tours. Alternatively, the **Countryside Ranger Services** of both areas provide an excellent 'walks and talks' service. They can be contacted at either the Regional Planning Offices, English Street, Dumfries (Tel 0837 61234, ext 4184), or at the Borders Regional Council offices, Newtown St Boswells (Tel 0835 23301). It should be noted that proposals are afoot at present to provide shorter loop walks from the main Southern Upland Way, particularly in the vicinity of towns.

The older **Pennine Way** from the south ends at Kirk Yetholm in the Borders. Throughout the main season there is a wide range of guided walks provided by countryside rangers, associated with both particular estates and the area in general. Walks and hikes cover everything from birdwatching to Border trails, and forestry to pond-dipping. A comprehensive leaflet is available from Information Centres. In addition the RSPB has published a comprehensive guide to birdwatching walks in the region.

Useful Local Contacts

There are a number of local groups concerned with maintaining the environment, heritage and culture of the area, and with using such assets to promote identity and economic benefit. The **Border Country Life Association** (Dr R Allan, Buskin Burn House, Coldingham, near Eyemouth. Tel 089 07 71215) has produced a practical strategy for countryside interpretation and aims to foster an interest in all aspects of past and present country life. At the more local level the **Liddesdale Heritage Association** (Michael Robson, Overshanks, Newcastleton. Tel 03873 75454) has developed its own Information Centre and linked facilities, including accommodation, eating places and local walks around the Newcastleton community. The **Upper Nithsdale Tourist Group** (contact Rachael Saville, George Hotel, Drumlanrig Street, Thornhill. Tel 0848 30326) is a consortium of local community councils and others, established to promote local tourism and provide information. Another group, **Peebleshire Environment Concern** (Mrs Martynoga, Kirkbride House, Traquair, Innerleithen. Tel 0896 830361) is interested in raising awareness of local environmental issues through its publication *Peebleshire Green Pages*. The **Scottish Wildlife Trust** has active branches in both the Borders and Galloway which administer a number of reserves, many of which are open to the public.

Museum interests throughout the Borders have joined together in a forum to promote museums and heritage exhibitions. In recent years there has also been a development of local groups to protect and manage other amenities such as local commons, and by-committees have been formed for events such as Common Ridings. Other areas benefiting from increased organisation are estates, tourist associations, recreational interests and co-operatives, and there is now a substantial volume of literature dealing with topics such as the environment, history and traditions of the area. Prepared by residents, inexpensive booklets can be obtained from local newsagents and Information Centres.

Geographical Breakdown of Region

The following centres and attractions represent the best of the many in this diverse area, and have been chosen to cover a range of landscapes and interests. All the main sights are listed plus a number of smaller towns and villages which still retain much of their vernacular charm. Emphasis has been placed on multiple facilities to cater for a range of visitors, including families. An important criterion is whether the attraction enables the visitor to become more aware of the local environment and culture, particularly through interpretation and quality information. For instance, there are many craft workshops in this region, which offer the visitor insight into traditions such as pottery and furniture-making (full details can be found in both *Crafts in the Scottish Borders*, produced by Borders Regional Council, and the Galloway Craft Guild's *Craft Trail*).

There is a general convention in Scotland that outside fenced farmland people are free to walk where they wish, provided they do no damage. In the Borders and Galloway however, it is not always easy to locate routes across open ground due to the lack of marked rights of way. For this reason, those trails that are marked clearly, especially by organisations and owners on their own land, are to be welcomed. Equally so however, visitors should take care not to displace any markers or pointers along the way.

Nature reserves, estates, forest walks and farms have been selected to cover geographical and ecological distribution.

Dumfries and Galloway

Wigtown District

Starting with the most westerly town in the area, **Stranraer** is mainly of significance as a port for the Northern Ireland ferry, but also as an important market centre. It serves as a gateway to the distinctive **Rhinns of Galloway** and has the rare advantage of being a railhead. Due south of Stranraer, the **Mull of Galloway RSPB Reserve** is located at the most southerly point in Scotland and offers spectacular cliff scenery and nesting seabirds. **Logan Gardens** (open April–October) on the same peninsula is located on the B7065 north of the picturesque harbour of Port Logan and contains a wide range of exotic plants. To the east of Stranraer, **Castle Kennedy Gardens** (open Easter–end September) specialises in herbs and their uses.

Newton Stewart, attractively situated on the River Cree, is a good centre for exploring this scenic hinterland. To the south of the town lie the open Moorlands and dairy farming country of the Machars, along with the historic town of **Whithorn**. One of the oldest Christian centres in Britain, it is a rich treasurehouse of early Celtic artefacts associated with church and monastery. The continuing **excavations** (Tel 098 85 508) are open to the public (open Easter–October). Nearby the **Luce Bay Shore Centre** (Tel 098 87 527; open July–August exc. Saturdays) offers nature trails, crafts and a shop.

Cairnsmore of Fleet National Nature Reserve occupies a typical Galloway sheep farm to the west of Newton Stewart, where there are a number of walks and spectacular views from the summit. This is also a good place for spotting wild goats. Following the River Cree northwards, the **Wood of Cree RSPB Nature Reserve** is located on the east bank and, as well as offering walks and waterfalls, is one of the few native broadleaf woodlands in this area. At **Palgowan Open Farm** (Tel 0671 84 231; open July–August exc. Saturdays, May–October mid-week only), four miles (6.5 km.) north of Glen Trool, animals and work routines of a Galloway hill farm are offered on afternoon tours.

Galloway Forest Park at Loch Trool is an important recreation area with a variety of walks and visitor facilities, including a goat park and access to Merrick summit. **Kirroughtree Visitor Centre** at Palmure on the A75 west of Newton Stewart offers an informative introduction to the forest.

Accommodation

The Dumfries and Galloway *Tourist and Accommodation Guide* lists a wide range of places to stay, many of which offer evening meals also.

First Class

Knockinaam Lodge Hotel, Portpatrick DG9 9AD (Tel 077 681 471). Bed and breakfast and evening meal in a country house hotel near Portpatrick. Resident proprietors, croquet lawn, golf nearby, cliff walks and beautiful gardens. Cuisine is French but the produce Scottish.

North West Castle Hotel, Seafront, Stranraer DG9 8EH (Tel 0776 4413). This was once the home of the 18th-century Arctic explorer Sir John Ross. Built in the shape of a boat it offers good food and accommodation. Swimming pool and sauna, but no credit cards are accepted.

Middle Range

Creebridge House Hotel, Newton Stewart DG8 6NP (Tel 0671 2121). Family run hotel in four acres (1.6 hectares) of garden near the town centre. Bed and breakfast and evening meal.

Corsemalzie House Hotel, Port William DG8 9RL (Tel 098 886 254). Situated between Port William and Mochrum, a country house set in forty acres (16 hectares) of wooded gardens.

Economy

Melvin Lodge Guest House, Portpatrick DG9 8LG (Tel 077 681 238). Scottish Tourist Board 'Approved' bed and breakfast, large Victorian villa with sea views.

Flower Bank Guest House, Minnigaff, near Newton Stewart DG8 6NP (Tel 0671 2629). Eighteenth-century house on the banks of the River Cree. Scottish Tourist Board 'Commended', B&B and evening meal.

There is a **Youth Hostel** at Minnigaff.

A wide range of self-catering properties is available in this area. Mention should be given to **Low Craiglemine Organic Farm**, Low Craiglemine, Whithorn DG8 8NE (Tel 098 85 730) where a self-catering cottage is available. The farm has goats, sheep, cows, geese and hens, and visitors are given the opportunity to be as self-sufficient as possible.

Eating Out

The area has many restaurants offering local specialities, but few of outstanding note and none which could be categorised as 'First Class'. Hotel restaurants and bars are usually a safe option, although local restaurants should not be avoided.

Middle Range

Kirroughtree Hotel, Newton Stewart (Tel 0671 2141). Wholesome cuisine at this well-known hotel. Wheelchair access.

Queen's Arms Hotel, Isle of Whithorn (Tel 098 85 369). Specialities include lobster, Galloway steaks and local fresh fish.

Economy

Bay House Restaurant and Bar, Cairnryan Road, Stranraer (Tel 0776 3786). Family owned and run restaurant in an old golf clubhouse. Children welcome.

Bladnoch Inn, Bladnoch, near Wigtown (Tel 098 84 2200). Family run inn offering fresh local produce and home baking (opposite Bladnoch Distillery)

Stewartry District

Gatehouse-of-Fleet, an attractive Galloway town with characteristic wide streets and well-kept whitewashed houses, is a good centre for exploring the Kirkcudbright coast and old oakwoods of the picturesque Fleet Valley. The area boasts many features of archaeological interest, including early Christian and Roman sites. At **Skyreburn**, near Gatehouse, there is an **underwater wildlife park** (Tel 077 182 204; open April–October, closed Friday April, May, Sept., Oct.), with over 50 different species of aquatic creatures. Southwest of Gatehouse, **Kirkcudbright** is a small old fishing port on the River Dee with a central castle, museum, art gallery and a centre for painters. The town hosts a wide range of events during its festival in July. Nearby is the impressive **Dundrennan Abbey**, noted for its fine medieval workmanship and as the last stopping place of Mary Queen of Scots before her exile to England. Just over two miles (3.2 km.) north of **Dalbeattie** off the B794 is the largest motte and bailey earth castle in Scotland at **Motte of Urr**. It was one of a series of Anglo-Norman defensive sites and is of international significance.

Castle Douglas is a busy market town and, although holding no special interest in itself, makes a good base from which to visit nearby attractions. These include **Threave Castle** (open 1 April–28 October) and its outstanding gardens (open all year), which are the training ground for gardeners of the National Trust for Scotland. There is also a visitor centre and ranger service here. The marshes of the River Dee to the north are notable for wintering wildfowl, which can be seen at **Ken-Dee Marshes RSPB Reserve** (Tel 064 45 236) by appointment with the warden.

North of Castle Douglas at the head of Loch Ken lies **New Galloway**, the smallest Royal Burgh in Scotland. Situated in scenic surroundings, it is also the meeting point for several roads, and is handy for **Galloway Forest Park** and as an access point to the **Southern Upland Way**. The nearby **Galloway Deer Museum** is worth visiting, and at **Blowplain** on the Balmaclennan road there is a historic steading, complete with farm animals (afternoon tours exc. Saturday). On the same route there is the **Galloway Farm Heritage Centre**, with displays of horses and 18th-century equipment. Following the A702 north from New Galloway, a stop can be made at

Moniaive, where the narrow winding main street provides the focus of this ancient burgh. With its delightful setting, it is a good base for exploring this lesser-known area of Dumfries, including nearby **Maxwelton House Gardens**.

Accommodation

First Class

Cally Palace Hotel, Gatehouse-of-Fleet DG7 2DL (Tel 0557 814341). Georgian mansion set in 100 acres (40 hectares) of parkland offering bed and breakfast and evening meal. Heated outdoor swimming pool and extensive leisure facilities.

Woodlea Hotel, Moniaive DG3 4EN (Tel 084 82 209) Small family run hotel in beautiful countryside offering bed and breakfast and evening meal, as well as indoor swimming pool, sauna and games room. Pony riding, clay shooting and golf also organised if staying three nights or longer.

Middle Range

Murray Arms Hotel, Ann Street, Gatehouse-of-Fleet (Tel 0557 814207). Bed and breakfast and evening meal at this one-time haunt of Robert Burns.

Longacre Manor Hotel, Ernespie Road, Castle Douglas DG7 1LE (Tel 0556 3576). Georgian house with lovely full-panelled lounge, set in its own grounds on the edge of town.

Economy

High Auchenlarie Farmhouse, Mrs Johnstone, Gatehouse-of-Fleet DG7 2ER (Tel 0557 24 231). Open between March and October, families welcome at this working farm, which was awarded the area Tourist Board's Good Service Award in 1987 and 1989.

Cairn Edward, New Galloway DG7 3RZ (Tel 06442 244). Spacious Victorian country house offering bed and breakfast, set in nine acres (3.6 hectares) and overlooking Loch Ken.

Eating Out

First Class

Auld Alliance Restaurant, 5 Castle Street, Kirkcudbright (Tel 0557 30569). Seafood and Galloway beef are just a couple of the local products used in this French/Scottish restaurant.

Granary Restaurant, Barend Properties, Sandyhills (Tel 038 778

663). The best of Scottish home-cooking is served in this converted cattle shed!

Middle Range

Ingle, St Mary's Street, Kirkcudbright (Tel 0557 30606). Family run restaurant specialising in seafood in the old station building. The kitchen is where the trains used to come in.

The Old Smugglers' Inn, 11 Main Street, Auchencairn (Tel 055 664 331). Eighteenth-century inn offering bar lunches and suppers served on the patio or lawn (weather permitting). Evening dinners in the restaurant, children's meals and vegetarian dishes available.

Economy

The Mad Hatter, Douglas Centre, 87–91 King Street, Castle Douglas (Tel 0556 4176). Local produce used in Scots baking and cooking for morning coffee, lunches and afternoon tea. Local paintings on display for sale.

Old School Tea-room, Ringford (Tel 055 722 250). Victorian tea-room and craft shop between Gatehouse-of-Fleet and Castle Douglas. Vegetarian dishes available.

Nithsdale, and Annandale & Eskdale Districts

Dumfries on the banks of the Nith is a county town and bustling market centre. Known as the 'Gateway to south-west Scotland', it is of considerable antiquity and has strong associations with figures such as Robert the Bruce, Prince Charlie and Robert Burns, whose memory is perpetuated in **Burns House**, **The Mausoleum**, and the **Robert Burns Centre**. The **Dumfries Museum** is also worth a visit. If you're in the town in June, the **Gude Nychburris Festival** is a week of celebrations commemorating the granting of the town charter and other historic events.

South of Dumfries the 14th-century **Sweetheart Abbey** at New Abbey is especially impressive, due to both its great red sandstone arches and as the resting place of Devorguilla Balliol, mother of King John Balliol. Also at **New Abbey** there is an 18th-century working corn mill where demonstrations are provided.

On the opposite bank of the Nith from Dumfries is **Caerlaverock Wildfowl and Wetland Centre** and **National Nature Reserve** (open mid-September–April). Nearby there is also the spectacular **Caerlaverock Castle**. The lonely marshland and great flocks of

Barnacle Geese and other wintering wildfowl provide an atmospheric setting.

Mabie Forest (Forestry Commission), four miles (6.5 km.) south-west of Dumfries, has an attractive picnic place and walks. On the A76, north of Dumfries at Thornhill, **Drumlanrig Castle** (Tel 0848 31682, open 15 May–19 August) and grounds (open 28 April–30 September) offer an adventure woodland, audio-visual theatre, shop, crafts and bicycle hire.

Almost in the exact centre of southern Scotland, **Moffat** is a small resort town in a spectacular mountain setting which offers woollen shops and leisure amenities. Although somewhat spoiled now by traffic, the wide main street is still attractive, dominated by a bronze ram monument which symbolises the importance of the local sheep trade. On the A708 north-east of the town, the **Grey Mare's Tail** (National Trust for Scotland) is a dramatic waterfall which appears from nowhere out of some of the most rugged hills in this area. It is possible to walk up the side of the waterfall, with guides if so desired. To the north-west of Moffat in the Lowther Hills lies **Wanlockhead**, one of the highest villages in Scotland. On the very edge of Dumfries and Galloway, this remote settlement is of particular relevance to industrial archaeology, including gold and silver mining, exhibits of which can be viewed at the museum (Tel 0659 74387, open daily Easter–mid-October). The **Border Collie and Shepherd Centre** at Tweedhopefoot (the source of the River Tweed), off the A701 north of Moffat, offers daily demonstrations of sheep herding and crafts.

Accommodation

First Class

Station Hotel, 49 Lovers Walk, Dumfries DG1 1LT (Tel 0387 54316). Refurbished Victorian hotel next to the station.

Hetland Hall Hotel, Carrutherstown DG1 4JX (Tel 0387 84201). Recently refurbished impressive mansion situated in its own grounds with magnificent views of the Solway coast. Bowls, badminton and games room, and sporting and mini-breaks offered.

Middle Range

Moffat House Hotel, High Street, Moffat DG10 9HL (Tel 0683 20039). Bed and breakfast and evening meal available in this charming 18th-century Adam mansion in the town centre.

Criffel Inn, 2 The Square, New Abbey, by Dumfries DG2 8BX

(Tel 038 785 244). Friendly bed and breakfast (and evening meal) in this pleasant town.

Economy

North Laurieknowe, Mrs Prentice, 3 North Laurieknowe Place, Dumfries DG2 7AL (Tel 0387 54136). Good value bed and breakfast in a substantial 19th-century townhouse with a large secluded garden, within walking distance of the town centre.

Ivy Cottage Guest House, High Street, Moffat DG10 9HG (Tel 0683 20279). 18th-century listed building in the town centre offering bed and breakfast and evening meal.

Youth Hostels can be found at Kendoon and Wanlockhead, and bunk house and dormitory accommodation at the **Walk Inn**, Wanlockhead (Tel 0659 74360).

Eating Out

First Class

Wellview Hotel, Ballplay Road, Moffat (Tel 0683 20184). Family run hotel and restaurant (reservations for dinner and lunch essential) serving fine cuisine made from local produce.

Auchen Castle Hotel and Restaurant, Beattock, Moffat (Tel 068 33 407). Nineteenth-century country house serving traditional Scots dishes prepared from local lamb, poultry, beef, pork, seafood and game in season.

Middle Range

Opus Salad Bar, 95 Queensberry Street, Dumfries (Tel 0387 55752). Quality salad bar in the town centre serving traditional and vegetarian dishes.

The Courtyard Restaurant, Eaglesfield, by Lockerbie (Tel 04615 215). Scottish lunch and dinner in this atmospheric and friendly restaurant.

Economy

Globe Inn, 56 High Street, Dumfries (Tel 0387 52335). Robert Burns described the Globe Inn as his favourite 'howff', and the tavern has retained its character. Bar lunches only, but worth a visit.

Abbet Cottage Coffees and Crafts, New Abbey (Tel 038 785 377). Home baking and freshly prepared light meals, coffees and teas in the garden, situated next to Sweetheart Abbey.

The Borders

Roxburgh and Berwickshire Districts

Hawick is the largest of the Border towns and supports the oldest established stock auction market in Britain, as well as being an important woollen manufacturing centre. Its **Common Riding** festival in June is, even by Border standards, especially lively. If you prefer to take the slower B6357 route south, you will pass through **Newcastleton**, which celebrates an annual music festival. At nearby **Kielder Forest** (Forestry Commission) there is a wide variety of open-air activities and visitor services in a forest of over 130,000 acres (52,650 hectares), while the Economic Forestry Group runs a **Deer Museum and Wildlife Centre** at Eskdalemuir, near Langholm.

Jedburgh Abbey, another of the great Border abbeys, has an excellent interpretative centre, while the town itself has retained much of its historic interest, accessible via a town trail. **Jedburgh Castle** and **Mary Queen of Scots' House** are special features which, apart from their architectural value, have some unusual exhibits. Mary Queen of Scots is also associated with **Hermitage Castle**, ten miles (16 km.) south of Hawick, a forbidding Border keep which, in its lonely position, conveys much of the atmosphere of the turbulent 'Debatable Lands'. Several miles north of Jedburgh near Ancrum, the **Woodland Visitor Centre** (Tel 083 53 306, open daily Easter–end October) provides imaginative interpretative services, with shop and tea-room and a range of woodland trails. Five miles (8 km.) south of Jedburgh (off the A68) the **Jedforest Deer and Farm Park** (Tel 083 54 364) has a large conservation collection of rare breeds of farm animals in addition to deer. The park is particularly suitable for children.

Kelso, at the junction of the Rivers Tweed and Cheviot, has a fine rural setting and, with its Georgian Square, is of considerable architectural charm. **Kelso Abbey**, founded in 1128, was once the most important ecclesiastical establishment in the land, while **Floors Castle**, on the outskirts of town, is a classic example of a large 18th-century country mansion, with fine collections of paintings and porcelain. Another historic home is **Mellerstain House** (Tel 057 381 225, open Easter and May–September, daily, exc. Saturdays), the residence of the Earl of Haddington seven miles (11.3 km.) north-west of Kelso. Considered one of Scotland's finest Georgian mansions, it is noted for its plasterwork and 18th-century furniture and paintings, and is set in meticulously landscaped grounds. **The Hirsel** near Coldstream comprises a country park, estate museum and craft shop/demonstrations, although the house is not open to the public. Especially informative is the interpretation of the activities of a Border estate.

Around **Duns** there are a number of attractions. **Duns Castle Loch**, a Scottish Wildlife Trust Reserve, provides lochside trails from the car park just within the Oxendean entrance (B6365). At **Crumstane Farm Park** (Tel 0361 83268, open May-September, exc. Tuesdays), on the A6105 west of Duns, some of the more unusual farm animals can be seen, as well as a working farm which has not given way to modern agricultural methods. Two miles (3.2 km.) east of Duns, **Manderston** (Tel 0361 83450, open mid-May-September, Thursdays and Sundays only) is considered one of the finest Edwardian country houses in Britain, in true 'upstairs-downstairs' tradition. It also has an impressive collection of rhododendrons in its formal gardens. North of Duns, the 4000 acre (1620 hectares) country estate of **Abbey St Bathans** (Tel 036 14 242) is of considerable historic (Bronze Age forts) and natural interest. It offers a variety of activities, including riding and walking.

The Borders coast, although short, is notable for spectacular cliff scenery, such as at **St Abbs Head National Nature Reserve** (open throughout the year). Although nesting sea birds are the most obvious feature of interest, the geology and flora are also notable. The inshore waters are protected by the first voluntary marine nature reserve in Scotland, and their clarity attracts divers from many parts of the country. On the nearby **Northfield Farm** (Tel 089 07 443), off the B4638, there is a tea-room and exhibits related to the area. A ranger service is also provided. The village of St Abbs itself is attractive with its fishermen's cottages, and has one of the few sandy beaches on this coast. The historic town of **Eyemouth** close by is a thriving fishing port, complete with a town trail and an interesting museum illustrating the fishing industry and marine life.

Accommodation

First Class

Marlefield House Hotel, Eckford, by Kelso TD5 8ED (Tel 05734 561). Seventeenth-century house in beautiful gardens, known for comfort and cuisine.

Sunlaws House Hotel, near Kelso TD5 8JZ (Tel 05735 331). Country house hotel owned by the Duke and Duchess of Roxburghe, set in 200 acres (81 hectares) of woodland and park. Log fires and fresh produce.

Glenfriars Hotel, The Friars, Jedburgh TD8 6BN (Tel 0835 62000). Large Victorian house above Jedburgh with good views, within walking distance of the town centre. Some bedrooms have four-posters.

Middle Range

Kirklands Hotel, West Stewart Place, Hawick TD9 8BH (Tel 0450 72263). Charming small hotel overlooking Hawick and the surrounding hills.

Ednam House Hotel, Bridge Street, Kelso TD5 7HT (Tel 0573 24168). Mid-18th-century Georgian mansion in its own grounds overlooking the Tweed.

Chirnside Hall Country House Hotel, Chirnside, by Duns TD11 3LD (Tel 089 081 219). Large Victorian mansion set in peaceful surroundings between Duns and Berwick-upon-Tweed.

Economy

Ferniehist Mill Lodge, by Jedburgh TD8 6PQ (Tel 0835 63279). Friendly and quiet hotel overlooking the river south of Jedburgh.

Blackadder Hotel, West High Street, Greenlaw TD10 6XA (Tel 03616 365). Small family run bed and breakfast in this attractive village near Duns.

Worth noting is the new address of **Whitchester Christian Guest House**, recently moved to Borthaugh, Hawick (Tel 0450 77477). Formerly near Duns, Whitchester is well known for its excellent home cooking and caring atmosphere.

Youth Hostels can be found at Coldingham, Ferniehirst (Jedburgh), Kirk Yetholm and Snoot. Bunkhouse and dormitory accommodation is available at **The Rest House**, Abbey St Bathans (Tel. 0361 4217).

Eating Out

First Class

The Old Forge Restaurant, Newmill-on-Teviot, by Hawick (Tel 0450 85298). Inventive Scottish cooking, including vegetarian dishes, at this award-winning restaurant, housed in the old village smiddy and complete with the original forge and bellows.

Octime Restaurant, High Street, Jedburgh (Tel 0835 63982). Small family run restaurant offering the best of local cuisine. Vegetarian and special diets catered for.

Four Seasons Restaurant, Wheatsheaf Hotel, Swinton, near

Duns (Tel 089 086 257). Village inn of character south of Duns serving excellent home-produced food and specialising in fine wines and spirits. Booking essential for restaurant, advisable for lounge bar.

Middle Range

The Penny Black, 2–6 North Bridge Street, Hawick (Tel 0450 76492). Bar and restaurant in the former GPO sorting office, still complete with telephone box, pillar box and sorters' tools. Local fish and best Border beef specialities.

The Wagon Inn, 10 Coalmarket, Kelso (Tel 0573 24568). Attractive inn serving special home-made dishes using local produce.

The Craw Inn, Auchencrow, near Eyemouth (Tel 08907 61253). Traditional country inn located in a quiet hamlet. Real ale and local food, beer garden and putting green.

Economy

Cross Keys Inn, Denholm, by Hawick (Tel 0450 87305). Popular pub and restaurant. Booking for dinner essential.

Templehall Inn, Morebattle, Kelso (Tel 05734 249). Small village inn located in the Cheviot foothills and offering light meals. Vegetarian dishes offered.

Black Bull, Etal, near Coldstream (Tel 089 082 200). Popular thatched pub offering real ale and a wide-ranging lunch and evening bar menu, including vegetarian dishes, in this tiny village east of Coldstream.

Ettrick & Lauderdale, and Tweeddale Districts

Selkirk overlooks Ettrick Water and is an old Royal Burgh well known for its Common Riding (June), commemorating the disastrous defeat of the Scots at the Battle of Flodden. The town has a distinctive triangular market place and is noted for its association with Sir Walter Scott and the African explorer Mungo Park, who was born nearby. **Halliwell's House and Museum** near the main square is worth a visit for its portrayal of the history of Selkirk through its buildings. **Bowhill Estate** (Tel 0750 20732, house open July, grounds 28 April–28 August) lies off the A708 west of Selkirk, and is the magnificent Border home of the Duke of Buccleuch. The house offers an outstanding collection of furniture and paintings while the estate and grounds are used for pony trekking and mountain-biking. There is also a woodland adventure playground here.

In **Melrose**, the centrally situated **Abbey** is considered to be the most beautiful of all the Border abbeys, while the attractive **Priorwood Garden** (open 30 April–24 December, National Trust for Scotland) is noted for its medieval orchard and herb collection. Nearby, picturesque **St Boswells** is the venue for its annual fair (July), a rendezvous for travelling folk throughout the country. **Mertoun Gardens** (Tel. 0835 23236, open weekends, April–September) near St Boswells has fine views of the Tweed, and a historic dovecot. It is notable for its arboretum and azaleas. **Dryburgh Abbey**, five miles (8 km.) away, is one of the most complete of all the abbeys in the area, beautifully situated on a bend of the Tweed.

The larger and busier town of **Galashiels** lies four miles (6.5 km.) north of Melrose and is strongly associated with the wool industry. At the **Borders Wool Centre** (North Wheatlands Mill, open April–October, exc. Sundays; November–March, exc. weekends) visitors can watch a sheep display and hand-spinning demonstrations. If you're particularly interested in this aspect of Border history, the **Woollen Trail** offers a complete insight into the trade (leaflets available from Tourist Information).

Visitors travelling on the A68 north to Edinburgh will pass through **Lauder**, a small town of considerable vernacular charm, with the advantage also of being close to the Southern Upland Way. On the outskirts of the town is **Thirlestane Castle** (Tel 057 82 430, open Easter–September), a fine Restoration building housing the **Border Country Life Museum**, and offering a number of walks. The castle is noted for its huge collection of historic toys. En route to Lauder it's worth taking the B6356 past **Scott's View**, one of the outstanding panoramas of the Borders. Sir Walter Scott spent so many hours gazing at this typical Border scene that, after his death, his horse stopped of its own accord at the marked point on the way to the funeral. At **Earlston, Legerwood Farm Trail** (Tel 0835 23301, ext. 433, open 1 June–30 September) allows visitors to wander over open farmland next to a working farm.

Like Moffat, **Peebles** is a spa town in a beautiful setting with an attractive wide main street. The town is a good place for walks along the Tweed or through the surrounding forests and hills, and has strong associations with John Buchan. During the summer a variety of events are held, from sheepdog trials in June to the Peebles Highland

Games in September. **Walkerburn** nearby has the **Scottish Museum of Woollen Textiles**.

Reputedly the oldest inhabited mansion in Scotland, **Traquair House** (near Innerleithen, Tel 0896 830323, open Easter and daily May–mid-September) is said to have been visited by twenty-seven kings. Today it is still lived in but is open to the public. The grounds have woodland walks, craft workshops and exhibitions. South of Peebles on the B712, **Dawyck Botanic Garden** (Tel 072 16 254, open daily April–October) is over 300 years old and has magnificent conifers and rhododendrons. During spring large areas are carpeted by thousands of daffodils. On the A702 at the south end of **Broughton** village, the recently established **John Buchan Centre** (Tel 0899 21050, open Easter–mid-October) celebrates the life and work of the Scottish novelist and one-time Governor General of Canada.

Accommodation

First Class

George and Abbotsford Hotel, High Street, Melrose TD6 9PD (Tel 089 682 2308). Tastefully restored 17th-century coaching inn in the centre of town, known for good cuisine.

Kingsnowes Hotel, Selkirk Road, Galashiels TD1 3HY (Tel 0896 58375). Nineteenth-century red sandstone mansion overlooking the River Tweed and Eildon Hills. Hard tennis court and beautiful conservatory.

Cringletie House Hotel, by Peebles EH45 8PL (Tel 072 13 233). Privately owned and personally run hotel in a Scottish baronial mansion, set in its own gardens and woodland.

Middle Range

Philipburn House Hotel, Selkirk TD7 5LS (Tel 0750 20747). A country house hotel on the outskirts of Selkirk (on the Bowhill road), set in delightful award-winning grounds.

Lauderdale Hotel, 1 Edinburgh Road, Lauder TD2 6TW (Tel 05782 231). Friendly family run hotel in Lauder town centre.

Venlaw Castle Hotel, Peebles EH45 8QG (Tel 0721 20384). Dating from 1782, this impressive building is family run with a reputation for good food.

Economy

Tibbie Shiels Inn, Cappercleuch, Selkirk TD7 5LH (Tel 0750 42231). Dating from 1823, this cosy inn has some illustrious names in its visitors' book, having been a popular meeting place and hostelry for some of Scotland's greatest poets. South-west from Selkirk, amongst some of the area's most stunning countryside.

Green Tree Hotel, 41 Eastgate, Peebles EH45 8AD (Tel 0721 20582). Family run hotel in the centre of town, attractive garden and private parking.

Damhead Farm, Traquair, Innerliethen EH44 6PZ (Tel 0896 830474). Bed and breakfast in an 18th-century farmhouse situated on a working hill farm adjacent to the Southern Upland Way.

Youth Hostels can be found at Broadmeadows and Melrose, while bunkhouse and dormitory accommodation is available at **Mountbenger Bunk House** (Gordon Arms Hotel, near Selkirk, Tel 0750 82232).

Comprehensive coverage of accommodation in the Borders can be found in the *Scottish Borders Holiday Guide*, available from Tourist Information offices.

Eating Out

First Class

Hoebridge Inn, Gattonside, near Melrose (Tel 0896 82 3082). Scottish, continental and vegetarian dishes offered in this friendly inn, situated in an attractive village five minutes from Melrose.

Horseshoe Inn, Eddleston (Tel 072 13 225). Relaxed and informal, but offering first-class local cuisine. Near Peebles.

Dolphinton House Hotel, West Linton (Tel 0968 82286). Inventive cooking using local produce at this high standard country house hotel, a short drive from Peebles.

Middle Range

Dryburgh Abbey Hotel, St Boswells (Tel 0835 22261). Excellent value Scottish cuisine in this impressive hotel, located in the beautiful grounds of Dryburgh Abbey on the banks of the River Tweed.

Redgauntlet Restaurant, 36 Market Street, Galashiels (Tel 0896 2098). Scottish dishes and baking made from local produce in what used to be an old wine shop.

Kailzie Garden Restaurant, Kailzie, near Peebles (Tel 0721 22807). No-nonsense Scottish cooking in this attractive restaurant, housed in converted stables and set in extensive grounds a couple of miles (3 km.) outside Peebles.

Economy

Cross Keys Inn, 25 Market Place, Selkirk (Tel 0750 21283). Friendly pub serving home-made bar meals.

Golden Bannock, High Street, Lauder (Tel 057 82 324). Welcoming village pub offering wholesome local fare.

Sunflower, 4 Bridgegate, Peebles (Tel 0721 22420). Restaurant and coffee shop serving home-made meals and baking.

ENGLAND

6 Northumbria

Northumbria is made up of four separate counties: Northumberland, Tyne and Wear, Durham and Cleveland.

Northumberland, England's most northerly county, stretches from Blanchhead and Allenheads in the south to Berwick-upon-Tweed in the north. First-time visitors will be struck by the emptiness of it; huge areas of countryside seem to be populated solely by sheep. Its best-known feature is Hadrian's Wall, a 73-mile (118-km.) stretch of earthworks and fortifications dreamt up by the Emperor Hadrian to separate the 'civilised' Romans in the south from the 'barbarians' in the north. The Wall extends into Cumbria but many of the most impressive sites are in Northumberland.

Lindisfarne, the off-shore island from which St Cuthbert set out to evangelise northern England in the 7th century, is also well known. A better kept secret is the heritage coast that runs south from Lindisfarne to Newbiggin-by-the-Sea, with unspoilt sand beaches and dunes overhung with cliffs and haunted by the mournful cry of wading birds.

The Northumbrian Tourist Board calls Northumberland 'England's Border Country', and this border status explains the castles dotting the northern fringes and west coast of the county. Alnwick and Bamburgh are giants, dwarfing everything in their vicinity and still inhabited today. Others, like Dunstanburgh and Norham, are ruins.

Northumberland has no really big towns. In contrast Tyne and Wear, a triangular wedge of land cutting in from the coast, is dominated by Newcastle-upon-Tyne. Tucked below Tyne and Wear, Cleveland has some depressing post-industrial landscapes. However, it too boasts some stunning coastal scenery which gets better the further south you travel.

County Durham, the Tourist Office's 'Land of the Prince Bishops', has been the heart of tourist Northumbria for decades, with Durham City rivalling York, Canterbury and Winchester in beauty and historic interest. Its castle and cathedral were amongst the first UK World Heritage Sites. In contrast, beautiful Teesdale and Weardale are relative newcomers to tourism.

Traditional Northumbrian culture has a Celtic tinge exemplified by its bagpipes. You may not be lucky enough to hear them in action, but the Morpeth museum explains how they differ from their Scottish and Irish cousins, and lets you listen to pipe recordings through headsets. Impossible to miss, 'Geordie' is a particularly distinctive regional dialect with its own vocabulary and idioms.

History

When Hadrian's Wall was built along the route of old Stanegate Road in the 2nd century, the surrounding area was occupied by Celtic farming tribes like the Brigantes. Although the Romans ventured further north, the Wall marked the Empire's effective limit. Periods of peace in the region were interspersed with outbreaks of fighting, particularly with the Picts, which grew more serious in the 4th century. The end, when it came, was with a whimper rather than a bang. After Constantine III left for the continent in 407 to assert his claim to the throne of Rome, silence descended on the Wall.

In his *Ecclesiastical History* the Venerable Bede recorded Northumbria's starring role in the spread of northern Christianity in the 7th century. In 634 the Anglo-Saxon King Oswald conquered what was then Bernicia. When St Aidan journeyed south from Iona, Oswald let him establish a Celtic monastery on Lindisfarne which became a bishopric until the 870s. After the 664 Synod of Whitby, Aidan returned to Iona and St Cuthbert took over at Lindisfarne. Following Danish raids the monks moved St Cuthbert's coffin and the illuminated Lindisfarne Gospels first to Chester-le-Street and then to Durham. It wasn't until 1081 that monks once again occupied 'Holy Island'.

Despite their destructive raids the Danes never dominated Northumbria as they did southern England. However, the Normans stamped their authority on the countryside, building massive stone keeps like those at Norham and Prudhoe. The Middle Ages saw constant demarcation battles between the Scots and the English; Berwick-upon-Tweed changed hands fourteen times before becoming a permanent part of England. Northern earls and barons had an importance in keeping with their role as border guards. The Percys with their stronghold at Alnwick were amongst the most powerful warrior families. Eventually over-estimation of their own importance led one of them, Harry Hotspur, to rebel against King Henry IV, a rebellion that ended with Hotspur's death at the Battle of Shrewsbury in 1403. In 1513 Henry VIII invaded France, and the Scots, in alliance with the French, retaliated by invading England. They were defeated at the Battle of Flodden just outside Wooler, where their king James IV was killed. The 1707 Act of Union finally linked Scotland with England and brought an end to such fighting.

From Roman times the Northumberland dales were mined for lead, zinc and silver, and today the landscape is strewn with redundant mine buildings. Nineteenth-century heavy industry bypassed northern Northumbria, but further south coal mines soon dominated towns like Ashington. The post-World War One slump was disastrous for southern Northumbria, and unemployed marchers, trekking to London to publicise their plight, replaced Bede as the symbol of Jarrow. Of seventy coal mines existing in 1948, only one remained by 1990. In the 1980s the iron and steel industries collapsed just as dramatically, leaving towns like Consett as deserts of unemployment.

Geography

Four major rivers drain Northumbria: the northern Tweed provides a natural border with Scotland along some of its route to Berwick-upon-Tweed; the central Tyne and Wear converge on Newcastle-upon-Tyne; and the southern Tees finally reaches the coast at Middlesbrough.

More than 621 sq. miles (1000 sq. km.) of Northumberland, including the Cheviot and Simonside Hills, are part of Northumberland National Park. The Pennine Way long-distance footpath also cuts across the Park from Greenhead in the south to Kirk Yetholm in the north. Beyond the Pennine Way the National Park becomes the Border Forest Park, a vast stretch of Forestry Commission land traversed by forest tracks. At its heart lies 2684-acre (1087 hectare) Kielder Water, western Europe's largest reservoir. The Cheviots, straddling the Scottish border north of Kielder Forest, are made of granite and older volcanic rocks whereas the Pennines, which cut into County Durham from Yorkshire, are formed from shale and gritstone.

Redesdale Forest, Wark Forest and Kielder Forest make up the Border Forest Park. Kielder, Europe's largest man-made forest, mainly consists of spruce trees, while Hamsterley Forest, further south in Teesdale, contains beeches and conifers. Inside Hamsterley, Bedburn Valley Forest Nature Reserve is home to deer and crossbills, and has meadows full of harebells, foxgloves and oak ferns. Extensive moorlands, including Hexhamshire Common, encircle Allendale.

Much of western Durham is peaty, poorly-drained moorland, often at a height of more than 2000 feet (610 m.). Spectacular waterfalls include High Force which falls for 70 feet (21 m.) over the Great Whin Sill escarpment, and Cauldron Snout, at 200 feet (61 m.) is England's highest waterfall.

Some parts of the North Pennine Area of Outstanding Natural Beauty are particularly fragile. Around Cow Green Reservoir in Upper Teesdale stretches of 'sugar limestone' soil support rare Arctic/alpine flora. Herb-rich hay meadows also offer spring and early summer wild flower displays, while dry-stone walls and stone barns make the area doubly picturesque. It is now a designated Environmentally Sensitive Area, with incentives to encourage traditional farming methods.

Climate

Northumbria's northerly position ensures that it bears the brunt of wintry conditions, with icy easterly winds blowing in from the North Sea and January temperatures averaging 4°C (40°F). Spring can be particularly pleasant but often arrives late. Summer temperatures rarely rise above 16°C (63°F), and cool coastal fogs accompanied by drizzle are common. Coastal areas are relatively dry with an average 25 inches (635 mm) of rain a year. However, the Cheviots can receive as much as 50 inches (1270 mm) of rain a year. Walkers in particular should check forecasts before setting out since mist can descend on the moors with alarming speed (Tel 0898 500 418 for north-east weather forecasts).

Attractions

Visitors come to Northumbria to enjoy the scenery of the Northumberland National Park, the Heritage Coast and the North Pennines. The long-distance footpaths, the Pennine and Cleveland Ways, can be very crowded in July and August. Popular natural attractions include the Farne Islands which draw 44,000 people a year, and the Washington Wildfowl Reserve which attracts 80,000.

History-lovers flock to the sites along Hadrian's Wall, particularly Housesteads, Vindolanda and Chesters. Durham Cathedral, Bowes Museum and Lindisfarne Castle are also very popular. The North of England Open Air Museum at Beamish brings turn-of-the-century Northumbria to life, while Darlington's North Road Station houses George Stephenson's 'Locomotion', the first fare-paying, passenger-carrying train. Other popular stopping places include Preston Hall

Museum in Stockton, South Shields Museum and Art Gallery, and the Captain Cook Birthplace Museum in Middlesbrough.

Northumbria has many remote, stone-built villages, ruinous castles, fortified manor-houses and medieval churches worth exploring. A Northumbria Tourist Board leaflet, *Just Off the A1*, promotes the quieter roads and attractions. Three of the most important churches are the Saxon edifices at Escomb, Jarrow and Monkwearmouth.

Cuisine

Northumbria is not noted for the originality of its cuisine. Instead traditional English cooking survives, unmodified by concern for weight or health.

Coastal restaurants and shops specialise in fresh fish; Craster's oak-smoked kippers are particularly popular. Some inland restaurants also feature game on their menus, while a few shops sell hand-made sausages; Peppermoor Farm, near Alnwick (Tel 0665 77255) even sells goat-meat sausages. For a list of farms where you can pick your own soft fruits, ask for the *Food from Northumbria* leaflet.

Lindisfarne visitors can sample locally-brewed mead. At St Aidan's Winery it's sold in hand-crafted ceramic decanters bearing motifs from the 8th-century Lindisfarne Gospels.

Level of Tourism

UK residents spend an annual average of four million nights in Northumbria, the majority of them in Tyne and Wear; the value of these trips is estimated at about £260 million. Overseas visitors spend another 320,000 nights in the region, worth approximately £86 million.

With heavy industry declining and sheep farming increasingly difficult, tourism has been seen as a way to revitalise the local economy. The Kielder area currently boasts a Tourism Development Action Programme aimed at kick-starting local projects. The villages of Ford and Etal are also spearheading the drive towards rural tourism, offering attractions as diverse as a steam railway, art gallery and craft workshops.

Northumbria could easily accommodate more visitors. In a few honeypot locations the number of tourists is a problem: at Lindisfarne Castle, with more than 70,000 visitors a year, the number of people admitted at any one time has to be controlled to stop them making it impossible to appreciate the site. Tourists to Hadrian's Wall are being encouraged to spread their visits further afield than Housesteads (121,000 visitors a year) and Vindolanda (77,000 visitors a year) to preserve the ruins' fragile infrastructure; and in peak season, finding accommodation in Durham, where the cathedral attracts more than 400,000 visitors a year, can be difficult. In contrast the Northumberland National Park attracts only one million visits a year compared with twenty million to the Peak District. Many beautiful beaches are currently deserted, and Cleveland had hardly any tourists until the Tourist Board dreamed up 'Captain Cook' country.

Beamish Museum attracts more than 485,000 people a year, but has a site large enough to absorb them. The award-winning Bowes Museum has about 90,000 visitors a year, and Preston Hall Museum in Stockton more than 400,000. In contrast the Bede Monastery Museum draws a mere 20,000 annual visitors.

Because of difficult trading conditions, the 1990 Gateshead Garden Festival had less impact on Northumbria as a whole than was expected. Nevertheless summer visitors to Tyne and Wear attractions rose by up to 50 per cent.

Industrial tourism is developing slowly and visitors are now welcome at Hartlepool's Nuclear Power Station (Tel 0429 869201) and Whitbread Brewery (Tel 0429 836431).

Northumbria is least crowded in winter. However, many attractions and tourist information centres either close altogether or have shorter opening hours from early October to late March. The Tourist Board leaflet *Places to Visit in Winter: England's North Country* available from the Northumbria Tourist Board, Aykley Head, Durham DH1 5UX (Tel 091 384 6905) lists winter opening hours for most attractions.

Good Alternatives

Meeting People

Activity holidays are perfect for meeting people and many new ideas have been pioneered in the Kielder Forest and reservoir area. The **Reivers of Tarset** watersports base at Leaplish (Tel 0434 250217) provides instruction in waterskiing, windsurfing and canoeing, hires out equipment to non-beginners, and organises 'Kielder Safaris' in four-wheel drive vehicles and cross-country skiing. The **Forestry Commission** offers orienteering courses near Kielder Castle (Tel 0434 250209). **Ravenshill Pony Trekking Centre**, Kielder (Tel 0434 250251) and **Brownrigg Pony Trekking Centre**, Bellingham (Tel 0434 220272) offer riding holidays.

There are also waymarked mountain-bike routes; see page 244 for cycling details.

The **Northumberland National Park Authority** offers 300 walks of between one and six hours' duration, and the leaflet, *Walking in Teesdale*, details routes for serious walkers. **Northern General Transport Company** and **Durham County Council** have a programme of 'Ride and Ramble' coach tours which combine scenic coach tours with short rambles (Tel 091 567 1471 for details).

Teesdale District Council offers **green weekends** when you can learn countryside crafts, including dry-stone walling and conservation methods; details from Anthony Seaman, 43 Calgate, Barnard Castle (Tel 0833 690000). Winter weekend courses on working with heavy horses are also available; details from Anthony and Pamela Dove, 13 Castle Drive, Kielder (Tel 0660 50319).

Discovering Places

It's possible to walk the length of **Hadrian's Wall** following signposted rights of way. The most attractive (and popular) stretch of the Northumbrian Wall runs from Greenhead in the west to Sewingshields milecastle in the east, taking in the three mile (5 km.) length from Steel Rigg to Housesteads and passing the sites at Carvoran (Roman Army Museum), Walltown Crags (wall and turret), Cawfields (milecastle), Great Chesters (infantry fort), Vindolanda (fort and museum) and Housesteads (fort). The booklet, *Hadrian's Wall Country*, details **Roman Heritage Breaks** (with admission to attractions included in the accommodation price); contact the Department of Leisure and Tourism, Tynedale Council, Prospect House, Hexham, NE46 3NH (Tel 0434 604011).

With more and more churches locked against thieves, the Tourist Board leaflet, *Christian Heritage in Northumbria*, lists opening hours for some of the most important and identifies key-holders for others.

Durham University heritage tourism specialists offer four- and seven-night fully escorted heritage holidays staying in university accommodation. Details from the Marketing Officer, Old Shire Hall, Durham (Tel 091 374 3454).

Communications

How to Get There

AIR: There are international airports at **Newcastle** (Tel 091 286 0966) and **Teeside** (Tel individual air lines). Domestic services to Newcastle are available from London (Heathrow and Gatwick), Belfast, Birmingham, Aberdeen and Manchester; and to Teeside from London (Gatwick), Aberdeen, Humberside, Norwich and Jersey.

International flights to Newcastle are available from Paris, Brussels, Amsterdam, Frankfurt, Oslo, Stavanger, Bergen and Dublin; and to Teeside from Amsterdam, Stavanger, Dublin and Bergen via Aberdeen and Paris.

RAIL: Rail connections to the region are good. The East Coast London to Scotland route stops at Darlington, Durham, Newcastle (Tel 091 232 6262 for all stations) and Berwick-upon-Tweed. There are 26 trains every day between London and Newcastle.

FERRY: There are direct ferries to Tyneside from Scandinavia, with **Scandinavian Seaways** operating from Esbjerg and Gothenburg, and the **Fred Olsen Line** from Bergen, Alesund, Molde and Maloy.

COACH: Regular **National Express** coaches connect the area with the rest of the UK. Contact either Durham (Tel 0325 431447) or Newcastle (Tel 091 261 6077) for full details.

When You're There

RAIL: Generally, provincial services to popular areas are (relatively) frequent and efficient. Northumberland however, is not overly-blessed with public transport for tourists. The nearest stations to the central area of Hadrian's Wall are Bardon Mill and Haltwhistle, both 3 miles (5 km.) from the actual Wall. British Rail's summer 'Freedom of the North-East' weekly rail-rovers are useful for visiting the coastal towns.

BUS: Bus services to most towns and villages are infrequent. Nevertheless Explorer North-East tickets are valid for a day at a time. Even the hourly bus service along the A69 from Newcastle to Carlisle does not have particularly frequent or convenient stopping places. No buses use the B6318 which is closer to the Wall. A special service to the main sites between Hexham and Haltwhistle is provided during school summer holidays.

CAR: Not surprisingly 75 per cent of all Northumbria's visitors travel by car. This does, of course, mean that roads can be very congested and visitors are urged to consider using public transport wherever possible.

CYCLING: The region is a popular cycling centre and there are a wide variety of routes detailed by Tourist Information Centres. Even greater in number are cycle hire firms, and cycling holiday companies. In the very north of the region (just into Scotland), **Coldstream Cycles**, The Lees Stables, Coldstream, Berwickshire

TD12 4NN (Tel 0890 2709) offer a range of bikes and can book a tour for you (including facilities for the disabled). Slightly further south, there is **Kielder Garage Cycle Hire**, Kielder Village (Tel 0434 250227), while **Kielder Bikes**, Hawkhope Car Park, Kielder Water, Falstone NE48 1BX (Tel 0434 220392), also offer a range of bikes (including mountain-bikes) and provide a useful leaflet detailing routes devised in conjunction with the Forestry Commission. Also in Northumberland, **Further Afield**, Warcarr, Greenhead CA6 7HY (Tel 06977 47358) organise themed tours around Northumbria in general, very much in keeping with Good Tourist philosophy, using local guest houses and B&Bs and helping clients really get to the heart of the area. In Durham, **Weardale Mountain-Bikes**, 39/41 Front Street, Frosterley DL13 2QP (Tel 0388 528129) offer bike hire and 'Wilderness Biking Tours and Holidays'. The **Cyclists' Touring Club** at 15 Wallington Court, Killingworth, Newcastle, offers advice on local cycling routes, and the **Northumbria Tourist Board**, Aykley Heads, Durham DH1 5UX (Tel 091 384 6905) produces a useful list of cycle companies throughout the region.

WALKING: There are many parts of Northumbria which are ideal for walking, and Tourist Information Centres carry details of trails and paths. **Durham County Council Environment Department**, County Hall, Durham DH1 5UF (Tel 091 386 4411, ext. 2354), aided by the Countryside Commission, produces a wide range of leaflets on the many and varied walks in this area. In Tyne and Wear, Tourist Information will be able to supply details of the **River Wear Trail**, while the booklet *Discover Cleveland* carries details of town trails and the **Cleveland Way**.

PUBLIC TRANSPORT: **Newcastle's** integrated network shows what could be possible in all big towns. Drivers can leave their vehicles in convenient car parks and take the bus or Metro even to suburbs like Jarrow. Tickets are not especially cheap, but the service is quick, clean and efficient. For details of travel and timetables contact: Northumberland (Tel 0670 514343, ext. 3347); Durham (Tel 091 386 4411); Cleveland (Tel 0642 210131), and Tyne and Wear (Tel 091 232 5325).

Useful Local Contacts

In Cleveland, visitors might like to contact the **Cleveland Naturalists' Field Club**, 11 Kedleston Close, Stockton-on-Tees TS19 0QW (Tel 0642 611967) who take an active interest in natural history and nature reserves, or the **Cleveland Wildlife Trust**, The Old Town, Mandale Road, Thornaby, Stockton-on-Tees TS17 6AW (Tel 0642 608405), who can advise on general conservation and countryside issues. On the environmental and planning side, the **Industry Nature Conservation Association**, Broadcasting House, Newport Road, Middlesbrough TS1 5JA (Tel 0642 232653) is a good place to start.

Visitors to Tyne and Wear have a large choice of organisations, and the following should suffice for making initial contact. The **Natural History Society of Northumbria** are at The Hancock Museum, Barras Bridge, Newcastle NE2 4PT (Tel 091 26386), while the **Derwent Valley Protection Society** can be contacted at 18 Glamis Crescent, Rowlands Gill NE39 1AT (Tel 0207 542377). As well as contacting the RSPB, bird-lovers could try the **Tyneside Bird Club**, 5 Bath Terrace, Tynemouth NE30 4BL (Tel 091 575928). **Newcastle University Botanical Society**, care of Department of Biology, Ridley Building, University of Newcastle, Newcastle NE1 7RU (Tel 091 232 8511) are up to date on the forestry and botany of the area.

Durham has a relatively large number of natural history and wildlife associations, and a good place to start might be the **Durham Wildlife Trust**, 52 Old Elver, Durham DH1 3HN (Tel 091 386 9797). Ornithologists could contact **Durham Bird Group**, 6 Whitesmocks Avenue, Durham DH1 4HP (Tel 091 384 3084). The well-known **Groundwork Trust**, dealing with arts and crafts and the environment in general, also has a base here: Thornley Station, Industrial Estate, Shotton Colliery DH6 2QA (Tel 0429 836533).

Lastly, in Northumberland try contacting the **Alnwick and District Natural History Society**, The Cottage, Roughcastles, Edlingham, Alnwick (Tel 066 574 646) who can advise on the area's nature reserves and flora, as can the **Northumberland National Park and Countryside Committee**, Eastburn, South Park, Hexham NE46 1BS (Tel 0434 605555). For information on conservation of the countryside, contact the **North Pennines Protection Group**, Unthank Hall, Haltwhistle NE49 0HX (Tel 0498 20500).

Geographical Breakdown of Region

Northumberland

Berwick-upon-Tweed

Berwick-upon-Tweed, England's most northerly town, is situated on the mouth of the river from which it takes its name.

Some of Europe's best preserved **medieval and Elizabethan walls** encircle the town. **Berwick Barracks**, the oldest purpose-built barracks in England, house a regimental museum and art collection.

Towerless **Holy Trinity church** is one of only two churches built during Cromwell's period of office. There's a **Wine and Spirit Museum**, and three bridges across the River Tweed. The **Town Hall** houses the Cell Block Museum, and **Tourist Information** is at Castlegate Car Park (Tel 0289 330733).

Seven miles (11 km.) west of Berwick, **Norham Castle** has a magnificent ruined Norman keep. Just off the A1, **Ancroft** village has a Norman church with a 14th-century fortified tower or 'vicar's pele'.

Holy Island (also known as Lindisfarne)

The island home of St Aidan and St Cuthbert is connected to the mainland by a causeway which can be crossed at low tide; times are posted at the start of the causeway. Very popular with visitors, Lindisfarne is often overcrowded in school holidays. A national nature reserve, the coastline is excellent for watching migratory birds.

The ruins of the 11th-century **Benedictine Priory** are open all year round; a brand-new **visitor's centre** explains the site. The **Castle** (closed in winter) dates from 1550 and was turned into a private house by Sir Edward Lutyens in 1903.

Bamburgh Area

Set around a green, Bamburgh itself is dominated by its magnificent medieval castle. The **Castle** (closed in winter) was extensively restored in the 19th century and has waxworks in the dungeons. The ramparts offer views of the Farne Islands and seemingly endless sandy beaches. The **Museum** is unusual in commemorating a woman, Grace Darling, who is buried across the road in **St Aidan's** church. Built on the site of one of St Aidan's mission churches, the present church dates mainly from the 13th century.

To the south, **Seahouses** is a pretty fishing village with sandy beaches. It's particularly popular at weekends and can get very crowded. From April to September boats go to Inner Farne and Staple Island in the **Farne Islands**, twenty-eight volcanic outcrops inhabited by cormorants, shags, kittiwakes, razorbills, gulls, terns, puffins and a large grey seal colony. Seahouses itself has a **Marine Life Centre and Fishing Museum**. At nearby **Dunstanburgh** the ruins of a 14th-century castle, once the home of John of Gaunt, stand on lofty cliffs dominating the landscape. One and a half miles (2 km.) further south is the picture-postcard fishing port of **Craster**.

Wooler

A typical small market town, Wooler has a ruined castle. From Langleeford, five miles (8 km.) to the south, a vigorous walk leads to panoramic views from the flat summit of the **Cheviot**.

Chillingham Castle, south-east of Wooler, dates from the 12th century, although most of what visitors see now is more recent. The grounds contain a lake and Italian garden. The wild cattle, the last of their kind, are descended from beasts enclosed inside the grounds in 1220; protected from diseases and pests they were able to survive into the 20th century. From **Dod Law** near the village of Doddington, there is a fine view of the Cheviots. The large Iron Age hill fort on top of **Yeavering Bell** may have been the capital of pre-Anglo-Saxon Northumbria.

North of Wooler, the twin 19th-century villages of **Ford** and **Etal** offer thatched roof cottages, a 14th-century ruined castle, the painted murals of **Lady Waterford's Hall**, the 19th-century **Heatherslaw Corn Mill, Heatherslaw Light Railway** and several craft shops.

Alnwick

The market town of Alnwick lies inland from the beaches and golf courses of Alnmouth. Bustling and lively in summer, it can be quiet from September onwards. To see it at its best, visit on Saturday market day or in late June/early July when locals don medieval costume for the fair. The **Tourist Information Centre** is at The Shambles, Northumberland Hall (Tel 0665 603129).

Alnwick Castle dates from the 11th century but was extensively restored in the 19th century when the guardian figures over the gateway were reinstated. Home to the Percy family since 1309, the castle has a lavishly decorated interior, with paintings by Titian, Canaletto and Van Dyck. The gardens were laid out by Capability Brown. A magnificent example of 15th-century architecture, **St Michael and All Angels** also has fine 14th-century effigies. **The House of Hardy Fishing Museum** is open all year round.

Warkworth Castle, another stronghold of the Percy family and the birthplace of Harry Hotspur, is 7.5 miles (12 km.) south of Alnmouth, overlooking the Coquet River. A 15th-century keep survives amid 12th-century ruins. Picturesque **Warkworth** village boasts a medieval fortified bridge. In summer a small 14th-century **hermitage** is also open. Nearby **Amble** is a fishing port with good beaches, where coal is sometimes washed ashore in winter. At **Low Hauxley**, a lake nature reserve, hides offer visitors the chance to watch migratory waders, terns and other nesting birds.

South of Druridge Bay's beautiful beach the scenery changes as rural Northumberland gives way to industrial Tyne and Wear. Slag heaps, colliery winding gear and terraced miners' cottages are reminders of a once-booming coal industry. **Ashington** has been called the biggest mining 'village' in the world but is really a small town full of traditional working-men's clubs, the place to go to get to grips with northern humour. The **Woodhorn Colliery Museum** records the industrial and social history of the region. A busy seaport, **Blyth** is a large town with Friday and Saturday markets. **Seaton Sluice** has an unusual 18th-century harbour built by the Delaval family. Nearby **Seaton Delaval Hall**, a fine example of northern Baroque, was designed by Sir John Vanbrugh in 1720.

Morpeth

On the Wansbeck River where the A1 meets the A697, Morpeth is much livelier than Alnwick, probably because it's closer to Newcastle. The Chantry area houses the **Tourist Information Centre** (Tel 0670 511323), the Northumbria Craft Centre, and Chantry Silver, which sells hand-made jewellery and paintings by local artists.

The **Bagpipe Museum** is upstairs from the Tourist Information Centre. **St Mary the Virgin**, a rare example (for Northumberland) of 14th-century architecture, has the county's most complete medieval stained glass, including a Tree of Jesse in the east window. The **Clock Tower** still sounds an eight o'clock curfew. Ruined **Newminster Abbey**, a 12th-century Cistercian abbey, lies just outside town to the west.

Morpeth is a good base for visits to the **Bedlington** conservation area and to **Bolam Lake** country park where the fine medieval church has a pre-Conquest tower. Waterfowl can be observed at **Cresswell Pond Nature Reserve, Druridge Bay Country Park** at Hadston, and **Druridge Pools Nature Reserve**. At Belsay a 14th-century tower-castle, a ruined Jacobean manor house and a Grecian-style Hall completed in 1815 stand in 30-acre (12 hectare) gardens. Twelve miles (19 km.) west, austere 17th-century **Wallington Hall** is set in 100-acre (40 hectare) grounds with woodlands and lakes; the house itself is closed from November to April but the grounds are open all year round. Nearby **Cambo** has stone-built picture-postcard cottages with neat gardens and a 19th-century church.

Bellingham

A small market town on the edge of the Northumberland National Park, Bellingham is an ideal base for visits to Kielder Water and the Border Forest Park, and for walking the Pennine Way.

St Cuthbert's Church dates from the 13th century; St Cuthbert's Well can be reached along a path behind the churchyard. **Black Middens Bastle House** is a 16th-century fortified farmhouse where animals lived on the ground floor with their owners on the floor above. A footpath northwards leads to a waterfall at **Hareshaw Linn**. **Otterburn** was the site of a battle between the English and Scots in 1388 which inspired 'The Ballad of Chevy Chase'; the mill now sells locally-manufactured tweeds. Nearby **Elsdon** has a seven-acre (2.5 hectare) village green, a fine medieval church, a fortified parsonage and Norman earthworks.

The road north to Alnwick passes through **Rothbury**, a market town on the banks of the pretty Coquet river. Two miles (3 km.) south a path leads from Lordenshaw to **Tosson Hill** (1447 feet/441 m.), highest point in the Simonside Hills. One mile (1.5 km.) east, **Cragside** was built in the 19th century by Sir Norman Shaw for Lord Armstrong, whose interest in electricity ensured his was one of the first UK houses with electric lights. Spectacular wooded grounds offer a 'Power Circuit' trail around reminders of his electrical experiments. Four and a half miles (7 km.) south-east of Rothbury, 12th-century **Brinkburn Priory** was extensively restored by Thomas Austin in 1858.

From **Alwinton** there's a tough fifteen mile (24 km.) round trip walk along **Clennell Street**, an old cattle-droving road, which leads north-west to **Windy Gyle** at 2036 feet (621 m.) in the Cheviots.

Hexham

Despite the off-putting factory chimneys and huge car parks confronting Hexham's visitors, enough of the old town centre survives to make it worth visiting. The **Tourist Information Centre** is at Manor Office, Hallgate (Tel 0434 605225).

The mainly medieval **Abbey** has a 7th-century crypt complete with Roman inscriptions. The south transept staircase once led to the monks' dormitory, while the 'frith' stool in the chancel offered sanctuary to criminals. The **Seal** used to be part of the Abbey grounds but is now a public park. A 14th-century manor house accommodates the **Middlemarch Centre for Border History**.

Three miles (4.5 km.) east of Hexham, **Corbridge**, one of the forts on Hadrian's Wall, later became the Roman town of Corstopitum. The **Tourist Information Office** at The Vicar's Pele (Tel 0434 632815) supplies a *Visitor's Guide to Hadrian's Wall* with site opening times. One and a half miles (2.5 km.) north-east of Corbridge is **Aydon Castle**, a fortified medieval manor house. A little further east are **Cherryburn** with the **birthplace museum** of 18th-century woodcarver Thomas Berwick, and **Prudhoe's** magnificent 12th-century castle. On the A69 just outside Newcastle, one room of the 18th-century cottage in **Wylam**, where railway engineer George Stephenson was born, is open in summer.

West of Hexham the B6318 skirts the North Pennines and follows the line of Hadrian's Wall. **Housesteads**, **Chesters** and **Vindolanda** are very congested and best visited out of season. Quieter sites include **Planetrees, Brunton Turret, Black Carts Turret, Winshields Crag** and **Carrawburgh** with the remains of a temple to the oriental god, Mithras.

The River Allen branches south from the Tyne near Haydon Bridge. A footpath winds past the ruined **Staward Pele Tower** and down to the **Allen Gorge** with its 250 feet (61 m.) high walls. The B6295 continues south through Allendale Town to **Allenheads** and the Visitor Centre for the North Pennines AONB. Over the New Year **Allendale Town** hosts a ceremony dating back to pre-Christian times, with men carrying tubs of blazing tar to a bonfire.

Accommodation

Surprisingly, Northumberland does not really offer any hotels which could be categorised in the First Class price range. The consolation is that there are many Middle Range hotels to choose from, some of which offer what could be called First Class service, but at extremely reasonable prices. For the visitor to the area this is good news as value for money is relatively easy to find.

Middle Range

King's Arms Hotel, Hide Hill, Berwick-upon-Tweed TD15 1EJ (Tel 0289 307454). Popular Georgian coaching inn now restored to original style.

Manor House Hotel, Holy Island, Berwick-upon-Tweed TD15 2RX (Tel 0289 89207). Friendly family run hotel set in its own grounds and with wonderful views of the Farne Islands and Lindisfarne Castle and Priory.

Victoria Hotel, Front Street, Bamburgh NE69 7BP (Tel 06684

431). Peaceful hotel in a pleasant location in the centre of Bamburgh, close to the castle, beach and golf course.

Blue Bell Hotel, Market Place, Belford NE70 7NE (Tel 0668 213543). Charming ivy-covered hotel offering high standards of comfort and service. Three acres (1.2 hectares) of gardens, out of which comes much of the fresh produce used in preparing the excellent cuisine.

Warren House Hotel, Warren Mill, Belford NE70 7EE (Tel 0668 4581). Set in delightful grounds on the edge of Budle Bay Nature Reserve two miles (3.2 km.) from Belford, this is a lovely hotel which offers outstanding value, providing country house accommodation in a peaceful setting at prices which might put other establishments to shame. Peace comes at a price however: children are not accepted here and there is no public bar.

Bamburgh Castle Hotel, Seahouses NE68 7SQ (Tel 0665 720283). Pleasant hotel with a wonderful position right above the harbour, offering excellent views of the Farne Islands, Bamburgh Castle and Holy Island. Extras such as a complimentary glass of sherry on arrival and free tour guide to the area are nice touches which don't go by unnoticed.

White Swan Hotel, Bondgate Within, Alnwick NE66 1TD (Tel 0665 602109). Traditional former coaching inn (with a modern extension) offering cosy accommodation.

Waterford Lodge, Castle Square, Morpeth NE61 1YD (Tel 0670 512004). Friendly local hotel with a pleasant conservatory and beer garden, close to the river. Horse-riding and golf available nearby.

County Hotel, Priestpopple, Hexham NE46 1PS (Tel 0434 602030). Traditional town centre hotel with a reputation for good food.

Economy

The Estate House, Ford, Berwick-upon-Tweed TD15 2QG (Tel 089082 297). Edwardian country house set in its own grounds in the peaceful village of Ford. Walking, fishing, gliding and riding offered by arrangement.

Lindisfarne Hotel, Holy Island, Berwick-upon-Tweed TD15 2SQ (Tel 0289 89273). Welcoming hotel offering bed and breakfast. An evening meal is available as well, but will put the price up by around one third (although the four-course dinner is worth it).

Sunningdale Hotel, Lucker Road, Bamburgh NE69 7BS (Tel 06684 334). Family run hotel with a reputation for good food, situated in a quiet village in an Area of Outstanding Natural Beauty.

Loreto Guest House, 1 Ryecroft Way, Wooler NE71 6EW (Tel 0668 81350). Family run bed and breakfast in an early Georgian house set in large grounds.

New Moor House, Edlingham, Alnwick NE66 2BT (Tel 0665 74638). Family run bed and breakfast offering accommodation full of character; wooden beams, open fires and good food.

Westfield House, Bellingham, near Hexham NE48 2DP (Tel 0434 220340). Charming guest house lovingly looked after by its owners, set in its own grounds and with good views. No smoking.

Eating Out

First Class

Waterford Lodge Hotel, Castle Square, Morpeth NE61 1YD (Tel 0670 512004).

Middle Range

Ravensdowne Hotel, 34–36 Ravensdowne, Berwick-upon-Tweed (Tel 0289 330770). Traditional fare served in pleasant surroundings.

John Blackmore's, 1 Dorothy Foster's Court, Narrowgate, Alnwick (Tel 0665 604464). Local produce and fare at this popular restaurant.

La Brasserie Gourmet, 59 Bridge Street, Morpeth (Tel 0670 516200). A mixture of local and continental cuisine at good value prices. More expensive in the evening.

Economy

Jackdaw, 34 Castle Street, Warkworth (Tel 0665 711488). No-nonsense cooking and baking, with particularly good fish dishes.

Harlequins, Queens Hall Art Centre, Hexham (Tel 0434 607230). Restaurant and cafe serving home-baked goodies.

Tyne and Wear

Northumbria's smallest county, Tyne and Wear constitutes little more than the city of Newcastle-upon-Tyne and its dormitories: Tynemouth, North Shields, South Shields, Gateshead, Washington and Sunderland. It is the transport hub for the area, with frequent trains and coaches from London and Edinburgh. The **Catherine Cookson Trail** links a church, two houses, a school, shops, a laundry and other South Tyneside sites associated with the author's life and novels. A good time to visit would be during the **Catherine Cookson Country Festival** between June and August.

Newcastle-upon-Tyne

Newcastle itself is sited at the mouth of the River Tyne and has an excellent integrated transport network (contact Travel Information, Bus and Metro, Tel 091 232 5325 for further details). **Bikes** can be hired from **Glenbar Hire** at 217 Jesmond Road. The **Tourist Information Centre** is at Blackfriars, Monk Street (Tel. 091 261 5367).

A **heritage trail** links sites of historic interest. The Tyne itself is a good starting point for city tours. The **Quayside** area north of Tyne Bridge is being revived and repays a visit, especially on Sunday morning for the outdoor market. The nearby **Castle** dates from the 11th century. Until 1882, when a new bishopric was created for the growing city, **St Nicholas' Cathedral** was a parish church; amongst other treasures it contains a rare pre-Reformation brass eagle lectern. Paintings by local artists are displayed in the **Laing Art Gallery** in Higham Place, while the **Museum of Antiquities** in the university quadrangle houses finds from Hadrian's Wall. City-centre streets have elegant early 19th-century architecture interspersed with attractive shopping arcades. However, a trip out to **Jarrow** to see St Paul's Church with its Saxon choir, and the Bede Museum in Jarrow Hall, quickly confirms that industrial dereliction continues to blight the suburbs. **Gibside Chapel** is a Palladian mausoleum to the south. Sea birds nest on **Marsden Rock** to the north.

Newcastle is the cultural heart of Northumbria, and the free listings magazine *Northern Events* gives full details of entertainment in the region. Over £9 million was spent on restoring the **Theatre Royal** (visited by the Royal Shakespeare Company every February and March; Tel 091 232 2061). Other theatres include the **Tyne Theatre**; the **People's Theatre** in Stephenson Road; **Live Theatre** in Broad Chare and the **Playhouse** and **Gulbenkian Studio Theatres** in Barras Bridge. **City Hall** in Northumberland Street hosts mainstream rock and pop concerts, while the **Riverside** in Melbourne Street offers an alternative venue for bands. Newcastle also has its own orchestra, the Northern Sinfonia of England.

The large Chinese community guarantees that Chinese New Year is celebrated in lively fashion. Festivals include the **Newcastle**

Jazz Festival (May), the **First Wave Festival** (June/July, youth arts), the **Great North Festival of Sport** (summer), and **Tyneside International Film Festival** (September/October, at Tyneside Cinema, Pilgrim Street). A huge fair takes place on the Town Moor every June.

Washington

Washington Old Hall, Washington Village is a mainly medieval manor house with tenuous links to George Washington and lively American Independence Day celebrations. **The Wildfowl and Wetlands Centre** (District 15) has 1250 swans, geese and ducks, and a flock of flamingos named after Catherine Cookson characters. Wild birdwatching from hides is possible and occasional canal boat trips to the Centre are available (Tel 091 416 5454 for details).

Gateshead

Visit the Metro Centre, if you're into American-style 'shopping entertainment'. More than 350 shops, an indoor theme park (Metroland) and a ten-screen multiplex cinema are on offer. Free parking for 10,000 cars and frequent buses to Newcastle centre.

Sunderland

The Sunderland Illuminations, from late August until early November each year, are the focal point of a string of events in all the coastal resorts from Roker to Seaburn (Tel Illuminations Hotline 091 567 9400 for more details).

Accommodation

Tyne and Wear offers a relatively good selection of hotels, although there are none suited to Good Tourist philosophy which fall into the First Class price range. Nonetheless, Middle Range hotels provide a perfectly acceptable alternative.

Middle Range

Whites Hotel, 38–42 Osborne Road, Jesmond, Newcastle NE2 2AL (Tel 091 281 5126). Pleasant, privately-run hotel situated in one of Newcastle's suburbs, but close to the bus route. Comfortable and homely.

Tunstall Lodge Hotel, Burdon Lane, Burdon, near Ryhope, Sunderland SR3 2QB (Tel 091 521 0353). Elegant 18th-century country house hotel set in lovely gardens, complete with tennis court and outdoor swimming pool.

Economy

Ye Olde Wagon Inn, Higham Dykes, Belsay Road, Ponteland, Newcastle NE20 ODH (Tel 0661 81286). Comfortable bed and breakfast in an 18th-century coaching inn in a quiet location.

Old School House, Kirkwhelpington NE19 2RT (Tel 0830 40226). No-smoking, vegetarian guest house in a convenient location. Vegans also catered for.

Eating Out

As with First Class hotels, Tyne and Wear offers little in the way of First Class restaurants. With Durham often just a short drive away however, it is easy to nip across the county border should you wish.

Middle Range

Tunstall Lodge Hotel, Burdon Lane, Burdon, near Ryhope, Sunderland (Tel 091 521 0353). The restaurant of this recommended hotel (see above) is well worth a visit, especially for the 4-course Sunday lunch, for which bookings are strongly advised.

Gibside Arms Hotel and Restaurant, Front Street, Whickham, near Newcastle (Tel 091 488 9292). Local hotel with a popular restaurant serving traditional food, overlooking the Tyne Valley.

Economy

Marquis of Granby, Streetgate, Sunniside, Gateshead (Tel 091 488 7813). Traditional pub offering wholesome home-cooked food. Good value.

The Red Herring, 3 Studley Terrace, Fenham, Newcastle (Tel 091 272 3484). Wholefood cafe and shop offering lots of healthy, home-made fare.

Durham

Durham City

Durham City is Northumbria's honeypot par excellence. A hilly town, it meanders upwards from the market square and high street to the cathedral close. An excellent time to visit is during the **Durham Miners' Gala** in the second week in July. The

Tourist Information Centre is on Market Place (Tel 091 384 3720).

The Norman **cathedral** stands in a dominating position, its twin towers overlooking the Wear Valley. The surrounding **close** is mercifully unspoilt, but gets progressively more crowded as the day wears on. Luckily the cathedral opens at 0730 so you can visit before the coach parties. Inside, the vast Norman pillars, each with a different pattern incised on them, dwarf everything else. Amongst the cathedral's treasures look out for the unique **Lady Chapel** at the west rather than the east end of the church, which has some fine murals, the **tomb of the Venerable Bede**, and the magnificent gorgon-headed **sanctuary knocker** (a copy; the original is kept in the cathedral treasury). The Norman Undercroft offers an audio-visual description of the cathedral's history. The Cloisters restaurant lets you contribute to the building's maintenance as you eat.

Durham University owns the 11th-century **castle**, and parts are open to the public. The **Museum of Archaeology** is housed in an old fulling mill near the cathedral. The **Botanical Gardens** in Hollingside Lane are open all year round. Sunday **river trips** are available (Tel 091 386 9525 for details).

Four miles (6 km.) south-west of Durham, **Brancepeth** has a reconstructed 12th-century castle and wonderful 17th-century woodwork in a medieval church. **Bishop Auckland** has two medieval churches. **Escomb**, one mile (1.5 km.) to the west, is home to one of England's few remaining pre-Conquest churches. The key hangs on a hook outside a nearby house, and the church makes visitors welcome with every feature meticulously labelled.

North of Durham, the **Beamish North of England Open Air Museum** should be a must on every visitor's itinerary. The site incorporates everything from a steam railway to colliery cottages, a drift mine, a turn-of-the-century farm and a reconstructed town centre with shops and pubs. Restored buses and trams link the various attractions which might otherwise be too far apart for the elderly or disabled.

Much of Durham's coast, and Easington beach in particular, has been ruined by industrial pollution. However, the **Castle Eden Denes** nature reserve, in native woodlands running through gorges to the coast, has rare plants and insects.

West of Durham, **Weardale** is accessible (on summer Sundays) by train and bus from Darlington on a 'Heritage Line' linking Heighington, Shildon, Bishop Auckland, Stanhope, Killhope, Alston and Gilderdale; details from Friends of the Heritage Line, Auckland New Business Centre, Bishop Auckland (Tel 0388 450505). High House Chapel in **Ireshopeburn** houses the Weardale Museum, near where John Wesley once preached. **Killhope Lead Mining Centre** is still being developed; visitors can see how 19th-century lead mines worked and then follow a beautiful woodland walk with interpretive boards explaining the industry's impact on the surrounding landscape. Phone Melissa Jones (0388 528449) for local pony trekking information.

Barnard Castle

Barnard Castle, an attractive hilly market town looking down on the River Tees, is perfect for exploring southern Durham and Teesdale to the east. The **Tourist Information Centre** is at 43 Galgate (Tel 0833 690909).

The **Castle** itself dates from the 12th century. John Bowes and his wife Josephine established the **Bowes Museum**, one of the greatest private collections of fine and decorative art (15th–19th century). Josephine's French ancestry explains how a chateau with formal gardens came to adorn the Durham countryside. The most popular exhibit, an 18th-century clockwork swan, is activated only once or twice a day to protect its mechanism. Ruined **Egglestone Abbey** is romantically isolated on the outskirts of town.

Just to the north-east is **Raby Castle**, mainly built in the 14th century by the Neville family, with a collection of horse-drawn carriages in its grounds. **Rokeby Park**, a Palladian house, is also open in summer. In **Bowes village** to the south-west a ruined Norman castle stands inside Roman earthworks.

Darlington is easily reached from Barnard Castle. **North Road Station** is now a museum devoted to the railways of north-eastern England, while **Darlington Museum** has exhibits about Tees valley social and natural history.

To the west of Barnard Castle, **Teesdale** has many villages of stone-built or whitewashed houses. **Romaldkirk**, which has an impressive medieval church is typical of the area. Near Newbiggin, at the **Bowlees Visitor Centre** there's a forest trail. Further north the **Low** and **High Force waterfalls** are easily accessible but **Cauldron Snout** requires a stiff walk. The **Cow Green, Selset, Grassholme, Balderhead, Blackton** and **Hury reservoirs** permit fishing and have shoreside nature reserves. Teesdale is being promoted as a tourist destination and local information centres have a detailed *Teesdale Accommodation Guide*.

Accommodation

First Class

Lumley Castle Hotel, Chester-le-Street DH3 4NX (Tel 091 389 1111). Imposing castle seven miles (11 km.) north of Durham, set in woodland grounds and looking down on the River Wear.

Hallgarth Manor Hotel, Pittington, near Durham DH6 1AB (Tel 091 372 1188). Delightful country house offering luxurious accommodation a short distance from the centre of Durham.

Walworth Castle Hotel, Walworth, near Darlington DL2 2LY (Tel 0325 485470). An 800-year-old castle set in extensive lawns and gardens, with golf and riding available nearby. Four-poster beds in some rooms.

Middle Range

Old Manor House Hotel, The Green, West Auckland, Bishop Auckland DL14 9HW (Tel 0388 832504). Charming old manor house set in lovely gardens, offering a range of outdoor pursuits in the surrounding countryside.

Headlam Hall Hotel, Gainford, near Darlington DL2 3HA (Tel 0325 730238). Historic mansion house set in delightful gardens seven miles (11 km.) west of Darlington. Traditional comfort and cuisine, good value.

Morritt Arms Hotel, Greta Bridge, Barnard Castle DL12 9SE (Tel 0833 27232). Lovely former coaching inn in the peaceful village of Greta Bridge. Privately owned and managed, it offers a real escape into rural Durham.

Economy

Bee Cottage Farm, Castleside, Consett DH8 9HW (Tel 0207 508224). Bed, breakfast (and dinner if required) on a working farm with wonderful views. Pleasant walks in the surrounding countryside.

Pennine Lodge, St John's Chapel, Weardale, near Stanhope DL13 1QX (Tel 0388 537247). Charming bed and breakfast in a 16th-century farmhouse next to the River Wear. Interesting bedrooms filled with items collected over the years.

Grove House, Hamsterley Forest, near Bishop Auckland DL13 3NL (Tel 0388 88203). Bed and breakfast (and dinner) in a former shooting lodge situated in the Forestry Commission's Hamsterley Forest. All food made from fresh produce; lots of walks and trails.

Eating Out

First Class

Ramside Hall Hotel, Carrville, Durham (Tel 091 386 5282). Excellent local and continental cuisine at this popular country house hotel, situated in its own grounds.

Middle Range

Bishops Bistro, 17 Cockton Hill Road, Bishop Auckland (Tel 0388 602462). Converted cottages now running as a restaurant serving English cuisine with a few French touches.

Crossways Hotel and Restaurant, Dunelm Road, Thornley, Durham (Tel 0429 821248). Traditional cuisine and wonderful home-made sweets in an attractive semi-rural restaurant.

Economy

Seven Stars Inn, Shincliffe Village (Tel 091 384 8454). Pleasant old-world inn serving good home-made food and offering an extensive choice of whiskies.

Punch Bowl Inn, Edmundbyers, Consett (Tel 0207 55206) Traditional local pub with log fires offering wholesome food (including vegetarian dishes) in a cosy atmosphere.

Priors, 7 The Bank, Barnard Castle (Tel 0833 38141). Vegetarian restaurant and take-away cafe at the same location as a craft shop and gallery.

Cleveland

The triangular wedge of country squashed in between Hartlepool and Saltburn and drained by the River Tees became the county of Cleveland in 1974. In the battle to attract tourists its greatest success story has been the **Captain Cook Heritage Trail**, which starts at the explorer's birthplace in Marton (with an excellent **Museum**) and follows the coast south to Whitby in Yorkshire. The English Tourist Board has even tried to market the safety floodlighting at Middlesbrough's ICI chemical works as 'illuminations'. Good times to visit Cleveland would be during **Saltburn's Victorian Celebration** in August or during the **Captain Cook Birthday Celebrations** in October. Further details are available from the **Tourist Information Centre**, 51 Corporation Road, Middlesbrough (Tel 0642 243425).

The Cleveland Way

The Cleveland Way runs for 107 miles (172 km.) through the North Yorkshire Moors National Park and along the North Yorkshire and Cleveland Heritage Coast, cutting across a part of Cleveland which makes nonsense of the county's industrial reputation. The route links the 1000 foot (305 m.) **Roseberry Topping**; the remains of a fine 12th-century priory at **Guisborough**; **Upleatham** church (possibly the smallest in England); **Tocketts working watermill**; **Saltburn**, with north-east England's only pier, and the **Tom Leonard Mining Museum** in Deepdale.

Stockton-on-Tees itself has a market around its old town hall on Wednesdays and Saturdays. The **Green Dragon Museum** houses an audio-visual exhibition on railway history. **Preston Park Museum** contains recreated Victorian shops and houses. There is also a **Georgian Theatre** in Theatre Yard (Tel 0642 674308 for performance details). **Yarm,** with an attractive 18th-century town hall and 'wynds' or lanes leading down to the Tees, hosts a three day street fair every October. Across the river, **Egglescliffe** has a pretty village green and a Norman church. The 3.5 mile (6 km.) **Castle Eden Walkway** nature reserve follows the route of the old Stockton-to-Castle Eden Railway. **Billingham** hosts an annual **International Folklore Festival** every August.

Accommodation

First Class

Rushpool Hall Hotel, Saltburn Lane, Saltburn TS12 1HD (Tel 0287 624111). Country house hotel set in extensive grounds and woodland close to Saltburn. Traditional in every way and offering clay pigeon shooting.

Larpool Hall Hotel, Larpool Lane, Whitby YO22 4ND (Tel 0947 602737). Eighteenth-century Georgian mansion situated in large grounds and overlooking Whitby and the Esk Valley.

Middle Range

Marine Hotel, 5–7 The Front, Seaton Carew TS25 1BS (Tel 0429 266244). Recently renovated hotel with wonderful sea views and good food.

The Grand Hotel, Swainson Street, Hartlepool TS24 8AA (Tel 0429 266345). Late Victorian hotel benefiting from a comprehensive refurbishment scheme carried out over the past few years.

Economy

Longlands Hotel, 295 Marton Road, Middlesbrough TS4 2HF (Tel 0642 244900). Large stone-built bed and breakfast close to the town centre, offering the unusual extra of a charter fishing boat for hire (with skipper) and deep sea wreck and reef fishing.

Laurel Hotel, 113 Borough Road, Middlesbrough TS1 3AX (Tel 0642 245861). Friendly pub and hotel offering cosy accommodation and handy for the centre of town.

Eating Out

Middle Range

Filberts, 47 Borough Road, Middlesbrough (Tel 0642 245455). Co-operative-owned vegetarian restaurant offering a good range of dishes. Also sells pictures by local artists.

Andersons, 3 Silver Street, Whitby (Tel 0947 605383). Steak and local fish dishes are a speciality at this popular informal bistro-style restaurant.

Economy

Rooney's, 23 Newport Road, Middlesbrough (Tel 0642 223923). Popular fish and chip restaurant serving cheap and filling meals.

Waiting Room, 9 Station Road, Eaglescliffe (Tel 0642 780465). Excellent vegetarian restaurant on the ground floor of an old Edwardian house.

7 Cumbria

From the boundaries of Lancashire in the south to the Scottish Border country in the north stretches one of England's most beautiful regions. Cumbria can offer a variety of superb landscape which includes the wildness of lake and fell, the fascination of sea and shore and the gentler farming land of crop and sheep.

Cumbria's Lake District is Britain's most popular National Park. A compact area of around 900 square miles (2331 sq. km.), it attracts thousands of people each year; climbing, riding, walking, water sports, wildlife study or just appreciation of the beautiful scenery, all have their own appeal. To the east of the region lies the valley of the River Eden, an area of unrivalled beauty. Here, rolling farmland and green meadows stocked with sheep and cattle edge the river (which is an angler's paradise), while the fells above are a haven for walkers.

Adding to its wealth of attractions, Cumbria has one of England's longest coastlines. Several estuaries and the spread of Morecombe Bay all lie along its southern boundaries. To the north there are sandy and shingle beaches, towering cliffs and stretches of flat coastal land against the backdrop of hills.

This north-west corner of England has much to offer. It boasts some of England's largest and deepest lakes, highest mountains and quietest valleys – a dramatic and diverse landscape.

But such beauty and tranquillity must come at a price and, unfortunately, Cumbria, and the Lake District in particular, have become victims of their own appeal. As in so many other parts of the country, too many feet are tramping the hill paths and mountain trails; the lakes themselves have reached saturation point during the summer, with every available stretch of water occupied; the local population has become frustrated and dissatisfied, and the environment is suffering. There is perhaps nowhere else in Great Britain that can lay claim to such an intensity of fauna, flora and environmental beauty in an area the size of Cumbria, and yet, if measures are not taken, the sheer numbers of visitors to the county may well destroy the attractions they come to see.

History

Cumbria is a region of north-west England formed in 1974 from the former counties of Cumberland and Westmorland, covering an area of 2628 square miles (6808 sq. km.). Human occupation of the land dates from the Neolithic period; there is a stone axe 'factory' of this time at Great Langdale, a settlement site at Ehenside tarn and the Eden area contains remains of Iron Age settlements and ancient stone circles, such as Castlerigg near Keswick, and Long Meg near Langwathby. Military occupation by the Romans resulted in the construction of several roads and the great wall complex (a defence against the peoples of Scotland) built by the Emperor Hadrian (reigned AD 117–138), stretching from Wallsend in Tyne and Wear to Bowness on the Solway Firth. The Romans were also responsible for the construction of a series of coastal and inland forts (for example, Brough and Birdoswald).

Christianity was established in the region by St Ninian, who founded Candida casa (Whithorn) in AD 397 and, as is seen in the many priories and abbeys (Cartmel, Furness, Lanercost, Holme Cultram, St Bees), religion has played its part in forming Cumbria's character.

In the 7th century Cumbria came under Northumbrian control and the importance of subsequent Scandinavian settlements is reflected in the numerous placenames containing Norse elements. These Norse invasions resulted in a period of forest clearance and the Cistercian abbeys of Furness and Byland, exploiting the area for wool production, continued the process of deforestation. This was accelerated by iron ore smelting and, later, by the extraction of lead and copper. These activities became uneconomic after the 1870s however, and labour was directed into slate and building-stone quarries. The Forestry Commission has planted some areas with conifers but has agreed to leave the central fell area in its deforested state with fragmentary deciduous woodland.

After 945 the northern part of Cumbria alternated between Scottish and English rule and was finally taken by the latter in 1157. The subsequent border skirmishing continued intermittently, as exemplified by numerous castles (Carlisle, Egremont and Appleby), and only ended after the Union of the Crowns in 1603 when James VI of Scotland became James I of England on Queen Elizabeth's death.

Industries of Cumbria's past are linked with mineral extraction – the mining of lead and silver in the 12th century at Alston and iron ore at Egremont. Coal was also extensively mined. Reminders of the region's industrial past, from silver mining to bobbin making, are housed in museums and a variety of visitor centres. Cumbria's maritime history is depicted at Mayport on the west coast.

No history of Cumbria is complete without mention of the Lake Poets or Lake School. The expression 'Lake School' seems to have appeared originally in the *Edinburgh Review* of August 1817, coined as a collective term to include William Wordsworth, Samuel Taylor Coleridge and Robert Southey. Coleridge was born in 1772 in Devon. In 1794 on an undergraduate walking tour he made the acquaintance of Southey and the following year he met and struck up an intense friendship with Wordsworth and his sister Dorothy, based on their mutual love of poetry, hillwalking and critical debate. Southey, who was born in Bristol in 1774, settled in the Lake District in 1800. Wordsworth, the only Cumbrian-born member of the trio, spent his young adulthood in the south of England and Europe, but returned to Grasmere in 1799, followed soon after by Coleridge. The early years of the 19th century saw the three men settled in the Lake District and producing some of their best poetry and prose. Coleridge eventually returned to London, but Wordsworth and Southey remained in Cumbria for the rest of their lives. The Lake Poets did much to popularise Cumbria in the 19th century and, since then, improved road and rail communications have stimulated a growing tourist industry.

Geography

Cumbria forms the north-west corner of England and, together with Northumbria in the east, borders Scotland to the north. It covers an area of 2628 square miles (6808 sq. km.) which, prior to 1974, constituted the counties of Westmorland, Cumberland and the detached Furness district of Lancashire.

The region includes the famous Lake District National Park, incorporating mountain peaks and lake-filled valleys formed from a dome of deeply dissected ancient volcanic and slate rocks. In the north the smoothly-rounded shapes of Skiddaw and the fells west of Derwentwater have formed from the soft Skiddaw slates. Southwards the harder Borrowdale volcanics give rise to the rugged peaks of the central Lake District. Still further south of Ambleside and Coniston, gently sloping lower hills are the result of Silurian slates and mudstones. Virtually ringing the Lake District proper, a broad band of carboniferous limestone provides impressive examples of limestone pavements, creviced expanses of bare rock. Subsequent glaciation during the Ice Ages scoured out deep valleys, formed rocky corries in the fells and dammed streams with moraines. The picturesque lakes of Windermere, Grasmere and the remote and wild Wast Water are among the most notable results of this process. The loftiest mountains in England overlook Wast Water, where Scafell Pike reaches 3210 feet (978 metres). To the east Helvellyn rises to 3118 feet (951 metres), and Skiddaw to the north, 3054 feet (931 metres).

To the east of the region lies the fertile Eden Valley, dividing the Pennines from the outlying lakeland fells, with the Solway plain to the north. Cross Fell (2930 feet, 894 metres) and Knock Fell (2604 feet, 794 metres) are the culmination of the long Pennine Range, the spinal ridge of north England.

The valleys of the Lune and Kent rivers provide much pleasant broken country in the south, with low hills and beautiful scenery formed, as in the north, from newer outcrops of limestone and sandstone. To the west a long and varied coastline stretches from the estuary of the Solway Firth in the north to Morecombe Bay in the south. Fine sand dune systems are found here and coastal marshes and mosses have been developed as nature reserves. St Bees Head is formed from high sandstone cliffs.

The main rural occupation of Cumbria is sheep farming on the rough grazing lands of the uplands and agriculture on the more fertile lowlands. The hardy Lakeland Herdwick sheep, renowned for their homing instincts, graze on the fells in many places, but the severe climate, steep rocky slopes and high winds prohibit agriculture and even forestry on the higher hills. Trees are scarce and stunted on exposed slopes over 1500 feet (450 metres) above sea level and selective grazing by mountain sheep has exacerbated this situation on slopes that were once wooded. As always in sheep raising areas, visitors should take care to keep dogs on leads, especially during lambing time, usually between March and June.

Apart from tourism, modern industry is rarely evident in the region; only around Carlisle, Barrow and the West Cumberland coalfield is industrialisation significant. Also noteworthy, and the subject of some controversy, is the nuclear reprocessing plant at Sellafield on the isolated coastal region south of St Bees Head.

Cumbria's two most populous centres are Carlisle in the north and Barrow-in-Furness in the south, lying at opposite extremities of the region. Situated on the River Eden and close to the Scottish border, Carlisle is located in an area with large stretches of forestry mixed with sheep and cattle farming country. Further south and at the northern extremity of the Lake District, Penrith has been a market town since 1223. Keswick, to the west and known as Queen of Lakeland, is a good centre for exploring the area, while Alston, on top of the Pennines at over 900 feet (275 metres) to the north-east, is reputedly the highest market town in England. Southwards the M6 motorway offers a scenic route to Kendal, the southern gateway to the Lake District.

On the west coast, both Whitehaven and Workington are significant urban centres. The latter is situated at the mouth of the Derwent River and the former is a seaport, notable for the extension of coal mining some four miles (6.5 km.) under the sea.

In the extreme south of the region lies the industrial and shipbuilding town of Barrow-in-Furness. This district, forming the jutting northern peninsula of Morecombe Bay, takes its name from medieval furnaces, the mineral rights of which were owned by the Monks of Furness Abbey and Cartmel Priory.

Climate

Although Cumbria's reputation for rain goes a long way before it, visitors will find that certain areas are more susceptible to wet weather than others. The central fells and valley heads in particular receive more than their fair share of rain, while at Seathwaite in the central Lake District, the annual rainfall is 122 inches (3100 mm). Away from the mountains however, there is a marked contrast, with the amount of rainfall decreasing rapidly to under 40 inches (1000 mm) along the Solway plain and southern coast. In terms of temperature variation, a similar difference is experienced.

Air frost is recorded on about 160 days of the year on the high fells, but down at Grange-over-Sands on Morecombe Bay in the south, there are only around 30 days a year when there is a definite nip in the air. In the mountains snow can be found in high gullies in June, but is rarely seen at any time around the southern estuaries.

Attractions

Cumbria's attractions are many and varied and offer visitors a surfeit of activities and entertainment or, if so desired, the solitude and tranquillity of the dark lakes and high fells. Sporting pastimes abound: walking, climbing, cycling, riding and water sports of all kinds. For the very energetic and fleet of foot there are fell races, when athletes run up seemingly impossible gradients and descend at a terrifying pace. Spectator sports include Cumberland and Westmorland wrestling and hound trailing. Anglers and golfers are also catered for, in the beautiful Eden valley and on the western 'Golf Coast' respectively.

For those interested in the traditional life of the area, there are numerous agricultural shows, festivals and fairs throughout the summer and autumn. There are also year-round programmes of films, exhibitions, theatre, music and art and craft workshops.

History lovers will find much to appreciate in this region. Iron and Bronze Age relics, Roman remains along Hadrian's Wall, medieval castles and pele towers, ruined abbeys and priories and a range of visitor centres and museums are all here.

This corner of England is one of the most famous (and developed) tourist centres in the world, yet possibly its main attraction remains its superb landscape, which is second to none.

Cuisine

Cumbria enjoys a fine reputation for traditional fare and can lay claim to being the 'gourmet region of England'. Until the end of the 18th century, Whitehaven was a major English port with a flourishing trade in rum and sugar. One local delicacy born out of these imports was Cumberland rum butter – Demerara sugar and butter beaten together with rum, nutmeg and cinnamon – served as a spread or eaten with Christmas pudding. Traditionally, rum butter was given by anyone visiting a new baby. Rum was said to give the baby spirit, butter to smooth its way through life, sugar to make it sweet and spices to add zest.

With a long coastline and many deep lakes, fish and seafood abound. Amongst the specialities are flukes (flatfish with a flavour similar to plaice), which are driven into nets on the sands around Flookburgh; silver, scarlet and olive-green char, which are found only in the deepest lakes; salmon from the Solway Firth, and shrimps from Morecambe Bay. All are favourite dishes of the region.

The hilly terrain of Cumbria lends itself to sheep farming and flocks of Herdwick, Swaledale and Rough Fell thrive on the high lands. Roast Herdwick lamb graces many a Sunday lunch table and recipes such as tatie pot (John Peel's favourite dish) use the local mutton.

Many acres of forest provide a home for a large number of red, roe and fallow deer, and some of England's finest venison is produced here. No Cumbrian menu would be complete without Cumberland sausage – sometimes over a yard long, containing 100 per cent meat flavoured with herbs, and delicious eaten with red cabbage or apple sauce. Sweet Cumberland ham is still cured in Carlisle and Waberthwaite and has its own special flavour. Successful dairy farming has resulted in a range of butter, ice-cream and yoghurt. Cheese is also produced, notably at Alston in the north Pennines, Wigton in the north and Calthwaite in the fertile Eden valley.

In the beautiful Lyth valley, south of Windermere, are found exceptionally fine damsons, known locally as Witherslack damsons. The fruit is used for making jam, wine, damson gin and desserts such as damson cobbler.

As travel was difficult in years gone by, many dishes became localised and even today bear the name of their town of origin: Kendal mintcake, Grasmere gingerbread, Borrowdale tea bread and Lamplugh pudding.

To ensure the continuation of Cumbria's high standards of traditional fare, a company was formed in 1988 by a number of regional producers. Cumbria Fine Foods, as it is known, aims to encourage the development of quality food production and respond to the growing demand for fresh natural food and the flavours of Cumbria.

Level of Tourism

In 1989 Cumbria received a combined total of 3.23 million visits from UK and overseas visitors. The area continues to be one of the most popular in the UK and is inevitably showing signs of stress and wear and tear, particularly at honeypot locations such as Windermere, and throughout the Lake District National Park in general. In response to the growing pressure to mount some sort of campaign to counteract the detrimental effects of visitors, a significant amount of research has been undertaken with the subsequent result of the creation of a number of Action Groups, aiming to minimise damage to the environment.

According to 1989 figures, Cumbria's top tourist attraction was the Windermere Iron Steamboat Company, which received 572,616 visits. Next in line was Talkin Tarn Country Park, with 200,000 visits, followed by Grizedale Forest Park with 160,000. Of the top twenty attractions, nine clocked up figures of 100,000 visits or over, and only one, Levens Hall, fell below the 50,000 mark, recording 47,907 visits. Not surprisingly, the busiest season of the year for both UK and overseas visitors was the third quarter, when 29 per cent of all UK visitors came to the area and 55 per cent of overseas visitors. Perhaps what is more surprising however, is that the seasonal spread of tourism in terms of UK visitors is remarkably even, with 22, 28, 29 and 21 per cent of visits being recorded in the first to fourth quarters respectively. It seems that when other parts of the UK are desperately trying to create a more continuous tourist flow throughout the year, Cumbria has already achieved this, at least with its home market. On the overseas front, there is still some way to go, with the third quarter showing a marked rise in numbers of tourists compared to the rest of the year (between January and March only 8 per cent of all visitors were here).

In financial terms, the revenue generated by tourism in this area is, of course, very considerable indeed. In 1989 UK residents spent a total of £262 million and overseas residents £34 million. The largest market comes from the North-West, where residents are obviously keen to make the most of the attractions on their doorstep, while the largest overseas market comes from the USA, which accounts for 26 per cent of all overseas visitors to the area, followed by Australia at 13 per cent.

The general conclusion, therefore, is that visitors would do well to consider Cumbria as a holiday destination at times other than the summer period. Given the continuity of visits by UK residents throughout the year, the area's infrastructure would seem to be such that even out of high summer season, Cumbria still has much to offer. Although this applies equally to overseas visitors, the problem becomes slightly more complex given the fact that few tourists from abroad, particularly from the USA and Australia, will be visiting Britain for the sole purpose of seeing Cumbria. Unless the infrastructure throughout the whole of the UK is such that low-season attractions can be made equally as appealing as high season ones, the seasonal spread of overseas vistors is unlikely to become more even.

Good Alternatives

Meeting People

Meeting the locals around Cumbria should be fairly easy, as long as visitors can discern between who is a tourist and who is a local. One of the most straightforward ways is offered at the village of Broughton-on-Furness, which is a participant in the growing scheme run by the **Country Village Weekend Breaks** organisation (address page 405). Visitors are invited to immerse themselves in village life for a weekend, staying at a local bed and breakfast, having dinner in a local restaurant, going on tours of the town and surrounding area with a local guide, and enjoying an introduction to the area's flora and fauna with a local author and naturalist. Direct contact can be made by calling either of the village co-ordinators, Anne Shepherd (Tel 0229 716676) or Audrey Dawson (Tel 0229 716224).

Local festivals and events are always good for meeting people, and there are many throughout the year. Everything from jazz evenings to furniture restoration demonstrations are included in the South Lakeland's *What's On and Leisure Guide*, available from the Cumbria Tourist Board. Smaller pamphlets are also available detailing specific town events, as in the *Events Around Allerdale Guide*.

In terms of finding places yourself, look out for Cumbria's many local pubs, often full of character (and characters) and bursting with local news. As in the rest of Britain, 'the pub' is very much a focal point where locals gather simply to enjoy the company, and where the attitude more often than not is simply 'the more the merrier'.

Discovering Places

Walking around the area is a good way of finding those little nooks and crannies often overlooked by visitors. Check with Tourist Information for details of any 'off the beaten track-type' places worth exploring.

Visitors to East Cumbria would be well advised to contact the **East Cumbria Countryside Project**, Unit 2C, The Old Mill, Warwick Bridge, Carlisle CA4 8RR (Tel 0228 61601) which has been set up to 'look after the land for the benefit not only of ourselves, but, more importantly, for future generations'. Covering an area from north of Longtown to south of Kirkby Stephen, the organisation is involved in conserving landscape and wildlife, from farm woodlands and hedgerows to large Areas of Outstanding Natural Beauty, and seeks to maximise the possibilities for enjoying the countryside without damaging the environment. This organisation is also a good starting point for meeting people.

In West Cumbria a similar organisation has been set up which is also worth contacting, as information is available about the best places to go to get away from the crowds, particularly in respect of areas which are able to cope with increased tourist numbers. Contact the **West Cumbria Tourism Initiative**, Thirlmere Building, Lakes Road, Derwent Howe, Workington CA14 3YP (Tel 0900 65656).

Final mention should be given to the **Lord Inglewood Conservation Award**, set up in 1990 by the Cumbria Tourist Board in memory of its first president, Lord Inglewood. Nominations were invited from around the county for tourism projects which have contributed most to the conservation of Cumbria's environment and heritage. In 1990 the winner was **Priest's Mill** at Caldbeck, which was originally built as a corn mill in 1703, but was derelict when acquired by Coryn Clarke in 1984. Over the past seven years the mill has been restored to working order and the buildings have been converted into a restaurant, craft workshops, museums on rural industry and gift and bookshops. Fifteen people are now employed at the mill, most of them from the immediate locality.

A parallel award, the Lady Inglewood Training Award, was presented to the **Glenridding Hotel** in Ullswater, where the training strategy had resulted in increased business turnover. Judges had also been particularly impressed by the hotel's staff appraisal system, along with the level of commitment made to training and the financial investment made by the owners, John and Doreen Melling.

Other projects which were nominated for the awards were the **Cistercian Way**, a 33 mile (53 km.) recreational walking route along existing public rights of way in the Furness area, which links several monastic sites and highlights the Furness area as a suitable place for gentle walking; **Fell End Barn**, at Thownthwaite Farm near Broughton, where a disused field barn has been converted to provide inexpensive, basic accommodation for walkers and climbers, subsequently bringing additional revenue to the farm business, and **Longlands**, on the outskirts of Cartmel. This was an 18th-century country house and adjoining outbuildings which have been converted to provide eight holiday cottages, a restaurant with small conference facilities and a family home. Virtually all the work was carried out by skilled local craftsmen and, in addition, the walled garden which has been saved from the weeds now provides pleasure and fresh produce for the guests and owners. Many other projects were also put forward for the awards, and all of them are places worth discovering, particularly given that these really are areas of the tourist industry instigated, executed and run by the locals. Contact the **Cumbria Tourist Board**, Ashleigh, Holly Road, Windermere LA23 2AQ (Tel 09662 4444).

Communications

How to Get There

RAIL: Connections between Cumbria and the rest of the country are good. InterCity trains run between London (Euston) and Windermere (via Oxenholme station in Kendal), Penrith and Carlisle, taking less than four hours. From Edinburgh the journey takes under two hours. Good services also operate between Newcastle and

Carlisle, while travellers from Yorkshire have the added bonus of the Settle-Carlisle railway, one of the most scenic routes in Britain. Also attractive is the route between Lancaster and Carlisle along the west coast. Train information is obtainable from British Rail at Carlisle (Tel 0228 44711).

COACH: **National Express** run coaches from London to Cumbria at cheaper prices than British Rail, but the journey takes almost twice the time and services are somewhat infrequent. Information is available from the Carlisle office (Tel 0228 48484).

Mountain Goat Bus (Tel 09662 5161) runs from York to Keswick, stopping at Skipton, Settle, Ingleton and Windermere.

When You're There

RAIL: British Rail services around the area are good, and there are frequent trains down the Carlisle–Barrow route. Also worth noting is the **Lakeside and Haverthwaite Railway** (Tel 05395 31594) which runs a steam train through the scenic Leven River Valley between April and October. Also available is the **Ravenglass and Eskdale Railway** (Tel 0229 717171), England's oldest and narrowest narrow-gauge railway.

BUS: Bus services around the area are frequent and efficient. **Cumberland Motor Services** (Tel 0228 48484) operate a good network, as do **Ribble Bus** (Tel 0539 33221). **Mountain Goat Bus** (Tel 09662 5161) services are particularly useful for reaching the less accessible parts of the area, while **Fellbus** (Tel 0596 72403) operate a route between Keswick and Seatoller.

CAR: Driving in the area may well offer the flexibility afforded by independent travel, but given the comprehensive public transport system, visitors might well consider leaving the car behind. Although roads are good, they are also extremely busy during the summer and can be treacherous during the winter.

BOAT: Boat trips on the Lakes are always a popular pastime, but their value should not be forgotten as a valid means of transport. Tourist Information offices carry full details of excursions and trips.

CYCLING: The **Cumbria Cycle Way** is a 259 mile (417 km.) round trip exploring the whole of the county. It is well worth looking into and details can be obtained from Tourist Information centres.

WALKING: This is one of the area's major pastimes, either in the country or in towns. Guided walks are offered around all the major towns and a number of companies specialise in walking holidays. Tourist Information centres carry full details of what is available.

274 The Good Tourist in the UK

Useful Local Contacts

The **Cumbria Wildlife Trust,** 22 Church Street, Ambleside LA22 0BU (Tel 05394 32476), which also includes the **Cumbria Trust for Nature Conservation** and **Cumbria Urban Wildlife Project,** is an excellent starting point for the Good Tourist. Also worth contacting are the **Association of Natural History Societies in Cumbria,** 5 Standings Rise, Whitehaven CA28 6SX (Tel 0946 3668) and the **Cumbria Countryside Conference,** 6 West Walls, Carlisle. The **Cumbria Bridleways Society,** Spigot House, Crook, Kendal LA8 8LJ is a good contact for walkers, while the **Groundwork Trust** has a West Cumbria office at The Old Flour Mill, Cragg Road, Cleate Moor CA25 5PT (Tel 0946 813088).

Geographical Breakdown of Region

Carlisle and the North

Lying on the River Eden roughly nine miles (14 km.) south of the Scottish border, Carlisle is a city steeped in history. It was a Roman station of some importance and even after the departure of the Romans in 383, it still dominated the area. Subsequently destroyed by Norse invaders, it was restored by the Norman-English King William Rufus in 1092, who initiated the building of the **castle** and the town walls. Carlisle's **cathedral**, begun in 1123 as a Norman church, is the second smallest in England. Between the castle and cathedral stands **Tullie House**, a museum and art gallery which contains Roman and prehistoric relics, as well as English porcelain and pre-Raphaelite paintings. The **Guildhall**, a splendidly-renovated early 15th-century timbered building, is found in Greenmarket and contains displays of guild, civic and local history. Another museum of note is housed in **Queen Mary's Tower** in the castle, the **Border Regiment and King's Own Royal Border Regiment Museum**, which offers exhibitions about 300 years of regimental history.

The area around Carlisle has stretches of forestry, but is mainly sheep and cattle country. There are many tiny hamlets and villages dotted around the unspoiled region to the north of Carlisle and below the Scottish border. **Wetheral** to the east is an attractive village, where peaceful walks can be enjoyed along the banks of the Eden. In the local church there are also sculptures by Joseph Nollekens.

Brampton lies in the Irthing Valley to the north-east of Carlisle and has been a market town since the 13th century. In the market place there is a Georgian **Moot Hall** and, outside it, the town **stocks**. After Bonnie Prince Charlie's defeat at Culloden, six of his supporters were hanged on the **Capon Tree** at Brampton; a memorial still remains. Two miles (3 km.) north-east of Brampton lies **Naworth Castle**, the seat of the Earl of Carlisle. This is a historic border fortress which was built by the Dacres in the 14th century and acquired by the Howard family 300 years later. Its Great Hall houses Gobelin tapestries, and of particular note are Lord William's Tower, the pre-Raphaelite library and the original 14th-century dungeons.

Nearby is **Lanercost Priory**. Built in 1169 with stones from Hadrian's Wall, much of the priory still stands, in spite of the fact that it was damaged many times during the Border Wars. The road from here to **Birdoswald** offers a glimpse of the Roman **Hadrian's Wall**. Just south of Brampton can be found **Talkin Tarn Country Park**, which boasts 183 acres (74 hectares) of woodland, open space and water in a beautiful setting at the foot of the North Pennines. Its many attractions include nature trails, coarse fishing, rowing boats for hire, sailing and windsurfing.

Eighteen miles (28 km.) south of Carlisle, the busy market town of **Penrith** is situated at the foot of **Penrith Beacon** (937 feet, 286 m.) at the junction of the M6 and A66. The Beacon itself is worth a visit for the views it offers of the Lakeland fells. In the 14th century **Penrith Castle** was built as a defence against Scottish raiders and was ruined during the Civil War in the mid-17th century. **St Andrew's Parish Church** is of Norman foundation, with a 13th-century tower, although the main body of the building dates from the 18th century.

One mile (1.5 km.) south-east of Penrith is one of the finest ruins in Cumbria, **Brougham Castle**. Situated by the River Eamont and close to the Roman fort of Brocavum, it was originally built in the 12th century as a moated Norman keep. During the Civil War it suffered along with many others, but was subsequently rebuilt at the instigation of Lady Anne Clifford in the 17th century, as the ancestral seat of her family. Today it is once more a ruin, but the impressive remains include a small keep, complete with a spiral staircase to the top, from where there are fine views. The tombs of the Clifford family are contained in **St Lawrence's Church** at **Appleby** (see below), where there is also a monument dedicated to Lady Anne.

A little further east on the A66 is the village of **Temple Sowerby**, where the National Trust Gardens at **Acorn Bank** offer a good display of wild plants and herbs. Another five miles (8 km.) along the road is **Appleby**, once the county town of Westmorland. Despite the changing of boundaries, it is still an important market town and Royal Borough, with charters dating from 1174. Its horse fair in June is always a popular event with gypsies, who gather from miles around. Situated beside the River Eden and on the Settle to Carlisle railway route, Appleby has an interesting castle and many old buildings. William the Lion of Scotland is said to have built the great **Norman keep** of the castle in the 12th century, and the grounds provide a tranquil riverside setting for a **Conservation Centre**. Rare breeds of British farm animals and unusual birds can be found here.

From Appleby, the road continues to **Brough**, which was a major coaching town in days gone by. It has had a market charter since 1331 and **Brough Castle** ruins are well worth a visit. They consist of the remains of a Norman keep and domestic buildings, which were built on the site of a Roman camp. It was originally one of William Rufus of England's royal castles but William the Lion later destroyed much of it. In 1660 however, Lady Anne Clifford came to the rescue once again and restored it. In mid-June, Brough hosts the Hound and Terrier Show, which features classes of hounds, terriers, gun dogs and beagles.

A few miles south of Brough on the Kirkby Stephen road lies the quiet village of **Winton**, which is the home of **Langrigg Pottery**. A wide range of stoneware is produced, from cooking pots and tableware to decorative plates and vases.

The small market town of **Kirkby Stephen** lies close to the River Eden and has an attractive market square, once used for bull-baiting. The **Cloisters**, now a butter market, were built in 1810 and stand between the church and the market place. The **Cathedral of the Dale**, St Stephen's Church, has an interesting 16th-century tower and, in the churchyard, the **Trupp Stone**, where money was given over in place of tithes. At **Crossfield Mill** is the Heredities Shop – the first people to commercially adapt the cold cast bronze to make figurines. Their showroom in Kirkby Stephen has a photographic storyboard showing the process, and discontinued lines and seconds can be purchased. Near Kirkby Stephen is **Pendragon Castle**, built in the 12th century, pillaged by the Scots in the 14th, and restored by the ever-faithful Lady Anne Clifford in the 17th. It is reputed to have been the home of Uther Pendragon, father of King Arthur.

Beyond Kirkby Stephen the road turns west through **Soulby** and **Orton** to **Crosby Ravensworth**. This village, in the vale of

Lyvennet, is an attractive peaceful settlement with a magnificent Norman church. High above the village stands a monument which was erected to commemorate King Charles II, who camped here in 1651.

A few miles westward lies **Shap** village at almost 1000 feet (305 m.) above sea level and, consequently, enjoying the finest of views across the fells. To the west of the village are the ruins of the 12th-century **Shap Abbey**, with its 90 foot (27 m.) nave and 16th-century tower.

Travelling northward from Shap, **Lowther Park** and the ruined **Lowther Castle** are situated four miles (6 km.) south of Penrith. The grounds offer an adventure park with miniature trains, boating, a 'Tarzan trail assault course' and many other attractions for a good family day out. Just outside Penrith to the south is **Eamont Bridge**, the site of King Arthur's Round Table and **Mayburgh Henge**. These early Bronze Age henge monuments remain a historical mystery.

For an alternative day out from Penrith, it is worth visiting **Alston** (on the A686), England's highest market town, with cobbled streets and its own narrow-gauge railway.

Accommodation

First Class

Farlan Hall Hotel, Hallbangate, Brampton (Tel 06976 234). Delightful family run hotel, partly dating from the 17th century. Set in large gardens, the house offers luxurious accommodation.

String of Horses Inn, Faugh, Carlisle CA4 9EG (Tel 0228 70297). Seventeenth-century country inn offering comfortable accommodation and a renowned restaurant. Leisure centre and outdoor heated pool also available.

Crosby Lodge, Crosby on Eden, near Carlisle (Tel 0228 73618). Secluded country mansion in extensive gardens. Antique beds in some rooms.

Middle Range

Lovelady Shield Country House Hotel, Nenthead Road, near Alston CA9 3LF (Tel 0434 381203). Comfortable Georgian house in lovely gardens high in the Pennines. Excellent cuisine using local produce.

Appleby Manor Country House Hotel, Roman Road, Appleby-in-Westmorland CA16 6JD (Tel 07683 51571). Delightful traditional hotel combined with indoor leisure club, offering a good base for a family holiday.

George Hotel, Devonshire Street, Penrith CA11 7SU (Tel 0768 62696). Privately owned old coaching inn with antique furniture and modern amenities. Convenient for the lakes and the Roman wall.

Economy

Bessiestown Farm, Cutlowdy, Penton, Carlisle CA6 5QP (Tel 022877 219). Award-winning farm with home cooking and residential licence. Also has an indoor heated pool.

Woodland House Hotel, Wordsworth Street, Penrith CA11 7QY (Tel 0768 64177). Elegant and spacious house at the foot of Beacon Hill. Wonderful library of books, maps and pamphlets for the benefit of the visitor. No smoking.

Prospect Hill Hotel, Kirkoswald, near Penrith CA10 1ER (Tel 076883 500). An attractively-converted group of 18th-century farm buildings set in the Eden Valley. A good value hotel offering the best of traditional living.

Wetheriggs Pottery, Clifton Dykes, Penrith CA10 2DH (Tel 0768 62946). This is a guest house and unique working Victorian pottery with beehive kiln. There is also a licensed restaurant and coffee shop.

Eating Out

First Class

The Courtfield Hotel, Bongate, Appleby (Tel 07683 51394). Converted vicarage offering traditional English fare at its best.

Middle Range

Crown Hotel, Wetheral, near Carlisle (Tel 0228 61888). Popular village pub in a Grade II listed building, serving nouvelle English cuisine.

Royal Oak, Bongate, Appleby (Tel 07683 51463). Highly-rated stone-built pub, offering both local and international dishes.

Economy

Shepherd's Inn, Langwathby, near Penrith (Tel 076881 217). Converted beamed barn serving both local and more exotic specialities. Vegetarians catered for.

Old Forge Bistro, 39 North Road, Kirkby Stephen (Tel 07683 71832). Small restaurant serving vegetarian and traditional fare.

Kendal and the South

Travelling south on the A6 from Shap, the thriving market town of **Kendal** is situated on the very edge of the Lake District National park. The town offers plenty to see and do and has excellent shopping facilities. Kendal's history can be traced throughout the town, from the Gothic five-aisled **Parish Church** in Kirkland to the ruined 14th-century **castle**, birthplace in 1510 of Katherine Parr, King Henry VIII's sixth and last wife. In the 14th century Flemish weavers settled in the town and established a successful wool industry, which lasted over 600 years. The **Lakeland Life and Industry Museum** reflects this trade and also has a good collection of farming memorabilia, while the **Arthur Ransome room** here depicts the life of this popular children's author. The **Abbot Hall and Art Gallery** next door houses paintings by Turner, Romney and Reynolds.

Webb's Garden Centre, home of the world famous Webb's Wonder lettuce, is found at Burneside Road, Kendal. There are acres of gardens in which to wander and thousands of plants for those with green fingers. **Levens Hall**, a few miles outside the town, is the magnificent Elizabethan home of the Bagot family. It has a famous topiary garden which was laid out in 1692 by Monsieur de Beaumont, and which is said to be haunted by three ghosts: a pink lady, a black dog and a grey lady. The National Trust's **Sizergh Castle** near Kendal reflects the history of Cumbria since the reign of Edward III. There are particularly fine Elizabethan wood carvings and a very colourful garden.

Leaving Kendal and travelling east, **Killington Reservoir** is on the right, and a few miles beyond lies **Sedbergh**, an attractive old town in the Yorkshire Dales National Park. The town has a famous public school founded in 1552 and the **Brigflatts Quaker Meeting House**, which was once used by the founder of the movement, George Fox. Just outside Sedbergh, **Farfield Mill** is the site of **Pennine Tweeds**. This is a working Victorian mill with a wide range of products, including exclusive wool tweed and mohair fabric. **Holme Farm**, also near Sedbergh, is a traditional Dales working farm with nature trails, including foxholes and a protected badger set. Holding and feeding baby animals is part of the guided tour around the farm and there are seasonal demonstrations of milling, shearing and sheepdog working.

South-east of Sedbergh along the valley of the River Dee, the tiny village of **Dent** has attractive cobblestone streets. This area is very popular with cavers and fell walkers. Not far from Dent runs the **Settle to Carlisle railway**, probably the most scenic line in England, which crosses high viaducts and wild expanses of moorland such as **Mallerstang Common**.

Barbon lies south-west of Dent, with **Kirkby Lonsdale** beyond. This is a busy little market town set in the superb scenery of the Lune Valley. The poet John Ruskin was inspired by the view across the River Lune, calling it 'one of the loveliest scenes in England and therefore the world'. At the beginning of September a Victorian Fair is held with a traditional street market and entertainment. Stallholders who fail to appear in Victorian dress may be fined. The **Cumbria Cycle Way** passes through Kirkby Lonsdale following its circular route and reaching parts of Cumbria rarely visited by tourists.

Along the southern boundaries of Cumbria lie three peninsulas and the estuaries of the Duddon, Crake, Levens and Kent rivers. On the most westerly peninsula is the small industrial town of **Millom**. This is ironstone mining country and Millom itself offers a **Folk Museum**, where there are fascinating exhibits with a full-scale reconstruction of a drift at **Hodbarrow Iron Ore Mine**. It also displays agricultural bygones as well as replicas of a blacksmith's forge and a miner's cottage kitchen.

Continuing round the coast, **Broughton-on-Furness** is situated on the Furness Peninsula. Overlooked by **Broughton Tower**, where there is the keep of a once substantial Norman castle, Broughton is an attractive town. To the south **Dalton-in-Furness** offers **Dalton Castle**, a 14th-century pele tower that contains a small museum, and **Tytup Hall**, a small Queen Anne house with original wood panelling and a Victorian-style greenhouse in the gardens. Dalton was the birthplace of the painter George Romney in 1734 and has an ornate drinking fountain in the market square.

Walney Island, part of which is a nature reserve, lies off the tip of the peninsula. Nearby, on the tiny **Piel Island**, are the remains of a **castle** used by the monks of Furness Abbey. The dramatic remains of the abbey itself, which was founded in 1123 by Stephen (later King of England), are romantically set in **The Vale of Deadly Nightshade**, an attractive wooded valley.

Barrow-in-Furness is an industrial port and shipbuilding centre. The 19th-century red sandstone **Town Hall** is the subject of considerable civic pride. The **Dock** is a new and exciting industrial maritime museum which is due to open in the early 1990s. Constructed within a Victorian ship repair dock, it will bring to life the story of steel shipbuilding. **Furness Museum** in Ramsden Square exhibits a collection of local ship models and Stone, Bronze and Iron Age relics. A little further round the coast is **Rampside** and nearby, **Ria Island** at the end of the causeway. This is the departure point for the boat crossing to Piel Island.

Bardsea Country Park is slightly further up the road, as is **Conishead Priory**, which is now a Tibetan Buddhist study centre. **Ulverston** is a bustling market town and was a port until the reclamation of land put it several miles inland. The comedien Stan Laurel was born here and there is an entertaining **Laurel and Hardy Museum**. Sir John Barrow (1764–1848), who was Under-Secretary at the Admiralty for over 40 years and a founder member of the Royal Geographic Society, is commemorated by a monument on nearby **Hoad Hill**, which is a replica of the Eddystone Lighthouse. George Fox, founder of the Quaker movement, lived at **Swarthmoor Hall**, a substantial Elizabethan house. A few miles outside Ulverston stands the **Stott Park Bobbin Mill**. Built in 1835 and virtually unchanged for 150 years, this mill has been restored as a working industrial monument – a turbine and steam engine still remain. At **Newby Bridge** near Ulverston lies **Fell Foot Park**, which contains 18 acres (7.3 hectares) of country park and offers a bathing area, fishing, sailing, adventure playground and National Trust information centre.

Finally, the Cartmel peninsula is the site of **Cartmel village**. Here there are many charming old cottages, although a warning should be heeded about trying to cross the estuary between tides: in the cemetery are the graves of those who tried and failed. It should not be attempted without a guide. **Cartmel Priory** was founded in 1188 as an Augustinian monastery and survived the Dissolution. It is architecturally interesting with its distinctive towers set diagonally to one another, and offers examples of 15th-century glass.

Just outside Cartmel is an attractive little racecourse known as **Cartmel Steeplechases**. It is situated in wooded parkland with the tower of Cartmel Priory and the hills bordering the Lake District as a backdrop. North of Cartmel is the **Cartmel Craft Centre**, with its resident print maker, wood turner, artist, fabric printer, potter and cane restorer keen to display their talents.

Grange-over-Sands on the west side of the Cartmel Peninsula is a popular seaside resort and combines with **Arnside**, on the opposite edge of the bay, to form what is affectionately known as Cumbria's Riviera. A few miles west at **Cark-in-Cartmel** is the **Lakeland Motor Museum**, displaying historic cars, tractors, motor and pedal cycles.

There is also a large collection of automobilia, including car badges, mascots, enamel signs and posters.

Accommodation

Middle Range

Hipping Hall, Cowan Bridge, Kirkby Lonsdale LA6 2JJ (Tel 05242 71187). Handsome 17th-century country house set in beautiful gardens between the Dales and the Lakes.

Whitewater Hotel, The Lakeland Village, Newby Bridge LA12 8PX (Tel 05395 31133). Pleasant hotel in a picturesque setting on the banks of the River Leven. Guests have free membership of the leisure club, with swimming pool, whirlpool, tennis and squash.

Uplands, Haggs Lane, Cartmel LA11 6HD (Tel 044854 248). Intimate turn-of-the-century country house hotel with just four bedrooms (all double), set in its own gardens and offering magnificent views over Morecombe Bay.

The Old Vicarage, Witherslack, near Grange-over-Sands LA11 6RS (Tel 044852 381). Peace and quiet in a Georgian vicarage set in five acres (2 hectares) of grounds.

Aynsome Manor Hotel, Cartmel, Grange-over-Sands LA11 6HH (Tel 05395 36653). Interesting 16th-century manor house with a cobbled courtyard. This is a family run hotel with magnificent public rooms and comfortable, traditional bedrooms.

Economy

Millers Beck, near Stainton, Kendal LA8 0DU (Tel 05395 60877). Converted 17th-century corn mill retaining many of its interesting features, combining old world charm with modern amenities.

Cobblers Cottage, Griffin Street, Broughton-in-Furness LA20 6HH (Tel 0229 716413). Seventeenth-century oak-beamed cottage situated in one of the quieter areas of the Lake District.

Stonegate Guest House, The Promenade, Arnside LA5 0AA (Tel 0524 761171). Beautiful Victorian house overlooking the Kent estuary. Of particular interest to ornithologists and fishermen.

Eating Out

First Class

Swan Hotel, Newby Bridge, near Ulverston (Tel 05395 31681). The Tithe Barn Restaurant and adjoining cocktail bar provide a pleasing venue for Sunday lunch in particular. The Mailcoach Wine Bar serves a more informal meal.

The Wild Boar, Crook, near Kendal (Tel 09662 5225). Seventeenth-century country house hotel with a popular and acclaimed restaurant, serving British cuisine.

Middle Range

Fat Lamb Country Inn, Newbiggin-on-Lune (Tel 05873 242). Imaginative range of restaurant meals or bar snacks beside the old kitchen range.

Bay Horse Inn, Canal Foot, Ulverston (Tel 02295 3972). Friendly inn making good use of local produce and offering marvellous views over Morecombe Bay.

Lupton Tower Vegetarian Country House, Lupton, Kirkby Lonsdale (Tel 04487 400). Mid-18th-century country house hotel with an innovative vegetarian restaurant.

Economy

At Home, Dunum House, Main Street, Grange-over-Sands (Tel 05395 34400). Popular with local residents and serving no-nonsense traditional food.

Copper Kettle, Kirkby Lonsdale (Tel 05242 71714). Varied menu of tasty and home-cooked meals prepared by the resident proprietors.

The Lake District National Park

History of the Park

The Lake District became a National Park in 1951, designated by Act of Parliament. It is administered by the Lake District Special Planning Board, an autonomous local government body commonly known as the National Park Authority (NPA), and combining the planning powers of District and County Councils. The Board consists of members appointed by Cumbria County Council, the Secretary of State for the Environment and District Councils who have territory in the Park.

With an area of 885 square miles (2292 sq. km.), the Park occupies the central part of Cumbria, constituting one third of the region's total area. The resident population (1981 census) was 40,674; the largest settlements being Windermere (5647), Keswick (4762), Ambleside (2671) and Bowness (1648). From London along the M1 and M6 motorways to the Lakes is roughly 300 miles (482 km.).

The Lake District is a compact area with scenery of incomparable beauty, including the highest mountains in England, together with some 60 lakes and tarns. Until the 18th century, travel in the area was mainly by packhorse through passes such as **Kirkstone** with its isolated inn, now served by minibus in the summer.

The largest of the lakes is **Windermere**, over 10 miles (15 km.) long, almost one mile wide (1.5 km.) and 204 feet (62 m.) deep, extending from Ambleside to Newby Bridge. Next in size is **Ullswater**, stretching from Pooley Bridge to Patterdale, followed by **Bassenthwaite** to the north and **Derwentwater** to the south of the important Lakeland centre of Keswick. For remote grandeur, **Ennerdale Water**, reached from Ennerdale Bridge, and **Wast Water**, with the road to the lowly **Wasdale Head** are unsurpassed.

Whilst much of the natural woodland which once covered all but the peaks of the area has mostly disappeared, in places remnants of oak/birch woodlands with hawthorn, hazel, holly and rowan remain. Even in the severe exposure of mountain tops, dwarf willow only one inch (2.5 cm) high, bearing minute catkins one tenth of an inch (2.5 mm) long, can be found in rocky crevices. Around the lime-rich perimeter, yew, whitebeam and lily-of-the-valley flourish beneath a canopy of ash. There has also been a considerable amount of planting of exotic conifer trees though the Forestry Commission is now aware of the need to have such plantations integrated into the landscape.

Wildlife attracted to the woodlands includes red deer, badger, red squirrel, fox and pine marten, although the latter two can also be found on the higher rocky slopes. Tree pipit, woodcock, pied flycatcher, wood warbler and redstart inhabit the broad-leafed woodlands, with wagtail and sandpiper in the vicinity of water. Mallard, teal and tufted duck breed around the lakes. Whilst gulls abound the most striking winter visitor is the wild whooper swan and the occasional Bewick.

Keswick

Situated on the River Greta by Derwentwater, with Bassenthwaite overlooked by Skiddaw to the northwest, Keswick provides the ideal northern starting point for a visit to the Lakes. Originally a small market town, it boasts a **one-handed clock** built in 1813, while the **museum** contains a model of the Lake District and relics of the author **Hugh Walpole. Coleridge** and **Southey** lived at **Greta Hall** and **Shelley** also stayed in the town. Southey is buried in the churchyard of the 11th-century **parish church. Castlehead** and **Friars Crag** with Ruskin's memorial are notable viewpoints.

Keswick **Tourist Information** is at the Moot Hall, Market Square (Tel 07687 72645).

Southwards from Keswick lies **Borrowdale**, arguably the most beautiful valley in the Lake District. **Lodore Falls** are located at the southern extremity of Derwentwater and a short distance further on is the curious **Bowder Stone**, balanced precariously on edge following a fall from nearby heights in ages past. There are magnificent mountain views from **Rosthwaite**, and by **Seatoller** is **Scathwaite Farm**, the wettest inhabited place in England, overshadowed by **Great Gable** (2949 feet, 900 m.) and **Pillar Rock** (2927 feet, 893 m.), where the annual rainfall is around 180 inches (4572 mm)! Over the **Honister Pass**, which reaches a height of 1000 feet (305 m.), lie **Buttermere** and **Crummock Water**.

Keswick to Ambleside

From Keswick the A591 leads southwards along **Thirlemere**. With **Helvellyn** rising to the east, the road reaches **Dunmail Raise**, the 'loveliest spot that man hath ever found', according to **William Wordsworth**, forever associated with this area; he lies buried in the churchyard at Grasmere. **Dove Cottage**, the poet's home from 1799 to 1813 (with the adjoining **Wordsworth Exhibition** building) and **Rydal Mount**, where he subsequently lived until his death in 1850, are both open to the public. **Grasmere**, which lies on an old pack horse route to Whitehaven, is the home of Grasmere gingerbread, made locally to a secret recipe. The local sports, held annually on the Thursday nearest to 20 August, feature Cumberland and Westmorland wrestling, fell races and hound trailing. Also in August, as in many lakeland towns, children take part in the rushbearing ceremony in the **church**, which has a 14th-century tower.

Ambleside

On past **Rydal Water**, the A591 leads to Ambleside at the head of Lake Windermere. Here, recollections of Wordsworth are rekindled by a memorial window in **St Mary's Church**, and amongst the many National Trust properties in the town is **Bridge House**, an intriguing little building spanning **Stock Beck. Stock Ghyll**, a fine waterfall, is just to the east.

Ambleside to Windermere

From Ambleside, the main A591 continues to Windermere, passing **Brockhole** National Park Visitor Centre (Tel 09662 6601), the main headquarters of the National Park. An attractive country house, it offers beautiful gardens and numerous exhibitions and events.

Alternatively, the A593 leading westwards provides a less direct route to Windermere. Shortly after leaving Ambleside, there is the option of taking the minor road which climbs to **Wrynose Pass** and on to the tortuous **Hard Knot** pass, before continuing to **Eskdale** and the west coast. Drivers should be warned that this route is not for the faint-hearted.

For those in search of an easier time, continue on the A593 to **Coniston**. Lying at the foot of the **Old Man of Coniston** (2633 feet, 803 m.) and at the north-west extremity of **Coniston Water**, this charming village has many artistic associations, not least of which being the inspiration it provided for a painting by Turner, which is now in the Tate Gallery in London. **John Ruskin**, buried in the churchyard, produced much of his finest work at his home, **Brantwood**, from 1871 onwards. He is celebrated in the **Ruskin Museum**. **Tennyson** stayed at **Tent Lodge**, while more recently in 1939, Sir Malcolm Campbell established a world water-speed record of 141 miles per hour (226 kph) in his boat *Bluebird*. Sadly, after setting four world records, his son Donald died on Coniston Water in 1967 during his attempt to set a new record. There are many National Trust properties in this area, which is also a centre for watersports; hiring facilities exist for launches, rowing boats, sailing dinghies and canoes. Windsurfing and bathing are popular.

Westwards around the head of Coniston Water is **Hawkshead**, a quaint little village where there is a 16th-century church and an old grammar school, originally founded in 1585 and attended by Wordsworth between 1779 and 1783. During his pupilage he is thought to have lodged at **Ann Tyson's Cottage**, off Red Lion Square.

South-west of Hawkshead lies **Esthwaite Water** and the villages of **Near** and **Far Sawrey**. The former is the location of **Hill Top**, a 17th-century farm which was the home of Mrs Heelis, otherwise known as **Beatrix Potter**. This famed children's author and originator of the Peter Rabbit classics, illustrated her books with drawings and watercolours of the surrounding hills and lakes. On her death in 1943 she bequeathed the whole of her property, extending to 4000 acres (1620 hectares) to the National Trust.

Windermere

The quickest way to Windermere from Far Sawrey is by means of the **car ferry** which crosses to the east side of Lake Windermere, from where it is a short drive up to Bowness and on to the town of Windermere itself. Lake Windermere is an island-studded lake and the largest in England. The Windermere/Bowness area is the centre of tourism in the Lake District, with a wide range of recreational activities on offer. During the holiday season **steamer trips** operate along the length of the Lake and connect with the **Lakeside and Haverthwaite Steam Railway**, offering a three mile (5 km.) trip through the valley of the River Leven. Just north of Bowness is the **Windermere Steamboat Museum**, with a fine collection of Victorian and Edwardian steam launches, occasionally seen puffing their way around the lake. **Power boat races** (a subject of some controversy) are held on the lake, with the biggest grand prix taking place in October. Well-greased swimmers take part in the Windermere swim, the length of the lake, in late summer. Although views of the lake from the town are difficult to find, the nearby countryside offers many viewpoints, including a short walk up **Orrest Hill** to the east.

Accommodation

First Class

Wordsworth Hotel, Grasmere LA22 9SW (Tel 09665 592). Luxurious hotel with attentive service and fine cuisine. Peace and quiet in beautiful surroundings.

Sharrow Bay, Ullswater, Penrith CA10 2LZ (Tel 08536 301). Winner of many awards, reputedly one of the best country house hotels in England. Comfort, cuisine and setting are all superb.

Armathwaite Hall, Bassenthwaite Lake, Keswick CA12 4RG (Tel 059681 551). Situated on the edge of the lake, this hotel offers fine food, opulent surroundings and a position of great natural beauty. Leisure club with a wide range of facilities also available.

Langsdale Chase Hotel, Windermere LA23 1LW (Tel 05394 32201). Situated in delightful grounds, and complete with an elegant restaurant. A chance to immerse yourself in gracious living.

Middle Range

Kirkstone Fort Hotel, Kirkstone Pass Road, Ambleside LA22 9EH (Tel 05294 32232). Excellent cuisine and convivial atmosphere at this hotel, set in secluded gardens.

Hallbeck Ghyll Country House Hotel, Hallbeck Lane, Windermere LA23 1LV (Tel 05394 32375). Nineteenth-century manor house overlooking the lake and offering excellent cuisine and warm hospitality.

Dalehead Hall Lakeside Hotel, Thirlmere, Keswick CA12 4TN

(Tel 07687 72478). Dating from 1557, charming lakeside hotel set in lovely gardens. Four-poster beds in some rooms.

Waterhead Hotel, Lake Road, Ambleside LA22 0ER (Tel 05394 32566). All home comforts and fine food overlooking the lake. Guests have free membership of the leisure club nearby.

Economy

Riverside Hotel, Under Loughrigg, Ambleside LA22 9LJ (Tel 05394 32395). High standards of comfort and cuisine in pleasant hotel with its own river frontage.

The Drunken Duck Inn, Barngate, near Hawkshead, Ambleside LA22 0NG (Tel 09666 347). An inn of old-fashioned hospitality set in extensive grounds.

Cottage in the Wood, Whinlatter Pass, Braithwaite, near Keswick CA12 5TW (Tel 059682 409). Small 17th-century coaching inn at the top of the pass, with superb views.

The Old Rectory Hotel, Torver, Coniston LA21 8AX (Tel 05394 41353). Country house hotel in secluded gardens close to the lake shore. Renowned for its imaginative cooking.

Eating Out

First Class

Fisherbeck Hotel, Lake Road, Ambleside (Tel 05394 33215). Attractive family run hotel, serving superb food and fine wines. Situated between the village and lake.

Rothay Garth Hotel, Rothay Road, Ambleside (Tel 05394 32217). Set on the edge of the village and with a relaxed and friendly atmosphere. Highly acclaimed restaurant.

Lindeth Fell Country House Hotel, Bowness-on-Windermere (Tel 09662 3286). Country house in beautiful grounds offering excellent cordon bleu cooking.

Middle Range

The Regent Hotel, Waterhead Bay, Ambleside (Tel 05394 32254). Situated in a peaceful bay, offering an elegant George IV restaurant overlooking the courtyard and commended for its good food.

Grizedale Lodge Hotel and Restaurant in the Forest, Grizedale, Hawkshead (Tel 09666 532). Former shooting lodge in the heart of the forest. Famed for its excellent food and wines and under the personal supervision of the management.

Gilpin Lodge, Crook Road, Windermere (Tel 09662 88818). A country house hotel and restaurant set in extensive woodland and gardens.

Economy

Stampers Restaurant, Church Street, Ambleside (Tel 05394 32775). Small cellar restaurant in Old Stamp House. Good local fare.

The Yew Tree, Honister Pass, Keswick (Tel 07687 77634). Built in 1628, the restaurant boasts oak beams and slate floors. Extensive and varied menu to suit all tastes.

Baldry's, Red Lion Square, Grasmere (Tel 09665 301). Plain, functional cafe with very good food. Traditional cooking using local produce.

The West Coast

Cumbria's west coast offers a variety of entertainment, places of interest and outdoor activities to suit all tastes.

Situated on the shores of the Solway Firth and facing the southern Galloway hills, **Sulloth**, the main seaside resort of West Cumbria, is noted for its mild climate. The town was originally established as a sea port to serve Carlisle, but subsequently became more popular as a tourist resort. Its wide elegant tree-lined streets and attractive green leading to the seashore and promenade make it a favourite with visitors. One of the most testing **golf courses** is to be found here and **sea fishing** is a popular pastime. An annual event is a **carnival** held on Bank Holiday Monday (August) which is attended by both locals and tourists. **Grune Point** is a peninsula projecting into Moricambe Bay (not to be confused with Morecombe Bay). Of keen interest to the ornithologist, it is a haven for seabirds and small migratory birds. This area offers glorious sea views and sunsets fine enough to have been painted by Turner, the famous landscape artist.

A few miles north lies **Skinburness**. This old harbour, which once belonged to Holme Cultram Abbey, was the gathering place of the English fleet in 1297 when Edward I launched his attack on Scotland. By 1302 however, it had been destroyed by the sea. Nearby **Abbeytown** is the site of **Holme Cultram Abbey**, which was the second Cistercian monastery in Cumbria. Parish worship is maintained in surviving parts of the abbey, which boasts a bell cast in 1465. The little village of **Allonby** is a few miles south of Silloth. It was established in the 18th century and, later, one of its famous visitors was Charles Dickens. Travelling southward,

Maryport is built on the site of a Roman fort and was a 'planned' town in 1749. In bygone days its harbour was filled with sailing ships, many built in local yards. Nowadays the harbour is silted up but plans are afoot for a redevelopment scheme, which will see the creation of a mixed leisure, commercial and residential project to revitalise the dockland area. There are town trails and a **maritime museum** displaying pictures, models and paintings to illustrate Maryport's past.

A slight diversion inland leads to the market town of **Cockermouth**, just outside the Lake District National Park boundary. **Wordsworth House**, birthplace of the poet in 1770, is a most impressive building open to the public. It is owned by the National Trust and displays many original features. **Cockermouth Castle**, built in the 13th century, is partially ruined, but a section is still lived in by Lady Egremont. It is not open to the public. Two famous sons of the town were Fletcher Christian of *Mutiny on the Bounty* fame and John Dalton, inventor of the atomic theory. The **Cumberland Toy and Model Museum** at Banks Court features mainly British toys from around 1900 to the present day. There is an educational toy quiz and the opportunity to handle some of the old toys.

Returning to the coast, **Workington** boasts a **sports centre** and **swimming pool**, as well as the **Carnegie Theatre and Arts Centre**. This 1904 listed building contains a gallery and coffee shop, art room, theatre and bar. The **Helena Thompson Museum** has displays of costume, furniture, glass and ceramics of the 18th century. Temporary exhibitions are shown in the former stable block. In the 19th century Workington was a booming industrial centre with coal mining, iron and steel making and shipbuilding. The town has two interesting churches. The **Church of St Michael** is late 19th century, rebuilt after a fire, although a church has stood on this site since the 8th century. **St John's Church**, built in 1823, is an exact copy of St Paul's, Covent Garden. The nearby **Workington Hall** is where Mary Queen of Scots sheltered for a night in 1568 after the Battle of Langside.

To the south lies the Georgian port of **Whitehaven**. In the 18th century it was a larger port than Liverpool and ranked third in national importance. Exporting coal to Ireland and importing tobacco from Virginia was its main trade for nearly 200 years. Today, because of its unspoiled state, the whole harbour has been declared a conservation area. The **South Harbour** is less than 50 yards from the shopping area and the **West Pier**, one of the finest in Britain, was built by the famous Scottish engineer, Sir John Rennie. The port is still busy with the activity of the fishing fleet and pleasure craft. In the town, many Georgian buildings have been restored to their former glory. **Whitehaven Castle**, once the home of the Lowther family, stands in its own grounds at the entrance to the town. For the literary-minded, **Michael Moon's Bookshop and Gallery** is the largest old bookshop in Cumbria, offering a choice of around 100,000 books on a mile (1.6 km.) of shelves and with room for 100 browsers. The **Rosehill Theatre** at **Moresby**, just outside Whitehaven, presents plays, concerts, films and children's shows. The area's maritime and social history is depicted in the **Whitehaven Museum** on Lowther Street.

A few miles further south, **St Bees** is a village of historical interest and character. The splendid priory church of **St Bega**, which is on the site of a church dating from Viking times, has a great 12th-century Norman doorway. The village has many traditional elements, with its ancient green, golf course, pubs and famous old public school. The nearby **St Bees Head** is an RSPB nature reserve, with one of the largest colonies of sea birds on the west coast of Britain. These include guillemot, razorbill, kittiwake and puffin.

A few miles east lies the small town of **Egremont**. Held continuously every year since 1267, **Egremont Crab Fair** is a popular event in September. There is a parade of apple carts through the main street when apples are thrown to the public and a 30 foot (9 m.) greasy pole smeared with fat is worth a prize for anyone who is able to scale it. In the evening the **World Gurning Championship** is staged, the prize going to the person who pulls the most grotesque face! There are also sporting events and hound trails during the day.

Continuing southward, near the coast are the ruins of **Calder Abbey**, founded by the Furness Abbey monks in 1134 and ruined at the time of the Dissolution. At nearby **Gosforth** are the **Gosforth Crosses** dating from Viking times. In contrast, the 20th-century Seascale area is the site of the **Sellafield Nuclear Processing Plant**. At the visitor centre there are screen presentations, life-size working models, computer games and quizzes, all helping to tell the nuclear story.

Ravenglass, a few miles beyond, has the highest standing Roman remains in Britain at the Bath House of **Walls Castle**. It is now just a tiny village and large boats can no longer use the silted-up estuary, but it remains popular with sailing enthusiasts and sea birds. The village is the starting point for the **Ravenglass and Eskdale Railway**, which is Britain's oldest narrow gauge railway and which runs from the coast to the foot of Cumbria's highest hills.

Accommodation

First Class

Scale Hill Hotel, Loweswater, Cockermouth CA13 9UX (Tel 090085 232). Early 17th-century restored farmhouse now running as a country house hotel which has been in the same family for almost 35 years.

Skinburness Hotel, Silloth-on-Solway CA5 4QY (Tel 06973 32332). Offering luxurious English hospitality and with an enviable reputation for fine food and exceptional comfort.

Washington Central Hotel, Washington Street, Workington CA14 3AW (Tel 0900 65772). Modern hotel, traditionally furnished and offering fine cuisine.

Middle Range

Low Hall, Lorton Vale, Cockermouth CA13 0RE (Tel 0900 826654). Secluded 17th-century guest house with a real country atmosphere. Vegetarians catered for, and no smoking.

Ellenbank, Birkby, Maryport CA15 6RE (Tel 0900 815233). Family run country hotel set in lovely gardens. Cuisine to interest and delight the most discerning palate.

Golf Hotel, Criffel Street, Silloth CA5 4AB (Tel 06973 31438). Comfortable hotel with excellent food overlooking the Solway Firth. Championship golf course 150 yards away.

Economy

Holly House Hotel, Main Street, Ravenglass CA18 1FQ (Tel 0229 717230). Situated in the centre of this picturesque village, a good base for ornithologists, anglers and steam train enthusiasts.

Stanger Farm, Cockermouth CA13 9TS (Tel 0900 824222). Comfortable 16th-century small working dairy farm with private fishing and old-fashioned hospitality.

The Chase Hotel, Inkerman Terrace, Whitehaven CA28 8AA (Tel 0946 693656). Situated near the town centre and attractively set in landscaped gardens.

Eating Out

First Class

Allerdale Court Hotel, Market Place, Cockermouth (Tel 0900 823654). Architecturally interesting listed building with period furnishings and an excellent à la carte restaurant.

The Shepherd's Arms Hotel, Ennerdale Bridge (Tel 0946 861249). Traditional village hotel. Menu includes local salmon and game in season.

Middle Range

Quince and Medlar, 13 Castlegate, Cockermouth (Tel 0900 823579). Intimate restaurant serving fine vegetarian food. Winner of the Vegetarian Society's Restaurant of the Year Award 1989–90.

Seacote Hotel, Beach Road, St Bees (Tel 0946 822777). Situated next to the beach and serving table d'hote and à la carte meals.

Economy

The Red Admiral Hotel, Gosforth (Tel 09467 25222). Small family run pub serving wholesome home-cooked meals.

Crossbarrow Motel, Little Clifton (Tel 0900 61443). A family run motel standing in extensive grounds and with a popular farmhouse restaurant.

Pennington Arms, Main Street, Ravenglass (Tel 0229 717222). Family run country inn in an attractive seaside village. Good food served from 7 a.m. to 11 p.m.

8 The North-West

The North-west of England makes the headlines in all sorts of ways. For one thing it contains two of Britain's premier tourist attractions: Liverpool's Albert Dock, with its complex range of exhibitions and activities; and the Pleasure Beach at Blackpool, which has everything that human beings can devise to stimulate and entertain. But then the region claims so much of the 'biggest and best': Blackpool illuminations, 'the greatest free show on earth'; Wigan's Trencherfield Steam Wheel, 'the largest in Europe', and Manchester, Britain's finest Victorian city. And it provides the throbbing heart of most forms of sport: the golf course at Lytham St Annes; famous football clubs, Manchester, Liverpool and Everton; Aintree, site of the Grand National and Old Trafford cricket ground. The emphasis seems consistently to be on activity, stimulation, entertainment, offering all (or almost all) possible diversions; high-key and rather garish in its self-advertisement.

But perhaps this is a misconception prompted by the inhabitants in order to revive those traditions which led to the region's prosperity – and urbanisation – in cotton-spinning days. The urban areas, consequences of the Industrial Revolution, stretch in a band from Merseyside past the Northern Peaks and into Yorkshire. Perhaps it is the pragmatism that turned muck into brass in previous centuries which energises present-day entrepreneurs and others. Yet, amid all the sophistication of theme parks and man-made attractions, Cheshire's countryside remains tranquil, and the Forest of Bowland in Lancashire is still wild and remote.

Whereas the Peak District National Park preserves its territory not as a museum piece, but as a place where people make their livelihood – putting up with the encroachment (like quarrying) which that involves – other parts of the region, less blessed with spectacular landscape, seem to strive after re-creating the past. The result is that much experience seems passive and second-hand. True, it may also be educational, or at least instructive, but nevertheless lacking in originality.

Natural assets include magnificent sandy beaches, many now

intensely commercialised, and the attraction of the coast and wetlands for a wealth of resident and migrant birds. It could be that the region really does have the balance between town and country pleasures; in some places you just have to block your ears a little to the strident clamour of high-level marketing.

All sorts of events take place in the three counties: floral festivals, tea dances at Blackpool Tower, and city tours in the company of a Roman soldier. No one should ever be at a loss for 'something to do'. The main cities of Manchester and Liverpool are centres of much splendid culture, including the Walker Art Gallery, the Free Trade and Philharmonic Halls, as well as intensively documented heritage sites and the more contemporary Science Centre at Jodrell Bank, home of the radio telescope.

The region's shape is not unlike a long corridor making a springboard for the Lake District. With their sights set farther north, and an excellent motorway to take them there, visitors are disinclined to linger on the way; which is a pity, for Lancashire has its own natural beauty. This, though confined to a smaller area than Cumbria's, is as yet under-developed in terms of tourism facilities. As for the people whose home it is, the Mersey sharply divides the Northerners from Cheshire's more traditional landowners. In the past this was a county of dairy cows and, even with industry spilling out from its northern boundary, remains on the whole a placid easy-going land. Lancastrians had among them fewer landed gentry and always expected to work hard in order to achieve. It was through this determination that their cities were built and flourished, and are still planning ahead for tomorrow's world.

History

An Iron Age camp on Helsby Hill is one of several forts on the wooded ridges of central Cheshire, which provided lookouts against invaders. The Romans established camps at Deva (now Chester) and Mancunium; their legionaries watched for Welsh tribesmen from the border hills or pirates from the sea. For the next thousand years Angles, Saxons and Norsemen (who bequeathed names like Kirby to the Wirral) formed some identity, so that when William the Conqueror became England's king, Chester was the last important town to submit to him (and was destroyed as a result).

During the reign of King John, who granted the fishing village of Liverpool its charter in 1207, people began to rebel against the royal requirement for hunting forests such as Delamere and persisted in ploughing the land for agriculture instead. The Isle of Man receives mention for its brief annexation by Robert the Bruce to Scotland; actually its history goes further back than any, since hunters were using flint implements there about 6000 BC. On the mainland, fighting continued for thirty years with rival claimants to the throne waging the Wars of the Roses between the Houses of Lancaster and York. Disagreements were settled when the Red Rose of Lancaster married the White Rose; Elizabeth of York, and the ordinary people, pleased with this outcome, sang:

> Both Roses flourish, Red and White,
> In love and sisterly delight.

The 'wiches' – Nantwich, Northwich, Middlewich – had been salt-producing centres, since before the Domesday Survey, but by Elizabeth I's reign this was central Cheshire's main industry. It was, after all, an essential product when animals with only summer fields to graze in had to be killed and salted for winter meat. The cloth trade, which thrived in these Northern areas with plentiful running water, received a boost when highly-skilled Flemish weavers were imported to share their secrets with English clothiers. The prosperity this brought encouraged more luxury living; manor houses were built in the elaborate half-timbering which reached a peak at Little Moreton Hall and continued to flourish especially in Northern counties.

People were superstitious in those days: everybody, educated or not, believed in witchcraft, and Pendle Hill was associated with magic long before the Romans performed religious rites there. In 1591 Mother Demdyke, walking in Pendle Forest, met somebody called Tibb. Regrettably she sold her soul to him, became a witch and, with nine other 'Lancashire Witches', was hanged near Lancaster Castle. Charles I reprieved a later band of Pendle Witches on grounds of insufficient evidence. It did him no good for, in 1645, he watched his troops' defeat at Rowton Moor from Chester's battlements. The Royalist town was then starved into surrender. After the Commonwealth, James I – unlikely though it sounds – was so pleased with the joint of beef served to him at Hoghton Tower that he knighted it 'Sir Loin'.

The 17th century brought a number of 'firsts'. Liverpool, a growing port, received its first cargo from America in 1648 – exporting slaves in return. In 1652 George Fox had a vision on ill-famed Pendle Hill, and subsequently founded the Society of Friends. Poorer people had difficulty obtaining books, and Humphrey Chetham, who died in 1653, bequeathed to Manchester the first public library in Europe. And about this time, in the Isle of Man, the first Manx cat was bred.

Liverpool opened docks in quick succession along the Mersey coastline to feed cotton to Lancashire's mills. The Duke of Bridgewater, an important colliery owner, employed Brindley to build a canal, thus ensuring his coal would reach Manchester. Other canals followed, forming a network of inland waterways and bringing the bonus of unaccustomed amenities for country people. By 1782 cotton was the 'in' fabric for fashion-conscious ladies, but the inventions of 'spinning jennies' and 'mules' transformed the craft of spinning from cottage industry to factory product, powered at the end of the 18th century by steam.

Meanwhile many city folk were growing rich on the proceeds of cotton, coal and foreign trade. Henry Tate, born in Chorley, having created his wealth from American sugar, used some of it to found the Tate Gallery in London. The present firm of Cammell Laird built the first iron ship, which operated from the developing port of Birkenhead; by the 1840s steamships brought more trade – and also Irish refugees from their own country's potato famine. Dissension was strong in the industrial North; indeed the Church's attempt to enforce a levy required troops with fixed bayonets to keep order in Rochdale. In 1844 twenty-four of the town's workmen, by founding the Co-operative Movement, began the process of democratising profits. Manchester, nicknamed 'cottonopolis', used its status for such cultural investments as the Free Trade Hall (home of the Hallé Orchestra), built on the site of the Peterloo Massacre, when yeomen charged and killed protestors against factory conditions.

Life did improve and, with the coming of the railways, the workers enjoyed an annual seaside holiday and Blackpool rose to the position of Borough. During this century air pollution became a problem in all industrial cities, and the first smokeless zones were introduced to Manchester in 1952, greatly improving the quality of the environment. More recently, Liverpool's out-of-use dockland has been resurrected, and now Albert Dock re-creates from the 1960s era the city's outburst of Beatles fame and the resultant Beatlemania.

Other famous natives include: George Stubbs, painter of horses and huntsmen, born in Liverpool in 1724; Samuel Crompton, who invented the spinning mule and revolutionised the cotton industry; Emma Hamilton from the Wirral, favourite of Lord Nelson; Mrs Gaskell, who portrayed her native town of Knutsford in her novel *Cranford*; Lewis Carroll, born as Charles Dodgson, at Daresbury near Runcorn; and in 1863 at Manchester, David Lloyd

George, the Liberal statesman (he was moved to Wales at the age of two).

Geography

Low-lying land, alluvial on the Cheshire plain, extends in a narrowing coastal corridor up to the sandy expanse of Morecambe Bay. In the middle of the northern Irish Sea lies the Isle of Man, about four and a half hours by boat from Liverpool. Beyond Morecambe Bay are the Cumbrian mountains and these join with the Pennines to form the eastern half of Lancashire and the edge of Cheshire. Two extra mini-counties were created out of the original two: Greater Manchester and Merseyside. The spreading conurbation of Manchester has managed to claw into its district the Higher Peaks to the North of Derbyshire, while Merseyside includes the almost equally-spreading city of Liverpool. Thus the once large county of Lancashire has been reduced; more serious, Cheshire's proudly advertised shape as either flying eagle or teapot has become just an amorphous blob.

The former county town of Lancaster in the extreme north of the region, with a population of 45,000, has been ousted by the much larger and more centrally placed Preston, while Chester, Cheshire's county town, once a port at the head of the now silted up River Dee, has 116,000 inhabitants. None of these can compete with Manchester's 450,000 and Liverpool's 545,000 (and growing). The cotton-milling towns of Oldham, Rochdale and Bolton, with a host of others, are partly absorbed into Greater Manchester. Blackburn, another important cotton town, spreads over the foot of the Ribble Valley, an Area of Outstanding Natural Beauty; for, of course, all these places were established just because they were close to running water from the fells.

On the seaboard, suburbia grew out of Lancashire's many miles of sandy beaches from Morecambe, across the Ribble estuary and down to the Mersey. Here Blackpool and its satellites have stretched their ribbon development along the whole coastline of the Borough of Fylde (derived from an Old English word for 'plain'). Southport, below the Ribble, has also spread, though less invasively since the coastal area of sand dunes is preserved in National Nature Reserves and National Trust property (this is where a local paler variety of the Bloody Cranesbill grows). Unfortunately the Irish Sea is amongst the most polluted in the world and so all these beaches, with the one exception of Formby, south of Southport, have failed to reach the European Community standard.

The Forest of Bowland, covering half the north of Lancashire, is a high wild area of fells reaching 1839 feet (560 m.) at Ward's Stone, in complete contrast with the development down the valleys to the south. Below the Mersey estuary the Wirral Peninsula forms what used to be the spout of Cheshire's teapot. Almost entirely covered by Birkenhead and adjoining towns on its Mersey edge, the Dee shoreline has been partly preserved from further urbanisation by Wirral Country Park. South of the Dee, Cheshire is a gentle county whose prosperity comes mainly from its rich pastureland. The area also profited for a while from the former silk town of Macclesfield, at the centre of the high land to the east where it borders the Derbyshire dales.

Canals are a distinctive feature of the region. The original Bridgewater Canal connecting with the Rochdale Canal and also the Trent & Mersey runs from near Runcorn in Cheshire to Manchester, while the great Manchester Ship Canal reaches the Mersey at Eastham. The network is extensive and intricate. Today, the three most suited to pleasure cruising are the Macclesfield, Leeds & Liverpool and Lancaster Canals.

The valleys north of Manchester are constantly under threat from urban and industrial development; wooded ravines and nature reserves with uncommon flowers (like wall rue near Middleton town centre) are battling to survive. Happily, various countryside management services promote better care of the country so that, all being well, to the east of Manchester's conurbation, herons and willow warblers will still nest by the Tame, and mountain hares will go on changing the colour of their coats amongst the conifers on the upland Peaks.

Climate

The west-facing coast, together with the high eastern hills, give the North-west more variations of climate than almost anywhere else in the British Isles. The Isle of Man, lapped by the Gulf Stream, is very mild throughout the year, while Blackpool and Southport have an average of five hours of sunshine per day (high for this county) and more in June, the sunniest month. Industrial Lancashire, on the other hand, has an annual average of about three hours. The clarity of the sunshine here is likely to be lower than on the coast, despite the disappearance now of smoke-belching chimneys; the concentration of industry around Greater Manchester and Merseyside does leave a haze in the air on all but the clearest days. The Wirral Peninsula, though, is an exception, being particularly mild and sunny. August is, on average, the hottest month on the coast; further inland it's July, but the best time to visit the hill country is in the spring.

As for rainfall, August is the wettest summer month in the Peakland area, which has the highest rainfall of almost anywhere in Britain, except the Scottish Highlands. The lush green grass of the Cheshire Plain is caused by the high rainfall there too. In fact, most Cheshire summers are cool, and the east of the county has a wet reputation. So does the Stockport area, at the foot of a network of valleys leading into the High Peaks. Here it can be very stormy in winter, with both rain and snow; winter snowfall can be heavy on all the higher ground, especially on the northern hills. Manchester itself however, despite its poor reputation, actually has much less rain than England's popular South-west.

Attractions

The emphasis of the top tourist attractions is certainly on fun, with Blackpool's Pleasure Beach at the head of the list. Unfortunately, for one of Britain's most popular beaches, it is far from reaching Blue Flag Status; 'one of the world's greatest amusement parks' will divert any visitor brave enough to venture there. Add to this the indoor Sandcastle (with giant wavepool) and Sealife Centres, and children anyway should be more than satisfied with Blackpool's 'sea, sand and fun'. There's the Tower too, and the illuminations to which millions crowd each autumn. Other high fliers in the attraction stakes are Southport's Pleasureland, and Frontierland on the beautiful bay at Morecambe; this is where the Wild West entertains from June to mid-September.

On Merseyside, the Maritime Museum instructs at the cleverly reconstituted Albert Dock amid the coster carts and bars, and Liverpool's arm of the Tate Gallery presents contemporary art. Here too the Beatles story is told, to the feel of the Cavern Beat. A little gentler, down in Cheshire, Stapeley Water Gardens is a hyper garden centre with fountains and Grecian porticos.

For history – Roman, medieval and Tudor – go to Chester, with its well-preserved walls, half-timbered 'Rows' and Cathedral (though the latter, together with the Visitor Centre and Zoo can all become overcrowded). Architectural gems include the intricate black and white timbering of Little Moreton Hall; Bramall Hall, near Stockport; Rufford Old Hall, with fine hammerbeam roof, and Speke Hall, currently under threat in the heart of Liverpool. Amongst many stately mansions, Tatton Hall is one of the most visited

National Trust properties, standing in over 1000 acres (405 hectares) of deer park, and Lyme Park has welcoming staff who reconstruct Edwardian 'downstairs' life. For castles, it would be difficult to beat Beeston on its crag-top with views over the whole county and a 2500 year history; or there's Clitheroe's Norman castle under Pendle Hill, and Lancaster's on the site of a Roman fort.

Reminders of our industrial heritage are found in Macclesfield, with its silk industry, the cotton mill at Quarry Bank or the working windmill at Garstang Discovery Centre. Back to the present day, Heysham Nuclear Power Station is open for visits and so is Jodrell Bank's Science Centre, complete with radio telescope. One much advertised must is a ferry cruise across the Mersey with views of the waterfront; but there are any number of canals and waterways to explore either by boat or on foot along the towpaths.

Nature reserves range from the Ainsdale dunes near Formby, with such unusual plant and animal species as dune helleborine and sand lizard, to Mere Sands Wood in disused gravel workings near Rufford. There are countryside centres like the Groundwork one at Oldham which is developing the Crompton Circuit Trail, or the Natural History Museum and Art Gallery at Towneley Hall, Burnley.

It seems that a good many of the region's obvious assets have already been exploited, some more sensitively than others. But there still remains the countryside, in particular Ribblesdale and the hill country, as well as the market towns and villages of Cheshire's Vale Royal. There's also the Lune Valley beyond the Bowland Fells, and the birdwatchers' paradise of salt marshes up at Silverdale.

Cuisine

A meal typical of the region is best eaten at Nantwich, where the museum tells the 'Cheshire Cheese Story'. It might begin with farmhouse Cheshire soup, a thick vegetable broth topped with cheese – with the alternative of shrimps from Morecambe. The main course ought to be Lancashire hotpot, using locally-grown potatoes and flavoured with Nantwich salt. For dessert it will be hard to choose between steamed Chester pudding with hot blackcurrant jam, or a speciality Cheshire and fruit flan. Whichever it is, you must leave room for some Sugbury's ice-cream from Park Farm nearby; it's made from Jersey milk and whole fruits. The meal will be rounded off, naturally, with Cheshire cheese – red, white or blue – which goes well with traditionally brewed beer. For afternoon tea there are, of course, Eccles Cakes. Lancashire people also like eating black pudding, tripe and fish-and-chips – the fish coming fresh from Fleetwood.

Vegetarians will do well in Cheshire, where there are a number of farmhouse cheesemakers and creameries. Nantwich holds an international Cheese Show annually at Dorfold Hall Park (the last Wednesday of July) and there is even a Cheshire Cheese kiosk on Crewe railway station. Delicatessens abound, among them the family run coffee-shop of A. T. Welch in Hospital Street, Nantwich, which sells regional cheeses and home-made sausages. As John Speed the map-maker and a native of the area said of Cheshire in the 17th century: 'The soil is fat, fruitful and rich . . . the Pastures make the Kine's udders to strout to the pail, from whom and wherein the best Cheese of all Europe is made.'

Level of Tourism

The number of tourists coming to the North-west is high. The total sum spent by holiday makers and tourists accounts for around 6 per cent of the total for England. Taking all types of tourism into account – that is to say, business visits, staying with friends and through trips – spending in the North-west is the highest anywhere, with the exception of the West Country. Quite a high proportion of the young to middle age range (25–44) and professional or managerial people come on business trips; Blackpool, after all, is a prime conference town and Manchester an important commercial centre. The ratio of UK visitors to those from overseas is about nine to one, but the actual number of visits made is considerably higher, since most British visitors come on day trips from other parts of the region. Seventeen per cent of overseas visitors come from the USA, closely followed by Germany, whose nationals seem to come to the North-west more than to any other part of England; this may well reflect its importance as a business destination. Spending here is above average, despite the lack of overnight expenditure. Apart from visits to friends or relatives, hotels are by far the most favoured type of accommodation, occupied mainly on short holidays of up to three or four nights. The peak holiday months for both British and overseas visitors are July to September, although a surprising number do come from abroad in the last quarter of the year. March would be a good month to come for fewer crowds.

More large hotels and leisure complexes are being built or are in the planning stage, often in competition with existing attractions. An ever-increasing volume of visitors to historic towns and cities inevitably causes congestion, especially as these people mainly travel by car on day visits. An effort is being made to plot the patterns of activity in these overcrowded places in order to protect them, their residents and those who come to enjoy them.

A good deal of the region is subject to mass tourism in a big way. Apart from the six top tourist attractions (Blackpool Pleasure Beach; Albert Dock, Liverpool; Pleasureland, Southport; Blackpool Tower; Stapeley Water Gardens; and Frontierland, Morecambe) which all had well over a million visitors in 1989 – Blackpool beach had 6.5 million – there are others where the volume of tourism is sometimes higher than the attraction can support. These are notably, Rufford Old Hall; the Botanical Gardens Museum at Southport; the Rossendale Museum, and Towneley Hall Art Gallery. Other popular draws with a greater capacity to absorb the crowds are Chester Cathedral and Zoo, the Tate Gallery and Museum at Liverpool and the parks at Croxteth and Knowsley, amongst many others.

On the whole tourists tend to congregate in the built-up areas at the sites of man-made attractions, leaving relatively undisturbed a large part of South Cheshire, the Ribble Valley leading up past Clitheroe into Yorkshire, the flat Fylde area around the banks of the Wyre, the fells Area of Outstanding Natural Beauty in the Forest of Bowland, the Lune Valley with its villages north of Lancaster, and a whole chunk of wetland and limestone scrub on Morecambe Bay.

Information about tourism's effect on the environment (both natural and man-made) is being collected through the work of a number of organisations in the region. For instance, the Lancashire Trust for Nature Conservation persuaded the Water Authority not to fill in a group of mill ponds at Oswaldtwistle which had become a haven for wildlife; instead the residents formed a management committee, tackling jobs like tree-planting and clearance. A Rural Enterprise award has gone to Old Hall Farm Conservation Centre in Cheshire, where children can learn about the natural world; and the Wildfowl Trust has gained RAMSAR status for Martin Mere. But the transformation of disused warehouses at Liverpool's Albert Dock is perhaps the biggest rescue story of recent years, with its present level of attraction at over five million visitors annually.

Of course, amidst all the claims of industry and commerce, there are numerous plans giving cause for concern to environmentalists and conservationists. Currently under consideration is British Aerospace's proposed expansion of Liverpool Airport. One of the most famous of all half-timbered houses, Speke Hall, is balanced precariously on Merseyside with the airfield as nextdoor neighbour – and for the moment has managed to preserve its rose garden and bluebell woods. The National Trust, as owner, accepts development needs, and discussions continue. On the other hand, schemes are under way to redevelop Manchester City Centre with provision for parks, riverside walks and a canal 'village'. On a smaller scale, Wyre Borough Council is planning to improve Poulton-le-Fylde's Market Place. Bolton business firms are also being encouraged to brighten the environment. Waterside improvements range from the Mersey Basin Campaign's measurement of Mersey water quality, to desilting a pond at Kirkby for recreational use. A 'Clean Watersides Campaign' hopes to involve both residents and visitors in tackling litter problems at lakes and canals; and an overgrown graveyard at Bolton has now been divided into plots, each tended by a local family, to create a wildflower meadow. In fact, there are numerous volunteer groups throughout the region, often targeting schoolchildren, as well as their parents, and working on a range of imaginative projects for the future.

Good Alternatives

Meeting People

A good way of meeting people is to work with them; the **British Trust for Conservation Volunteers** provides several opportunities of doing this in Lancashire, where those you meet are likely to be young people living locally. On Hilbre Island in the Dee estuary, a feeding ground for wading birds, you could construct a boardwalk saving them – and the seal colony – from disturbance by random wanderers. Alternatively, work is needed on a woodland trail in parkland near Wigan, now a wildlife haven reclaimed from mining spoil. Rochdale's **Community Leisure Department** also welcomes the enthusiastic to help restore a Victorian riverside park at Heywood. Local volunteers are planting trees, turning a paddling pool into a butterfly and bee garden and carrying out other imaginative schemes. The Restoration Group would be glad of extra hands.

Cheshire College of Agriculture demonstrates the county's best-known product in the milking parlour at Reaseheath, near Nantwich – a meeting place for Cheshire farmers; it's best to go on Wednesday, between 3.30 and 5 p.m. You could learn more about Nantwich's history by joining a walk, followed with tea at the town museum. This is one activity of the lengthy programme organised by **Cheshire County Council**; another is a bicycle treasure hunt through the countryside around Crewe.

It's a challenging experience to visit **Droylesden's Water Adventure Centre** in the middle of Manchester; here different groups in the community are encouraged to develop unknown skills. Team leader, Lilian Pons, would be encouraged by interested and well-qualified help in her work. **Fox Howl Outdoor Education Centre** in Delamere Forest, amongst other activities, initiates beginners in orienteering. The Sandstone Trail runs through pinewoods here and for 32 miles (51 km.) to the Shropshire border. Another Easitrail has been specially made for wheelchair users.

There's a nature reserve in Princess Park, Chadderton, an oasis on Manchester's outskirts, where Oldham and Rochdale Groundwork Trust have a study centre. Here, near the disused canal is a varied habitat of meadows and marshland. The edge of Rochdale Jubilee Colliery, long since closed, is now a haven for plants and animals.

If you are in Manchester on Whit Sunday or spring Bank Holiday Monday, you could join a religious procession on their Walking Day through the city; while on Easter Monday the people of Preston perform the ancient custom of egg-rolling down one of the Ribblesdale hills. At Clitheroe further up the valley, where many shops have been in the same family for generations, a busy open-air market is held on Tuesdays and Saturdays. There's also a livestock market here, and big car-boot sales on Sundays; less frenetic, you can listen to concerts in the Castle grounds. Another branch of the **Groundwork Trust – Macclesfield and Vale Royal** – gives monthly exhibitions at their Discovery Centre in a Victorian cotton mill at Bollington on the edge of the Peak District. They have a craft shop by the canal and a place for hiring canoes or bicycles. Helsby, rising out of the Mersey marshes, can be climbed in the company of a National Trust Warden, who will show you the Iron Age fort and the area's geology, flora and fauna.

Exciting things are happening in Lancashire, linking artists and sculptors with the environment, using the creative processes to enhance awareness. The **Lancashire Trust for Nature Conservation** has sponsored the making of a sculpture in a wildflower garden at Cuerden Park near Preston, in which local children played an important part. Other plans are under way; to hear more, contact the Voluntary Sector Network.

Several shows take place through the summer: the Lord Mayor's Parade and a two-day Police Horse Show in Liverpool during June, and a big flower show at Southport in August. But it's South Cheshire which is known as the floral heart of England, with various events happening in early summer. Bridgemere Garden World and Cheshire

Herbs at Little Budworth are venues for some of them. Budworth Mere nearby is a good birdwatching spot, and wildlife can also be found in Marbury Country Park.

Discovering Places

Water plays an important role in the region and the Boat Museum at Ellesmere Port is a good place to learn the history of canal transport. The museum charity rescued the site and volunteers are sorting its collection of artefacts; more help is needed. You can now walk across South Wirral to Parkgate on public footpaths (an all-day expedition) and along the Dee marshes. Caldy Hill gives views of at least 20,000 oystercatchers roosting across the estuary, and Thurstaston Common is rich in insect life.

The Romans mined salt in the 'wich' towns; Northwich Salt Museum tells the story – ending with the last open pan salt works, currently being restored, at Marston. Through Northwich town, with its perpendicular style church, the River Weaver flows to be joined to the Trent & Mersey Canal by the remarkable Anderton lift. Beyond this a riverside footpath runs down a rural valley to Sutton Weaver Bridge. The towpaths of six canals make the Cheshire Ring Canal Walk, starting at Marple, on the edge of the High Peaks. Astbury village in quiet countryside near the Macclesfield Canal is known for its springtime daffodils and lovely church with its carved vaulting and fine timber roof.

Close to the M66 in industrial Rossendale, public footpaths crisscross agricultural land and woods full of interesting flowers to reach Holcombe Moor. Numerous bird species, including wildfowl, live on the moorland and reservoirs around. Steam trains run along the Irwell Valley from Rawtenstall to Bury, while up in the fells is Goodshaw Chapel, built for Baptist worship in 1760 and home then to the 'Larks of Dean', local musicians who wrote their own hymns and music. **Rossendale Groundwork Countryside Centre** in converted farm buildings makes a good start for walks and has all kinds of information about the area; the café serves herbal teas and home-made cakes.

In Southern Cheshire, Bournes (The Bank, at Malpas) allow visits – by at least two people at a time – to watch traditional cheese-making, and nearby Oakcroft Organic Gardens sell seasonal vegetables and fruit. The Post Office Stores at Cholmondeley, an old-fashioned country grocery, sells its own whisky as well as cheeses, and on Cholmondeley Castle estate you can see how woodland is being regenerated, and discover an ancient chapel in the park.

There are various ways of enjoying the Lancaster Canal. You can explore all 59 miles (94 km.) of the towpath from Carnforth to Preston, giving views of sea, moors and castle. Boating is easy on this lock-free canal, and you can hire craft for a day or longer. Canoeing and angling are popular, but you need a licence for both. Waders often shelter near the northern reaches and further south white water lilies grow. Railway enthusiasts will appreciate the Steamtown museum at Carnforth and everyone will be impressed by the big Keer viaduct. Robin and Nell Dale paint collectable figures in their craft workshop at Bank House Farm, Holme Mills, via Carnforth (Tel 0524 781646); you will need to phone for directions.

The pastoral Valley of the Lune leads through Lancaster to Kirkby Lonsdale and the Yorkshire hills; Turner enjoyed painting the river's wooded banks near Crook O'Lune. Burton Wood is a Site of Special Scientific Interest with bluebells growing in deep ravines. Scots raided this land in the 14th century, as you can see from the defensive pele tower on Gresgarth Hall. Near Lancaster, in the churchyard at Hallow village is a 10th-century preaching cross, carved with both Christian and pagan symbols; beyond, the five-arched Lune Aqueduct carries the canal over the river.

Cheshire also has rare Saxon crosses, carved with dragons and biblical scenes, in the cobbled market square at Sandbach, a town of Tudor buildings famed for its strong ale. For industrial archaeology, the **Countryside Office** at Hassall will direct you to the Salt Line, a once busy railway, or the Canal Centre at Hassall Green. While Jodrell Bank's giant radio telescope dominates the countryside, Swettenham Water Mill, a good deal smaller, is still working in Daffodil Dell. **Countrywide Holidays**, 42 Cromwell Range, Manchester M14 6HU (Tel 061 257 2055) organise walking and activity holidays.

Communications

How to Get There

AIR: **Manchester International Airport** (Tel 061 489 3000) connects with thirty-five countries as well as airports throughout the UK. **Speke Airport, Liverpool** (Tel 051 486 8877) connects with London Heathrow and Ireland.

RAIL: Trains run hourly from London, taking three hours to Chester and Liverpool, two and a half to Manchester. Crewe is an important junction with lines running north, south and south-westwards beyond Chester to North Wales.

COACH: **National Express** run daily services, connecting locally, to Chester, Liverpool, Manchester, Southport, Birkenhead and Wirral.

When You're There

RAIL: Liverpool and Manchester have connecting lines around the area, and the North-west Rover Ticket offers bargain travel. The only areas not served by rail are Clitheroe and the Ribble Valley, and Fleetwood in the northern half of Fylde. There is a **Travel Centre** at Lime Street Station, LIVERPOOL for trains in the city area and under the Mersey to Wirral. In MANCHESTER there are two stations – Piccadilly in London Road (Tel 061 832 8353) and Victoria in Chapel Street, where there is also a **Travel Centre**. East Lancashire steam railway runs from Bury to Rawtenstall; information from Bolton Street Station, Bury BL9 0EY (Tel 061 764 7790).

BUS: Local bus services are good and frequent, but fewer north of Manchester. **Cheshire Bus** operates a Sunday service on the Sandstone Trail (Busline Tel 0244 602666). **Merseytravel Line** covers the Wirral and offers Savaway tickets (Tel 051 236 7676), and a Wayfarer ticket can be used on bus or rail. In LIVERPOOL, Ribble Bus Station, Skelhorne Street, is opposite the rail station (Tel 051 709 6481). For transport within the city (Tel 051 236 7676). There is a comprehensive city service in MANCHESTER, with a **Centreline** mini-bus connecting the two rail stations. Greater Manchester Passenger Transport Executive (Tel 061 228 6400) will give further information. There are fifteen County Information Centres in Lancashire and a transport enquiry line (Tel 0772 263333). The Marketing Department, North-west Tourist Board, Last Drop Village, Bromley Cross, Bolton BL7 9PZ (Tel 0204 591511) will give information on the numerous coach trips available.

CAR: Motorways approach the region from all directions. The M6 runs north and south, while the M62 connects Liverpool and Manchester with all points east. Merseyside and South Lancashire are covered by linking motorways. The **Mancunian Way** runs east and west across Manchester, with the outer motorways linking a network of roads which converge at the city centre in a maze of one-way streets.

BOAT: A network of canals – Lancaster, Leeds & Liverpool, Bridgewater, Macclesfield, and Trent & Mersey – ensures a wide range of boating, from a restaurant boat hired at Hassall Green Canal Centre (Tel 0270 762266) to narrow boats and day hire craft, including canoes. For information on Leeds & Liverpool Canal contact **British Waterways Leisure**, Swan Meadow Road, Wigan WN3 5BB (Tel 0942 323895). Mersey Ferries run an hourly service between Liverpool Pier Head and Birkenhead or Wallasey;

they also have boats for private hire. Narrow-boat trips in Manchester are operated by **Bridgewater Packet Boat Service** at Castlefield, and **Egerton Narrow Boats**, the Boatyard, Worsley (Tel 061 793 6767).

Sunday afternoon trips are also run from Worsley and Castlefield by **Lorunz & Co**, 26 Worsley Road, Worsley (Tel 061 794 1441) and **Castlefield & Tiller** (Tel 061 748 2680). There are many more small boat hire firms within the region; tourist centres will give particulars. There are also various marinas or sailing centres: Hollingworth Lake, Visitor Centre, Hollingworth Country Park, Rackwood Road, Littleborough OD15 0AQ (Tel 0706 73421); Trafford Water Sports Centre, Riffle Road, Sale M33 2LX (Tel 061 962 0355) and others on the River Weaver; Glasson Dock by the Lune estuary; Winsford Bottom Flash; Fairhaven Lake, Lytham St Annes; and West Kirby Marine Lake on the Wirral. Most have facilities for sailboarding, windsurfing and canoeing. For the use of reservoirs, contact Northwest Water, PO Box 30, New Town House, Buttermarket Street, Warrington WA1 2QG (Tel 0925 53922).

CYCLING: Cheshire offers excellent cycling country and **Macclesfield Groundwork Trust** has cycle hire centres at Bollington, Tatton Park near Knutsford, and Linmere, Delamere Forest. They also give information on cycle tours and repairs shops. Their address is Adelphi Mill Gate Lodge, Grimshaw Lane, Bollington (Tel. 0625 7268). The **Cheshire Cycleway** around Vale Royal covers 155 miles (248 km.); for information contact Heritage and Recreation Service, County Hall, Cheshire CH1 1SF (Tel 0244 602424). The **Middlewood Way**, only ten miles (16 km.), is on a former railway line at the edge of the Peak Park. The **Adventure and Discovery Programme** organised by Cheshire County Council includes cycle rides and treasure hunts. **Oldham Countryside Ranger Service** has similar events through the summer. Other good Lancashire cycling areas are the Ribble and Lune Valleys; but there are plenty more. You can rent from **Greenbank Cycle Shop**, 232 Smithdown Road, Liverpool (Tel 051 733 6666), which is three miles (5 km.) from the city centre. **Manchester Cycling Campaign** is a local group at 1 Seedley Avenue, Little Hulton, Manchester M28 6LZ.

WALKING: North-west Water and local authorities run joint visitor centres at seven sites in the region. Here Countryside Rangers supply information on walks (group or individual) in the 120,000 acres (48,600 hectares) owned by the Board. In Cheshire, there is **Macclesfield Forest Ranger Centre**, Macclesfield Forest, Langley, Macclesfield (Tel 02605 2832), while in Lancashire you should contact Jumbles Information Centre, Water Fold Car Park, off Bradshaw

Road, Bradshaw, Bolton (Tel 0204 853360), and for Merseyside, Pex Hill Visitor Centre, 1 Pex Hill, The Avenue, Cronton Way, Widnes (Tel 051 495 1410). All the canals offer towpath walking over at least part of the way. There are footpaths in the Forest of Bowland, the Lune Valley, and the Sefton coast on Merseyside. Other tracks are the **Pendle Way**, **Cheshire Ring Canal Walk**, and **Weaver Valley Way**. Cheshire County Council organises discovery walks and the National Trust also has guided walks. Special tours of Nantwich and South Cheshire are arranged through **South Cheshire Blue Badge Guides Association** (Tel 0270 623914). **Lancashire Trust for Nature Conservation** will give details of public access to nature reserves, where guided tours are sometimes available.

RIDING: Vale Royal is a favourite riding area, with several hiring stables. Little Budworth Common is pleasant and so is Whitegate Way leading to Delamere Forest. For riding in Delamere, you need a permit from the Forestry Commission. Marbury Country Park has a waymarked bridle path and adjustable jumps, while the Middlewood Way can also be used by horse-riders. The moors above Oldham are also good riding country. For bridleway information around the reservoirs, contact North-west Water (Recreation and Conservation), PO Box 30, New Town House, Buttermarket Street, Warrington WA1 2QG (Tel 0925 53922).

Useful Local Contacts

Mersey Basin Voluntary Sector Network, The Building Centre, 115 Portland Street, Manchester M1 6DW (Tel 061 228 6924). **Stream Care Co-ordinator**, c/o BTCV, 24 Seymour Grove, Old Trafford, Manchester, M26 OZH (Tel 061 876 7148). **Tidy Britain Group**, The Pier, Wigan, WN3 4EX (Tel 0942 824620). Lilian Pons, **Water Adventure Centre**, Fanfield Locks, off Maddison Road, Droylesden, Manchester, M35 (Tel 061 301 2673). **Water Watch**, 23 New Mount Street, Manchester, M4 4DE (Tel 061 953 4081). **Heywood Queens Park Restoration Group**, c/o 48 Queens Park Road, Heywood, OL10 4LQ (Chairman Sheila Hill). **Oldham Countryside Ranger Service**, Tandle Hill Country Park, Tandle Hill Road, Royton, Oldham, OL2 5UX (Tel 061 627 2608). **Cheshire County Council**, Heritage and Recreation Service, County Hall, Chester, CH1 1SF, for programme of walks and events. **Caring for the Countryside**: Medlock Valley Warden Service, The Stables, Park Bridge, Ashton-under-Lyne, OL6 8AQ (Tel 061 330 9613). **Peak District National Park Ranger Service**, Peak National Park Office, Aldern House, Baslow Road, Bakewell, Derbyshire (Tel 062

981 4321). **Greater Manchester Countryside Information Project:** Marie Mohan, Project Officer, Greater Manchester Countryside Unit, West End Offices, Jowetts Walk, Ashton-under-Lyne, OL7 OBB (Tel 061 343 3138). **Northwich and District Heritage Society,** The Rosary, Cinder Hill, Whitegate, Northwich (Tel 0606 882418). **Oldham and Rochdale Groundwork Trust,** Bank House, 8 Chapman Street, Shaw, Oldham (Tel. 0706 842212). Project Officer, **British Waterways Leisure,** Aldcliffe Road, Lancaster, LA1 1SU (Tel. 0524 63448). **Blue Badge Guide Services:** Merseyside – Tourism Board, Atlantic Pavilion, Albert Dock, Liverpool (Tel 051 709 2444). South Cheshire – Tourism Action Programme, Crewe Library, Civic Centre, Prince Albert Street, Crewe (Tel 0270 588645). D. Cookall, **National Federation of Anglers** (Tel 061 225 9768). Kenneth Oultram, Clatterwick Hall, Little Leigh, Northwich, CW8 4RJ (Tel 0606 891303 in office hours) organises tours and accommodation for **choirs**.

Geographical Breakdown of Region

Cheshire

Considering the extent of industrialisation to the north, Cheshire is remarkably untouched – due partly, no doubt, to traditional dependence on pastureland, and partly because many of its inhabitants are deliberate refugees from suburbia. Quick and easy commuting leaves plenty of time for environmental concerns.

Towns do encroach on villages and countryside, but planners often try to preserve their original atmosphere or create new central parks. **Norton Priory's** excavated ruins on a Runcorn industrial estate are surrounded by woodland, and at nearby **Danesbury** the church stands in meadowland – a church unusual for its stained glass window depicting Alice and the Mad Hatter; this was Lewis Carroll's birthplace. Although **Warrington** has spread there is pastureland beyond the **Bridgewater Canal**; here the family-run farm at Kenyon Hall, Croft, has open afternoons and pick-your-own facilities, while **Risley Moss**, Birchwood, is a woodland nature reserve.

The mainly Georgian town of **Knutsford**, with steep narrow alleyways, achieved fame through Mrs Gaskell's *Cranford*; her grave is behind the Unitarian Chapel. The **Heritage Centre** in a 17th-century building has changing exhibitions on wildlife and local history. The ancient custom of sanding pavements in coloured patterns marks Knutsford's May Day celebrations as unique. Several county families used to live hereabouts; many of their stately homes are open to the public. **Tatton Park**, very popular, is preserved as a museum piece; Victorian **Arley Hall**, in a variegated garden, though lived in, can be visited. At John Chalmers-Brown's workshop in the grounds you can watch the furniture-making process from tree to finished product; and **Peover Hall's** Tudor manor has interesting stables and topiary work.

Nether Alderley Mill near the foot of Alderley Edge, still working, has an overshot tandem wheel, and sometimes gives demonstrations of flour grinding. The wooded escarpment of the Edge, once the home of Neolithic people, now has foot and wheelchair paths running along it, and a pub is named after the legendary wizard who appeared by its holy well 300 years ago. **Hare Hill's** walled garden at Over Alderley is colour-themed in blue, white and yellow. North of Wilmslow, on the edge of Greater Manchester, 'Lindow Man' was discovered in the peat bogs of Lindow Common, one of the last remaining lowland heaths and a nature reserve.

Although wooded **Styal Country Park** is all too near Manchester Airport, **Quarry Bank Mill** there won a Tourist Board award in 1991 for its attractive restoration. Two hundred thousand people visit it annually to see the unique record of the life of mill apprentices around 1830. The weaving and cotton-spinning methods of that time are demonstrated and the 19th-century kitchen garden cultivates appropriate food plants. Numerous footpaths cover the Bollin River valley, and interesting birds and butterflies – Orange Tips and Large Commas – live in park and woodland close to suburbia. **Arlington Hall**, a half-timbered mansion in wilderness gardens contains an old organ once played by Handel.

Marple is a post-industrial cotton town in a beautiful setting under the High Peaks; regrettably it's one of the wettest parts of Britain. The **Middlewood Way**, a traffic-free walk, skirts the Peak District from Marple to Macclesfield. The **Gritstone Trail**, another upland walk (for which you need stout boots) starts near the National Trust's Lyme Park (nine miles, 14 km., round). Inside the house four Chippendale chairs are believed to be covered with material from the cloak Charles I wore at his execution. On a much smaller scale, **Mellors Gardens** at Hough Hole House, Rainow, have water and trees on different levels, best seen in May and June. East of Macclesfield the moors are really high and wild, with woodland reflected in Ridgegate and Trentabank Reservoirs. The Cat and Fiddle Inn stands at the road's highest point under Shining Tor, but **Teggs Nose Country Park**, with wide views and walks and peaceful woodlands, is the real gateway to this edge of the Peak District.

Macclesfield, once a great silk-making town and where cobbled streets climb the hills, retains its memories in three museums, while another at **West Park** contains work by Charles Tunnicliffe, painter of birds; perhaps he took his subjects from the ones round Redesmere Lake at Siddington. The frontage of Victorian **Capesthorne Hall** is longer than Buckingham Palace's, and in the gardens there are woodland walks, a chain of lakes and a Georgian chapel. At **Gawsworth**, the church, old hall and rectory date from medieval times, and the 13th-century church, built of both sandstone and gritstone, stands at the dividing line between upland rocks and sandy plain. In the sunken garden operas and Shakespeare plays are performed from June to August. **Danes Moss** reserve near Gawsworth, a Site of Special Scientific Interest on a former peat extract area, is now restored as a peat bog and hosts numerous bird species. So too do Sutton and Bosley Reservoirs where you can ramble by the **Macclesfield Canal**. The hills behind Oakgrove provide more energetic walking to the county border and beyond. Up at Wincle, **Danebridge Fisheries** have a farm shop with speciality foods, and a fishing lake as well. **Tall Cloud Hill** towers above **Congleton**, where **Biddulph Valley Way** takes the route of a former railway into Staffordshire.

Little Moreton Hall's moated manor is so breathtaking one almost doubts it's genuine. It is, but the beautiful timber framing had to be extensively repaired in 1991. The Knot Garden and Yew Tunnel were copied from designs in 17th-century gardening books. You can escape the tentacles of the Potteries at Alsager by taking the **Merelake Way**, a disused railway line which used to carry coal. On the **Trent & Mersey Canal**, designed for the same purpose, boats had to be 'legged' through Harecastle Tunnel, one and three quarter miles (2.8 km.) long.

Sandbach, with its Saxon crosses (actually only their shafts – the crosspieces have disappeared) has a large open market on Thursdays, and an annual Marathon. All round this area the flashes – stretches of water where salt mines used to be – attract flower species and rare wading birds. The grassland meadows and woodland round Swettenham Mill are nesting areas in summer and home to winter visitors such as Fieldfares and Bramblings. A beautiful stretch of the Trent & Mersey Canal passes through the Dane Valley to **Northwich**, and **Whitegate Way** makes a pleasant walk or ride alongside it. Beyond this, in **Delamere Forest**, Black Lake reserve is managed by the Cheshire Conservation Trust, which gives access only to members because of this floating bog's delicate nature. However, within the Forest there are numerous paths and public picnic sites, like Barnesbridge Gates. Near **Kelsall** you can pick fruit and vegetables or buy local honey at Hawarths Fruit Farm. **Bunbury's** attractive collection of villages has a working watermill, selling stoneground flour. The Peckforton ridge runs from the Iron Age fort of **Maiden Castle** to the dramatically sited **Beeston Castle**, and the Sandstone Trail follows its Western slopes. **Cheshire Workshops** at Burwardsley have an interesting candle-making factory, with demonstrations, while at next-door **Tattenhall** you can visit a farm manufacturing Cheshire ice-cream, watch the cows being milked or eat a clotted cream tea. The medieval market town of **Malpas** has a fine 14th-century church, containing an even earlier parish chest. The River Dee wriggles down this side of the county, marking the Welsh border, and crossed at **Farndon** by a nine-arched medieval bridge. On the Cheshire side it's called the Farndon Bridge but over the border the Welsh villagers of Holt know it as Holt Bridge.

Accommodation

First Class

Broxton Hall, Whitchurch Road, Broxton, Chester, CH3 9JS (Tel 082 925 321). Half-timbered hotel, filled with antiques and a friendly atmosphere.

Longview Hotel, 51–55 Manor Road, Knutsford, WA16 0LX (Tel 0565 2119). Comfortable hotel in Victorian terrace, central but with good views and warm welcome.

Middle Range

Burland Farm, Wrexham Road, Burland, near Nantwich, CW5 8ND (Tel 027 074 210). Comfortable working dairy farm with welcoming owners.

Cholmondeley Arms, Cholmondeley, SY14 8BT (Tel 082 922 382). Pub converted from a schoolhouse, serving excellent home-made food.

Economy

Park Vale Guest House, 252 Park Lane, Macclesfield, SK11 8AA (Tel 0625 34521). Central, clean and comfortable B&B.

Beechwood House, 206 Wallerscote Road, Weaverham, Northwich, CW8 3LZ (Tel 0606 852123). Working stock farm in peaceful area near town.

Eating Out

First Class

Crabwall Manor, Parkgate Road, Mollington (Tel 0244 85166). Good value meals (in large portions) served graciously.

Middle Range

La Belle Epoque, 60 King Street, Knutsford (Tel 0565 3060). Popular and relaxing restaurant, used as *Brideshead Revisited* set.

White House, New Road, Prestbury (Tel 0625 829376). Healthy eating in converted farmhouse.

Randalls, 22 High Street, Old Market Place, Bollington (Tel 0625 575058). Friendly welcome and popular with local people.

Economy

Dusty Miller, Wrenbury, near Nantwich (Tel 0270 780537). Canalside millhouse, with Innkeeper of the Year award.

Roebuck, Town Lane, Mobberley (Tel 056 587 2757). Popular pub in quiet lane, with home-made food.

Chester

Chester is a blend of antiquity (two miles, 3 km., of partly Roman walls surround the old city) and modernity, with up-to-date shops trading in the medieval 'Rows'. Yet some of these half-timbered galleries, reached from the street by outside steps, are deceptive, being Victorian 'Olde English' replacements of the originals. The effect however, is entirely genuine, unique, and attractive to the many thousands of visitors who throng here.

A walk round the ramparts built in the red sandstone which is Chester's prevailing colour reveals Roman, medieval and later additions, as well as views across the city and the Welsh hills. **King Charles's Tower**, built into the walls, contains a small exhibition about the Civil War; the **Water Tower** has another exhibition of medieval Chester; and **Pemberton's Parlour**, named after the ropemaker who used to work there, was rebuilt in 1898.

The **Rows** are probably Chester's main tourist draw; the oldest houses date from Tudor times and in places form continuous tunnels at first-floor level, supported by wooden pillars – ideal shopping arcades, acknowledged even in the 16th century as 'keeping a man dry in foul weather'. Under the most famous shop, Brown's, there is a rib-vaulted crypt, and Watergate Street contains some of the most authentically ancient buildings. **Bishop Lloyd's House** has especially fine carving and the reconstructed **God's Providence House** includes the original inscribed beam. This is the black and white face of Chester; the **Cathedral** returns to the red sandstone theme. Built as a Benedictine Abbey, the Norman arches remain in the North transept and the choir stalls are medieval, although a great deal of the building was restored last century by Sir George Gilbert Scott.

The **Grosvenor Museum** gives a summary of the town's history and is rich in coins and Roman remains; there is also a Georgian townhouse furnished in period styles. Other museums are housed in **Agricola's Tower** (all that's left of the medieval castle) containing military exhibits; in former St Michael's church, now the Heritage Centre; and at St Mary's Centre. A **Toy Museum** has the largest collection of matchbox cars in the world.

Outside Newgate the Roman amphitheatre would have seated about 9000. There are relics of Roman occupation underneath houses in Northgate Street, leading from the central Cross, the intersection of the four Roman roads.

Accommodation

First Class

Ye Olde King's Head, 48/50 Lower Bridge Street, Chester (Tel 0244 324855). Historic inn, with distinctive rooms, serves hearty farmhouse meals.

Middle Range

The Redland, 64 Hough Green, Chester CH4 8JY (Tel 0244 671024). Victorian hotel a mile (1.5 km.) out of town, with large bedrooms, reception area and small garden. No evening meal.

Green Bough Hotel, 60 Hoole Road, Chester CH2 3NL (Tel 0244 32624). Homely guest house on main road, serving traditional food.

Castle House, 23 Castle Street, Chester CH1 2DS (Tel 0244 350354). Family run guest house in quiet central street. No evening meal but use of kitchen.

Egerton Lodge Hotel, 57 Hoole Road, Chester CH2 3NJ (Tel 0244 320712). Cheerful hotel, close to centre and station, run by friendly couple.

Holly House Guest House, 1 Stone Place, Hoole, CH2 3NR (Tel 0244 328967). Bright house in quiet street, serving large and/or vegetarian breakfasts.

Eating Out

Middle Range

2 Abbey Green, Northgate Street (Tel 0244 313251). Vegetarian restaurant, popular with local people, offering wide wine choice.

Blue Bell Restaurant, 65 Northgate Street (Tel 0244 317758). Five-hundred-year-old inn, offering high quality English cooking.

Economy

Falcon, Lower Bridge Street. Seventeenth-century building with upstairs restaurant which can get crowded.

Latymer House, 82 Hough Green (Tel 0244 675074). Comfortable small hotel with welcoming restaurant.

Entertainments

On **Chester Racecourse**, outside the walls, the oldest horse-races in England are run. Within the city, characterful **shops** provide a range of goods in the fascinating setting of the Rows; here on summer Saturdays, although it's traffic-free, there's hardly room to move. Chester is justly celebrated for its many antique shops, though it has modern boutiques as well; to stock up with Christmas presents try the Twelve Month Christmas shop. If you want a professionally guided history tour you can be escorted by an armoured Roman soldier or even, at night, by a Ghosthunter.

The country's largest **zoo** is two miles (3 km.) out of town, in gardens which won the Regional Britain in Bloom competition; children might also enjoy a visit to **Grosvenor Garden Leisure** in Wrexham Road. It's a garden centre but has a play area, with pets and aquarium. There are river cruises on the Dee, and you can take a canal trip in a horse-drawn barge, or hire dinghies for short excursions. Annual events include the **regatta** in May, and a **Sports and Leisure fortnight** running from June into July, with river carnival and wild raft races. During the third week in July the **Summer Music Festival** hosts national orchestras and groups. The programme is available in May from Chester Summer Music Festival Office, Gateway Theatre, Hamilton Place, CH1 2BH (Tel 0244 340392). The **Gateway Theatre** itself has a variety of shows during the summer, with alternative events at the Chester Fringe. The **Tourist Office**, Town Hall, Northgate Street (Tel 0244 324324) will give details of all events in the town.

To meet residents in their own homes for after-dinner coffee or tea, contact the **Chester at Home** scheme. The chairman is Keith Butcher, Change Hey, Change Lane, Willaston, South Wirral L64 1TE (Tel 051 327 5191), who will arrange a visit free of charge.

The **National Trust** has a number of local voluntary groups which carry out projects at Trust properties, in addition to a social programme. Chester's active group work on alternate Tuesdays as well as at weekends; more information from the Regional Volunteer Co-ordinator, The National Trust, Attingham Park, Shrewsbury SY 4TP.

Merseyside, Lancashire and Greater Manchester

The National Trust owns extensive farmland on the Wirral, from which you can look across the Dee estuary, with its varied bird life. The rare natterjack toad breeds in reedbeds at **Red Rocks**, under careful protection from the Cheshire Conservation Trust. At the old **New Brighton** fairground, now a conservation area, the local primary school have planted trees and are constructing a cockleshell path. **Port Sunlight Heritage Centre** tells the story of this century-old industrial village, where an outstanding collection of English art is displayed in Lady Lever's Gallery.

Liverpool

The ferry-crossing brings you face-to-face with the spectacular Merseyside waterfront. Though there are two road tunnels the river route is the best way to arrive to appreciate the vista – the Liver (with a long 'I') Building's tall towers and the domed Cunard Offices.

Once ashore, Albert Dock is the city's premier attraction, and high on the national list as well. Formerly derelict warehouses have a new role, combining past history with present entertainment and culture. The **Maritime Museum** has floating exhibits, while another warehouse is the home of the **Northern Tate Art Gallery**. At **New Quay** a strange variety of Large Objects has been collected – anything from horse-drawn vehicles to a Blue Streak rocket. The **Liverpool Museum** near Queensway Tunnel has natural history collections and a planetarium, while the **Walker Art Gallery** next door houses important works of art, especially from early Italian and Flemish schools. The **Sudeley Art Gallery** contains works by famous British painters, and yet another museum, that of Labour History, is close by.

The two modern and distinctive **cathedrals**, Anglican and Roman

Catholic, overlook the city. The Anglican one, designed as a vast hall, is the largest church in Britain, completed only in 1978, while a lantern tower crowns the **Metropolitan Cathedral**, lit with John Piper designed stained glass. Parks include **Sefton**'s palm-house and tropical gardens, the **Botanic Gardens** at Harthill, adjoining Calderstones Park, and **Croxteth Hall** and Country Park, where special events are held. Within the city boundary, **Knowsley Safari Park** is roamed by lions and elephants. Back at Albert Dock the **Beatles Story** is told in three dimensions and, in addition to front-of-house performances, you can tour behind the scenes of Liverpool Playhouse. **Bluecoat Arts Centre**, attracting 500,000 visitors annually to the oldest city-centre building, exhibits contemporary work, houses concerts, and also has workshops for local craftspeople.

Close to the airport **Speke Hall**, the famous Tudor house, is converted inside to the standards of Victorian comfort. Sadly, it's the object of conflicting interest: conservation and airport expansion. The National Trust and the City Council are hoping to balance commercial need and heritage preservation. **Stocktons Wood** in the land which still surrounds the Hall harbours a variety of insects, because it has never been cultivated. **Seaforth Reserve** also, near the entrance to the Free Port of Liverpool, attracts seabirds in passage, and sixteen different butterfly species. The **Tourist Office** is at Atlantic Pavilion, Albert Dock (Tel 051 708 8854).

Accommodation

First Class

Trials Hotel, 52–62 Castle Street, Liverpool L2 7LQ (Tel 051 227 1021). Privately owned and magnificent, in a former bank building. Twenty suites, all very Edwardian, with friendly professional service.

Middle Range

Antrim Hotel, 73 Mount Pleasant, Liverpool L3 5TB (Tel. 051 709 5239). Twenty rooms in a friendly family run hotel in city centre.

Church End Farm, Church End, Hale Village, Liverpool L24 4AX (Tel 051 425 4273). Conveniently situated converted farmhouse on city outskirts, near Speke Hall.

Ullet Lodge, 77 Ullet Road, Liverpool L17 2AA (Tel 051 733 1680). Victorian family home near Sefton Park.

Economy

New Manx Hotel, 39 Catherine Street, Liverpool L8 7NE (Tel 051 708 6161). Characterful building, ten minutes from city centre, with interesting owner who serves excellent breakfasts.

Hardman House, Hardman Street, Liverpool L1 9AS (Tel 051 708 8303). Near Philharmonic Hall, offers free jazz sessions twice a week.

Atlantic Hotel, 9 Lord Nelson Street, Liverpool (Tel 051 709 1162). Close to station, clean and welcoming for bed and breakfast.

Eating Out

Middle Range

Armadillo, 20–22 Matthew Street (Tel 051 236 4123). Imaginative food served informally, with good range of wines.

La Grande Bouffe, 48A Castle Street (Tel 051 236 3375). Basement bistro, favouring vegetarian menu.

Jenny's Old Ropery, Fenwick Street (Tel 051 236 0332). Business restaurant in downtown Liverpool, specialising in fresh fish.

Economy

Munchy's, Myrtle Parade (Tel 051 709 7896). Serves vegetarian and vegan food. Non-alcoholic wines available.

Everyman Bistro, Hope Street (Tel 051 708 9545). Student resort near theatre, serving some home-made food.

Entertainments

Many of the attractions listed previously also offer entertainment. The **Royal Liverpool Philharmonic Orchestra** plays at the Philharmonic Hall, bought for the purpose by the City Council. As well as the **Playhouse**, the **Everyman Theatre** presents contemporary plays, and there are about four more theatres. A Beatles 'Magical History Tour' leaves from the Tourist Office each afternoon. A summer **Festival of Comedy** takes place annually. For sport, you can choose from the two major **football** grounds at Everton's Goodison Park, or Liverpool's at Anfield; alternatively, in April, you can watch the **Grand National** at Aintree Racecourse. **Soccer City Weekends** can be arranged as package tours. Visits to local homes can be arranged through **Merseyside Hospitality** (Tel 051 336 6699).

Lancashire

Formby town is separated from the sea by two miles (3 km.) of accumulating dunes, high enough to be called hills and partly grown over with pines. Red squirrels have preserved their colour here and sanderlings wade along the shore; all visitors should keep to the tracks, near which masses of yellow irises flower in June. A craft centre at **The Old Post Office**, Haskayne, just inland, sells locally-made wooden toys and hand-painted silks, while in the disused railway cutting at nearby **Downholland** are interesting flora and fauna. The sands at **Southport**, a family resort, are growing as the sea recedes; its pier was the first built in Britain for pleasure and the **Botanic Garden** is bright with Victorian flower beds. **Rufford Old Hall**, beautifully decorated outside and in, stands in farmland by the canal running close to the River Douglas. Here intersecting lanes (once infested by highwaymen) cross flat land as far as Wrightington Bar. The canal towpath stops by **Tarleton** near Mere Brow's boating and fishing lakes; you can pick-your-own at the Fruit Farm here.

Wigan has upgraded its image since George Orwell's day; canal-side buildings now house the excellent **Heritage Centre**, and 'The Way We Were' opposite the Pier illustrates how local people lived, worked and played 100 years ago. Elizabethan **Astley Hall** at Chorley contains an enormous gaming-table for playing shovelboard; it also gives period costume displays on some evenings. The town is overlooked by moors, ideal for walking, with Rivington Reservoir and Rivington Pike at their southern limit. A marina has been made from the dock at **Preston** – distinguished by its many church spires and known for founding the teetotal movement in 1834! Here the **Lancaster Canal** starts (through farmland which yields free-range eggs) while you can see birds of passage like shelduck along the River Ribble.

Fylde used to be covered in windmills; one survivor at Lytham St Annes was built in 1805. **Lytham**'s miles of sandy beach are used for sand-yacht championships in May; other championships are played on the town's four golf courses. The **'Golden Mile'** in Blackpool's six mile (10 km.) promenade is filled with thrills; here trams run along the sea front past the mighty Tower to **Fleetwood** at the mouth of the River Wyre. This used to be an important fishing port; now it has a harbour village, a yacht marina and holds regattas for model yachts. It's also a summer departure point for the shortest boat trip (three hours) to Douglas, **Isle of Man**. This is an independent sovereign country with a Lieutenant Governor but its own parliament – the oldest in the world; a lovely place for walking, with warm sea all round to swim in but, unless you want to watch motor-cycle races, best not visited in June, July or August.

Back to the mainland; **Beacon Hill's** great hump stands between the flat Fylde area and the moors. You can walk up from Preston along a maze of little roads – in company, probably, with many others. Turning back from hills to shoreline, the tiny port of **Glasson** still trades with coastal and foreign vessels, though the Basin is used for pleasure craft. The River Lune runs out past **Overton** and the saltings beyond Sunderland Point to the open sea with, just to the north, Heysham Nuclear Power Station.

August is the month for Lancaster's County **Agricultural Show**; the annual **regatta** is in May. You can take an escorted tour around **Lancaster Castle** and its grey Norman keep – though the prison occupies most of the building – or visit the neighbouring priory church. The **Custom House** on the quay dates back to the time when Lancaster was a more important port than Liverpool. On a hill above **Morecambe** (which holds a Bowling Festival in September) graves are carved into the rock beside the remains of a Saxon church. The sun sets beautifully beyond the treacherous expanses of Morecambe Bay, where local fishermen dig for lugworms. It's possible to walk at low tide from Hest Bank to Grange-over-Sands, but only with an official guide. However, there is public access at all times to the National Trust owned cliffs and foreshore, known as Jack Scout which have much to interest botanists and birdwatchers.

The beautiful **Lune Valley** leads into the high Cumbrian hills, hiding villages like Aughton (pronounced 'Afton'), which celebrates a plum pudding festival every twenty-one years – the next is in 1992 – and **Gressingham**, with crosses like the Halton one, carved under Scandinavian influence. The medieval Old Rectory at **Warton**, near Carnforth, was the home of some of George Washington's ancestors, and on the Crag above it a **Local Nature Reserve** protects the limestone terraces and grassland. Stony footpaths run north to Yealand Redmayne and the coastland around **Silverdale**, a breeding ground of the High Brown Fritillary butterfly. The National Trust owns much of this area, from the saltmarshes and low limestone cliffs to the patchwork fields filled with springtime daffodils. The Royal Society for the Protection of Birds is responsible for **Leighton Moss**, a wetland reserve where rare bitterns, marsh harriers and bearded tits live in the reed-beds. A permit is needed to visit **Gait Barrows**, an expanse of limestone pavement brought to the surface during the Ice Age. Before English Nature's protection, stone was used for various products, completely destroying part of the pavement's unique structure; some is still being removed and sold for rockeries. This is a botanist's dream; among many other plants, rare types of Solomon's Seal and St John's Wort grow in the rock fissures and scrubland. **Haweswater** is yet another Reserve; in late spring Bird's-eye Primroses flower by the lake, and in **Eaves Wood** on the Cumbrian border, sycamores grow among the ferns and mosses.

The **Forest of Bowland** is one of England's largest Areas of Outstanding Natural Beauty, high and rather treeless, though with Forestry Commission woodlands, notably at Gisburn. Here, those who like formal picnicking can do it on Cocklet Hill above Stocks Reservoir. Plenty of other paths criss-cross the moors, down Bottoms Beck, or at Dunsop Bridge, entrance to the Trough of Bowland and through which the Lancashire witches were taken from Pendle on their way to trial at Lancaster. Countryside Officers here ensure that the unique environment is managed for its own benefit and for those who visit it. **Scorton**, dissected by the M6, is a good starting point for fell walks, over to **Tarnbrook** for instance, standing under Ward's Stone, the highest point of all. At the centre of the grey stone village of **Slaidburn** is the Hark to Bounty Inn, so named, it's said, after the vicar-owner of a dog called Bounty heard its worried barking. **Chipping** is another delightful village with cobbled pavements and a rural furniture factory beside the mill-wheel, which used to provide its waterpower, while **Button Row** in Inglewhite recalls that this isolated spot was once a button-making centre.

The Ribble runs from the Pennines through **Ribblesdale**, where you can hire bicycles or canal barges, go canoeing or visit ancient markets. On the church font at **Bolton-by-Bowland** is Robert Thompson's 'mouse' trademark, as seen on much northern church furniture. Incidentally, churchyards often provide an undisturbed habitat for plants and birds. **Downham**, under Pendle Hill, has an unconventional grey pillar-box, painted to match the ancient stone village. Footpaths lead from Clitheroe to the summit of **Pendle** with extensive views, and from the church tower of **Newchurch-in-Pendle** the sculptured Eye of God stares out. The area was famous for its persecution of witches, who were believed to transform themselves into hares. Whalley and Salley are ruined Cistercian abbeys; still in working order, the mid-19th-century railway viaduct nearby was constructed from hand-made bricks. At **Hodder Bridges** a riverside walk passes near the old Roman road to **Ribchester**, which has a Museum of Childhood and another containing objects found in excavations of the fort – amongst them charred barley from its granary. Try to avoid visiting the village at summer weekends; it's very popular.

At **Blackburn** on the edge of cotton mill country, working mills jostle with heritage sites. The Cathedral contains a large and striking metal sculpture, and **Witton Park** to the west has nature trails, rhododendrons and butterflies. This end of the Ribble Valley was heavily industrialised, but moors like Blacksnape Ridge are always in the background. By the Leeds & Liverpool Canal are the beehive-shaped coke ovens of **Aspen Colliery**, scheduled an Ancient Monument. Weekend courses are held in textiles and embroidery at **Jacobean Gawthorpe Hall**, housing a collection of costumes and accessories. There are walks, some quite strenuous, on **Worsthorne Moor** around Hurstwood Reservoir and through rocky Cliviger Gorge. A 19th-century weaving mill at Queens Museum in **Burnley** is now working again, powered by a steam engine called Peace; and even Duckpits sewage works have another use as a haven for birds and plants.

At the **Weavers Triangle** industrial history is preserved while **Pendle Heritage Centre** (in the former home of athlete, Sir Roger Bannister) displays the area's textile industry. The **Liverpool & Leeds Canal** begins its descent towards Liverpool at Barrowford Locks and just above them **Foulridge Reservoir** is the resting-place of various swans and an occasional smew. Birdwatchers share Lower Foulridge with anglers and sailors; boats are for hire at Lower Park Marina, **Barnoldswick**. Paths wind around Thieveley Pike above Bacup, and in the Spodden Valley further south, the **Nature's Ways Trail** is designed to study nature's regeneration of former millponds; the **Rossendale Groundwork Trust** will supply information. At **Healey Dell**, where a high stone railway viaduct crosses the valley, the Spodden cuts through slate and sandstone to form waterfalls amongst the woodland. **Turton Moor** north of Bolton offers more remarkable walking country, in which Turton Tower, a 15th-century pele tower contains a museum of weapons; there's a folk museum too at **Hall i' th' Wood**, a half-timbered manor house in Bolton town.

Within the boundary of Greater Manchester lies environmentally conscious **Middleton**, where Oldham and Rochester Groundwork Trust are active. Alkrington Woods near the town centre are preserved as a Local Nature Reserve, while young schoolchildren and friends developed **Thornham Lane Trail** to explain the area's history. The woods round 16th-century **Hopwood Hall** form another reserve including old clay pits and mining areas. These conditions encourage the Lancastrian Asphodel, so named because 16th-century local girls used it to dye their hair. **Oldham**, with a traditional textile market, gives its name to a circular way, 42 miles (67 km.) long across the Medlock and Tame Valleys, linking with the Crompton Circuit. This includes heather-clad Denshaw moor and Brushes Clough quarry, perfect for walking or riding. The **Summit Circuit** covers both moorland edge and Rochdale Canal towpath, and still nearer to Manchester's sprawl Tandle Hill Country Park gives views of Pennine hills and urbanised valleys.

Manchester

Manchester has absorbed its satellite towns, creating an enormous complex of industry, commerce and culture. The art scene in drama and music especially is internationally known, and its expanding airport makes it easily accessible from places throughout the world. Throughout this country 70 per cent of the population are within two hours' drive of this city of Victorian architecture and 20th-century ambition.

Castlefield on the site of a Roman fort is possibly the largest of many redevelopments in the city centre. Here an **Urban Heritage Park** includes a Visitors Centre, a reconstructed Roman fort, and an Urban Studies Centre, where local schoolchildren learn about their city, past and present. The **Castlefield Gallery** displays contemporary art, while the expanding **Museum of Science and Industry** on the site of the world's oldest passenger railway station recreates the 1830s booking hall, has galleries on Air and Space, and exhibitions from paper-making to the poor sanitation of Victorian Underground Manchester.

Prominent buildings include the Gothic **Town Hall** (where guided tours are given) and the columned rotunda of the **Central Library**, the largest municipal one in the world. Of Tudor buildings in the centre, only the half-timbered **Wellington Inn** in the Market Place survives. Eighteenth-century **Heaton Hall**, Prestwich, has a collection of furniture and paintings and holds chamber concerts of the period; **Platt Hall**, Rusholme, is home to a fine English costume collection, and **Wythenshawe Hall** at Northenden displays Elizabethan furniture in a 16th-century manor house.

The **City Art Gallery** is a Classical building specialising in English painting schools; **Whitworth Art Gallery** holds permanent collections and temporary exhibitions and at **Salford Lowry Centre** the city commemorates its native painter. The Perpendicular Gothic cathedral was much rebuilt last century and had to be further reconstructed after Second World War bombing; but the carved roodscreen and stalls with misericords are mostly original. The

University's **Manchester Museum** contains natural history collections, and other museums include the **National Museum of Labour History** and Salford's **Mining Museum**.

The Bridgewater, Rochdale and Manchester Ship Canals all pass through the city and the earliest Bridgewater Canal is carried over the Manchester Ship by means of the remarkable Barton Steel Swing aqueduct. There are towpath walks at **Trafford**, and in this built-up area **Dark Lane Reserve** attracts various birds to breed. Cheshire Conservation Trust issue permits if you want to explore beyond the footpath. Farther along the canal is the 18th-century estate village of **Worsley**, where the canal system began. The half-timbered Court House and Lantern Gallery stand at the edge of water which is coloured orange from the iron ore here. The old canal basin is still in use, showing the entrances to mine tunnels, previously navigated underground by a special boat called a 'starvationer'. On the other side of town the Marple Aqueduct carries the **Lower Peak Forest Canal** over the River Goyt on a structure scheduled as an ancient monument. At Portland Basin where three canals join, an old warehouse has been turned into a Heritage Centre; and the Ashton Canal towpath passes through **Tameside Leisure Park**. In the heart of urbanisation you can see numerous birds, including some rare ones, at **Audenshaw Reservoirs**. In **Didsbury**, rare plants are grown at **Fletchers Moss Botanical Gardens**, while demonstrations and talks are given at **Wythenshawe Horticultural Centre**, and tropical insects fly at **Queens Park Butterfly Centre**.

Accommodation

First Class

Etrop Grange, Bailey Lane, Etrop Green, Ringway, Manchester M22 5NR (Tel 061 499 0500). This is a bit out of town (near the airport) but worth recommending. Small country house hotel run by caring couple, offering excellent menu.

Moss Nook, Ringway Road, Manchester M22 5NA (Tel 061 437 4778). Small cottage attached to pleasant Victorian restaurant.

Middle Range

Needhams Farm, Uplands Road, Werneth Low, Gee Cross, near Hyde, SK14 3AQ (Tel 061 368 4610). Also on the edge of the city but within easy reach of airport and centre. Mrs Walsh serves wholesome food in 16th-century farmhouse.

White Lodge Private Hotel, 87–89 Great Cheetham Street West,

Broughton, Salford, M7 9JA (Tel 061 792 3047). Small family run hotel close to centre.

Avoca Guest House, 69 Edge Lane, Chorlton-cum-Hardy, M21 1JU (Tel 061 881 0736). Mrs Mulkeen serves big breakfasts only, in warm friendly house, near centre and airport. Vegetarians catered for.

Economy

Rembrandt Hotel, 33 Sackville Street, Manchester M1 8LZ (Tel 061 236 1311). Friendly helpful hotel near coach station, serving good breakfasts.

Shire Cottage, Benches Lane, Chisworth, Hyde, SK14 6RY (Tel 0457 866536). Mrs Sidebottom offers home-from-home accommodation in peaceful countryside, with city centre easily reached.

The Black Lion, 65 Chapel Street, Blackfriars (Tel 061 834 1974). Rooms above cheerful pub, not far from station.

Eating Out

First Class

Worsley Old Hall, Old Hall Lane, Worsley (Tel. 061 799 5015). Award-winning restaurant in 16th-century hall near canal bank.

Moss Nook, Ringway Road, on B5166 (Tel 061 437 4778). Competent cooking of varied menu in comfortable surroundings.

Middle Range

Woodlands, 33 Shapley Road, Audenshaw (Tel 061 336 4241). Popular with local people. Range of vegetables served with main course. Good wine list.

Blinkers French, 16 Princess Street (Tel 061 228 2503). European cooking in comfortable basement near Chinatown, with good service.

Terrace Restaurant, The Gardens, St Ann's Square (Tel 061 834 6399). Fine view and convenient for theatres.

Economy

Market Restaurant, 104 High Street (Tel 061 834 3743). Very friendly atmosphere and wide menu. Separate Starters and Pudding Clubs.

Lime Tree, 8 Lapwing Lane, West Didsbury (Tel 061 445 1217). Informal, but sometimes slow service, and good adequate food.

Cornerhouse Cafe, 70 Oxford Street (Tel 061 976 2947). In Arts Centre; popular with students and cheap.

Wellington Inn, Shambles Square, off Market Street (Tel 061 832 7619) Old pub with small restaurant; very busy at lunch time.

Duke of York, Stockport Road, Romiley (Tel 061 430 2806). Welcoming pub with large helpings of good food in upstairs restaurant.

Entertainments

There are concerts at the **Free Trade Hall** by the Hallé, BBC Philharmonic and other famous orchestras. More musical treats are offered at the **Opera House**, by touring companies, and the Royal Northern College of Music, as well as at the Cathedral, where concerts and organ recitals are often given. For theatres you are spoiled for choice. The **Royal Exchange Theatre** on the trading floor in the old cotton exchange is the spectacular venue for a programme of theatre-in-the-round events, while the Edwardian style **Palace Theatre** specialises in opera and ballet; then there is the company playing at the **Library** and **Forum Theatres**; a professional company at the **University** – and several more. There are shows and night clubs of every kind as well as cinemas – and the leisure pool, the **Water Place** at Bolton. The old **Central Station** is now a vast Exhibition Centre, **G-Mex**, putting on all sorts of events from boxing, to rock concerts and trade fairs. **Granada Studios Tour** is a major entertainment item, giving behind-the-scenes insights into most television series. Modern shopping facilities include **Manchester Craft Village** in Tib Street where designers' work is made and sold.

Sport is an important priority; **Lancashire County Cricket Club** play at Old Trafford – so do **Manchester United Football Club**; here too is a comprehensive **Water Sports Centre**, with angling and nature trails in the surrounding park. Added to this are other major football clubs, the Northern Lawn Tennis Club and Haydock Park for racing; there is almost no sport unrepresented. At **Longford Park**, Stretford, you can play tennis or bowls, or walk in the parkland. **The Tourist Office**, Town Hall Extension, Lloyd Street (Tel 061 234 3157) will give details of these and other events.

John Rylands University Library contains rare books and manuscripts (including the St Christopher woodcut dated 1423) and holds changing exhibitions; there is also **Chetham's Hospital School and Library** and, of course, the **Central Library**. The city is almost awash with pubs, where small-scale entertainment features regularly, while annual events include the **Manchester-Salford University Boat Races** in May; a vintage and veteran **car run** to Blackpool in June; the **Hallé Proms** during the first fortnight in July; and also in July a **Summer Waterways Festival** at Portland Basin.

9 Yorkshire and Humberside

In 1974 English local government was reorganised and the historic 'ridings' (or divisions) of North and West Yorkshire became North, South and West Yorkshire, while the East Riding was lumped with part of Lincolnshire to create the new county of Humberside. Together Yorkshire and Humberside now stretch from the North Sea coast in the east to the borders of Cumbria, Lancashire and Greater Manchester in the west, with Durham and Cleveland to the north, and Derbyshire, Nottinghamshire and Lincolnshire to the south. The majority of Yorkshire and Humberside's five million population live in West and South Yorkshire.

North Yorkshire consists of the Vale of York, with the Yorkshire Dales National Park to the west and the North York Moors National Park to the east. York itself and the picturesque towns of Knaresborough, Harrogate, Ripon, Northallerton and Richmond all lie in the Vale of York. In contrast to these primarily rural areas, South and West Yorkshire are heavily industrialised; West Yorkshire is dominated by the conurbations of Leeds, Bradford, Halifax and Huddersfield, and South Yorkshire by Sheffield, Doncaster, Rotherham and Barnsley. Northern Humberside is dominated by the Yorkshire Wolds, while the south is flatter windmill country. The largest town, Kingston-upon-Hull (or just plain Hull), is an important port with ferry connections to Scandinavia.

Yorkshire folk are renowned for their strong sense of regional identity. Local dialects can be almost as incomprehensible to outsiders as Geordie and are exemplified by the song which has become a virtual anthem, 'On Ilkla Moor baht at' ('On Ilkey Moor without a hat').

The split between rural north Yorkshire and the industrial south is reflected in its 20th-century political allegiances; the north may be solidly Conservative but Sheffield is so strongly Labour that it was once dubbed the 'Socialist Republic of South Yorkshire'. The textile industries in particular have attracted a large immigrant population to South and West Yorkshire.

History

Standing stones and ceremonial circles in the Vale of York and on the Moors and Dales are evidence of prehistoric settlement in an area which eventually became home to the Brigantes tribe in the west and the Parisi in the east. The Romans founded the city of Eboracum (later York) on the banks of the River Ouse. At first primarily a military base, in time it became their most important northern town, where the Emperors Septimius Severus and Constantius died, and where Constantine was crowned.

Following the retreat of the Romans and Saxon attacks Eboracum was captured by the Vikings in AD 867. Renamed Jorvik, it became the capital of the Danelaw established in eastern England the previous year. Excavations in the Coppergate area of York in the 1970s uncovered remains of the Viking settlement, now incorporated in the award-winning, innovative Jorvik Viking Centre. The Scandinavian occupation is also commemorated in local place names ending in '–thwaite' (a clearing or meadow), '–thorp' (secondary settlement) and '–by' (village).

Eric Bloodaxe, Jorvik's last Danish king, was expelled in 954. In 1066 Harold Hardradda defeated the Scandinavians and drove them out of England altogether at the Battle of Stamford Bridge (in the Wolds). He himself was defeated at the Battle of Hastings, which established the Normans in England. Once again York became the northern capital. In 1073 an archbishopric of York, second only in importance to Canterbury, was established there. However, resistance to the Conquest resulted in 'the harrying of the north' and such widespread retaliation that many villages, particularly on the Moors, are recorded as 'wasted' in the Domesday Book. The Normans then fortified most towns to forestall further trouble.

In the Middle Ages Cistercian monks in particular settled in Yorkshire, building superb abbeys and priories and creating huge sheep farms; by the 13th century Fountains Abbey alone owned one million acres (405,000 hectares) of land and its monks were the north's largest wool producers. Nevertheless times were unsettled; in one particularly unpleasant incident in 1190, 150 Jews were burnt to death inside Clifford's Tower in York. During the Wars of the Roses when Yorkists were represented by a white rose, the bloodiest battle ever fought on English soil claimed 30,000 lives at Towton, near Tadcaster. The victor, Edward Duke of York, became King Edward IV.

After dissolving the monasteries in 1536, Henry VIII gave their land to important families like the Scropes, Cliffords and Percys. Their ruthless exploitation of local villagers resulted in the 1539 Pilgrimage of Grace led by Robert Aske of Gilling, who was eventually hanged for treason in York. Another uprising followed in 1569 when northern nobles rebelled in favour of Mary Queen of Scots, then imprisoned in Bolton Castle. Their defeat led to the execution of 700 Dalesmen.

During the Civil War most Yorkshire nobles supported Charles I, and after his defeat their castles were 'slighted' (partially demolished). Fortunately Colonal Fairfax, Cromwell's deputy in the north, treated Yorkshire leniently, sparing the Minster the iconoclasm common elsewhere.

Archaeologists have found traces of pre-Roman lead mines and forges in Yorkshire. In the Middle Ages lead mining continued, and textile industries sprang up round the sheep farms. In the 18th century however, the industrial landscape was irrevocably changed. Cottage-based production gave way to textile mills and the West Riding gradually sucked business away from traditional centres such as Doncaster, Hull, York, Richmond and Wensleydale. West and South Yorkshire also had coal seams and plentiful water supplies. Once the Industrial Revolution brought the necessary machinery, heavy industry quickly developed and cities sprang up in its wake. Early 18th-century Sheffield had just 5000 people; by 1893 there were 350,000 and the town gained city status. Bradford's wool market was soon the UK's largest. During the Luddite Riots of 1811–13 West Riding factory machinery was wrecked as a reaction to the changes in people's working lives. Titus Salt designed the model village at Saltaire to give his workers better living conditions.

In the late 20th century West and South Yorkshire, like other industrial areas, suffered from a collapse in manufacturing and consequent mass unemployment. Towns like Bradford hope to use tourism to replace the jobs lost.

Geography

The western Yorkshire Dales, limestone hills with millstone grit caps sometimes reaching 2000 feet (610 metres), resulted from Ice Age activity. Uplands are interspersed with fertile 'dales' or valleys drained by rivers like the Nidd, Wharfe, Swale and Ure. Some are broad and open like Wensleydale, others enclosed and remote like Swaledale. In the villages greystone cottages rub shoulders with fine Georgian houses. Hardy Swaledale sheep roam remote churchyards. Cotton grass, heather, bilberries and crowberries grow on the hills, and curlews, lapwings, golden plovers and red grouse are common. The landscape is decorated with drystone walls and occasional stretches of layered limestone, sandstone and shale, as at Yoredale between Arncliffe and Kilnsey.

The Pennines and the River Ribble cut across the western Dales and provide some of England's most spectacular scenery, including the Ingleborough, Whernside and Pen-y-Ghent peaks, Malham Tarn and Gaping Gill, a cavern big enough to house York Minster. The Craven Faults created the Aire Gap, the only true gap in the Pennines, which passes through Ingleton, Clapham and Settle to Giggleswick Scar, a huge roadside cliff.

The North York Moors are bleaker than the Dales. To the north are the Cleveland Hills, to the west the Hambleton Hills, to the east Fylingdales Moor and in the centre Wheeldale Moor. Much of the Moors lies at or above 1000 feet (305 m.), with Black Hambleton reaching 1257 feet (383 metres). The River Esk, Yorkshire's only salmon river, flows from Westerdale Moor to Whitby, while the Leven flows from Kildale Moor north to the Tees. Smaller streams, called 'gills' or 'becks', drain the southern moors. Common wild flowers include great hairy willow-herb, sweet cicely, meadowsweet, marsh marigold and lady's smock.

The Moors lack the spectacular limestone scenery of the Dales, but still have impressive features, including the Hole of Horcum, a natural amphitheatre near Pickering. The Moors eventually reach the sea and three stretches of designated heritage coastline. The North Yorkshire and Cleveland section to the north has stretches of fine, firm sand interspersed with steep cliffs, into which are cut the picturesque villages of Staithes and Robin Hood's Bay. Flamborough Headland, north of Bridlington, where chalk cliffs soar to 400 feet (122 m.), is also protected, as is Spurn Head, east of Hull, a stretch of coastline with sand-bars which constantly change shape.

The Vale of York itself is sandstone overlaid with boulder clay to the north, and clay, sand and gravel to the south. Most of the Dales rivers, including the Swale, Ure and Nidd, drain into the Ouse and thence into the Humber. Fertile soil permits mixed farming, but the prosperity of villages around York owes more to proximity to the city than to traditional rural activities.

The Yorkshire Wolds form an arc sweeping north from the Humber to the coast at Bridlington. Enclosed inside them to the east, Holderness is an area of chalk overlaid with clay left behind by retreating glaciers. Two miles (3 km.) inland from Hornsea, Hornsea Mere is the only remaining glacial lake. Five miles (8 km.) in circumference, it is also Yorkshire and Humberside's largest lake. Holderness is wheat-growing land, with farms right up to the cliff edges and tidy red-brick villages. Smooth, rounded hills, the Wolds rise to an average of 800 feet (244 m.), absorbing rain which then flows south into the Humber.

Climate

The Pennines act as a natural barrier, protecting much of the area from south-westerly winds. Consequently Yorkshire and Humberside are England's driest counties, receiving about 25 inches (635 mm) of rain a year. Although the Vale of York and much of the east coast can be hot in summer, reaching temperatures of up to 31°C (87°F) on good days, cold north-easterly winds also hit the coast from the North Sea and can bring rough winter weather.

Attractions

The city of York itself is Yorkshire and Humberside's biggest honeypot, especially for overseas visitors and coach parties who come to see the Minster, the Jorvik Viking Centre, York Castle Museum, the National Railway Museum, Clifford's Tower, the York Dungeon and other sights as well.

Visitors also flock to the many ruined abbeys and priories, especially Fountains, which is now a World Heritage Site, but also to Rievaulx, Jervaulx, Bolton, Roche, Kirkstall, Kirkham, Byland and Mount Grace. Castles at Richmond, Knaresborough, Scarborough, Conisborough, Middleham and Skipton (still in one piece) are also very popular. Amongst the most popular stately homes in the area are Castle Howard, where *Brideshead Revisited* was filmed, Harewood House, Beningborough Hall, Sewerby Hall, and Burton Agnes and Burton Constable Halls.

Of the five cathedrals, York Minster is architecturally and historically the most important. Ripon is also interesting however, and the ex-church cathedrals at Sheffield, Wakefield and Bradford at least repay brief visits. Other important churches include Beverley Minster, and Selby and Howden Abbeys.

South and West Yorkshire's industrial past ensures a wealth of industrial heritage sites, including Abbeydale Industrial Hamlet in Sheffield, Halifax's 'Horses at Work' exhibition, and the Yorkshire

Mining Museum in Wakefield. Humberside also has several preserved windmills.

Cuisine

Yorkshire is world famous for its pudding, a batter dish generally served with roast beef, but also available as a pub snack with onion gravy or with a meat-based filling like steak and kidney. In the past Yorkshire pudding was cooked on an open fire beneath the spitted roast and was sometimes served as a starter. Nowadays it is even found as a sweet with jam or fruit.

Locally-produced cheeses include Wensleydale (and the rarer Blue Wensleydale), sometimes eaten with apple pie, gingerbread or fruit cake; Cotherstone, which has a sharp, slightly acid taste and a natural crust which matures from a gold colour to pink; and Botton which is made in Danby and tastes quite like Cheddar.

Cafes often serve fish and chips with mushy peas. Harry Ramsden's Fish Restaurant in Guiseley reputedly sells England's best fish and chips (Tel 0943 874641). Humberside boats bring in cod, haddock and whiting in such quantities that the National Federation of Fish Friers runs local courses for would-be fish and chip vendors.

Much of the cuisine reflects the harshness of life in the past, using basic ingredients and ingenious methods of using up the least appealing cuts of meat. Tripe, faggots, potted meat and black pudding are readily available, as are oats-based cakes.

Yorkshire's greatest surprise is Bradford, where the number of Indian restaurants reflects the population's ethnic mix and has led to the creation of special 'Curry Weekends'. Brontë Yorkshire liqueur is honey-based and flavoured with herbs, spices and brandy. Local beers include Samuel Smith's and Timothy Taylor's.

A culinary footnote. It was William Strickland, a Humberside man, who first imported turkeys from America to England, a deed commemorated by the turkey-shaped lectern in Boynton church.

Level of Tourism

UK residents make over 9 million trips to Yorkshire and Humberside annually, spending an estimated £838 million. Overseas visitors make another 800,000 trips, spending £153 million. Tourism supports over 100,000 full-time and many more part-time jobs in the area.

York itself is the most popular destination. One of the established 'milk run' cities for coach tours, it is the fourth most popular town for staying visits in the UK, and the narrow medieval streets around the Minster can be unpleasantly crowded during peak holiday periods. To reduce the disturbance caused by crowds (and generate much needed cash) the Minster now charges coach parties for admission. In summer, signs are posted along the queues for the Jorvik Viking Centre (which receives more than 900,000 visitors a year) telling people how long they must expect to wait.

Of the many ruins, Fountains Abbey, a World Heritage Site, is the most popular, receiving more than 285,000 visitors a year. Unfortunately its entrance is awkwardly positioned on a bend in a road, the car park, restaurant and cafe are too small, and the site layout encourages congestion around the actual ruins. The National Trust plans to move the car park away from the Skell Valley and to provide new facilities in a camouflaged site at nearby Swanley Grange.

Both the Dales and Moors have areas with too many tourists and others which are virtually empty. The long-distance footpaths, and the Pennine Way in particular, are the most overwalked, but even the Lyke Wake Walk, once a quiet backwater, is now so busy that the North York Moors National Park Authority discourages large groups from using it; the Coast-to-Coast Walk to the north offers a good alternative. Wharfedale is close enough to the big towns of South and West Yorkshire to get very congested, especially on summer weekends when the Ingleborough/Malham Tarn area is also extremely busy. However, Littondale, upper Nidderdale and parts of Wensleydale are virtually deserted.

Most Vale of York towns also receive large numbers of visitors, with Richmond, Harrogate and Knaresborough especially popular for their combinations of scenic beauty and historic attractions. In contrast the conurbations of South and West Yorkshire and Humberside receive relatively few visitors. Bradford is in the forefront of efforts to change this. In 1979 unemployment there reached 16 per cent as the textile and engineering industries declined. The UK's first local Economic Development Unit decided to turn Bradford into the first inland industrial city that was also a successful tourist destination. 'Themes' were used to promote the city. Amongst the most successful were 'Herriot' (Thirsk area); 'Emmerdale Farm' (Leeds/Bradford area); 'Last of the Summer Wine Country' (Holmfirth area), and the marketing of the city's industrial heritage attractions and its contemporary Indian culture, the 'Flavours of Asia' programme. The Alhambra Theatre was expensively refurbished and new museums, including the award-winning National Museum of Photography, Film and Television, the Colour Museum and Treadwell's Artmill, were set up. Local tourist information centres now handle 285,000 annual enquiries and the Film Museum receives more than 730,000 visitors a year. Hull also marketed itself as a tourist destination, focusing on its renovated dock area. Bradford, Hull and Leeds eventually joined another fifteen British cities in the Great British Cities Marketing Group, which offers Gold Star city breaks.

The development of ex-industrial areas for tourism (so-called 'smokestack tourism') has been criticised on the grounds that it replaces 'real' jobs with 'candy-floss' work which is frequently seasonal and low-paid, and because it tends to romanticise the reality of harsh working and living conditions. However, where the educational as well as the entertainment value of the new attractions is taken into account, as in Sheffield's Abbeydale Industrial Hamlet, then such developments can be more successful than traditional museums in bringing the past to life. Clever marketing, particularly of weekend city breaks, can also ensure year-round trade. And it is debatable whether the factories and mines were really much better places to work.

Some Bradford marketing concentrated on the appeal of Brontë Country, centred on the parsonage at Haworth where Charlotte, Emily and Anne grew up. The building has already had to be extended to cope with more than 200,000 visitors a year, and in 1990 the Brontë Society announced controversial plans for a further extension.

The coastal villages of Staithes and Robin Hood's Bay receive more than their fair share of visitors and are prevented by their geography from dispersing them. In both places drivers must leave their cars away from the sea front. Whitby and Scarborough are better able to absorb large numbers of visitors without damage to their social and environmental fabric.

In 1990 the Commercial Members Group of Yorkshire and Humberside Tourist Board set up a working party on 'Tourism and the Environment'. A Tourism Visitor Management Initiative covering the Dales and North York Moors areas with ETB funding is also planned.

Good Alternatives

Meeting People

Yorkshire and Humberside have a busy **festival** calendar, with several events offering 'meet the locals' opportunities. For example, visitors to the **St Leger** horse-race meeting at Doncaster; the **Harrogate Flower Festival**; **Filey's Edwardian Festival** in June; the famous **Scarborough Fair** and the even older **Hull Fair** are bound to get chatting. The **Egton Bridge Gooseberry Show** offers the chance to sample locally-grown produce at the same time. The free leaflet, *What's On in Yorkshire and Humberside*, available from Tourist Information Centres, includes up-to-date details of dates and places. **Market days** also offer chances for informal exchanges, and are often the best days for visits.

Trips to industrial sites and craft workshops listed in the free *Working Guide to Yorkshire and Humberside* are another possibility. At Hebden Bridge the Maude Walkley Clog Factory (Tel 0422 842061) offers tours during which visitors can discuss the clog-making process. A **Dales Country Workshop Trail** suggests places to watch candle-making, glass-blowing, brewing, weaving, sculpture, ropemaking, pottery, farming and woodworking. The free leaflet, *Craft Centres and Workshops in Yorkshire and Humberside*, gives addresses of businesses which welcome visitors, including a rocking horse shop in Holme-upon-Spalding Moor (Tel 0430 860563); Samuel Smith's Old Brewery in Tadcaster (Tel 0937 832225), and Swillington House Farm near Leeds (Tel 0532 869129).

The **British Trust for Conservation Volunteers** (Tel 0491 39766) has a range of local projects and runs a skills training centre at Hollybush Farm, Broad Lane, Kirkstall, Leeds (Tel 0532 742335), where techniques for countryside conservation are taught. Courses are also available on angora farming (The Mohair Farm, Barmby Moor, York, Tel 07595 308) and corn-dolly making (Primrose Hill Farm, Cawood, Selby, Tel 075786 270). Younger tourists can also help restore York Minster at a summer 'cathedral camp'; contact Manor House, High Birstwith, Harrogate (Tel 0423 770385) for details.

Activity holidays offer opportunities to meet people while also exploring beautiful and remote countryside. The free leaflet, *Activity and Special Interest Holidays in Yorkshire and Humberside*, details these and many other possibilities; a separate leaflet lists companies offering riding and pony trekking holidays.

To find out about Bradford's many religions and to visit its places of worship contact the **Interfaith Education Centre**, Listerhills Road (Tel 0274 731674).

Discovering Places

Yorkshire and Humberside local authorities have created many **trails** to encourage tourists to spread their visits more widely;

the **Yorkshire Mining Heritage Trail** in the Barnsley/Wakefield area starts at Caphouse Colliery, while a **Turner in the Dales** tour links up Wensleydale, Swaledale and Teesdale sites visited by the artist. In the Hambleton area (north of York) there are **In Herriot's Footsteps, Hambleton Historic Houses, Famous People from the Past** and **Craft Workshop** trails (details from local tourist information centres). Bedale and Northallerton offer **town trails** and Leeds has a **Cloth Trail** (details from Leeds City Tourism. Tel 0532 462631). Ilkley Moor and Middleton Woods also have **nature trails**. The **Captain Cook Heritage Trail** continues south from Cleveland along the coast to Whitby.

Of many new and imaginative tourist attractions, the **Jorvik Viking Centre** is probably the best known. In 1990 the York Archaeology Trust also opened **ARC** – the Archaeological Resource Centre – in St Saviour's church, to explain archaeological processes to the many visitors. In 1990 the National Railway Museum was completely refitted and a new **Museum of Automata** was opened. Having discovered tourism so recently, the industrial south and west have many new attractions. Typically **Halifax** has several innovative museums, including **Piece Hall Pre-Industrial Museum and Art Gallery**, housed in a converted Cloth Hall, and the **National Museum of the Working Horse**. In 1992, **Eureka**, Britain's first museum to interpret everything from a child's perspective will also open in Halifax.

Communications

How to Get There

RAIL: Connections between the region and the rest of the UK are good, with main stations at York (Tel 0904 642155), Sheffield (Tel 0742 726411) and Leeds (Tel 0532 448133). York is on the main east coast London–Edinburgh route and there are regular trains both south and north. The town has been a major railway junction for almost a century. Travelling to Hull (Tel 0482 26033) by train, passengers usually have to change at Doncaster. There are direct trains from London however, which also go through Newark and Doncaster (Tel 0482 225678 for a recorded timetable).

COACH: Sheffield (Tel 0742 754905), York (Tel 0532 460011) and Hull (Tel 0482 27146) are all connected to the rest of the country by regular **National Express** coaches.

FERRY: Ferries from and to Zeebrugge and Rotterdam leave from Hull (Tel 0482 795141).

When You're There

RAIL: A rail route passes through Aire Gap in the Pennines. The Settle to Carlisle railway also passes through the Gap. In 1990 British Rail tried to close the line on the grounds that maintenance of its infrastructure, including the spectacular Ribble Viaduct, was too costly; the fate of some stations along the route remains uncertain even though BR eventually lost its case. Regular trains run from York to Hull.

Of several preserved steam railways, the most popular are the Keighley and Worth Steam Railway which runs through Haworth, and the North Yorkshire Moors Railway which travels across the Moors from Pickering to Grosmont carrying over 250,000 people a year. At Grosmont the preserved trains connect with British Rail's Esk Valley line, joining Middlesbrough and Whitby along a particularly scenic route. The Keighley and Worth Railway also links into the British Rail line from Leeds to Carnforth at Keighley, another scenic route, much of it following the Leeds and Liverpool Canal. The Embsay Steam Railway from Skipton and the Lincolnshire Light Coast Railway are smaller preserved railways.

BUS: The area is well served by regional buses. Tourist Information offices carry information on local routes and times.

CAR: The A1, or Great North Road, follows the route of the old Roman Dere Street, along a ridge of limestone to the west of the Vale of York. Travelling the eastern coastal route used to involve a major diversion until the Humber Bridge, the world's longest single-span suspension bridge, opened in 1981 (tolls charged). The M62, or Trans-Pennine route, links Hull to western cities but is often closed during bad winter weather.

BOAT: The Leeds to Liverpool Trans-Pennine canal preserves striking engineering structures like Bingley Five Locks which raise the canal level some 120 feet, one of the seven wonders of the waterways world and easily accessible from Leeds and Bradford. At Hebden Bridge the Rochdale canal has also been cleared to offer horse-drawn barge trips.

WALKING: Walking is popular in this area, either casually on the Moors or Dales or along the three National Trails: the Pennine Way, which crosses the Dales; the Cleveland Way which crosses the Moors and follows the coastline, and the Wolds Way, which heads north from Hull to the Humberside coast. Also popular are the Lyke Wake Walk, which traverses the Moors from west to east and the Coast to Coast

Walk, devised by A. Wainwright, which enters the Dales west of Keld and crosses Yorkshire to Robin Hood's Bay.

An alternative route for walkers is the Ebor Way, which runs from Ilkely to York/Helmsley. The free leaflet *Walking in Yorkshire and Humberside* (available from Tourist Information Centres) outlines local walks and where to get further information.

Useful Local Contacts

In Yorkshire, visitors could contact the **Yorkshire and District Field Naturalists' Society**, 53 Bootham Crescent, York YO3 7AJ (Tel 0904 53953) for information on the natural history of the area, or the **Yorkshire Archaeological Society**, Claremont, 23 Clarendon Road, Leeds LS2 9NZ (Tel 0532 457910) for details of ruins and remains. **Yorkshire Dales Conservation**, 6 Hallgarth, Airion, Skipton BD23 4AQ might be a good place to start for visitors interested specifically in the Dales, as would be the **Yorkshire Dales National Park Authority**, Yorebridge House, Bainbridge, Leyburn, Richmond DL8 3BP (Tel 0969 50456). For information on field centres, contact **Yorkshire Field Studies**, Church Farm House, High Street, Thornton Dale, and for wildlife issues try the **Yorkshire Wildlife Trust**, 3rd Floor, 10 Toft Green, off Micklegate, York YO1 1JT (Tel 0904 659570).

Visitors to Humberside could contact the **Hull Natural History Society**, 678 Beverley High Road, Hull HU6 7JH (Tel 0482 851798) or the **Spurn Bird Observatory**, Kilnsea, near Patrington, Hull HU12 0UG.

Geographical Breakdown of Region

York

The administrative and tourist centre of Yorkshire and Humberside, York is very compact, its old parts enclosed within walls and best explored on foot. **Yorktour**, 8 Tower Street (Tel 0904 64137) provides guide services and tours. Evening 'ghost' tours are also available; contact the **Tourist Information Centre**, Rougier Street (Tel 0904 620557) for details. The best time for a visit might be during the February **Jolablot Viking Festival**, when many hotels offer special rates (Festival Office, 37 Micklegate. Tel 0904 611944).

The **Minster** is one of the UK's most impressive medieval cathedrals: its east transept has been restored and rerooofed after the 1984 fire and an exhibition in the undercroft displays finds made while the central tower was being strengthened. There are good views from the tower. Thirteenth-century **City Walls** enclose most of the city. The **Jorvik Viking Centre** recreates 9th-century York down to its sounds and smells; in 'time cars', tourists travel past fibreglass repro-Vikings. The **Castle Museum** contains reconstructed Victorian streets and shops and a condemned cell where Dick Turpin spent his last night. **Clifford's Tower** is a ruined 13th-century keep. **The National Railway Museum** houses many famous preserved locomotives. The **Shambles** and **Stonegate** are narrow, medieval streets with novelty shops. **York Dungeon** is only for those with a taste for the macabre. The **York Story** offers an audio-visual introduction to the city's history in a redundant church. The **Merchant Adventurers' Hall** is a 14th-century half-timbered building. **The Treasurer's House**, a 17th/18th-century townhouse with formal gardens, is reputedly haunted. Twenty of York's forty-one pre-16th-century churches also survive: most interesting are **All Saints, North Street** and **Holy Trinity, Goodramgate** (redundant but retaining an unspoilt, higgledy-piggledy 18th-century interior). Ouse river trips are available from **White Rose Line** (Tel 0904 28324).

York Arts Centre, Micklegate (Tel 0904 627129) has a programme of cabaret, music, dance and art. **Theatre Royal** (Tel 0904 623568). The **York Mystery Plays** are staged in the **Merchant Adventurers' Hall**, and, once every four years, in the grounds of St Mary's Abbey. Every July there's a week-long early music festival.

Around York

Castle Howard is a 17th/18th-century country house in 1000 acre (405 hectare) grounds. **Beningborough Hall**, an 18th-century house, contains paintings from the National Portrait Gallery collection. Attractive villages in the area include **Stillington, Easingwold, Coxwold** and **Sutton-on-the-Forest**. **Sutton Park**, a small Georgian house, can be visited in summer.

Accommodation

First Class

Middlethorpe Hall, Bishopthorpe Road, York YO2 1QB (Tel 0904 641241). Charming 17th-century country house offering traditional comfort and luxury, set in extensive grounds and parkland.

Lady Anne Middleton's Hotel, Skeldergate, York YO1 1DS (Tel 0904 632257). Family-run hotel in a lovely building set in pleasant gardens close to the town centre.

Beechwood Close Hotel, 19 Shipton Road, Clifton YO3 6RE (Tel

0904 658378). Pleasant family run hotel about one mile (1.5 km.) from York Minster.

Middle Range

Arndale Hotel, 290 Tadcaster Road, York YO2 2ET (Tel 0904 702424). Large Victorian house overlooking the race course. Four-poster and half-tester beds.

Blue Bridge Hotel, Fishergate, York YO1 4AP (Tel 0904 621193). Private hotel offering a friendly welcome and good food, a short walk from the town centre.

Skeldergate House Hotel, 56 Skeldergate, York YO1 1DS (Tel 0904 635521). Mid-18th-century Georgian town house right in the town centre.

Economy

Annjoa, 34 Millfield Road, York YO2 1NQ (Tel 0904 653731). Family run hotel with a good reputation.

The Hollies, 141 Fulford Road, York YO1 4HG (Tel 0904 634279). Family run guest house convenient for the city centre.

Gill House Farm, Tockwith Road, Long Marston, York YO5 8PJ (Tel 0904 83379). Five hundred acre (202 hectares) mixed working farm offering bed and breakfast (and evening meal) on the site of the Battle of Marston Moor. Good views, peace and quiet and lots of healthy country living.

Youth Hostel, Haverford, Water End, Clifton, York (Tel 0904 53147).

Eating Out

Middle Range

St William's College, 3 College Street, York (Tel 0904 634830).

Plunket's, 9 High Petergate, York (Tel 0904 637722).

Miller's Yard Cafe, Miller's Yard, Gillygate, York (Tel 0904 610676).

The White Bear, Stillington (Tel 0347 810338).

Economy

Jazz Cafe and Bar, Arts Centre, Micklegate, York (Tel 0904 642582).

Betty's, St Helen's Square (Tel 0904 659142).

Taylor's, 46 Stonegate, York (Tel 0904 622865).

Southern Vale of York

Harrogate is a spa town oozing gentility, with Victorian streets radiating from the **Stray**, 200 acres (81 hectares) of city centre commonland. The **Pump Room Museum** houses local history and costumes in an original 19th-century spa building. The **Valley Gardens** are pinewoods with formal floral displays. **Tourist Information** is at the Royal Baths Assembly Rooms, Crescent Road (Tel 0423 525666).

One mile (1.5 km.) west, the 60 acre (24 hectare) **Harlow Car Gardens** are run by the Northern Horticultural Society. **Ripley**, to the north, is an unspoilt 19th-century Gothic village; the mainly 16th- and 18th-century **Castle** has grounds laid out by Capability Brown. **Fountains Abbey** is also north of Harrogate, in wooded Skeldale. English Heritage is still restoring the medieval ruins, but the National Trust has completed work on the surrounding Studley Royal estate, providing marvellous walks. There's a fine 19th-century church by William Burges.

Ripon cathedral, isolated in the middle of a traffic junction, which makes it difficult to appreciate its austere Early English west front, dates from the 12th century and has particularly fine misericords and a Saxon crypt. Nearby, the **Prison and Police Museum** is in a 17th-century building. Every night the hornblower still sounds a medieval curfew in the market-place. Ripon **Tourist Information** is in Munster Road (Tel 0765 4625).

South of Harrogate is 18th-century **Harewood House**, with Adam and Chippendale fittings. To the east, **Knaresborough** has a superb setting on a cliff overlooking the River Nidd, ruins of a 14th-century castle, a medieval church with fine monuments and Mother Shipton's Petrifying Well, where lime in the water turns objects hung from a rock into stone; **Tourist Information** is at 35 Market Place (Tel 0423 866886).

Aldborough has remains of a Roman town built over the Brigantes' capital.

Accommodation

First Class

Grants Hotel, Swan Road, Harrogate HG1 2SS (Tel 0423 560666). Friendly town-centre hotel now benefiting from refurbishment.

Ripon Spa Hotel, Park Street, Ripon HG4 2BU (Tel 0765 2172). Privately owned country house hotel set in delightful gardens and close to the town centre.

Middle Range

Scotia House Hotel, 66 Kings Road, Harrogate HG1 5JR (Tel 0423 504361). Cosy private hotel now under new ownership.

The Yorkshire Lass, High Bridge, Harrogate Road, Knaresborough HG5 8DA (Tel 0423 862962). Traditional Yorkshire hospitality in a characterful pub with pleasant rooms.

Economy

The Langham Hotel, 21 Valley Drive, Harrogate HG2 0JL (Tel 0423 502179). Family owned hotel with a reputation for good food, and offering golf breaks.

Hutton Grange, Hutton Moor, Ripon HG4 5LX (Tel 0765 84520). Traditional Yorkshire farmhouse, tastefully refurbished and with an indoor heated swimming pool.

Riverside, 21 Waterside, Knaresborough HG5 8DE (Tel 0423 865714). Small, family run guest house overlooking the River Nidd.

Eating Out

Middle Range

Dr B's Kitchen, 5–13 Knaresborough Road, Harrogate (Tel 0423 884819). Good food and provides training for young people with special needs.

Tiffin's on the Stray, 11A Regent Parade, Harrogate (Tel 0423 504041).

Economy

Betty's, 1 Parliament Street, Harrogate (Tel 0423 502746).

Northern Vale of York

Thirsk, Masham and **Bedale** are attractive market towns with fine medieval churches. Isolated **Jervaulx Abbey**, once a Cistercian monastery, is being strengthened and restored by its private owners. The picture-postcard village of **East Witton** has 19th-century stone cottages lining a long green. Ruined **Snape Castle** was home to Henry VIII's last wife, Catherine Parr. **Northallerton** has Georgian houses and a fine market square. Picturesque, hilly **Richmond** on the River Swale has a dramatic Norman castle, a regimental museum in redundant Holy Trinity church and the Georgian **Theatre Royal**, the oldest theatre still staging performances in its original shape (Tel 0748 3021 for performance details). **Easby**, one mile (1.5 km.) south-east, has extensive ruins of a Premonstratensian abbey. The main **Tourist Information Centres** in the area are at Applegarth Car Park, Northallerton (Tel 0609 776864), and Friary Gardens, Victoria Road, Richmond (Tel 0748 850252).

Accommodation

First Class

King's Head Hotel, Market Place, Richmond DL10 4HS (Tel 0748 850220). Traditional hotel in an attractive Georgian building overlooking Richmond's cobbled square. Some rooms with four-posters.

Middle Range

Sheppard's Hotel, Front Street, Sowerby, Thirsk YO7 1JF (Tel 0845 523655). Seventeenth-century farmhouse on the edge of the village green close to Thirsk centre.

Frenchgate Hotel, 59-61 Frenchgate, Richmond DL10 7AE (Tel 0748 2087). Converted Georgian town house near to the original gates of the old walled town.

Economy

High Paradise Farm, Boltby, Thirsk YO7 2HT (Tel 0845 537353). Attractive old farmhouse in a wonderful setting on the Hambleton Hills.

Alverton Guest House, 26 South Parade, Northallerton DL7 8SG (Tel 0609 776207). Victorian town house offering traditional Yorkshire comfort and cuisine.

West End Guest House, 45 Reeth Road, Richmond DL1 0EX (Tel 0748 4783). Bed and breakfast (and evening meal) in a 19th-century house with a large garden.

Eating Out

Middle Range

The Angel Inn, Long Street, Topcliffe, Thirsk (Tel 0845 577237).
The Green Dragon, 16 Market Place, Bedale (Tel 0677 22902).

Economy

Betty's, 188 High Street, Northallerton (Tel 0609 775154).

The Yorkshire Dales

The Dales stretch from Ilkley in the south to Ingleton in the west, Langthwaite in the north and Kirkby Malzeard and Winksley in the east. Roads usually follow the rivers: the Ribble, Aire, Wharfe, Nidd, Skell, Ure and Swale. Not surprisingly the quietest areas tend to be at the furthest ends of the valleys; **Arkengarthdale** in the north is particularly peaceful.

A market town at the start of the Aire Gap, **Skipton** has a magnificent intact medieval castle with banqueting hall, kitchen and dungeon, a fine 14th-century church, the Craven Museum and the George Leatt Industrial and Folk Museum. The **Embsay Steam Railway** starts just to the west.

Wharfedale

Ilkley, a spa town, has Saxon crosses in its churchyard. The Cow and Calf Rocks are climbable. The **Swastika Stone** and other prehistoric carved stones can be seen on Ilkley Moor to the south and west. Part of 12th-century ruined Augustinian **Bolton Abbey** is now a parish church in a lovely riverside setting. A pleasant walk along the river to Appletreewick passes 15th-century ruined **Barden Tower**, the Stridd gorge, hump-backed bridges and stepping stones. **Grassington** and **Linton** are pretty villages, partly medieval; Grassington has a National Park Interpretation Centre. From picturesque **Kettlewell** a steep moorland road passes between Buckden Pike (2302 feet, 702 m.) and Great Whernside (2310 feet, 704 m.) to reach Coverdale and Wensleydale. Three miles (4.5 km.) south, Kilnsey Crag marks the start of **Mastiles Lane** leading to Malham Tarn. Peaceful wooded **Littondale** flows west from Kilnsey through the unspoilt villages of Arncliffe and Linton. From **Halton Gill** a path heads north across Horse Head Moor to join Langstrothdale, an extension of Wharfedale. **Malham**, to the west of Linton, is a mile (1.5 km.) south of **Malham Cove**, a natural amphitheatre, 240 feet (73 m.) high. Within walking distance is **Gordale Scar**, with cliffs and waterfalls, and **Malham Tarn**.

Wensleydale

Middleham Castle has a massive ruined 12th-century keep. **Wensley's**

beautiful medieval church, overlooking the Ure and with sheep cropping its grass, is one of the best in the Dales. **Aysgarth Force** is a series of attractive waterfalls in woodland. North-east is ruined medieval **Bolton Castle**, where Mary Queen of Scots was once held prisoner. At **Bainbridge**, where a medieval evening curfew is still sounded, the River Bain flows south to the Dales' largest lake, Semerwater. A five mile (8 km.) path follows the route of an old Roman road. North of Hawes is **Hardow Force**, a 100 foot (30 m.) waterfall. A road over **Buttertubs Pass** leads north to Swaledale.

Swaledale

At **Reeth** a tributary river flows through remote **Arkengarthdale**. **Grinton** has a magnificent, austere, mainly 15th-century church, 'the Cathedral of the Dales'. From **Keld** a footpath joins the Pennine Way. Four miles (6 km.) north-west, **Tan Hill Inn** (1732 feet, 528 m.) is one of England's most remote pubs.

Ribblesdale and the West Dales

Settle is a market town at the start of the scenic Settle–Carlisle railway. The A65 turns westwards past the roadside cliff of **Giggleswick Scar** to **Clapham**, where a path along the beck leads to **Ingleborough Cave** and **Gaping Gill**, the largest limestone cave in Britain. Four miles (6 km.) north-east of **Ingleton**, **Ingleborough Hill** (2373 feet, 693 m.), with its natural limestone terrace, can be climbed from Hill Inn. North of Settle the B649 follows the Ribble, with access to **Pen-y-Ghent** (2273 feet, 693 m.) from **Horton-in-Ribblesdale**.

Tourist Information Centres in the area are at Pen-y-Ghent Cafe, Horton-in-Ribblesdale (Tel 07296 333); Station Road, Ilkley (Tel 0943 602319); Town Hall, Cheapside, Settle (Tel 07292 5192), and 8 Victoria Square, Skipton (Tel 0756 792809).

Accommodation & Eating Out

First Class

Randell's Hotel, Keighley Road, Snaygill, Skipton BD23 2TA (Tel 0756 700100). Modern hotel offering comfort and good service, as well as a leisure centre, squash courts and swimming pool.

Middle Range

The Old Station, Brackenber Lane, Giggleswick, Settle BD24 0EA (Tel 07292 3623). Traditional Yorkshire inn offering comfortable accommodation and providing a convenient base.

Moorgarth Hall, New Road, Ingleton LA6 3HL (Tel 05242 41946). Family run Victorian house offering the best of Yorkshire hospitality and cuisine.

Secret Garden House, Grove Square, Leyburn DL8 5AE (Tel 0969 23589). Peaceful Georgian house in the centre of Leyburn with a pleasant walled garden and good food.

Economy

Langber Guest House, Ingleton LA6 3DT (Tel 05242 41587). Friendly bed and breakfast (evening meal if required) with a superb hilltop setting offering fine views of the surrounding countryside.

Youth Hostels can be found at Aysgarth Falls (Tel 09693 260); Ingleton (Tel 0468 41444); Malham (Tel 07293 321), and Stainforth (Tel 07292 3577).

The North York Moors

The North York Moors form an arch shape around the Vale of Pickering, stretching from the coast to Osmotherley, Kilburn and Sheriff Hutton in the west, and Commondale and Runswick in the north. The **Ebor Way** footpath runs from York to Helmsley, connecting the Dales Way to the Cleveland Way.

Malton and the Southern Moors

Malton has a lively Friday and Saturday market. Four miles (6 km.) south-west, early 18th-century **Castle Howard** was designed by Vanbrugh with extensive parklands. The 13th/14th-century ruins of **Kirkham Priory** stand in peaceful woods. Remains of the deserted medieval village of **Wharram Percy** lie south-west of Wharram-le-Percy.

Hambleton Hills/Cleveland Hills area

Rievaulx Abbey, two miles (3 km.) north-west of the market town of Helmsley, is one of Yorkshire's most beautiful ruined Cistercian abbeys; Rievaulx Terrace offers panoramic views of the magnificent 12th-century ruins and of Ryedale and the Hambleton Hills. At the **Kilburn** workshops of Robert Thompson's Craftsmen, every item has a wooden mouse carved on it. From **Hawnby** a path leads to an old drove road up to **Black Hambleton** (1257 feet, 383 m.). **Hutton-le-Hole**, a particularly picturesque village, has the Ryedale Folk Museum and a 17th-century Quaker cottage. Five miles (8 km.) north-west, **Farndale Nature Reserve** on the River Dove has one of the country's best wild daffodil displays. West of Kirkbymoorside are **Kirkdale Woods** and **St Gregory's Minster**, which retains Saxon features. One mile (1.5 km.) north of **Osmotherley** is **Mount Grace Priory**, a ruined 14th-century Carthusian monastery.

Central Moors Area

The market town of **Pickering** on the edge of the Moors has a ruined 12th-century castle, and a church with impressive 15th-century frescos. One mile (1.5 km.) north-west of Goathland, **Beck Hole** hamlet sits in a hollow surrounded by woods and waterfalls. A path leads to Hunt House and then to visible remains of a Roman road crossing Wheeldale Moor to Stape. East of Goathland on Fylingdales Moor are the huge space-age golf-balls of a ballistic missile early warning system. South of Goathland is a natural amphitheatre, the **Hole of Horcum**. The **Dalby Forest Drive** passes through the Dalby and Bickley forests with red squirrels and goldcrests. **Danby** to the north has a visitor centre and a 14th-century castle, now a farmhouse; Danby Ridge is covered in prehistoric tumuli. From **Sleights** a path leads to bluebell-filled Littlebeck Valley via Falling Foss waterfall.

Tourist Information Centres are at The Moors Centre, Lodge Lane, Danby (Tel 0287 60654); and Old Town Hall, Market Place, Malton (Tel 0653 600048).

Accommodation

First Class

The White Swan, Market Place, Pickering YO18 7AA (Tel 0751 72288). Welcoming coaching inn situated in the centre of Pickering offering comfort, good food and a fine selection of wines.

Middle Range

Oakdene House Hotel, 29 Middlecave Road, Malton YO17 0NE (Tel 0653 693363). Victorian country house set in beautiful gardens in a pleasant area of Malton.

Economy

The Brow, 25 York Road, Malton YO17 0AX (Tel 0653 693402). Large Georgian house offering bed and breakfast and fine views.

Vivers Mill, Mill Lane, Pickering YO18 8DJ (Tel 0751 73640). Converted watermill in peaceful surroundings; full of character and comfort.

Youth Hostels are at Helmsley (Tel 0439 70433) and Goathland (Tel 0947 86350).

Eating Out

Economy

Camphill Book and Coffee Shop, 91 Saville Street, Malton (Tel 0653 695265).

South Yorkshire

The smallest district of Yorkshire and Humberside, South Yorkshire is dominated by the university city of **Sheffield**, with its thriving nightlife and cultural activities. In 1990 a tourism development initiative was expected to result in improvements to several city sites.

Despite rather grim approaches, Sheffield is sited in a southern Pennine hollow and countryside is distantly visible from most parts of the city. The area's declining manufacturing industries are recalled in the **Kelham Island Industrial Museum** and in **Abbeydale Industrial Hamlet**, a late-18th/early-19th-century steel and scythe works, three miles (5 km.) south-west. Two miles (3 km.) west at Whiteley Woods, **Shepherd Waterwheel** drove grindstones for the cutlery industry. The **Cathedral** was a parish church until 1913.

Rotherham, north-east of Sheffield, has a surprisingly impressive medieval church, while the bridge over the Don has one of only four medieval bridge chapels left in England. The Doncaster road passes **Conisbrough** with its romantic 12th-century ruined castle; the ruins of contemporary **Roche Abbey** lie to the south-east. **Doncaster** is best known for the September St Leger races.

To the north-east of Sheffield are **Barnsley**, a struggling coal-mining town, and **Penistone**, with a 13th-century church. Two miles (3 km.) north is **Gunthwaite Hall**, a 15th-century half-timbered barn. Directly west of Sheffield the Howden Moors overlap the edge of the Derbyshire Peak District. There is a **Tourist Information Centre** at the Town Hall Extension, Union Street, Sheffield (Tel 0742 734671).

Accommodation

First Class

Grosvenor House Hotel, Charter Square, Sheffield (Tel 0742 7200421).

Middle Range

Middlewood Hall Hotel, Mowson Lane, Worrall (Tel 074286 3919).

Economy

Fell House, 354 Barnsley Road, Hoylandswine (Tel 0226 790937).

For **university rooms** contact **Holiday Information Office** (Tel 0742 768555, ext 4080).

Eating Out

Middle Range

Beauchief Restaurant, 161 Abbeydale Road (Tel 0742 620500).
Just Cooking, 16–18 Carver Street (Tel 0742 27869).
Fat Cat, 23 Alma Street (Tel 0742 28195).
Nirmal's, 189–93 Glossop Road (Tel 0742 724054).

West Yorkshire

West Yorkshire is dominated by the conurbations of Leeds, Bradford, Halifax, Huddersfield and Wakefield, which together form England's third largest urban area. In 1990 a Tourism Development Action Programme aimed at improving facilities and the environment along the Leeds and Liverpool Canal was launched.

Leeds

Despite some ugly post-industrial and 1960s buildings, Leeds also has fine Victorian architecture, with several covered shopping arcades including the **Victorian City Market** in Vicar Lane. **Abbey House Museum** has reconstructed period streets. **Armley Mills** has an excellent industrial museum. Three miles (5 km.) north-west, the ruins of 12th-century **Kirkstall Abbey** stand beside the Aire. Three miles (5 km.) east, partially Jacobean **Temple Newsam House** has grounds designed by Capability Brown and a Home Farm Rare Breeds Centre. The **Museum of Leeds Trail** follows an eight mile (12 km.) stretch of the Leeds and Liverpool Canal.

Bradford

Today Leeds and Bradford are almost continuous and share an airport.

However, Bradford has promoted tourism even more vigorously than Leeds. The **National Museum of Photography, Film and Television** has free admission, although there are charges for films on its giant IMAX screen. The **Colour Museum** illustrates the history of dyeing. The **Little Germany** merchant area of the city and the **Wool Exchange** are being restored to their Victorian grandeur. A Victoria and Albert Museum of the North will soon open in Manningham Mill. **Tong**, on the city outskirts, has a fine church with unrestored 18th-century interior. Bradford offers easy access to the Pennine village of **Haworth** with the **Brontë Parsonage** and a **Museum of Childhood**, and to **Five Rise Locks** on the Leeds and Liverpool Canal at Bingley.

Halifax

Most of Halifax's buildings are Victorian, but **Piece Hall** is an 18th-century Cloth Hall, now housing a **Pre-Industrial Museum and Art Gallery**. Shire and other heavy horses can be seen at the **Horses at Work: National Museum of the Working Horse** in Dobbin's Yard, South Parade. Twenty different industries are explained at the **Calderdale Industrial Museum** in Square Road. **Hebden Bridge** on the Calder preserves mills and workers' cottages; horse-drawn barge rides are available. The **Maude Walkley Clog Factory** on Burnley Road has lots of extras like a bee museum and art gallery. A mile (1.5 km.) out of town, pretty **Heptonstall** has weavers' cottages, 13th-century church ruins and a museum in a 17th-century Grammar School.

Huddersfield

Another primarily Victorian city, Huddersfield has a particularly impressive railway station. At **Holmfirth** to the south is a Postcard Museum.

Wakefield

The primarily 13th-century cathedral has a dramatic spire, while the medieval bridge retains a much-restored bridge chapel. At the **Yorkshire Mining Museum** at Caphouse Colliery (Overton) visitors are shown round a real mine. **Wakefield Art Gallery** houses important 20th-century paintings.

Tourist Information Centres in the area are at 19 Wellington Street, Leeds (Tel 0532 462454); City Hall, Hall Ings/Channing Way, Bradford (Tel 0274 753678); and Piece Hall, Halifax (Tel 0422 368725).

Accommodation

First Class

Queen's Hotel, City Square, Leeds (Tel 0532 431323).
Victoria Hotel, Bridge Street, Bradford (Tel 0274 728706).
Leeming Wells Hotel, Long Causeway, Leeming, Oxenhope, near Haworth (Tel 0535 42201).

Middle Range

Rydings Country Hotel, Bridgehouse Lane, Haworth (Tel 0535 45206).
PLS Hotel, Shearbridge Mill, Bradford (Tel 0274 306775).

Economy

Avalon Guest House, 132 Woodsley Road, Leeds (Tel 0532 432545).
Carlton House Guest House, Thornton Road, Thornton, Bradford (Tel 0274 833397).
Redacre House, Redacre, Mytholmroyd, Hebden Bridge (Tel 0422 883019).
There is a **Youth Hostel** at Haworth (Tel 0535 42234).

Eating Out

Middle Range

Strawberryfields Bistro, 159 Woodhouse Lane, Leeds (Tel 0532 431515).
Byrams, 3 Byram Street, Huddersfield (Tel 0484 530243).
Weavers, 15 West Lane, Haworth (Tel 0535 43822).

Economy

Saltaire Boathouse and Victorian Restaurant, Victoria Road, Saltaire, Bradford (Tel 0274 590408).

The Yorkshire and Humberside Coast

The coastline stretches from Staithes, a pretty fishing village with Captain Cook associations in the north, to Cleethorpes on the mouth of the Humber in the south.

The **Captain Cook Heritage Trail** can be picked up at Staithes, a narrow street of tiny cottages, where Cook worked in a merchant's shop. Occasionally village women wear old-fashioned lace headdresses. Two miles (3 km.) west, 700 foot (213 m.) Boulby Cliff is England's highest perpendicular cliff. South of pretty **Runswick** are remains of a Roman lighthouse, a sea viewpoint at Kettle Ness and **Sandsend**, another pretty fishing village.

Whitby is a large fishing town where the Esk meets the sea. The 13th-century ruins of **St Hilda's Abbey** are wonderfully positioned on a cliff at the top of 199 steps, beside unrestored **St Mary's church**. A whalebone arch commemorates the lost whaling trade. There's a Captain Cook Memorial Museum, while a Dracula Experience and a Dracula Heritage Trail build on the town's links with author Bram Stoker. The north side of town is all amusement arcades and fish and chip shops, the south a jumble of narrow streets with shops selling locally-made jet jewellery.

Robin Hood's Bay is a bigger version of Staithes but just as attractive. The Smuggler's Experience recalls a past trade other than fishing and tourism. Three miles (4 km.) south there are fine views from Ravenscar headland. Once a fishing village, then a spa, **Scarborough** is now a fading Victorian resort, its streets lined with stalls selling cockles, mussles and crab sticks. There are ruins of a 12th-century castle, and **Anne Brontë** is buried in St Mary's church nearby.

From **Filey** sands stretch south to **Flamborough Head**, past the Iron Age **Danes' Dyke** earthwork and the 400 foot (122 m.) chalk **Bempton Cliffs** with breeding colonies of gannets, kittiwakes, fulmars, puffins, guillemots and razorbills. Local fishing 'cobles' can sometimes be seen. At the popular resort of **Bridlington**, the medieval church of St Mary developed from the nave of an Augustinian priory. At **Rudston** to the west a huge Neolithic standing stone dominates the churchyard. To the south-west in beautiful **Burton Agnes** village an Elizabethan Hall forms a group with a partly-Norman church. **Hornsea** is another popular resort, attached to a pretty village; visitors are welcome at the Pottery. A path leads to **Hornsea Mere**, a nature reserve. Inland from Aldbrough is Tudor **Burton Constable Hall** with grounds by Capability Brown. Drivers can reach the **Spurn Head** lighthouse and walkers can continue to the sandbar tip to watch migratory birds, waders and terns.

South of the Humber, **Grimsby**, once an important fishing port, is now in decline; the new **Fishing Experience** recreates busier days. There's also a restored 13th/14th-century church. **Cleethorpes** is a popular holiday resort with fine old houses. St Peter's church at

Barton-on-Humber to the north-west is especially important since its Saxon tower reproduces earlier wooden structures in stone.

Tourist Information Centres in the area are at New Quay Road, Whitby (Tel 0947 602674); St Nicholas Cliff, Scarborough (Tel 0723 373333); and Prince Street, Bridlington (Tel 0262 673474).

Accommodation

First Class

Larpool Hall, Larpool Lane, Whitby YO22 4ND (Tel 0947 602737). Peace and quiet in an 18th-century Georgian mansion set in lovely grounds roughly one mile (1.5 km.) from Whitby.

Esplanade Hotel, Belmont Road, Scarborough YO11 2AA (Tel 0723 360382). Period-style house with a good position on South Cliff.

Middle Range

Harcourt Hotel, 45 Esplanade, Scarborough YO11 2AY (Tel 0723 373930). Comfortable hotel with good sea views and catering for vegetarians.

Economy

Birtley House, Station Road, Robin Hood's Bay, near Whitby YO22 6RL (Tel 0947 880566). Victorian guest house offering comfortable accommodation. Moorland views and close to the beach.

Inkwells Guest House, 1 Eskdaleside, Sleights, Whitby YO22 5EP (Tel 0947 810959). Bed and breakfast (and evening meal) in a converted early-19th-century school.

Glen Alan Hotel, 21 Flamborough Road, Bridlington YO15 2HU (Tel 0262 674650). Family-run hotel offering comfort and good food.

Youth Hostels are at Whitby (Tel 0947 602878) and Scarborough (Tel 0723 361176).

Eating Out

Middle Range

Shepherd's Purse, Sanders Yard, 95 Church Street, Whitby (Tel 0947 820228).

Downe Arms, Wykeham, Scarborough (Tel 0723 862471).
Vittles, 64 Quay Road, Bridlington (Tel 0262 604826).
Brit's, 29 Abbey Road, Grimsby (Tel 0472 354442).

Economy

Magpie Cafe, 14 Pier Road, Whitby (Tel 0947 602058).
The Square Cat, Stephen Joseph Theatre, Valley Bridge Parade, Scarborough (Tel 0723 368463).
Gemini, 13 Victoria Road, Scarborough (Tel 0723 360054).

Hull, the Wolds and South Humberside

Still a major ferry port, **Hull** has old docks, now restored and providing a marina and maritime heritage trail. Other attractions include the **Old Town conservation area**, with renovated merchants' houses and warehouses, and museums, including the Wilberforce and Town Docks Museums. Medieval **Holy Trinity** is England's largest parish church (restricted opening hours). Also worth seeing is the **Old Grammar School** where Andrew Marvell and William Wilberforce were students. There's a working windmill at **Cottingham**. Good times to visit would be during the August Regatta or the October Fair, the biggest in England. Hull **Tourist Information** is on Corporation Road, King George Dock (Tel 0482 702118).

Just outside Hull is **Beverley**, whose beautiful twin-towered Minster is regarded as one of Europe's finest medieval buildings. Beverley also has a Heritage Centre, Art Gallery and Museum of Army Transport. The 'King and Queen of Holderness' are the fine medieval churches of St Augustine at **Hedon** and St Patrick in **Patrington**.

South of the Humber, **Scunthorpe** is a large industrial town. **Goole**, where the Humber meets the Don, is one of England's most inland ports. To the south-west, John Wesley was born at **Epworth** in 1703, in an old rectory now preserved by the World Methodist Council.

Accommodation

Middle Range

Kingstown Hotel, Hull Road, Hedon, Hull HU12 9DJ (Tel 0482 890461). Family owned hotel, traditional, comfortable and a real 'home from home' atmosphere.

Economy

May's Guest House, 16 Albany Street, Spring Bank, Hull HU3 1PJ (Tel 0482 212457).
Eastgate Guest House, 7 Eastgate, Beverley HU17 0DR (Tel 0482

868464). Victorian guest house which has been run by the same owner for almost 25 years.

There is a **Youth Hostel** at Beverley (Tel 0482 881751).

Eating Out

Middle Range

Fagin's Restaurant, Scale Lane, Hull (Tel 0482 225212).

Gainsborough Fish Restaurant, Anlaby Road, Hull (Tel 0482 225619).

Economy

Ferens Art Gallery, Carr Lane, Hull (Tel 0482 222752).

10 The East Midlands

The area called the East Midlands covers such diverse landscapes as the limestone Derbyshire Peaks and Dales; Nottinghamshire's Trent Valley; the fertile fenland of Lincolnshire; rocky Charnwood Forest in Leicestershire; and neighbouring Northamptonshire, where the iron in the soil turns fields and stone buildings a distinctive reddish-ochre. The region contains not only the industrial conurbations of Nottingham, Derby, Leicester and Northampton, but also spreading countryside, the long coastline of Lincolnshire and, inland, the Shires which typify, more than anything else, the life of county gentry in the 18th and 19th centuries.

Derbyshire is best-known for its Peak District, but outside the over-frequented spots is a network of old packhorse ways across the uplands, which link former lead-mining villages. Navigation systems running off the Trent and Mersey Canal to the east and north of Derby provide rich vegetation in the water meadows, and a variety of plant and bird life. Around Chesterfield there is rolling countryside, as well as a wealth of historic houses and castles.

Nottingham is famous for lace-making, though the county is most renowned perhaps for Robin Hood's adventures in Sherwood Forest. This region also has its canals running through quiet farmland, contrasting with the much busier tidal River Trent. Delightful villages once formed coaching stops for journeys on the Great North Road; indeed, market towns, working farms and country parks may give a truer picture of the county than the big commercial centre of Nottingham.

Lincolnshire is noted for bulb fields and its associations with the reclaimed areas of the Netherlands. But the fens form only part of this large county, where the land rises abruptly to the Wolds before dropping again to the coast and a string of sandy beaches. This seaboard offered easy access for invaders, via the Humber and the Wash, filling the region with relics of history as early as Neolithic times. South of the popular resort of Skegness lies a rich area of sand dunes, while unexpected tranquillity is found in the woodlands of Kesteven Forest between the originally Anglo-Saxon towns of Stamford and Grantham.

Leicestershire is one of the Shire counties, where Quorn, Belvoir and Pytchley hunts have traditionally fought other battles than the 15th-century one at Bosworth Field, while the former county of Rutland, now officially absorbed by its neighbour, retains a gentle individuality. For centuries Charnwood Forest has contained more slate and stone than trees but, though disturbed by quarrying, there are still the remains of ancient forest and a lot of fine parkland around the county. Canals intersect the countryside which is rich in peaceful ironstone villages.

Northamptonshire is known for the boots and shoes made in the county town. But this 'Rose of the Shires' is dotted with ancient churches (such as Saxon-towered Earls Barton), historic homes and manor houses. The River Nene and Grand Union Canal play an important role in the county; once used commercially, now enjoyed by boatpeople, naturalists and anglers. The land is primarily agricultural. Reservoirs fill the sites of former quarries and gravel pits, while earlier inhabitants foreshadowed the M1 by building Watling Street.

People in the East Midlands see their environment as a vulnerable resource. Visitors have increased in numbers recently, so a balance is needed in order to protect the countryside. Midlands dwellers would rather emphasise heritage attractions than simply provide entertainment for their visitors.

History

Neolithic people lived and died in this area. They were buried in the many long barrows, and Willy Howe, one of the largest, is reputedly enchanted after a reveller reported seeing fairies feasting inside. There are Bronze Age stone circles in Derbyshire, and Iron Age hill forts in Northamptonshire.

The Romans bequeathed roads, notably Ermine and Watling Streets, which are still in use. Also utilised today, at Laxton, Nottinghamshire, is open-field strip-farming, as mentioned in the Domesday Book. During the Crusades, in the 11th-13th centuries, land owners carved out new estates, with fortified manors such as Haddon Hall and Oakham Castle. Gradually the relationship of lord of the manor and serf was replaced by an early form of 'poll' tax. Discontented townspeople and farmers were supported by outlaws in forests like Robin Hood's Sherwood.

The Wars of the Roses ended in 1485, when Welsh Henry stripped Richard III's dead body and found his crown in a hawthorn tree, whereupon the new House of Tudor took the crown in a bush as their emblem. Many 'county' families established themselves during Henry VIII's reign, through commerce or royal favour; Burghley House, near Stamford, was built by the Cecils, and its park laid out two hundred years later by Capability Brown.

The Pilgrim Fathers set off from Boston in 1607 for pastures new, though their first attempt ended in imprisonment. However, in 1620 they founded Boston, Massachusetts, and with it the beginnings of our continuing link with the USA. When the Great Plague of 1665 reached Eyam in Derbyshire the villagers isolated the place to protect their neighbours from contamination. Sadly, they then proceeded to die themselves, all 250 of them.

In 1630 the drainage of the Fens began. Till then fen villages were separated from one another and the rest of the country. New land was reclaimed for cultivation, though water had to be pumped up by wind-powered mills. Throughout the 18th century inland navigation progressed, alongside the improving road system, and canals like the Grand Union transported goods and boosted the new tanning and malting industries. At the same time lead mining, carried out in the Peaks for 2000 years, became increasingly industrialised.

The 19th century ushered in the age of romantic poets and writers. Byron moved into his ancestral home at Newstead Abbey, accompanied by a tame bear; Tennyson was born in Somersby rectory; Peveril Castle inspired one of Walter Scott's novels; and Charles Dickens wrote *Bleak House* in Rockingham Castle. In 1841 Thomas Cook ran the first package tour as a train trip from Leicester to Loughborough.

In this century another 'first' was the Peak District's designation as a National Park. Lincolnshire's bulb fields, a feature of the rich soil from the reclaimed fenland, became focused in 1965 at Springfields as an annual spectacle. Boundary changes saw Rutland's demise as a county in the eyes of all but its inhabitants.

Among many famous natives are the poet, Dryden, and Sir Isaac Newton, who theorised about gravity at Woolsthorpe Manor.

Geography

The East Midlands, as defined by their Tourist Board, are also called the Shires of Middle England. Nottingham is the largest county town (population 300,000) with Leicester a close second. Here lies the region's manufacturing and industrial heart (including coalfields) mainly in the neighbourhood of the M1. Mining and quarrying are carried out, especially in Derbyshire, but there are extensive areas of rural countryside, broken only by villages, market towns and many stately homes. Lincolnshire, because of its fenland, is sparsely populated and relatively unexplored.

Mostly the Midland Plain is low-lying, though the rolling slopes of Leicestershire and Northamptonshire actually mark the tail end of the Cotswolds. Dramatically different is the limestone Peak District, the southern culmination of the Pennines. The Wolds, the only other higher ground, rise out of the fens in North-east Lincolnshire. On the other side of the region, the Peaks climb progressively until they reach the High Peaks and Kinder Scout's 2088 feet (637 m.).

Important to these eastern counties are the rivers and associated canal systems. The largest, the Nene and the Welland, flow into the Wash, while the Trent flows northwards to the Humber. Man-made Rutland Water has twenty-four miles (39 km.) of shoreline.

A 'forest' means not only woodland, but also open space, and this is what Charnwood and Sherwood Forests mainly are. Charnwood contains primitive forms of seaweed in some of the oldest (pre-Cambrian) rocks, which form craggy outcrops, unlike Sherwood's sandy soil, where medieval workers on neighbouring manors deposited agricultural rubbish. Wolves roamed here in the 12th century, but the present ancient oaks are survivors from 18th-century parks called the Dukeries because of the numerous noble families once living there.

Crops grow on half the agricultural land, with more wheat than barley, and a good deal of oil-seed rape. Although some small farms use their rich pastureland for fattening cattle and lowland sheep, the trend continues to create larger co-operatives. However, increasing calls for more environmentally sensitive farming have encouraged the re-use of farm buildings.

Natural vegetation ranges from the varied plants of limestone Derbyshire, through Nottinghamshire's riverside flowers to Lincolnshire salt-marsh flora, and meadows where pyramidal orchids grow. The infrequent herb Paris blooms in ancient woodland in Leicestershire, while wood-warblers nest in Charnwood Forest, and long-eared owls near Grantham. There's at least one wood here where you'll see badgers, if you are lucky and very quiet. Rare butterflies like the White Letter Hairstreak breed in grassland near Nottingham (and lots of mosquitoes in the woodlands fringing the Wolds). Foxes naturally flourish in the Shire counties.

The Peak District National Park contains spectacular hill country, caves and mines, and stately homes, while the Wolds have been designated an Area of Outstanding Natural Beauty. Conservation is practised in numerous Nature Reserves. There's a swan sanctuary near Southwell and a Site of Special Scientific Interest in Dimminsdale, with old lime kilns alongside flooded quarries which host a fascinating variety of plants. The National Park Environmental Service is constantly guarding against attempted quarry encroachment, and the Joint Planning Board has won several battles in the interests of the landscape and the local community.

Climate

Apart from the Peak District, the East Midlands are much drier than the western side of the country, with average annual rainfall of only about 26 inches (660 mm.), decreasing to 22.4 inches (569 mm.) on the coast. Average annual rainfall in central and North Derbyshire is 48.5 inches (1232 mm.). There is likely to be more frost and snow than farther west, and spring comes late, with temperatures staying below 14°C (58°F). However, from about May it's warmer than Southern England, with a July average of 22°C (71°F). Lowland Lincolnshire and Nottinghamshire are more prone to thunderstorms. September is a good month to holiday in the eastern counties, as the winds, usually south-westerly then, have already dropped their moisture.

Attractions

The region has a wealth of stately homes to offer the visitor; Chatsworth House in its beautiful riverside setting is the most visited of them all. However, it's the country parks which attract the greatest number, top of the list being Bradgate Park with 1,300,000 visits in 1989. This is a large area of natural parkland near Leicester, which includes the ancient trees of Swithland Wood, now preserved for the nation. The enormous National Trust estate of Clumber Park, together with Sherwood Forest and Shipley Country Parks each received a million visitors that year, closely followed by the park at Elvaston Castle. These are all near major population centres and obviously provide a welcome outlet for surrounding town-dwellers.

Sherwood Forest is scenically attractive but its principal appeal is in its associations with Robin Hood; the Country Park makes full use of them – though it also relates the history of the woodland.

The only indoor attractions which brought in a high number of visitors were Nottingham Castle and Museum; and Rufford Craft Centre within the Country Park – a place which stages year-round events. About half a million people enjoyed the outdoor pleasures of Rutland Water – water sports, fishing, trips in a passenger cruiser, cycle rides round the perimeter, waterside picnics. Twycross Zoo is also in the much-visited category with well over 400,000 visitors. Top of Northamptonshire's list are the country parks at Irchester and Barnwell; the Derbyshire reservoirs at Ogston and Upper Derwent are also very popular.

Although overall numbers are fewer, historic houses also draw the crowds. The National Trust's Calke Abbey, called 'the house that time forgot', receives so many that entry is by timed ticket only, with long delays on busy days. Haddon Hall, reflecting the life of medieval England, is another very popular Derbyshire home. On a smaller scale, numbers admitted may sometimes have to be restricted at Woolsthorpe Manor in Lincolnshire, the farmhouse birthplace of Sir Isaac Newton.

Dovedale is certainly a holiday hotspot. The River Dove flows through a limestone gorge with dramatic rock formations on each side, in a two mile (3.2 km.) stretch of beauty visited by many sightseers. The traditional well-dressing ceremonies are famous now, so that some small Derbyshire villages almost reach breaking-point during May and June, with Tissington perhaps the best-known. The Peak District National Park in general attracts walkers, cyclists, riders and climbers, as well as those interested in its caves and industrial heritage sites like Arkwright's Cromford Mill and the Crich Tramway Museum. Of the many caves in this county the one most likely to require patient queuing is the Speedwell Cavern, with its mile-long (1.6 km.) boat journey underground. You will find queues of traffic around Matlock Bath, and at Bakewell during show-time in early August.

Other draws, for racing-car enthusiasts anyway, are Silverstone, and the collection of Grand Prix cars at Castle Donington. Springfields at Spalding is another crowded place, particularly during the May Flower Festival, but in the summer rose season too.

Cuisine

Close contenders for the most famous food of the region are Melton Mowbray pork pies and Bakewell Pudding (it's wrong to call the native version a tart). In 1859, in the Rutland Arms

Hotel in Bakewell (where, incidentally, Jane Austen wrote *Pride and Prejudice*), the cook misunderstood instructions, put the jam at the bottom of the baking tin – and the famous pudding was born. Savoury specialities from Lincolnshire are the haslet (stuffed chine of pork) and distinctive sausages. Regional desserts are Mansfield Gooseberry Pie and Nottingham Pudding – made of Bramley apples, which orginated at Southwell. Leicester, Derby and Sage Derby are among the excellent cheeses from the area, while there are claims that Stilton was first made in Leicestershire. All this good food will need to be washed down with mineral water from Buxton, or Ashbourne's table water. Ashbourne also makes its own gingerbread, as does Grantham. Many Derbyshire villages boast that they serve real ale. In Northamptonshire you can buy yoghurt and ice-cream concocted from local sheep's milk, while at one Derbyshire pub marmalade flavoured with rum is made.

Vegetarians will enjoy the variety of cheeses and the organically grown fruit and vegetables. Plenty of restaurants around the region serve vegetarian food.

Level of Tourism

The East Midlands seem to be level pegging with the rest of the country in numbers of visitors, with an average 7 million trips for all types of tourism (national average 7.4 million) and for holiday tourism approximately 4 million trips (national average 4.2 million). The holiday figure is considerably boosted however by the inclusion in the region of the Peak District National Park. Fewer than average overseas visitors come to this region – a total of 3.5 per cent when the average is 5.58 per cent; the majority are from Germany (19 per cent) followed by France (15 per cent) and USA (14 per cent). Expenditure is lower than average at £460 million when the national average is £668 million; or, for holiday tourism only, £320 million with a national average of £448 million. There is more take-up of budget accommodation (or perhaps visits to friends and relatives) than of hotels, inns or guest houses. Excepting Lincolnshire, which is well away from major developments, the existence of large towns within fifty miles (80 km.) of anywhere in the area means that a good many holidaymakers pay day visits only. This obviously results in weekend traffic snarl-ups, especially at the well-known and publicised sites. On the other hand, weekday congestion inside the Peak District is aggravated by large cement lorries, both in and outside the National Park.

A specifically tourism-created problem is erosion of footpaths and tracks, in the Peak District (the most visited of all the National Parks) and also along canal towpaths and riverside walks elsewhere. The Peak National Park Authority carefully monitors this danger, and has set up traffic management schemes to separate visitors from their cars so that the weight of heavy footsteps round the car parks is dispersed. Traffic-free routes have been provided on disused railway lines, to allow people to cycle or walk in peace.

Another Peak District problem, recently become apparent, is pollution in the form of dust caused by rock-climbers, for instance in Millers Dale, drilling holes into the rock faces. More permanently polluting are the metal spikes they leave behind, in the interest of greater safety for their sport.

Teams of volunteers work throughout the year repairing and constructing improved access for the benefit of visitors and residents alike. Most notable is the nationwide network of the British Trust for Conservation Volunteers, who do such work as building a footbridge and hedge-laying on the Cossall Canal in Nottinghamshire. This canal, originally built to carry coals, is now a wildlife reserve, much appreciated by local townspeople and villagers.

The Countryside Commission is aware of the need to deal with traffic congestion, and hopes to improve public transport and co-ordinate local services. Rural railways are being developed, something local people will also welcome, and cycle paths created, together with promotion of cycle hire. Probably the worst traffic jams occur within a twenty-five mile (45 km.) radius of the M1, and certainly reach seasonal peaks (July/August – school holidays), but in general the region welcomes its tourists. The advertised sites of special interest seem to be contained within their boundaries, with not too much adverse overspill. In fact, in a region which would otherwise be suffering from EEC directives towards reduced agricultural output, tourism has brought definite assets, primarily in the re-use of redundant farm and other buildings. Conversion into camping barns, for instance, was the brainchild of the East Midlands Tourist Board. Farmers are now branching out into such activities as tours to watch sheepshearing or horseshoeing, and they have an incentive to preserve and display rare breeds and free-range creatures – as well as selling their eggs and other by-products. The Farm Holiday Bureau promotes farmhouse accommodation, where the welcome for visitors into the local environment benefits both hosts and guests.

All sorts of features which would have fallen into decay are being revived – canals and associated buildings, steam railway lines, the Derbyshire mines and their workings. And it's not only tourists who gain from these ventures. Traditional crafts are being reintroduced – for instance, framework knitting in Nottinghamshire; regional food is being rediscovered; Lincoln cathedral and the many churches around the Shires receive donations which help enormously in their upkeep. The money that tourism generates has brought a whole range of Nature Reserves to new life and a high level of preservation. These amenities are certainly appreciated by those who live locally. One other development should be mentioned as an example of good practice: that of the Center Parcs holiday village in Sherwood Forest, where people and cars are successfully absorbed into an extensive landscape of newly-improved woodlands and water.

Each county has active Wildlife Trusts and other voluntary groups for protecting the countryside and heritage sites. The Tourist Board itself is concerned to strike a balance between entertainment and education, in order to avoid heritage attractions being trivialised by the current delight in technological effects. The open space of the Wolds, an Area of Outstanding Natural Beauty, is due to have its profile raised. Information provided by Centres in nearly fifty towns tends to emphasise the attractions of the farm as the way forward for the region's rural economy.

Good Alternatives

Meeting People

Traditional events in villages are often a good way of getting to know local people. There's a unique contest at Ashton, near Oundle, on the second Sunday in October, when the world conker championship is decided. Or you could join the villagers of Hallaton, Leicestershire, on Easter Monday, when the rector presides over a bottle-kicking race, followed by necessary refreshment at the Bewicke Arms.

County Wildlife Trusts organise working parties from 'Wildlife Wanderings' to habitat clearance for rare flora, to which all are welcome. **Northamptonshire Countryside Services** will tell you about volunteering opportunities in that county, and also about their guided walks (see page 370 for address). Natural Breaks, the programme devised by **BTCV**, offers opportunities throughout the year to protect the environment, in groups of about 12, sleeping in basic accommodation like village halls. In one of these groups you might learn wildlife management with country park rangers, or get gloriously muddy clearing a canal. Contact Paulette Cohen (address on page 61). Another worthwhile reason for getting wet can be found with the **Waterway Recovery Group**, who co-ordinate volunteers to help restore neglected waterways. John Glock (address on page 62) will give details.

For the slightly less energetic, **Losehill Hall**, Castleton, runs environmental activity days, farm visits, and week-long or weekend field courses. These can range from birdwatching or exploring the background of Derbyshire villages and Bronze Age settlements to alternative medicine or botanical illustration. There's a smaller Field Study Centre at Brailsford, five miles (8 km.) south of Ashbourne.

Discovering Places

Woodlands flourish throughout the three midland counties, and several Sites of Special Scientific Interest (the habitats of a wealth of plants, birds and butterflies) are being successfully managed. You should see **Terrace Hills Woods** on the **Belvoir Estate** in rhododendron time (May and June), or visit **Spa Ponds** beside the River Mann, near Mansfield. In these medieval ponds you may see kingfishers as well as many dragonfly species. Prehistoric sites abound, especially in Derbyshire, like the huge stone circle at **Arbor Low**, or the much smaller and lesser known one at **Upper Oldhams Farm**, also near Monyash. These are both on private land, and the farmer may charge for a visit. You will find stalactite grottoes in **Treak Cliff Cavern** at Castleton, while the **Peak District Mining Museum** illustrates the region's industry over the last two thousand years.

For an alternative day by the sea you could visit **Gibraltar Point**, only four miles (7 km.) south of bustling Skegness. This is a National Nature Reserve which includes both seashore and freshwater habitats, where there are seals offshore and nesting little terns on the beach. The Field Station here runs residential courses. Then there are inland reserves such as the one at **Attenborough Pits** near Nottingham where you can wander round flooded gravel pits – a paradise for botanist and birdwatcher alike.

Among less-frequented historic buildings **Lyddington Bede House**, converted to an almshouse from its original role as Bishop's palace, stands in one of the many picturesque villages in Leicestershire – **Horninghold** is another. Alternatively, **Fulbeck Hall**, also in a charming village, has craft workshops in the manor stables. Other man-made features are Rutland's stone villages, and the hundreds of listed churches – for instance, **Ashbourne**'s with its 212 foot (64.7 m.)

high spire, the Pride of the Peak, which soars above the churchyard daffodils in spring.

Also man-made is the fascinating turf maze at **Wing** and the topiary at **Clipsham**. Windmills and watermills abound, especially in the flat wetlands of Lincolnshire where **Heckington Windmill** has eight sails and at weekends sells stone-ground wholemeal flour. The churchyard at **Bugbrooke**, Northamptonshire, has been used to create a nature reserve of wild flowers, including some less common ones.

Besides canoeing on **Rutland Water** you can take boat trips at **Stoke Bruerne** on the Grand Union Canal which passes through an interesting flight of locks at **Foxton**, near Market Harborough. Dinghies and sailboards are available for hire at the **Bosworth Water Trust** in Nuneaton. A quite different cruise, on the **Chesterfield Canal**, in the *Norwood Packet*, is operated by the Chesterfield Canal Society; and if you're in **Chesterfield** on Monday, Thursday, Friday or Saturday, you can visit the market there. Then you can go on to plant a tree in **Heritage Wood** at **Brailsford**, five miles (8 km.) south of Ashbourne.

For naturalists, English Nature has gained public access to National Nature Reserves at three Lincolnshire salt-marsh sites. Part of the reserve at **Barnack Hills and Holes** near Stamford is leased to the Northampton Naturalists Trust; here you will find limestone plants in former quarry workings. Local branches of the Royal Society for the Protection of Birds organise walks to see spring migrants or listen to the dawn chorus. Anglian Water issues permits for a nature reserve, with birdwatching hides, at **Brixworth**, near **Pitsford Water**, and for walks round the reservoir to see newly-hatched birds. **Boughton House** estate has extensive park and farmland, with river, lakes and a stables area, all run by the Living Landscape Trust. There are open days with farming demonstrations at **Plum Park Farm**, **Paulerspury**, while **White Post Modern Farm Centre** near Newark has free-range animals on a working mixed farm.

You can hunt for the site of **Fotheringham Castle** in a field near Oundle. The Castle itself is no more, but the church is beautifully floodlit on summer evenings. The Countryside Commission initiated a scheme to turn disused railway lines into cycleways so that wide stretches of countryside can be explored; for the **Tissington** and **High Peak Trails** contact the National Park Officer. Northampton Steam Railway Preservation Society plans to re-open the old Northampton to Market Harborough line for those interested in steam and diesel locomotives. Another local enterprise, **North Leverton Windmill** in Retford, grinds regularly for neighbouring farmers. Avoid the overcrowded **Framework Knitters' Museum** at **Ruddington**, and see the survival of this 19th-century craft at **Wigston**, near Leicester. The **Lace Centre** in Nottingham gets very crowded too, so you might prefer to watch lace-making demonstrations at the **Lace Hall** instead. For concerts and drama, it's worth contacting the National Trust regional office for their programme of events in historic houses like **Sudbury Hall**. In the **Museum of Childhood** here chimneys can be climbed by adventurous children. And don't miss the unique open-air theatre at **Tolethorpe Hall** where Shakespeare's plays are performed by a highly professional amateur company from mid-June to mid-August.

Communications

How to Get There

AIR: **East Midlands International Airport** at Castle Donington has flights connecting with other UK airports, and Birmingham Airport also feeds visitors into the region.

RAIL: Regular train services from London to Derby or Nottingham take an hour and forty minutes; other main line stations at Leicester, Kettering and Loughborough are all only about an hour from London; the journey to Lincoln takes two hours more. As well as the main lines radiating from London various routes operate across the region, Lincolnshire being the most sparsely served of the five counties. Skegness, however, can be reached from Nottingham via Sleaford and Boston. Detailed information is available at Tourist Centres or main line stations.

COACH: **National Express Coaches** run regular services throughout the region. Derby is four hours from London; the journey to Leicester or Northampton is rather shorter. Allow eight to nine hours between Edinburgh and Derby. **Midland Fox** and **United Counties** are other large operators within the area.

When You're There

RAIL: As well as main line trains, several steam-hauled passenger services operate. The Peak Rail Rambler takes a scenic route from Buxton Steam Centre to New Mills. Also in Derbyshire the Midland Railway Centre runs a service with gala days and wine-and-dine trains. In Leicestershire, the Battlefield Line operates between Market Bosworth and Shackerstone, and the Great Central Railway largely run by volunteers connects Loughborough and Leicester; this too has a programme of special events.

BUS: The **Sherwood Forester** tours – of course – Sherwood Forest. **Saunterbus** runs various trips in Northamptonshire between visitor attractions. For instance, the Sulgrave Saunter takes you from Northampton via Daventry Country Park, Sulgrave Manor and Canons Ashby House to the Old Dairy Farm at Upper Stowe, and back again. Services within the National Park are covered by the **Peak Park Travel Club**. Contact Martin Smith at the Peak District National Park (Tel 0629 814321, ext. 208).

CAR: The M1 runs diagonally across Northamptonshire from junction 15 near Northampton and then due north into Yorkshire. Numerous roads cross it and a network of roads converge on the main towns. There is a coastal road, but apart from that Lincolnshire is short on main routes, which are concentrated on the western half of the region.

BOAT: The main navigable waterways are the Rivers Trent and Nene; the Grand Union Canal running all the way from Nottingham to the Thames, and its offshoot, the Erewash Canal originally built to carry coal from the Nottinghamshire/Derbyshire coalfield; and the two canals leading off the Trent – the Chesterfield, and Fossdyke & Witham Navigation, which links the inland system to Boston and the sea.

Dayboats can be hired on the Erewash Canal at **Davisons Sawley Marina**, Trent Lock, Long Eaton (Tel 0602 734278); other cruise boats are available on the Grand Union and Fossdyke Canals, as well as the Rivers Soar, Witham and Trent; details of these can be had from any Tourist Office. The **British Canoe Union**, Mapperley Hall, Lucknow Avenue, Nottingham, NG3 5FA (Tel 0602 691944) runs canoeing holidays, and you can go weekend canoeing on the Rivers Nene and Soar through **Mobile Adventure**, Bridge Works, Knighton Fields Road West, Leicester, LE2 6LG (Tel 0533 440165). Nottinghamshire County Council Leisure Services Department, Trent Bridge House, Fox Road, West Bridgford, NG2 6BJ (Tel 0602 824425) can give details of water sport activities at the National Watersport Centre, Holme Pierrepont Country Park, and with East Midlands Windsurfing and Water Sports.

CYCLING: The Peak District is a favourite cycling area, from seven centres in and near the National Park. Each has bicycles for hire and the **Peak Park Joint Planning Board** (Tel 0629 814321) will supply details. Tourist Offices have lists of hire outlets. The Cyclists' Touring Club gives details of tours and cycle events to its members – they always welcome new ones.

WALKING: By far the longest footpath is the **Viking Way** covering

140 miles (224 km.) from the Humber to Oakham in Leicestershire, with views from the Wolds towards Lincoln. Another extensive track, the **Nene Way**, covers 70 miles (112 km.) of undulating countryside in Northamptonshire. Shorter but more demanding trails are found in Derbyshire: the **Monsal Trail** on the former Midland rail line, and the beginning of the **Pennine Way** at Edale. In Leicestershire the **Jubilee Way** runs from Melton Mowbray to join the Viking Way. Linking the larger bridleways is a network of smaller tracks, making the whole area excellent walking country. Many of the woodlands too have nature trails. Details of these and many other walks can be obtained from the County Wildlife Trusts.

RIDING: There are several riding stables in the Peak District; **Northfield Farm**, Flash, near Buxton, SK17 OSW (Tel 0298 22543) runs a riding and trekking centre. You can hire horse-drawn carriages at **Red House Stables**, Old Road, Darley Dale, Matlock (Tel 0629 733583); comprehensive information can be had from the leaflet, *Riding and Trekking*, obtainable from the Peak Park Authority. **Shortwood Lodge Equestrian Centre**, Apethorpe Road, Nassington, Peterborough, PE8 6QX (Tel 0832 280845) has all kinds of facilities in the Northamptonshire countryside. For riding opportunities elsewhere, contact local stables.

Useful Local Contacts

Derbyshire Wildlife Trust, Elvaston Castle, Derby, DE7 3EF (Tel 0332 756610). **Leicestershire and Rutland Trust for Nature Conservation**, 1 West Street, Leicester, LE1 6UU (Tel 0533 553904). **Lincolnshire and South Humber Trust for Nature Conservation**, The Manor House, Alford, Lincolnshire, LN13 9DL (Tel 0507 463468). **Northamptonshire Trust for Nature Conservation**, Lings House, Billing Lings, Northampton, NN3 4BE (Tel 0604 405285). **Nottinghamshire Wildlife Trust**, 310 Sneinton Dale, Nottingham, NG3 7DN (Tel 0602 588242). Lincolnshire has a regional branch of the Ramblers Association, which organises regular walks, and a Naturalists Union. Ask for a *What's On* guide at one of the Tourist Offices.

Northamptonshire Countryside Services, Northampton House, Northampton, NN1 2HZ (Tel 0604 233389). **Derbyshire Countryside Centre**, 23 Market Street, Clay Cross, S45 9JE (Tel 0246 866960). These last two centres co-ordinate the work of local groups. The **Peak National Park** runs an Environmental Education Service at Losehill Hall, Castleton, S30 2WB (Tel 0433 20373).

Specialised societies include the **Arkwright Society**, currently restoring the first successful waterpowered cotton-spinning mill at Mill Lane, Cromford, DE4 3RQ (Tel 0629 824297). In Lincolnshire, the county branch of the Civic Trust has recently restored Lincoln's last surviving windmill, while the **Society for Lincolnshire History and Archaeology** has its home in the medieval Jews' Court, Steep Hill, Lincoln, LN2 1LS (Tel 0522 521337).

Geographical Breakdown of Region

Derbyshire

The **Peak National Park** covers a good deal of Derbyshire, lying like an island surrounded by spreading cities. This makes certain areas very overcrowded at popular times and seasons. The National Park Authority provides easily accessible information on most things you may want to know, including how to get away from it all. The nerve-centre of the NPA, **Losehill Hall**, near Castleton, is located between the Dark (High) Peak and the White Peak where gritstone gives way to limestone. Nearby is the spectacular landmark of **Mam Tor**, on which stands an Iron Age fort. Deep caves here can be explored under supervision, or just visited because you want to escape the rain. At **Monk's Dale**, one of the small valleys branching off the Wye, the woodland is quite unspoiled; in contrast quite a lot happens at the thriving spa town of **Buxton**. You can swim year-round in its warm spring water, as well as drinking it. For more solid refreshment, try Pugson's shop which specialises in British farmhouse cheeses, including Buxton Blue.

Bakewell

This is a busy town during Carnival Week in June; indeed, being centrally placed, it always attracts visitors, who appreciate its good locally-owned shops, among them several butchers who sell traditional pork pies.

The 14th-century church has a collection of medieval monuments, while the museum, restored by Bakewell Historical Society, has exhibits in the 16th-century **Old House**. Take a riverside walk to the start of the **Monsal Trail** – and leave time to watch trout in **Lathkill Dale**, part of which is a National Nature Reserve.

You'll need a whole day for **Chatsworth House and Park**, but be prepared for crowds in fine weather. Amongst the many mines which can be visited it's possible to explore the old galleries at **Holme Chert Mine**, while the local limestone at **Ashford** used to be polished to resemble black marble. From the packhorse bridge here you may still see sheep being dipped.

Accommodation

First Class

Hassop Hall, near Bakewell, DE4 1NS (Tel 062 987 488). Country home with farmer owner; all very impressive. Not in Bakewell itself but two miles (3 km.) out.

Riverside Country House, Fennel Street, Ashford-in-the-Water, DE4 1GL (Tel 062 981 4275). Also two miles (3 km.) outside Bakewell. Come here for real self-indulgence.

Croft Country House, Great Longstone, near Bakewell, DE4 1TF (Tel 062 987 278). Also two miles (3 km.) out. Small comfortable country hotel, with cooking by owner.

First Class to Middle Range

Milford House, Mill Street, Bakewell, DE4 1DA (Tel 062 981 2130). Homely Georgian house near centre with traditional home cooking.

Rutland Arms, Bakewell, DE4 1BT (Tel 062 981 2812). Slightly larger hotel in town centre, but friendly and welcoming.

Middle Range

Everton, Haddon Road, Bakewell, DE4 1AW (Tel 062 981 3725). Homely, comfortable and near the park.

Economy

Avenue House, Haddon Road, Bakewell, DE4 1EP (Tel 062 981 2467). Comfortable large Victorian house, near centre.

Bourne House, The Park, Haddon Road, Bakewell, DE4 1ET (Tel 062 981 3274). Accommodation in former manse, near park, river and town centre.

There is also a **Youth Hostel**; and, at Bank Top House Farm, accommodation in a **camping barn**. Losehill Hall, near Castleton, S30 2WB (Tel 0433 20373) will give details.

Eating Out

First Class

Rutland Arms, Bakewell (Tel 062 981 2812). Four Seasons restaurant has excellent menu and comprehensive wine list.

Middle Range

Lathkil, Over Haddon (Tel 062 981 2501). Village inn just outside the town. Friendly and informal; welcomes walkers.

Economy

Green Apple, Diamond Court, Water Street, Bakewell (Tel 062 981 4404). Serves organic food with a vegetarian slant.

Aitch's Wine Bar, 4 Buxton Road, Bakewell (Tel 062 981 3895). Varied menu in warm spacious bar.

Entertainments

Carnival Week in June is also the time for well-dressing – and raft racing too on the Wye. For possibly less crowded well-dressing ceremonies, try **Hope** or **Youlgreave**. In August there is a major agricultural show, and sheep-dog trials at **Eyam** each September.

Useful Addresses

Tourist Office: The Old Market Hall, Bridge Street (Tel 0629 813227). **Post Office** (Tel 0629 814427). Hospital: **Newholme Hospital** (Tel 0629–812525).

Peak National Park Information Centre, Aldern House, Baslow Road (for written enquiries). For details of the **Field Study Centre** at Eyam Youth Hostel, contact YHA Regional Office, Peak Area Office, Bank Road, Matlock (Tel 0629 4666). **Rock Lea Activity Centre**, Hathersage (Tel 0433 56345) provides guides for various activities.

Transport Options

'Wayfarer' bus tickets offer good value; Park Information centres have timetables; and details of guided walks are published in the *Peakland Post*. The nearest cycle hire centre is at **Parsley Hay**, once a station on the railway which now forms the High Peak Trail. (Tel 0298 84493).

North-eastwards from Bakewell, near the bridge over the Derwent, is the largest craft centre in the county, which also serves Egon Ronay recommended food. Passing through **Baslow** notice the church clock face, on which the numerals have been replaced by 'VICTORIA 1897'; from here you can walk over the meadows to Chatsworth. Beyond the river precipitous 'Edges' mark the moorland's end;

the rocks on **Baslow Edge** are named Victory, Defiant and Royal Soverin. Do wear strong boots though, if you go 'bog-trotting' on the waymarked paths.

One feature of **Chesterfield** is its twisted church spire; another is the 800-year-old market (England's largest) which attracts browsers, especially to the Thursday flea-market. English Heritage recently reprieved the ancient square from demolition, so the area is now traffic-free, with new shops opened in restored buildings. South of the town is **Five Pits Trail**, a pleasant cycle route across rolling countryside. Beyond the M1 access to **Hardwick Hall** may be limited at peak times but you can walk in its country park.

The county town of **Derby** provides a good shopping centre for the surrounding districts and its Industrial Museum sets out the town's varied history. Outside the Peak District boundary **Ogston Reservoir**, hemmed in by plantations, is a good place for birdwatching. The Derwent flows down from the Peaks through the rather urbanised valley round **Matlock** and **Matlock Bath**, but **High Tor Grounds** up above have walks with fantastic views beside a 400-foot (122 m.) drop to the river. Home-made patés and ice-creams are sold in **The Coach House Craft Shop** at **Lea**, and **Lea Gardens** blaze with rhododendrons in late spring. The **Whistlestop Centre** in old station buildings, managed by Derbyshire Wildlife Trust, has a countryside exhibition. This Trust also looks after the **Cromford Canal** (a Site of Special Scientific Interest) which begins near **Arkwright's Mill** and has a wealth of 18th- and 19th-century industrial machinery, as well as the flora and fauna which you can see from the towpath. While there you could take a horse-drawn boat trip on the canal; Cromford Canal Society will give details of this and of the **Steam Museum** at the wharf. At **Leawood Pumping Station** a 19th-century beam engine is periodically steamed. The **Black Rocks Trail** dropping down to the canal provides a challenge to rock climbers. Another trail, the **High Peak**, starts here along the former railway bed. To find more about local customs and industries, visit the **Heritage Centre** in the old silk and velvet mill at **Wirksworth** which has recently undergone a programme of conservation.

Ashbourne has been described as a perfect Georgian town. As it is also the gateway to Dovedale it can be extremely crowded. The Black's Head Inn sign stretches the width of the street with, farther up, the **Old Grammar School** and 17th-century almshouses. Some of the town's more unusual shops are: the 15th-century **Gingerbread Shop**, whose products are made to a secret Napoleonic recipe; **Fosters** world-famous fishing tackle shop, selling locally made rods and flies; **Mr Haycock**, only survivor of the town's clock industry; and **Derwent Crystal**, where glass blowing and decorating is demonstrated. Probably the best-known attraction is the Shrovetide football match – short on rules but with its goals three miles apart.

A tramp across **Ilam Tops** takes you above the wooded depths of the **Dove and Manifold Valleys** – places seen better in wintertime. Ashbourne's well-dressing is in June, and its Carnival in July. There is a Youth Hostel at **Ilam** and a National Trust Information Centre (Tel 033 529 245); from here too you can take a course in hang gliding. If you want to hire a bicycle and take the **Tissington Trail**, go to Ashbourne Cycle Hire, Mapleton Lane, Ashbourne (Tel 0335 43156).

Much of the south-west corner of the Park lies in Staffordshire, whose border follows the Dove to its source in the bleak gritstone hills in which **Flash** is the highest village in England. **Northfield Farm** here is a centre for outdoor activities including riding. These heights form the watershed from which the **River Goyt** runs north towards the Mersey (visible on a clear day) through **Errwood** and **Fernile Reservoirs**. Too many walkers have trodden the footpath up to **Shining Tor**, but in the **Goyt Valley** woodlands are various other lovely walks.

Nottinghamshire

A tour of Nottinghamshire inevitably starts in the **Royal Forest of Sherwood**. Reminders of Robin Hood crop up along the 88-mile (141 km.) route to Nottingham, named after him, which has been eroded by many feet and occasional flooding from the River Mann. Paths fan out from the **Edwinstowe Visitor Centre** (with the **Major Oak** the chief attraction) leading to plenty of other elderly and younger oak trees. There's village cricket here and a summer fair, while the **Farm Park** specialises in rare farm animals and home-made cakes. **Rufford Country Park** on the other hand in its ruined abbey grounds has fine sculpture in the formal gardens. Seventeenth-century cottages overlook a tall maypole on **Wellow** village green, and at **Laxton** medieval strip-farming is practised. A walk round the **Laxton Trail** passes a motte and bailey castle and the pinfold for impounding cattle, besides the surviving fields using this rotational (and non-chemical) system.

You can gain some impression of the former Dukeries estates from those country parks that survive. **Clumber** has a Conservation Centre, a lake designed by Capability Brown, the 18th-century landscape architect, and a two mile (3 km.) avenue of limes. The **National Mining Museum** at **Lounde Hall** depicts the mining heritage of the area; here, in the colliery town of **Worksop**, the **Chesterfield Canal** begins to be navigable. Downstream, **Steetley** has a perfect Norman chapel, while at **Ranby** a local landowner donated the waterside willow trees. To escape the noisy A1 take the towpath where old pit heaps have been landscaped over, and you may discover the **Osberton Hall** estate. The canal also bypasses **Blyth**, once on the Great North Road and still boasting four coaching inns; the Angel dates from 1274. Ruined **Mattersey Priory** stands in river-encircled farmland; in this low-lying country it's pleasant to climb the ridge where **Gringley-on-the-Hill's** mellow red-brick cottages command views from Yorkshire to Lincoln cathedral. **West and East Stockwith**, at the canal's confluence with the Rivers Idle and Trent, stand only fifty yards (45 m.) apart without connecting bridge or ferry; only barges come and go on the tidal river in this back-of-beyond landscape. **East Retford**, a market town with annual fairs in March and October, is surrounded by quiet farmland, and nearby **Daneshill Gravel Pit** and **Eaton Wood Nature Reserves** have specially fine spring and early summer flora. The Trent here forms the boundary with Lincolnshire, with power-stations dominating the scene. However, birdwatchers will enjoy the water meadows around **Dunham**, and also the towpath walk at **Sutton-on-Trent**.

Newark at the junction of the Fosse Way and the Great North Road is an old market town which has survived much siege and plunder. Choose a market day to wander in the elegant market place, where the 15th-century **White Hart** offers a wide range of food and drink; also in the market, Gladstone made his first political speech at the **Clinton Arms**. In the tall-spired church you can see the Treasury and beautiful East window. The **Castle**, a Royalist stronghold, was dismantled by Roundheads when they took the town, so now only the riverside wall remains, though tower and dungeon can be visited. The **Governor's House** in the Market Place is the prestigious half-timbered building which was once the home of Prince Rupert, dashing supporter of his uncle Charles I in the Civil War. At the fine Georgian **Town Hall** the civic plate is displayed, including the set called the Newark Monteith; and a 16th-century schoolroom houses the museum and art gallery.

You can walk along the riverbank to **Farndon** village and its waterside Rose and Crown. **Winthorpe** is a quieter village, bypassed by the main road, with an air museum outside. It was Elizabeth I who granted Newark its original May Day Charter from which the **Newark and Nottingham Show** has developed. If you want to take a boat trip from the **Town Wharf** contact Lock & Castle Line, Lock Entry Cottage, Castlegate (Tel 0636 707939).

The wooded Trent hills overlook the flat valley between Newark and Nottingham, and the beautiful twin-towered minster at **Southwell**. Naturalists can identify the amazingly accurate carvings of foliage in the 13th-century **Chapter House**. The original Bramley apple tree grows in a cottage garden here. Although 24 miles (38 km.) separate Nottingham and Newark only one road bridge spans the river – at **Gunsthorpe**, backed by dramatic tree-covered cliffs, where the riverside is crowded on fine summer days. The **National Sports Centre** at **Holme Pierrepont Country Park**, constructed from worked-out gravel pits, has an international rowing course; it's a good place for birdwatching too.

Nottingham

Although a big industrial centre, Nottingham is an interesting and also a forward-looking town. The **Lace Hall** tells the story of Nottingham lace; the **Lace Centre** too gives hand lace-making demonstrations. The town has several museums; the main one, together with the **Art Gallery**, is housed in the sandstone **Castle** overlooking the town, whose 'secret' underground passages can be explored. Others have various exhibitions including a waterways one below the **Castle Lock**, while **Green's Windmill and Centre** tells the story of milling. **Wollaton Hall** in a deer park contains a **Natural History Museum**, a theme continued in nature trails around the lake. Another nature trail has been specially adapted for wheelchair users at the **Skylarks Nature Reserve**, Holme Pierrepont. Indeed Nottingham County Council launched an experimental project to bring the countryside nearer to 'disadvantaged' groups, especially from inner city communities. Their Spadework Trust clears urban eyesores and creates wildlife areas; **Martins Pond**, three miles (5 km.) from the city centre, makes a surprising sanctuary for wetland plants. **Patchings Farm** has a pottery workshop and art studio at nearby **Calverton**, home of organically produced English fruit wines.

Accommodation

First Class

Walton's, North Lodge, North Road, The Park, Nottingham NG7 1AG (Tel 0602 475215). Excellent accommodation in park lodge with modern extension.

Rufford, 53 Melton Road, West Bridgford, NG2 7NE (Tel 0602

814202). Fairly large hotel, family owned and managed, near county cricket ground.

Bestwood Lodge Drive, Arnold, NG5 8NF (Tel 0602 203011). Victorian hunting lodge with attractive accommodation in country park.

Middle Range

Cambridge Hotel, 63–65 Loughborough Road, West Bridgford (Tel 0602 811455) is an efficient hotel, a mile (1.6 km.) from Nottingham centre.

Milford House, Pavilion Road, West Bridgford, NG2 5FG (Tel 0602 811464). Family run hotel with fourteen bedrooms, convenient for centre and Trent Bridge.

Grantham Hotel, 24–26 Radcliffe Road, West Bridgford, NG2 5FW (Tel 0602 811373). Modern, comfortable, family run hotel.

Economy

Firs Guest House, 96 Radcliffe Road, West Bridgford (Tel 0602 810199). Close to Trent Bridge cricket ground; offers bed and breakfast only.

Eating Out

Middle Range

Les Artistes Gourmands/Café des Artistes, 61 Wollaton Road, Beeston (Tel 0602 228288). Popular with local people; serves vegetarian dishes.

Ben Bowers, 128 Derby Road, Canning Circus (Tel 0602 413388). Ambitious food, pleasantly served.

Economy

Ben Bowers, as above. Victoria Bar offers good value home-cooked food.

Jack Sprat's, 23–25 Heathcote Street (Tel 0602 410710). Victorian corner shop near Lace Market. Serves fish and vegetarian dishes; also organic wines.

Entertainments

A satisfying trip can be made round the modern Broad Marsh. Shopping Centre; the **Playhouse Theatre** and **Concert Hall** have also been recently built. Even if it's not Test Match time, cricket fans will want to visit **Trent Bridge**; and for anglers, Stoke Bardulph is the place. The River Leen originally formed the Castle moat and the **Leen Valley Way** north of the town is used by cyclists and walkers. If you're in the town at the beginning of October you can take part in the **Goose Fair**; plenty of local flavour – but prices double on Saturday.

Useful Addresses

Tourist Office: 14–16 Wheeler Gate (Tel 0602 470661) and County Hall, Loughborough Road, West Bridgford (Tel 0602 823558). **Hospital**: Nottingham General, Low Pavement (Tel 0602 590052) and Queen Street (Tel 0602 474463). **Post Office**: 1 Brook Street (Tel 0602 585585).

Transport Options

BUS: Forest & City Transport Depot is at Broad Marsh bus station. The Sherwood Forester serves Sherwood Forest and Rufford Country Parks.

BICYCLE: Cycles can be hired at Bestwood Country Park.

BOAT: *Maid Marion* starts at University Park Lake. Contact Recreation Department, Nottingham County Council, Woodthorpe Grange, Sherwood, Nottingham (Tel 0602 691666). A larger cruise boat operates from Victoria Embankment; details from Tamar Belle River Cruises, 1c Holborn Avenue (Tel 0602 400181).

There are plenty of countryside footpaths where you can watch birdlife; for instance, around **Stanford-on-Soar** and **West Leake**; near **Colston Bassett** in the Vale of Belvoir; or at canalside **Cossall** close to Nottingham. Afterwards you could call at D. H. Lawrence's birthplace in the mining town of **Eastwood**; his house, now a museum, is furnished in 1885 style. If **Newstead Abbey** is too crowded, **Ravenshead Pottery** at the gates might make a pleasant alternative; so would **Longdale Rural Craft Centre** where artists and craftsmen work in re-created 19th-century workshops. In the park at **Portland Training College for the Disabled** rare fauna and flora flourish inside a disused lime quarry; and **King's Mill Reservoir** is a sailing centre. **Cresswell Crags**, a prime archaeological site, should certainly be seen; caves in this limestone gorge were inhabited a hundred million years ago. Nowadays it's a popular picnic spot.

Lincolnshire

The tidal Trent flows between the flatlands of Nottinghamshire and Lincolnshire's woods which rise steeply from the riverside.

Gainsborough is Britain's most inland port, its former importance indicated by warehouses along the banks. At the centre stands the 15th-century **Old Hall**, a beautifully preserved manor house; here the future Pilgrim Fathers met before their escape from persecution. Weekend reconstructions at the Hall bring this and similar historical events to life – after which you could sample a wide range of ciders at the **Brandy Wharf Cider Centre**, a traditional riverside inn.

Ermine Street runs ruler-straight through the fen country near **Kirton-in-Lindsey**'s craft shop and pottery; but at **Market Rasen** the wooded slopes of the Wolds begin. Here almost deserted drove roads, once used for herding cattle, link stone-built villages. Opposite the golf course at **Linwood Warren** lily-of-the-valley grows in heath-surrounded woodland; ask for a permit to visit from the Nature Conservation Trust. To the west of the Wolds **Louth** is a charming Georgian town with narrow winding streets. Nearer the sea a National Nature Reserve of dunes, saltmarsh and mudflats at **Saltfleet by Theddlethorpe** is managed by English Nature. A little way on down the coast you might like to pay your respects to injured and orphaned wild creatures at **Mablethorpe Animal Gardens**, where rescued baby seals and oiled seabirds are treated. It's a good coast for swimming; **Sutton-on-Sea, Chapel St Leonards** and **Skegness** all have safe, sandy beaches.

The millpond trout are tame at **Claythorpe**, near Alford, and rare waterfowl flourish by the restored watermill, while **Rigsby Wood** at the edge of the escarpment is a place of ancient ash and oak-trees. South of Alford, the **Lincolnshire Sculpture Project** operates from workshops in converted farm buildings surrounded by woodland. Tennyson captured the atmosphere of his birthplace at **Somersby** in the words of 'In Memoriam', and he is remembered in the church here, where leafy lanes lead to **Old Bolingbroke**'s unexpected, though ruined, castle. If you come at fruit-picking time you can pick your own at **Glebe Farm** in fenlands near **Spilsby** while at **Candlesby** herbs are sold from the garden of **Cross Keys Cottage**. Another cottage, **Whitegates**, on the **Gunby Hall Estate**, is National Trust property; it can be visited by written appointment with the tenant, who will show you its rare mud and stud walling, recently restored using traditional methods and materials. **Gunby Hall**, also inspiring Tennyson, holds occasional concerts, but check opening times beforehand. Do include **Gibraltar Point**, the sea-shore nature reserve, in any tour of this area. At **East Kirkby**, in windmill-dotted countryside, is Lincolnshire's **Aviation Heritage Centre**; as an alternative, listen to the dawn chorus in **Snipe Dales Country Park**, a Nature Reserve oasis of woods surrounded by farmland. Also worth exploring is Forestry Commission woodland at the entrance to **Woodhall Spa**, a pleasant town with good sports facilities; cycles can be hired at **Jubilee Park**. The massive keep is **Tattershall Castle**'s outstanding feature; various sports are encouraged in the park.

Boston Stump, the tower of Britain's largest parish church, dominates countryside and town, including the medieval **Guildhall's** museum. You might like to buy prints or home bakery at the tea-room in the nearby village of **Swineshead**. The Waterway Recovery Group is restoring the 18th-century canal around **Kyme Fen**, which was originally opened to connect Sleaford with the Witham. Beyond Spalding and Holbeach the **Butterfly Park** at **Long Sutton** is a place to enjoy even in bad weather; and the saltmarsh near **Lutton** is another National Nature Reserve with open access – or you can feed rare waterfowl on the lakes and waterways of the **Wildfowl and Wetlands Trust's Centre** at **Peakirk**, near Market Deeping.

Stamford, a fortress constructed against Danish invasions, is a beautiful golden-coloured town, with locally-tiled rooftops; on Fridays you will find a street market here. The **Steam Brewery Museum** is worth a visit, and don't miss **Barnack Nature Reserve** – mentioned under *Good Alternatives* (page 367). These quarries, once owned by Benedictine monks, provided stone for the Saxon church, but you can learn more of Stamford's long history at the museum. For more contemporary entertainment the **Burghley Horse Trials** take place in September; both house and park are a big attraction. You can best see **Castle Bytham**, tucked away under a limestone edge on the road to Grantham, from the hilltop earthworks; look out for 18th-century humour on the churchyard sundial.

Grantham, an old coaching-stop, is now bypassed, but its various inns remain. **St Wulfram's** is an outstanding church containing a chained library, dated 1598, and a spire that's a landmark for miles around; it also holds occasional concerts. The gardens of the National Trust's **Grantham House** run down to the river and with **Sedgwick Meadows** opposite make a pleasant open space in the town centre. The **Museum** surveys local history, while changing exhibitions are held at **Willoughby Memorial Trust Gallery**, once the Grammar School which Isaac Newton attended. **Harlaxton Manor**, a Victorian extravaganza, has regular open days; also, beyond **Woolsthorpe Manor**, the mock-medieval pile of **Belvoir Castle** stages numerous demonstrations and events, and all kinds of fruit concoctions are produced by fruit farms in the grounds.

Another National Trust property, **Belton House**, is a specially fine example of Restoration architecture. Due east from Belton, **Oasby** with its pottery is an attractive conservation village, and **Folkingham's Old Correction House** is also worth seeing; then at **Boothby Pagnell** the **Norman Manor** has an unusual outside staircase. Before leaving the Grantham area have a walk from stone-built **Croxton Kerriall** through the fields to the spired church and windmill at **Waltham-on-the-Wolds**.

Lincoln

This city, established in Roman times, is crowned by **Cathedral** and **Castle** which oversee it from their hilltop. The central tower of the Cathedral is the highest in England, and the whole building is dramatically floodlit at night. Inside, look for the Decorated style **Angel Choir** and the violet-blue stained glass in the rose window. Walk round the walls of the Castle too, built soon after William conquered England. You will find more interesting Norman buildings at **St Mary's Guildhall** and the **Jew's House**. The **City and County Museum** holds a model copy of the Magna Carta, while the **Usher Gallery** has, amongst much else, a permanent collection of Peter de Wint paintings. For more information on what you will, consult the large neo-Classical library.

Accommodation

First Class

D'Isney Place, Eastgate, Lincoln (Tel 0522 538881). Almost next door to the Cathedral, offering only the best in bed and breakfast accommodation.

Washingborough Hall, Church Hill, Washingborough, LN4 1BF (Tel 0522 790340). Small-sized hotel in Georgian mansion just outside Lincoln.

Hillcrest, 15 Lindum Terrace, Lincoln LN2 5RT (Tel 0522 510182). Victorian former rectory, high up near Cathedral with good views.

Middle Range

Carline Guest House, 3 Carline Road, Lincoln LN1 1HN (Tel 0522 530422). The breakfast part of this B&B accommodation includes free-range eggs from garden chickens.

Winnowsty House, Winnowsty Lane, Lincoln LN2 5RZ (Tel 0522 528600). Pretty Victorian family house near Cathedral.

Mayfield Guest House, 213 Yarborough Road, Lincoln LN1 3NQ (Tel 0522 533732). Small homely guest house near Cathedral, with views.

Economy

ABC Guest House, 126 Yarborough Road, Lincoln (Tel 0522 543560). Fifteen minutes' walk from town centre. Views over the common, and willing to provide vegetarian breakfast.

Birchside, 7 The Grove, off Nettleham Road, Lincoln LN2 1RG (Tel 0522-528769). Victorian house in quiet cul-de-sac near Cathedral.

The Copse, Brigg Road, Scampton, Lincoln LN1 2SY (Tel 0522 43870). Four miles (6.5 km.) out of Lincoln, opposite showground, with views and homely atmosphere.

Eating Out

Middle Range

Wig and Mitre, 89 Steep Hill (Tel 0522 535190). Serves modern food in a very old building.

Harvey's Cathedral Restaurant, 1 Exchequergate, Castle Square (Tel 0522 510333). The proprietor-cum-chef, who also caters at Doddington Hall, offers excellent value food and drink.

Green Dragon, Waterside North (Tel 0522 524950). Tudor building by river. Attractive, comfortable and friendly.

Entertainments

Concerts and exhibitions are held at **Doddington Hall**, an Elizabethan mansion with beautiful gardens and a turf maze; and the recently reopened **Old Bishop's Palace** is included in a tourist trail. Within the city boundary you can go for a proper country walk in **Hartsholme Park**. There are three theatres and three sports centres, and the county showground stages various exhibitions. Look out for displays and festivals at the Castle, and at **The Lawn**, Union Road, which presents a continuous programme.

The Civic Trust has restored the last surviving windmill in Lincoln, where wheat is ground and wholemeal flour sold. The Ramblers Association organises regular walks, and the Naturalists Union also has outdoor meetings. An Arts Festival takes place in May, and annual pony races in August, while in September oarsmen row from Lincoln to Boston for the world's longest rowing event.

Useful Addresses

Tourist Office: 9 Castle Hill (Tel 0522–529828). **Lincolnshire & South Humberside Tourism**, Lincoln Castle (Tel 0522 526450). **Hospitals**: County Hospital, Greetwell Road and St George's, Long Leys Road. **Post Office**: Guildhall Street.

Transport Options

BUS: **Lincoln City Bus Company** (Tel 0522 534444) and **Roadcar** (Tel 0522 532424).

BICYCLE: Cycle hire at F & J, 41f, Hungate (Tel 0522 545311).

Leicestershire

The M1 carves the county in half, but away from the industrial overspill of larger towns are wide stretches of countryside. On the Northamptonshire/Warwickshire borders, close to the Saxon settlement of Lutterworth, **Stanford Hall** has been in the same family for 300 years; attractions include rose-garden and motor-cycle museum. In farmland at **Eaglesfield** you can pick your own soft fruit, after which a horse-drawn carriage, hired at **Hinckley**, will take you round the lanes. You can idle down the **Ashby Canal** too, by narrowboat, to visit the **Market Bosworth battlefield**. Although only a small market town it's crammed with tourist inducements; you can 'relive the battle' at the **Visitor Centre**; talk to chimps at **Twycross Zoo**; sail at **Bosworth Leisure Park**; have steam-train rides on **Cadeby Light Railway**, or **Shackerstone** railway; and buy hand-made leather goods from **Bosworth Crafts**.

On the **Moira Trail** near Ashby-de-la-Zouche, a well-preserved 19th-century blast furnace illustrates our industrial heritage as you follow the route that the old coal barges took. The disused lime kilns in this area enable chalk and acid-loving plants to grow together at **Dimminsdale Reserve**. At **Staunton Harold** you'll find craftspeople working in a Georgian courtyard; beyond that is a limestone bluff from which **Breedon-on-the-Hill's** church surveys the village and its 'lock-up' down below. In **Loughborough**, a bell-making town, the **Bell Foundry Museum** tells the story of bell-casting within a working factory. You can travel either on a steam-driven stretch of mainline track, or by boat on the **River Soar** from **Sileby Mill**. Special weekend events demonstrate farm life at **Whatoff Lodge Farm** with its country trail, quite close to the town. On the other hand **Broombriggs** in **Charnwood Forest** is a hill farm, with woodland areas created as fox coverts. There are deer roaming in **Bradgate's** parkland and the trees of **Swithland Wood** where slate used to be quarried.

History lingers in the major commercial centre of **Leicester**, on which a spider's web of roads converges from all directions. You can see the **Roman Jewry wall** which has been preserved, and in **Castle Park** there are not only the castle remains but **St Mary de Castro's** church, the 14th-century **Guildhall** and a unique **Jain Temple**. Museums range from one housing the **Art Gallery** (specialising in contemporary German art) to the **Gas Museum**. At **Waterside Centre** in **Abbey Meadows** you can hire a boat or picnic on the riverbank. The city is certainly enhanced by the tree-lined canal running through it, crossed by ornamental iron bridges. Leicester's environmental awareness is seen at **Eco House**, a show home set up by the Ecology Trust; and at **Belgrave Hall**, a small Queen Anne house, you can see an amazing range of plant species. The **Framework Knitters' Cottage** at **Wigston** is small and so gets crowded; more peaceful and also on the edge of town, you could watch the milking or have a cart ride at **Stoughton Farm Park**.

Moated **Kirby Muxloe Castle** is west of Leicester, and beyond that tropical birds fly round in **Desford Bird Garden's** natural woodland. **Halstead House Farm**, Tilton-on-the-Hill, has a well-stocked farm shop and also serves lunches and teas. **Market Bosworth** offers brass-rubbing facilities, while **Rutland Railway Museum** has its steam days. Various events happen too in Leicester's **Castle Park**, including guided walks. You can go to the theatre, to concerts in the **Cathedral** or **De Montfort Hall**, and to exhibitions at **Castle Donington**. There's racing at **Leicester Racecourse**, and athletics at **Saffron Lane Stadium**, while in autumn you may see Hindu festivals being celebrated.

Accommodation
(Leicestershire and Northamptonshire)

First Class

Vine House, 100 High Street, Paulerspury, Towcester, NN12 7NA (Tel 032 733 267). Family owned farmhouse in village with home-made food.

The Boultons, 4 Catmose Street, Oakham, LE15 6HW (Tel 0572 722844). Seventeenth-century cottage with bedroom extension. Friendly owners, cooking with local ingredients.

Middle Range

The Red Cow, Hinckley Road, Leicester Forest East, Leicester, LE3 3PG (Tel 0533 387878). Modernised old pub with cheerful staff and bedrooms across lawn.

The Maltings, Main Street, Aldwincle, Oundle, NN14 3EP (Tel 080 15 233). Family run B&B farmhouse with welcoming owners.

Dairy Farm, Cranford St Andrew, Kettering, NN14 4AQ (Tel 053 678 273). Small farmhouse in peaceful setting, with food from the garden.

Rutland House, High Street, Uppingham, LE15 9PY (Tel 0572 822497). Homely service in town centre guest-house with large rooms.

Economy

Wold Farm, Old, Northampton, NN6 9RJ (Tel 0604 781258). Old working farm with spotless rooms and home-produced food.

Saxelbye Manor House, near Melton Mowbray (Tel 0664 812269). Old house in lovely village, serving home-grown produce.

Boot & Shoe, South Luffenham, near Stamford (Tel 0780 720177). Welcoming pub with log fire.

Eating Out (Leicestershire and Northamptonshire)

First Class

Restaurant Roger Burdell, 11–12 Sparrow Hill, Loughborough (Tel 0509 231813). Traditional food in first-floor restaurant, with bistro below.

Hambleton Hall, near Oakham (Tel 0572 756991). English country house, comfortable atmosphere and excellent menu.

The Hind, Sheep Street, Wellingborough (Tel 0933 222827). Coaching inn with extensive menu.

Middle Range

Boat, Stoke Bruerne, near Towcester (Tel 0604 862428). Delightful old thatched pub on canal bank. Possibly crowded, with tricky parking at peak times.

Old Bakery, Countesthorpe, near Leicester (Tel 0533 778777). Traditional food and good choice of wines.

Roadhouse Restaurant, 16–18 High Street, Roade, south of Northampton (Tel 0604 863372). Family run country restaurant offering favourite dishes, generously served.

Economy

Mill-on-the-Soar, Sutton-in-the-Elms, south-west of Leicester (Tel 0455 282223). Converted mill which can be busy at peak times.

Burrough Hill, topped by an Iron Age fort, has extensive views over to **Melton Mowbray** where, on Tuesday, Thursday or Saturday, you will find a bustling street market (mentioned in the Domesday Survey). Try buying local pork pies and Stilton cheese here – and learn more about them at **Melton Carnegie Museum**. At the six-storey **Wymondham Mill** you can enjoy a cream tea and the panorama of the Wolds, whose rolling pastureland is crossed by **Jubilee Way**, following the Roman road past Belvoir Estate. Children will enjoy visiting **Lodge Farm, Plungar**, where young animals are reared in a Victorian-style farmyard. The large church in the red-brick village of **Bottesford** is called 'The Lady of the Vale', and a notice on the bridge asks 'Please drive slowly – ducks cross here'.

Oakham at one corner of Rutland Water still clings to its former county town status. **Rutland County Museum** reflects local history; there's a collection of horseshoes in the Norman banqueting hall of ruined **Oakham Castle**; and an old buttercross and stocks in the **Market Place**. There are birdwatching hides at **Egleton Nature Reserve**, and **Prior's Coppice** nearby is managed by the local Nature Conservation Trust; it's wet woodland, rich in flora. Much-visited **Rutland Water** offers all sorts of attractions, including the animals in **Rutland Farm Park**. Or you could try exploring **Kesteven Forest** around **Clipsham Yew Avenue**, a quite secluded place. Go quietly through the woods until you reach **Pickworth**, where an archway is all that remains of a lost medieval village. From **Edith Weston** you can't miss **Normanton Church**, like a miniature cathedral, jutting into Rutland Water.

The **Railway Museum** at **Cottesmore** lays on summer season events, with free train rides, and **Uppingham School** has concerts during term-time. You might like to watch indoor bowls at **Melton Mowbray**, or polo with the **Rutland Polo Club**; and **Belvoir Castle**'s Sunday events include such things as Morris dancing. May is the month for **Rutland's agricultural show**, while **Market Harborough Museum** sets out the area's history and also houses the **Symington Collection of Corsetry**. You will find some original local work at **Frank Haynes's village Gallery** in **Great Bowden**. There are narrow-boats for hire at **Kilworth Marina**, while **Foxton Locks** with a ten-lock staircase form a feature at the Canal junction, after which the Grand Union continues through farmland into Northamptonshire.

Northamptonshire

Rockingham Forest probably used to extend across the county, providing deer with cover from royal hunting parties; nowadays only scattered woodland is left. Iron and steel industries developed but, without coal resources, Northamptonshire's landscape remained mostly rural. Leather manufacture began in medieval times and today is Northampton's best-known product. The other three large towns are **Wellingborough**, **Kettering** and **Corby**. Everywhere are historic reminders.

Northampton's central position in England makes it a more probable seat of government (as it once was) than London; sadly, much of the city was burned in the 17th century. However, the circular **Holy Sepulchre Church** dates from Crusader times, while **Derngate** (now a modern shopping centre) was an exit from the ancient walled town. The grieving king, Edward I, erected an **Eleanor Cross** near the outskirts, to mark the passage of his wife's body to Westminster. Displays in the six museums concentrate on leathercraft, including footwear through the centuries. You may need waterproof footwear to follow trails through **Salcey Forest**, where ancient oaks form a Site of Special Scientific Interest. The Grand Union Canal passes through the longest navigable tunnel in the country at **Blisworth** and emerges at **Stoke Bruerne**. This village, with its **Canal Museum** and thatched houses, is the starting point of several boat trips. The **Saracen's Head** at **Towcester** (where there's a national **racecourse**) was mentioned by Dickens in *Pickwick Papers*.

The **Grafton Way** partly follows the towpath for twelve miles or so (19 km.) and from here quiet roads run westwards. **Aynho** in hillier country is one of many attractive villages; here apricot trees once provided toll for the lord of the manor. **Canons Ashby** belongs to the National Trust, who organise terrace tours with the chief gardener. Then there's the **Knightley Way**; but it's the **Nene Way** that is the really long trail, on which a cycle track is planned beside the riverbank as far as Bedfordshire. (Incidentally, the river's name is pronounced Nen in Northampton, but with a long E farther north.) If you need refreshment after all this walking, call at the Red Lion in picturesque **Hellison**, or the Countryman in **Staverton** – a village which once sheltered highwayman, Dick Turpin. Another long-distance footpath is being constructed from London to Birmingham, following the Canal. **Althorp**, family home of the Princess of Wales, which contains priceless paintings, is open to visits, but might have to be closed without notice. Gardeners will appreciate the flowering borders at **Coton Manor**, where flamingos are flying freely; other rare waterfowl live in **Guilsborough Wildlife Park**. Climb **Honey Hill** at **Cold Ashby** to see seven counties – and look out for the church here, with a verse inscribed near its North window. The Battle of Naseby (1645) is commemorated at **Purlieu Farm Museum**, and a nearby railtrack has been designated as a bridleway for walking and cycling from **Kelmarsh tunnels** northwards. **Lamport Hall** is known as the birthplace of the garden gnome among its alpine rockeries; the house has fine collections of furniture and paintings, and an agricultural museum in the outbuildings. Don't miss the rare **Saxon church** at **Brixworth** which dates from the 7th century; Anglia Water Authority issues fishing permits for the nature reserve here. **Earls Barton**, whose church is another Saxon treasure, and **Castle Ashby**'s parkland, designed by Capability Brown, are both close to Northampton.

In **Wootton**, outside the town, if you happen to want to, you can dance to the Wurlitzer at **Turner's Musical Merry-go-Round**, which has a fantastic show of mechanical musical instruments – or, a little farther away, watch motor racing at **Silverstone**; you can also receive advanced driving instruction here. **Billing Aquadrome** offers all kinds of water-based amusements; and there's sailing or fishing at the extensive reservoir of **Pitsford Water**.

In Northampton itself, concerts and shows are performed at the **Derngate Centre** with a changing programme at the **Royal Theatre**. Go to the **County Ground** for some exciting cricket, while events like hot air ballooning take place on the **racecourse**, horse and sheep-dog trials in **Belapré Park**, and the **Countryside Centre** organises Family Nature Days and outings.

You can get accommodation lists from Northamptonshire Enterprise Agency, Elgin House, Billing Road, Northampton (Tel 0604 37401); also from Northamptonshire Farm Holidays, c/o Drayton Lodge, Daventry (Tel 0327 702449). Northampton Transport (Tel 0604 51431) run a Saunterbus service in the area.

Kettering's contemporary Leisure Park at **Wicksteed** provides every kind of spectacular fun event; at the **Manor House Museum** you can see thatchers actually at work. The second of the three surviving **Eleanor Crosses** is in the centre of **Geddington** village, and farther down the lane **Rushton's Triangular Lodge** is an architectural curiosity. Built in the 16th century with three of everything, it symbolises the Trinity. Industrial **Corby** has spread into the original Rockingham Forest, but **Kings Wood** has a welcome Nature Reserve; try too to visit the **Castle Gardens** above **Rockingham** village at rose-time. Rockingham Forest Association organises various journeys; on the **Queen of Scots route** you will be guided from **Kirby Hall** to **Fotheringhay**; and **Planter John's** passes the enormous beech tree in **Wakerley Great Wood**. **Harringworth**, as well as having the longest viaduct in England, is also home to **craft workshops** where you can, if you wish, learn the craft of stencilling.

Oundle is an interesting market town, with wide streets, dormer-windowed houses, and a 16th-century church. The town also has a **marina** on the River Nene. Also on the riverside, **Barnwell Country Park** preserves well-tended meadows and a kingfisher hide. Beyond Barnwell a farm shop in the **Tithe Barn, Thurning**, sells cakes and organically grown produce. In Oundle the **Stahl Theatre** puts on a continuous programme and **Oundle School** is open to the public for concerts and plays. The church here and also the neighbouring villages host **Music in Quiet Places**. Then there are guided walks, organised by Northamptonshire Wildlife Trust, while morning entertainment is offered each Thursday at the **Women's Institute Market** in **Victoria Hall**. On the last Thursday of the month, if you enjoy jazz go to the **Shuckburgh Arms**; and if you want to book a tennis court, ask at the Tourist Office.

The Nene curves past **Aldwincle** (where Dryden lived) and the fine church tower at **Titchmarsh**, determining the character of the countryside. This is the place – at **Ringstead Grange Trout Fishery** – to learn fly fishing. Further upstream, the **Heritage Centre** at **Wellingborough**, beside a medieval fish farm, displays 2000 years of local history.

For *Accommodation* and *Eating Out* in Northamptonshire see p.385 and p.386.

11 The Heart of England

The Heart of England is indeed just that. The geographical centre of the country lies in Warwickshire, a county whose landscape seems typically English. Here too is the industrial heartland, in the country's second city of Birmingham with all the urban conglomeration that surrounds it. And then there is something less definable, a sense that the region is not only heartland but backbone too. The people in each of the original six counties (five, since the merger of Herefordshire and Worcestershire) developed a sturdily independent identity – arising perhaps from rearing England's principal source of wealth, Cotswold sheep and their wool. It is also a wholly inland region, with no part touching the sea, although the broad Severn estuary reaches up almost into Gloucestershire and the river continues its tidal influence as far as Tewkesbury.

Each county has a perceived characteristic. Staffordshire, to most people, means the Potteries; Birmingham and the West Midlands belong to the Black Country; Gloucestershire implies the Cotswolds; orchards and fruit-growing are associated with Hereford and Worcester; and finally Shropshire, least known of all, where hills climb gently towards the Welsh mountains. Certainly industry plays a dominant role in the West Midlands and northwards into South Staffordshire. But the rest of that county includes Cannock Chase, an Area of Outstanding Natural Beauty, and quite a chunk of the Peak National Park as well.

The regions producing those goods which increased Birmingham's 19th-century prosperity are more often than not today's tourist 'heritage sites'. The canals which run like veins through the city's interior are a case in point. Stratford is quite the most world-famous town in Warwickshire yet, despite its numerous visitors, that 'typically English' landscape remains in parts much as Shakespeare knew it. Golden Cotswold stone characterises Gloucestershire's villages and towns; well known as pretty countryside, some areas can easily become visitor-saturated. But Gloucestershire extends the other side of the Severn valley into the beautiful but less-frequented Forest of Dean – which leads imperceptibly into Herefordshire, a Welsh-bordering county that has managed to remain essentially English, with its crisply black and white farmhouses and a feeling that it firmly turns its back on the bustle of big cities and the panic scramble down the M5. Worcestershire spans both the lovely Malvern Hills and the Western tentacles of the Black Country; so it provides a natural outlet for urban-dwellers' overspill. Back to Shropshire, which is a large county, half hills, half plain, and bisected dramatically by the Severn Gorge.

As always traditionalists live in country areas while the townspeople (on the whole) are go-ahead and forward-looking, though nowadays trying where possible to marry rapid expansion with environmental concern. The many attractions of the region are almost equally divided between town and countryside. The concentration of three cathedral cities within a fairly small triangle appeals to historians and culture-seekers as well as to beauty-lovers; but urban developments like the Potteries have much of interest, and policy in the more recent industrial townscapes is enthusiastic in promoting their growing opportunities. As for the countryside, where because of the reduction in farming income change is inevitable, there's a feeling that discovery of the under-explored heartlands is something even to be welcomed.

History

The Long Mynd in Shropshire, a hill which is itself shaped like an ancient burial mound, is one of the best-known prehistoric sites in the region. Hill-forts stand on high moorland here, while in Gloucestershire there's a massive standing-stone. It was once believed that this stone turned and ran whenever a clock struck twelve. Later, Celtic tribes inhabited the forests and cut a Red Horse into the Warwickshire turf as protection and a focus for worship.

During Roman colonisation, fortress towns were established at Gloucester, Worcester and Cirencester, and villas built along Fosse Way and Watling Street. Municipal baths bear witness to successful imposition of civilisation on the locals. Offa, an Anglo-Saxon chieftain who followed the Romans, ruled most of the land and erected the Dyke named after him to protect his subjects against Welsh invaders. The threat from Wales remained in the counties bordering it – the Marches – which are lined with the ruins of defensive castles.

Simon de Montfort tried to define a Parliamentary system but was killed at Evesham in 1265 by royalist enemies, who rather nastily mutilated his body; a miraculous spring bubbled up where he died. Cartographers were devising maps of the world about this time; Mappa Mundi in Hereford Cathedral is one of the oldest.

In 1381 a man born in Malvern foreshadowed the Puritans in his indignation at the wrong-doing of others; this was William Langland, author of the visionary poem, 'Piers Plowman'. During that century the wool trade prospered in the Cotswolds, and wealthy clothiers built stone houses to establish themselves and their products in the eyes of the world.

One of England's most famous natives was born in Stratford in 1564: young Will Shakespeare is said to have poached for deer in the grounds of Charlecote Park. At the same time Elizabeth I was visiting nearby Kenilworth Castle, where her favourite Earl, Robert Dudley, welcomed her with fireworks and pageantry. Another castle, Ludlow, saw a quite different performance when Milton's *Comus* was acted there in 1634.

Meanwhile the iron trade was growing in Birmingham and westwards, while the Staffordshire manufacture of glass and the developing salt-pans (hollows by the sea where salt was obtained by evaporation) burned quantities of wood. Coal was mined to replace it and the coalfields spread across the Midland counties. By the 18th century Josiah Wedgwood, a rising captain of industry, created a market for pottery and promoted canal transport to cut down costs. Earthenware replaced pewter for household vessels, and 'common Wedgwood' was contrasted with the more aristocratic 'china trinkets'. The future Industrial Revolution began in Ironbridge Gorge when iron was smelted with coke in 1709. The Severn here was later spanned by the world's first iron bridge.

The 19th century saw the introduction of the game of rugby union football at Dr Arnold's public school at Rugby, scene of *Tom Brown's Schooldays*; balls have been manufactured in the town since 1842. With all this civilising influence, yet 'there were enough witches in Long Compton (Warwickshire) to push a wagonload of hay up Long Compton Hill'; that was in 1875. It's still associated with witchcraft today.

In our own century, the 1940 blitz devastated the town and cathedral of Coventry; its successor built from the ruins is a symbol of hope. This belief in the future is shown in several imaginative projects like the National Exhibition Centre in Birmingham. Following this an International Convention Centre was completed in 1991, and the region is now planning for the 21st century.

Besides famous natives already mentioned, Dr Johnson, the essayist, was born in Lichfield in 1709, while the 19th-century naturalist,

Charles Darwin, hailed from Shrewsbury, and Elgar, the composer, from Worcester.

Geography

The Heart of England runs from England's estimated centre at Meriden to the Welsh border. Going clockwise, Staffordshire is in the north, Warwickshire east, Gloucestershire south, while Hereford & Worcester, together with Shropshire, meet Wales on the Marches. The West Midlands is surrounded by them all and, being densely populated, to a great extent influences them. Birmingham plus satellites occupies almost the whole West Midlands area, apart from a strip that was once the edge of the Forest of Arden. The county towns are not always the largest; Newcastle under Lyme and Stoke-on-Trent with a combined population of 300,000 are bigger than Stafford, and formerly elegant Cheltenham Spa will soon equal Gloucester's population of 90,500. Worcester (population 80,000) is nearly twice as large as its sister city, Hereford, while in Shropshire Telford's spreading complex has a population topping 115,000; the Birmingham area has well over a million inhabitants. So urbanisation is at the region's core, with provincial pockets round the Staffordshire Potteries and in manufacturing Gloucester. Elsewhere is mostly rural countryside, with AONBs on Cannock Chase, the Cotswolds, the Wye Valley in Herefordshire, Worcestershire's Malvern Hills, and a chunk of southern Shropshire.

The River Cherwell forms a natural boundary to the east; the foothills of the Cambrian Mountains in the West. The highest spots are in the North Staffordshire Peaks (1658 feet, 506 m.) and at Stiperstones in Shropshire (1760 feet, 537 m.). The River Avon branches off the Severn above Gloucester and, while its parent carves a passage down from the Welsh mountains, it meanders across the Vale of Evesham to flow peacefully through Warwickshire.

The Forest of Dean survives as natural forest, tucked away beyond the Severn – home of independently-minded Freeminers since Roman times. About 6000 acres (2430 hectares) in Worcestershire's Wyre Forest remain under Forestry Commission management. Warwickshire is well wooded too in patches. Limestone-loving trees clothe the steep valleys on the Cotswold escarpment but the high plateau is bleak and infertile; little but turf grows on the shallow soil, ideal for sheep-rearing. Hops are a favourite crop in Herefordshire where hop fields are called yards and conical-roofed oast houses still feature in the landscape. The lush orchards here and in Worcestershire produce quantities of fruit, and are best seen in blossom-time (usually early May). The Vale of Evesham is especially rich in the production of market-garden crops.

A phenomenon of the Severn is its periodic 'bore' which rushes upstream in tidal waves. Supplementing the rivers, an important canal system was developed for coal delivery and the prosperity of Stoke-on-Trent.

Where Worcestershire, Herefordshire and Gloucestershire meet is the lovely Daffodil Crescent, where these flowers grow in wild carpets, multiplying in Dymock Forest, and even blooming on the central reservation of the M5. The limestone Cotswolds have their own species, including the rare orchid, Red Helleborine; and beechwoods host a variety of autumn fungi. Four species of deer are found here and on Cannock Chase, where crossbills and nightjars can be seen or (more likely) heard. The Slimbridge Reserve near the Severn estuary is a winter feeding ground for ducks and geese. The river is famous too for lampreys, salmon and elver. The country's only elver collection depot traps many of these travellers from the Sargasso Sea in cheesecloth nets. As for lampreys, Gloucester's privilege is to present the sovereign with lamprey pie at coronation time. In Warwickshire, sadly, several conservation areas and Sites of Special Scientific Interest are threatened by development.

Climate

The region has a fairly low rainfall (annual average 26 inches, 660 mm.). On the Cotswolds, in Herefordshire, and the higher ground of Shropshire this increases to about 30 to 40 inches (762 to 1016 mm.) annually. Summer rainfall is highest on the hills in August, but July is wetter in the lowlands. However, when the wind is in the south-west (its prevailing quarter) the Marches are often comparatively dry, escaping the showers falling on the mountains. May and June are normally the driest and sunniest months, but early autumn is also pleasant. Average July temperature is about 23°C (74°F), possibly a little lower in Shropshire; temperature variation throughout the year is less than on the East coast. Winters however can be quite cold; counties on the leeward side of mountain masses tending to be wetter then, with heavier snowfalls. It's also both windier and cloudier on the hilltops. A Worcestershire adage warns:

> When Bredon Hill puts on his cap,
> Ye men of the vale beware of that!

Attractions

There is much to appeal to any visitor in this area aptly named 'England's richest heritage region'. The most popular tourist attraction is undoubtedly Alton Towers, advertising itself as Europe's premier leisure park. It obviously appealed to the 2,382,000 people in 1989 who visited it for a family-fun day out. As it's also conveniently close to Ashbourne, 'Gateway to Dovedale', it can offer needed contrast to the Peaks and Dales.

Country parks are a major draw, especially those close to the Birmingham conurbation, Clent Hills and Drayton Manor, with its amusement park and zoo. Warwick Castle continues to be the most visited stately home in Britain, with well over 600,000 visitors; Birmingham Museum and Art Gallery fall few short of that total. All these places are near the ever-fascinating centre of Stratford-upon-Avon with its unique status as Shakespeare's birthplace.

Although far from the West Midlands complex, Queenswood Arboretum near Hereford brings in about 400,000 visitors annually to enjoy the woodland views. Rather more man-made attractions are the illuminations at Walsall's Arboretum back in the Birmingham area, and also Birmingham Science & Industry Museum.

Ironbridge Gorge intrigues everyone interested in our industrial heritage and – since family tickets are available – that includes most children too. Coventry Cathedral attracts about the same number, though prompted possibly by rather different motives. On the other side of Birmingham, Himley Country Park offers fishing, golfing and sailing facilities, and also a miniature village. Also topping the 300,000 mark are Tittesworth Reservoir in the Peak District National Park, a never-failing magnet for all who enjoy natural beauty; Birmingham Nature Centre for exhibitions indoors and out; and Worcester Cathedral, on one of the recognised overseas tourist routes. Gloucester Cathedral is in a similar category.

Runners-up, at well over a quarter of a million visitors each, are Slimbridge Wildfowl Trust – which can be comfortably combined with a visit to historic Berkeley Castle – and the Black Country Museum at Dudley, with its open-air displays and underground mining features. Other parks with around a quarter of a million attendances, both in the West Midlands, are Trentham Gardens and Byrkley Park, with farm animals, garden centre and children's play area. Robinswood Hill, three miles (5 km.) out of Gloucester, is simply open countryside with nature trails and views.

Of the many glass and pottery manufacturers in the Potteries area, the Georgian Crystal Company seems to attract most visitors to its glass-blowing demonstrations. However, there are numerous opportunities here for touring china factories like Coalport, Royal Doulton and Spode, and to watch the processes, sometimes with opportunities to buy.

Other sites which reach maximum capacity at certain times are: Ford Green Hall at Stoke-on-Trent, a reconstructed 16th-century farmhouse; Kiftsgate Court Gardens, near Chipping Campden, where unusual plants are grown and sold; the Jenner Museum, by Berkeley Castle, also in Gloucestershire; and, at the Staffordshire Peak Arts Centre, the Regimental Museum. In these cases overcrowding is mainly due to their more limited accommodation. However, it's well to remember that each of these crowded pockets is acting as an overspill from other nearby attractions. The whole Cotswold AONB is extremely popular in summertime. Chipping Campden, being about the largest of its idyllically pretty villages (and also a quick drive from Stratford-upon-Avon down the A46) is nearly always thronged, providing a focus for the various impressive houses and gardens in the neighbourhood.

All around the region are places worth visiting, man-made sites like Gloucester Docks or else the beautiful scenery of, for instance, the Wye Valley and the Marches, currently being promoted by the Tourist Board.

Cuisine

On the whole the region seems to favour drinking rather than eating! Hereford and Worcester are renowned for their range of ciders and perry – though the latter, made from locally-grown pears, was dismissed in Elizabethan days as 'a counterfeit wine, both cold and flatulent'; an opinion certainly not held today. Staffordshire is the beery heart of England, with its Bass Museum of Brewing. And English wines are being more and more produced, especially from Three Choirs Vineyards, covering the three fruit-producing counties.

For a meal representing different parts of the region however, you could try a starter of Gloucester Cheese and Ale (cheese spread with mustard on ale-soaked toast), or baby eels from the Severn. Then there is a choice of high quality Hereford beef, pork from the sandy-coloured Tamworth pigs of Staffordshire, or Shropshire Pie – rabbit, with oyster, bacon and liver dumplings. Any of these items should of course be accompanied by Worcestershire Sauce – derived originally from an Indian recipe, bottled and shaken twice a day for a fortnight. Those with a sweet tooth could try Pershore plums in season (though the town was actually named after its pear orchards), or Cadbury's Dairy Milk Chocolate from Bournville, a suburb of Birmingham.

Level of Tourism

The Heart of England comes a good second in the league tables for visitor popularity, only beaten by London and the South-east; indeed over the last ten years it has received the biggest increase of visitors of anywhere in the country (64 per cent). This reflects the richness of its heritage in terms of history, towns, cathedrals, castles and much older archaeological remains, and in the special events held to bring the past to life; in countryside where every view is a picture post-card one; in its many literary associations; in its survey of industry from the Industrial Revolution to the present day, and in a host of man-made recreational centres.

About 14 per cent of visitors come from overseas, with North America, followed by Germany, easily topping the list, and it seems that many overseas tourists have Stratford-upon-Avon as the principal goal of any English trip. It's these tourists who spend a higher than average amount either in Stratford or in other parts of the area. On the other hand, expenditure in the region generally is well below average, indicating perhaps that most visitors have enjoyment of the countryside more in mind than the payment of entry fees. People tend to stay for about a week and to use the economy range of hotels.

The Tourist Board is trying to draw the impact of tourism away from the well-publicised centres by strengthening the image of less developed destinations. The Potteries area has great potential and a campaign is being mounted for short-break holidays there. The Marches, Shropshire's uninterrupted border country with Wales, are receiving similar treatment, in conjunction with the Welsh Tourist Board. These and other campaigns are designed to spread tourism throughout the region, especially by providing the central concentration of city-dwellers with a great variety of breathing-holes in the not-too-distant countryside.

This policy obviously has its dangers but there are dozens of others under way designed to encourage people's concern about the environment in general and their own back-yard in particular. For instance, the Warwickshire Nature Conservation Trust instigated community action to create a wildlife lake out of disused land in Coventry, and the Wildlife Trust is promoting a Local Education Authority-sponsored Village Nature Trails competition. At the intensively visited Warwick Castle, although rope barriers and warning signs are necessary, conservation is carried out in full public view, and guides take trouble to explain the work. In Worcestershire, Nature Reserves with Visitor Centres are being developed by the Nature Conservancy Trust, and the Shropshire Wildlife Trust is devising working holidays in partnership with the British Trust for Conservation Volunteers. The Waterway Recovery Group is another organisation which aims to reverse heritage destruction, in this case the canal network and, through voluntary working holidays, restore the waterways. Similarly, the National Trust practises various public awareness schemes, balancing conservation with access. Visitors and schools are encouraged to plant a tree as replacement for those lost in recent storms; one elegant country house is being dedicated to a corporate hospitality scheme to entertain visiting business people, while the Cotswolds have a team of volunteer wardens who plan informative walks.

Carefully landscaped car parks have to be located in strategic spots so as to guard against the concentrated impact of heavy footsteps (and wheel-treads). Local people want to preserve their environment despite the pressure of movement outwards from the expanding urban areas. Public outcries are made against insensitive development proposals, such as the hyper-size leisure complex near Birmingham International Airport. At the same time however, this 'environment' is not simply a 'green belt' concept, but includes much of interest within towns and cities. The National Trust is also involving itself in concerned urban tourism (together with the Tourist Boards) by, amongst other ideas, its exhibition in major cities, called The Countryside comes to Town. So it is the total cultural heritage which it is intended to preserve and develop for the benefit of visitors to the region, whatever their original motives for coming may have been.

Good Alternatives

Meeting People

A good way of meeting local people is to join one of the many voluntary groups in the area. The British Trust for Conservation Volunteers combines conservation work such as constructing bridges and stiles for footpaths in the Forest of Dean with activities like tree maintenance, followed by instruction from the Greenwood Trust in how to turn wood into useful tools. The Waterway Recovery Group offers other conservation opportunities; for instance, clearing a hundred years of undergrowth from Hereford & Gloucester Canal. A social event arranged annually by the Inland Waterways Association is a Waterways Festival and boat rally around August Bank Holiday. This is attended by many thousands of visitors and requires much preparation, as well as help with displays on the day. The museums, and in particular Worcester City Museum, are often looking for volunteers for archaeological work; it would be worth applying to the appropriate County Council for details. The Countryside Wildlife Trusts are glad of volunteers and can be contacted directly. Events run by smaller local organisations (like the Knowle Society, who go rambling on Knowle Nature Reserve in the West Midlands) will be listed in the public libraries. Tourist Centres supply information on local festivals and village fêtes.

Courses which might not be widely advertised include those at **Straw Crafts Centre**, The School House, Much Cowarne, Herefordshire HR7 4JQ (Tel 0432 820317). This is in a quiet village where informal tuition is given by an enthusiast in straw work, with family accommodation and home cooking. Another uncommon craft can be learnt at the **Rag Rug Workshops** run by Jenni Stuart-Anderson, The Birches, Middleton-on-the-Hill, Herefordshire HR6 0HZ (Tel 056 887 229).

At Shortwood Working Dairy Farm, Pencombe, Bromyard, Herefordshire (Tel 0885 400205) you can meet the farmer and his family – which includes George and Bonny, the donkeys. You can also feed the calves, follow the farm trail with views stretching from the Malvern Hills to Wales, admire the distinctive Jacob sheep, watch cider-making during the third week in October, eat home-made cakes, and enjoy much more as well.

In the Black Country district of South Staffordshire a local club sails model boats in a rural park. Once one of the largest coal mines in the world, it has been converted for walking or fishing in its woods, meadows and pools; this is Baggeridge Country Park, Gospel End, near Sedgley, Dudley. Or you might like to visit a small family run vineyard in the Severn Valley, where you can wander round and taste the wine. Another country concern is **Rowlstone Pottery**, a craft centre near the beautiful Golden Valley in Herefordshire, where you can see the potter at work. The address is Rowlstone, Pontrilas HR2 0DW. For companionable exploration of the Cotswolds, you could join **Lord Winton's Walking Tours**; details from The Manor, Moreton Pinkney NN11 6SJ (Tel 029 576 342).

Discovering Places

Tourist Centres all have lists of farm or activity holidays. In each county farming families have formed groups offering a range of accommodation, a warm welcome and wholesome food. Activity holidays cover anything from hot-air ballooning over Shakespeare's countryside or the Earl of Lichfield's home, to residential leisure courses visiting exhibitions and galleries in the Shrewsbury area. For a cruising holiday aboard a 'hotelboat', contact **Willow Wren Cruises**, Junction Wharf, London Road, Braunston, near Daventry NN11 7HB (Tel 0788 891356). Tourist Centres will give details of these and other waterway trips, for the day or longer. For land-borne excursions, try a horse-drawn gypsy caravan, which will take you through picturesque countryside, with evening stops at farmhouses or coaching inns. Contact Equitana Holidays, The Plough at Kelmscott, Lechlade GL7 3HG (Tel 036 785 489).

Black Country Breaks give you a town holiday in which you can nevertheless 'get away from it all'; either 'Step Back in Time', with visits to museums and a steam railway journey in the Severn Valley; or 'Crafts Galore', touring centres of craftsmanship like Royal Brierley Crystal Works. Information from: Beryl Woodhouse, Accommodation Unit, Wolverhampton Polytechnic, Wolverhampton WV1 1SB (Tel 0902 321000). Bristol University Extra-Mural Department, Senate House, Tyndall Avenue, Bristol BS16 3SJ (Tel 0272 303629) also run programmes of exploration in the Cotswold area. While in the Cotswolds you could join a guided walk by a Volunteer Warden. Send a stamped addressed envelope to the Cotswold Warden Officer, Gloucester County Council Planning Department, Shire Hall, Gloucester GL1 2TN, for details. Heart & West of England Country Tours, Yew Tree House, Ombersley, Worcestershire WR9 0JX (Tel 0905 620848) also supply guides and have a list of manor houses and privately owned stately homes which groups may visit for coffee, tea or a meal with the owners.

The region is rich in cathedrals and abbeys, and each of the larger ones has an Education or Visitor Officer to welcome visitors and tell them what they want to know. All towns of any size have a Tourist Information Centre, which can give details of local clubs, such as the Gloucestershire Gliding Clubs, or events like those at the attractive village of Painswick with its Civil War connections. Here the Guild of Craftsmen's Exhibition and the Annual Show are held in August, while the 14th-century custom of 'Clipping the Yews' takes place around 19 September.

Day trips can be made for a nutshell-view of rural England to Hatton Country World, near Warwick, where a craft village sells unique items, a farm shop is stocked with local produce, rare breeds are displayed, and a nature trail takes you to Hatton Locks. Hollybush Farm Country Centre offers similar countryside products in a less developed setting at Astley, Nuneaton, in Warwickshire. At many English Heritage properties events are organised, such as re-enactments of the various battles that have taken place in the region's past.

The Tourist Centres are excellent sources of local information, but a local paper will also give you an insight into the day-by-day happenings in the community; the public library too is usually festooned with notices about what is going on.

Communications

How to Get There

AIR: **Birmingham International Airport** is a centre for international and domestic flights servicing all parts of the British Isles.

RAIL: InterCity train services cross the region, so that London can be reached in one and a half hours and Glasgow in four. Express trains run between the South Coast and Liverpool or Manchester, via Hereford and Shrewsbury. Rail enquiries to **Birmingham** (Tel 021 643 2711), who should be able to give details of main line routes in the region.

COACH: **National Express** (Tel 021 622 4373) run coaches every two hours to London, and operate tours to all parts of the country.

CAR: The motorway network crosses the region and London can be reached by car on the M40 in about one and a half hours; Glasgow on the M6 in four hours. The M5 runs down the west of the region, and to the east there is quick access to the M1.

When You're There

RAIL: The only area without an excellent train system is the Wye Valley and Western Herefordshire in the hilly Welsh border country. A funicular railway operates at Bridgnorth in Shropshire and the Severn Valley Railway runs from there into Worcestershire, via Bewdley as far as Kidderminster. Here services link with British Rail trains. Foxfield Light Railway runs rides for five miles (8 km.) through the Staffordshire countryside on summer Sundays.

BUS: **Midland Red Bus Company** operates throughout the region; details from Midland Red West, Heron Lodge, London Road,

Worcester WR5 2EW (Tel 0345 212555). **Gloucestershire** has a good network of cross-country services; contact Gloucestershire County Council Public Transport Information (Tel 0452 425543). Tours are run in the Cotswolds and Forest of Dean, for which you should apply to Public Transport Team, County Surveyor's Department, Shire Hall, Gloucester GL1 2TH. **Midland Fox** is a useful company in the West Midlands and Warwickshire, connecting with Midland Red South and offering Explorer tickets. Details of other services in Hereford & Worcester are available from County Engineer and Planning Officer, Hereford & Worcester County Council, County Hall, Spetchley Road, Worcester WR5 2NP.

To find out about the **Shropshire** Bus Wayfarer, apply to Public Transport Section, Shropshire County Council, The Shirehall, Abbey Foregate, Shrewsbury SY2 6ND (Tel 0345 056785). You can take a Chaserider to enjoy the heathland of Cannock Chase; for enquiries (Tel 0543 466124).

In **Staffordshire**, PMT offer an *Out and About* leaflet, detailing scenic routes and bargain tickets. A central organisation which passes on bus enquiries during the off-peak season (October to March) is **Scenic England and Wales by Bus**, 4 Station Road, Knowle, West Midlands B93 0HT.

CAR: The main motorway from the north is the M6 running through Staffordshire to the West Midlands, joining at West Bromwich with the M5. This continues southwards through Worcestershire and Gloucestershire towards Bristol and the West Country. The M6 and M42 between them ring the Birmingham area, connecting it with the M1 to the east. The M54 links Shrewsbury with the West Midlands and the M50 leaves the M5 to run as far as Ross-on-Wye. This leaves Herefordshire and Shropshire largely unserved by motorway, but the A49 is a good road running north to south through these counties.

A 'leisure drive' of approximately 50 miles (80 km.) suggested by the Tourist Board runs from Bromyard to Tenbury Wells along the Teme Valley in Herefordshire. Leaflets are available from Tourist Centres on drives through Warwickshire and the Cotswolds, or, in Worcestershire, on the Elgar and the Cider Trails.

Here are a few less formalised country drives. Starting at Ross-on-Wye, you can explore the AONB between that river and the Severn in the Forest of Dean; or from Shrewsbury, tour over Shropshire's uplands past the Long Mynd; or north across the Shropshire Plain, a rural landscape scattered with half-timbered farms.

BOAT: The two main rivers, Severn and Avon, have various cruise lines operating on them, including a restored narrow-boat which can be hired from **Time and Tide Ltd**, Tolsey Wharf, Tewkesbury (Tel 0684 29656), and larger cruisers on the higher reaches of the Severn. Rowing boats, canoes and punts can be taken out by the hour from **Rose's Boat Yard**, Swan's Nest Lane, Stratford-upon-Avon (Tel 0789 67073). There is also a comprehensive canal network linking the cities of the West Midlands with Droitwich in the west, and northwards to Staffordshire and the Shropshire Union Canal. On all these canals different kinds of trips are run, including a horse-drawn boat along the Ashby Canal to visit Bosworth battlefield. Details of trips and operators are available from Tourist Centres.

CYCLING: **Waywalks**, 23 Southfield Road, Westbury-on-Trym, Avon BS9 3BG (Tel 0272 623586) gives information or arranges guided tours for cyclists and walkers in the Cotswolds. **Intrepid Cycle Tours**, Manor Farm, Napton, Rugby CV23 8NF (Tel 0926 812253) provide bikes and holidays to meet all requirements. **Cadence Cycling and Cycle Hire**, Foregate Street Station, Worcester WR1 1DB (Tel 0905 613501) hires out bikes and suggests routes; send SAE for leaflet. Otherwise Youth Hostels can supply information about local hire firms.

There is a cycleway on Kingswinford Railway between Wolverhampton and Dudley, and parts of a number of the long-distance paths such as the Cotswold Way or Wychavon Way through Worcestershire include bridleway sections for cyclists. The Countryside Commission or the Cyclists' Touring Club will give details of specific cycle routes.

WALKING: **Cotswold Rambling**, Ludlow House, Berralls Road, Tetbury GL8 8ED (Tel 0666 54340) arrange self-guided walking holidays. In addition to the **Wychavon and Cotswold Ways**, the **Heart of England Way** links the latter with the Staffordshire long-distance path at Cannock Chase. A similar 172 mile (277 km.) way crosses Shropshire, and in the Wye Valley sections of a footpath between Chepstow and Hereford are now complete. For further details on this, contact Wyedean Tourist Board, Ross-on-Wye. The **Severn Way Path** starts at Tewkesbury and follows the river down to Berkeley. Cotswold Guided Tours are mentioned under *Discovering Places* (page 401). The **Worcestershire Way**, running into the Malvern Hills, is managed by Hereford & Worcester Countryside Service, while Offa's Dyke Centre, Old Primary School, West Street, Knighton (Tel 0547 528753) gives information on the Offa's Dyke Path stretching the length of the Marches, as well as details of other walks in the area. Short trails run through various Nature Reserves managed by the County Wildlife Trusts, from whom details can be obtained. For a host of other waymarked walks, such as the one at Crackley Wood, near Kenilworth, where the delicate balance needed for successful plant and animal life is demonstrated, or trails in Sutton Park, an AONB at Sutton Coldfield, see the local Tourist Centre.

RIDING: **Lea Bailey Riding School**, Ross-on-Wye HR9 5TY (Tel 0989 81360) offer hacking and jumping holidays and courses. For horse-drawn caravan holidays, contact **Uley Carriage Hire**, Weaver's House, Uley, Dursley GL11 5TB (Tel 0544 318548).

Useful Local Contacts

Gloucestershire Trust for Nature Conservation, Church House, Standish, Stonehouse GL10 3EU (Tel 045382 2761). **Herefordshire Nature Trust**, 25 Castle Street, Hereford HR2 2NW (Tel 0432 56872). **Shropshire Wildlife Trust**, Old St George's School, New Street, Shrewsbury SY3 8JP (Tel 0743 251691). **Staffordshire Nature Conservation Trust**, Coutts House, Sandon, Stafford ST18 0DN (Tel 08897 534). **Warwickshire Nature Conservation Trust**, Montague Road, Warwick CV34 5LW (Tel 0926 496848). **Worcestershire Nature Conservation Trust**, Hanbury Road, Droitwich WR9 7DV (Tel 0905 773031). **Wildfowl Trust**, Slimbridge GL2 7BT (Tel 045 389 333). **Peak National Park Centre**, Losehill Hall, Castleton S30 2WB (Tel 0433 20373). **Droitwich Canal Trust**, 1 Hampton Road, Droitwich (Tel 0905 774225) operates cruises on restored canal. **Heart of England Tourist Guides Association**, 9 Arrow Grange, Arrow, Alcester B49 5PJ (Tel 0789 764282) offer registered guide services in various languages. **Guild of West Midlands Artists and Craftsmen** (Tel 021 501 2391) stage craft exhibitions and fairs. **Heritage in Action** (Tel 0242 570481) promote craft fairs in the region. **Lyneal Trust**, The Shirehall, Abbey Foregate, Shrewsbury (Tel 0743 25100) operate a canal boat for disabled and their helpers. **Country Village Weekend Breaks**, The Cruck House, Eardisley, Herefordshire HR3 6PQ (Tel 05446 488219). **Multi-Active Holidays Ltd**, 90 Sandown Drive, Hereford HR4 9TB (Tel 0432 357336). **Water-colour Weeks at Weobley**, The Old Corner House, Weobley HR4 8SA (Tel 0544 318548). **Wineweekends**, Upper Orchard, Hoarwithy HR2 6QR (Tel 043270 649). **Acorn Activities**, 5A King Street, Hereford HR4 9BW (Tel 0432 357335) for all kinds of activity holiday. **Moorside Activity Centre**, Moorside Farm, Hollingsclough, Longnor, Staffordshire SK17 0RF (Tel 029883 406), activities with farmhouse accommodation. The Farm Holiday Groups also operate in the region; details from Tourist Centres.

Geographical Breakdown of Region
West Midlands

Birmingham and its satellites occupy almost all this county, created in the 1970s boundary changes. Both the M5 and M6 'fly over' the city, which is currently using its central position to develop as a major exhibition and conference venue. At one time the area called the Black Country justified its name when, for many miles around, the air was literally black with soot residue. No longer so – and the county is reshaping its image; now the very factors which were seen as defects are being turned into leisure attractions, and you can trace here the history of England's industrial development.

Birmingham

Birmingham is an important destination for business travellers and has tailored its amenities accordingly. The city centre is being upgraded so that pedestrians can appreciate its spaciousness.

The city's 'highest profile' building is probably the **National Exhibition Centre (NEC)**, where a variety of local events are held as well as international ones. In June there is the International Horse Show, followed by the International Motor Show in October, and in April the Centre is the venue for the International Antiques Fair. Complementing this, an International Convention Centre and National Indoor Arena were completed in 1991. The NEC, on the outskirts of Birmingham, is near the airport and on a direct bus route from the city centre. Nearby is the **National Motorcycle Museum**; enthusiasts can experience vintage nostalgia here in specially built premises.

There is good shopping in the city centre, where there are also various museums. The popular **Birmingham Museum and Art Gallery** specialises in pre-Raphaelite work; for a smaller, but wide-ranging collection of paintings, visit the **Barber Institute of Fine Arts** at the University. The **Science and Technology Museum** is also centrally placed, while a little out of town but easily reached by bus is the **Railway Museum**, offering rides and guided tours. The **Patrick Collection** covers motor-car history amid landscaped gardens.

Once famous for pens, pins, toys and brooches, the city is now celebrated for its chocolate manufacturer. At **Cadbury World** in Bournville you can follow the chocolate trail from Central American rainforests to the finished product.

The city has a noteworthy **Cathedral**, whose Education Adviser, Alan Lamb, will gladly discuss the stained glass windows. Victorian Gothic **St Chad's Roman Catholic Cathedral** is less central, but contains interesting carved work. Older buildings which have survived surrounding developments are Jacobean Aston Hall (near Aston Villa football ground); Blakesley Hall, a 15th-century farmhouse at Yardley; Sarehole Mill, a working water-mill; an 18th-century dovecote at Moseley; Selly Manor, a beautifully half-timbered house, near Cadbury World; and another old manor still standing in central Birmingham, Stratford House.

Accommodation

First Class

Asquith House, 19 Portland Road, Edgbaston Bl6 9HN (Tel 021 454 5282). Ten bedrooms in friendly and comfortable Victorian-style house, not far from University.

Norton Place Hotel, 180 Lifford Lane, Kings Norton B30 3NT (Tel 021 433 5656). Ten ground floor rooms in walled garden of the Patrick Collection.

Health Lodge Hotel, Coleshill Road, Marston Green B37 7HT (Tel 021 779 2218). Small private hotel close to motorway junctions and NEC, offering warm hospitality.

Middle Range

Copperfield House Hotel, 60 Uplands Road, Selly Oak B29 7JS (Tel 021 472 8344). Friendly 14-bedroom Victorian house close to University and Pebble Mill TV studios.

Willow Tree Hotel, 759 Chester Road, Erdington B24 OBY (Tel 021-373-6388). Conveniently placed 7-bedroom hotel in large garden, in north-east of city.

Robin Hood Lodge Hotel, 142 Robin Hood Lane, Hall Green B28 OJX (Tel 021 778 5307). Tourist Board approved family run guest house with home cooking, in South Birmingham.

Bilthoven, 1253 Stratford Road, Hall Green B28 9AJ (Tel 021 777 3324). Small multi-lingual guest house in its own grounds.

Economy

The Kennedy, 38 York Road, Edgbaston B16 9JB (Tel 021 454 1284). Friendly family run guest house not far from Edgbaston Reservoir.

Grasmere Guest House, 37 Serpentine Road, Harborne B17 9RD (Tel 021 427 4546). Pleasant rooms in residential area.

Lyby, 14–16 Barnsley Road, Edgbaston B17 8ED (Tel 021 429 4487). Good accommodation in house not far from University.

Eating Out

The city is well-endowed with Indian and Chinese restaurants but it's difficult to find traditionally English ones.

First Class

Swallow, 12 Hagley Road, Five Ways (Tel 021 452 1144). Langtry Restaurant offers regional specialities in Edwardian surroundings.

Middle Range

Lyndhurst House, 135 Kingsbury Road, Erdington (Tel 021 373 5695). Family owned hotel and restaurant serving English food.

Nutters, 422 Bearswood Road (Tel 021 420 2528). Excellent range of mainly vegetarian food in simple surroundings.

Economy

Wild Oats Restaurant, 5 Raddlebarn Road, Selly Oak (Tel 021 471 2459). Serves vegetarian food.

Bartons Arms, High Street, Aston (Tel 021 359 4853). Edwardian pub close to the city centre with excellent food, including salads and seafood.

The James Brindley, Bridge Street (Tel 021 643 1230). Attractive canal-side pub in city centre, also offering well-served seafood.

Entertainments

The **Alexandra Theatre**, John Bright Street (Tel 021 643 1231), with cafe-bar, and **Hippodrome**, Hurst Street (Tel 021 622 7486), home to Birmingham's Royal Ballet, have continuous programmes, while the new **Symphony Hall** at the Convention Centre puts on concerts with internationally famous names. The box office is in the Town Hall, Victoria Square (Tel 021 236 3889). The excellent **Central Library**, also in Victoria Square has a newly-opened cafe-bar. The Birmingham Super Prix motor race is held in August; a more gentle pastime would be a canal-side walk round Gas Street Basin, or along the Titford Canal, part of the old Birmingham Navigation system. At **Edgbaston Reservoir** in Cannon Hill Park you can fish, sail, row or canoe; festivals are held here, there's a restaurant, and it's home to the **Midlands Arts Centre**. The Nature Centre here keeps wild animals in natural enclosures. Also in Edgbaston are the **Botanical Gardens**, with the largest collection of plants in the Midlands. One of Birmingham's traditional trades is carried on in the Jewellery Quarter, a conservation area near the centre.

Useful Addresses

Tourist Information Centre, City Arcade (Tel 021 643 2514). **Airport Information Desk** (Tel 021 767 5511). **General Hospital**: Steelhouse Lane (Tel 021 236 8611). **Post Office**: Victoria Square (Tel 021 644 8652).

West Midlands and Warwickshire

It may be surprising to find how interesting Birmingham's outer suburbs are. At West Bromwich, **Sandwell Valley's** 400-acre (162 hectares) Country Park has a farm museum and opportunities for riding, fishing and boating. It's worth exploring the intricate canal system, either by boat hired from **Brummagem Boats**, at Sherborne Street Wharf, or at Galton Valley Park's Canal Heritage Area. You can continue by canal to Dudley where Dudley Canal Trust operates trips through man-made caverns in about two miles (3.2 km.) of underground waterway. Here is the open-air **Black Country Museum**, much publicised, which reconstructs the area's history; also the **Zoo** and castle ruins – or you may like to have a country walk in Cotwall End Nature Centre. There are even vineyards at Halfpenny Green on the county border.

The **Leasowes** is an early example of natural landscape gardening, while for indoor interest you can watch the skilled manufacture of **Royal Doulton Crystal** at Stourbridge. To the north of the city is an interesting example of William Morris decor at **Wightwick Manor**, Wolverhampton, and **Bantock House Museum** has a collection of Staffordshire portrait figures and 18th-century enamels. At Walsall there is a working leather centre, while in the former Boatman's Rest at Top Lock you can see a recreated boatman's cabin in **Birchills Canal Museum**. Beyond Sutton Park with its varied flora, **Kingsbury Water Park** has woodland walks and twenty lakes for sailing and fishing. Moving westwards towards Atherstone, the nature reserve at **Alvecote Pools** was developed from a former mining area and harbours over-wintering wildfowl. Pooley Fields is open to the public, but the Pools can only be visited by members of the Warwickshire Nature Conservation Trust. **Nuneaton** is a walking centre, from

Hartshill Hayes Country Park with woodlands overlooking the Anker Valley to Galley Common where wild flowers grow profusely in ridge and furrow meadows; there is even a small urban wetland near Bedworth town centre. The estate of Arbury Hall, Elizabethan on the outside and Gothic Revival within, was George Eliot's birthplace.

Coventry's highlight is its Cathedral, destroyed during the Second World War, completely rebuilt by 1962, and now a treasure-house of contemporary art. There are still medieval buildings in this manufacturing city. For a countryside walk, the **West Midlands Way** passes through Meriden, with its market cross at the supposed centre of England. Alternatives are **Coombe Abbey** or the Local Nature Reserve at Stonebridge Meadow on the River Sowe, managed by Warwickshire Nature Conservancy Trust, while the **Organic Gardening Centre** at Ryton-on-Dunsmore has come to fame through television. Where the M45 finishes, **Draycote Water Country Park** near Rugby is another open area; the nearby folk museum of Country Bygones at Marton is worth visiting too. Also organic, Church Leys farm at Napton-on-the-Hill has superb views and a ridgetop windmill; rather more noisy is the mechanical music at Napton Nickelodeon. Continuing westwards, look out for the Old Mint Inn at Southam and Chesterton Mill, used as an observatory, at Harbury.

The red sandstone bulk of **Kenilworth Castle** stands high over the meadowland; Elizabeth I's exhibition is sited in the Barn (she would not have approved!). **Crackley Wood** nearby is a reserve for spring flowers, birds and Muntjac deer, with more formalised woodland walks at **Stoneleigh National Agricultural Centre**, site of the Royal International Show in July. Only the gateway remains of a Cistercian abbey, while the Children's Farmyard provides contemporary attraction. Bishops Bowl Lakes, a commercial fishery in a disused lime quarry near Leamington Spa, is threatened by development, despite its special beauty and scientific interest.

Immensely impressive is **Warwick Castle**; but any visit to the town's many historic buildings should include the **Museum** and **Lord Leycester's Hospital** for 16th-century old soldiers – followed by cream tea in the Brethren's kitchen. **Guy's Cliffe** on the Avon is associated with a sad and complicated Saxon romance.

Stratford-upon-Avon is perhaps the most concentrated centre for attractions (mostly derived from Shakespeare) of any provincial town. Once immersed in it you can't avoid them, nor will you want to. To see a summer performance at the **Royal Shakespeare Theatre** (Tel 0789 295623) on the banks of the swan-crowded Avon you normally need to book in April, or join a lengthy queue for unreserved seats. On

23 April there is a Birthday Procession through the streets; the local market is a more frequent event. The **Butterfly Farm** (which includes spiders) makes an interesting variation on Shakespeare, as does the **Falconry Centre** at Mary Arden's house. When visiting **Charlecote Park** (with deer) five miles (8 km.) away, near Wellesbourne, you should look for the watermill producing stone-ground flour; but there's no missing the charming thatched roofs of Shottery or the half-timbering at Wilmcote.

Nearer the Oxfordshire border lies **Edge Hill**, site of an indecisive Civil War battle, with a **Battle Museum** at Farnborough Hall, and three stately homes: moated **Broughton Castle**; **Upton House**, with fine painting and tapestry collections, and **Compton Wynyates**, a Tudor masterpiece, which, though seen from the Upper Tysoe footpath, cannot normally be visited. Among surrounding stone-built villages, Warmington and Radway have village greens and duck-ponds, or you could explore Ilmington (on foot only, though).

Ragley Hall, south of Alcester and magnificently set in parkland, contains a fascinating modern mural and much more, while **Coughton Court** is a historic Elizabethan house. Try to visit Oversley Wood on the A422, an isolated remnant of the Forest of Arden. The name survives anyway at Henley-in-Arden, with its Guildhall and a pottery workshop, Torquil Pottery, in a Tudor coaching-inn. **Umberslade Farms** at Tanworth-in-Arden encourage visits from schools and young children; and Clowes Wood, also at Tanworth, is one of many sites designated by West Midlands County Council as a nature reserve. Farmer Ted at Earlswood sells delicious home-produced ice-creams, not far from Packwood House, with its remarkable yew garden. **Baddesley Clinton** is a well-preserved moated manor at Knowle, where an Elizabethan building houses the local library.

Accommodation

First Class

Mallory Court, Harbury Lane, Bishop's Tachbook, Royal Leamington Spa CV33 9QB (Tel 0926 330214). Luxury manor house, where food is imaginatively served.

Stratford House, Sheep Street, Stratford-upon-Avon, CV37 6EF (Tel 0789 68288). Georgian house with walled courtyard in town centre, and adventurous menu.

The Dun Cow, The Green, Dunchurch, near Rugby CV22 6NJ (Tel 0788 810233). Rambling old-world inn in pretty village with traditional food.

Middle Range

Shrewley House, Shrewley, near Warwick CV35 7AT (Tel 092 684 2549). Warm family welcome in Georgian farmhouse.

Chapel House, Friars' Gate, Atherstone CV9 1EY (Tel 0827 718949). Small family run town house, with good-value food.

Blackwell Grange, Blackwell, Shipston-on-Stour CV36 4PF (Tel 060 882 357). Working farm which is peaceful and homely. Meat-eaters are encouraged.

Economy

Pear Tree Cottage, Church Road, Wilmcote, Stratford-upon-Avon CV37 9UX (Tel 0789 205889). Quietly situated 16th-century farmhouse run by enthusiastic local couple.

Maxstoke Priory, Maxstoke, near Coleshill B46 2QW (Tel 0675 462117). Beautifully converted 13th-century priory situated in rural surroundings not far from NEC. Good breakfasts but no other meals served.

Templar House, Temple Grafton, Alcester B49 6NS (Tel 0789 490392). Small, comfortable and welcoming.

Eating Out

First Class

Mallory Court, Harbury Lane, Bishop's Tachbrook, Leamington Spa (Tel 0926 330214). Gourmet food on fixed-price menu, with supplements.

Nuthurst Grange, Nuthurst Grange Lane, Hockley Heath (Tel 0564 783972). Cheerful welcome and a good range of food.

Arrow Mill, Arrow, near Alcester (Tel 0789 762419). The Mill-stream Restaurant offers lovely surroundings, friendly service and a lengthy menu.

Middle Range

Sir Toby's, 8 Church Street, Stratford-upon-Avon (Tel 0789 68822). Tiny central restaurant where couple cooking and serving food also enjoy theatre-talk.

Fanshawe's, 22 Market Place, Warwick (Tel 0926 410590). Run informally by an efficient couple, who serve huge portions and also vegetarian menu.

Feldon House, Lower Brailes, near Shipston-on-Stour (Tel 060

885 580). Welcoming and friendly, offers simple menu, excellently cooked; but you must book.

Economy

Cafe Natural Wholefood Vegetarian Restaurant, Unit 1 Greenhill Street, Stratford-upon-Avon (Tel 0789 41574). Cafe behind health food shop, serves elaborate vegetarian food.

Old Red Lion, 42 Church Street, Shipston-on-Stour (Tel 0608 61002). Friendly service in ancient building.

The Thatch Restaurant, 24 Cottage Lane, Shottery, Stratford-upon-Avon (Tel 0789 293122 or 0789 750502). Traditional English food, all home-made, in half-timbered cottage.

Gloucestershire

Here is the traditional landscape of rural England. The Cotswolds sweep up to east and north, their underlying stone used to build golden villages in the 16th-century heyday of the wool trade. The River Severn slices through the west of the county, creating the Gloucester plain, and giving rise to industry along its banks, as tidal rivers usually do, but also to wildlife, and the once secret community of the Forest of Dean. It wasn't till 1966 that the Severn could be crossed by road at a lower place than Gloucester – hence this little-known land beyond the river.

Gloucester

The name itself means 'a shining fortress' which once, doubtless, it was. Founded near the meeting-point of Roman roads, the town is dominated now by the 14th-century Cathedral, with its high central tower.

Any visit to Gloucester starts, for most overseas tourists anyway, with the **Cathedral**. The present building, constructed around a Norman Abbey, demonstrates the flowering of Perpendicular architecture in intricate fan vaulting, especially round the North cloisters. You can't miss the East window (the size of a tennis court) with its luminous stained glass. Here too is the tomb of Dr Edward Jenner, discoverer of smallpox vaccination.

Much of the Roman and medieval remains can be seen in the **City Museum**. Gate-towers and moat are preserved in an underground exhibition at Eastgate, and a **Folk Museum** in Westgate Street reconstructs Gloucester's history in a group of half-timbered houses. The city walls were largely demolished, not by modern developers but by Charles II in 1662, to repay a grudge against its citizens. However, there are old buildings tucked away, near where the four main streets meet at **Gloucester Cross**. Look for jutting medieval houses in New Inn Lane and St Mary's Gate, and St Bartholomew's Almshouses near the Folk Museum. Blackfriars, once a priory, and Greyfriars are both in the town centre, as is the house Beatrix Potter chose to illustrate her *Tailor of Gloucester* story.

The **dockland** area is another attraction, demonstrating the city's status as a port since Roman times. Currently being restored as a museum centre, old warehouses are now home to the **National Waterways Museum**, displaying the story of water transport, housing as well as the large Antiques Centre, the Opie Collection of Packaging, which sets out the contents of a century of shopping baskets, and the **Gloucestershire Regimental Museum**. Here too is a floating restaurant and various other amenities.

Outside the city, **Hucclecote Meadows** Local Nature Reserve preserves the hay meadows that once covered Gloucester Vale. **Robinswood Hill** Country Park is three miles (4.8 km.) from the centre and offers walking or riding in 250 acres (101 hectares) of countryside. **Llantony Priory** in Castle Meads also gives respite from town traffic. A little outside but on a bus route is the **International Centre for Wildlife Art** at Twigworth, a unique collection, with artists in residence. Near the A40 dual carriageway is **Over Farm Market** with on-site farm animals, where local produce is sold. Thomas Telford designed the single-arch bridge spanning the river here.

Accommodation

First Class

Hatton Court, Upton Hill, Upton St Leonards GL4 8DE (Tel 0452 617412). Seventeenth-century country house in large gardens with beautiful views.

Bowden Hall Resort Hotel, Bondend Lane, Upton St Leonards GL4 8ED (Tel 0452 614121). Private hotel with 23 bedrooms in large secluded grounds beyond the motorway.

Middle Range

Rotherfield House Hotel, 5 Horton Road, Gloucester GL1 3PX (Tel 0452 40500). Friendly and comfortable, specialising in good food.

Westville Guest House, 255 Stroud Road, Gloucester GL1 5JZ

(Tel 0452 301228). Small and friendly, in residential area, close to all amenities.
Notley Guest House, 93 Hucclecote Road, Hucclecote GL3 3TR (Tel 0452 611584). Modernised cottage offering homely accommodation.

Economy

Clovelly Guest House, 68 Tewkesbury Road, Longford, Gloucester GL2 9EH (Tel 0452 26380). Small comfortable guest house on frequent bus route to centre.
Silvercroft, 7 Barnwood Road GL2 0RZ (Tel 0452 306618). Pleasant Edwardian family house with comfortable rooms.
Melbourne House, 7–9 Heathville Road, off London Road GL1 3DS (Tel 0452 418089). Large Victorian house close to stations and centre.

Eating Out

First Class

New Country Hotel, Southgate Street (Tel 0452 307000). Centrally placed pub serving home-made traditional country food.
Twigworth Lodge Hotel, Tewkesbury Road, Twigworth, Gloucester (Tel 0452 730266). Coach house restaurant offers traditional English food in friendly atmosphere.

Middle Range

The Judge's Lodgings, Spa Road (Tel 0452 309713). Good range of food in elegant surroundings, close to docks development.

Economy

College Green, 9 College Street (Tel 0452 20739). A half-timbered house, conveniently central and favoured by local people.
Down to Earth Wholefoods and Vegetarian Restaurant, 11 The Forum, Eastgate Shopping Centre (Tel 0452 305832). Good value, home-cooked, traditional food.

Entertainments

Gloucester Civic Trust provides guides for **tours** of historic Gloucester on Wednesday and Sunday afternoons through the summer, and every day in August. These can be booked through the Tourist Centre, St Michael's Tower, The Cross (Tel 0452 421188). In dockland you can also take a guided walk, or a narrow-boat trip. The annual

Three Choirs Festival will be held in the Cathedral in 1992, and in Worcester and Hereford the following years.

Transport Options

The bus station (Tel 0452 27516) off Market Parade and Bruton Way, and rail station (Tel 0425 29502) also off Bruton Way, are both near the centre. Trains go north, south or west, and Cheltenham & District buses cover surrounding areas. Shoreline Ltd, Gloucester Docks (Tel 0452 308018) run ferry trips around the docks and canal.

The extensive grassland and beechwoods of Crickley Hill Country Park cover the edge of the escarpment, with magnificent views towards the Severn estuary, and the remains of a large Roman villa with luxury bath-house. Long before the Romans, an Iron Age fort was built on the site of a yet earlier Neolithic camp. Close by, at Prinknash Park and Abbey you can watch local craftsmen making the famous pottery or visit the bird park where, besides water fowl, you will find trout and pigmy goats.

At **Ashleworth**, on the other side of Gloucester, there is a group of 15th-century buildings: a tithe barn, an E-shaped manor, and Court House. The church, a geologist's joy, was built with stone from a range of geological periods. The manor's original owner eloped with a nun and had to hand Ashleworth over to the monks of Bristol Abbey as a penance! Near the river, at Westbury Court, is a Dutch-style 17th-century water-garden, planted with species from that era. The church there has an unusual detached tower.

West of the Severn lies the **Forest of Dean**, where coal and iron may have been mined even before the Romans came. The mining tradition is strong; indeed, after working in a mine for a year and a day, any native may become a Freeminer and dig under royal licence. Six waymarked trails run through the woodlands, some needing stouter footwear than others, all testifying to previous human occupation, and offering spectacular views. The Forest's social and natural history is displayed at **Soudley's Dean Heritage Centre. Dene Rise Fruit Farm** near Blakeney has pick-your-own facilities, while Dean Forest Railway offers short rides.

Downstream, **Chepstow** has Britain's first stone-built castle. Turn right here to follow the River Wye, beside which stands **Tintern Abbey** – praised in paint and poetry; if possible, see it in autumn, winter or spring. In summer you may escape the crowds by taking a fairly taxing but beautiful walk through the woods: Offa's Dyke Footpath starts here. The splendid 12th-century castle of **St Briavels** is now a Youth Hostel. At **Clearwell Mining Museum** the caverns of ancient iron mines are open for caving trips and guided tours, while in **Puzzle Wood** paths landscaped in the 1800s intertwine in an intriguing maze. The **Speech House**, built in 1680 as a court house, is a hotel surrounded by woodland, where the Verderer's Court still meets quarterly; nowadays the Verderers protect forest amenities instead of royal deer. The Rock at Symonds Yat offers unbeatable views down the gorge; unfortunately too many people want to see them. Try to visit it in October when the beech-leaves are brilliantly flame-coloured.

For more wonderful views walk through the pine-trees to the top of May Hill in **Newent**, where young people used to meet on May Day to stage a mock battle between winter and summer. Newent has 18th-century Shambles, and an earlier Market House, while at the **Falconry Centre**, containing one of the largest collections of birds of prey in the world, you can watch the skill and precision of these hunters. Also at Newent the **Butterfly and Nature World Centre** is worth visiting. Besides Three Choirs Vineyards, **St Anne's Vineyard** at Wain House, Oxenhall, has a large collection of vines and produces its own marmalade too. In springtime you will see the wild daffodils in Dymock Wood – while trying to ignore the M50 traffic driving past.

Before reaching Tewkesbury, you'll pass **Odda's Chapel**, an Anglo-Saxon rarity attached to a half-timbered farmhouse. The great Norman pile of **Tewkesbury Abbey** supervises the black and white town at the angle where Severn and Avon rivers join. The townspeople saved their church from Henry VIII's Dissolution by paying him £453. In a medieval house here the **John Moore Countryside Museum** interprets farming and conservation activities. On the county border you can watch hand-printing and dyeing processes at **Beckford Silk Factory** and in the particularly pretty village of **Conderton** domestic pottery is made.

Cheltenham reached its glory as a spa town in the 18th and 19th centuries, and spa waters can still be taken at **Pittville Pump Room**, where there is also a Museum of Fashion. Despite the town's more recent development, it retains elegant wrought-iron Regency terraces and little parks. Up on the hillslope are the chamber tombs of Belas Knapp Long Barrow. **Cotswold Water Park** has been extensively tailor-made for various sporting activities, and for birdwatching too; it's a popular place. Instead you might explore the more peaceful village of **Guiting Power** and the woods where the River Windrush has its source. At **Greet**, near Winchcombe, a team of potters produce practical pots; here along the Cotswolds' western edge runs a row of castles and manor houses. Queen Katherine Parr lived and died at **Sudeley Castle** with its Tudor rose garden, while **Hailes Abbey**, in wooded pastureland, was built in 1246 by King John's son in thanksgiving for escape from shipwreck. **Snowshill Manor**, an attractive Tudor home on the exposed Northern slopes of the range, contains a curious collection of artefacts from Japanese armour to mousetraps. The two picturesque villages of **Stanway** and **Stanton** have Jacobean manor houses, with a medieval tithe barn in Stanway's parkland.

Braving the crowds in **Chipping Campden**, you may like to visit Smith's family-run garden centre, or **Hoarston**, a family farm at Charingworth, where fruit and vegetables are for sale. If you're here on the first Friday after Spring Bank Holiday you can watch the 'Olympick Games' on Dover's Hill, a re-enactment of 17th-century rural contests. **Hidcote Manor Garden** is a series of small gardens, famous for interesting plant species, and Batsford Arboretum contains rare trees in a lovely setting over **Evenlode Vale**. In the village, Evenlode pottery specialises in slipware.

The Windrush stream runs through **Bourton-on-the-Water**, its houses reached by footbridges; Chestnut Gallery here sells craft work. The Model Village at the Old New Inn is Bourton in miniature, while beyond the river banks exotic birds roam in Birdland, and Folly Farm has more rare water-fowl and endangered species. Still beside the Windrush valley, you can follow waymarked walks through **Sherborne Park**, off the A40, while an 18th-century prison at **Northleach** houses the Cotswold Countryside Collection. **Chedworth Roman Villa** stands in a woodland reserve which gives an overview of Cotswold wildlife, including the deer; alternatively take one of the trails at **Denfurlong Dairy Farm** and study milking-parlour procedure. The Mill Inn at Withington offers further refreshment; its church was commended in Cobbett's *Rural Rides*.

Bibury has been called 'the most beautiful village in England'. Try to visit it off-season to appreciate the cloth mill, cottage almshouses and Saxon church; it will be worth it. Bibury has a trout farm too, where fish may be fed – or caught. Aldsworth and Barnsley are quieter less self-conscious villages; notice the stone monsters carved round Aldsworth church walls. The Thames is a recognisable river at **Lechlade**, where the proposed (and much-needed) bypass threatens flooded gravel-pits of particular interest for wildlife, especially dragonflies.

Life in Roman Britain is reconstructed at the **Corinium Museum** in **Cirencester**; for more Roman remains, see the grass-covered amphitheatre near the town. At **Rodmarton**, where the Thames rises, is Windmill Tump, an enormous Neolithic long barrow, with yet another archaeological site on Minchinhampton Common. The grassland tilts steeply down here towards the Stroud Valley and Princess Anne's home, **Gatcombe Park**, where in August the British Open Trials Championships are held. Tetbury Festival, at Spring Bank Holiday includes traditional Woolsack Races, while spring and autumn are the seasons to visit world-famous **Westonbirt Arboretum**. There's a nature trail from here through Silk Wood, damp underfoot but full of butterflies. Starting at **Wotton-under-Edge** you can walk past ruined Kingswood Abbey and the tower commemorating the martyrdom of William Tyndale, translator of the Bible into English. Not far away, **Hunts Churt Nursery Garden** in Dursley has a large collection of old roses. There's a hill-fort and more long barrows above Uley on the edge of the escarpment, the longest being Hetty Pegler's Tump.

The Berkeley family have lived in **Berkeley Castle** for twenty-four generations. You can tour its dungeons where Edward II was murdered, or visit the tropical Butterfly House. The **Gloucester Canal** with swing bridges and lock-keepers' cottages runs by the river at Sharpness. Nearby, the **Wetlands Trust Centre** at Slimbridge has created ponds where visitors can feed tame breeding wildfowl or watch the over-wintering swans, geese and ducks. **Frampton-on-Severn**, actually on the canal, has the longest village green in England. Its Court and historical garden were made more famous through Richard Mabey's presentation of 'The Frampton Flora', and the Orangery here has been converted to holiday accommodation. Surrounded on three sides by the Severn, **St Augustine's Farm and Country Centre** is near the elver-collecting depot at Epney.

The **Stroud Valleys** with their mill-streams and canals are being developed as an industrial heritage area. The Medieval Hall and classical-style Subscription Rooms are amongst many old buildings in **Stroud**. Nearby, **Selsley Herb Farm** keeps goats in the paddock at all times, and serves cream teas on Sundays. There are woods for walking on Stroud Common or at Cranham, South of Birdlip Hill. On **Cooper Hill**, where the Cotswold Way is almost too well signposted, an annual cheese-rolling ceremony happens every Whit Monday. It's bleak up here; Bizley used to be called 'Bisley-God-help-us'; on Ascension Day it has well-dressing at its seven springs. In Painswick churchyard there is a clipped yew-wood, and the streamside walk is one of many set out by Gloucester County Council in a booklet, *Walking around*

Painswick. The stables here have an unusual rococo garden as well as woodland walks.

Accommodation

First Class

Calcot Manor, near Tetbury GL8 8YJ (Tel 0666 89 0391). Comfortable 15th-century farmhouse in rolling countryside with Michelin star cooking.

Middle Range

Halewell, Withington, near Cheltenham GL54 4BN (Tel 024289 238). Family home, part of 15th-century monastery, where guests are treated as friends.

Malt House, Broad Campden, Chipping Campden GL55 6UU (Tel 0386 840295). Family atmosphere and ample, ambitious meals.

Tudor Farmhouse, Clearwell, near Coleford GL16 8JS (Tel 0594 33046). Fourteenth-century, but newly refurbished house, run by friendly couple.

Economy

Lamb Inn, Great Rissington, Bourton-on-the-Water GL54 2LJ (Tel 0451 20388). Seventeenth-century inn serving traditional beers and home-cooked food.

The Old Vicarage, Awre, Newnham GL14 1EL (Tel 0594 510282). Warm welcoming house run by enthusiastic cooks.

Drakestone House, Stinchcombe, near Dursley GL11 6AS (Tel 0453 2140). Friendly welcome in Edwardian family home.

Eating Out

First Class

Epicurean, 1 Park Street, Stow-on-the-Wold (Tel 0451 31613). Short but quality menu.

Oakes, 169 Slad Road, Stroud (Tel 0453 759950). Comfortable welcome and fine cooking.

Middle Range

Savery's, The Green, Frampton-on-Severn (Tel 0452 740077). Country restaurant serving simple but satisfying food.

Le Champignon Sauvage, 24–26 Suffolk Road, Cheltenham (Tel 0242 573449). Small smart restaurant with set price varied menu.

Calcot Manor, Beverston, Tetbury (Tel 0666 890391). Family hotel with modern cooking.

Economy

Corner Cupboard Dining Room, Corner Cupboard Inn, Gloucester Street, Winchcombe (Tel 0242 602303). Tiny restaurant serving varied food.

Kingshead House, Birdlip (Tel 0452 862299). Unpretentious cooking in informal 16th-century house.

Hereford and Worcester

The flat Vale of Evesham covers a good deal of Worcestershire but the contours are broken by the Clent Hills in the north and by the Malvern range which rises quite abruptly from the surrounding countryside. These are embryo foothills of the Welsh mountains, whose border Marches were fiercely fought over for centuries. The Severn splits Worcestershire in two and the Wye winds a tortuous course through wooded gorges in Herefordshire, but this now-amalgamated county is characterised chiefly by its orchards.

Malvern

The curative spring waters of Malvern have been sampled for 300 years but the complex of towns which go under this name grew up largely in the last century, and are linked by a switchback of hills. Great Malvern nowadays includes Malvern Link, North and West Malvern, with Malvern Wells and Little Malvern just to the south; what they have in common is steep gradients and panoramic views.

The 15th-century **Priory Church** formerly belonged to a Benedictine monastery; inside, massive Norman columns reveal a building of earlier date. In the Priors Hall and surrounding rooms there are collections of paintings and religious vestments; old-fashioned roses grow in the gardens outside. There is a Victorian walled garden at **Madresfield Nursery** with the original Vine House, while the **Museum** in the Abbey Gateway features the town's history. At **Welland**, near Little Malvern there is an Animal and Bird Garden, which has a creepy-crawly house and puts on daily snake demonstrations. Principally though, if you come to Malvern you have come to see the hills, over which there are various walks and trails. The highest point, **Worcester Beacon** is 1114 feet (425 m.), and there is an Iron Age Fort on Hereford Beacon.

Entertainments

The **Three Counties Agricultural Show** takes place in June on the showground where a range of leisure activities can be enjoyed. In Priory Road there is also the Malvern Splash Leisure Pool with various entertainments. Malvern has a **Festival Theatre** (Tel 0684 892277), and the Tourist Office is in the Winter Gardens, Grange Road (Tel 0684 892287).

From Malvern you can do no better than go walking on the hills, and from **Midsummer Hill** there are views from the Cotswolds to the Welsh Mountains. Down in the marshes of **Knapp and Papermill Reserve** in the Leigh Brook Valley kingfishers are nesting; the warden will tell you more. Midsummer Weavers in **Upton-upon-Severn** produce a range of cloths in their workshop, using all British yarn on fifty-year-old looms called Bertha and George.

Pershore's name comes from the pear orchards which were there in Saxon times, and the Royal Horticultural Society continues tree culture in the ornamental grounds of Pershore College. The **Abbey's** decorated vaulting and carved bosses are the work of medieval craftsmen; in the High Street Jennie Hill's Gallery encourages young artists of today. Various events are held throughout the year in Abbey Park at **Evesham**; all that is left of the Abbey is an isolated archway and some ruined walling. The town has Tudor houses though, and the **Almonry Museum**, which is filled with historical memorabilia. Greenhill Farms to the North have pick-your-own produce in the heart of fruit-producing country, while for craft shops and lakeside walks, visit **Twyford Country Centre. Annard Woollen Mill** demonstrates the arts of mohair winding and rug-making, and also sells natural fibre wools.

The 13th-century tithe barn at Middle Littleton is still in use, as is the Fleece Inn, a medieval farmhouse in Bretforton village. At the Domestic Fowl Trust in Honeybourne you can learn anything you need to know about poultry. Golden-coloured **Broadway**, too charming for its own good, is now a tourist stronghold, and from its 'Folly' Tower, built in 1793 in the Country Park, you can enjoy views over twelve counties. **Elmley Castle**, below Bredon Hill, is a pretty village, not yet over-run, with a brook at the side of the street. A path from the 'No Through Road' here continues up Bredon Hill, once an Iron Age settlement, and at **Bredon** itself a lengthy medieval barn was restored with traditional materials after a fire in 1980.

Somewhere here is the lost boundary of what was the county of

Herefordshire. **Ledbury** makes a good introduction to this half of the county, surrounded by hopfields and orchards, and distinguished above all by its 17th-century Market House; the chevron-timbering is supported on oak pillars, under which an open market is still held. The Old Grammar School, whose first floor overhangs the cobbles of Church Lane, now houses a Heritage Centre. Another track here – possibly muddy – leads into the Malvern Hills, with glorious views from the 19th-century Monument. Below that stands pseudo-medieval **Eastnor Castle** and deer park, with collections of armour and tapestry inside and arboretum outside – also a thatched Post Office. **Bronsil Castle**, genuinely medieval, has only a moat and two gatehouses left.

It's worth seeking out The Bounds at Much Marcle for H. Weston and Sons, Cider and Perry Makers. You might also hunt round Ross-on-Wye for **Leeping Stocks**, a reserve of limestone grassland and woods, harbouring butterflies, birds and a rich flora. **Ross** is built on a wooded spur over the river, best seen from the Prospect public gardens near the church; in the churchyard itself a Plague Cross commemorates the townspeople who fell victim to the disease. At **How Caple Court** unusual plants and old-fashioned roses grow in the Edwardian riverside garden, and one of the country's leading candlemakers operates in the Market House. Down the Wye Valley the huge sandstone remains of **Goodrich Castle** stand guard above the river, with fine views from the battlements; here William Wordsworth wandered and was inspired. **Wye Valley Farm Park** has a collection of rare farm animals, which children are encouraged to touch and get to know, and woodland walks by the river.

Hereford is more like an enlarged market town; only the solid grey cathedral marks it as a city. Originally built where the Wye joins the River Lugg, Hereford has remained compactly snuggled around its centrepiece. A church has stood on the same site since the 7th century, and the present **cathedral** dates from Norman times. It has a **chained library**, and its most famous treasure, the **Mappa Mundi**, one of the oldest maps known which depicts Jerusalem in the centre of a flat world. The **Old House**, near the High Street, is Jacobean, and furnished in 17th-century style, as Nell Gwyn, born near the Wye bridge, might have known it. The **Natural History Museum** includes a bee-keeping display, while **King Offa Distillery** demonstrates the manufacture of all kinds of cider. **Bulmers Cider Mill** also has a Visitor Centre, with appropriate refreshment included in the admission fee.

The wooded hills above the village of **Mordiford** once harboured a green dragon, slain eventually by a convict in return for his freedom (so the story goes). More recently, the Petty Sessions Court met at **Fownhope's** Green Man Inn; the Judge's bedroom is still there, as are the iron bars for chaining prisoners. One of the finest Norman churches in Britain, **Kilpeck**, preserves more early history in its Romanesque carving and grotesque sculptures. Nearby is the road to lovely **Golden Valley**, and the great **Abbey Dore** which guards it; the wall paintings there show a medieval preoccupation with death. Home-made lunches and teas are served in the conservatory of Abbey Dore Court's walled garden. Further west is **Longtown Castle** with the fifteen-foot thick walls of its keep still standing. The Black Mountains can be seen from the woodland garden of The Weir at Swainshill on the Wye – best at snowdrop or daffodil time. At **Yarsop Dams** the British Trust for Conservation Volunteers are improving two lakes as a wetland habitat. The gardens of **Dinmore Manor** at Wellington have wonderful views eastwards to the Malvern Hills, and the house itself contains 12th-century Commandery, cloisters and a music room. **Lea and Pagets Wood** near Hereford is worth searching out for its rich woodland flora (twayblade for instance), while at the end of Golden Valley is the prehistoric burial chamber called **Arthur's Stone**. **Moccas Court** by the river here was designed by Robert Adam and is set in parkland laid out by Capability Brown.

Hay-on-Wye, where three counties, several rivers and as many roads converge, was once called The Hay. Nowadays it's known as a bookworm's paradise for its wealth of antiquarian and other bookshops. There's an old railway track from Hay to **Eardisley** (you can walk along it now) which at one time was used to bring coal by horse-drawn truck from Brecon. The black and white cottages behind the Tram Inn at Eardisley used to be their stables. One of the carved figures on the church's Norman font represents Christ snatching Adam from the devil. Further on is the last Great Oak, thirty feet (9 m.) round its trunk, in an area once all forestland. **Hergest Croft Gardens**, by Kington, has a magnificent collection of more recent trees and flowering shrubs, beautiful at any time of year, and in early summer **Park Wood** is walled with flowering rhododendrons. At the top of **Hergest Ridge**, 1397 feet (426 m.) high, there are more fine views northwards. It's difficult to trace the line of Offa's Dyke here, but you can climb **Bradnor Hill** to find the highest golf course in Europe.

Lugg Valley Field Centre is a wildlife sanctuary with old world gardens on a beautifully situated working farm, and the quiet village of **Wigmore** has a 16th-century hall, together with a ruined castle and Augustinian priory. Go to **Mortimers Cross**, where the last Wars of the Roses battle was fought, to see the more peaceful process of corn-milling at the 18th-century water mill. Just up the road are the rounded corner towers of **Croft Castle** and an avenue of 350-year-old Spanish chestnuts between flower-filled meadows. From the grounds a footpath climbs to Croft Ambrey's Iron Age fort, where hawfinches sometimes feed on the hornbeam seeds. Local people still exercise their grazing rights on Bircher Common, and at **Yarpole** village (mentioned in Domesday Book), The Old Bakehouse has also served as gaol and illegal Quaker meeting-house. Summertime concerts are held at **Berrington Hall**, whose elegant interior includes nursery, dairy and Victorian laundry.

Herbaceous plants are sold at Willows Nursery, West of **Leominster**, a town surrounded by half-timbered villages. One of them, **Eardisland**, whose charming houses line each riverbank, has a whipping-post in the 17th-century school-house, once used to chastise the women-folk but not the pupils. You can eat a delicious farmhouse tea at The Elms country garden here, or drink their home-made lemonade. **Pembridge** looks much as it did when New Inn Hotel was built as a coaching stop, beside the 16th-century Market House on its eight pillars. Nearby **Weobley** is equally picturesque.

At **Broadfield Court Estate**, Bodenham, old English gardens and a vineyard are open for tours and wine-tasting, while at **Shortwood Dairy Farm** in the maze of lanes south-west of Bromyard, the Leggs will invite you to feed the pigs or walk amongst the bluebells in Broxash Wood; their Jacob sheep have four horns. Madge Hopper sells specialist plants from her herb garden at nearby **Stoke Lacy**, and just down the road, Cowarne Hall Cottages have been beautifully converted for weekly letting, with angling in the Wye included. At **Hop Pocket Farm**, Bishops Frome, you can see the process of hop-growing, as well as visit the craft-shop in a converted hop kiln, admire the topiary in the gardens, and eat a home-baked tea.

The downs sweep up behind the quiet market town of **Bromyard**, with walks through the woods on Bringsty Common. The half-timbered manor and gatehouse at **Lower Brockhampton** are reflected in the water of the moat, while at **Edvin Loach**, on a hillside to the north, there are the lonely remains of an 11th-century church.

By the time you reach Tenbury Wells you are back in Old Worcestershire. The town is no longer an active spa, though salt springs were discovered here in 1839. Further down the river, **Clifton-upon-Teme**, perched above a wooded valley, has a huge hollow yew in the churchyard. Georgian **Stourport-on-Severn** grew round its 18th-century canal, designed to connect Severn and Trent; today the Basin, with the old brick warehouse and clock-tower beside it, is filled with narrow-boats and other craft. If you feel like sampling wines, a family-run vineyard at **Astley** has a record of 'tasting' awards. Beyond the river, **Hilditch Pool** at Hartlebury Common is a nature reserve with especially interesting plants and insects, and **Bewdley** (corrupted from the French Beaulieu – a 'beautiful place') has some fine riverfront houses. There's a chance to try making a clay pipe at its museum which demonstrates country crafts. Behind the town lies what's left of the **Wyre Forest**, whose trees were cut to make charcoal for the iron industry. Here there are nature reserves where you can walk by the streamside, starting perhaps at Sturt Common; look out for the Hawkhatch picnic site, with views over the Severn valley.

Kidderminster developed its silk trade in the 17th century, followed by the carpet-weaving industry for which it's known today. From here the Severn Valley Railway runs steam trains as far as Bridgnorth. Also beginning here is the North Worcestershire Path in quiet woodland at **Kingsford Country Park**; more dramatic is the steep wooded ridge of **Kinver Edge**, over the border in Shropshire. The path is waymarked and passes through three more country parks on its way over the Clent and Lickey Hills, at whose foot **Hagley Hall** is a riot of ornate 18th-century decor. The **Stour Canal** opened in 1776 through the encouragement of the local glass industry. Staffordshire and Worcestershire Canal Society volunteers reopened it in 1967 and traffic now passes through wooded countryside to reach the Black Country. Still well outside the Black Country sprawl, **Feckenham** is a neat village from which you can walk over the fields to the **Nature Reserve** made out of peat marsh on Wylde Moor, while **Abbots Morton**, not very near anywhere, has a thatched pillar-box attached to one of the black and white cottages. The **Avoncroft Museum of Buildings** is off the Bromsgrove bypass; here in the open air, buildings rescued from destruction recreate English history up to pre-fab times. In **Bromsgrove** itself Daub and Wattle's brick-floored pottery once housed a button factory, and ancient woodland threatened by encroachment is preserved round **Chaddesley**.

Droitwich has the saltiest springs in Europe, and you can float weightless in its brine baths. At **Hanbury** nearby (identified as the BBC's 'Ambridge' in *The Archers*) a community of craftspeople work in converted barns at the Jinney Ring Craft Centre. **Ombersley**, now happily bypassed, contains a Plague Stone where fearful traders left their wares at the village boundary to avoid contamination. At Clacks

Farm garden, well-known through television, you can seek expert advice on open days. **The Wychavon Way** starts not far from Shrawley's pink lopsided church, where native lime trees grow in the woods. At **Sankyns Green** is Eastgrove Cottage's colourful old-world garden and nursery, while a vast but ruined Victorian mansion at **Great Witley** has a unique Baroque church in the grounds.

Worcester is filled with memories of the past, standing side by side with present day industries. Perhaps best known is the **Royal Worcester Porcelain** factory where visitors see the manufacturing processes and museum. The **Lea and Perrins Sauce factory** is also open to the public. But the glory of this Royalist city is the **cathedral**, with its architecture spanning three centuries. The original Norman chapter house was circular, while from later times fan tracery decorates the chantry chapel. A carving of Cromwell's head is nailed by the ears over the doorway of the handsome Guildhall, beside statues of the two King Charles. Among many other medieval buildings **Greyfriars garden** offers a city-centre haven.

Woodlands creep up to the city's eastern edge: ancient bluebell woods at Warndon, and oakwoods and open fields in the Country Park behind County Hall. **Spetchley Park** down the road has a big informal garden with unusual shrubs and fallow deer. Edward Elgar was one of Worcester's famous natives; born at Broadheath, his birthplace is now a museum and contains some of his manuscripts. You can follow the Elgar Trail for 42 miles (67 km.) around the county that he loved.

Accommodation

First Class

Hope End, Ledbury HR1 1JQ (Tel 0531 3613). Set in wooded parkland and offering home-cooking in stylish 18th-century house.

Collin House, Collin Lane, Broadway WR1 7PB (Tel 0386 858354). Small, friendly and informal, well away from crowds.

Grafton Manor, Grafton Lane, Bromsgrove B61 7HA (Tel 0527 579007). Run by the Morris family who serve imaginative food.

Middle Range

The Steppes, Ullingswick, near Hereford HR7 3JS (Tel 0432 820424). Country guest house with old-world atmosphere.

Nether Court, Stoke Lacy, near Bromyard HR7 4HJ (Tel 0432 820247). Peaceful Victorian farmhouse with fishing in the lake.

Green Man, Fownhope, near Hereford HR1 4PE (Tel 0432 77243). Popular country pub with rooms, serving tasty food.

Economy

Rhydspence Inn, Whitney-on-Wye HR3 6EU (Tel 04973 262). Traditional hospitality in a half-timbered inn.
Butchers Arms, Woolhope HR1 4RF (Tel 043277 281). Comfortable pub with rooms, serving excellent food.
Caldewell, Pershore Road, Stoulton WR7 4RL (Tel 0905 840894). Country home in large grounds, with friendly owners and farm animals.

Eating Out

First Class

Poppies, The Roebuck, Brimfield (Tel 058 472 230). Varied menu in elegant and comfortable surroundings.

Middle Range

Brown's, 24 Quay Street, Worcester (Tel 0905 26263). Converted corn mill with simple healthy cooking.
Brockencote Hall, Chaddesley Corbett (Tel 0562 777876). Country house hotel in parkland with extensive menu.
Penrhos Court, Kington (Tel 0544 230720). Cooking from fresh local produce served in converted barn.

Economy

Glewstone Court, Ross-on-Wye (Tel 098 984 3071). Meals served informally in hospitable 18th-century house.
Jule's Cafe, Portland Street, Weobley (Tel 0544 318206). Organic meals much enjoyed by the locals.
The Marches Health Shop and Restaurant, 24–30 Union Street, Hereford (Tel 0432 355 712). Centrally placed, serves good vegetarian food.

Shropshire and Staffordshire

Shrewsbury

The sandy-coloured **Castle** stands guard to Shrewsbury at a bend in the river, leaving only the north undefended. Built in the 12th-century, it has been destroyed, restored and rebuilt, and now houses various regimental museums. Thomas Telford, stone mason turned county surveyor, redesigned it inside, and built Laura's Tower as a summer house for the 18th-century owner's daughter.

Amongst several museums in high and low town, **Rowley's House**, a 17th-century mansion, contains local history galleries and treasures from Roman Wroxeter, like a chemist's eye-lotion label.

The Civic Society has restored medieval buildings at Bear Step Hall, and the Council House is another example of fine Jacobean architecture. The oldest building of all, the **Abbey**, was founded in 1083; refurbished by Victorian renovators, the Norman style remains. **St Mary's Church** is full of original Flemish glass, and an enormous 'Jesse' window, showing that patriarch with all his descendants round him. Another of Shrewsbury's many churches is circular St Chad's, while at St Julian's, now deconsecrated, there is a craft centre with working studios, and exhibitions in the 13th-century tower. Exploring the town, you can find streets like Wyle Cop, named five centuries ago, with narrow passages called 'shuts'. Indeed, Charles Dickens, staying at the Lion Hotel, described the view of 'the crookedest black and white houses'. Representing more modern times, the **Victoria Arcade** creates a 19th-century atmosphere, while, over the river, **Longden Coleham Pumping Station** has restored beam pumping engines on view. The town library is in the old grammar school attended by Charles Darwin, who probably developed his interest in botany there. At **Frankwell**, his birthplace, a waterside path follows the river's loops. BBC personality, Percy Thrower, designed formal gardens at the **Dingle**, Quarry Park, the site of the August Flower Show.

Entertainments

The **Shropshire and West Midlands Agricultural Show** is in May, in July there is the **International Music Festival**, and **ploughing trials** take place in October. From May to October there are guided tours of the town. St Julian's Centre, where there's a vegetarian restaurant, holds a craft fair every Saturday. Besides regular events like these, Shrewsbury is noted for its many antique shops and bookshops. The Shrewsbury Gateway on Chester Street (Tel 0743 55159) holds leisure courses, concerts and plays, and has a riverside coffee shop. The **Tourist Office** is in The Square (Tel 0743 50762).

For information on **local bus services** send a stamped addressed envelope to Public Transport Section, Shropshire County Council, Shire Hall, Abbey Foregate SY2 6ND. You can take a bus to Haughmond Abbey and on Haughmond Hill there are woodland walks. Attingham Park, another short bus ride away, is an elegant 18th-century house with an enormous columned portico and cedars in the park. While there you could visit Home Farm at Attingham Atcham, to watch the Jersey herd being milked.

Close to Shrewsbury, life as it was in AD 150 is recreated in **Wroxeter's Roman City Museum**. Towards **Pitchford** a single-span iron bridge crosses Cound Brook; designed by Thomas Telford, it's the little brother of Derby's masterpiece at Ironbridge. Ancestors of American General Robert E. Lee were buried in **Acton Burnell** church, while the next village, **Acton Scott** gives butter-making demonstrations. The monuments in Condover Church include one carved by Reginald Cholmondeley of his wife after their year-long marriage. Mary Webb, who set her novels in this area, lived at **Pontesbury**, above which Earls Hill is topped by an Iron Age fort and nature reserve. If you continue to **Minsterley**, you will see the 'death's-head' doorway on its 17th-century church. **Merrington Green** north of Shrewsbury is a place of heathland and pools, while **Pimhill Organic Farm Centre** contains rare breeds, and country furniture. If you walk steeply up from Clive church you will reach Corbet Woodlands grown over disused quarry workings, with wide views. Down below, **Moreton Corbet** has a ruined medieval castle, and although the Parliamentarians in the Civil War removed the roof of the mansion enough remains to be able to visualise its splendour.

The Powys Eisteddfod is held each July in **Oswestry**, near the Welsh border. From here you can climb to an Iron Age hill-fort amongst gorseland and bracken, and look down on Offa's Dyke. Contrasting with the hills, at the edge of the Shropshire plain **Ellesmere** is a Georgian market town. On the canal which bypasses it, pleasure boats can be hired. **Colemere** is one of the beautiful meres round about, as well as Blake Mere, surrounded by steep wooded hills. The mere at the edge of town provides fishing opportunities and water sports. **Whixall Moss**, almost entirely uninhabited, lies between Ellesmere and Whitchurch; here peat left after the Ice Age is still being cut. Apply to English Nature for access to its rich plant and insect life. At **Grindley Brook** the canal passes through a tricky set of staircase locks; if landborne, you can watch manoeuvres from the bridge. **Brown Moss Nature Reserve** beyond Whitchurch is an area of heath, woods and pools, with uncommon plants and breeding birds; fishing permits are available. Seasonal flower displays are held in Hodnett Hall Gardens, whose former owner spent thirty years transforming the marshy valley into landscaped lakes and lawns. At **Fordhall Organic Farm**, after walking amongst freely ranging animals, you can have tea in their flower garden.

Market Drayton, rebuilt after fire in the 17th century, claims to be the home of gingerbread; it was certainly the home, in a rather rebellious childhood, of Clive of India. A small garden on a hillside near Willoughbridge, named Dorothy Clive, has rhododendrons and views, both of which are worth seeing. If you are looking for fruit, you can pick your own at Hungersheath Farm, Ashley. Organic vegetables, cheese, and home-made ice-cream are sold at New House Farm, Acton, nearby.

Downs Bank, only a little south of industrial Stoke-on-Trent (and given to the National Trust in 1946 in thanksgiving for the ending of the war) has a stream and moorland scenery. The countryside is also preserved at Trentham Gardens, with its wildfowl reserve near the edge of town. **Stoke** is the centre of the Five Towns of the Potteries; here you can tour china factories, travel in underground mines, ride on the Foxfield Steam Railway, visit museums, and see the signs of past industry preserved in the bottle kilns beside the canal. The Spode Works in the town centre show china-making processes, and Wedgwood is the largest china factory in the world; the City Museum also contains a fine ceramics collection. **Stoke** is the venue of the National Craft Fair in June. **Biddulph Grange**, to the north of the town complex, has an interesting Victorian garden offering a world tour in miniature.

The **Staffordshire Way** starts at Mow Cop, an 18th-century 'folly' on a crag, and passes Rudyard Lake before continuing South to Kinver. At **Consall Nature Park**, where the hills rise towards the Peak District, you can study natural history, while **Hawksmoor Nature Reserve**, through which the River Churnet flows, is a refuge for badgers and birds. Upstream, **Coombes Valley** is thick with rhododendrons, while on Ipstones Edge, Moorlands Farm Park welcomes children to play with rare farm breeds. Over the hill, in another Peakland valley, **Staffordshire Peaks Arts Centre**, with crafts and an excellent wholefood restaurant, is sited in an old village school. Just by Waterhouses is **Brown End Quarry**, visited by geologists from round the world. The porous limestone here causes the River Manifold to flow underground for much of its course. Staffordshire Wildlife Trust manages these spectacular hillslopes, among them **Castern Wood Nature Reserve** which is rich in butterflies, notably the Northern Brown Argus. Another lesson in geological history can be read on Apes Tor in a gorge below Hulme End.

The vast neo-Gothic mansion of **Alton Towers**, once the largest private house in Europe, with fountains and lakes in the gardens, now uses its fun park to attract visitors throughout the year. If you are in **Abbots Bromley** early in September you will meet a twelve-strong team of Horn Dancers beating the bounds round the village; you will have no trouble recognising them as all six will be wearing reindeer antlers. This dance, performed annually since pre-Norman times, symbolises the struggle of light and darkness, and may have been used to emphasise villagers' rights in nearby Needwood Forest. Mary Queen of Scots must have looked across the Forest during her captivity in **Tutbury Castle**, on its steep rock above the Dove Valley.

The Bass Museum and Shire Horse Stable at **Burton-on-Trent** make an intriguing venue for an indoor day, especially if you are over eighteen and thirsty. Just outside the town, you can walk in **Branston Water Park**, and near the centre of Tamworth, Warwickshire Moor has open grassland, though it does get flooded. **Hodge Lane Local Nature Reserve** offers varied wetland habitats, while Ash End House Farm, Middleton, is especially suitable for children. Here they can have pony rides, feed the animals and picnic in the barns. **Drayton Manor Park and Zoo** is a rather more stereotyped place, attracting many hordes of visitors. **Alrewas**, on the other hand, is a quiet village worth exploring for its thatched and timbered cottages. The Trent, in flooding the valley also watered the alders from which the villagers used to weave baskets.

Lichfield's sandy-brown Cathedral is unique in its three spires, known as the 'Ladies of the Vale'. There are carved figures covering the west front (over a hundred of them) and lovely Flemish glass in the Lady Chapel. The city has been the birthplace of several famous people. On 18 September, Dr Samuel Johnson's birthday, an annual commemoration service is held; his house in the market place is now a museum. Erasmus Darwin, grandfather to Charles of *Origin of Species* fame, also lived here and founded the Lunar Society whose 'Lunatic' members met every full moon to discuss current scientific and similar issues. For an out-of-town shopping trip, try the group of 'country shops' at Home Farm, Swinfen, in a farmyard setting, with restaurant and specialist crafts.

The Romans set up a staging post off Watling Street at the place now called **Wall**. Here there is a complete bath-house and the foundations of an inn. Beyond this, **Cannock Chase** covers 3000 acres (1215 hectares) of wild heath and woodlands, once one great oak forest; here you can walk or ride for miles on the different trails. The Visitor Centre is over at Rugeley but, to see green woodpeckers, foxes and deer among the pine trees, stay to the south of the Chase, or cross birch scrubland to Brocton in the North. At **Milford Common**, attractive paths lead to the **Shugborough Estate**; when the big hall was built and altered in the 18th century the family of the Earls of Lichfield bought and demolished the village to allow themselves more space and privacy. Lord Lichfield still lives there but now it belongs to the National Trust. The County Museum housed in the stables gives a comprehensive re-creation of 19th-century life, and there are demonstrations at the farm. Neo-classical monuments are scattered around the park, where special events are often held. A child-oriented 'Noah's Park' has a games gallery in the corn mill, a farm quiz book, and activity days during August.

In May the County Show is held in **Stafford**, where there are plenty of old buildings around the Market Square and in the back alleys, while the 12th-century castle overlooks it all. **Doxey Marshes Reserve** is almost surrounded by the town, yet from viewing platforms in the damp meadows and reedbeds you can see waterfowl and migrating waders. Charles I, after his defeat on Worcester battlefield, joined friends at **Boscobel House**, a hunting lodge north of Wolverhampton. Cromwell's soldiers, looking for him, walked right under the oak tree where he was hiding; Royal Oak pubs have celebrated that escape ever since.

White Ladies Priory, a 12th-century church, also sheltered the fleeing King, who probably passed through **Claverley** as well. In the village he would have seen the black and white cottages that are still there today; it's worth visiting the church to see a very early frieze of mounted knights painted along the north wall. In nearby **Highgate Common Country Park** the birds in the birch woods compete with Halfpenny Green airfield. Nearer still to urbanisation, **Kingswinford Railway Walk** provides a rural cycleway. Just to the south, where Kinver Edge juts up in a sandstone ridge, the last troglodyte dwelling in Britain at Holy Austin Rock was inhabited up until the 1950s. On the minor road to Bridgnorth, Rays Farm at Billingsley, has free-range farm breeds, as well as red and fallow deer, and at Quatt on the main road **Dudmaston Hall** houses fine furniture and 17th-century Dutch flower paintings.

Bridgnorth is built each side of the Severn, with a steeply graded railway connecting higher and lower town. The **Midland Motor Museum** has a collection of racing-cars and motor-cycles, and the Severn Valley Railway runs from here to connect with British Rail trains at Kidderminster. The castle keep leans at a surprising angle, greater than the Tower of Pisa. On the **Clee Hills**, an Area of Outstanding Natural Beauty, there are forest trails with magnificent views. Small brooks run down the hillslopes, and remote little villages like Neenton and Clee St Margaret have timbered manors and churches dating back to Norman times.

In 1779 the world's first iron bridge was built across the Severn Gorge near Coalbrookdale. Now the **Ironbridge Gorge Museum** is a major tourist attraction where, as well as enjoying the scenery, visitors learn about the Industrial Revolution. Beautiful woodland clothes the Gorge, which contains various museums on iron and china themes. **Buildwas Abbey** on the riverside has lost its roof but the arcade of sturdy Norman pillars is perfectly preserved. The industrial town of **Telford**, which began life in 1963, now surrounds on three sides the high conical outcrop called The Wrekin. From Junction 7 of the M54 there's an easy path through beech trees to the summit. North of Telford **Lilleshall Abbey** is rather attractively ruined amid lawns and ancient yew trees.

Much Wenlock is a delightful market town at the start of the long ridge called Wenlock Edge. In the town centre you can buy local pottery, or see the oak panelling in the 16th-century Guildhall. Unusual are the three-seated stocks on wheels for displaying victims to the populace. Ruined **Wenlock Priory** has some lovely carving on its remaining walls. Leaving the town, you can travel by the lonely hilltop road along the Edge to **Wilderhope Manor**, a stone built house looking down to Corvedale and largely unaltered since 1586; it's said that the Great Chamber is haunted.

Ludlow is unbeatable for its setting on a sudden hill above the river, dominated by both the tall tower of St Laurence's Church and the pale stone **castle**. This is the most central of all the Marches strongholds and a long history is preserved there and in the Museum. Following in the tradition of Milton's *Comus*, plays are performed in the grounds during the Festival (end of June and beginning of July). The Feathers Hotel, with its half-timbered patterning and original iron-studded door, is the best-known of Ludlow's many medieval buildings. In the large 13th-century church, look out for the droll carvings on the misericords. Regular guided tours save you from missing anything. Near the castle **Dinham House** is now an exhibition centre with working studios; alternatively, if you have an interest in poultry, stop at the Wernlas Collection in Onibury, where other farm animals too enjoy life in lovely surroundings. **Stokesay Castle**, little altered since the 13th century is a perfect example of a fortified manor beside its moat. Roman Norton Camp looks down from the steep hillside opposite.

Beyond Craven Arms you really begin to face the massif of the

Welsh hills. If, on 29 May, you happen to be in tiny **Aston-on-Clun**, you may see an oaktree decorated with national flags, commemorating the wedding in 1786 of John Marston, a local land-owner. Another quiet village (according to A.E. Housman) is **Clun**, though it has been the scene of many battles, as the ruined castle shows. If you climb to the Norman keep a game of bowls might be in progress on the flat grass there. The town (which has Bronze Age relics in the Georgian Town Hall) gave its name to a special breed of thick-fleeced sheep. You can see them everywhere in this perfect walking country, designated an AONB.

Bishops Castle is another half-timbered town; look out for the medieval 'House on Crutches' here. On wild moorland above Hope Valley to the north fifteen of the original stones in **Mitchells Fold Stone Circle** are still visible among the gorse. The jagged rock crests of the **Stiperstones**, now a National Nature Reserve, were formed in the Ice Age; it's said that Shropshire witches used to meet around the Devil's Chair. The **Long Mynd**, the county's other well-known hill formation, is a high ridge, crossed by the ancient Port Way. Brow Farm Tea Room at Ratlinghope makes a good centre from which to explore it by foot, as the steep roads here are crowded with traffic in summer. Off-peak season is also the best time to visit the tiny valley of Ashes Hollow and Little Stretton with its thatched roofs. Carding Mill Valley, another AONB East of the Mynd, is also very popular.

Accommodation

First Class

Haydon House, Haydon Street, Basford, Stoke-on-Trent, ST4 6JD (Tel 0782 711311). Small Victorian hotel on western edge of Stoke, family owned for forty years and increasingly popular.

Pen-y-Dyffryn Hall, Rhydycroesau, near Oswestry, SY10 7DT (Tel 0691 653700). Welcoming and family run 19th-century rectory in rolling landscape.

Middle Range

The Old Rectory, Hopesay, Craven Arms, SY7 8FD (Tel 058 87 245). Gracious family home and garden with wholesome English cooking.

Stoke Manor, Stoke upon Tern, Market Drayton, TF9 2DU (Tel 063 084 222). Bed and breakfast in very friendly farmhouse on working farm.

Pethills Bank Cottage, Bottomhouse, near Leek, ST13 7PF (Tel

0538 304277). Comfortable modernised cottage in Peak National Park, with good ample food (including vegetarian) and warm hospitality.

Economy

Angel Croft, Beacon Street, Lichfield, WS13 7AA (Tel 0543 258737). Old-fashioned Georgian townhouse, homely and comfortable.

Bridge House, Buildwas, Telford, TF8 7BN (Tel 095 245 2105). Attractive old house run by friendly owners. Bed and breakfast only.

Guest House designed for the disabled: **Corndene**, Coreley, Ludlow, SY8 3AW (Tel 0584 890324). Run by Clare and David Currant.

Eating Out

First Class

Dinham Hall, Ludlow (Tel 0584 876464). Town house restaurant near castle, with willing service.

Old Beams, Waterhouses (Tel 053 86 254). Hospitable restaurant with good cooking in scenic setting.

Old Post Office, 9 The Square, Clun (Tel 058 84 687). Inventive cooking for walkers in beautiful surroundings.

Middle Range

Park Cottage, Jopton Castle (Tel 05474 351). Not far from Clungunford Station in lovely countryside. Small dining-room and honest local cooking.

Wharf, Foxt Road, Froghall (Tel 0538 266486). Imaginative cooking by vegetarian, with range of approved organic wines.

Economy

Mynd House, Little Stretton (Tel 0694 722212). Good value food, vegetarian catering, and friendly service.

Crown Inn, Hopton Wafers, Cleobury Mortimer (Tel 0299 270372). Coaching inn in peaceful surroundings offers good food with fresh ingredients.

12 East Anglia

The most often repeated observation about East Anglia is 'It is flat', which is meant to imply that it is also boring. As with many stereotypes there is an element of truth, but to a great extent reality does not fit this idea of a featureless, low-lying, flat plain. Parts of the area are very flat, such as the Fens and the Broads. The Broads, however, have recently been designated the eleventh National Park in England and Wales, and are far from lacking in interest. But this stereotype does have advantages for the discerning tourist, as mass tourism has had a limited impact, except in a number of important honeypots.

It is the amount of sky – often the full 180 degrees from horizon to horizon – that visitors to Norfolk, Suffolk, Cambridgeshire and northern Essex really notice. It is no coincidence that artists such as Constable and Gainsborough did much of their work in East Anglia. Not only is there more light, but it is of a special quality and it has been captured in the works of the Norwich School artists.

Most of East Anglia consists of low undulating hills, rarely exceeding 328 feet (50 m.), but reaching over 164 feet (100 m.) in the Cromer–Holt ridge of North Norfolk. Geologically speaking the region is young, being composed of glacial material overlaying chalk and sandstone. The sea surounds Norfolk on three sides and runs the length of the east coast of Suffolk and Essex and this has contributed to the character of a people who look outwards – to the near continent of Europe as well as south and west to the urban centres of England.

Some of the major settlements of East Anglia such as Norwich, King's Lynn and Bury St Edmunds exhibit in their architecture links with the continent, made via the wool trade between England and the Dutch. The wealth generated is evident in the huge churches that were built in places such as Worstead in Norfolk, which was once a major centre for the wool industry, but is now only a small village with its church as a landmark of past prosperity. East Anglia has settlements such as Colchester, the major Roman town of southern England before the development of London, and Cambridge both of which date from Roman times. Many of the larger settlements are expanded market towns and, in the case of Norwich and King's Lynn, were once important ports. Despite several important cities however, East Anglia remains a predominantly rural area.

The topography, climate and fertile soil have helped to make this a major agricultural area for at least ten centuries, but the rural landscape has changed enormously since the Second World War. Much of the area now deserves the title 'the English Prairies' as it contains huge windswept fields, dusty in spring and early summer and swaying with yellow cornstalks in mid to late summer. Hedgerows have been ripped up and copses razed to create these vast grain-producing fields, but there is still some woodland, particularly in the Brecklands on Thetford Chase, in north-west Norfolk and close to the Suffolk coast. The Norfolk Broads are also a mixture of woodland and wetland.

East Anglia has remained unaffected by much that has happened in England in the last 200 years. It is not on the way to anywhere – except the North Sea and continental Europe – so change has tended to pass it by. But part of the attraction for the visitor also lies in the fact that it is not far from London and the South-east and therefore is not inaccessible.

History

Nelson and Boadicea are major historical figures who represent certain aspects of the East Anglian character: leadership, bravery, strength and possibly foolhardiness. But Robert Kett, who led the Norfolk rebellion in 1549 against the enclosure of common land and got hanged for his trouble, reveals another trait; revolt against authority in pursuit of a popular cause. On a more prosaic level centuries of working the land and the sea are more likely contributers to the regional character. The sea has also had an impact in that it was by this route that most invaders of the region arrived. Many East Anglians are descended from invaders, be they Romans, Angles, Saxons, Vikings, Normans or Dutch.

The name East Anglia is derived from 'the land of the East Angles'. The names Norfolk and Suffolk come from the North and South Folk of the Angles, whilst Essex is derived from the East Saxons. The Angles and the Saxons reached the region between 400 and 900, although at this time the Romans had already settled the area, despite the attempts of Boadicea, leading the Iceni, to repel them. Colchester, once a Celtic settlement under Cunobelin (Shakespeare's Cymbeline), became the first Roman colony in Britain in AD 43. It was here, in AD 60, that Boadicea sacked the town and forced the Romans to retreat to London, although she and the Iceni were later defeated. Concerned about invasion themselves, the Romans built defensive forts on the coast, and a well-preserved example can be seen at Burgh Castle, near Breydon Water.

Following William the Conqueror in 1066, the Normans gradually took control of the area in the early 12th century. From around 1100 to 1400 the area was part of a European wool trading region, maintaining links with the Dutch and the Flemish in what is now Holland, Belgium and northern France. Towns and villages such as Worstead in Norfolk and Lavenham in Suffolk became locally and even nationally important centres for wool production. Work on the cathedrals at Norwich and Ely began in this period and some of the colleges that form part of Cambridge University were also built at this time. Evidence of links with the Dutch can be seen in the style of buildings dating from the period 1300–1700. The Dutch came not just for the wool trade, but helped to drain the Fenland and protect it from the sea. Dutch-derived surnames in the Fens are not uncommon and Fenland place names, such as Nordelph, are a reminder of these past links.

Nelson's home area was North Norfolk; he came from Burnham Thorpe, but went to school in Norwich. The church at Burnham Thorpe contains many momentoes of Nelson and numerous public houses throughout Norfolk, with names such as The Hero, The Victory, The Battle of Trafalgar and The Nelson, are reminders of the county's most famous son.

The Industrial Revolution largely bypassed East Anglia as there are few natural resources useful for industry. The railways reached the region in the second half of the 19th century and helped to accelerate a process begun in the late 18th century: the exodus from the countryside. This was particularly acute in more remote areas such as North Norfolk, the Fens, Breckland and the Sandlings area of the Suffolk coast. Gradually exodus became rural depopulation and evidence of a more populous past can be seen in the numerous very large churches which now serve a greatly reduced congregation. The railways did however, contribute to the growth of resorts such as Great Yarmouth, Cromer, Sheringham, Clacton and Lowestoft. Wroxham on the Norfolk Broads also expanded and the Broads in general were subsequently developed for yachting by the Victorians in the 1880s.

The 20th century has seen the continuation of depopulation from the more isolated areas and this has contributed to a decline in services, including retailing and transport. Large towns such as Norwich, Ipswich, Cambridge and Colchester have benefited from this loss of population from rural areas and have expanded quite rapidly. It is only in the past fifteen years or so that more remote areas have shown signs of a turn-around in the earlier population trend, and this is partly a result of second homes, people retiring to the area and the expansion of tourism.

Geography

East Anglia is a predominantly low-lying region of undulating hills with a highest point of only just over 328 feet (100 m.). The rocks of the area are sedimentary, with much of the underlying material being chalk. There are also major areas of sandstone. The surface material is commonly glacial in origin, deposited during past Ice Ages and mixed by natural and human activity. There is a variety of soil types, some of which are very fertile and have long been used for agricultural activity. The poorer soils, often sandy, are usually forested, as at Breckland and the Sandlings of the Suffolk coast.

Despite the generally low-lying land and the soft rocks, the coastal areas exhibit a large number of different features. Blakeney, Great Yarmouth and Orford Ness are examples of well-developed sand spits. These are long, curved extensions of the land formed at the mouth of estuaries, causing the river in the estuary to be diverted in its course. Blakeney and Orford spits are important bird habitats, whilst much of Yarmouth's urban development has taken place on its spit. Behind the spit at Blakeney and extending to Morston and Stiffkey to the west and Cley and Salthouse to the east are salt marshes which provide a wonderful environment for waders, ducks and geese. Similar marshland environments, but where the water is fresh or merely brackish, can be found at Minsmere and Walberswick on the Suffolk coast.

There are low cliffs, made of glacial sands and drift material at Weybourne, Cromer and Overstrand in Norfolk and Dunwich in Suffolk. Southwards of the cliffs, from near Overstrand to Yarmouth is a sand dune coast. In 1953 these dunes were breached by a combination of unusually high tides and northerly gales, with the result that thousands of acres were flooded and cattle, sheep and more than thirty people drowned. The dunes are now planted with maram grass and the beaches backed with concrete sea defences.

The Essex coast is the location of the major North Sea ferry port of Harwich. Across the Deben estuary is Felixstowe (in Suffolk), the

UK's largest container terminal. Much of the Essex coast is low-lying marshland adjacent to estuaries such as the Stour and Blackwater.

The Broads are the most distinctive area for wildlife in East Anglia and in recognition of their national and European importance as a wetland environment they became the eleventh National Park in England and Wales in March 1989, the only low-lying area in the UK to be recognised in this way. The Fens, located in west Norfolk and north Cambridgeshire are an almost completly man-made landscape. They are now intensely cultivated, with an emphasis on market gardening and horticultural produce and can be attractive in spring and early summer, when tulips and other bulbs are in bloom. The Fens also attract migrant birds in autumn and winter.

Climate

The eastern side of Britain is much drier than the west – or at least under average conditions. It is not just that the west receives the weather from the Atlantic first but also that the east is generally low-lying and this means that there is little relief rainfall. Despite the generally drier conditions, with the period from June to September being the driest time of the year, East Anglia is not necessarily as sunny as places to the west since there can be many cloudy days. These are often a result of anticyclonic haze and on occasions sea mists rolling in from the North Sea.

June and September are often the best months to visit as they have the most sunshine and temperatures can be higher than in July and August. East Anglia is however, much colder than the rest of the country during the winter months and dry, cold, crisp weather can be expected at any time in the period December to March. Most rain falls between October and March but heavy rain, often associated with thunderstorms, can occur at any time from May to September.

Distinctive local climatic features include sea mists along the east coast. These are caused by onshore breezes that bring banks of fog and mist, and which may lead to temperatures dropping between five and ten degrees centigrade in a matter of minutes. In the Fens area in early spring, Fen Blows can occur, accompanied by dust storms as the fine dry top soil, unprotected by crops, is carried by the wind.

Attractions

Most visitors to the region are attracted by the coastal scenery, the Broads and the historic and cultural heritage of places such as

Norwich, Cambridge and Ely. The Broads is the most important ecological area in East Anglia and, until quite recently, was one of the great wetland regions of Europe. The area was once a wildlife paradise but has been under serious threat since the Second World War. The area is made up of marshes, navigable rivers and lakes (fifty two in total), known as broads. About a dozen of the broads are linked by almost 125 miles (200 km.) of rivers and artificial waterways but virtually none of the broads is natural, being in the majority the remains of medieval peat diggings. Peat was an important source of fuel from around 900 to 1400 and according to records, the amount used for cooking and heating during the 1300s at Norwich Cathedral exceeded 300,000 turves per year. The peat was dug from marsh areas adjacent to the rivers Yare, Bure, Waveney, Ant and Thurne and, as most of the diggings were close to or at sea level, and since the coastal area was protected only by a low ridge of sand dunes, invasions from the sea were not uncommon. During the last quarter of the 14th century it appears inundation of the area became more frequent and by the early 15th century most of the diggings had been abandoned. These subsequently became the broads.

Another inland area of interest is Breckland, a partly forested, sandy heathland. Most of the area is now managed by the Forestry Commission and there are a number of small lakes known as meres. These appear to be glacial in origin, but the water level in them seems to fluctuate erratically and independently of changes in the water table. Several of these meres have been designated as nature reserves.

The coast of East Anglia, although low lying, offers a great range of scenery and one of the most distinctive areas is North Norfolk. Here there is a mixture of sand spits, maram grass-topped islands and salt marsh. Cliffs of chalk and glacial material are found at Weybourne, West Runton, Beeston, Cromer and Overstrand and there are sand dunes at Winterton and Waxham. In Suffolk the coast from Dunwich to Minsmere, with low cliff and brackish marsh land, has little evidence of 20th century development. Orfordness and the Alde estuary are most easily visited by boat so show few of the signs of the impact of mass tourism. In Essex the Blackwater Estuary has the advantage of being close to London, as does Dedham Vale in Constable Country, although this can be a serious disadvantage on summer weekends.

Norwich and Cambridge are the chief historic and cultural cities of the region, whilst King's Lynn and Bury St Edmunds are smaller, more local towns. Ely has a magnificent Cathedral. Ipswich has the reputation of being much less interesting than the other county capitals but it does have notable features, such as Silent Street, Christchurch Mansion and the Ancient House.

Cuisine

Food from East Anglia that is known outside the region comes mainly from the sea. Herring from the North Sea and lobster, crabs, oysters, cockles and whelks have been enjoyed since Roman times (herring has now largely gone, but curing of herring still continues in the region). At the Smoke House at Cley in North Norfolk, Norwegian herring are oak-smoked and sold in the adjacent shop. Many local shops and roadside stalls sell fresh crabs (locally known as Cromer Crabs) in the summer season. Stiffkey in North Norfolk produces 'Stukey Blues' (cockles) and these can be obtained free, on a pick-your-own basis, on the nearby salt marshes north of Stiffkey and Morston. Samphire, sometimes known as poor man's asparagus, is another saltmarsh product from this area. Frumenty, a fruity porridge made from wheat soaked in water, is a famous Suffolk dish.

During the 1970s much of East Anglia was a desert in terms of regional beers. The Watney empire had largely reduced consumer choice but two very distinctive local breweries survive: Adnams at Southwold in Suffolk produce a distinctive bitter, claimed by many as their favourite beer, and Greene King at Bury St Edmunds produces the strong bitter, Abbott Ale. Both of these breweries expanded their output in the 1980s and their beers can be obtained in many tied and free houses throughout the region. Some small independent breweries developed during the 1980s. Woodforde, now serving over fifty outlets and recently relocated to Reepham in Norfolk, is helping to add to choice in this previously Watney-dominated area, with brews which include Norfolk Pride, Wherry Best Bitter and Norfolk Porter. A distinctive non-alcoholic drink is Original Norfolk Punch made from a medieval recipe using thirty herbs at Upwell Manor in Norfolk.

Level of Tourism

Most of the region has a fairly low level of tourism, but there are several honeypots that the discerning tourist will wish to avoid at certain times. The main ones are those on the coast such as Great Yarmouth and Hunstanton, the historical/cultural centres, particularly Cambridge, and the Broads villages of Wroxham, Horning and Potter Heigham. The Broads area has its maximum influx of visitors in the period June to August and the waterways of the northern Broads, particularly around Wroxham, Horning, Potter Heigham, Thurne and Acle can be very busy at this time. Great Yarmouth, which is a meeting place for boats from the northern and southern Broads, can also be a bottleneck. The southern Broads in the Waveney valley area are generally quieter, although Oulton Broad can be extremely busy.

Local planning bodies such as the Norfolk County Council Planning Department recognise the importance of tourism to the regional economy. Their documents indicate that they wish to confine new tourism development to exisiting holiday areas and 'other places where they will not conflict with Norfolk's heritage'. The existing holiday areas where tourism expansion is allowed to take place include Great Yarmouth, Cromer, Sheringham, Hunstanton and Wells. The Norfolk County Planners make specific reference to the Broads area and indicate that they wish to protect and enhance its landscape, waterways, wildlife and built environment. They are opposed to new development in open marsh land and where it would affect woodland or lead to an increase in motor craft on the Broads. They also state that new holiday accommodation has to meet certain criteria.

The majority of locals in East Anglia are in favour of tourism in terms of the economic benefit they personally derive or the gains generally to the region, but residents of the central area of Cambridge and Norwich may be less welcoming during the summer months. In the main holiday centres of Great Yarmouth and Hunstanton there has been an overdevelopment of tourist activities and facilities, which is evident in the preponderance of amusement arcades, souvenir shops, funfair style entertainment and cheap take-away food establishments. In parts of the resorts where these tourist facilities are located, particularly in Great Yarmouth, virtually no local character or atmosphere remains. Such localities are impossible to distinguish from similar areas in holiday resorts found in other parts of Britain. Many of those working in such localities obviously benefit in terms of economic gain from tourism, but some appear to be motivated by a desire simply to exploit the visitor.

Good Alternatives

Meeting People

Norfolk people have the reputation of not being easy to make meaningful contact with in formal, or even informal, situations.

The same could be said for inhabitants of Suffolk. Such claims are, naturally, gross generalisations, but it still may be difficult to strike up a lengthy conversation in the more rural parts of the region and it may be even more difficult for the visitor to understand responses if they are in broad Norfolk dialect or the slow, singsong Suffolk drawl.

Major festivals are not that common in East Anglia. One exception is the **Aldeburgh Music Festival** which is held at Snape Maltings near Aldeborough. **Norwich** has a fortnight of festival activities, usually in the first half of October and this attracts some national and international figures from the theatre, music and the arts. **King's Lynn** also has a locally important festival. **Norwich Arts Centre** puts on a variety of events throughout the year both in Norwich and in other parts of the region. Contact the Arts Centre (Premises), Reeves Yard, St Benedict's Street, Norwich.

Discovering Places

The first regional wildlife group in Britain was established in East Anglia when the **Norfolk Naturalists** (NNT) was set up in 1926. There are now 40 NNT sites in Norfolk and Suffolk and many of these are in Broadland, with others on the coast or in woodlands such as Thetford Chase. NNT produce a guide covering all their sites and leaflets for individual sites, available from NNT, 72 Cathedral Close, Norwich NR1 4DF.

Birds can be seen not just at NNT sites but also at sites run by the **Royal Society for the Protection of Birds (RSPB)**. The RSPB have three marsh and a woodland site in Norfolk; two coastal, one heathland and a woodland site in Suffolk; two wetland sites in Cambridgeshire, and a woodland site in Essex. For information contact RSPB East Anglian Office, Bethel Street, Norwich NR2 1NR.

There are 32 **Country Parks** in the region: five in Norfolk, four in Suffolk, four in Cambridgeshire and nineteen in Essex. Details of these can be obtained from County Council Offices in each county.

Communications

How to Get There

RAIL: Rail access to the area is generally good in terms of journey time, if travelling from London. Cambridge and Ipswich can be reached in about one hour from London and King's Lynn and Norwich in just over two hours. Rail services within the region, however, are far from satisfactory. Norwich is the focus for routes to and from Great Yarmouth, Lowestoft, Wroxham, Cromer and

Sheringham but the major disadvantage is the lack of a line heading west from Norwich to King's Lynn.

COACH: Connections between Norwich and London are fast and efficient, as are those between Norwich and Cambridge. Full information on coach services to the area can be obtained from the **Norfolk Bus Information Centre (NORBIC)**, 4 Guildhall Hill (Tel 0603 613613).

ROAD: Access to the area by road is rather poor as the sole motorway in the region (M11) extends only to Cambridge. There is a dual carriageway extension (A45) from the M11 and this leads eastwards via Bury St Edmunds to Ipswich, Felixstowe and Harwich but it is a very busy trunk road with heavy goods vehicles heading for the container port of Felixstowe. North of Cambridge and Newmarket the main route, the A11, is inadequate for the volume of traffic. The A12 is a fairly fast dual carriageway which extends from London passing close to Colchester and Ipswich before reaching Lowestoft. It is, however, plagued with many roundabouts in the London area and close to Colchester and Ipswich, and is very congested on Friday evenings with traffic heading out of London. It can also be very busy on summer weekends.

Recent improvements to the A11 north of Newmarket include the Thetford bypass, which has shortened journey time from Norwich to London considerably. Access from the Midlands/North to the region via the A47/A17/A1 has been traditionally slow with holdups at Sleaford, Long Sutton, Sutton Bridge and also upon entering the region at King's Lynn and Swaffham. All of these places have now been bypassed, and the journey is far more tolerable although there are still few stretches of dual carriageway.

When You're There

RAIL: Rail connections around the region are good, and it is generally advised that visitors make as much use of the trains as possible. Details for the area can be obtained from British Rail in Norwich (Tel 0603 632055).

BUS: Bus services operate from Norwich, to Great Yarmouth, the Broads area, the East Coast and south to Ipswich, Bury St Edmunds, Cambridge and west to King's Lynn. Links along the east coast of Norfolk are few in number and slow whilst access to North Norfolk, Breckland and the Suffolk coast is possible, but difficult.

CAR: Traffic on the A47 between Great Yarmouth and Norwich; is a problem, especially on Saturdays and in particular during July and August. There are new stretches of dual carriageway on this part of the A47 and they are helping to speed up traffic but the major problem occurs when traffic reaches the inner ring road in Norwich. This road is a headache at the best of times but during the summer season it can take anywhere from one to three hours to get through Norwich. Coastal roads are extremely busy throughout the summer. Those on the east and north coast of Norfolk are of a low standard in terms of width and the frequency of bends. It is best to keep out of Cambridge during the summer months and at weekends throughout the year, unless on foot or two wheels. The A12 has stretches of dual carriageway and can be a fast road but tends not to be so during the summer. Likewise the A11 and A47 leading into or out of the region are likely to be congested, particularly at weekends and during the summer season.

CYCLING: Cycling is another activity well suited to East Anglia. **Norfolk Cycling Holidays** of Sandy Lane, Ingoldsthorpe, King's Lynn offer cycling holidays in North Norfolk, the Fens, Breckland and the Broads area. A number of other cycle hirers exist in Norfolk, including **Dodgers**, Trinity Street, Norwich; **Langfords Cycles**, 24 Northgate Street, Great Yarmouth, and the **New Inn** at Roughton, near Cromer. Cambridge also has several cycle hirers including **Geoff's Bikes** at 65 Devonshire Road and **Armada Cycles** of 45a Suez Road. Ipswich, Southwold and Lowestoft in Suffolk, and Colchester in Essex all have cycle hirers.

WALKING: Most of the region is ideal for walking, and Norfolk County Council (NCC), in conjunction with the Broads Authority, publish details of eight short circular walks and twelve heritage coast walks (details from NCC, County Hall, Martineau Lane, Norwich NR1 2DH). Recently a number of long distance paths have been set up including **The Weavers Way** (56 miles, 90 km.) which starts at Great Yarmouth and passes through Broadland via Worstead, Blickling Hall and North Walsham to Cromer. This is linked to the **Angles Way** which is a riverside walk from Great Yarmouth following the Waveney and Little Ouse valleys (the Norfolk/Suffolk border) from Broadland to Breckland. This way is approximately 77 miles (130 km.) in length and The Ramblers Association of 150 Armes Street Norwich, NR2 4EG, produces a guide for it. These two routes are linked by the **Peddars Way/North Norfolk Coast Way** (93 miles, 150 km.). The Peddars Way is an old Roman road which passes Grimes Graves, while the North Norfolk Coast Way passes through Blakeney and Cley to meet the Weavers Way at Cromer. This completes a 220 mile (350 km.) circular path around the Norfolk/Suffolk borders. Guides to parts of these Ways are also available from NCC (see address above).

Useful Local Contacts

The **Field Studies Council** has a centre at **Flatford Mill** on the Stour (in Constable country). A wide variety of courses are on offer, including study of aquatic wildlife, birds in different seasons, architectural heritage, drawing, painting and even cycling through Constable country. Details of courses are available from Flatford Mill Centre, East Bergholt, Colchester, Essex (Tel 0206 298283).

Those not afraid of hard work could be well satisfied joining the **British Trust for Conservation Volunteers (BTCV)** in one of their activities. BTCV offers 'Natural Breaks' which are conservation holidays involving footpath repair, fencing, coppicing woodland, marshland management and treeplanting. Work takes place throughout the year both at weekends and during the week, and is usually tough and tiring, but for those interested, very rewarding. Many young people (18–30) enjoy this type of break as much for the social life as the environmental focus of the work. Accommodation varies from the very basic (village hall standard) to the equivalent of a Field Study Centre but costs are fairly low for all types of accommodation. There are heathland, woodland and marshland sites in Norfolk and Suffolk.

Working Weekends on Organic Farms (WWOF) offer a similar type of experience to BTCV. The major difference is that those who give their labour for a weekend working on an organic farm will receive in return food and accommodation for free. There are a number of organic farms in the region that accept weekend workers.

Geographical Breakdown of Region

Most tourists to the region head first for Norwich or Cambridge. Both are excellent starting points for exploring their respective hinterlands but are well worth visiting in their own right.

Norfolk

Norwich

Three hundred years ago Norwich was the second largest city of England. At the turn of the century it was reputed to have a pub for every day of the year and a church for every week. Today there are fewer of both, but Norwich remains very much a historic city. Despite a charmless, usually crowded inner ringroad, the heart of the old medieval city has been conserved.

The Market Place is the largest open air daily market in the country and it is possible to buy almost any small household goods, and items of food here. Snack stalls are plentiful, and tend to serve hot cheap food such as mushy peas and chips. At the top end of the Market is the **City Hall**, an impressive brick edifice built in the 1930s, and to the right of the Market when facing the City Hall is the **Guildhall**, built 600 years ago. It was once a prison, previously a magistrates court, and now the Norwich **Tourist Information Centre** – address: Gaol Hill, Norwich (Tel 0603 666071). Part of the building is open to the public. From the steps at the foot of the City Hall, looking across the Dutch gabled rooftops, **Norwich Castle** can be seen. There was originally a wooden Norman castle here with a moat, but the present building was faced with Bath stone in the 1830s so it looks much younger than the 12th-century stone keep that can be found inside the castle walls. The castle was once the main gaol of Norwich and the dungeons – open to the public – provide an idea of what it must have been like to be a prisoner here. It is now a museum with displays of local archaeology and natural history, and also houses paintings by the Norwich School of artists, such as Crome and Cotman.

Norwich has two other museums of interest. The **Bridewell Museum**, located in Bridewell Alley, provides a history of the things Norwich has made as well as of the people who made them. **Strangers Hall** at Charing Cross is a labyrinth of period rooms and provides a glimpse into the lives of both prosperous and poor Norfolk folk from the medieval period to the 1950s.

The **Cathedral** was begun in 1096, completed in 1125, but not consecrated until 1278. Despite frequent fires, occasional riots and attempts by Hitler's Luftwaffe to destroy it, it remains a distinctive and impressive landmark. The area around it, the **Cathedral Close**, is remarkably peaceful, given that it is very close to the city centre. **Tombland**, the original medieval market place, is close to the main gate to the Cathedral.

Norwich pioneered pedestrian precincts and one of the first streets in the city to be pedestrianised was **London Street**. This runs from the Market Place towards the Cathedral. Several other streets in the area are now permanently pedestrianised and the area at the lower end of the Market place, **Gentleman's Walk**, is in the process of being thus transformed. The best way to explore the city is on foot as this allows access to the many narrow alleys, such as **Upper** and **Lower Goat Lane**, **Swan Lane** and **Bridewell Alley**. The Tourist Office provides a town trail with an accompanying booklet. One of the most photographed streets in the city is **Elm Hill** which is cobbled, and boasts pink and cream painted half-timbered houses. The tree that gave the street its name has sadly succumbed to Dutch Elm disease and has been replaced by a young plane tree.

A city centre **riverside walk** has recently been created. This starts near the Cathedral at Fye Bridge, follows a loop in the River Wensum and passes Cow Tower (a medieval boom tower) to Bishop's Bridge. The walk continues passing Pull's Ferry, on to Foundry Bridge, near the main rail station, then to Carrow Bridge adjacent to Norwich City Football ground. The walk also extends in the opposite direction from Fye Bridge along the Wensum to Hellesdon, a suburb of the city. A new walk along the River Yare valley to the University of East Anglia is currently being created.

Norwich has several parks, with **Wensum Park** and **Earlham Park** being two of the larger ones. The largest wildscape area in close proximity to the city is **Mousehold Heath** which is a remnant of an old heathland. It is now completely surrounded by housing, but is accessible by a relatively short walk from the city centre via **St James's Hill** or **Ketts Hill**. Mousehold was given to the people of the city in 1880 by the Dean and Chapter of Norwich Cathedral to be used for 'lawful recreation'. Although little of the natural heath remains, late summer brings mauve heather and yellow gorse. The area is under minimal management and has much scrub and bracken interspersed with birch and mature oak woodland, as well as many species of birds, including spotted woodpeckers, willow warblers, red poll and linnet. There are also common lizards in the open areas and a wide variety of fungi in the wooded parts.

Norwich has a wide range of entertainment for a town of only 150,000 inhabitants. The **Theatre Royal**, Theatre Street (Tel 0603 623562) operates throughout the year, hosting touring companies with plays, musicals and ballet as well as one-nighters. There are several cinemas, but **Cinema City**, St Andrews (Tel 0603 622047) shows art films and imported foreign films.

Norwich Arts Centre, Reeves Yard, St Benedict Street (Tel 0603 660352) operates throughout the year offering mainstream but also alternative theatre and art.

Norwich City Football Club offers First Division soccer, at Carrow Road, while for **Cricket**, Norfolk play in the Minor Counties League. Their ground is at Lakenham in the southern part of the city.

Useful addresses

Norwich City Council Amenities Dept. 130 Ber Street NR1 3EH (Tel 0603 622233). **Tourist Information Centre**, Guildhall, Gaol Hill NR2 1NF (Tel 0603 620679). **Norwich Wildlife Group**, 69 Bethel Street (Tel 0603 664327). **Bicycle Hire** Dodgers 69 Trinity Street, and Magpies Nest, 112 Magpie Rd.

Accommodation

First Class

Maids Head Hotel, Tombland, Norwich (Tel 0603 628821). Part of this hotel is 700 years old. The Maids Head has a good reputation, notably for its English and French cuisine.

Sprowston Hall, Wroxham Road, Norwich (Tel 0603 410871). Traditional family run hotel set in pleasant gardens, situated on the east side of the city about three miles (5 km.) from the town centre.

Middle Range

Kimberly Home Farm, Wymondham, near Norwich (Tel 0953 603137). Eight miles (13 km.) south-west of Norwich, a four-bedroom farmhouse offering bed and breakfast, and welcoming anyone who wants to help out on the farm.

The Georgian House Hotel, 32–34 Unthank Road, Norwich (Tel 0603 615655). Lovely hotel offering traditional comfort in two Georgian houses connected together. Upper end of the Middle Range price bracket.

Economy

Edmar Lodge, 64 Earlham Road, Norwich (Tel 0603 615599). Four bedrooms in a pleasant house ten minutes' walk from the city centre. Bed and breakfast and lots of literature on Norwich and the surrounding area.

Salamanca, Stoke Holy Cross, near Norwich (Tel 0508 62322). Five miles (8 km.) south of Norwich, a working dairy farm offering bed and breakfast in a comfortable, four-bedroomed house.

Eating Out

Middle Range

Brasteds, St Andrews Hill, Norwich (Tel 0603 625949).
Green's Seafood, St Giles, Norwich (Tel 0603 623733).

Economy

Ferry Boat Inn, King Street, Norwich (Tel 0603 613553).
Adam and Eve Inn, Bishopgate, Norwich (Tel 0603 667423).

The Broads

From about 1400, after the flooding of the peat diggings, the area now known as the Broads developed its unique character. The landscape is a mixture of navigable waterways, reedbeds, marsh, woodland and the lakes that are known as broads. Windpumps, and there are many of them, are a distinctive human contribution to this landscape. They look like windmills, but were once used for pumping water, not grinding corn, although some pumps had a dual purpose.

Until the early part of this century the Broads were managed carefully, to extract resources such as reeds and fish, and the navigation of waterways was maintained. For about fifty years, until the 1960s, the Broads were becoming neglected as their resources were extracted less and less. The area has subsequently been one of conflict between the main protagonists: farmers, birdwatchers, conservationists, anglers and tourists in sailing and motor-boats. Farmers are contributing to the effects of pollution through the use of chemical nitrates on their fields, which get washed into the rivers and broads. Sewage from local and tourist sources also adds to pollution. The result of nitrates from the land and phosphates from sewage has been to stimulate the growth of algae that eventually lead to the destruction of other life forms. Almost 300,000 tourists visited the Broads area in the summer of 1989. Most tourists using the waterways hire motor-boats and these cause bank erosion, destroy reed beds, drive away birds and mammals and annoy other visitors. The decline of reed cutting has allowed woodland to invade the fringes of broads and alter wildlife habitats. The broads are also shrinking as a result of natural processes in which water-loving plants take over at the edges and gradually spread towards the centre. Without human intervention and management all the broads would eventually disappear.

It is not a totally depressing story as the realisation that the Broads could suffer irreparable damage has led to conservation groups, such as the RSPB and the Norfolk Naturalists, pressing for a stronger environmental emphasis in planning. The recent establishment of the Broads as a National Park, partly as a result of conservation group pressure, is a recognition of the need to preserve this major wetland area.

Attempts at conservation include the restoration of some broads to the conditions that prevailed before the motor-boat era, the establishment of nature reserves, the reintroduction of fish stocks and the raising of visitor awareness through the establishment of visitor centres.

Cockshoot Broad has been set up by the Broads Authority as an experiment to restore a dead broad. It has been isolated from the polluted water of the River Bure by a dam, and between 1982 and 1984 plant species reappeared or were reintroduced. These plants encourage wildlife, particularly birds, to return. The broad has a bird hide which can be reached by a boarded riverside walk from Woodbastwick, and a guide is available from the Broads Authority, 18 Colegate, Norwich.

Ranworth Inner Broad is close to Cockshoot Broad, with access from Ranworth village. The Norfolk Naturalist Trust has its Broadland Conservation Centre here, housed in a thatched roof pontoon, floating on the reed beds. The Centre is reached via a boarded walk through marshland reed beds and contains an exhibition explaining interests and problems of the Broads. The Centre also has a gallery for views of the broad and its bird life. Ranworth village is attractive with several circular walks beginning near the quay, and it is possible to climb the **parish church**, which contains a fine 14th-century rood screen, to gain magnificent views of Broadland. On a clear day it is possible to see the North Sea.

Hickling Broad is the largest stretch of open water in Broadland with extensive reed and sedge beds, grazing marsh and woodland. It is a most important site for wildlife but is, however, heavily used for leisure and tourism activities. Rare species such as the swallow tail butterfly and the bittern are still found here and Hickling provides a site for many migrant birds, including warblers, terns, sandpipers, osprey, and spoonbills, as well as a home for rare plant species and more common birds and animals. A water trail operates from May to September and visitors are taken to bird hides, reed beds and a 65-foot (20 m.) high observation tower. The Water Trail Information Centre is near the Pleasure Boat Inn at Hickling. Alternatively, contact Norfolk Naturalists at 72 Cathedral Street, Norwich.

Horsey Mere is east of Hickling Broad and has waterside walks and a windpump which is open to the public. **Upton Fen**, near Acle and **Alder Fen Broad** near Irstead are relatively isolated broads, closed off from major rivers. They are both small and offer a great diversity of plants including water lilies, milk parsley and yellow flag irises. Both broads can be reached by footpath and Upton Fen has a nature trail (further details from Norfolk Naturalist Trust).

Sailing is the least damaging of Broadlands waterborne activities and boats can be hired in most of the Broadland towns and villages. Sailing at Hickling and Horsey Mere offers a large area of open water with the backdrop of a wide variety of Broadland flora and fauna, although Hickling Broad does become very crowded with motor cruisers and other sailing boats in the summer months. Many of the tourists to Broadland do not reach the Waveney Valley, hence the **Beccles to Oulton Broad** stretch is often quieter than the Northern Broads area. Sailing along the Yare, the Bure from Wroxham to Acle, and the Thurne from Potter Heigham to Thurne Mouth in June, July and August can be more stressful than the rush hour on the M25!

Accommodation

Norwich is an excellent base for exploring the Broadland (see accommodation list page 451). In addition, **Regency House** at Neatishead, near Coltishall (Tel 0692 630233) has 5 rooms and offers B&B. Large breakfasts including vegetarian choice. Economy.

The Norfolk Coast

Some of the best beaches on the Norfolk coast are between **Overstrand** and **Caister**. The beaches at **Winterton**, with a large car parking area in the dunes, and **Waxham**, received the thumbs up from the local FOE group in the summer of 1990, whilst Yarmouth, Cromer and Hunstanton failed to come up to FOE standards. Both Winterton and Waxham have wide sandy beaches backed by dunes and swimming is fairly safe, although there may be dangerous rip currents. The beaches at **Sea Palling** and **Happisburgh** (pronounced Haysbro') are also pleasant. The places to avoid, unless you like crowds, amusement arcades, caravan parks and holiday camps, are Hemsby and Caister.

Cromer is one of the least spoilt of the Norfolk seaside resorts and is known for its crabs. Access is possible by train from Norwich and visitors can obtain an excellent view from the 160 ft. (50 m.) high parish church tower of St Peter and St Paul. The privately operated, steam-driven, **North Norfolk Railway** runs west from Cromer to **Sheringham** and **Weybourne**. Sheringham, a little more commercialised than Cromer, is backed by heath and woodland, part of which is known as **Pretty Corner** and which extends to the **Roman Camp** at West Runton. This is a hilly area with fine views of Sheringham, Beeston and the North Sea. It is, in fact, a natural feature, being a mixture of glacial deposits and not, as previously thought, a site of a Roman encampment. The cliff path from **Sheringham** to **Weybourne** is particularly attractive.

Holt is the major inland town of the area with several interesting 18th- and 19th-century buildings and most of the town has been designated a conservation area. **Cley**, once on the coast, is now a mile inland and NNT have one of their most important reserves at **Cley marshes**, where there is a Visitor Information Centre. Sitings of rare migrant birds are not uncommon here, so the beach, marsh and even the village area can be crowded with twitchers! It is possible to walk along the shingle spit across the River Glaven estuary to **Blakeney Point**, another NNT reserve, and in the summer months boat trips leave from Blakeney Quay to this reserve.

The marshes at **Blakeney**, **Morston** and **Stiffkey** are a maze of muddy creeks and are well worth exploring at low tide. An excellent walk (on top of the raised sea defence) begins at **Burnham Overy Staithe**, and goes along the estuary and salt marshes via the beach and sand dunes to **Holkham**. Holkham beach is one of the best in the whole region with wide expanses of sand at low tide backed by sand dunes and pine woods. Much of this area is a nature reserve. The beach can be reached by a car park at the end of a long drive opposite the entrance to **Holkham Hall**, once owned and lived in by the Coke family. The gardens and interior of the Hall are open to the public and there is a pottery adjacent. Between Holkham and **Brancaster** there are six places prefixed with Burnham; **Burnham Thorpe**, the birthplace of Nelson, is the largest, with a broad green crossed by a seasonal beck, and has several fine Georgian houses. From Brancaster it is possible to gain access to **Scolt Head Island** (National Trust Nature Reserve), and **Holme-next-the-sea**, where the Peddars Way meets the North Norfolk Coast Path, is an AONB with several nature reserves.

Accommodation

Economy

Cobblers, South Creake, near Fakenham (Tel 032879 200). Two beds. Home-made jams, marmalade and bread. B&B.

Holland House, Docking (Tel 0485 518295), open fires, B&B.

Eating Out

First Class

Congham Hall, Gruiston, King's Lynn (Tel 0485 600250). Quality English and French food.

Medium Range

The Dukes Head, King's Lynn (Tel 0553 774996). Good traditional food at reasonable prices.

Economy

The Moorings, Wells (Tel 0328 710949). Specialises in fish dishes.

Breckland

This is the area around **Thetford**, **Swaffham** (both in Norfolk) and **Brandon** (in Suffolk) and much of it is naturally sandy heathland, which was extensively forested in 1922 by the Forestry Commission. There are some good forest walks, and distinctive features of the area are the small lakes or meres. The underlying rock is chalk, containing much flint, which was mined in prehistoric times at **Grimes Graves**, near Thetford. Flint knapping (shaping of flints) was once significant at **Brandon** and a little knapping still continues, with exports to Africa and the USA. **Swaffham** has a splendid 15th-century church and a large market place, whilst **Thetford** is the home of Thomas Paine, the radical political writer.

Close to Thetford is **Kilverstone Wildlife Park**, with a varied collection of animals and an emphasis on South American species. **Oxburgh Hall**, a fine 15th-century brick building, is open to the public at certain times of the year and there is a good five mile walk around the village of Oxborough. At nearby **Cockley Cley** there is a re-creation of an Iceni village.

Suffolk

The Suffolk Coast

The area from the south of **Lowestoft** to **Southwold** is the Suffolk Heritage Coast and most of it is well worth visiting. Southwold is a traditional seaside resort with a pier, but with few amusement arcades. The beach is shingle and sand but shelves steeply and could be dangerous for young children to swim. Southwold also has the Sole Bay Brewery, home of Adnams beer. There is a lighthouse set in the town, and excellent walks to the estuary of the **River Blyth** and **Southwold harbour**. Across the river, by footbridge or ferry (in summer), is **Walberswick**. Here there are marshes and reed beds and the area is favoured by artists, whilst inland is gorse and heathland which is good for blackberry picking.

Dunwich was once the foremost port of the east coast and also the centre of Christianity in the region. Its harbour has, however, silted up and the soft cliffs where most of the town once stood have been washed away by the sea. The **Dunwich Museum** has an exhibition that shows how the town has disappeared over the last 600 years. The **Heath**, to the south of Dunwich, is owned by the National Trust and bird lovers should ensure that they visit **Minsmere Reserve**, which is the main RSPB site on the east coast. There are a number of hides on the beach which are open to the public, but access to the Reserve is by permit only.

Aldeburgh, with a good shingle beach, is the home of the **Aldeburgh Music Festival**, which was established by Benjamin Britten. Most of the music now takes place in the nearby **Snape Maltings Concert Hall** on the banks of the River Alde. The Alde has been diverted eight miles (12.8 km.) south by a shingle spit known as **Orford Ness** and the marshes around here, where access is possible, are much favoured by birdwatchers and naturalists. **Orford** has an interesting castle, which is open to the public and provides excellent views of the Alde and Orford Ness, but much of Orford Ness is owned by the Ministry of Defence. **Havergate Island** is a RSPB reserve and access is by permit only. Between the **Orwell** and the **Stour** is the **Shotley Penninsula**, which is an AONB. There are good walks around **Pin Mill**, but this is a very popular spot with the yachting crowd in the summer.

Inland Suffolk

Ipswich is often neglected as a visitor attraction, but as the county town of Suffolk it has much to offer. It is still an important port with coastal and European trading links. The **Tourist Information Centre** at the Town Hall in Princes Street (Tel 0473 258070) provides an interesting town trail. **Bury St Edmunds** is the only cathedral town in Suffolk and the present cathedral dates back to the 16th century. There was originally an abbey here and this was the place where the Magna Carta was drawn up in November 1214, before King John was made to sign it. There is an interesting square of buildings at

Angel Hill, and **Moyse Hall**, once a Norman dwelling house, is now a museum. At **Stowmarket** is the **Museum of East Anglian Life** with various exhibits relating to rural life of the area over the past three centuries. At **Woolpit**, near Stowmarket is the **Bygones** museum depicting life in a Suffolk village. At **Giffords Hall**, Hartest, near Bury St Edmunds, there is a small country park with ten acres (4 hectares) of vineyards, a winery, rare sheep breeds, wild flower meadows, an organic vegetable garden and an apiary.

Accommodation

Economy

The Old Rectory, Monks Eleigh, Ipswich (Tel 0449 740811). Regency building in two acres of grounds. Three comfortable beds. B&B.

The Old School House, Saxtead, Woodbridge (Tel 0728 723887). Vegan catering. Home-made produce. Dinner as well as B&B.

Eating Out

Medium Range

The Butley, Orford Oysterage, Market Hill, Orford (Tel 039 45277). Oysters are the speciality, quite reasonably priced, and fresh local fish. Guinness, on draught, is a good alternative to the wine.

Mortimers, Bury St Edmunds (Tel 0284 60623). Seafood specialities.

The Crown, Southwold (Tel 0502 722275) Adnams beer, excellent wine list, good local fish and seafood.

Cambridgeshire

Cambridge

Cambridge has the highest concentration of buildings of architectural interest of any city in East Anglia and it needs at least two or three days to see most of the worthwhile sights. The best way to see the centre of the city is on foot, but at least three quarters of the city's population appear to travel by bicycle. Bicycles can be hired at several places including **Mikes Bikes** at 28 Mill Road. Cambridge Friends of the Earth produce a booklet *Cycle City*.

A major problem with Cambridge is that it is one of the main honeypots for British and foreign tourists, and although the city has a resident population of just over 100,000 there are in excess of 3 million visitors each year. Traffic congestion and parking problems are major disincentives to bringing a car near to the city centre, but at the same time bicycles and other visitors are a serious hazard in the supposedly pedestrian precincts around the colleges.

Cambridge University is arguably the town's main attraction. Many of the students who have passed through the university have helped shape world events; they include Darwin, Newton, Wordsworth, Milton, Byron, Tennyson, Pepys and Cromwell, and countless statesmen. Oliver Cromwell was, in fact, the MP for Cambridge and attended Sidney Sussex College.

The university is made up of a number of colleges, the oldest of which is **Peterhouse**, established in 1284. Other colleges from a range of historical periods of architectural interest include Queens', King's, Trinity, Clare, Magdalen, Christ's, Pembroke and St John's.

The **Backs** is an area of well-kept lawns that are adjacent to the **River Cam** and which can be reached from King's College or **Clare Bridge**. It is possible to walk from the university area to **Grantchester Meadows**, a favourite summer picnic spot on the banks of the Cam. Being a seat of learning Cambridge is not short of museums and good bookshops. The **Cambridge and County museum** in Castle Street has displays showing three centuries of the Cambridgeshire way of life.

Fenland

Probably the most fertile arable land in Britain is found in the Fens, although once the area was useless marshland. The Fens were extensively drained, with Dutch help, from the 16th century onwards and were transformed into an area specialising in market gardening produce and cut flowers. **King's Lynn** (in Norfolk) is the largest town in the Fenland area, standing at the mouth of the **River Ouse**, and it has an annual festival, the focus of which is the **Guildhall of St George**, the oldest medieval merchant's house in the country. There are two market places in the town, one for the Tuesday market and the other for use on Saturday. **Ely** was once an island in the Fens and the **Cathedral**, begun in 1063, dominates the skyline for miles around. It has several chapels and a long nave (540 feet, 165 m.). **Wisbech**, although ten miles (16 km.) from the sea, still has strong trading links overseas, and it has two of the best preserved Georgian streets, in **North** and **South Brinks**. It also has the 18th-century **Elgoods Brewery**. **Denver Sluice**, a flood control point in the Fens, has an interesting six-storey windmill and there is a farm museum at **Haddenham**, near Ely.

Accommodation

First Class

Garden House, Granta Place, Cambridge (Tel 0223 63421). 117 rooms.

Middle Range

University Arms, Regent Street, Cambridge (Tel 0223 351241). Traditional family run hotel. 115 rooms. Close to city centre.

Blue Boar, Trinity Street, Cambridge (Tel 0223 63121). Traditional city-centre hotel. 48 bedrooms. Close to city centre.

Economy

Kirkwood House, 172 Chesterton Rd, Cambridge (Tel 0223 313874). Edwardian house, 5 Bedrooms. 15 mins. city centre. B&B.

11 Glisson Rd, Cambridge (Tel 0223 311890). University town house. 7 rooms. Close to main College area. B&B.

7 Water Street, Chesterton, nr. Cambridge (Tel 0223 355550). Sixteenth-century cottage once a coaching house. 3 Bedrooms. Small garden and views of river. B&B.

The Old Rectory, Swaffham Bulbeck. (Tel 0223 811986). 4 beds. Large gardens. Views of hayfields. B&B.

Eating Out

As Cambridge is a town of many students there are a large number of places to eat reasonably cheaply.

First Class

Xanadu, Jesus Lane (Tel 0223 311678).

Middle Range

Jean Louis, Magdalene Street (Tel 0223 315232).

Economy

The Arts Theatre, St Edwards Passage (Tel 0223 35246). There are two self-service restaurants here, The Roof Garden and The Pentagon.

Hobbs Pavilion, near Parkers Piece, (Tel 0223 67480). Excellent pancakes and salads.

Free Press, Prospect Row (Tel 0223 368337). Greene King pub.
Fitzbillies, Trumpington Street (Tel 0223 352500). Reputed to make the best sweet cakes in the world.

North Essex

Constable country

This is the area around the **Stour** and **Brett** valleys on the border of Suffolk and north Essex. Constable was born at **East Bergholt**; *The Hay Wain* was painted at Willy Lotts Cottage and he went to school in **Lavenham** and **Dedham**. Dedham and **Flatford Mill** are the inspiration for several of Constable's paintings and the **Sir Alfred Munnings Art Museum** is at Dedham, whilst **Stoke by Nayland** church is featured in several paintings. **Hadleigh**, on the River Brett, is an old wool town and is also the headquarters of the **East Anglian Tourist Board**, (Topplesfield Hall, Hadleigh, Suffolk IP7 5DN. Tel 0473 822922). **Sudbury**, also a wool town, was the home of another famous East Anglian painter, Gainsborough.

13 Thames and Chilterns

The Thames and Chilterns region extends out from the north and west of London and includes the counties of Hertfordshire, Bedfordshire, Buckinghamshire, Oxfordshire and Berkshire.

As part of the 'Home Counties', the area has more than its fair share of expanding commuter towns and red-brick housing estates along with an over-burdened public transport system and congested motorways. Although it might be necessary to work in London, not everyone wants – or can afford – to live there. The attraction of smaller towns, neat villages and gentle rolling countryside, combined with easy access to the capital, makes the Thames and Chilterns a highly desirable area to live.

Despite the expanding new towns and fast motorways, this compact region is extremely beautiful and varied. It is the contrasts and not the distances that are great; ranging from the tourist honeypots of Windsor, Oxford and St Albans, to quiet, seemingly unknown areas of outstanding natural beauty often overlooked by coach tours and day-trippers.

In many ways, this region distils the essence of England. Impressive stately homes and castles, elegant riverside towns and canal walks, extensive woodlands and open countryside, and hidden villages and ancient sites are all here. There are three major hill ranges: the Oxfordshire Cotswolds to the west; the Berkshire Downs in the south, and the Chilterns which cross Oxfordshire and Buckinghamshire to the south-east. Several long-distance walking trails cross much of the countryside within the area. There are nature reserves, wildlife sanctuaries, wetland sites and lakes, heathland and meadows, providing year-round interest.

River life is a major feature of the region, and there is a particular Englishness about the Thames: gentle and understated, with no great waterfalls or dramatic gorges. Originating in a field near Cirencester in Gloucestershire, it neatly cuts southern England in half as it makes its way for some 170 miles (273 km.) to the estuary beyond London where it meets the open sea. Throughout the journey it is fed by tributaries with names like Evenlode,

Windrush and Glyme in Oxfordshire, and the Kennet, Pang and Lodden in Berkshire. As a result of this – and the countless other streams that feed the main river – the Thames widens from 150 feet (45.75 m.) at Oxford to over 750 feet (228.75 m.) at London Bridge.

Boating is a very popular pastime. In 1889 Jerome K. Jerome wrote his famous book *Three Men in a Boat*, and this amusing account of adventures and mishaps between Kingston and Oxford contributed much to the river's popularity. Today, Thames-side towns like Windsor, Maidenhead, Pangbourne, Goring, Henley, Abingdon, Oxford and Lechlade are all exceptionally busy (and frequently congested in high summer) with private boats, dinghies and river cruisers, indicating that 'messing about in boats' is still as popular as ever.

The region has been home to many powerful and influential people who built their country residences and palaces in the grand style like Blenheim, owned by the Duke of Marlborough and the largest private palace in the country. The Rothschilds created Waddesdon – a French château set in rolling Buckinghamshire countryside – and filled it with extravagant furnishings and works of art. In addition there are some of the country's finest examples of gardening in the grand manner, created by the most talented landscape architects and gardeners. They range from the splendid gardens at Stowe, the birthplace of English landscape gardening, or Rousham Park, where William Kent created his greatest romantic landscape, to small and equally beautiful gardens like the seven-acre (2.8 hectares) garden at Benington Lordship and the physic gardens at Chenies Manor with its hundreds of medicinal and culinary herbs.

Beyond Oxford, the Cotswolds offer highly attractive walking country. Although many of the small towns and villages have sold out to the tourist dollar, it is still possible to find places off the beaten track that are worth exploring. Similarly, there are unspoiled stretches of riverside and woodland walks along the banks of the Lee in Hertfordshire and the Ouse in Bedfordshire.

Many overseas visitors who set out to 'do' England in three or four days start their holiday in London and then bolt-on one-or two-day trips out of the capital that take in Windsor, Oxford, Blenheim Palace and Stratford-upon-Avon. This chapter aims to help you further explore (or look again) at a region that embraces some of the loveliest parts of England.

History

The earliest recorded settlers in the region were the hunter-gatherers, followed by Neolithic, Bronze Age and early Iron Age man. The Rollright Stones in North Oxfordshire date from Neolithic times, and cut into the hillside near Uffington is the famous 350 foot (106 m.) White Horse, made by the Celts.

During the Roman period, Verulamium (St Albans) became one of the most important cities in England. It was connected by road to London, Colchester and westwards through Dorchester and Alchester to Cirencester. By the 6th century, the Saxons had settled in the area, then known as Mercia, although Berkshire was part of the kingdom of Wessex. During the 9th century, the region was invaded by the Danes who suffered a decisive defeat at the hands of Alfred the Great. Wallingford in Oxfordshire became a strategic town during this period, and the fortifications built by Alfred can still be seen today.

After the battle of Hastings, William I led his cavalry in a broad sweep across the south, sending infantry down as far as Winchester and north and east towards Oxford and Hertfordshire. He founded castles at Oxford, Wallingford, Bedford and Great Berkhamstead. He also built Windsor, the oldest royal residence and longest-inhabited castle in the country.

On 15 June 1215, King John signed the Magna Carta at Runnymeade, a field beside the Thames near Windsor. This was a significant turning point in history as the document presented a bill of rights which set out the liberties of the individual and opened the legal system to the common man.

The true origins of Oxford University are unknown. It is generally accepted that it was founded in the 12th century during the reign of Henry II, largely as a result of the exodus of English scholars from Paris. Early studies were based around theology, the Arts and Science, and Oxford, along with its rival Cambridge, became one of the most distinguished seats of learning in the country. In 1642, Charles I set up his headquarters in Oxford, where the city became a Royalist stronghold. Many of the colleges were plundered for their gold and silver, and the Royal Mint was established in New Inn Hall. Guns were mounted throughout the city and it is still possible to see one of the cannon earthmounds in the grounds of New College.

Further south, Newbury was the scene of two major battles. In 1644, Donnington Castle to the north of the town was garrisoned for King Charles, and the siege lasted for over twenty months. The castle was largely destroyed in the process, with the exception of the great gatehouse which still stands today.

West Oxfordshire was an important centre for the wool trade which flourished until the last century. Witney still manufactures wool blankets and exports on a worldwide basis. Woodstock was famous for gloves (there is still a small cottage industry there), and parts of Bedfordshire for lace-making. Farming and agriculture are still major economic activities in all five counties.

In 1974, many of England's county boundaries were redrawn, and as a result Berkshire lost almost one third of its acreage. In April of the same year, the Queen granted the use of the term 'Royal County of Berkshire'. This title is quite unique among English counties, and perhaps some compensation for the loss of land.

The Thames and Chilterns region has reflected centuries of man's quest for domination and control of the land. The battle still continues today as the armies from the capital move out into the surrounding countryside and more protected greenbelt is released to the developers. The price-tag is high: increased levels of generalised congestion and pollution; alterations to the natural landscape, and changes in the ecological balance. The key is for a well-planned programme of development with a concern to maintain the unique, irreplaceable natural fabric of the area.

Geography

The Thames and Chilterns countryside is without extremes. It is a largely unspectacular, but highly attractive landscape of low rolling hills and flat plains, woods and meadows with picturesque villages scattered here and there. The shape of the land was formed by the southward pressure of ice at the end of the last Ice Age, reaching its southern limit in Berkshire. Starting in the north of the region, the area from Oxfordshire across to Bedfordshire lies upon the lias formation of compacted limestone. It is a hilly region, somewhat bare, but interspersed with wooded valleys. Moving southwards, a broad band across from the Gloucester border in the west to Buckinghamshire in the east consists largely of bare uplands, although there is a good deal of woodland, stretching from the old Forest of Wychwood to the slopes of the Chilterns. The highest ridge of these uplands forms part of the main watershed of England. The marlstone here provides rich loamy soils for what is regarded as some of the best cereal growing land in the country.

To the west, the Cotswolds, once renowned for sheep rearing, is now mostly arable land, with the distinctive honey-coloured drystone walls dividing the fields. The limestone of the Cotswolds is a calcareous rock formed from small grains of carbonate of lime, and various layers of this are used for the building of both walls and roofs. Further south, a broad band of gault clay covers the region from the Thames to the Ouse. Because of the lack of building stone, many of the older houses here are timber-frame with thatch roofs. Brick was also widely used from an early date. The clay gives way to a great belt of chalk which stretches across all five counties. The finest chalk scenery is to be found at Uffington in Berkshire, above which rises the slope of White Horse Hill, 856 feet (261 m.). Generally speaking however, the slopes of the Downs are gentle and bare of trees, whereas those of the Chilterns are much bolder and thickly wooded. Here extensive beechwoods formerly supported a flourishing furniture industry and other wood-using crafts. Blocks of chalk have sometimes been used for building in the Chilterns, but grey and red brick and flint are more widely used.

This century has witnessed a massive acceleration in the pace of change and shape of the land. Changes in agriculture since the Second World War have seen the decline of the small farm, the redundancy of traditional farm buildings and the destruction of hedgerows. Changes in forestry management have resulted in the spread of conifer plantations, and the decline of the canals and railways has been counterbalanced by an extensive motorway network that neatly carves up the region. The extent and use of built-up land has been intensified, with new towns and 'garden cities' created to attract the large mobile population.

A section of the Berkshire Downs and pockets in the Chilterns have been designated Areas of Outstanding Natural Beauty (AONB) and many of the Country Parks have been designed around flooded gravel pits creating lakes, often attracting large numbers of ducks and other waterfowl in winter, and holding birds like nesting grebes and kingfishers in summer. In recent years, an interest in the region's waterways has seen a regeneration in riverside development, particularly along stretches of the Ouse in Bedfordshire and the Lee in Hertfordshire, along with the Stort Navigation and Grand Union Canal projects. The Kennet and Avon Canal in Berkshire has recently been restored into a very attractive cruiseway linking the Thames to Bath.

Wildlife reserves are scattered throughout the five counties and include a great diversity of habitats, plant and animal communities.

County wildlife trusts like The Berkshire, Buckinghamshire and Oxfordshire Naturalists' Trust (BBONT) and the RSPB are active in the management of protected reserves and details of open access sites are given in this chapter.

Climate

Recent years have seen somewhat dramatic shifts in climatic patterns in this region. Winter temperatures that have averaged around 6–7°C have dropped to −15°C, and the usual summer temperatures of 20–22°C have maintained a steady 25–27°C, often for weeks on end. In the main however, the climate is mild, though the weather very changeable and unpredictable. The air in the Chilterns up to the north-east of the region can be sharp and bracing, but moving into the Thames Valley the moisture and damp of the winter, and in the summer the humidity, make for an oppressive atmosphere. Oxford, for example, lies below a circle of hills at the bottom of a shallow dip, and parts of the city are surrounded by extensive watermeadows, which contribute to the dampness and lack of stringency in the air. Chest ailments and asthma are common in the area.

Localised fog is widespread throughout the winter and spring, bringing hazardous driving conditions to major roads.

Although traditionally April is a showery month, spring is usually the driest season of the year. Even if the weather is cold, it is unlikely to last much beyond the middle of the month and warm spells are common. June, July and August are usually the sunniest months, but pockets of low pressure build up from time to time, causing depressions which can result in mild wet-and-windy weather, followed by a warm dull period. Thunderstorms are common during these months. Long spells of dry sunny weather often continue into September and October and this can be a very pleasant time to see the countryside as many areas are quiet and uncrowded.

Attractions

Many visitors to the Thames and Chilterns are attracted initially by the historical, cultural and architectural splendours of famous towns like Windsor, Oxford and St Albans, and the palaces and grand houses of Blenheim, Hatfield and Waddesdon. But the region also boasts many smaller, yet equally distinctive country towns and houses, that are often omitted from the standard tourist itinerary.

The gentle undulating countryside offers excellent walking opportunities and there are plenty of waymarked routes to choose from. The Ridgeway, one of the oldest highways in Britain, passes through four counties: Wiltshire, Berkshire, Oxfordshire and into Hertfordshire along the line of the prehistoric Icknield Way. The Oxfordshire Way links the Chilterns to the Cotswolds, while the North Bucks Way crosses the centre of the region and the Greensand Ridge Walk runs from Leighton Buzzard to Sandy in Bedfordshire.

For those interested in industrial heritage, the canal network of the region is fascinating, ranging from the famous Grand Union Canal to the newly reopened Kennet and Avon, providing one of the best and easiest ways to see the countryside.

Although much of the original forest cover disappeared from the region centuries ago, Wychwood Forest between Leafield and Charlbury in Oxfordshire, was one of England's great medieval forests. Covering well over 50,000 acres (20,250 hectares) and stretching as far as Witney and Burford, this was one of the largest royal hunting forests in the country. An Act of Parliament in 1857 altered its status from forest to ordinary land and considerable acreages of coppice and heathland were cleared and farmed, and trees were felled to make way for cereal land. As a result, there are only about 2000 acres (810 hectares) left today, but the area is extremely atmospheric and little visited by tourists.

Buckinghamshire is well known for the beech-clad Chiltern Hills which run like a spine across the southern half of the county. These attractively wooded hills with their ridges, valleys and panoramic views offer some of the most spectacular scenery in the region and are at their best in spring and autumn. The rich farming land, spreading from the Vale of Aylesbury into Bedfordshire is delightful touring country, and many of the country villages have cottages of timber and thatch. Some of the villages here (notably Haddenham), feature the traditional creamy witchert walling peculiar to the area.

The much neglected Hertfordshire, often dismissed due to its close proximity to London, has much to attract the visitor. Among the many open areas to enjoy are the Colne Valley Park near Rickmansworth; the Lee Valley Regional Park in the east, where leisure facilities have been developed along the river valley as far as London; Aldenham Country Park near Elstree, home of the Aldenham herd of rare longhorn cattle, and Northaw Great Wood near Potters Bar, a 290-acre (117 hectares) Site of Special Scientific Interest comprising ancient forest and interesting flora and fauna.

Cuisine

Although specialist local food and produce has largely given way to the convenience of the hypermarkets, many of the county towns still hold regular weekly markets that sell quality home-produced food. In recent years, the growth of farm shops and pick-your-own fruit and vegetable sites has been quite phenomenal, and there is a definite shift towards more wholesome eating. Almost every type of restaurant is represented in the region, but the emphasis still tends to be on traditional English cooking.

Oxford is famous for Frank Cooper Marmalade. Originally made for the colleges, it is now produced, using the same recipes, from a small factory in Wantage. Oxford also markets its own brand of sausage. Breadmaking and baking is excellent across the region and lardy cakes, Banbury cakes and Olney pancakes are well known. Oxo bread is one of the more unusual specialities: slices of fresh bread are soaked in an Oxo mix, pan fried and eaten hot. Game in season, and in particular, game pie, is a popular and widely available dish. Trout is the most popular fish dish, with the majority of the specimens raised on local trout farms.

Regional breweries produce distinctive bitters that are worth trying. Names like Hook Norton, Halls and Morrells are well known throughout the Thames and Chilterns. Surprisingly, the area is not noted for dairy produce, but the village store in Streatley, Berkshire, offers over 150 different types of cheese and has been in business for longer than anyone can remember.

Level of Tourism

The Thames and Chilterns has more than its fair share of honeypots. The level of tourism is high in certain areas and visits do need to be planned with care. Oxford has its main influx of tourists from Easter to September, but the city is busy all year round. It is not uncommon to find five- to six-mile tailbacks of cars on the A40 through the city on Saturdays. Sundays and Bank Holiday Mondays can be good days to see the sights, as many of the stores are closed and the visitor does not have to compete with local shoppers. Oxford City Council has invested a great deal of time and money on redesigning the complicated one-way traffic system, and it is frequently upheld as an example of how a tourist centre has coped successfully with this problem. Despite this, Oxford still remains an exceptionally busy city and drivers are encouraged to use the new Park and Ride schemes or travel in by train.

The Thameside towns, particularly Henley and Marlow, can be real bottlenecks in peak-season weekends and Bank Holidays, and should be avoided during these times. Windsor is best visited out of season, between November and March. The town has a very attractive shopping centre which draws crowds from Bracknell, Wokingham and Reading in addition to the coachloads of tourists who come to see the castle. St Albans is similar, although changes in the one-way traffic system and extended parking facilities have eased the pressure somewhat.

Most of the major stately homes and palaces arrange special events over holiday periods and it would be wise to avoid visits over Easter Weekend, and during the May and August Bank Holidays.

Burford, labelled as the Gateway to the Cotswolds, is a favourite meal and shopping stop for many visitors. The main street can quickly become congested as the traffic has to cross a narrow bridge before continuing on to Stow-on-the-Wold and Bourton-on-the-Water. This can become very frustrating for the casual visitor and the continuous flow of vehicles through the centre of this old market town does little to enhance the overall attraction of the place.

It must be said though, that many visitors to the Thames and Chilterns do tend to follow well-worn routes and rarely go off the beaten track. It is still possible, therefore, even in the height of the season, to find peaceful, rural places well away from the crowds.

At present, the region is paying increased attention to 'environmentally friendly' tourism, with farm, country and walking holidays at the forefront. Their Rural Tourism Strategy has three main aims. It seeks to strengthen the rural economy through tourism development, to conserve the natural countryside as a tourism resource and to provide for visitors' enjoyment of its attractions. This strategy is currently being promoted through a series of Local Area Initiatives (LAIs) in each county, and along environmentally sensitive lines. The Beautiful Berkshire Campaign, Bucks Tourism, Hertfordshire Leisure Marketing and Bedfordshire Tourism are already in operation, leaving Oxfordshire, who have not yet indicated their policy for the county. Although the LIAs are funded directly from each county council, all liaise and work closely with the regional tourist board and the local tourist information centres.

The National Trust is well represented in the Thames and Chilterns and at the forefront of conservation issues in the region. Many of the parks, gardens, and extensive areas of woodland were severely damaged in the devastating storm of January 1990, and it is estimated that it will take two to three years to clear some woodland stretches.

The majority of local people are generally in favour of tourism as it brings economic benefit to the region as a whole. In some of the busier centres like Oxford and Windsor, however, tolerance levels can become low during the summer months and tempers frayed; very often tourist behaviour leaves much to be desired, and it is not unknown for visitors to invade private homes in some of the prettier Oxfordshire and Buckinghamshire villages.

In many respects, though, the Thames and Chilterns does not suffer from some of the more unpleasant side effects of the tourism industry that have afflicted other parts of the country. There are no theme parks as such, and even the more commercial tourist attractions are restrained and in keeping with the local environment. Tourist erosion – the wearing down of footpaths, soil, natural habitats and even buildings – and effective methods of coping with ever increasing hordes of visitors are major problems, and it only remains to be seen what effect the new Rural Strategy issues will have on these areas.

Good Alternatives

Meeting People

The **Berkshire, Buckinghamshire and Oxfordshire Naturalists' Trust** (BBONT) is a registered charity set up in 1959, who maintain and protect over ninety nature and wildlife reserves that are widely distributed throughout the three counties. Most of these reserves are key sites with high wildlife value, but the Trust also conserves a variety of habitats including mixed deciduous woods, chalk downland, wet meadows, hay meadows, bogs and heaths, hedgerows and even disused railway lines and gravel pits. BBONT produce a comprehensive guide covering all their reserves and members and volunteers are encouraged to assist with the maintenance of individual sites. Further information can be obtained from BBONT, 3 Church Cowley Road, Rose Hill, Oxford OX4 3JR (Tel 0865 775476).

The newly formed **Wildlife Trust of Bedfordshire & Cambridgeshire** also manage over ninety wildlife and nature reserves, and are currently purchasing new ones at the rate of four per year. The Trust works closely with local communities and runs an active educational programme involving both adults and children. Further details may be obtained from the Trust at 5 Fulbourn Manor, Fulborn, Cambridge CB1 5BN.

Set in 104 acres (42 hectares) of woodland and open heathland, the national headquarters of the **Royal Society for the Protection of Birds** at The Lodge at Sandy in Bedfordshire, is a wonderful place to watch the many bird varieties attracted to the reserve. More information is available from RSPB, The Lodge, Sandy, Bedfordshire SG19 2DL (Tel 0767 80551).

Most of the region offers superb walking and this can provide good opportunities to meet other people. The **Ridgeway Path** is one of the great walks of the region. It runs for eighty-five miles (136 km.) from Avebury in Wiltshire to Ivinghoe Beacon in Buckinghamshire. Further details are available from the Ridgeway Officer, Department of Leisure and Arts, Countryside Section, Library Headquarters, Holton, Wheatley, Oxford OX9 1QQ. If you're interested in riding, Berkshire is the main county for equestrian pursuits. Riding can be arranged at **Highclere Castle** on 5000 acres (2025 hectares) of private land including many cross-country jumps. Further details from Jenny Phillips (Tel 0635 27240). At the heart of the West Berkshire Downs is **Lambourn**, home of some of the best racehorses in the world. Lambourn Trainers Association hold annual open days and escort visitors around the stables, giving a fascinating insight into the racing world not normally seen by the public. For further details (Tel. 0293 25313).

One of the first projects of the Hertfordshire Leisure Marketing Initiative was to put together a **Roman Trail** linking county-wide Roman sites and objects. A free guide is available and more information can be obtained from Melanie Burton, The Town Hall, Market Place, St Albans, Herts AL3 5DJ.

Discovering Places

For those interested in active countryside conservation and a budget holiday, the National Trust in association with the Countryside Commission have produced the **Acorn Project** and **Working Holidays** brochures. There are volunteer projects for every age range (starting from sixteen), from Bio-Survey Projects to hedge planting and drystone walling. Accommodation ranges from converted stable blocks on country estates to village halls, and this is also an excellent way to meet with other like-minded people. All projects allow free time and outings are usually arranged to local places of interest. To obtain a brochure, write to the National Trust, Volunteer Unit, PO Box 12, Westbury, Wiltshire BA13 4NA (Tel 0373 826826). The prices are extremely low and it is possible to choose from a weekend to seven-day projects.

There are a number of low-impact holiday and tour groups in the region worth considering.

Thames Valley Farm and Country Holidays in Bampton, Oxfordshire (Tel 0993 850162) is an association of farms and country homes. They offer reasonably priced accommodation with a warm personal service. The **Bedfordshire Farm and Country Holiday Group** is similar. For information on the North Bedfordshire area Tel 0234 870234; for South Bedfordshire Tel 0525 712316.

For a unique way to tour the Cotswolds, the **Cotswold Romany Caravan** company offer traditional-style horse-drawn caravans combined with overnight farmhouse accommodation. No previous experience of horses is necessary. Contact the company at Friars Court Farm, Clanfield, Oxfordshire (Tel 036781 226). On the waterways, **Grebe Canal Cruises**, Ivinghoe, Bucks (Tel 0296 661920) rent narrow-boats for holiday hire on the Grand Union Canal, while the **Kennet Horse Boat Company** in Newbury (Tel 0635 44154) offer traditional horse-drawn and motorised barges on the Kennet and Avon Canal. On the Thames, the best people to contact are the **Thames Hire Cruiser Association**, 19 Acre End Street, Eynsham, Oxford OX8 1PE (Tel 0865 880107).

Walking Tours of Windsor provide excellent on-foot trips around the town but Easter to November only (Tel 0753 852010). **Official Walking Tours of Oxford** can be arranged from the Tourist Information centre several times a day. For more information Tel 0865 726871.

The **Thames and Chilterns Tourist Board** stock a good range of material from regional area guides to farmhouse listings. Contact them at The Mount House, Church Green, Witney, Oxfordshire OX8 6DZ (Tel 0993 778800). Final mention should be given to **Friars Court**, at Clanfield in Oxfordshire, where John and Frances Willmer open the grounds of their part-moated farmhouse to the public. Nature trails, a Farm and Romany folklore display and delicious cream teas are all on offer.

Communications

How to Get There

RAIL: The rail network into Bedfordshire, Berkshire, Hertfordshire and parts of Oxfordshire is comprehensive and efficient, and major centres can be reached within forty minutes to an hour from

London. Information is available from **British Rail** at Oxford (Tel 0865 722333).

COACH: The area is well served by coach networks. The main company is **National Express** (Tel 071 730 0202).

CAR: Access by road is excellent, but local traffic and motorway conditions do cause serious problems. The M40 is a reasonably fast route from London to Buckinghamshire, Oxfordshire and the Cotswolds, but is notorious for what seem like continuous road works and contraflow systems. Traffic build-ups near Oxford are common at weekends and it is hoped that the M40 extension will ease the pressure once completely open.

The M4 motorway out of London provides easy access to Berkshire and south Buckinghamshire. Once the busiest motorway (that label has now gone to the M25), it can still be problematic at weekends and on public holidays.

When You're There

RAIL: Regional services are, on the whole, relatively comprehensive. Within Oxfordshire and Buckinghamshire however, rail travel becomes more difficult, and there is no direct line south to Berkshire without a detour via Reading.

BUS: Local bus networks are comprehensive and offer good links between all parts of the region. In many areas, strong competition between companies has led to high standards of efficiency and service. Contact local Tourist Information centres or bus stations for details.

CAR: The major routes through Hertfordshire are the A1 and A1(M). Both roads are very busy and this is further compounded by the slow-moving M25 traffic that circles the capital and feeds down to the main seaports. This can be extremely frustrating and it is usually essential to allow plenty of time when planning a journey. As with roads in many parts of the country, peak rush-hour times should be avoided.

The A34 which runs through the region can also be a bottleneck, suffering from an excess of roundabouts and heavy goods vehicles. One of the most congested sections is from Woodstock to Birmingham via Stratford-upon-Avon, and it is hoped that the M40 extension will eventually take most of the through-traffic off this busy route.

BOAT: *Cruising on the River Thames* is a useful leaflet produced by the National Rivers Authority and available from Tourist Information centres which provides an introduction to enjoying the 'non-tidal'

River Thames, inland at places such as Reading, Wallingford, Abingdon and Oxford. Also available is the excellent publication *Holidays Afloat*, produced by the National Tourist Boards of England, Scotland and Wales in conjunction with the British Marine Industries Federation. This guide includes details of holidays on the canals in the Thames and Chilterns Area, as well as a wide variety of other useful facts relevant to holidays on the water.

CYCLING: This is a particularly pleasant area in which to cycle, although summer crowds inevitably mean that roads can be very busy. The **Oxfordshire Cycle Way** is the main route of the area, stretching for around 200 miles (322 km.) and encircling the outskirts of the county of Oxfordshire, as well as crossing the centre of the county. The route takes in all the best-loved places, and some of the less well known ones, and a leaflet available from Tourist Information offices points out things to see and do en route.

WALKING: Long-distance footpaths in the area include the **North Buckinghamshire Way**, which runs northwards from the Ridgeway Path (see *Meeting People*, page 471) near Great Kimble (Buckinghamshire) to join up with the **Grafton Way** in Northamptonshire. The **Two Ridges Link** joins the Buckinghamshire Ridgeway Path with the **Greensand Ridge Walk** in Bedfordshire; and the newly-opened **Chess Valley Walk** follows the course of the River Chess from Chesham through to its confluence with the River Colne near the Grand Union Canal at Rickmansworth.

The recently opened footbridge at **Temple** on the River Thames now provides the last link needed to enable the walker to follow the Thames Path from the source at Kemble in Gloucester through to Greenwich in London.

For the newcomer to walking and rambling, Buckinghamshire County Council, in association with the Countryside Commission, publishes details of **10 circular walks** averaging about five to six miles each. Most of the routes pass through areas of archaeological, historical and nature conservation interest and further information can be obtained from the Recreational Paths Officer, County Engineer's Department, County Hall, Aylesbury, Buckinghamshire HP20 1UY.

RIDING: Riding is extremely popular in Buckinghamshire, particularly in the southern half of the county. The keen rider will be interested to learn about the **Swans Way**, the county's first long-distance bridleway and one of the few in England. The sixty-five mile (104.5 km.) route traverses a wide range of scenic landscape as it runs southwards from Salcey Forest in Northamptonshire through the Ouse Valley to the Vale of Aylesbury, where it joins up with the Ridgeway Path near Bledlow. The **Bledlow Circular Ride** covers a ten-mile (16 km.) circuit through the Chilterns with some fine open views. Details from the Recreational Paths Officer as above.

Useful Local Contacts

In Hertfordshire there is the **Hertfordshire Groundwork Trust**, 29a Mill Green, Hatfield AL9 5PE, working to improve the environment, and the **Hertfordshire Society**, 29a Mill Lane, Welwyn AL6 9EU (Tel 043871 7587), which maintains a general overview of developments in the area. The **Hertfordshire Bird Club** is at 61 Pondfield Crescent, St Albans AL4 9PA (Tel 0727 34853).

Contacts for Bedfordshire include the **Bedford Society**, 61 Church Road, Aspley Heath, Woburn Sands MK17 8TJ (which is actually in Buckinghamshire!) and the **Urban Studies Centre** of Bedford College, 13 The Crescent, Bedford (Tel 0234 51671). In Buckinghamshire there is the **Buckinghamshire Bird Club**, 319 Bath Road, Chippenham, Slough SL1 5PR and the **Buckinghamshire Geology Group**, The Climb, Gold Hill North, Chalfont St Peter SL9 5PR.

Visitors to Oxfordshire could contact the **Oxford Fieldpaths Society**, Grenfell, Hazeley Road, Little Milton, Oxford OX9 7OE; the **Oxford Forestry Institute**, University of Oxford, South Parks Road, Oxford OX1 3RB (Tel 0865 275000); **Oxford Ornithological Society**, care of Edward Grey Institute, Zoology Department, South Parks Road, Oxford OX1 3PS, and the **Oxford Urban Wildlife Group (BBONT)**, 3 Church Cowley Road, Rose Hill, Oxford OX4 3JR (Tel 0865 775476). This is also the BBONT headquarters, from where visitors may also obtain information about Bedfordshire.

Geographical Breakdown of Region

Berkshire

Although one of the smallest of the English shire counties, Berkshire is extremely varied and has much to offer the visitor. Admittedly, the rapid expansion of business parks and light industrial developments in the east of the county does little to enhance the region, but there are still many areas that remain unspoiled and well worth exploring.

Windsor

Windsor falls into the category of a 'must see' destination for almost every visitor who tours England. Situated just off the M4 motorway in the heart of commuter territory, the castle dominates the skyline as it rises above the town.

It is important to appreciate that Windsor is always busy. Coach parties begin arriving from 9.30 a.m. and this continues through to early evening. In addition to overseas visitors, literally hundreds of school children from this country and abroad descend on the town adding to the general congestion. For those who wish to avoid crowds, try visiting after 6.00 p.m. The town is less busy then as many of the excursionists have moved on and the souvenir shops have closed for the day.

The castle and the surrounding parks are the main focus of interest, but the old town is attractive and it is worth wandering through the narrow streets.

Windsor Castle has been the home and burial place of English kings and queens for over 900 years. Built by William the Conqueror as a stronghold to guard the western approaches to London, its purpose was to serve as a military fortress and it continues to do so to this day. Visits should also include the **State Apartments** containing many treasures from the Royal Collection, and **St George's Chapel**.

One of the very best vantage points from which to view the town is the river. Local boat companies offer short trips along this stretch of the Thames and there are easy walks along the river banks. Often overlooked by tourists is **Windsor Great Park** with its ancient oak trees and miles of walks. This can offer a welcome escape from hordes of tourists who pack the town centre at peak times of the day.

A worthwhile visit is to **Duffey's Old Bakery** in Oxford Road. This is an authentic Victorian Bakery and it is still possible to see food being prepared in a traditional coal-fired oven. The **Guildhall** in the centre of Windsor should not be missed.

Just across the Thames and within the shadow of the castle lies **Eton** and one of Britain's most famous public schools, **Eton College**, founded by Henry VI in 1440. The college is open to the public in the afternoon and there is a small **museum** of 'Eton Life' depicting the history and lifestyle of the college from its earliest beginnings to the present day. The best view of Eton

College and the famous playing fields is from the battlements of Windsor Castle.

Accommodation

First Class

Oakley Court Hotel, Windsor Road, Water Oakley, Windsor SL4 5UR (Tel 0628 74141). Elegant Victorian country house on the Thames in thirty-five acres (14 hectares) of gardens. Excellent French cuisine. This hotel has often doubled as a film set due to its location near Bray Studios.

Sir Christopher Wren's House Hotel, Thames Street, Windsor SL4 1PX (Tel 0753 861354). Designed and built by Sir Christopher Wren in 1676, this unique and dignified hotel is rather special. Furnished with fine antiques in keeping with the magnificent architecture, it offers superb quality and service.

Middle Range

Castle Hotel, 18 High Street, Windsor (Tel 0753 851011). Georgian hotel with country house atmosphere. Good location opposite Guildhall.

The Manor, Village Green, Datchet, near Windsor SL3 9EA (Tel 0753 43442). Period hotel on historic village green. Good access to area.

Economy

The Union Inn, 17 Crimp Hill, Old Windsor (Tel 0753 861955). Comfortable accommodation in character inn. Good restaurant.

Bear Farm, Binfield, Bracknell, near Windsor RG12 5QE (Tel 0734 343286). Attractive, low-beamed farmhouse in an area that used to be part of Windsor Forest.

Eating Out

First Class

Montmorency Restaurant, Windsor Bridge, Eton, Windsor (Tel 0753 854479). Fish restaurant on the banks of the Thames with good views of Windsor Castle.

Oscars, South Hill Park Arts Centre, Bracknell (Tel 0344 59031). English and international cuisine (including some vegetarian dishes) at this popular arts centre. Bar meals during the day, plus à la carte in the evening.

Middle Range

Ye Hare and Garter, High Street, Windsor (Tel 0753 863426). Tudor inn serving good value English cuisine.

Eton Wine Bar, 82 High Street, Eton (Tel 0753 855182). Informal wine bar offering a limited range of dishes, but all of excellent quality.

Economy

The Duke of Windsor, Woodside Road, Windsor (Tel 0344 882736). Former hunting lodge in Windsor Great Park. Fish dishes a speciality, but also serving meat and vegetarian alternatives.

Jolly Farmer, Cookham Dean, near Maidenhead (Tel 0628 482905). Small pub serving excellent value meals, especially good on Sundays.

Around Windsor

Beyond Windsor is **Cliveden**, near Taplow, on the Berkshire/Buckinghamshire border. Set on cliffs rising 200 feet (61 m.) above the Thames, this National Trust property was once the home of Nancy, Lady Astor, and is now let as an hotel to Blakeney Hotels Ltd (three rooms are open to National Trust visitors). The 375 acres of gardens and woodlands offer unusually dramatic views of the Thames. Nearby is **Thames Valley Vineyard**, Twyford, one of the largest vineyards in Britain, set in a vale overlooked by an Elizabethan manorhouse. The wines are produced in a winery situated in a clocktower barn that dates from the time of Oliver Cromwell. Red, white and sparkling wines are usually available and winery walkabouts and tastings can be arranged.

Reading

Reading is the county town of Royal Berkshire. A university town since 1926, it is an uneasy blend of new and old. Major companies have their headquarters in the town and stand side by side with the traditional red-brick buildings for which Reading is known. Plans are under way to enclose the town centre and part of the Thames under a glass canopy, creating a gigantic covered mall.

In 1990, the Queen officially re-opened the Kennet and Avon Canal which runs from Reading to Bath. **Blake's Lock Museum** of the town's waterways and industries, features reconstructions of canal life and includes a printer's workshop, a bakery and a barber shop.

Try and visit the **Museum of English Rural Life**. This houses an important national collection of agricultural artefacts depicting the farming, crafts and way of life of the countryside over the last 150 years. The museum is situated on the main university campus and is open from Tuesday through to Saturday, 10.00 a.m. to 1.00 p.m. and 2.00 p.m. to 4.30 p.m.

Reading **Tourist Information** is in the Civic Offices (Tel 0734 592388), behind Broad Street shopping centre.

Although Reading itself is frequently dismissed as an unattractive urban sprawl, there is plenty to see in the surrounding countryside. **Mapledurham House and Watermill** just to the north of the town on the Oxfordshire border, is the last working watermill on the Thames still producing wholewheat flour. A river launch is available when the house is open (Saturday, Sunday and Bank Holidays from Easter). A few miles away is the **Herb Farm**, near Sonning Common. It contains the most exhaustive collection of herb plants and herbal products in the country, all available for purchase. There is a restored 19th-century granary housing a small collection of agricultural hand tools and a children's play area.

Sonning is a delightful picture-book Thames village, popular with weekend visitors. Although the narrow road that feeds through the village is usually bumper-to-bumper with traffic, most cars do not stop as parking can be difficult.

The **Child-Beale Bird Park** at Lower Basildon, near Reading is a worthwhile family visit. Attractions include an extensive bird collection, rare breed sheep, Highland cattle, llamas and Shetland ponies. Set beside the Thames, Beale Bird Park makes an ideal and undisturbed mooring for visitors arriving by boat. Just a few minutes away is **Basildon Park**, a classical 18th-century house built by John Carr of York, in beautiful surroundings overlooking the Thames Valley. Completed in 1776, it stands in over 400 acres (162 hectares) of park and woodland. Both the house and the gardens are open to the public and maintained by the National Trust.

Accommodation

First Class

Caversham Hotel, Caversham Bridge, Reading (Tel 0734 391818). Situated on the Thames within easy access to the countryside around Reading. Excellent facilities including room for disabled.

The Great House at Sonning, Thames Street, Sonning, near Reading (Tel 0734 692277). Beautiful hotel in splendid setting. Bedrooms are situated in various cottages surrounding the main building. Most contain four-poster beds, with river views available. Two good restaurants and bistro.

Middle Range

Upcross Hotel, 68 Berkley Avenue, Reading (Tel 0734 391573). Victorian mansion set in two acres (0.8 hectares) of gardens. A family run hotel with an elegant restaurant and good menu. Quietly situated, yet only ten minutes' walk from the city centre.

Abbey House Hotel, 118 Connaught Road, Reading RG3 2UF (Tel 0734 590549). A small family run hotel with a warm welcome. A varied menu including vegetarian dishes.

Economy

Tudor House, Maidenhatch, Pangbourne, near Reading (Tel 0734 744482). Attractive listed family bed and breakfast in beautiful location. Two rooms.

Kennet House, Burghfield Bridge, Reading (Tel 0734 571060). Conveniently located family bed and breakfast. Three rooms.

Eating Out

First Class

New Mill Restaurant, Eversley, near Reading (Tel 0734 732277). Highly attractive 16th-century mill on the River Blackwater, with working mill wheel, and stream running through the middle. Excellent cuisine.

Cantley House Hotel, Milton Road, Wokingham (Tel 0734 789912). Victorian mansion offering both fine cuisine in its restaurant and cheaper meals in two converted 17th-century barns.

Middle Range

The Bull, Bisham Village, near Marlow (Tel 0628 482675). 650-year-old inn that has played host to many a dignitary, including Henry VIII and Elizabeth I. Good value cuisine and quality bar meals.

Old Boot Inn, Stanford Dingley, near Pangbourne (Tel 0734 744292). English cuisine covers just a small selection of the dishes available on the comprehensive menu at this extremely popular inn.

Economy

The Crown, Reading Road, Lower Basildon, near Reading (Tel 0491 671262). Situated near Basildon Park and the Child-Beale Bird

Park. Spacious well-appointed inn serving good home-cooked food. Family room available.

The Beehive, Upper Basildon, near Reading (Tel 0491 671269). Set in rolling wooded countryside with loyal local following. Superb home-cooked food and highly pleasant atmosphere. Children's menu.

Around Reading

Further west is **Newbury** on the southern border of the county (**Tourist Information** at The Wharf, Tel 0635 30267). Newbury is a natural crossroads leading to Winchester, Bath, Oxford and London, and although the fringes of the town have been developed for high-tech industry, the central area has still retained its market town atmosphere. The countryside here is possibly the most attractive in the county and is largely overlooked by the casual visitor who tends to quickly pass through the area en route to somewhere else. Cycling is a good way of exploring the area, and cycles can be hired from **Trents**, at 25 Cheap Street (Tel 0635 46004). **Snelsmore Common** to the north of Newbury, is the only country park in West Berkshire. The extensive common and woodland contains varied habitats including some rare species. Guided nature walks can be arranged with the warden during the summer months.

Thatcham Moors, three miles (4.8 km.) to the east, is a Site of Special Scientific Interest (SSSI), and covers an area of 150 acres (60.75 hectares). The site contains a variety of wildlife habitats but its most important feature is the largest area of freshwater reedbeds in England. Access is along the canal tow path or from Lower Way, Thatcham. Crossing over the River Kennett, toward Bury's Bank Road is **Baynes Reserve** consisting of a forty-acre (16.2 hectares) ancient woodland dating back to the end of the last Ice Age. Roe and muntjac deer are present and up to fifteen different species of dragonfly have been recorded.

To the west of Newbury is **Inkpen Common** near Hungerford. An SSSI, the reserve is on lease to BBONT. This is excellent walking country and amongst the highest downland slopes of the district.

Highclere Castle is four miles (6.5 km.) south of Newbury. It is the seat of the Earl and Countess of Carnavon and renowned for its priceless display of Egyptian treasures, some discovered only a few years ago behind concealed panels. It was the fifth Earl who with Howard Carter discovered the tomb of Tutankhamen. The castle was designed by Sir Charles Barry, architect of the Houses of Parliament. There are walled and secret gardens, yew walks and tropical conservatories. For opening times and further information Tel 0635 253210.

East of Newbury through the villages of Hermitage, Yattendon and Hampstead Norreys is **Lardon Chase** and **The Holies** near the village of Streatley on the west side of the Goring Gap. The small car park at the top of Streatley Hill provides access to the sites, from which there are magnificient views and easy walks. At Lardon Chase, the chalk grassland is managed for its nature conservation interest, while The Holies comprises grassland, heathland and woods. This is exceptional countryside under the care of the National Trust.

Accommodation

First Class

The Chequers Hotel, Oxford Street, Newbury (Tel 0635 38000). Attractive conveniently-located hotel in town centre. Good restaurant.

Foley Lodge Hotel, Stockcross, Newbury RG16 8JU (Tel 0635 528770). Luxury country house hotel in a former hunting lodge, set in landscaped gardens and complete with Victorian-style conservatory.

Middle Range

Bacon Arms Hotel, Oxford Street, Newbury (Tel 0635 31822). Sixteenth-century coaching inn offering comfortable accommodation.

Pilgrims Rest Guest House, Oxford Road, Newbury RG13 1XB (Tel 0635 40694). Charming family run guest house near Donnington Castle.

Economy

Hart Hill Farm, Hart Hill Road, Thatcham (Tel 0635 63242). Period farmhouse set in an acre (0.4 hectares) of lawns and mature garden. Supervised tour of 200-acre (81 hectares) mixed farm, and wholesome cooking.

St Mary's House, Kintbury, near Newbury RG15 OTR (Tel 0488 551). Picturesque guest house in a former Victorian school on the Kennet and Avon Canal.

Eating Out

First Class

Regency Park Hotel, Bowling Green Road, Thatcham (Tel 0635 71555). Country house hotel locally renowned for its excellent cuisine.

Middle Range

Royal Oak, The Square, Yattendon (Tel 0635 201324). Sixteenth-century village inn north of Newbury serving high quality bar meals.

The Swan, High Street, East Ilsley, near Newbury (Tel 063528 238). Sixteenth-century coaching inn situated in a scenic village in the Berkshire Downs. Good food and an impressive wine list.

Economy

The Five Bells, Wickham, near Newbury (Tel 048838 242). Eyecatching thatched inn set in lovely rolling countryside. Excellent reputation.

The Blackbird, Bagnor, near Newbury (Tel 0635 40638). Charming pub close to Snelsmore Country Park.

Oxfordshire

Oxfordshire lies close to the centre of the English plain, equidistant from London, Southampton and Bristol. It is a county of great historical interest and has many attractive features.

Oxford

A magnificent university town containing some of the most distinctive buildings in the region. Within one square mile (2.59 sq. km.) alone the city has more than 900 buildings of architectural or historic interest. For the visitor, this presents a real challenge. Although the city centre is compact, there is no single building that dominates. Even the University is spread throughout thirty-five different colleges, often hidden behind walls, locked gates, shops and offices. Perseverence is essential as the worthwhile sights are not always obvious to the first-time visitor.

Like its rival Cambridge, Oxford is extremely popular with British and overseas visitors and this results in horrendous parking problems and severe congestion on a year-round basis. To help alleviate this problem, Park-and-Ride facilities have now been set up on every main entrance road to the city and drivers are strongly recommended to use them.

The city is best explored on foot. Bicycles can be a real danger around the colleges during term, so exercise care – especially if you are accompanied by young children.

Carfax Tower in the city centre is a good place to start and one of the best points from which to view the city. One of the most atmospheric areas is **Merton Street**, just off the High Street. From here it is possible to reach **Christ Church Meadows** and walk along the banks of the Cherwell and Thames. Nearby is the **Botanic Gardens**, the oldest in the country and well worth a visit. Opposite is **Magdalen College** with its huge deerpark and riverside walks. **Radcliffe Square** contains some of Oxford's most beautiful buildings, particularly the domed **Radcliffe Camera**, built in 1736. Nearby is the **Sheldonian Theatre**, designed and built in the manner of a Roman theatre by the young Christopher Wren. Today it is used for university occasions including matriculation and degree ceremonies. There are many museums, including the **Ashmolean**, the oldest public museum in Britain, dating back to 1683, the **Museum of Modern Art** and the **Frank Cooper Museum of Marmalade** (a famous Oxford export), in the High Street.

College visits are a must, but many colleges do not open to the public until after 2.00 p.m. Times are clearly displayed at the entrance gates. Worcester and St John's have particularly beautiful gardens, and the grounds of New College contain part of the old city walls.

It is almost a forgotten fact that Oxford is a Cathedral city. **Christ Church Cathedral** can be found at St Aldates, just south of Carfax Tower. Oxford has an excellent **covered market** just off the High Street containing many speciality shops. The main shopping centre is also of a high standard, although the design of the new shopping malls has little in common with the rest of the city architecture.

Iffley Meadows, an ancient wet meadowland occupying 32 acres (13 hectares), can be reached from Iffley village, just two miles (3.2 km.) from central Oxford. The meadows are crossed by old river channels and willow-lined ditches. Plants found here include adder's tongue, great burnet, common meadow-rue, pepper saxifrage and creeping jenny. Also of interest is the **Henry Stephen/C.S. Lewis Reserve**. This is a large man-made pond with mixed woodland surrounds, covering an area of seven and a half acres (3 hectares). The ground was once owned by C.S. Lewis, the writer and friend of J.R.R. Tolkein. It is said that the worlds of Narnia and Middle Earth were dreamed up here. The site was bought as a nature reserve by BBONT in 1976 and remains a memorial to imagination as much as wildlife interest. Access is from the A40 ring road, taking the first turn on the left and then right into Kiln Lane. After 300 yards turn right into Lewis Close. The reserve is at the end of the path.

Oxford **Tourist Information Centre** is at St Aldates (Tel 0865 726871). It is possible to book local walking tours and accommodation from here. Unofficial university tours may be arranged with undergraduates. Look for the information boards at key points throughout the city centre.

Accommodation

First Class

The Randolph Hotel, Beaumont Street, Oxford OX1 2LN (Tel 0865 247481). Very attractive Victorian style hotel in city centre. Good restaurant.

Linton Lodge Hotel, Linton Road, Oxford OX2 6UJ (Tel 0865 53461). Country house hotel in north Oxford, one mile (1.6 km.) from city centre. Delightful setting.

Middle Range

The Old Black Horse Hotel, 102 St Clements, Oxford (Tel 0865 244691). Close to city centre, the High Street and Magdalen Bridge.

The Victoria Hotel, 180 Abingdon Road, Oxford (Tel 0865 724536). Family run Victorian hotel, twelve minutes' walk to city centre.

Economy

Casa Villa Guest House, 388 Banbury Road, Oxford (Tel 0865 512642). Extremely comfortable family home with à la carte menu. Good area.

Middle Farm, Old Wootton, Boars Hill, near Oxford (Tel 0865 739290). Bed and breakfast at a working farm just three miles (4.8 km.) from city centre.

Eating Out

First Class

The Well House Restaurant and Hotel, 34–40 High Street, Watlington (Tel 049161 3333). Period country house hotel with a locally-renowned restaurant serving English and French cuisine. Separate vegetarian menu.

Studley Priory, Horton-cum-Studley, near Oxford (Tel 086735 203). Twelfth-century nunnery now converted to a charming hotel and restaurant serving English and French cuisine.

Middle Range

The Cherwell Boathouse, Bardwell Road (Tel 0865 52746). Attractively situated on the River Cherwell (punts available for hire), and serving excellent food made from fresh produce. Wide choice and vegetarian options. Booking essential.

Gee's Restaurant, 61 Banbury Road (Tel 0865 58346). Good menu offered in a delightful setting in an old conservatory.

Economy

Brown's Restaurant, 7 Woodstock Road (Tel 0865 511995). Arguably Oxford's most popular eating place. Wide selection including vegetarian dish of the day. Can be very busy during the evenings and at weekends. No reservations accepted, just turn up and take your chance.

The Nose Bag, 6 St Michael's Street (Tel 0865 721033). Highly attractive for just a bite or a main meal. Very good food, reasonably priced, vegetarian options.

North of Oxford

Just eight miles (12.8 km.) north of Oxford is the attractive market town of **Woodstock** and **Blenheim Palace**. This splendid building was designed by John Vanburgh and was a gift from Queen Anne to the first Duke of Marlborough after his victory over the French. Winston Churchill was born at Blenheim and a selection of his paintings are on display. Often overlooked are the 2000 acre (810 hectares) gardens landscaped by Capability Brown. There are miles of secluded walks around the estate and it is possible to escape the crowds as most of the visiting coach tours only allow enough time to view the palace.

Villages of interest in the area include **Wootton**, two miles (3.2 km.) north of Woodstock. This is a very attractive and unspoiled village. Look out for the 'Toads Crossing' sign as you enter: every year, hundreds of toads migrate from the shallow river across the main road, to the fields beyond the village. **Stonesfield** with its narrow streets of cottages and houses is worth a visit along with **Spelsbury**, **Charlbury** and **Chipping Norton** – a typical Cotswold market town. One of the most beautiful drives in the area is from **Charlbury** to **Burford**. The route offers some of the very best (and least known) sightseeing in the county, and there are ample opportunities for walking and hiking. The backdrop of the ancient **Wychwood Forest** provides an added attraction.

Burford is an ancient and picturesque wool town beautifully positioned in the Windrush Valley. The entrance to the town is quite dramatic and the honey-coloured Cotswold stone buildings are well preserved. There are superb walks along the Windrush to **Swinbrook**, a truly idyllic village untouched by the majority of visitors who come to Burford. In the Swinbrook churchyard, the author Nancy Mitford and her sister Unity are buried side by side.

The village of **Filkins** between Burford and Lechlade, is the home of the **Cotswold Woollen Weavers**. This is a working weaving mill in a splendid 18th-century barn. There is a small exhibition gallery and it is possible to purchase a wide range of woollen products. No admission charge.

Minster Lovell is one of the loveliest villages on the River Windrush. Attractive stone cottages in a wooded setting and the ruins of the 15th-century manor house provide a truly romantic environment in which to wander at leisure. Nearby is the thriving market town of **Witney**: head for **Church Green** to see the row of almshouses and the 17th-century buttercross. An interesting visit is to **Cogges Manor Farm Museum**, a nineteen-acre (7.7 hectares) Edwardian farm museum. There are regular demonstrations of sheep shearing, butter churning, hand milking and blacksmithing. Cattle, horses, pigs and sheep typical of the period can be seen, and nature and history trails take the visitor around the site. Picnics can be eaten in the orchard area.

South-east of Witney on the road to Stanton Harcourt is **Vicarage Pit**. There is a colony of flowering spotted orchids to be found here, but the reserve's main attraction is the waterfowl, including greylag and barnacle geese. The snow goose has also been recorded. The lake has been stocked with a variety of fish by the angling club which has private fishing rights.

Further west is **Bampton**. A beautiful, little-visited Cotswold village, Bampton has a sophisticated air with many elegant houses, a market place and a fine church. Morris dancing has long been popular here, and the annual festival brings hundreds of visitors from all over the country.

South of Oxford

The village of **Dorchester** was an important settlement before Roman times. The Abbey is well worth a visit. Nearby is **Wittenham Clumps**, site of an Iron Age fort that is visible for miles around. This is excellent walking country and the view from the top of the clumps is quite superb.

Continuing south, **Henley-on-Thames** is an elegant Georgian town, famous for the Royal Regatta which is held annually during the first week of July. The town is also the site of Britain's second oldest theatre, **The Kenton** on New Street (Tel 0491 575698). Henley contains over 300 buildings of architectural or historic interest. The very first Oxford and Cambridge boat race was held here in 1829. There are miles of easy riverside walks in Henley, but be prepared for crowds. This is an extremely popular area for local dog-walkers and visitors alike. **Tourist Information** is at the Town Hall, Market Place (Tel 0491 578034). Try and visit **Grey's Court** just out of the town. This 14th-century fortified house retains its medieval kitchen and a Tudor donkey wheel, in use up to 1915. The walled gardens contain an Archbishop's maze (National Trust).

A few miles north is **Stonor Park**, the historic home of the Stonor family for over 800 years. Stonor has been a centre for Catholicism, and the medieval chapel is still used for the celebration of Mass. **Stonor Valley** is one of the most untouched parts of the Chilterns and the deer park is possibly the most beautiful in southern England. The house, gardens and park are open to the public during the summer.

Accommodation

First Class

The Bear Hotel, Park Street, Woodstock OX7 1SZ (Tel 0993 811511). Beautiful coaching inn dating to the 12th century. Excellent cuisine.

The George Hotel, High Street, Dorchester OX10 7HH (Tel 0865 340404). Charming hotel conversion of a coaching inn, particularly notable for its two fine dining-rooms and traditional cuisine.

Middle Range

Morar Farmhouse, Weald Street, Bampton OX8 2HL (Tel 0993 850162). Attractive family farmhouse in a pleasant village location. Good use made of home produce.

Regency House, River Terrace, Henley-on-Thames RG9 1BG (Tel 0491 571133). Bed, breakfast and dinner on the banks of the Thames in a quiet and secluded position in Henley.

Economy

Swalcliffe Manor, Swalcliffe, near Banbury OX15 5EH (Tel 029578 348). Interesting manor house, parts of which date from the

13th century, offering bed, breakfast and dinner. Excellent cuisine and delightful decor.

Portwell House, Market Place, Faringdon SN7 7HU (Tel 0367 20197). Seven bedrooms with bed, breakfast and dinner in the centre of this pretty Cotswolds village.

Eating Out

First Class

King's Arms, Horse Fair, Deddington, near Banbury (Tel 0869 38364). Informal restaurant in a 16th-century coaching inn, serving traditional home-made English fare.

The Little Angel, Remenham, Henley-on-Thames (Tel 0491 574165). Bar and restaurant serving seafood specialities and some meat dishes, with an excellent wine list and good local beers.

Middle Range

The Clanfield Tavern, Clanfield, near Witney (Tel 036781 223). Sixteenth-century listed building in a pretty Cotswold village. Superb cuisine, fresh local produce and extensive wine list.

The Angel on the Bridge, Thameside, Henley-on-Thames (Tel 0491 573060). Superbly located restaurant offering wholesome food and bar snacks.

Economy

Nutters, 10 New Street, Chipping Norton (Tel 0608 641995). No-nonsense home cooking catering for meat-eaters, vegetarians and vegans. Situated below a health/spa centre.

Waterperry Gardens Tearoom, Waterperry Gardens, near Wheatley (Tel 0844 339254). Home-baking, afternoon tea and light snacks served amongst the formal gardens and adjoining garden centre.

Buckinghamshire

Buckingamshire is the rural heartland of the Thames and Chilterns. Ranging from the beechwoods of the Chilterns to the gentle rolling landscape of the Vale of Aylesbury, it offers the visitor some of the best touring country in the region. Woodland trails and countryside paths are numerous, and all are well signposted and maintained. Currently Buckinghamshire County Council administers some 2500 miles (4022 km.) of recreational footpaths which await discovery by the walker and rambler.

A few miles down river from Henley-on-Thames is **Marlow**. This lovely riverside town is famous for the 19th-century suspension bridge which spans the Thames. The buildings are mostly Georgian. **Albion House** in West Street was once the home of the poet Shelley. Many of the narrow backstreets are quite atmospheric and worth a wander: **St Peters Street, Cuckoo Alley** and **Spittal Street** in particular. **Tourist Information** is at the Court Garden Complex (Tel 0628 43597).

High Wycombe is situated just four miles (6.5 km.) away at the foot of the Chilterns. It is the surrounding area that is really of interest to the tourist, but a visit to the **Chair Museum** (Tel 0494 23879) is worthwhile. Chair-making has been practised in the Wycombe Chilterns since the 1720s. This small museum records the early development of the industry, with particular emphasis on the history of the Windsor chair. **Tourist Information** is at 6 The Corn Market (Tel 0494 461000).

North of the town is **Hughenden Manor**, bought in 1847 by Disraeli, who refashioned the house and grounds and lived here until his death in 1881. The house has been extensively refurbished by the National Trust. **Millfield Wood** (an SSSI bought by BBONT in 1983), is just across the road from Hughenden and up the hill. The nineteen-acre (7.7 hectares) reserve is a rare example of a semi-natural Chiltern beechwood growing on chalk – high forest in profile – with tall trees, mainly beech but also ash and wild cherry.

The charming village of **Bradenham** belongs almost entirely to the National Trust. There are over 1000 acres (405 hectares) of Chiltern beech woodland, hills and farmland to be explored. A series of well-marked paths provides easy access for the rambler. The 17th-century manor house (not open to the public), was once the home of Isaac Disraeli, father of Benjamin, who lived nearby.

West Wycombe Hill and Village is situated two miles (3.2 km.) west of High Wycombe. The village has an exceptional collection of 15th-17th century houses and all are maintained by the Trust. The hill affords fine views of the surrounding countryside and **West Wycombe Park**, a palladian house with frescos and painted ceilings. The house is beautifully set in a landscaped garden complete with a small lake and classical temples, including the recently constructed Temple of Venus. Look out for **St Lawrence Church** with the unusual golden ball on top of the tower. Halfway up the hill to the church are the **West Wycombe Caves**. This is the site of the infamous Hellfire Club and the caves are open to the public. It should be noted that the caves and church are privately owned and not part of the National Trust. Before leaving the area, visit the small village of **Fingest**. This is just four and a half miles (7.2 km.) west and one of the prettiest villages in the region.

East of High Wycombe is the **Chalfont Shire Horse Centre** near the town of **Chalfont St Giles**. There are daily demonstrations and visitors have the opportunity to see these giant animals at close range (Tel 02407 2304). A visit to **The Jordans**, south of Chalfont and famous for its links with the Quaker community, is a worthwhile excursion. The **Quaker Meeting House** was built in 1688 and is still in use today. Adjacent to the Meeting House is **Old Jordans Mayflower Barn**, built in 1624, reputedly from the timbers of the *Mayflower*, the ship in which the Pilgrim Fathers first sailed to America.

The Chilterns Open Air Museum at Newland Park, Chalfont, contains a collection of historic buildings that have been dismantled at their original site and re-erected in this beautiful forty-five acre (18 hectares) park. Farming and rural life is the main focus of attention, and many of the buildings date back to the 16th century (Tel 02407 71117).

Aylesbury (**Tourist Information** at County Hall, Walton Street, Tel 0296 395000) is a modern town that has lost much of its market origins, but five miles (8 km.) north-west is **Waddesdon Manor** (National Trust), a magnificent French Renaissance-style château built for Baron Ferdinand de Rothschild between 1874 and 1899. The furnishings are lavish and nowhere outside France are you likely to see such an extensive collection of French furniture and porcelain. The landscaped gardens are delightful and there is a flock of freeflying macaws which inhabits the trees around the château. Extensive refurbishment of the property is currently under way and it is advisable to check for further information before setting out (Tel 0296 651211). The Rothschild family also owned **Ascott House** (National Trust), a delightful half-timbered house that was originally a Jacobean hunting lodge. Look out for the outstanding collection of Oriental porcelain and the Victorian garden with its fine collection of unusual trees and attractive flower borders (Tel 0296 688242).

For something completely different, **Borstall Duck Decoy** (National Trust), near the Oxfordshire border at Brill, is a rare, 18th-century duck decoy in full working order – one of three such constructions in the country. An information centre and regular demonstrations by the warden illustrate how wild duck were caught for the table (Tel 0844 237488).

Stowe Landscape Gardens (National Trust) near Buckingham, is one of the supreme creations of the Georgian era. The 18th-century mansion, formerly the home of the Dukes of Buckingham and Chandos, but now one of the country's top independent schools, is set in over 250 acres (101 hectares) of beautifully landscaped gardens created by Charles Bridgeman, William Kent and Capability Brown. The gardens contain no less than six lakes and thirty-two follies or temples, and its sheer scale must make it Britain's largest work of art. The house is open to the public during school holidays only. Visitors should allow at least two and a half to three hours to circuit the gardens, and many paths are unsuitable for prams or wheelchairs. Comfortable walking shoes recommended. For further information (Tel 0280 822850).

Accommodation

First Class

Compleat Angler Hotel, Marlow Bridge, Marlow SL7 1RG (Tel 0628 484444). Picturesque 17th-century inn on the banks of the Thames, world renowned for its excellent restaurant and extensive cellar.

The Bell Inn, Aston Clinton, near Aylesbury HP22 5HP (Tel 0296 630252). Beautiful 17th-century coaching inn with an excellent reputation for its hospitality and cuisine.

Middle Range

The Fox Country Hotel, Ibstone, near High Wycombe HP14 3GG (Tel 049 163 722). Low-beamed 300-year-old inn set in the Chiltern Hills.

The Wheatsheaf, Weedon, near Aylesbury (Tel 0296 641581). Comfortable accommodation in a small family run hotel in a historic building.

Economy

Old Jordans, Jordans, near Beaconsfield HP9 2SW (Tel 02407 4586). Good value accommodation in a fascinating building, surrounded by orchards and fields.

Wallace Farm, Dinton, near Aylesbury HP17 8UF (Tel 0296 748660). Bed and breakfast in an attractive 16th-century farmhouse, complete with orchard, livestock, ponds and a croquet lawn.

Eating Out
First Class

Burnham Beeches, Grove Road, Burnham (Tel 06286 3333). Early 18th-century hunting lodge now functioning as a country house hotel and combining English and French cuisine in its dining-room. Booking recommended.

Hartwell House, Oxford Road, Aylesbury (Tel 0296 747444). Elegant listed 16th-century country house serving excellent nouvelle British cuisine.

Middle Range

The Blue Flag, Cadmore End, near High Wycombe (Tel 0494 881183). People travel from all over the Chilterns to dine here. Superb food prepared by a master chef.

Seatons, 5 Market Square, Aylesbury (Tel 0296 27582). Extremely popular spot in the town centre serving quality food which is both imaginative and fairly priced.

Economy

George and Dragon, West Wycombe Village (Tel 0494 23602). Home-cooked meals in a National Trust-owned village.

The Pheasant Inn, Windmill Street, Brill (Tel 0844 237104). Pleasantly situated next to a 300-year-old windmill, this inn boasts one of the best views in the county. Good value home-made food.

Bedfordshire

Bedfordshire is a surprisingly rural county ranging from the water-meadows and embankments along the River Ouse in the north to the Dunstable Downs in the south.

North Bedfordshire

The county town of **Bedford** is often dismissed as an urban sprawl, but the local council has invested a considerable sum of money in restoration and area enhancement projects. Stretches of the **River Ouse** have been opened up with the creation of miles of marked riverside walks and gardens, the restoration of locks and the construction of a marina.

Worth seeing is **Bedford Museum**, located in a restored brewery, with a collection which covers much of the agricultural and natural history of the area. The preacher and writer John Bunyan lived in Bedford, and the **Bunyan Meeting Library Museum** in Mill Street houses a large collection of his work and personal effects. Nonconformist chapels, many dating back to Bunyan's time, are much in evidence throughout the area. **Tourist Information** is at 10 St Paul's Square (Tel 0234 215226) while if you want to go cycling, contact **Lawes** at 64 Tavistock Street (Tel 0234 52257).

Three miles (4.8 km.) west of Bedford is **Bromham Mill** on the banks of the Ouse. This 17th-century mill with working machinery houses a natural history museum and exhibitions of work by local artists. **Elstow Moot Hall** is a restored medieval market hall just south of Bedford. It is a beautiful example of a timber-frame building and contains exhibits about the life of Bunyan. The **Stewartby Lake Country Park**, six miles (9.6 km.) south of Bedford, has the largest expanse of water in the county. The lake covers 287 acres (116 hectares) with 31 acres (12.5 hectares) of bank for walking and birdwatching. West of the lake is **Stagsden Bird Gardens**, a breeding centre for over 200 species of birds, including rare pheasants, birds of prey and cranes. Birdwatchers and nature lovers should also head for the **Harrold/Odell Country Park** on the north bank of the Ouse between the villages of Harrold and Odell. The 144-acre (58 hectares) site contains extensive marked walks through the river meadows and nature reserve. The habitat attracts a wide variety of birdlife from rare geese to the kingfisher. To the north of Bedford is **Sundon Hills Country Park**, a SSSI, set in an Area of Outstanding Natural Beauty (AONB). Here there are extensive waymarked walks across the open chalk meadowland, which is one of the highest points in the county.

There are many attractive villages in the area including **Podington** and **Felmersham**. Try and visit **St Mary's** 14th-century church in Felmersham, considered to be the finest in the county. Other places of interest to see are **Stevington Windmill**, a 200-year-old post mill, fully restored in 1951. Keys are available from the Royal George Inn, centre of the village.

The **RSPB Nature Reserve** lies to the east of Bedford, close to Sandy and the A1. Set in 104 acres (42 hectares) of open heathland and woodland, The Lodge is the headquarters of Europe's largest voluntary wildlife conservation body. Over 150 species of birds have been recorded here. Excellent nature trails and hides. For information (Tel 0767 80551).

Accommodation

First Class

Woodlands Manor, Green Lane, Clapham, Bedford MK41 6EP (Tel 0234 363281). Privately run Victorian manor-house in wooded gardens. Elegant restaurant and attractive à la carte menu.

Flitwick Manor, Church Road, Flitwick MK45 1AE (Tel 0525 712242). Georgian manor house south of Bedford offering traditional English country house hospitality and fine cuisine, particularly seafood.

Middle Range

Melford Lodge Hotel, 528 Goldington Road, Bedford (Tel 0234 43335). Small family run hotel offering good facilities.

Anchor Inn, High Street, Great Barford (Tel 0234 870364). Very attractive village location. Excellent facilities and good food.

Economy

Church Farm, 41 High Street, Roxton MK44 3EB (Tel 0234 870234). Charming family run bed and breakfast, parts of which date from the 16th century, located in a peaceful village north of Bedford.

Newton Park Farm, Turvey (Tel 023064 250). Family run farmhouse close to all major attractions. Very good value.

Eating Out

Although this part of Bedfordshire has a good number of restaurants, finding First Class cuisine can prove difficult.

Middle Range

The Knife and Cleaver, The Grove, Houghton Conquest, near Bedford (Tel 0234 740387). Conservatory-style restaurant serving nouvelle English and French cuisine in a local hotel.

Barns, Cardington Road, Bedford (Tel 0234 27004). Comprehensive menu in a pleasant setting.

Economy

Red Lion, High Street, Elstow (Tel 0234 59687). English carvery and bar snacks.

Royal George, Stagsden (Tel 02302 2801). Pleasant inn serving good home-made meals.

South Bedfordshire

Leighton Buzzard was a thriving town at the time of the Domesday Book. It still retains its market town character and there are many fine Georgian buildings lining its wide High Street. The town is famous for its sand, which is even exported to the Sahara Desert. The three and a half miles (5.6 km.) of railway built to carry the sand is now run by **Leighton Buzzard Narrow Gauge Railway** at Page's Park. Walkers and ramblers should head for the **Greensand Ridge Walk** which commences off Linslade Road. This is a waymarked 40-mile (64 km.) walk across mostly rural countryside to Gamlingay Cinques in Cambridgeshire.

Dunstable, a natural crossroads on what was once a prehistoric site at the foot of the Downs, has been transformed from a small market town into a thriving commercial centre. The market is still held on three days a week in the tree-shaded Queensway Market Square. **Tourist Information** is at the County Library on Vernon Place (Tel 0582 471012). A worthwhile visit is to the **Dunstable Downs**, a steep slope of Chiltern Hills rising from the surrounding farmland and offering lovely views to the Vale of Aylesbury. The 300 acres (121.5 hectares) of downland is managed by Bedfordshire County Council who have provided an Interpretation Centre and picnic site. Nearby is the village of **Totternhoe**, an area of exceptional antiquarian interest, with its Norman castle and ancient walkways.

Luton Hoo, set in a 1500-acre (607.5 hectares) park laid out by Capability Brown, is an 18th-century classical stone-built mansion. The house is famous for its priceless collection of art treasures, which includes Fabergé jewels, paintings by Titian and Rembrandt, rare tapestries and old porcelain.

Woburn Abbey, home of the Dukes of Bedford, is a very popular 'commercial' stately home. Set in a 3000-acre (1215 hectares) deer park, it incorporates Europe's largest drive-through safari park. There is plenty to do and see, and the attraction copes well with the large crowds who arrive on daily excursions from London. Enjoyable to a point, but not to everyone's taste.

Whipsnade Park Zoo near Dunstable was established in 1931 as a country retreat for animals from the London Zoo. At present, over 2000 animals live in 500 acres (202.5 hectares) of parkland on top of the Chilterns. The zoo is acclaimed for its breeding programme of threatened or rare species.

An interesting visit near Luton is the **Stockwood Craft Museum**

and Gardens. This houses a varied collection of rural life and crafts including a reconstructed thatched cottage and old forge. Craft skills displayed include saddler, miller, blacksmith and brickmaker. For more information Tel 0582 38714.

Before leaving the area, a visit to the **Barton Hills**, the northernmost tip of the Chilterns near Barton-le-Clay is recommended. This is the largest and most important grass chalkland area in the county, now a national reserve and managed by the Nature Conservancy Council. The views are spectacular and the footpath follows the ancient Icknield Way.

Accommodation

First Class

Swan Hotel, High Street, Leighton Buzzard LU7 7EA (Tel 0525 372148). Beautifully-appointed Georgian hotel with high standard of service. Good restaurant and very helpful staff.

Old Palace Lodge, Church Street, Dunstable (Tel 0582 662201). Lovely period building thoughtfully furnished. Good restaurant offering a wide range of English-style dishes.

Middle Range

The Bell Inn, 34–35 Bedford Street, Woburn MK17 9QD (Tel 0525 290280). Delightful Georgian hotel (some parts Elizabethan) close to Woburn Abbey.

Cock Horse Hotel, Woburn Road, Heath and Reach, near Leighton Buzzard (Tel 052523 7816). Good value, small character hotel in excellent location.

Economy

Town Farm, Milton Bryan, near Woburn (Tel 0525 210001). Surrounded by open countryside, this farm has been run by the same family for over forty years. Good value bed and breakfast.

Spinney House, 15 Horton Road, Slapton, near Leighton Buzzard (Tel 0525 221905). Friendly family run bed and breakfast.

Eating Out

First Class

As with North Bedfordshire, the area boasts few restaurants of note.

Middle Range

Leaside, 72 New Bedford Road, Luton (Tel 0582 417643). English cuisine served in relaxed and comfortable surroundings.

Norman King, Church Street, Dunstable (Tel 0582 61603). À la carte menu offering a good range of quality meals.

Economy

The Harrow Inn, 85 Hitchin Road, Luton (Tel 0582 24284). Good value home cooking.

Stable Yard Craft Gallery and Tea-Room, Mentmore, near Leighton Buzzard (Tel 0296 668660). Converted stable block housing attractive tea-room and craft shop. Wide choice of home cooked food in traditional country surroundings.

Hertfordshire

Although one of the most compact county shires, Hertfordshire's population has increased dramatically, partly due to the creation of Britain's first two garden cities, Welwyn and Letchworth, and more recently the new towns like Hemel Hempstead, Hatfield and Stevenage. There is plenty to see in the surrounding countryside, and the county has something to offer everyone.

St Albans

One of the most important Roman cities in Britain, named after Alban, a Roman soldier who was beheaded in 209 for his Christian beliefs and became Britain's first martyr. The Saxons built an abbey in his memory and it was later rebuilt and enlarged by the Normans in the 13th century. The **Cathedral** as it is seen today was built around the Norman abbey and is constructed largely of stone from the old Roman remains. The only English Pope, Nicholas Breakspear, was educated at the **Abbey School**. The abbey achieved cathedral status in 1877 and is now the only church in the world that is an abbey, a cathedral and a parish church in daily use.

Close to the abbey in the High Street stands the five-storey **Clock Tower** dating back to 1402. There are fine views from the top and the 19th-century clockworks can be seen. The **Museum of St Albans** is worth a visit. Look out for the large collection of trade and craft tools. The **Verulamium Museum** exhibits evidence of everyday life, work and death through four centuries of Roman occupation, and this should be combined with a visit to the **Verulamium Roman Theatre**, the only completely exposed Roman theatre in Britain.

Much of the city centre has been improved with the development of pedestrian shopping areas and the removal of the loathed one-way traffic system. With London just 20 miles (32 km.) away, St Albans suffers from a heavy tourist influx, but as many of the attractions are spread over a wide area, this seems more bearable than in other honeypot cities.

The **Herts and Middlesex Wildlife Trust** is based in Grebe House, St Michael's Street, and provides information on local countryside and wildlife issues (Tel 0727 58901). **Tourist Information** is in the Town Hall on Market Place (Tel 0727 64511).

Just nine miles (14.5 km.) north-east of St Albans is the village of **Ayot St Lawrence**. The Irish dramatist, critic and essayist George Bernard Shaw lived here at Shaw's Corner (National Trust), until his death in 1950. The house remains unchanged, right down to his desk and the summerhouse where he used to write, and even his hats in the hall (Tel 0438 820307).

In **Chiswell**, south of St Albans, are the **Gardens of the Royal National Rose Society** which contain over 30,000 roses displayed in twelve acres (4.8 hectares), making it one of the most important collections of roses in the world.

Six miles (9.6 km.) east is **Hatfield House**. This Jacobean house, which stands in its own great park, has been the home of the Cecil family since 1611. The state-rooms are rich in world-famous paintings and fine furniture. Within the gardens stands the surviving wing of the Royal Palace of Hatfield (1497), where Elizabeth I spent much of her girlhood and held her first Council of State in November 1558. Some of her personal effects can be seen in the house. This is a very popular and somewhat commercialised heritage attraction that is often combined with a mock Elizabethan Banquet in the Old Palace. Spring or autumn visits are best.

Rest of Hertfordshire

To the west of the county, north of Berkhamsted, lies the **Ashridge Estate** (National Trust) covering some 4000 acres (1620 hectares) of unspoiled open spaces, commons and woodland. This runs along the main ridge of the Chiltern Hills from Ivinghoe to Berkhamsted. Wildlife is well represented in the area; some 300 fallow and muntjac deer roam freely, along with foxes, badgers and squirrels. Unique to the area is the glis glis, or edible dormouse.

To the east is the pleasant county town of **Hertford**. The town dates back to Saxon times when it was founded on a ford across the River Lee, which formed a boundary between Saxon and Viking England. The twenty-eight-mile (45 km.) **Lee Navigation Canal** runs from here through some of the loveliest parts of the Lee Valley (boats for hire from Broxbourne Boat Centre, Tel 0992 462085). Fishing from the towpath is popular with anglers. Hertford is a paradise for antique lovers and bargain hunters, and **St Andrews Street** is virtually full of antique shops. Look out for the **Old Vergers House**, dating from 1450. The **Friends Meeting House** in Railway Street is the oldest surviving, purpose-built Quaker meeting house in the world, in continuous use since its erection in 1670. **Hertford Castle** is now occupied by the East Herts District Council and is also the location of **Tourist Information** (Tel 0992 655261) for the area.

East of Hertford are the busy market towns of **Ware** and **Bishop's Stortford**. This stretch of the Lee is a special attraction with its many narrow-boats and towpath walks. An unusual excursion in Ware is to **Scott's Grotto**, adjoining 28 Scotts Road. This remarkable folly of underground passages and chambers was created by Quaker poet John Scott over a period of thirty years and completed in 1773. No one knows why Scott had the Grotto constructed but it became a fashionable meeting place for London society on weekend excursions. Admission is free but as the Grotto is not lit, you must bring a torch. Contact Hertford Castle for more information, or Mrs Watson in Ware (Tel 0920 4131).

Just south is **Rye House Marsh Bird Reserve** at Hoddesdon. This is an excellent marshland reserve owned and maintained by the RSPB and well worth a visit.

If you want to go **cycling** in the Hertford area, contact Highway Cycles at 1 New Road, Ware (Tel 0902 61488). Alternatively, **riding** is offered from Petasfield Stables, Hangrove Road, Hertford (Tel 0992 587989).

Accommodation

First Class

St Michael's Manor, Fishpool Street, St Albans (Tel 0727 64444). Beautifully refurbished manor house set in five acres (2 hectares) with a private lake.

The White Horse, Hertingfordbury, Hertford (Tel 0992 586791). Character hotel with warm atmosphere. Attractive conservatory restaurant.

Middle Range

Sopwell House, Cottonmill Lane, Sopwell, St Albans (Tel 0727 44741). Georgian country house set in twelve acres (4.8 hectares) of parkland. Some rooms have four-poster beds.

The Salisbury Arms, Fore Street, Hertford (Tel 0992 583091). Attractive medium-sized period hotel in town centre.

Economy

Beechwood Home Farm, Roe End Lane, near St Albans (Tel 0582 840209). Bed and breakfast in a secluded setting amongst privately owned woodland, complete with stables, piggery, carpenter's dairy and cheeseroom.

Chequers, Nasty, Great Munden, Ware (Tel 092084 280). Peaceful rural retreat offering bed and breakfast.

Eating Out

First Class

Diomides, 97 St Peter's Street, St Albans (Tel 0727 33330). À la carte and set menu in a friendly atmosphere.

The Clock House, 251 East Barnet Road, East Barnet Village (Tel 081 449 6010). Popular restaurant serving traditional English (and some vegetarian) dishes. À la carte and set menus available.

Middle Range

Rose and Crown, St Michael's Street, St Albans (Tel 0727 51903). Excellent home-cooking and wide vegetarian selection.

The Crown and Falcon Inn, Puckeridge, near Ware (Tel 0920 821561). Historic 15th-century coaching inn where Samuel Pepys resided in 1662. Good restaurant with reasonably priced food.

Economy

Brocket Arms, Ayot St Lawrence, near St Albans (Tel 0438 820250). Snacks, light lunches and à la carte evening meals.

Sunflowers, 7 Amwell End, Ware (Tel 0920 3358). Pleasant restaurant serving superb, generously-portioned wholefood and vegetarian dishes produced from organic produce.

14 London

London is without doubt one of the world's great cities. The capital of Britain, it is also the country's political and economic centre, and arguably one of the most significant cultural meccas in Europe. The world's first megalopolis, it is still within the top ten largest cities, covering an area of 620 square miles (1605.8 sq. km.) and housing – in one form or another – a population of around 7 million: roughly 6,735,000 in Greater London and 5300 in the City of London.

Daniel Defoe described London in the 18th century as being 'stretched out in buildings, straggling, confused . . . out of all shape, uncompact and unequal; neither long nor broad, round or square.' Two hundred years later the description still fits, and visitors will soon realise that, were it not for the convenience of the Underground railway system, finding your way around this city would be a confusing and disorientating experience. Even as it is, it is possible to spend a week here riding the 'tube' between stations and districts, and still have little idea of the overall structure of the city's layout.

The answer lies in viewing London as it really is: as a mass conurbation encompassing a wide variety of towns and villages, rather than as a single entity. The name 'London' originally applied to the area now known as 'the City', the main business district which opens its doors to around 350,000 commuters every day. Districts such as Chelsea, Battersea and Westminster all evolved separately from the city itself, but have now been absorbed into its bulk, yet without having lost their original character. Visitors are likely to spend much of their time exploring north London, or at least, the area north of the River Thames, for the city as a whole is divided by England's primary river. The south bank is mainly an area of industry and commerce, although there are some attractions here worthy of note.

Londoners themselves are a mixed and diversified group of people, on the whole friendly although not always as welcoming as might perhaps be wished (try catching the tube during rush hour and you'll soon adopt the 'every man for himself' policy). The city has seen such massive immigration in the last fifty years that people of all creeds and colours have now become an integral part of London life. Those who arrived after the Second World War have raised families and grandchildren, and these new generations, regardless of origins, consider themselves Londoners. The cultural benefits that such a marriage of races has brought are immense, but there remains the problem of housing, more acute today than ever before, with thousands of homeless youngsters wandering the streets, living in the infamous 'Cardboard City', and scraping together whatever living they can in whatever way possible.

Contrasting sharply with this is the London of the high-fliers: the socialites, aristocracy and politicians. In the residential areas of Belgravia and Knightsbridge elegant buildings grace tree-lined streets and gardens, Bentleys and Porsches are two-a-penny, and life is fairly rosy.

Such are the two faces of London. Both offer something of interest to the visitor and, indeed, any visitor who leaves without experiencing something of each has not really seen the city.

History

London's first settlement was founded after the Romans invaded England in AD 43. Having landed in Kent, their progress was temporarily thwarted by the River Thames, but this was overcome by the construction of a bridge at the river's narrowest point, roughly sixty feet (twenty metres) from today's London Bridge. A site of primarily military importance was established, but trading rapidly developed and 'Londinium' became the commercial and military centre of Roman England.

After the Romans left, London lost its significance until it was reoccupied by King Alfred in 886. The city grew throughout the Middle Ages, while merchants thrived and the population expanded outside the city wall. The docks spread to the east of the city, and the aristocracy and legal and ecclesiastical settlements developed out into the west. Movement to the west escalated when Edward the Confessor rebuilt Westminster Abbey in 1050, laying the foundations for London's other city, the 'City of Westminster'. When Henry VIII was crowned in 1509, the population had reached 50,000. During the 16th century this number continued to grow and, combined with booming trade, enclosures and the dissolution of the monasteries, the city expanded rapidly. By 1600 the population stood at 220,000.

Further expansion during the 17th century was checked only by the Great Plague in 1666, followed in the same year by the famous London fire ('London's burning, London's burning') which razed 436 acres (176 hectares). Due to the subsequent urgency for housing, ambitious planning schemes proposed by Sir Christopher Wren were turned down, and the city was rebuilt largely on the existing medieval layout.

William III moved away from both the City and Westminster to Greenwich and to Henry VIII's old palace at Hampton Court. Ever since, the area between these two landmarks has been slowly filled, particularly during Georgian times when property speculation was at a peak. This was when the first of the London squares (houses around an open garden space) were laid out and many villages were incorporated into the city as a whole.

By 1801 London's population had increased to 969,000, and with the industrial growth of the Victorian era the town mushroomed. Sanitation had not been substantially improved and epidemics of cholera and typhoid broke out frequently. London became increasingly overcrowded and unhealthy, and segregation between rich and poor more marked. At the same time railway and Underground facilities enabled people to move outwards, instigating the start of the new suburbs which have continued to grow throughout this century.

The Second World War further changed the face of London, claiming the lives of 20,000 citizens and wiping out huge areas of the city, particularly in the East End. In the aftermath, rehousing and rebuilding were a main priority of post-war policy, leading to the development of housing blocks and slum clearances in the 1950s and 1960s, with much of the population being relocated to new towns. Today the idiosyncratic nature of this development has become apparent and, as in other major Western cities, problems have arisen due to urban decay and racial tension, and have been aggravated by economic conditions.

Urban rejuvenation has occurred in some areas, although controversy has arisen over a number of cases. Redevelopment of the dockland area for example, carried out under the auspices of the London Dockland Development Corporation, has encountered firm opposition from local people and authorities. New movements in all fields of day-to-day living are continually arising however, and the combination of modern and old has led to an exciting heterogeneity.

Geography

Divided by the River Thames running from west to east, London is built on an alluvial basin of sandy gravel and dark brown or grey clay ('London Clay') and surrounded by hills to the north and south. After 1965 and recognition of the city's rapidly expanding boundaries, London came under the administration of the newly-formed Greater London Council (GLC), which administered the area created at that time which is still known as 'Greater London'. From Charing Cross, the official centre, Greater London reaches for almost 20 miles (32 km.) in every direction, and is composed of 33 boroughs, also created in 1965 from the previous pattern. The Greater London Council no longer exists however, and administration falls to the borough councils.

Confusion for the visitor is likely to arise over London names, since many of the previous district names are still in use, even though each separate area has been incorporated into a new borough. Thus Hampstead has retained its name, even though it is now part of the borough of Camden. Most visitors are unlikely to reach further than the centre of the city and the boroughs immediately surrounding it. North of the Thames these are 'the City' (of London), Westminster, Camden, Kensington & Chelsea (one borough), and Hammersmith & Fulham (one borough), and south of the Thames, Lambeth and Southwark. Virtually all the city's most famous sights and sounds are to be found in these areas, although if in any doubt, the easiest way to clarify a location is simply by referring to the Underground stations. These frequently provide a clearer indication of where to find a specific attraction, although they are of little use in distinguishing boroughs. Most tourist literature lists the nearest tube stations to wherever you want to go, and a London A-Z street atlas, available from bookshops and news stands can also help.

The city boasts an incredible 3500 acres (1417.5 hectares) of heath and common (of which Londoners are very proud), as well as enjoying the benefits of an official 'green belt' area surrounding the capital, much of which is open to the public. In Inner London, most of the open space is comprised of public parks, and in the City alone there are 190 gardens. Urban fauna and flora are easily found in places such as Kensington Gardens and Hampstead Heath, while boating and other water sports are available in Hyde Park. London cemeteries also contain a significant proportion of the city's wildlife, and foxes, squirrels and mice are not unknown in many areas.

Large areas of open parkland are found at Hampstead Heath, Putney Heath, Greenwich Park, Blackheath and Battersea Park. In addition there are woodlands such as Crystal Palace and Burgess Park in the south, and Epping Forest (once a royal hunting lodge) in the east. More centrally, Victoria Park in Bow is the oldest municipal park; Lea Valley has been recently developed as recreational land, and Hackney Marshes provide an interesting wetland habitat. Some boroughs however, are sadly lacking in public space, notably Newham, Islington and Lambeth.

The Royal Botanical Gardens are found at Kew in the west, and also in this direction are Syon, Queens, Osterley and Ham Parks. Outwards from Richmond Deer Park are Hampton Court Park and Bushey Park. In the north there are Alexandra Palace, Harow-on-the-Hill, Barn Hill Waterlow, Wanstead Flats and Finsbury Park, as well as more natural wildlife areas at Kenwood, Highgate Wood and Hampstead Heath. Walthamstow has areas of wetland. Smaller nature areas and centres can be found at High Elms, Bromley and Snuff Mill and Merton. Camley Street Natural Park and Holland Park are more central.

In the green belt there are country parks at Romford, Epping Forest, Brent, Redbridge, Hillingdon, Norwood and Coulsdon Common. At the same time it should be noted that there are also areas in the green belt under threat from developers, notably in Bromley, Beckenham and Enfield. Most London boroughs however, have a commitment to safeguard open urban spaces and wildlife areas.

Climate

London's climate is basically moderate and the natural cycle of seasons can go past with little effect. The warmest months are usually July and August, when the average temperature is around 17°C (61°F); the coldest are January and February with an average of 5.5°C (41°F). Warm days during the summer see hordes of Londoners stripping off and heading for the nearest park or garden, and this can be a pleasant time for visitors to explore the streets. On the rare occasions when the temperature reaches the mid-20°C (70–80°F) however, threading your way around buildings and shops can be particularly fatiguing and sights and attractions tend to be very busy.

August, September and November are the capital's wettest months, while February and March are driest. Visiting London at the beginning of the year can be rewarding as visitor numbers are relatively low and the climate, although slightly cold, is often sunny and suited to walking and being outdoors. Generally there is little snow during the winter months, although recent years have seen more in the south of England than in Scotland. Even when there is snow it rarely lies for any length of time, and only after prolonged periods of continual snow does it impede exploration of the city. In such cases, it has to be said, the consequences can be serious, with rail and bus services running on a limited basis, if at all, and travel in general becoming virtually impossible.

Attractions

London's diversity is its greatest attribute. The city really does offer something for everyone, and there are few who will be pushed to find something of interest to occupy them for a week at least. Significantly, it is this reputation which has spread throughout the world and which attracts millions of visitors each year. No tourist comes to London specifically to see a single feature, and any visitor will soon realise the immense wealth of history and culture that the city boasts.

Attractions range from small and seemingly inconsequential aspects of everyday life, such as red doubledecker buses, to magnificent and enduring tributes to the city's past, such as St Paul's Cathedral. On a less tangible level, entertainment in London is amongst the best in the world, with high-tech cinemas showing the latest releases, theatres producing the newest and best musicals and plays (not to mention the oldest), and music venues offering everything from the most outrageous sounds of the day to the harmonies of Beethoven and Brahms.

For shoppers, the windows of Bond Street and Regent Street host some of the most fashionable names in the designer world, while Covent Garden, Kensington High Street and Camden Market offer goods of a less serious nature, although not always at less serious prices.

And for something completely different . . . museums, galleries and exhibitions of anything that's exhibitable (even a pile of bricks at the Tate Gallery) are all on offer, not to mention historic buildings and bequeathed collections scattered throughout the city. London has both the modern and the old, the punks and the beefeaters, Buckingham Palace and the Lloyds Building. The city's many facets are intriguing, disturbing, astounding and surprising; their interest is undeniable and their value priceless.

Cuisine

When it comes to cuisine, any attempt to identify London specialities will inevitably fall short of the mark. With the huge influx of foreigners into the city over the past forty years, there has been a massive increase in the number of restaurants serving food from all over the world. Spanning all budgets and offering every conceivable atmosphere, the choice is phenomenal.

European food is well represented, particularly Italian, French, Spanish and Greek. All are served in establishments ranging from cheap, lively places, such as pizza and pasta joints, bistros and tapas bars, to more intimate and exclusive hide-aways offering haute cuisine. In addition there are a number of restaurants from Eastern European countries, especially Poland.

London reputedly has some of the best Indian restaurants in the world outside India itself. These are mainly from Bangladesh, Bengal, Punjab and Kashmir. The main concentration of Indian restaurants is in the West End, although there are also clusters in Westbourne Grove and around Spitalfields, Limehouse and Southall. There are huge numbers of Chinese restaurants of varying quality, most of which serve Cantonese cuisine. China Town in Soho is the main area. Japanese restaurants are growing in number, but still tend to be expensive. South-East Asian cuisine is popular, particularly Indonesian, Thai and Malaysian. African and Caribbean food of excellent quality is available in Brixton and Stroud Green, while North American restaurants are prolific throughout the city. Mexican food is available from a comparatively small number of places.

British restaurants have undergone a revival in the last ten years. The success of 'New English Food' has been encouraged by a number of innovative chefs. Traditional London food served at pie, eel and mash shops can be found in east and north-east London. Some of the best British teas can be sampled at traditional London hotels, while the store Fortnum and Mason and the Cafe Royal both offer magnificent spreads.

Level of Tourism

Tourism to Britain from abroad is largely concentrated on London (9.7 million overseas visitors in 1990), and the city receives a total of 21.4 million tourists each year. It is the No. 1 'long weekend' destination for the British themselves and is therefore busy throughout the year. London has a long history of tourism, and its development has been gradual, with locals increasingly responding to demand. The Greater London Council had no overall tourism policy, but since administration has been handed over to the boroughs, some action has been taken. Westminster and Kensington & Chelsea, which have the most hotels and largest number of tourist attractions in the city, have developed local pro-housing policies, 'safeguarding character and amenities of residents', and curtailing attempts to build new hotels and convert housing.

In 1990 a Tourism Strategy for London – a three-year action plan – was drawn up in preparation for the single European market and the Channel Tunnel. It aims to promote economic growth, create employment and generate income from tourism, and requests that the London Tourist Board, in conjunction with local authorities, identifies sites for development. The strategy intends to minimise the effects of visitor pressure on those who live and work in London, and proposes to contribute to environmental improvement and increase the range of amenities for London residents. The LTB has pinpointed problem areas in communications, congestion, and pressure on the most popular sites. In 1990 the LTB and Tidy Up Britain Campaign drew up an environmental charter, 'London Against Litter', although much evidence of this is yet to be seen.

The huge number of tourists London receives causes problems in honeypot areas. Westminster Abbey is the second most visited site (after the British Museum), with 3.25 million visitors in 1990. As well as the noise and disruption caused by so many people, physical damage is also a major problem. Most visitors enter by the West Door with the result that this area in particular, and especially where queues form, has become seriously worn. The 13th-century Cosmati pavement in front of the high altar is now starting to disintegrate, and structural damage has been sustained by many of the abbey's monuments, largely due to the theft of small pieces of statuary, heraldic shields and crowns. In response, protective floor coverings have been laid in areas of severe stress and barriers have been installed in front of some of the most important artefacts, but an overall solution has still to be found. Similar problems are experienced in St Paul's Cathedral, where one inch of stone is removed each year due to the sheer weight of the number of visitors, and in the Tower of London, which is filled to capacity during the summer season with a portion of its 2.2 million annual visitors.

Museums and galleries are also sites of concentrated numbers. An average 3.4 million people visit the National Gallery each year, while the Tate, with 1.2 million, is still amongst the top ten sites in London. The Victoria and Albert Museum received 996,000 visitors in 1990; the Natural History Museum 1.3 million, and the Science Museum 1.2 million. All three have introduced entrance fees in an effort to generate further revenue, and visitor numbers have dropped.

The problems facing attractions such as these extend beyond the immediate dilemma posed by tourists (and tourism) themselves, to a question of basic funding. The decline in public subsidies to support museums, the introduction of entrance fees, staff redundancies and trustee influence in exhibitions and advertising have all received considerable media coverage. At the end of the day it has become clear that these institutions are largely expected to pay for themselves, thus aggravating more than ever the conflict between the need to keep visitor numbers high and the necessity of conservation and preservation.

As far as resident opinion goes, 87 per cent of Londoners take pleasure from the fact that their city is attractive to outsiders, although 25 per cent would like to see a reduction in the number of summer visitors (only 4 per cent feel this at other times). Of perceived problems, more than 50 per cent believe that tourists increase the cost of living and 20 per cent feel that tourism is a major cause of petty crime. The biggest complaint is traffic, and roughly half the population of London claim that tourist coaches congest the streets and make it more difficult to get around.

Good Alternatives

Meeting People

Getting to know Londoners and meeting local people should, in theory at least, be easy. But in a city so large, the inevitable problem of anonymity can sometimes be hard to overcome. Londoners themselves would be the first to admit that they could travel on the 'tube' with the same person every day for fifty years and never know it, let alone strike up a conversation. For visitors with a genuine interest in London people therefore, it is not always a matter of simply addressing a casual remark to the person nearest to you and letting things develop from there. A concerted effort may well have to be made to find the right place and time if progress is to be made. Festivals are usually a good starting point. At least you'll know that everyone else attending a certain event has similar interests. The **Proms**, one of the world's greatest classical music festivals, are also one of the most sociable events of the year on the music-buff's calendar. They usually take place from around 20 July until 15 September and the lively 'Last Night of the Proms' is one of the greatest shows of British nationalism that you're likely to experience. Having said that, obtaining tickets for the Last Night is virtually impossible, unless you're lucky enough to know someone with the right connections.

A slightly more unusual gathering takes place on Ascension Day (usually in May) between All-Hallows-by-the-Tower and St

Dunstan's, Idle Lane. **Beating the Bounds**, as it is known, is carried out by the boys of St Dunstan's School, thus continuing the old tradition of marking out parish boundaries (something akin to the Common Riding tradition of the Scottish Borders, but no longer on horseback). The proceedings start at 3 p.m. from the Tower of London.

Trooping the Colour, perhaps the world's finest military ceremony, takes place each June (check with Tourist Information for the date) to mark the Queen's official birthday (her real one is in April). The royal procession to the parade makes a wonderful spectacle, leaving from Buckingham Palace at 10.40 a.m. and heading down the Mall towards Horse Guards Parade. The best views are enjoyed by those who have tickets, obtainable for around £8.00 from The Brigade Major (Trooping the Colour), Household Division, Horse Guards, London. To stand the best chance of getting tickets, write before the middle of January. If that fails, try and grab standing room on the actual day.

Mixing with the 'real' Londoners is what's on offer at the **Costermongers' Pearly Harvest Festival**. Pearly Kings and Queens, representing the costermongers (the men and women of London who run street-side fruit and vegetable stalls) gather at St Martin-in-the-Fields, Trafalgar Square for a day of glittering 'pearly' costume and cockney rhyming slang (a language of its own; for example, 'pork pies' means 'lies'). This is an event which really does need to be experienced to be appreciated. It usually takes place around the beginning of October; check with Tourist Information for details.

The **London to Brighton Veteran Car Run** is a delight for anyone, whether interested in cars or not. The date is usually the first Sunday in November (check with Tourist Information), when vintage cars (only cars which were built before 1905 can take part) and their owners/drivers gather at Serpentine Road (Hyde Park) before setting off on a sedate drive to Brighton. The occasion commemorates the abolition of the act which stipulated that cars must be proceeded by a runner with a red flag at a maximum speed of 2 miles per hour.

There are many other festivals which take place in London throughout the year, and the chances are that there will be something on whenever you visit. Check with Tourist Information for details of other festivals.

London pubs are also a good place for meeting people. Most City pubs tend to be frequented by businessmen during the day and a less 'approachable' crowd in the evening. **Covent Garden** is always a good place to try, although, it has to be said, not the cheapest place to while away a few hours drinking. The **Flask Tavern**, 77

Highgate West Hill (Archway tube) is popular, especially on summer evenings, while the **Admiral Codrington**, 17 Mossop Street (South Kensington tube) caters for a lively younger crowd and offers over 100 different whiskies. The **Sherlock Holmes**, 10 Northumberland Street (Charing Cross) is filled with Sherlock memorabilia and, while always popular with visitors, also has a loyal local clientele. If your sights are set on intrigue and daring, then try **Saint Stephen's**, 10 Bridge Street (Westminster tube), which is frequented by Members of Parliament nipping out to wake themselves up in between sessions!

Finally, get to know London's parks and you may well end up getting acquainted with London people. During the winter this obviously isn't such a good idea, but in the summer the parks are usually full, especially on Sundays. Many parks also have bandstands where brass bands give free concerts, as well as hosting 'street-theatre' events and providing a refuge for buskers 'moved on' from the tube stations.

Discovering Places

Straying from standard tourist routes can be one of the most rewarding, not to mention environmentally sound ways of finding places not spoiled by large numbers of people. In London there are plenty of possibilities, if you know where to look.

The city has a wealth of ecclesiastical buildings, many of which, like St Ethelbergas in Bishopsgate, built in 1430, provide satisfying alternatives to the usual examples quoted in all the guidebooks. Equally so, there are considerable numbers of historic buildings largely overlooked by the public. Marlborough House in Pall Mall was designed by Sir Christopher Wren and can be visited by prior arrangement (contact the Tourist Board), while Leighton House in Holland Park is run by the Victorian Society (11 a.m. – 5 p.m. Monday–Friday). Fenton House in Hampstead was built in 1693 and is now run by the National Trust (open weekends).

Special-interest museums abound throughout the city and many boroughs have their own local history museums. There are also alternative art galleries, especially around Cork Street near Piccadilly, and Portobello Road in Notting Hill. In Kensington Gardens there is the Serpentine Gallery which exhibits contemporary art.

One of London's more surprising features is the number of city farms which are in existence. Regarding themselves as 'open-air social clubs', London's eighteen farms provide an entertaining morning or day out, as well as being of immense educational value. Most are located on areas of wasteland which would otherwise be derelict, and depend heavily on financial support from local and visiting people in order to survive. Differences in organisation, funding and administration mean that each has its own identity, but all have the same basic aim: the development of vacant land for the use of the local community. Events are organised when possible, particularly during spring and summer, and take the form of anything from a small jumble sale to the larger annual sheep and wool fair. Goods on sale at the farms include eggs, cheese, goat's milk, fleeces, honey, compost, pot and bedding plants, shrubs, herbs and animal feed. Further information is available from the National Federation of City Farms (see page 586).

Finally, mention should be given specifically to West London. Since June 1990 the London Tourist Board has been actively promoting this part of the city as a tourist destination, notably through its 'Welcoming West London' roadshow which has been on display at selected Tourist Information Centres in Britain and France. Sources of funding for this promotion have included the EEC, as well as the six boroughs within the area: Brent, Ealing, Hammersmith & Fulham, Harrow, Hillingdon and Hounslow. West London has a wealth of historic houses, open countryside and a wide range of entertainment and events, yet is often overlooked by tourists who are either anxious to get into town from Heathrow, or who enter the city from a different direction. The area is only forty minutes by tube or rail from the centre of town and is an ideal alternative for anyone keen to continue their exploration of the city, but wishing to leave behind the crowds of the city centre.

Communications

How to Get There

AIR: London has two major and two minor airports. Most international flights come into either **Gatwick** (Tel 0293 535353) or **Heathrow** (Tel 081 759 4321). Getting into town from Gatwick (and vice versa) is easily done on the Gatwick Express, a special train service which runs frequently to Victoria Station and takes only half an hour, while the most convenient transport from Heathrow is the tube, Piccadilly Line, which takes roughly one hour from the centre of town and stops at all airport terminals. Alternatively, coach services are available from/to either airport to/from Victoria Coach Station.

London City Airport (Tel 071 474 5555) and **Stansted Airport** (Tel 0279 502380) operate mainly intra-European flights and have rail or bus connections into town.

RAIL: Almost all rail lines in Britain eventually converge in London, and travelling by train to the capital is straightforward. If travelling either to or from the north, a recent survey carried out by a television travel programme concluded that train travel was the most economical means of reaching Scotland from London. In terms of finance, time and environmental impact, the four and a half hour train journey between the centre of London and the centre of Edinburgh will do less damage to the combined factors of your wallet, schedule and surroundings than any other means of transport. Similarly, with the completion of the Channel Tunnel, travelling to London by train from Europe is an alternative to flying that should be given serious consideration.

London's mainline stations are **Paddington** (for the West); **Victoria** (for the South-east); **Waterloo** (for the South-west); **Euston** (for the Midlands), and **King's Cross** (for the North and Scotland). Information for all services can be obtained from King's Cross: for the North (Tel 071 278 2477); the South (Tel 071 928 5100); the West (Tel 071 262 6767), and the Midlands (Tel 071 387 7070).

COACH: All coaches to London arrive at **Victoria Coach Station**, a few minutes' walk from Victoria Railway Station and the tube (if you're carrying heavy bags it's worth taking a taxi). For Information on coach times and routes contact **National Express** (Tel 071 730 0202).

When You're There

RAIL: The tube (Underground) is easy to follow on colour coded maps. If possible, avoid early morning (8–10) and mid-afternoon (4–6) which are the rush hours, when the transport infrastructure is already overstretched and passengers are literally squashed in like sardines. Prices vary according to a 'zone' system, marked on maps actually on the tubes. The cheapest rate in central London is currently 80 pence. Day, week and season tickets are available (interchangeable with buses) and usually work out cheaper. Explorer tickets are designed for off-peak travel for visitors. Prices are due to rise again and services to be cut as London Transport continues to run at a loss. Late at night it is not advisable for women to travel alone as the number of attacks has risen. According to a report by *Time Out* magazine, the most dangerous lines are the western end of the Metropolitan Line; southern section of the Northern Line, and at Oxford Circus and Baker Street where many people have to change trains. The worst time is between 10.30 and 11.00 p.m.

BUS: Using the existing transport infrastructure is the Good Tourist option, but in London this can also be problematic. The top deck of a London bus is one of the best ways to see the city, but if you're in a hurry go by tube – the average speed of traffic in London is 11 miles (17.7 km.) per hour. Buses come into their own late at night however, as they continue to run after the tube has closed (all late-night buses go through Trafalgar Square). Route maps are available from **London Transport** at Victoria and King's Cross train stations and Piccadilly tube, and from Tourist Information offices. A twenty-four hour information line is available on 071 222 1234.

CAR: As the public transport system has become increasingly underfunded and overcrowded, more people have taken to their cars. Far from helping communications in London, this has exacerbated the problem even further. Traffic jams are now an integral part of everyday life and congestion is no longer solely confined to the rush hours; hold-ups occur frequently throughout the day. This has led to a rise in pollution levels (especially during the recent hot summers), which is harming the city and residents alike. Driving is therefore not a recommended option in London and, indeed, should be avoided at all costs if you're on holiday and trying to get away from stressful situations.

BOAT: Water transport is an excellent option during the daytime. **River buses** run from Charing Cross to Docklands, Greenwich, the Tower and Chelsea Harbour from 10.30 a.m. to 4.30 p.m. (Tel 071 512 0555). River trips also run from Westminster Pier to Greenwich, Hampton, Kew, Putney and Richmond (Tel 071 730 4812). Trips along the Grand Union Canal are available from Little Venice; contact **Jason's Trips** (Tel 071 286 3428) and **The Water Bus Company** (Tel 071 482 2550).

CYCLING: Cycling can be a good way to explore off-the-beaten-track areas, but is unhealthy and dangerous wherever there is more traffic. Bikes can be hired from **Rent-a-Bike** at Kensington Student Centre (Tel 071 937 6089); **On Yer Bike**, 52–54 Tooley Street in Southwark (Tel 071 278 5555); **Cycle Logical**, 136 New Cavendish Street (Tel 071 631 5060); and **Riders**, 481 Hornsey Road (Tel 071 263 56091). The **London Cycling Campaign** is based at 3 Stamford Street (Tel 071 928 7220). They produce a book of cycle routes in London, *On Yer Bike*.

WALKING: If you have time, the best way to see London is undoubtedly on foot. Walking tours are an excellent way to combine sightseeing with an educational experience. The **City Corporation** has laid down two heritage walks shown by studs in the pavement. One is around Bank, Leadenhall and Monument, while the other includes St Paul's, Barbican and Guildhall. Both take around an hour.

Specialised tours covering Dickens, Sherlock Holmes, Royalty, and theatres, as well as more general area tours are offered by **Discovering London** (contact Alex and Peggy Cobban, Tel 0277 213704); **London Walks** (Tel 071 435 6413); **Historical Tours** (Tel 071 668 4019); **Exciting Walks** (Tel 071 624 9981); and **Citysights** (Tel 071 739 2372). Individual tours are offered by **Can Be Done** (Tel 071 907 2400), while **Regent's Canal Walks** are arranged by the Inland Waterways Association (Tel 071 586 2510).

Useful Local Contacts

Contact with some of London's many ecologically-sympathetic groups will bring visitors into touch with projects and people involved with preserving London's heritage. The **London Society** (The City University, Northampton Square EC1, Tel 071 251 1590) aims to promote knowledge of London by arranging lectures and visits. The **London Appreciation Society** (17 Manson Mews SW7) also arranges visits, as does the **London Archaeological Society** (28 Rothesay Avenue SW20). **London Ecology Centre** (45 Shelton Street, Covent Garden WC2H 9HJ, Tel 071 379 4324) has an information centre and cafe, and is run by the London Ecology Centre Trust, a registered charity and limited company. Also at 45 Shelton Street are the **Council for Environmental Education** (Tel 071 240 4936) and **Council for National Parks** (Tel 071 240 3603). The centre has another branch at 80 York Way, King's Cross (Tel 071 278 4736), where you can also find **British Trust for Conservation Volunteers – London Region** (Tel 071 278 4293); **Council for Environmental Conservation** (Tel 071 837 5399); and **London Wildlife Trust** (Tel 071 278 6612/3).

Geographical Breakdown of Region

West End

Westminster

The tourist route par excellence runs from **Westminster**, along **Whitehall**, **Trafalgar Square**, ending at **Covent Garden** for food and a well-deserved rest. In Westminster, for a glimpse of the UK's political system in action, the **Houses of Parliament** can be visited by way of the **Stranger's Gallery** (open from 2.30 p.m. Mon–Fri); overseas visitors need a card of introduction from their embassy, British citizens should apply to their MPs. **Westminster Abbey** is the most visited ecclesiastical building in London (open 8 a.m.–6 p.m., 7.45 p.m. on Wednesdays). It is often less overcrowded on Wednesday evening. Beside it is the small church of **St Margaret's**, the parish church of the House of Commons. Less visited is **Westminster Catholic Cathedral**, a late Victorian building based on a Byzantine style (open 7 a.m.–8 p.m., daily), at the far end of Victoria Street.

Along Whitehall are many of the government offices. The Treasury and the Foreign Office are on the left when approaching from Westminster. Churchill's underground **Cabinet War Rooms** are open to the public daily. **Downing Street**, where the Prime Minister lives at number 10, is on the left. The Ministry of Defence is on the right, as is Whitehall Palace, and the **Banqueting Hall** which, designed by Inigo Jones, contains a magnificent ceiling by Rubens (open 10 a.m.–5 p.m. Tue–Sat; 2 p.m.–5 p.m. on Sunday). **Horse Guards Parade** is where the Changing of the Guard can be seen daily at 11 a.m. (10 a.m. on Sundays during the summer). Admiralty Arch looks down the Mall to Buckingham Palace, with St James's Park in front. On the right of the Mall is the **Institute of Contemporary Arts**, which holds exhibitions, lectures and has an entertainment programme. Wren's **Marlborough House** is also in Pall Mall by St James's Park and can be viewed by arrangement.

In the centre of **Trafalgar Square** is Nelson's Column, surrounded by four bronze lions made from captured French cannons. The **National Gallery** covers different periods of European art, of note are the works of Rembrandt and Rubens. The new series of exhibitions showing the techniques of great artists is particularly illuminating, (open 10 a.m.–6 p.m. Mon–Sat; 2 p.m.–5 p.m. on Sundays). In the summer the gallery is open to 8 p.m. It receives a substantial number of visitors but crowds tend to cluster around the main exhibits and the shop. The new Sainsbury Wing will extend its displays.

The **National Portrait Gallery** is around the corner in St Martin's Place (open 10 a.m.–5 p.m. Mon–Sat; 2 p.m.–6 p.m. on Sunday). **St Martin-in-the-Fields**, the parish church for the Royal Family, is opposite. Lunchtime and evening concerts are often held in the church. A Brass Rubbing Centre is in the Crypt (open 10 a.m.–6 p.m. Mon–Sat; 12–6 on Sunday). The Crypt also contains an inexpensive restaurant.

Behind St Martin's is the area of **Covent Garden**. This changed from a fruit and vegetable market in 1974 into a fashionable shopping centre with a number of restaurants and winebars. It is a very lively place with street entertainers and a daily craft market. **St Paul's**, the actors' church, is a design by Hawksmoor in the Baroque style. Covent Garden **Opera House** is at the end of the market as is the **London Transport Museum** (open 10 a.m.–6 p.m. daily). Just off the Piazza, **Spitting Image** have recently opened a museum of puppets. Nearby, in Great Queen Street, is the magnificent art deco

Freemason Hall, while the **Theatre Museum** is at 1 Tavistock Street (open 11 a.m.–7 p.m. Tues–Sunday).

Another route to explore in the centre of the West End is **Mayfair**, around **St James's**, down **Piccadilly** and across to **Soho**. Mayfair is a very exclusive area, dotted with squares and gardens. The auction houses, designer shops and car show rooms are based here. It is interesting to wander around the small alleys off **Shepherd Market**. **Grosvenor Chapel** is a little gem in this area, and going along Farm Street, the unusual Farm House can be seen, as well as the beautifully ornate church of the **Immaculate Holy Conception**. Crossing Piccadilly, the Tudor **St James's Palace** can be seen. Once the site of a leper colony and later a hunting lodge for Henry VIII, it is now the official Court to which ambassadors are accredited and houses a number of offices. The beautiful **Queen's Chapel** with Holbein's coffered ceiling is open occasionally and is well worth a visit.

The area is rich in Georgian and Regency architecture. Many of London's gentlemen's clubs are located in this area. There is an abundance of impressive aristocratic mansions and small alleyways around St James's Palace.

On Piccadilly (named after the ruffled Elizabethan collar, the Picadil, whose designer built a house nearby), one of the best examples of Regency architecture can be seen in the **Burlington Arcade**, full of expensive shops. Nearby is the **Museum of Mankind**, the anthropology museum, with static collections and first-class changing exhibitions (open 10 a.m.–5 p.m. Mon–Sat; 2.30 p.m.–6 p.m. on Sunday). On Piccadilly, the **Royal Academy of Arts** is based in Burlington House. This has changing shows, including the famous Summer Exhibition. It can be very crowded when there are popular exhibitions and is best visited on weekdays (open usually 10 a.m.–6 p.m.). Opposite is **Fortnum and Mason** with its unusual chiming clock (displaying the figures of its two founders on the hour). The church of **St James's** was designed by Wren and was hit by a bomb during the war, as a result of which the steeple is fibreglass. The **London Brass Rubbing Centre** is based here. There is a craft market on Fridays and Saturdays in the courtyard. The cafe, The Wren, at the back sells wonderful vegetarian food, and is exceptionally cheap for this area.

At the end of the road is **Piccadilly Circus** with the statue of Eros, god of love, erected for Lord Shaftesbury, the Victorian reformer who did much to abolish child labour in Britain's factories. On Piccadilly Circus, the new Trocodero Centre, Guinness World of Records and The Rock Circus (with models by Tussauds) attract lots of tourists. **Regent Street**, to the left, has many prestigious shops including

Liberty's, and Hamleys which advertises as the largest toy shop in the world. **Carnaby Street** became famous for its fashion lead in the 1960s, but has now declined. **Shaftesbury Avenue** and its environs contain many of the West End theatres. **China town** is around Gerrard Street.

The area of **Soho** has hundreds of small restaurants differing in cuisine, price and quality. These small outlets are under threat due to the greatly increased rates and rents. **Oxford Street** is the longest and most crowded shopping street in London; there are a couple of big department stores (Selfridges and John Lewis) but practically all the shops are chain stores that can be found elsewhere.

The area behind Oxford Street, heading towards **Marylebone**, is an attractive business area. The **Wallace Collection** is found in Manchester Square. The **Sherlock Holmes Museum** is, of course, at 221B Baker Street (Tel 071 935 8866). Up towards Bloomsbury, in Scala Street, is the tiny but popular **Pollock Toy Museum** (open 10 a.m.–5 p.m. Mon–Fri).

Regent's Park is an area of imposing Regency buildings bordering the large park which contains an open-air theatre and **London Zoo**. The **West London Mosque** stands on the edge of the park. **Regent's Canal** has a towpath along its banks. The **English Folk Song and Dance Centre** is on the Outer Circle and hosts concerts and lectures.

St John's Wood is a residential area with interesting shops and restaurants in the High Street. To the west is **Lord's Cricket Ground**, home of MCC (Marylebone Cricket Club) and Test cricket. There is a museum of cricket here. **Primrose Hill** offers good views over the centre of London.

East of Westminster

Westminster to the City

From the West End to the City there is an interesting walk that passes through the **Strand**, **Holborn** and **Fleet Street**. The **Courtauld Institute** in the Strand has recently opened its collection in the new galleries of Somerset House; **St Mary-le-Strand** and **St Clement Danes** are both in the Baroque style.

The **Civil Courts of Justice** (the Law Courts, popularly) are fascinating from a historical and architectural, as well as functional viewpoint. The public are allowed in to view the legal system in action (10.30 a.m.–1 p.m. and 2–4 p.m. Mon–Fri). For the most part, **Lincoln's Inn, Gray's Inn, Middle and Inner Temple** are closed to the public; but some gardens, halls and chapels can be viewed on prior arrangement. Nonetheless, the surrounding streets and squares are a pleasure to explore. Of particular note is **Staple Inn**: an original Elizabethan wool warehouse. **Charles Dickens' House** is open at 48 Doughty Street (10 a.m.–5 p.m. Mon–Fri). There is a lunchtime market in Leather Lane. **Sir John Soane's House**, with its idiosyncratic art collection, is open at 13 Lincoln's Inn Field (10 a.m.–5 p.m. Tues–Sat). On Lincoln's Inn Fields, the signs of London's problem of homelessness are all too evident, with many makeshift sleeping covers and beds.

Opposite the Law Courts are **Twinings Tea Shop** (the smallest shop in London) and the **Old Wig and Pen Club**, an interesting, half-timbered building. The house of **Dr Samuel Johnson** (who compiled the first English dictionary) is a classical Georgian town house and is just off **Fleet Street**. The former **Daily Mail** building in Bouverie Street has the only mother-of-pearl ceiling in the world; this is visible from the outside. Wren's **St Bride's Church** is also in Fleet Street: its steeple is said to be the inspiration for the design of the wedding cake. The church has an excellent choir, which can be heard during Sunday services at 11 a.m. and 6.30 p.m. There are often lunchtime concerts. Across Ludgate Circus the **Old Bailey** is the central Criminal Court; the public gallery is entered from Newgate Street, site of the infamous prison (open 10.30 a.m.–1 p.m. and 2 p.m.–4 p.m. Mon–Fri).

The City

There is a wide range of buildings of interest. **St Paul's Cathedral**, designed by Wren, has a magnificent dome; the famous Whispering Gallery and Stone Gallery are at the top of the cupola, the latter providing spectacular views over London. The public can visit the Great Hall (15th-century but much restored after war damage) in the **Guildhall**, where the self-governing body of the City meets. Also here is the **Guildhall Museum**, Gresham Street (open 10 a.m.–5 p.m. Mon–Sat and on Sundays in the summer). **St Bartholomew's the Great** is the only church with Norman traces left in London (open 8.30 a.m.–dusk). **Smithfield** wholesale meat market is held daily, early mornings. The small, winding streets around this area are interesting to explore. The **Barbican Centre** holds the Royal Shakespeare Company, who had to close their doors from Nov 1990–March 1991 due to lack of funds.

The excellent **Museum of London** is highly recommended. In the most imaginative way possible it follows the history of London from the Romans to the 1950s (open 10 a.m.–6 p.m. Tues–Sat, 2 p.m.–6 p.m. on Sundays). Remains of the Roman Wall can be seen.

The area around the **Bank** is marvellous to explore and offers futuristic giants juxtaposed with 17th-century churches. The narrow streets hold a wealth of surprises. The **Stock Exchange** can be entered on Old Broad Street in trading hours; the **Royal Exchange** has its own museum, and the **Bank of England** also has a museum, entered on Bartholomew Lane. This is near the Roman remains of the **Temple of Mithras**. Lunchtime concerts are held in **St Mary Woolnoth**, a Hawksmoor church, and in the new amphitheatre at **Broadgate** (which also has an ice-skating rink in winter). The new **Lloyds Building**, designed by Richard Rogers, contains a museum of insurance history open free to the public. The beautiful Victorian, glass-covered market at **Leadenhall** is well worth visiting. Towards the Thames and London Bridge is the **Monument** to the Great Fire of London in 1666. This can be climbed for amazing views over the City and river.

The **Tower of London** is one of Britain's honeypot sites due to its continuous connections with national history. A segment of the original Roman Wall can be seen clearly near here. **All-Hallows-by-the-Tower** has a medieval crypt and a colourful yet macabre history, being linked with Tower Hill, the public execution site for traitors. Currently a new museum is being planned, underground at Tower Hill, which will take tourists through the history of the city in pull-carts in twelve minutes. **Tower Bridge** is one of the most popular picture-postcard subjects of London; visitors can see the working of the drawbridge, and an art gallery, with fantastic views down the Thames, has just opened here. **St Katherine's Dock** has been redeveloped and turned into a marina, surrounded by expensive bars, restaurants and a hotel. A few Thames barges and other interesting boats are usually moored.

West of Westminster

Westminster to Kensington & Chelsea

Belgravia, **Knightsbridge** and **Kensington** are close enough together for convenient exploration. **Buckingham Palace** is one of the most popular tourist attractions in London, whatever the weather; the **Queen's Gallery** (open 11 a.m.–5 p.m. Tues–Sat, 2 p.m.–5 p.m. Sunday) gives all entrance fees to selected charities while the collection of state carriages can be seen in the **Royal Mews** (open 2 p.m.–4 p.m. Wed & Thur). Belgravia is a prosperous residential area behind the Palace, with a stately square laid out by Thomas Cubbitt in 1825. In the back streets heading to Knightsbridge and Sloane Square there are a number of exclusive galleries and shops and restaurants. Knightbridge's most famous shop is **Harrods** with its beautiful interior decor and its suffocating crowds. Nearly opposite on the Old Brompton Road is the stunning, Baroque **Brompton Oratory**. The major National Museums are located around Exhibition Road: the **Victoria and Albert Museum**, with its decorative collections; the modern **Boiler House**, with its design exhibitions; the **Natural History Museum** in its beautiful, recently-cleaned building; the **Science Museum**, and the **Geology Museum** (all open from 10 a.m.–6 p.m. Mon–Sat, 2 p.m.–6 p.m. Sunday). Baden-Powell House contains the **Brownie and Cubs Museum** (open 10 a.m.–5 p.m. Tues–Sat). In Exhibition Road is the **Museum of Sound Archives**. In Kensington Gardens is the **Serpentine Gallery** of modern art. The **Royal Albert Hall** and **Albert Memorial** are supreme monuments of Victorian architecture. The nearby **College of Organists** is also an unusually beautiful building.

Kensington & Chelsea

The 19th-century architecture of Kensington, with its broad streets and gardens, is a pleasure to explore. All over London, famous former residents are shown on blue plaques placed on the buildings they inhabited. **Kensington Palace**, the London home of the Prince and Princess of Wales, has a section of State rooms once inhabited by William and Mary, and a costume collection of 18th-century court dress (open 9 a.m.–5 p.m. Mon–Sat, 1–5 p.m. on Sunday). The **Orangery** has recently opened as a delightful tea-room which is highly recommended (open in the summer months only).

The local shopping area is along **Kensington High Street**. There are interesting young designer collections in HyperHyper. Kensington Market has unusual and second-hand clothes. In the summer, nature walks for children are conducted around **Holland Park**. The **Commonwealth Institute** is on the edge of Holland Park (open 10 a.m.–5.30 p.m. Mon–Sat, 2–6 p.m. Sunday). On Sundays, there are free performances of ethnic dance and music. **Holland Park** has a small gallery with changing exhibitions and in the summer an open-air theatre which offers some very impressive opera and drama. **Leighton House**, opened by the Victorian Society, is at 12 Holland Park Road (open 11 a.m.–5 p.m. Mon–Sat).

On the other side of Holland Park and Kensington Gardens is **Notting Hill Gate**, a younger, more fashionable area. **Portobello**

Market (on Friday and Saturday) has bric-à-brac, antiques, fruit and vegetables and second-hand clothes for sale – in that order. There are many private galleries around this area which are open to browsers. The **Electric Cinema** on Portobello Road was one of the first cinemas and has an interesting programme of alternative films. The **Coronet Cinema** in Notting Hill was an old theatre and has a lovely interior. Nearby, in Bayswater, is the **London Toys and Model Museum**, 23 Craven Hill (open 10 a.m.–5.30 p.m. Mon–Sat, 1–5 p.m. on Sunday).

Hammersmith & Fulham and Richmond

Kew, Chiswick, Richmond and **Ham** are close in vicinity. The **Royal Botanical Gardens** are the most famous attraction in Kew (they are usually known as Kew Gardens), with an amazing collection of rare plant species and famous hot houses. Along the High Street at Brentford are the **Musical Museum** at 368 and the **Steam Museum** on Green Dragon Lane. **Syon House**, with gardens landscaped by Capability Brown and a vintage car collection, is in Kew. **Chiswick House**, in Burlington Lane, was another fashionable, 17th-century, out-of-town house in the English Palladian style (both open April–Sept, 10 a.m.–4 p.m.). Richmond is an attractive area by the river, with a variety of shops and restaurants. **Marble Hill House** was built in the 1720s, an incredible testimony to Gothic revivalism, and now holds riverside concerts in the summer (open Easter–October 10 a.m.–6 p.m.). **Richmond Park** is open all year round during daylight hours. Riding in the park is arranged by Manor Farm Stables, Petersham Road, Richmond (Tel 081 940 8511). **Ham House** is a fine example of Jacobean architecture; the parkland extends along the river and is owned by the National Trust.

North of Westminster

Camden

Eastwards from Regent's Park is **Camden**, where there is a lively and popular Sunday market, selling individual clothes, bric-à-brac and crafts. **Hampstead Heath** offers a good habitat for wildlife, while **Parliament Hill** (319 feet, 97 m.) offers one of the finest panoramas of the City. There are two sizeable English country houses in Hampstead: **Kenwood House**, which is experiencing problems of erosion due to the popularity of its grounds and the open-air concerts in the summer; and **Fenton House** (open April–Oct, 10 a.m.–5 p.m. Sat–Wed). Hampstead also has literary and intellectual connections: **Keats House**, Keats Grove (open 1–5 p.m. in winter, 2–6 p.m. in summer) and the **Freud Museum** (open 2–5 p.m. Wed and Sun). **Burgh House** houses the **Local History Museum** at New End Square. To discover more about the area, Hampstead Walking Tours can be contacted (Tel 071 435 0259). Nearby, **Highgate Village** is attractive. The **Victorian Cemetery** holds the grave of Karl Marx. In Highgate West is **Waterlow Park**, with its small lakes and the 17th-century Old Hall.

Bloomsbury is famous for a set of intellectuals who lived there in the 1930s – the most famous being Virginia Woolf. The crypt of **St George's**, Bloomsbury Way, houses an art gallery. The **October Gallery** is at 24 Old Gloucester Street and has interesting contemporary exhibitions. London University and the **British Museum** are close to Russell Square. The **Jewish Museum** is in Woburn House, Tavistock Square (open 10 a.m.–6 p.m. Tue–Thur).

Islington and Hackney

Further east is **Islington**, a younger, more fashionable area. A lot of streets with Victorian, middle-class, town house architecture still remain. **Camden Passage** holds an antique market. There is a wide variety of restaurants around Upper Street.

Hackney has mixed housing and great cultural diversity. This is the real non-postcard London. **Hackney Museum** of local history is at the Central Hall, Mare Street (open Tues–Fri 10–12.30 a.m., 1.30–5 p.m.). There is a **city farm** on Goldsmiths Row. **Hackney Marshes** and **Victoria Park** are the largest open spaces in East London. There is a new river walk along The Lea. **Sutton House**, a Tudor building in Hackney Marshes, is occasionally opened by the National Trust.

East End

Tower Hamlets

For exploration around the East End, start in **Spitalfields**. With its long history of immigration, East London has diverse cultural roots. The Huguenots settled here in the 17th and 18th centuries. Evidence of their occupation can be seen from the fine Georgian houses of the area. Later came the Jews, who laid the foundations of the rag trade, which is still in operation. The most recent wave of immigrants came from Bangladesh and Bengal. This has given the area an exotic flavour, with calls to prayer and a thriving restaurant scene.

Spitalfields Flower Market is for wholesalers. The area is slowly becoming 'gentrified' due to its proximity to the City and interest in the architecture displayed by the Georgian Society. The **Ragged School Museum** is at 46-48 Copperfield Road. Shoreditch and Bethnal Green are poor residential areas with substantial 1950s and 1960s housing estates and Victorian terraces. The renowned **Bethnal Green Museum of Childhood** is on Cambridge Heath Road (open 10 a.m.-5 p.m. Mon-Thur, 2.30-5.30 p.m. Sat & Sun). **Wesley's House, Chapel** and **Museum** are nearby at 49 City Road (open 9 a.m.-6 p.m. Mon-Sat, 2-6 p.m. Sun). **The Geffrye Museum** is on Kingsland Road in Shoreditch, (open 10 a.m.-5 p.m. Tues-Sat, 2-5 p.m. Sunday).

The foundation of the London Docklands Development Corporation (LDDC) has been surrounded by controversy, particularly regarding its funding and planning powers direct from central government. What has caused most outrage is the concentration on luxury developments, while the local boroughs suffer from serious housing problems. The area is still like a huge building site. **Canary Wharf** has interesting new buildings and historical pockets. There is a **city farm** at **Mudchute**, Pier Street and another just outside the LDDC in Stepney Way, **Stepping Stones Farm**. LDDC tours can be arranged (Tel 071 512 3000). The Docklands Light Railway can be taken from Tower Hill; it has raised lines offering brilliant views, but avoid it at rush-hours as it has proved hopelessly inadequate in meeting demands, and the narrow platforms make it dangerous.

South of the Thames

Lambeth

The **South Bank Centre** is the largest arts complex in London. The **Royal Festival Hall** and **Queen Elizabeth Hall** have a programme of concerts. The **National Theatre** has three stages: the Cottesloe, Littleton and Olivier. The **National Film Theatre** has three screens showing a number of rare, early and foreign films. The **Museum of The Moving Image** has many interesting exhibits from the world of film and TV (open 10 a.m.-8 p.m. Tues-Sat, 10 a.m.-6 p.m. Sunday). It is very popular and best visited during school term time. **Jubilee Gardens** hold a number of events in the summer. Next to Jubilee Gardens is County Hall, the old offices of the GLC and the Inner London Education Authority, now standing empty. Plans for the building's conversion into a mega hotel have been mentioned. Within **St Thomas's Hospital** on Lambeth Palace Road is the **Florence Nightingale Museum** and an old **Operating Theatre**, both open to the public.

The Tudor **Lambeth Palace** is the London home of the Archbishop of Canterbury, the premier of the Church of England. The gardens are opened on occasions. Next door is the **Museum of Garden History** in St Mary's at Lambeth. On the other side of the river is the **Tate Gallery**, with its collections of contemporary art (open 10 a.m.–5.30 p.m. Tues–Sat, 2 p.m.–5.30 p.m. Sunday). The **Imperial War Museum**, which won the 1990 Museum of the Year Award, is in Lambeth Road.

Southwark

Southwark has a concentrated tourist area in Bankside on the south side of the river, which has stunning views of the Tower of London and Tower Bridge. This part of London has the new **Design Museum**, the **Space Adventure**, the **London Dungeons** and the smart **Hays Wharf** shopping centre. **HMS Belfast**, a cruiser which saw service in the Second World War including bombardment of the Normandy invasion beaches, is moored by Tower Bridge. The **Clink Museum** at 1 Clink Street tells the history of prisons (open 10 a.m.–6 p.m. daily).

The towered Gothic **Southwark Cathedral** is very impressive (open 7.30 a.m.–6 p.m. daily). Nearby is Southwark **Visitors Centre**, which tells of the borough's historic development. The area was the centre of the Elizabethan theatrical scene, and Shakespeare's **Globe Theatre Museum** is due to open later in 1992 in Bear Gardens. Archaeological remains of the original Rose Theatre were discovered in 1989 by Southwark Bridge, only to be built over by developers amidst much public protest. The back regions of Southwark are mainly poor residential, though there are prosperous pockets.

Accommodation

Prices in London hotels have increased rapidly during the last few years. They have remained seasonal however, and winter is often a cheaper option.

First Class

Blakes, 33 Roland Gardens, London SW7 3PF (Tel 071 370 6701). Individual hotel in South Kensington with less than forty rooms and a good restaurant.

Beaufort Hotel, 33 Beaufort Gardens, London SW3 1PP (Tel 071 584 5252). Managed by the owner, a small hotel in the Chelsea area.

The Fenja, 69 Cadogan Gardens, London SW3 2RB (Tel 071

589 7333). Fourteen bedrooms in the atmosphere of an Edwardian townhouse, just a few minutes' walk from Knightsbridge.

The Pelham, 15 Cromwell Place, London SW7 2LA (Tel 071 589 8288). Luxury townhouse hotel offering high standards of comfort, elegant and opulent surroundings and traditional service.

Middle Range

Knightsbridge Green Hotel, 159 Knightsbridge, London SW1X 7PD (Tel 071 584 6274). Family run hotel with six bedrooms and sixteen suites.

Colonade Hotel, 2 Warrington Crescent, London W9 (Tel 071 286 1052). Comfortable accommodation in a grade two listed building.

Goring Hotel, 15 Beeston Place, London SW1W 0JW (Tel 071 834 8211). Eighty-four rooms and five suites in this exclusive hotel, built by the owner's grandfather.

Merryfield House, 42 York Street, London W1H 1FN (Tel 071 935 8326). Seven bedrooms just round the corner from Baker Street.

Economy

St Margaret's Hotel, 26 Bedford Place, Russell Square, London WC1B 5JH (Tel 071 634 4277). St Margaret's has been run by the same family for the past forty years. Part of an estate owned by the Duke of Bedford, it is situated close to Russell Square in Bloomsbury and offers comfortable accommodation in spacious rooms.

Ebury Court Hotel, 26 Ebury Street, London SW1W 0LU (Tel 071 730 8147). Mrs Topham has been running Ebury Court for almost fifty years. Initially one house bought by her brother, it has now expanded to five and provides a real 'home from home' for many visitors.

Oxford House Hotel, 92–94 Cambridge Street, London SW1 (Tel 071 834 6467). Eighteen bedrooms in a quiet location close to Victoria Station.

London Friendship Centre, Peace Haven, 3 Creswick Road, London W6 (Tel 081 992 0819). Beds for around £10 a night.

Tent City, Old Oak Common Lane, East Acton, London (Tel 081 743 5708). Large dormitory tents for under £5 a night. Open May–October.

Youth Hostels can be found at Hampstead Heath (Tel 081 885 3234); Holland Park (Tel 071 937 0748); Oxford Street (Tel 071 734 1618); Earl's Court (Tel 071 373 7083); Highgate (Tel 081 340

1831); Wood Green (Tel 081 881 4432); and White Hart Lane (Tel 081 885 3234).

Homestays

Homestays with resident families are run through the following organisations, all in the Economy price range. Guests are usually expected to stay at least three nights.

At Home in London, 70 Black Lion Lane, Hammersmith, London W6 (Tel 081 748 1943). Contact Maggie Dobson.

Host and Guest Service, The Studio, 635 King's Road, London SW6 (Tel 071 731 5340).

Home Hosts, 48 Heathfield Road, London W3 (Tel 081 992 5752).

London Homes, 66 Hyde Park Mansions, Cabbell Street, London NW1 (Tel 071 262 0900). Contact Heather Kassell.

Further information is available in *Stay with a London Family*, published by the British Tourist Authority.

Servas, an international network of hosts and guests is easy to join. There are four regional co-ordinators covering the London area:

West and South-west: Jenny and Ken Sturt, 34 Balfour Road, London W13 (Tel 081 567 5181).

South-east: David Sharman, 55 Mayhill Road, London SE7 (Tel 081 858 7297).

East: Lynn Saad, 13 Hurst Road, London E17 (Tel 081 520 7621).

The North and **Middlesex** are covered by Melora Davis, 8A Northdown Close, Ruislip (Tel 0895 677790).

Eating Out

First Class

The Savoy Grill, Savoy Hotel, Strand, London WC2 (Tel 071 836 4343). Traditional cuisine in one of London's top hotels.

Alastair Little's, 49 Frith Street, London W1 (Tel 071 734 5183). Chef Alastair Little's 'nouveau cuisine' is renowned.

The Greenhouse, 27a Hay's Mews, London W1 (Tel 071 493 3331). The best of English nouvelle cuisine, imaginatively served in an interesting and pleasant atmosphere.

Julie's Restaurant, 137 Portland Road, London W11 (Tel 071 727 7985). Wine bar/conservatory, leek and potato soup and Cumberland sausage!

English Garden, 10 Lincoln Street, London SW3 (Tel. 071 584 7272). The name says it all!

Middle Range

Green's, 36 Duke Street, St James's, London SW1 (Tel 071 930 4566). Unpretentious restaurant serving interesting English nouvelle cuisine dishes.

Kensington Place, 201 Kensington Church Street, London W8 (Tel 071 727 3184). Bistro-style restaurant making excellent use of fresh produce, and offering a wide range of meat and fish dishes.

Tiddy Dols, 55 Shepherd Market, London W1 (Tel 071 499 2357). Old-fashioned British cooking a speciality.

Millward's Restaurant, 97 Stoke Newington Church Street, London N16 (Tel 071 254 1025). Family run vegetarian bistro.

Good quality food at moderate prices is offered in many museum and theatre restaurants. Of particular note is the one at the Tate Gallery, which specialises in 17th- and 18th-century dishes.

Economy

Cherry Orchard, 241 Globe Road, London E2 (Tel 081 980 6678). Vegetarian restaurant run by a Buddhist co-operative.

Mrs Beetons, 58 Hill Rise, Richmond (Tel 081 940 9561). Co-operative run with alternating chefs.

Food for Thought, 31 Neal Street, London WC2 (Tel 071 836 0239). Vegetarian restaurant in a former banana warehouse!

Hungry's, 37A Crawford Street, London W1 (Tel 071 258 0376). Excellent value sandwich bar/cafe with an astounding range of fillings. Soups and snacks also served.

Most pubs serve food at lunchtime, although it's best to avoid the ones in the City and around the West End business districts as they become very crowded.

Entertainment

London boasts one of the most lively entertainment scenes in the world and there is something to satisfy all tastes and budgets.

The major **theatres** and **cinemas** are concentrated in the West End around Shaftesbury Avenue, Leicester Square and Covent Garden, and many theatres offer long-running musicals which usually require advance booking of anything from one week to over a year. Last-minute and return tickets are sometimes obtainable however, either from the box office (if you're willing to queue for a couple of hours) or from one of the independent ticket booths around the streets (if you're willing to take the chance of being ripped off).

The **Coliseum**, St Martin's Lane (Tel 071 836 3161 Information; 071 240 5258 Reservations) is home of the **English National Opera** and **London Festival Ballet**, and offers a frequently changing programme. It is also considerably cheaper than the **Royal Opera House**, Bow Street (Tel 071 240 1066) in Covent Garden, which is the base for the **Royal Opera** and **Royal Ballet Companies**.

The **South Bank Centre**, South Bank (Tel 071 928 3002 Information; 071 928 8800 Reservations) is London's largest arts complex, followed by the **Barbican Centre** (Tel 071 638 4141 Information; 071 638 8891 Reservations), home of the **London Symphony Orchestra** and London base of the **Royal Shakespeare Company**. Both venues offer classical concerts and drama. The **Royal Albert Hall**, Kensington Gore (Tel 071 589 3203 Information; 071 589 8212 Reservations) also holds concerts. The usual venue for **pop concerts** (as well as sporting events) is **Wembley Stadium and Arena**, Lakeside Way, Wembley (Tel 081 902 1234).

Sadler's Wells, Rosebery Avenue (Tel 071 278 8916) houses the famous dance company and regularly offers performances of varying dance forms. **Almeida Theatre**, Almeida Street (Tel 071 359 4404) offers a number of high quality theatre companies, while the **National Theatre**, South Bank (Tel 071 928 2252) presents both modern and classical drama. For something completely different and slightly less formal, try the **King's Head**, 115 Upper Street, Islington N1 (Tel 071 226 1916), which is the oldest pub theatre in London and still has one of the best reputations.

Nightclubs and **discos** abound throughout the city. **Annabel's**, 44 Berkeley Square (Tel 071 629 2350) is one of the most chic places in town (with prices to match), as are **Raffles**, King's Road (Tel 071 352 1091) and **Tramp**, Jermyn Street (Tel 071 734 3174). Slightly less upmarket are **Crazy Larry's**, 533 King's Road (Tel 071 376 5555) and **Camden Palace**, 1A Camden High Street (Tel 071 387 0428). Finally, for what is considered by some to be the most fashionable night out in town, the **Hippodrome**, Charing Cross Road/Leicester Square (Tel 071 437 4311) is loud, enormous and extremely lively.

London's thousands of **pubs** all offer a relatively sociable night out and popping into the nearest local is almost guaranteed to bring you into contact with Londoners themselves. For live music on Friday and Saturday nights, try the Camden area which has a large Irish population intent on educating the English about the joy of Irish song. Alternatively Chelsea, as fashionable now as ever, still boasts a wide range of local haunts favoured for their company and ale.

Up-to-date information on London's arts and entertainment scene is available in *Time Out* and *City Limits* magazines, available from news stands and bookshops.

Useful addresses

London Tourist Board, 26 Grosvenor Gardens (Tel 071 730 3450). A **Tourist Information service** is available on 071 730 3488, and main information offices can be found at Victoria Station and St Paul's Churchyard (both open 9.30 a.m–5.30 p.m. Monday–Friday). In addition there are offices in Harrod's basement (open 9 a.m.–6 p.m. and 7 p.m. on Wednesday) and Selfridges basement (open 9 a.m.–6 p.m. and 8 p.m. on Thursday). Other offices are at Kew Gardens (open 9.15 a.m.–5.15 p.m. Monday–Friday) and Hampton Court (open 9.30 a.m.–4.30 p.m. daily).

For finding out what's on in and around London, call the **British Travel Association** (Tel 071 730 3400); **Online Leisure Information** (Tel 071 222 4640); **Sportsline** (Tel 071 222 8000 for sporting activities); and **Kidsline** (Tel 071 222 8070), 9 a.m.–4 p.m. during school holidays, 4 p.m.–6 p.m. during term time.

London Regional Transport offer transport information (Tel 071 222 1234). **British Rail** has a recorded service with details of travel problems (Tel 071 222 1200).

London's main **post office** is at King Edward Building EC1 (Tel 071 239 5047), open 8.30 a.m.–6.30 p.m. Monday–Tuesday, Thursday–Friday, 9 a.m.–6.30 p.m. Wednesday). Far more convenient however, is the branch at Trafalgar Square, 24–28 William IV Street WC2 (Tel 071 930 9580), open 8 a.m.–8 p.m. Monday–Saturday, 10 a.m.–5 p.m. Sunday and Bank Holidays. Post restante will be held at Trafalgar Square for one month if addressed Poste Restante, Trafalgar Square PO, London WC2N 4DL. If a post office isn't specified, all poste restante will go to the main office at King Edward Building.

Advice on **health problems** of a minor nature can be obtained on **Healthline** (Tel 081 681 3311). **Chemists** opening late and on Sundays include Boots, 114 Queensway (Tel 071 229 1183), open 8.30 a.m.–10.00 p.m. daily; and Bliss Chemists at 149 Edgware Road (Tel 071 723 2336), 5 Marble Arch (Tel 071 723 6116), and 33 Sloane Square (Tel 071 730 1023). Depending on where you are, **emergencies** are taken to **Guy's Hospital** SE1 (Tel 071 407 7600); **St Thomas's** SE1 (Tel 071 928 9292); **London Hospital**, Whitechapel (Tel 071 377 7000); **St Bartholomew's**, Smithfield (Tel 071 601 8888); **Middlesex Hospital** W1 (Tel 071 636 8333); **Royal Free Hospital** NW3 (Tel 071 794 5000); **St Mary's** W2 (Tel 071 725 6666); and **Charing Cross Hospital** W6 (Tel 071 846 1234).

15 The South-East

The South-east region consists of the counties of Kent, Surrey, East and West Sussex, Hampshire (with the Isle of Wight), all areas that have been influenced specifically by their proximity to London, and to the Continent.

Successive invaders, entering Britain along the south-east coast, have each left their distinctive mark in architecture, industry, communications, and in the formation of the landscape itself. The area has been settled by the Celts, Romans, Jutes and Belgae, and most decisively by the Normans. The need for defence has been evident and consequently there are a large number of fortresses and castles in the region. A legacy has also been left by its diverse inhabitants – the Huguenots introduced the most characteristic buildings of the region, the famous oast houses, and from the Low Countries the Flemish imported their windmills. All these features now characterise the area.

The second influence has manifested itself with the growth of London, for the South-east has prospered as supplier to the capital of cereals, hops and fruits. Communications between London and the Continent have marked this region with ports, coaching towns, railway stations, ferry terminals, motorways, airports and now the Channel Tunnel. The almost continual development of London's suburban sprawl has meant that much of the north of Surrey and Kent have been engulfed.

Ask most people what image is conjured up of the South-east and they will say prosperity, commuters, pretty patchwork countryside, and the old seaside resorts. But traditionally this area has also had an industrial base, in the past with the iron industry, and presently with coal mining, still operational in Kent.

Altogether the region has many intriguing facets and is interesting, as well as rewardingly picturesque, to explore. Discerning tourists can look behind the stereotyped image and find much to surprise them.

History

The area has been settled by different peoples throughout the ages. Kent boasts the earliest human remains found in England: the Swanscombe Woman dating back 250,000 years, who was discovered near Dartford. The first signs of habitation are from Palaeolithic times, and early post-Ice Age sites have been found at Midhurst (Sussex), Aylesford and Ightham (Kent), while the first preserved dwelling in England was discovered at Abinger (Surrey). Neolithic sites are ubiquitous – with particularly fine examples such as the long barrow at Badshot Lea (Surrey) and the Bronze Age disc barrows at Flindon, Itford Down (Sussex), near Lightwater and at Reigate Heath in Surrey. In later periods the Wield was populated by the Celts, with Iron Age hill forts best preserved at Cissbury, Chanctonbury (Sussex) and Weybridge, Holmbury Hill and Lingfield in Surrey.

At the dawn of the Christian era, the recently settled Belgae had made Canterbury their capital and established provincial settlements at Selsey and Chichester (Sussex). The Romans, under Claudius, landed at Richborough (Kent) in AD 43 and returned in AD 55 to Deal (Kent). Evidence of Roman occupation is found all over the region, but particularly in Kent and Sussex. Long straight Roman roads were constructed, fortresses built or extended (at Pevensey for example), as well as Mithraic temples (at Burham) and many villas, the best preserved of which can be found at Fishbourne. After the Romans withdrew to beleaguered Rome the Jutes colonised Hastings, leaving the rest of the region to the Saxons, whose settlements are evident all over the South-east.

The many individual kingdoms that existed in the area were eventually conquered by the Kingdom of Wessex and by King Offa of Mercia. Christianity was introduced to England by Augustine who converted King Ethelbert in AD 587. Many Saxon churches survive, and there are notable examples at Worth, Bishopstone and Sompting (Sussex). The land-seeking Danes invaded throughout this period, and the coastal defences were strengthened by King Canute, who unified England in 1017 and whose daughter is buried at Bosham (Sussex).

The Normans invaded and settled after the decisive Battle of Hastings in 1066 (a piece of history embodied in the name of the town of Battle). They built profusely and left notable fortifications at Dover and Rochester, cathedrals at Rochester, Chichester and Canterbury, and many churches throughout the region. The famous Cinque Ports were established to help defend the coast, but the French still raided Rye, Hastings, Shoreham and Seaford during the 14th-century.

In the Middle Ages, the Weald iron industry (at Buxted and Hartfield, Sussex) and coal mining (in Kent) expanded rapidly. Also at this time, the weaving industry gained prominence in the area.

The South-east plays a major part in national history. It was in Surrey that the Magna Carta was signed, ending absolute monarchy. Sussex was the site of the foundation of parliamentary government after de Montford's victory in the battle at Lewes in 1264. The Church of England itself was founded due to the influence of a Kentish girl, Anne Boleyn, on the reigning monarch, Henry VIII. The resulting Dissolution of the (Catholic) Monasteries is evident throughout England. In the South-east, Henry built coastal forts and inland castles as a response to the Catholic threat from France and Spain. The (later Royal) navy used the Weald forest's timber for shipbuilding, with main building and repair yards established at Chatham and Sheerness. With the increasing spread of Britain's interests under the Tudor and Stuart monarchies, and the need to communicate with and protect those interests, the local industries of papermaking and gunpowder production rapidly expanded.

During the Georgian period fears of a Napoleonic invasion increased the influence of the Cinque Ports, and the distinctive Martello Towers were constructed to help defend the coast. In the late 18th-century agriculture prospered while the iron industry declined. Another important source of revenue (and of popular mythology!) for the region was the rise of smuggling. Less prosaically, the importance of the sea to health was stressed by the influencial Dr Russell, whose papers on the virtues of bathing in sea water (and drinking it!) greatly impressed the Prince Regent and led to his patronage of Brighton, which subsequently surged in popularity as a prototypical seaside resort. Almost by osmosis, Bognor Regis benefited from the same popularity, as did the spa town of Tunbridge Wells. With the Victorian period and the subsequent expansion of the railway network, the popularity of the seaside grew, expanding Brighton, as well as the towns of Margate, Ramsgate, Eastbourne and Worthing. Due to the railways and easier commuting, much of the northern parts of the counties of Kent and Surrey were gradually subsumed into the new Greater London.

In 1914 the first ever mainland bombing experienced by the British was a raid on Folkestone and Chatham. Later, in the 1930s airbases were established in the South East, while the coast in general was closed for the duration of World War II. The decisive Battle of

Britain took place over Kent, and Canterbury and Maidstone were both badly damaged by bombing. After the war the new town of Crawley was built and urban reconstruction became widespread throughout the area. Suburbanisation claimed more of the region and the commuter belt spread – this at the time of a decline in agriculture and an expansion of the service sector. Recently many areas of the countryside have been under threat of development.

Geography

The River Thames forms the northern boundary of the region, with the Channel to the south. The North and South Downs (of chalk and sandstone) provide the most distinctive topology, running horizontally across the area, enfolding the rich clay Weald. The countryside is divided into wetlands, downlands, woodlands, heathlands and agricultural meadows and fields. Each of these terrains has its own distinctive flora and fauna.

There is a high proportion of protected areas, in the form of green belt, nature reserves, country parks, Sites of Special Scientific Interest (SSSIs) and the substantial protected Areas of Outstanding Natural Beauty. There is still a high percentage of commonland and woodland, but the areas close to London become crowded at weekends and holidays and effective dispersion policies are badly needed.

The descriptions listed below will serve as a guide to the exploration of the many and varied natural habitats still to be found in this highly populated area.

Wetlands

Many of these areas are wildfowl reserves and of particular interest to ornithologists. The largest area of 12,000 acres (4860 hectares) is run by the Royal Society for the Protection of Birds (RSPB), but is unfortunately near the nuclear power station at Dungeness, Kent. Elmley Marshes near Sittingbourne, and a large proportion of Rye and Chichester harbours are also notable sites for birdwatchers. The RSPB have a heronry at Northward Hill (Spring Hill), and wildfowl sanctuaries at Forest Row and Bentley Park (near Lewes). The Wildfowl Trust is based at Mill Road in Arundel (Tel 0903 88 3355).

Downlands

Chalkland areas have many rare flowers, orchids and butterflies. Both

Rye Downs (250 feet (76 m.) above sea level) and Bluebell Hill near Aylesford (site of a mesolithic tomb called Kits Coty), offer wonderful vistas. Leith's Hill is the highest point in the South-east at 965 feet (295 m.) and also in Surrey there are good views from St Ann's Hill, Chertsey. The Hackhurst and Mickleham downs (Surrey), the Seven Sisters Country Park (in Sussex, with 700 acres (283.5 hectares) boasting no less than 45 plant species) and Ditchling Beacon (with its good views from a height of 813 feet (248 m.)) – all offer excellent walking terrain.

Woodlands/Forest

Unfortunately the area was badly hit by the storms of 1987 (Sevenoaks lost six of its namesake trees). The largest woodland area is the Ashdown Forest, Sussex, covering 6500 acres (2632 hectares). Hurtwood near Cranleigh, Surrey has 4000 acres (1620 hectares) and the Devils Punchbowl is in a mixed area of wood and heath near Hindhead, covering 1400 acres (567 hectares). The Alice Holt forest in Surrey and St Leonard's Forest near Horsham, Sussex are in the care of the Forestry Commission. Staffhurst Wood Nature Reserve near Limpsfield (Surrey) has a concentration of indigenous oaks. There is also Winkworth Arboretum and Bedgebury Pinetum near Gouldhurst, Kent. Many smaller areas of woodland are open as reserves or can be either encircled or crossed by means of public footpaths.

Heathlands

In Kent, Hathfield Common extends to 140 acres (56.7 hectares). In Surrey, Blackheath (near Chilworth) and Chobham Common (with 1600 acres, 648 hectares) are both open to the public. Puttenham Common is an area of sandy heathland and in Sussex Ditchling Common extends to 188 acres (76 hectares).

Mixed Commonland

There are many Commons in Surrey, and a significant number are owned and well maintained by the County Council. These include Ranmoor, Bagmoor, Wotten and Abinger (which also contains Mesolithic sites). Witley Common is well known for its wide variety of insect species.

Ordnance Survey maps show areas of different habitats, as well as public footpaths and bridleways. Use of these excellent information tools can enhance your exploration of the natural environment of the South-east.

Climate

The region has a very mild climate with good sunshine records – an average of 4.3 hours a day. It also has a low rainfall of 25–30 inches (635–762 mm) a year. March, April and May are the driest months. Snow falls mostly in February and March – especially in Kent, the most easterly county. While the climate is not extreme, it can be windy, especially along the coast.

Attractions

An interesting and varied landscape makes this area perfect for visits by the nature lover, walker, artist and photographer. There is a good deal of open and public space, nature reserves, open farms and rare breed animal centres. The coast is also varied, with dramatic chalk cliffs and sand and pebble beaches for family bathing. All along the coast (and on the Thames) there are centres for sailing where regular yachting regattas are held.

In addition there are beautiful villages, many built around greens or commons. The characteristic local styles of building are evident, including tile hanging (in Sussex), and weather boarding (along the coast), while there are many two-timbered weaving houses. All the variegated historical styles are evident in this region from the Saxon and fine Norman buildings, through medieval, Georgian, and Victorian Gothic and neo-Classical styles, to the rather more prosaic styles (mock-Georgian, mock-Tudor, International Style, Council House, Basic Bungalow) of the 20th century.

There are varied and interesting museums and tourist attractions and a wide range of day and evening entertainments in the region. The countries pride themselves on their cricket and for anyone who loves horse racing there are major and local race courses.

Cuisine

Kent is famous for its hops, apples and vines, producing much of Britain's beer, cider and wine. Since the Middle Ages the region has grown a great variety of fruit, particularly apples and pears, the most popular being Conference Pears, Bramley cooking apples, and Golden Delicious eating apples, to meet foreign competition). Strawberries, raspberries and Victoria and Czar plums are also grown in Kent. For gourmets (or gourmands) the local cuisine speciality is seafood, notably Dover Sole and Whitstable Oysters. There are many trout farms throughout Sussex and Kent.

Level of Tourism

Tourism in the South-east has traditionally been concentrated in the seaside resorts. Over the last ten years these resorts have declined in popularity with their old clients increasingly opting for holidays abroad (although this trend has recently reversed). The proximity of London, and the dominance of the car as a means of personal transport, has led to the South-east becoming a popular destination for 'the day out'. This is a trend that the local councils and tourist boards are trying to manage more successfully, as it tends to bring congestion, polarisation around honeypot sites and few lasting financial benefits to the region.

The prime 'day out' destination, institutionalised by many of the major tour operators, is Canterbury. This tiny city has 2.1 million visitors a year, and the resulting traffic influx causes road congestion, excessive parking restrictions and many associated environmental and social problems for the city's population. Other honeypot sites of the area also tend to be visited by car for only a few hours and many of the picture-postcard villages become overcrowded on Sunday afternoons and Bank Holidays. Historic country houses and gardens – such as Leeds Castle (with 529,000 visitors a year), Knole, Chartwell, Wisley, Sissinghurst and Hever – are perennially popular with motorists and coach tour trippers.

Other major attractions are the Thorpe Leisure Park (with 1,300,000 visitors a year) and the Chessington World of Adventure. This type of day-tripper tourism to overcrowded sites is particularly problematic in a region that already suffers from chronic traffic congestion.

In 1989 (the last year for which there are figures) the South-east region received £1,087,800 from the English Tourist Board. The County Councils are trying to promote overnight stays, and Surrey is promoting 'weekend breaks'. The old tourist resorts and areas of high unemployment are also being promoted to lure back lost markets or to encourage new investment. Tourism is definitely seen as a panacea to many of the region's financial problems.

All the local councils are trying to encourage the use of public transport in order to combat congestion, and this is to be greatly commended. West Sussex seems to have the most thorough and systematic tourism development policy, granting planning permission only to low impact developments. Larger scale projects are permitted only in existing resorts – and preferably on the urban fringes – in order to provide a buffer between urban and rural land use. Surrey and Kent have both initiated programmes with locally-organised tours of picturesque villages. However, money has also been allocated in order to increase the available hotel accommodation by 1000 beds, mainly for transit and conference traffic.

All the administrative areas in the South-east are promoting the cultural and environmental diversity of the region, from theme parks to wildlife habitats, which is all to the good. But many local people, especially in the popular tourist areas, are worried about the increasing problem of traffic congestion.

Good Alternatives

Meeting People

Unfortunately there are no formal arenas for meeting locals. This is probably best done in the time-honoured way, in the relaxing atmosphere of the local pub. The like-minded can meet up at special interest groups. One such is Friends of the Earth. They have thirty-two groups in the South-east and the best way of establishing contact with these is through their national headquarters in London. The **National Trust** have their regional base at Scotney Castle, Lamberhurst, Kent (Tel 0892 890651). **South East Arts** is at 9–10 Crescent Road, Tunbridge Wells, Kent (Tel 0892 41666). **Holiday Care Service** offers free advice to people with special needs (2 Old Bank Chambers, Station Road, Horley, W. Sussex, Tel 0293 7745357). Around the coast, sailing clubs accept temporary membership.

Discovering Places

Getting away from the most concentrated tourist sites, even a cursory exploration can lead to the discovery of many places of interest, while at the same time promising the intense satisfaction of making a special 'personal' discovery. The older resorts with their neo-classical Regency and Victorian gothic architecture, and well-established 'seaside' entertainments, make for delightful family holidays and outings. Outside the towns, the countryside is varied, and mostly accessible by minor roads and footpaths.

The region is interlaced by a network of public footpaths and there are many long-distance walking routes. The **North Downs Way** from Farnham to Gravesend stretches for 150 miles (241 km.) across some of the most beautiful rural land in Britain. The **South Downs Way** runs from Buriton to Beachy Head, with views over the coastal plain to the ever-changing Channel and Straits of Dover. The **Saxon Shoreway** goes from Gravesend to the ancient and now land-locked seaport of Rye. The **Weald Way** (from Eastbourne to Gravesend), the **Greensand Way** (from Surrey to Kent), the **Downs Link** (between Shalford and Steyning) the **Forest Way** and **Vanguards Way** – some ancient paths, some recently established – all offer a diversity of terrain that is a delight to the experienced walker.

For those who prefer less energetic strolls, the region contains many waterway paths, including those along the Arun and Wey Canal, the Basingstoke Canal, and the Wey, Arun, Ouse, Medway, Darwent and Thames riverbanks.

A cycle holiday is run from Maidstone with routes of up to a week's duration; contact Mrs Spree, Barn Cottage, Boxley Rd, Harbourland, Boxley ME14 3DN (Tel 0622 675891). There are the **Cycle Touring Company**, Cotterell House, 69 Meadowrow, Godalming (Tel 048 68 7217) and **Harman Hire**, 1 Surrey Street, Brighton (Tel 0273 603021) from which cycles can be hired. Brighton sensibly promotes a cycling campaign.

Horse riding is also offered throughout the region, and information on equestrian centres and livery stables can be obtained from Tourist Information offices. One place that runs short riding breaks is **Hayne Barn**, Saltwood near Folkestone (Tel 0303 265512). Sailing can be enjoyed at many resorts, estuaries and harbours all around the coast and at some of the large reservoirs.

For nature lovers there are specialist holidays throughout the region; **Barn Owl Travel** organises birdwatching and natural history day courses and holidays. Contact Mr Tutt, 27 Seaview Road, Gillingham, Kent (Tel 0634 56759). **Wildlife and Environment Ltd** organises countryside and farming tours from Warren Farm, Boxley, Maidstone, Kent (Tel 0622 52524).

Communications

How to Get There

AIR: Including the domestic market, three quarters of all visitor arrivals and departures in the UK occur in the South-east. In terms of air travel, in 1989 a total of 21.2 million people passed through Gatwick airport and 40.3 million through Heathrow.

Travelling to the South-east from either airport is easiest by transferring first to London (See *London* Chapter), and then onwards by either rail or coach.

RAIL: From London the South-east is reached via Waterloo, Victoria and Charing Cross stations. British Rail's **Network South-East** offers 'Away-Break' tickets for short holidays of up to five days duration. Information is available from main stations.

Trains are very busy during rush hour periods (7 a.m.–10 a.m. and 5 p.m.–7 p.m.) and at Woking alone up to 14,000 passengers pass through the station every day. Train services to Kent are not particularly fast (or clean) and tend to be less efficient than those in Surrey and Sussex. With the completion of the Channel Tunnel near Deal, along with a new terminal as Ashford, visitors from the Continent have the option of arriving by train and alighting at Ashford, from where they may continue by bus or train, or travel onwards to London.

FERRY: Main ports of entry to the country are situated at Dover and Folkestone, both of which offer rail and bus connections to the rest of the area.

COACH: Coach services to the area are run from London's Victoria Coach Station (see *London* chapter).

When You're There

RAIL: Travel by train around the South-east can be problematic, with most routes involving at least one change of train. This often means it is more convenient to travel via London even if you would prefer not to. Massive railway improvements are needed and it is to be hoped that the new infrastructure created to service the Channel Tunnel will offer some sort of solution.

BUS: The area's bus network is very good with a comprehensive system covering most of the major towns. Larger companies include **Maidstone and District Bus Company** (Tel 0634 47334) and the **East Kent Bus Company** (Tel 0227 472082). In Surrey local bus information can be obtained from 0483 575226 and in Sussex the **South Downs Bus Company** is on 0243 783251.

CAR: The major roads that run through the South-east are the M2/A2 to Dover; M20 to Folkestone; M23/A23 to Brighton; A21 to Hastings, and A3 through Guildford to Portsmouth. A section of the notoriously busy M25 runs through the north of the region.

Heading south from London all routes pass through seemingly endless suburban high streets until eventually reaching the motorways. All routes are congested, especially at peak time rush hours and on Friday and Sunday evenings. The route along the coast (A27/A259) is slow-moving during the summer months due to an overload of holidaymakers and, in fact, all coast bound routes suffer on summer days when tourists and locals alike head for the beach. At such times, it is recommended that public transport be used when possible.

Useful Local Contacts

In KENT there are a large number of local groups concerned with conservation issues and keen to promote the type of sustainable tourism issues relevant to the Good Tourist. For information about the countryside contact either the **Environment and Wildlife Society**, JCR, Wye College, Ashford TN25 5AH or the **Kent Trust for Nature Conservation**, The Annexe, 1a Bower Mount Road, Maidstone ME16 8AX (Tel 0622 53017). On urban issues, there is the **Urban Heritage Centre**, Napier Primary School, Napier Road, Gillingham ME7 4HG (Tel 0634 570392) and the **North-West Kent Urban Wildlife Group**, St Theresa, Watling Street, Gravesend DA12 5UD (Tel 047482 3800).

Visitors to SURREY could do worse than contact the **Surrey Wildlife Trust**, The Old School, School Lane, Pirbright, Woking GU24 OJN (Tel 0483 797575), or the **Reading Urban Wildlife Group** (BBONT), 2 Victoria Road, Reading RG4 7QY (Tel 0734 4786265). Other groups include the **British Association of Nature Conservationists**, 24 Appletree Close, Godalming GU7 1TY (Tel 04868 52333) and the **Juniper Hall Field Centre**, Dorking RH5 6DA (Tel 0306 883849).

SUSSEX groups include the headquarters of **Beautiful Britain**, Bostel House, 37 West Street, Brighton, East Sussex BN1 2RE (Tel 0273 23585); the **Sussex Wildlife Trust**, Woods Mill, Shoreham Road, Henfield, West Sussex BN5 9SD (Tel 0273 492630), and, for ornithologists, the **Sussex Ornithological Society**, 4 The Poplars, Yapton, Arundel, West Sussex BN18 OEQ (Tel 0243 552833). Walkers might be interested in contacting the **Sussex Rights of Way Group**, 4 Crown Street, Eastbourne, East Sussex BN21 1NX.

Down in HAMPSHIRE there are good contacts at the **Hampshire Field Club and Archaeological Society**, King Alfred's College, Winchester SO22 4NR and at the **Lymington and District Naturalists' Society**, 11 Southern Road, Lymington (Tel 0590 72573). If you're also heading over to the Isle of Wight, it's worth getting in touch with the **Hampshire and Isle of Wight Naturalists Trust**, 71 The Hundred, Romsey SO51 8BZ (Tel 0794 513786). Actually on the Isle of Wight are **Islandwatch**, Marsh Haven, Marsh Road, Gurnard (Tel 0983 525041), who are concerned with conservation of the countryside, and the **Medina Valley Field Centre**, Dodnor Lane, Newport (Tel 0983 522195).

Geographical Breakdown of Region

Kent

Maidstone

Kent's County Town is an old market and garrison town that is traditionally associated with brewing, but now relies on mixed light industry. Within the town the **Archbishop's Palace** (Mill Street) and environs are worth exploring, as well as the **Tyrwhitt-Drake Museum of Carriages**, the largest of its kind in the country. The **local museum** and **art gallery** are housed in an old manor house on St Faith's Street (open 10 a.m.–5.30 p.m, Monday–Saturday, 2 p.m.–5 p.m. Sunday). **Tourist Information** is at The Gatehouse, Old Palace Court, Mill Street (Tel 0622 602169).

Outside Maidstone, the **Museum of Kent Rural Life** is at Lock Land, Sanding (open Easter–October), while **Brattle Farm Museum** (Five Oak Lane, Staplehurst) looks at 200 years of rural skills and crafts. **Allington Castle** (open 2 p.m.–4 p.m. daily) dates from the 13th century, is moated and now serves as a Carmelite conference and retreat centre. **Stoneacre** is a 15th-century manor owned by the National Trust. The nearby villages of Staplehurst, Aylesford, Bearsted, Boxley, Loose, Ightham and Charing are all worth visiting. They contain many buildings of historic interest and are surrounded by hop fields and orchards.

Dartford and Gravesend

The Dartford Tunnel, linking Essex and Kent, has been overcrowded since it was opened. A new bridge is now being constructed.

The area around **Dartford High Street** is a conservation zone, within which can be found the **local museum**. Nearby is the **Rare Breeds Survival Centre**, particularly suitable for children. **Keithley Light Railway** is run by enthusiastic volunteers. **Tourist Information** is at Home Gardens (Tel 0322 343243)

Gravesend, at the mouth of the Thames, used to be a maritime centre for Thames pilots. Today it has an interesting riverfront conservation area. **Tourist Information** is at 10 Parrock Street (Tel 0474 337600).

Rochester

Founded by the Romans in AD 604, Rochester has a Norman **Cathedral** which is the second oldest in England after Canterbury Cathedral. The **Castle** is a fine example of Norman fortress architecture, with a keep that stands 113 feet (34.5 m.) high and offers good views over the Medway. The **High Street** contains a **local museum** in the Guildhall, as well as the **Tudor Poor Traveller's House** and **Eastgate House**, where the **Charles Dickens Centre** is housed. If you feel like being energetic, details of interesting **city walks** are available on 0634 46043. Nearby is **Upnor Castle**, built in 1559, as well as a ruined castle at Eynesford and **Knights Templar Manor** at Strood.

The Medway Towns

Surrounding Rochester, the Medway Towns have gradually been linked together by the spread of urbanisation, with a number of housing estates now overlapping outskirt areas. Rainham, Chatham, Sittingbourne, Faversham and Gillingham have become more or less one conurbation, although each town remains interesting within its own right. Collectively they are marketed as 'Maritime Kent', for Chatham and Gillingham were once the major shipbuilding areas for Elizabeth I's navy. These are now the industrial areas of Kent, although their history has been well maintained in places such as **Chatham Dockyard**, and at the **Dolphin Yard Sailing Barge Museum** (open Sunday, Easter–October), a working museum in Sittingbourne. At Chatham, and of more general historic interest there is also **Fort Amherst** (open April–October), with its intricate maze of tunnels.

Faversham

The centre of the old gunpowder and brewing industries, Faversham is home to **Old Court Hall Museum** (Abbey Road); **Gunpowder Mills** (off Stonebridge way), and the family run **Shepherd Neame Brewery** (Tel 0795 532206, call first to arrange a tour). Close at hand there is also **Ospringe**, site of a stone chapel built on a pagan shrine. **Tourist Information** is at Fleur de Lis Heritage Centre, 13 Preston Street (Tel 0795 534542).

The **Isle of Sheppey** is a heterogeneous area. The main town of Sheerness is an old seaside resort and container port. An older historic site is **Minster Abbey**. **Tourist Information** is on Bridge Road (Tel 0795 665324).

Canterbury

Canterbury is famed for being the seat of the Church of England. Its **Cathedral**, built in the Norman Perpendicular and Gothic styles, is the oldest in the country, while the town itself still contains medieval streets and buildings.

During high season Canterbury is thronged with visitors. Off season however, the town is quieter and tourists are welcomed, especially for longer stays. **Guided walks** (Tel 0227 454779) are offered from Amett House, Hawks Lane, and the town's **Heritage Centre** explains the area's history. Also of interest are the old **Augustian ruins** and **Pilgrim's Centre**, although the latter is usually very busy. Less busy but nonetheless worth a visit is the **Ethnic Doll and Toy Museum** on St Margaret's Street. In the evening, the **Gulbenkian** and **Marlowe Theatres** offer a variety of performances. **Tourist Information** is at 34 St Margaret's Street (Tel 0227 766567).

Close to Canterbury are the pretty villages of **Wye**, with its Agricultural College and race course, and **Whitstable**, an old fishing village famed for its oysters, as well as **Bishopsbourne, Ash**, and the delighfully-named **Wickhambreaux**. **Chilham** has an impressive castle with terraced gardens and offers jousting and falconry on Sundays and Bank Holidays and Chilham May Fair (held in May), when locals gather in period costume. **Herne Bay** is an old resort, somewhat run-down, but still boasting some good examples of Regency and Victorian architecture amidst its amusement arcades and cafes. From Herne Bay there is a **cliff-top walk** (and ideal picnic spot) to Whitstable.

Margate

Margate is a popular family holiday spot. The town is characterised by fine Victorian architecture, and offers all the traditional seaside attractions: a promenade, lido, funfair, ballroom, ice-rink and cinema, along with an eight mile (12.8 km.) beach which won the Clean Beach Award in 1988. Social history is chronicled in the **Tudor House Museum** and local history in the **Old Town Hall**. **Drapers Trust Windmill** is a good example of the many smock mills of the area. From Margate there is a **cliff-top walk** to Birchinton. **Tourist Information** is on Marine Terrace (Tel 0843 220241).

Ramsgate

Ramsgate has seen better days, although its **Royal Harbour**, built in

1794, is still rather special. Its high sea wall is perfect for a stroll, or a good spot to join the local anglers and watch the coming and going of the fishing boats and yachts. This is also the site of the Dunkirk Cross-Channel Ferry. Details of the **Harbour Trail** can be obtained at **Tourist Information**, Argyll Centre, Queen Street (Tel 0843 591086). For the history of Ramsgate visit the **Library** (open 9 a.m.–5 p.m. Monday–Saturday) at Guildford Lawn. Close by, **Broadstairs** is an attractive resort which holds an annual folk week, usually in August.

Deal

Deal's Old Town runs along the beach, from where narrow lanes lead to **Middle Street** and rows of former fishermen's houses. Throughout the town there are a large number of Flemish weaving cottages. The **Castle** (open 10 a.m.–4 p.m. daily, 6 p.m. in summer) was built in 1540 as one of the Tudor bastions against Catholic Europe. Close by there is also **Walmer Castle** (open 10 a.m.–4 p.m. daily, 6 p.m. in summer), once home to the Duke of Wellington.

East Kent Field Centre is situated at Great Mangeham, while **Sandwich**, once a thriving port until the River Stour silted up, retains many 16th-century buildings. Of particular interest are the old **Toll Bridge, Quay Gatehouse** and the **Guildhall**. Local-style windmills can also be seen here. Further along the river are the Roman ruins of **Richborough Castle**, once the first port of call for Roman legions arriving in Britain.

Dover

This is the region's major ferry port. The town has recently spent huge amounts of money on promotion, fearing the possible impact of the Channel Tunnel on cross-channel ferry services. Known as 'White Cliff Country', the area boasts **Dover Castle** (open all year) and a traditional Regency seafront. The **Roman Painted House** (open 10 a.m.–5 p.m. daily) is worth a visit, as is **Dover Gaol** with its audio-visual displays. **St Margaret's Bay**, which has been awarded an EEC Blue Flag, is nearby and can be reached along the **cliff-top walk**. **Barfreston Church** is well known for its stone masonry. **Tourist Information** is at Dover Town Hall (Tel 0304 206941).

Folkestone

Since the last century, Folkestone has changed from a small fishing village to a cross-channel ferry port. Ferries leave for Boulogne, Calais and Ostend. It is a thriving holiday centre with sandy beaches, a promenade and cliff-top walks, and is ideal for picnics. The Leas Cliff Top and old Cliff Sands are Victorian resort areas. The area surrounding the **harbour**, the bustling **High Street** and the old **fish market** are all worth exploring. The **local museum** is at Grace Hill. Nearby are the villages of **Barham** and **Elham**. **Tourist Information** is at Harbour Street (Tel 0303 58594).

Romney Marsh

This is a Regional Development Area and contains interesting wildlife in its wetland areas. **Lymphon** and **Saltwood Castles** are open to the public all year. The villages of Pluckley, Appledore and Hythe are delightful. The **Romney, Hythe and Dymchurch Steam Railway** runs through this romantic area.

Tenterden

Tenterden is an old weaving centre and its **High Street** has many original Georgian and Elizabethan façades. Characteristic of the town are its ship-lapped timber frontages. The towered 15th-century church dominates the town, and from the top there are fine views across the Weald to the Channel.

Tenterden is a good base from which to explore the lovely surrounding area. **Cranbrook** has a local history museum (at **Bailiffs House**, open March to October), and Hawkhurst, Smarden, Sissinghurst and Biddenden are villages that are very characteristic of the area. **Ashford** is the local shopping town and the planned destination of a terminal for the Channel Tunnel.

Royal Tunbridge Wells

This classic Regency spa town has the lovely collonaded **Pantiles**, the **Bath House** and **Chalybeate Springs**. The **Royal Victoria Theatre** is a beautiful example of the grand architecture of Victorian theatres. Mount Pleasant, Mount Ephraim and Mount Sion are where the Regency gentry stayed when visiting. **Tourist Information** is at the Town Hall (Tel 0892 26121).

Nearby is the village of Herstmonceux, home of the **Royal Observatory** and of trug making (gardeners' wooden baskets). **Finchcocks House** at Goudhurst has musical tours and recitals and **Scotney Castle Gardens** at Lamberhurst have an open-air theatre in the summer (can become overcrowded on public holidays). **Chiddingstone** is in the care of the National Trust; the castle is mock Gothic and contains many unusual collections of Stuart and Egyptian and Oriental artefacts. **Horsmorden** is an old iron town. Close by is the magnificent **Bodiam Castle** (open March–November) which stands in a lake-like moat surrounded by water lilies.

Tonbridge

A small country town on the river Medway, Tonbridge has many attractions in the surrounding area. These include the **Whitbread Hops and Shire Horse Centre** at Beltring; the Georgian and Tudor High Street at West Malling; the **Coldrum Stones** in the Manor Country Park, Yalding; and the pretty villages of **Offham** and **West Farliegh**.

Sevenoaks

To a large extent a commuter town, Sevenoaks nevertheless retains a strong sense of community. Nearby there are some special places to visit, including **Ightham Mote**, a fairytale-like medieval moated manor and a good alternative to other more crowded country houses open to the public.

Accommodation

First Class

Chilston Park, near Lenham, Maidstone ME17 2BE (Tel 0622 859803). Tudor manor south of Maidstone, set in one of the most romantic locations in the South-east. Open fires in every room and candle-light only downstairs.

Royal Victoria and Bull Hotel, 16–18 High Street, Rochester (Tel 0634 846266). A 400-year-old coaching house offering true comfort. Queen Victoria once stayed here.

Gordon Hotel, High Street, Rochester (Tel 0634 842656). Seventeenth-century building providing all facilities and a secluded walled garden.

Finchden Manor, Appledore Road, Tenterden (Tel 05806 4719). Bed and breakfast in a 15th-century manorhouse.

Spa Hotel, Mount Ephraim, Royal Tunbridge Wells TN4 8XJ (Tel 0892 570575). Traditional hotel established in 1766, also offering a health and leisure centre.

Middle Range

Rock House Hotel, 102 Tonbridge Road, Maidstone (Tel 0622 51616). Small, comfortable guest house close to the city centre.

Whitefriars, Boley Hill, Rochester (Tel 0634 409995). Georgian house in a quiet mews near the Castle.

Cathedral Gate Hotel, 36 Burgate, Canterbury CT1 2HA (Tel 0227 464381). Small hotel, recently renovated, set next to Canterbury Cathedral. Very atmospheric, exposed beams and creaking stairways.

Tancliff Hotel, 20 Wellington Crescent, Ramsgate (Tel 0843 593016). Regency terraced hotel offering fine views of the harbour and beach.

Castle Guest House, 10 Castle Hill Road, Dover CT16 1QW (Tel 0304 201656). A listed building dating from around 1830, located on the foothills of Dover Castle and offering bed and breakfast.

West Cross House, High Street, Tenterden TN30 6JL (Tel 05806 2224). Excellent value bed and breakfast (and dinner if ordered in advance) in an impressive Georgian house in the centre of town. Seven bedrooms, all different (closed in winter).

Economy

Willington Court, Willington Street, Maidstone (Tel 0622 38885). Comfortable accommodation in a listed Tudor house.

University of Kent, Conference Office (Tel 0227 769186, contact Peter Jordan). Rooms available on the hillside campus during university holidays.

Walnut Tree Farm, Lynsore Bottom, Upper Hardres, Canterbury CT4 6EG (Tel 0227 87375). Farmhouse bed and breakfast in a 14th-century thatched farmhouse set in its own grounds. No smoking.

Alma Tavern, 126 West Street, Deal (Tel 0304 360244). Family run establishment offering rooms above a pub.

King's Arms, Strand Street, Sandwich (Tel 0304 617330). Bed and breakfast in pleasant rooms over a pub in this quiet seaside town ten minutes from Deal.

Dell Guest House, 233 Folkestone Road, Dover CT17 9SL (Tel 0304 202422). Small, family run guest house close to the docks and station.

Self-Catering Cottages

Freedom Holiday Cottages, Weavenden Cottage, Frittended, Cranbrook (Tel 0580 80251) and **Kent Farm Holidays**, Mrs R Bannock, Court Lodge Farm, The Street, Teston (Tel 0622 812570) both arrange self-catering cottages.

Eating Out
First Class

Restaurant 74, Wincheap, Canterbury (Tel 0227 767411). One of the best restaurants in the South-east, serves nouveau British cuisine, close to Canterbury.

Walthams Restaurant, The Old Poor House Hotel, Kake Street, Petham, Canterbury (Tel 022 770 413). Vegetarian gourmet menu in this delightful country house hotel just ten minutes from Canterbury.

Sankey's, 39 Mount Ephraim, Royal Tunbridge Wells (Tel 0892 511422). Excellent fish restaurant in an old Victorian house.

Middle Range

The Duck, Pitts Bottom, Canterbury (Tel 0227 830354). Home-made food and local cider a speciality.

Cliffe Tavern Hotel, High Street, St Margaret's-at-Cliffe, Dover (Tel 0304 852749). Excellent menu of local produce and some vegetarian dishes in this old-fashioned inn set in a walled rose garden just outside Dover.

The Captain's Table, Cliffe Road, Kingsdown, Deal (Tel 0304 373755). Home-cooked fish, steak and vegetarian dishes in this village at one end of a cliff walk from Dover.

Economy

Old House at Home, 10 Pudding Lane, Maidstone (Tel 0622 52363). Fresh fish, poultry and meat dishes in a friendly atmosphere.

Alberry's, 38 St Margaret's Street, Canterbury (Tel 0227 452378). Cheap and filling pizza and vegetarian dishes.

Marlowe's 59 St Peter's Street, Canterbury (Tel 0227 462194). Vegetarian and international food.

East Sussex

Rye

One of the Cinque Ports, Rye is very picturesque but can be very busy in the summer, with crowds ruining an atmosphere that is best experienced during off-peak periods, when the 18th-century romance of the town is more apparent. Of interest on Mermaid Street are the **Old Mint, Town Hall** and **Fletchers House. Ypres Castle and Museum** and **Bamber Castle** (built in 1539) are worth visiting. Pevensey has a ruined fortress, the **Court House Museum** and two very picturesque and interesting churches.

Battle

This is where the famous Battle of Hastings was fought and where

William fulfilled his vow to build an **Abbey** (the ruins can still be seen). There is a pilgrims rest and a 12th-century church. The old **Pharmacy** is interesting to visit. Nearby many water sports can be enjoyed at **Bewl Bridge Reservoir**, and **Bodiam Castle** (12th-century and moated), run by the National Trust, is open to the public.

Hastings

The town has an interesting variety of architectural styles. The Victorian area of **St Leonards** is promoted by a local conservation group, while on the beach the **Net Sheds** are unique. Walk along the **High Street** and **All Saints Street** and visit **Stade Hill**. The **Old Town** is dominated by the ruined **Castle** (open April to September). There are a number of cliff walks and a cliff railway, going past **St Clements Caves** which were once used by smugglers. The **Fishermans Museum** tells of Hastings' former livelihood. For evening entertainment try the **Stables Theatre**. **Tourist Information** from 4 Robertson Terrace (Tel 424242).

Nearby is **Bexhill**, an old fishing town and Victorian seaside resort. The beaches are good but do not reach EEC Blue Flag standards. The **Manor Costume Museum** is open Easter to September. The villages of Ninfield, Sadlescombe, Icklesham and Burwash are interesting to explore. **Horam** is the home of the **Merrydown Wine Company**, which opens its vineyards to the public. Near Etchingham there is a **Shire Horse Centre**, which promotes the use of horses in modern farming.

Eastbourne

This old resort is now largely inhabited by the retired. It has a Blue Flag Beach, a promenade, a Napoleonic fort (the **Redoubt**) and the **Lifeboat Museum** on Green Parade. The Grand Parade band stand seats 3500 people, and performances are held throughout the summer. Also worth visiting is the **Towner Gallery**. **Tourist Information** on Lower Parade (Tel 0323 27474).

Beachy Head Park contains the white chalk cliffs of the Seven Sisters, and offers exhilarating walks and good views over the Channel. Close by is the **Wilmington Man** (carved into the chalk downs and thought to be medieval, but looking primeval). **Ditchling Beacon** is also good walking ground, with clear views. **Bishopstone** has a Saxon Church, and **Glyndebourne** is famous for its opera festival. Two fine country houses are at **Firle Place** and **Glynde Place** (June–September). The coast going westward is almost a continuous conurbation through Newhaven, Seaford and Rottingdean.

Brighton

In contrast to the rather elderly population of the rest of this stretch of coast, Brighton is a young and lively town – fuelled by the Polytechnic, the nearby University of Sussex at Falmer, and other Further Education colleges. A Regency resort, there is plenty of fine architecture with many period squares and crescents. There is also the incredible **Brighton Pavilion**, built by the Prince Regent, which is open to the public – the stables house a museum and the Dome is open for concerts. The **Lanes**, a concentrated area of little alleys which were once the homes of local fishermen, are now filled with antique jewellery shops, and become very crowded in the summer. There are two classic Victorian piers, one now sadly neglected. The beaches are pebble and unfortunately quite polluted. The old **Volks Railway** runs along the seafront eastwards from Kemptown with it's atmosphere of decayed elegance.

Westwards is Hove, traditionally the smarter area. Here, at **Sussex County Cricket Ground** there is a museum of county cricket, found at Eaton Road. Brighton offers a very wide variety of entertainment with many theatres and cinemas, and an annual arts festival. There are also the Brighton races and the races at nearby Plumpton. **Stanmer Museum** (of country life) is within easy reach, as are the **Thomas Stanford Museum** at Preston Park; **The Grange**, Rottingdean (which houses a toy museum) and the **Devil's Dyke**, which offers good walking and views. **Tourist Information** is at 54 The Old Steine (Tel 0273 23755).

Lewes

Now the county town of East Sussex, Lewes has a fascinating history. The **castle** is Norman (open 10 a.m.–5 p.m. April–October), and has the **Sussex Archaeology Museum** housed within it. The town grew up on the hillside between the castle and the River Ouse. Near the castle is the house where Anne of Cleves lived after Henry VIII divorced her; it is now a **folklore museum** (in Southover High Street). The town has an attractive compact centre, and the narrow streets of the old town are locally called 'twittens'. Outside the town, there is **Raystede Animal Welfare Centre** (open 10 a.m.–6 p.m.), as well as **Ditchling Common, Hickstead**, which has show jumping events in season. There is a good **theatre** at **Sussex University** in Falmer. **Alfriston** is a picturesque village, although it is very popular and crowded in the high season. **Drusilla Zoo** is nearby.

Accommodation

First Class

Netherfield Place, near Battle TN33 9PP (Tel 042 46 4455). Small country house hotel set in its own grounds. Fresh produce in the restaurant from the vegetable garden.

Shelleys Hotel, High Street, Lewes BN7 1XS (Tel 0273 472361). Comfortable accommodation in a grand Georgian townhouse with a delightful garden.

The Grand, King's Road, Brighton BN1 2FW (Tel 0273 21188). Following refurbishment in 1986, Brighton's grand old lady is more luxurious than ever before; 125 years old and offering tradition at its best. On the sea front.

Middle Range

The Old Vicarage Guest House, 66 Church Square, Rye TN31 7HF (Tel 0797 222119). Bed and breakfast in an old vicarage by the Church of St Mary. Some bedrooms have four-posters, and part of the house is used for semi-permanent art exhibitions.

Southcroft Private Hotel, 15 South Cliff Avenue, Meads, Eastbourne BN20 7AH (Tel 0323 29071). Small hotel with seven rooms in a quiet residential area not far from the beach and town centre.

Topps, 17 Regency Square, Brighton BN1 2FG (Tel 0273 729334). Friendly family run hotel close to the sea front. Restaurant and bar in the basement.

Economy

Winchelsea Tea-Room, Hiham Green, Winchelsea, near Rye TN36 4HB (Tel 0797 22679). Bed and breakfast (and evening meal) above an Edwardian-style tea-room, not far from Rye in Winchelsea, one of the area's best kept secrets.

Burnt Wood, Powdermill Lane, Battle TN33 0SU (Tel 042 46 2459). Good value bed and breakfast (and evening meal), also run as a language school for overseas businessmen. Swimming pool in garden, as well as a resident peacock in the rose garden. Six miles (9.6 km.) from Hastings.

Braemar Guest House, Steyning Road, Rottingdean, Brighton BN2 7GA (Tel 0273 304263). Welcoming family run bed and breakfast with fourteen bedrooms, close to Rudyard Kipling's house.

Eating Out

First Class

Flackley Ash, London Road, Peasmarsh, near Rye (Tel 0797 21381). Traditional food prepared by the owner/chef of this cosy hotel, who also organises jazz weekends during the winter.

English's Oyster Bar and Seafood Restaurant, 29–31 East Street, Brighton (Tel 0273 27980/25661). High-standard fish restaurant which has been a family business for over 200 years.

Middle Range

The Pub at Beachy Head, Beachy Head, Eastbourne (Tel 0323 28060). Restaurant and pub serving British and international cuisine, and with a children's play area.

Annie's, 41 Middle Street, Brighton (Tel 0273 202051). Homemade English cooking with a good value children's menu.

Economy

Swan Cottage Tea-Rooms, 41 The Mint, Rye (Tel 0797 222423). Rustic tea-room offering the best of British.

Slims Healthfood Restaurant, 92 Churchill Square, Brighton (Tel 0273 24582). Well-established vegetarian/vegan restaurant offering a wide range of dishes.

West Sussex

Shoreham, Worthing and Littlehampton

These towns join together in a stretch of suburban development along the coast. Like the other side of Brighton they are largely retirement areas. All have promenades and are classically old-fashioned resorts. Worthing has the **Sussex Folklore Museum** on the High Street (open Tuesdays–Saturdays, March–December). Nearby are the Iron Age earthworks of **Cissbury Ring** and **Chanctonbury Ring**, while from **Truleigh Hill** there are incredible views. The Elizabethan **Parham House** at Storrington is open Easter to September. Littlehampton has a harbour and is a popular sailing centre.

Arundel

Dominated by its spectacular **Castle** (open 1 p.m.–6 p.m., April–October ex. Saturdays), Arundel has an attractive town centre. There are good walks along the river, where the Wildfowl Trust looks after the meadows. The **Museum of Curiosity** is open in the summer. The pretty village of **Amberley** is close by and has a ruined castle, Norman church and marshes. **Pulborough** is built over a Roman village, and pretty **Petworth** has a grand house and parkland owned by the National Trust (open April–October). **Midhurst** on the River Rother is also attractive. There are races at **Fontwell Park**.

On the coast there is the once elegant resort of Bognor Regis, now unfortunately marred by poor town planning. A large Butlins holiday camp is based there.

Chichester

Chichester **Cathedral** – with its unusual detached bell tower – and **Close** are the highlights of the town. Unfortunately the atmosphere in the Close is marred by the main road that runs close by. The elaborate **old market cross** is rather unique. In the centre of the town are the **Buttermarket, Pallant House Gallery** and the **local museum**. The shopping area of Chichester has few distinctive features, but offers plenty of chain stores. For entertainment there is the highly regarded **Festival Theatre**.

Chichester Harbour is away from the town, although it was once connected by a canal. This natural harbour covers 27 square miles (70 sq. km.) and is often busy with yachtsmen, windsurfers and dinghy racers. Nearby villages to visit are **Appledram** on the edge of the harbour; **Birdham** and **Chidham**. **Bosham** is a pretty village with a couple of nice pubs, one by the water's edge. Unwary visitors leaving their cars parked on the dry mud flats can get a horrible shock when they return to find the tide has come in! The village often gets overcrowded in the summer. Selsey Bill – promontory at the end of the peninsula – is interesting to explore, but is usually busy due to one of the largest caravan parks in Britain being situated here.

Out to the east of Chichester, **Singleton Weald Open Air Museum** has reconstructed historic buildings and provides demonstrations of old skills and crafts (open 11 a.m.–5 p.m., April–September and Wednesdays & Sundays only November–April). **Fishbourne Roman Palace** (open May–November) and **Bignor Roman Villa** (open March–October) are also in the vicinity. **Goodwood races** are nearby and **Goodwood House** is open from Easter to October (afternoons only).

Accommodation

First Class

Bailiffscourt, Climping, near Littlehampton BN17 5RW (Tel 0903 723511). Warm country house hotel built in medieval style in the 1920s. Lovely furnishings, 20 acres (8 hectares) of grounds and a pleasant courtyard.

The Dolphin and Anchor, West Street, Chichester PO19 1QE (Tel 0243 785121). Old town centre hotel full of chintz and atmosphere.

Middle Range

Mill Stream, Bosham, near Chichester PO18 8HL (Tel 0243 573234). A charming traditional hotel in this rural village near Chichester.

The Royal Norfolk, The Esplanade, Bognor Regis PO21 2LH (Tel 0243 826222). Traditional Regency seaside hotel, civilised and relaxed.

Economy

Gratwicke House, 9 Gratwicke Road, Worthing BN11 4BH (Tel 0203 213000). Small bed and breakfast with four rooms, noted for its tasteful decor and friendly welcome, setting it apart from run-of-the-mill establishments.

Rock Windmill, The Hollow, Washington, near Worthing RH20 3DA (Tel 0903 892941). Bed and breakfast offered in this converted windmill (the sails are no longer there), once the home of composer John Ireland. Close to Chanctonbury Ring.

Eating Out

First Class

The Chequers, Slaugham, near Handcross (Tel 0444 400239). A restaurant with bedrooms, The Chequers specialises in fresh fish, oyster and lobster, as well as serving traditional English fare.

Spread Eagle Hotel, South Street, Midhurst (Tel 073 081 6911). Highly-rated restaurant serving the best of British cuisine in a 15th-century tavern and coaching inn.

Middle Range

Findon Manor, Findon Village, near Worthing (Tel 090 671 2733). Bar and restaurant meals in this old Rectory dating from the 16th century.

Micawber's Restaurant, 13 South Street, Chichester (Tel 0243 786989). Good value fish restaurant with a Dickensian theme.

Economy

Clinch's Salad House, 14 Southgate, Chichester (Tel 0243 788822). A small restaurant/cafe offering home-cooked traditional meals.

Cafe Violette, 67 High Street, Arundel (Tel 0903 883702). Friendly cafe where almost all food, including the bread, is prepared on the premises.

Inland Sussex

Horsham and **Crawley** are the two main towns of this area. Horsham is now mainly a modern town, although it still remembers its origins as an Assize village. The **local history** museum in **Causeway House** is a reminder of, amongst other things, the iniquities of the Assize system, for in times gone by Horsham was frequently the site of mass hangings. It was also the starting point for many a wronged citizen on their way to the colonies, often banished for crimes that were little more than the result of hunger or cold. On the south-west of the town stands the school **Christ's Hospital**, where students still model the traditional long-gowned uniform. Nearby are the villages of **Rusper**, offering some good pubs, and **Warnham**, site of an interesting church.

Crawley is a 1950s new town and offers little of notable interest. The **Barn Theatre**, known for quality entertainment, is situated in the attractive suburb of Ifield. To the north lies Gatwick Airport, as well as the village of **West Hoathley**, where there is a **Folk Museum** in the **Old Priest House** and the **Sharpthorne Museum of Leather Tanning**. **Bayham Abbey** ruins can be found in Hartfield, and the **Blue Bell Steam Railway** runs through the area.

Surrey

Guildford is the compact attractive country and market town. It has a well-preserved cobbled and traffic-free **High Street**, adjoining a traditional **street market**. The modern **Cathedral**, designed by

Edward Maufe, has a stunning interior. The pretty waterfront is worth a stroll, as is the Norman **Castle**, now in ruins but also the site of a **Brass Rubbing Centre**. The **local museum** is at the Castle Arch and there is a gallery at 155 High Street. A **cattle market** is still held at **Slyford Green**, and guided walks around here and the rest of town are held on Wednesdays and Sundays from June to August. For entertainment, the **Yvonne Arnaud Theatre** has a good reputation and receives a few London previews. **Tourist Information** is at the Civic Hall, London Road (Tel 0483 67314).

Nearby **Loseley House** and organic farms (the famous yoghurt and ice-cream producers) are open May to September (Wednesdays–Saturdays). The **Watts Gallery** is at Compton. There are many pretty villages set around greens in this area, including Shere, Shamley Green, Elstead on the Wey and Ewhurst near Pitch Hill. **Nowerwood Nature Reserve** and Chilworth's St Marthas Hill are both nearby. Cranleigh has a modern centre, but around it the villages are pretty – especially Bromley and Wonersh. The Guildford–to–Farnham road goes along the Hog's Back which has good views of the surrounding countryside.

Leatherhead, a once attractive town on the North Downs, is now dominated by modern development. There are many narrow streets around the centre. The **Fire and Iron Gallery** on Oxshot Road displays metal work by artists. For entertainment there is the **Thorndyke Theatre**. Nearby are lots of good places for country walks; Bookham and Banks Common; the **Druids Grove Yews** at Norbury Park, and the crowded Box Hill.

Dorking, now largely a commuter town, has a market on Fridays. The local museum is at the **Old Foundry**. Nearby Ranmore Common has many interesting scenic walks. **Chapel Farm Animal Trust** is open to the public, in West Humble, Polesden Lacey, Bookham, (open March to October). It can get crowded at peak times. It has an open-air theatre in summer. Ockley has a good pub – the Cricketers Arms – specialising in country pies. Betchwood is on the River Mole and Bletchingley has a ruined Norman Castle.

Godalming was once a leather, wool, and coaching town. The **High Street Museum** tells its story well. Nearby you can take punts, canoes or dinghies out on the river from Farncombe Boat House, Cotteshall Lock (Tel 0486 821306). Visit the Lockwood Donkey Sanctuary, Hatch Lane, Sandhills, Wormley and the nearby Hascombe Iron Age Fort. Chiddingford has a family run walking stick factory, Cooper & Sons, Combe Lane, Wormley.

Haslemere and **Hindhead** are two small towns surrounded by forest, in the South of Surrey. The **Dolmetsch Musical Instrument**

factory is at Haslemere; all the instruments are hand-made and visitors can arrange in advance to see them being made. The town hosts a festival of early music, held annually in July. Hindhead lies close to Gibbets Hill, at 894 feet (273 m.), overlooking the **Devil's Punchbowl**.

At **Farnham**, the park and **castle** cover 300 acres (121.5 hectares). The River Wey runs through the town. The town centre has mixed architecture, and particularly of note are the buildings of the Georgian period. There is a Norman **church** in the town centre. The **New Ashgate Gallery** at Wagon Yard displays lots of local artists' work. **Willmer House Museum** of local history is in West Street. **The Maltings** is the arts centre on Bridge Street, while the **Redgrave Theatre** has concerts and drama and the Bach festival is held annually. Nearby there is the **Old Kiln Agricultural Museum** at Reeds Road, Tilford (open April to September, Tuesdays–Sundays). **Waverley Abbey Ruins**; the **Badshot Lea Longbarrow**, and **Rowhill Nature Reserve** are close. **Tourist Information** is at South Street (Tel 0483 444007).

Chobham and **Woking** are both now mainly 'dormitory' towns for commuters into London. Woking has a light Industrial estate and new civic centre, and incidentally boasts the largest cemetary in the UK! Chobham has an **RSPCA Centre** (at Millbrook) and the **London Bus Preservation Trust** at Redhill Road. Nearby are the Horsell and Wisley Commons and Bagshot Heath. Wisley is the home of the **Royal Horticultural Society**, and the gardens are usually very crowded.

Chertsey lies on the Thames with lots of open space and woodland surrounding it, including the pretty Chertsey Mead and the old Abbey Ruins. **Runneymead** was the site of the signing of the Magna Carta in 1215. It is also on the river, with open spaces owned by the National Trust. The **John F. Kennedy Memorial** is placed on high ground halfway up Coopers Hill, standing on an acre of land given by Britain to the United States. At the top of the hill, the **Air Forces Memorial** stands in memory to the 20,000 airmen who died in the Second World War with no known grave. Being close to London these open areas can get crowded during holiday times.

Esher, Cobham, Staines and **Epsom** are now practically absorbed into London but each keeps its individual 'village' centre. Esher is a very prosperous area with a lot of exclusive houses, shops and restaurants. It has a large Common and nearby Ardbrook Common and Claremont Woods; all contain good footpaths. The famous race course, **Sandown Park** is near Esher (Tel 0372 460372 for details of the meetings). Epsom also has races throughout the season, the most famous being the annual **Derby** (Tel 0372 726311). **Kempton Park**, near Staines, is another popular racing venue (Tel 0932 782292). The riverside at Staines has a Regency glamour and a tangible atmosphere of days past.

Accommodation

First Class

Angel Coaching Inn, High Street, Guildford GU1 3DR (Tel 0483 64555). High standard traditional comfort in the centre of town.

Trevena House Hotel, Alton Road, Farnham GU120 5ER (Tel 0252 716908). Comfortable and spacious hotel in a late-19th century mansion, close to Jane Austen country.

Middle Range

Bulmer Farm, Holmbury St Mary, Dorking RH5 6LG (Tel 0306 730210). Bed and breakfast in the North Downs on this peaceful farm south of Dorking.

Knaphill Manor, Carthouse Lane, Woking GU21 4XT (Tel 0276 857962). Bed and breakfast in a delightful 18th-century family home. Croquet lawn and tennis court in garden.

Economy

Clandon Manor Farm, Back Lane, East Clandon, Guildford GU4 7SA (Tel 0482 222357/222765). Bed and breakfast on the edge of this charming village east of Guildford. Riding lessons available from the farm.

Crossways Farm, Abinger, Dorking RH5 6PZ (Tel 0306 730173). Bed and breakfast and evening meal in an atmospheric and historic old farmhouse from around 1620.

Eating Out

First Class

Clandon Park Restaurant, Clandon Park, Clandon, near Guildford (Tel 0483 222502). Excellent English cooking in this stately house set in peaceful parkland.

Middle Range

The Refectory, 6 Church Walk, Richmond (Tel 081 940 6264). Traditional home-cooked fare in buildings connected to Richmond Church (vegetarian dish usually available). Prices are really 'Economy' but the service and value is definitely Middle Range.

The Swan Inn, Petworth Road, Chiddingfold (Tel 042 879 2073). Up-market bar meals served in this pleasant inn situated in the peaceful village of Chiddingfold.

Economy

Jeffries Wine Bar, 7 Jeffries Passage, Guildford (Tel 0483 505311). Cosy wine bar in the centre of town serving traditional fare. Some vegetarian dishes.

Sun Inn, The Common, Dunsfold, near Godalming (Tel 0486 49242). Filling home-cooked food, open fires, exposed beams and views of the village green; unpretentious English hospitality at its best.

Hampshire

Hampshire sits in the centre of southern England and, strictly speaking, comes under the jurisdiction of the **Southern Tourist Board** (40 Chamberlayne Road, Eastleigh SO5 5JH; Tel 0703 620006). The county covers an area of 1382 square miles (3580 sq. km.) and can be divided into four physical areas: a belt of chalk downland rising in some places to over 800 feet (240 metres), which stretches across the middle of the county from east to west; tertiary (up to 65 million years old) clays, sands and gravels in the north and south, often covered by heath and woodland; the scarps and vales in the east of the area known as the Weald; and, also in the Weald, the Lower and Upper Green sands and Gault clays, which constitute some of the oldest rocks in the area, dating from around 100 million years ago. Bronze Age farmsteads exist throughout the county, notably at **Quarley**, while hill forts at **Danebury** and **Hengistbury Head** are relics of the Iron Age. The first written records of Hampshire are in the Anglo-Saxon Chronicle of AD 755, at which time the most important town in the area was **Winchester**. Unlike many parts of the country, Hampshire was relatively untroubled by invaders (apart from attacks by Norsemen during the Middle Ages), with the result that with the exception of castles at Winchester, Odiham and Portchester, the area has few significant fortifications.

Monastic remains can be found at Beaulieu, Netley, Romsey and Winchester, while good examples of local architecture include Norman houses in **Southampton**, a medieval palace at **Bishops Waltham**, and 16th-century (and later) buildings in the Vyne at **Sherborne St John**. Hampshire's main area of outdoor interest is the **New Forest**. Once a royal hunting ground, today it is an interesting 103 square miles (269 sq. km.) of woodland, heath and bog.

Winchester

Winchester's fame stems more from its magnificent cathedral and historic associations than from its present status. King Arthur made Winchester his capital and William the Conqueror, not content with his first coronation at Westminster, arranged a second here. Winchester was also the fifth largest Roman settlement in Britain, and became the capital of Wessex in 519, followed 300 years later by promotion to the capital of England in 827. In addition, Winchester was the site of the compilation of the **Domesday Book**. Today the town no longer claims the limelight, although it remains a popular tourist centre, due largely to its cathedral, and is known to many as the home of Winchester College, one of England's most renowned public schools. The town's **Tourist Information** centre is at the Guildhall, The Broadway (Tel 0962 840500).

Notable sights within the town include the **City Cross** on the High Street, close to the Archway which was partly made from Norman stones originally used in building William the Conqueror's palace. **Winchester Cathedral** is the longest (556 feet, 169 metres) Gothic cathedral in the world and was built between 1079 and 1093. Inside are the tombs of Saxon kings of England and a memorial marking Jane Austen's sepulchre. The marble font dates from around 1180 and the stalls, with 60 misericords, from around 1320. There is also an extensive medieval tiled floor, medieval paintings and a fine Norman crypt. Architecturally, the cathedral provides good examples of Norman and Perpendicular styles.

Looking over the town are the remains of the **castle**, built by William the Conqueror in the 11th century. Here the **Great Hall** is open for viewing, as well as a number of museums with exhibits of regimental life through the ages.

Around Winchester there is the village of **Chawton**, where Jane Austen lived in the early 19th century, and **Romsey**, a small market town with a fine Norman abbey, which is also where Lord Mountbatten is buried. Lord Mountbatten's home, which at one time was also the home of Lord Palmerston, is close to Romsey. Known as **Broadlands,** it is open to the public.

The New Forest

The New Forest lies 18 miles (29 km.) south of Winchester and is an area of particular interest to the Good Tourist. One of the most extensive tracts of oak woodland in England, it is interspersed with heathland grazed by half-wild ponies, and modern plantations of conifers. William the Conqueror designated the New Forest an area which was outside the common law of England in 1079, when he used it as a royal hunting reserve. Since that time the area of the forest has been increasingly reduced by surrounding farmland, although the natural amenities remain under the care of a number of planning bodies.

Today the problem, as in so many areas of beauty, is how best to preserve the forest without encroaching on the public's right to enjoy the area as their own. Recent problems have included proposals to develop **Cranford Heath**, which is home to rare indigenous plants and wildlife, and the decision to cover the paths and tracks of **Hengistbury Head** with a layer of tarmac, in order to prevent further erosion. In the case of the latter, the project was undertaken successfully, but amidst protest from locals and frequent visitors to the area, who, justifiably, were worried about the visual impact of stretches of tarmac. The Local Council has given assurances however, that paths will have a further covering of grit (or similar) in order to make them blend in with their surroundings.

Other bones of contention include the problem of increased traffic in the area, which has led to a rise in the number of animals being killed by motorists, the age-old problem of litter, and the difficulties of preventing damage in general.

The situation is not helped by the fact that, in finding solutions, there are essentially three parties to be taken into account, as well as the welfare of the forest – and its associated attractions – itself. Inhabitants of the area are becoming increasingly frustrated by tourists, while tourists themselves have to be split into their categories of day-trippers (residents from areas within easy distance of the forest) and longer-term visitors, either from abroad or further afield in the United Kingdom. Inevitably, the revenue generated by all parties is instrumental in maintaining the natural balance of the forest, yet a solution needs to be found which will satisfy all parties without threatening the area's future.

One of the main sights of interest in the forest is the **Rufus Stone**, where King William II was killed in a hunting accident.

Portsmouth

A major naval base and, with **Southsea**, a popular seaside resort, Portsmouth dates from 1194, when Richard I realised the strategic importance of Portsea Island and decided to establish a settlement in the area, granting at the same time a charter, fair and market. The town was the birthplace of Charles Dickens and today offers the usual seaside-town attractions, and an impressive range of maritime exhibitions and museums. The **dockyard** dates from 1496 and was greatly expanded after 1698; it is still a significant source of employment and covers an area in excess of 300 acres (120 hectares). Portsmouth **Tourist Information** can be found on the Clarence Esplanade, Southsea (Tel 0705 8232464); there is also an office at the Continental Ferryport, and another at 102 Commercial Road.

Tourism in Portsmouth tends to focus primarily on the 'town' of Southsea, now incorporated into Portsmouth's overall structure. The other main attractions are the excellent maritime displays, which include Henry VIII's ship, the *Mary Rose*, which set sail from Portsmouth in July 1545 to do battle with the French, but sank even before leaving the harbour. In 1982 the ship was raised from the seabed and is now on display in the **Ship Hall**, at the **Naval Heritage Centre**.

Also of considerable note is **HMS Victory**, Nelson's flagship, on board which he died during the Battle of Trafalgar in 1805 (a plaque marks the spot). The **Royal Naval Museum** offers a comprehensive history of life at sea and the development of the navy on land, while the **Royal Marines Museum** provides good insight into the history of this brave group of navy soldiers. Also in the town itself, the **Guildhall** was seriously damaged during the Second World War – as indeed was much of Portsmouth – but reopened in 1959. Today it houses concert and conference quarters and is used as the civic headquarters. Portsmouth's **cathedral** used to be the parish church and dates from the 12th century. In terms of travel, Portsmouth is the departure point for **ferries** to the Channel Islands, France and the **Isle of Wight**. Along at Southsea, **Southsea Castle** has an interesting round tower and point battery.

Accommodation

First Class

Careys Manor, Brockenhurst, New Forest, Hampshire SO42 7RH (Tel 0590 23551). Former 17th-century hunting lodge which was frequently used by King Charles I. Eighty bedrooms, some of which are in a new extension but also open directly onto the lawns or have a balcony; fine British and French cuisine and a leisure centre.

Chewton Glen, New Milton BH25 6QS (Tel 04252 5341). Highly acclaimed early 18th-century country house hotel set in 30 acres (12–15 hectares) of private gardens. Luxurious, opulent and traditional in every way.

Lainston House, Sparsholt, Winchester SO21 2LT (Tel 0962 63588). Late 17th-century house with elegant public rooms, two fine dining-rooms, and 32 bedrooms, including a number of suites. Also available are two all-weather tennis courts, a croquet lawn, clay-pigeon shooting and endless walks.

Middle Range

Belmont, Middle Road, Tiptoe, Lymington SO41 6EJ (Tel 0590 682979). Pleasant vegetarian guest house in the New Forest, also offering special interest courses such as bee-keeping, small-flock management and yoghurt-making.

Church Farm House, Barton Stacey, Winchester SO21 3RR (Tel 0962 760268). Intriguing house – part 15th-century, part Georgian, part modern – offering bed, breakfast and dinner if required. Accommodation is available in self-contained cottages, but guests are welcome in the main house when they want.

Avenue House Hotel, 22 The Avenue, Fareham PO14 1NS (Tel 0329 232175). Friendly and pleasant hotel close to the town centre and railway station, and with mature gardens.

Economy

Abbots Law, Abbots Ann, Andover SP11 7DW (Tel 0264 710350). Charming country house in the north of the county set in three acres (1.2 hectares) of grounds and offering large rooms, cordon bleu cooking, tennis court, swimming pool, croquet and sauna. Good value.

Long Candovers, Hartley Mauditt, near Alton GU34 3BP (Tel 0420 50293). Lovely 17th-century house set in peaceful gardens and paddocks and offering bed, breakfast and delicious dinners.

Forest Gate, Denmead, near Portsmouth PO7 6EX (Tel 0705 255901). Late 18th-century house with a lovely interior, lots of antiques and pleasant gardens. Bed and breakfast available, and dinner if ordered in advance.

Eating Out

First Class

Fifehead Manor, Middle Wallop, Stockbridge (Tel 0264 781565). Country house hotel and restaurant in a charming manor, parts of which date from the 11th century. British and French cuisine, with good use made of local ingredients.

Middle Range

Old Chesil Rectory and Restaurant, 1 Chesil Street, Winchester (Tel 0962 53177). Home-made traditional English fare at its best in Chesil's oldest (1450) house.

Moortown Lodge Hotel and Restaurant, 244 Christchurch Road, Ringwood (Tel 0425 471404). Pleasant country house hotel with a restaurant offering excellent British cuisine and a good range of wines.

The Town House, 59 Oxford Street, Southampton (Tel 0703 220498). Innovative vegetarian restaurant, extremely popular with locals so booking is advised. Lunch is cheaper than dinner.

Economy

Cart and Horses Country Inn, Kingsworthy, near Winchester (Tel 0962 882360). Cosy country inn dating from the 15th century and offering wholesome fare close to Winchester.

Barnaby's Bistro, 56 Osborne Road, Southsea, Portsmouth (Tel 0705 821089). Small and friendly bistro serving good English and French cuisine, and catering for vegetarians.

Harrow Inn, Steep, near Petersfield (Tel 0730 62685). Old-world pub with a great atmosphere serving straightforward, value-for-money fare.

Isle of Wight

An island county unto itself, the Isle of Wight also comes under the jurisdiction of the Southern Tourist Board, along with Hampshire (page 561 for address). Separated from the mainland by the Solent and Spithead, the diamond-shaped island stretches 22.5 miles (36 km.) from east to west and 13.5 miles (22 km.) from north to south. An irregular range of chalk hills – which constitute the thickest bed of chalk in the British Isles – runs from Culver Cliff in the east to the Needles, three detached chalk masses, in the west. In the north there is considerable woodland and in the south a range of downs rises to 787 feet (240 metres) on St Boniface Down. The Eastern Yar, Medina and Western Yar rivers all flow northwards into the Solent, with the Medina all but cutting the island in two. Chines – ravines running into the land – add to the attraction of the island, as do the rolling downs of the interior.

The Isle of Wight is divided into two counties: **Medina**, covering most of the northern half of the island and incorporating the towns of Cowes, Ryde and Newport (the county town), and **South Wight**, accounting for the rest of the island and including Bembridge, Sandown, Shanklin, Ventnor, Totland and Yarmouth. As a whole, the Isle might be considered a microcosm of England at its most typical, although at the same time it displays a unique air of its own, at once both pastoral and nautical. Access is by ferry from Portsmouth, Southampton and Lymington.

Evidence of human occupation dates from early times, with relics from the Bronze Age testifying to this in particular being a period of significant activity. Great numbers of bronze weapons have been found at **Arreton Down** and **Moon's Hill**, and there are many Bronze Age mounds. At **Mottistone** there is a **Long Stone** which is believed to be a Neolithic monolith. The Romans, who named the island 'Vectis', held it for 400 years before it was taken by the Saxons in the 6th century. At **Brading, Shide** and **Carisbrooke** there are the remains of **Roman villas**, while around the coast at Cowes, Sandown, Freshwater and Yarmouth there are forts, built between the 14th and 16th centuries as a result of fear of invasion by the French who, in 1377, had devastated the town of Newport.

The island offers all the expected delights of a seaside county and is also a walker's paradise, in as much as a network of footpaths leads apparently everywhere, including around the circumference. **Ryde** is, for most visitors, the first port of call, functioning as the island's gateway and known as one of, if not the main resort town. **Cowes** is the principal port and an international yachting centre, while Freshwater, Yarmouth, Sandown and Ventnor are typical holiday resorts which gained their popularity in Victorian times, partly as a result of Queen Victoria's patronage to the island. The grand old lady did in fact spend her last days here at **Osborne House**, near Cowes, while Alfred Lord Tennyson spent many years at Farringford.

Inland, the island is dotted with small villages, all of which are worth exploring. At **Godshill** there are delightful thatched cottages, as there are at **Calbourne**, which also has one of the best examples of a 17th-century water mill in the country, still in working order. Close to Newport, **Carisbrooke Castle**, which is said to be built on the site of a Roman fort and parts of which date from the 12th century, was once home to a reluctant Charles I when he was taken prisoner during the English Civil War in the mid-17th century.

The Isle of Wight is the site of no less than fourteen nature reserves, scattered on the south-east coast between Sandown and Ventnor, on the western peninsula between Brightstone and Totland, and in the centre of the island to the south, between Newport and Cowes. These cover everything from ancient pasture with mature and pollarded oaks to a circular walk taking in downland plants and a former mill pond which is now freshwater marshes and provides a habitat for breeding wetland birds. Details should be obtained from **Tourist Information**, Western Esplanade, Ryde (Tel 0983 62905). Other Tourist Information offices are located in the main towns around the island, but only those at Ryde and Sandown are open all year.

Accommodation

First Class

Braemar Hotel, Broadway, Sandown (Tel 0983 403358). Traditional hotel converted from a Victorian town house and now offering delightful accommodation, quiet gardens and fine cuisine.

Middle Range

Apse Manor, near Shanklin PO37 7PN (Tel 0983 866651). Lovingly restored by the owners, who are your hosts for the duration of your stay, this Tudor mansion offers elegant and comfortable accommodation in pleasant surroundings.

Woody Bank, St Lawrence, near Ventnor PO38 1XF (Tel 0983 852610). Mid-19th-century house with fine sea views over terraced gardens and excellent four-course dinners.

The Nodes Hotel, Alum Bay Old Road, Totland Bay PO39 0HZ (Tel 0983 752859). Traditional country house hotel set in lovely grounds, good for walking and close to the beach.

Economy

Edgecliffe Hotel, Clarence Gardens, Shanklin PO37 6HA (Tel 0983 866199). Family run hotel offering homely accommodation and close to the beach. No smoking.

Quinces, Cranmore Avenue, near Yarmouth PO14 0XS (Tel 0983 760080). Modern bed and breakfast (evening meal if required) set in lovely gardens close to a vineyard and dairy farm.

Eating Out

Middle Range

Seaview Hotel and Restaurant, High Street, Seaview (Tel 0983 612711). Traditional fare from the Isle of Wight in this popular local hotel.

New Inn, Shalfleet (Tel 0983 78314). Seafood in a wide range of shapes and forms is the speciality at this charming old-world inn.

Culver Lodge Hotel and Restaurant, 17 Albert Road, Sandown (Tel 0983 403819). Family run hotel with a restaurant which offers a welcome change from the host of establishments specialising in seafood. Traditional fare is served in a pleasant atmosphere.

Economy

Wight Mouse Inn, Clarendon Hotel, Chale (Tel 0983 730431). Traditional fare, good seafood, and an extensive range of whiskies. Particularly suitable for families with children as there are well thought-out play areas.

16 The West Country

The West country, consisting of Avon, Wiltshire, Dorset, Somerset, Devon, Cornwall and the Isles of Scilly, is the most popular destination in England and Wales for domestic tourists. In 1990 more money was spent in the region by British tourists than in any other region of England (including London) amounting to three quarters of that spent in the whole of Scotland. The region has been the major destination for British holidaymakers since the mid 1950s and is also becoming increasingly popular with overseas visitors, particularly those from nearby European countries such as France, the Netherlands and Germany. The region is thus one of the most visited parts of Britain and this suggests that there are certain locations, as well as times of the year, that are best avoided. There are several coastal honeypots ranging in size from locations such as Torquay, Newquay and Weston-super-Mare to the small fishing ports of Cornwall and Devon such as Mousehole, Mullion, Polperro and Boscastle. Whatever their size it appears that few of these coastal locations have escaped the impact of tourism. Inland areas may be less busy, but not necessarily those on or close to the moors. The main tourist season is from April to early September, with a concentration in the school holiday period.

The West Country attracts such large numbers of visitors due to a combination of physical and human aspects. The region has natural beauty in its varied landscape and is often termed the South-West Peninsula, which provides a clue to one natural attraction – the sea. Cornwall is almost completely surrounded by sea and Devon has both a southern Channel coast and a north coast facing across to Wales and Ireland. Somerset and Avon also have coastlines and only Wiltshire is landlocked. The coastlines of the region are varied with high, granite cliffs at Land's End and along much of the Cornish coast; limestone and sandstone cliffs on the East Devon coast, and 800 ft (244 m.) near-vertical cliffs on the northern boundary of Exmoor. There are long sandy beaches and bays such as at Exmouth and Torbay and secretive coves such as Cadgwith in Cornwall and Woody Bay in North Devon. Wide estuaries are to be found on the Exe south of

Exeter and on the Taw and Torridge and there are even sand dunes at, for example, Woolacombe. The region also has the great advantage of a very attractive interior with two major upland areas, reaching almost 2000 ft (600 m.). These are Dartmoor and Exmoor National Parks. Other upland areas include Bodmin Moor, the Quantocks and the Mendips, complete with rivers such as the Dart and the Exe.

Much of the area appears to be natural, or at least semi-natural and there are few large towns. Bristol is the largest metropolis and along with Bath is in the only predominantly urban county of Avon. The other large towns of the region are well spaced out, in a generally sparsely populated area. These centres include Exeter, which is a regional market centre, has a university and is the county town of Devon; Plymouth, the naval port and most important centre west of Exeter; Taunton, regional market centre and county town of Somerset, and Salisbury, the cathedral town of Wiltshire. There are still many traditional villages both inland and on the coast and these are significant attractions for many visitors. Much of the area appears to be virtually uninhabited and this is particularly the case with the moorlands, which are as close to wildscape as one can find in the region. But even here close inspection reveals a long history of land management as there is much evidence of prehistoric activity, particularly on Dartmoor and Bodmin Moor. Pastoral farming with previous emphasis on sheep and more recently cattle, has meant the preservation of fairly small fields, and many hedgerows still exist. This is, in other words, the type of farmed landscape that most visitors tend to see as 'typically English'.

Much of the West Country is well managed by people who are themselves little evident in that landscape and there is, at most times of the year and in most places, a blending of the human with the natural landscape, resulting in a fine balance being maintained. The sheer number of tourists however, during the peak holiday season and at certain popular destinations, can throw this balance into a state of temporary chaos.

History

Legends abound in the West Country and probably the most well known is that concerning King Arthur. Arthur's name is linked particularly with Tintagel, his supposed birthplace, and Glastonbury, the centre of the Kingdom of Avalon. Other places with Arthurian legend include South Cadbury and the Badbury Rings in Wiltshire.

Before Arthur's time however, if indeed he existed, there were certainly prehistoric, Roman and Celtic people in the region. Cornwall has more prehistoric monuments than any other county in Britain, with the greatest concentration being located on Bodmin Moor. These include stone circles, forts, barrows and chamber tombs. Wiltshire has almost as many prehistoric remains as Cornwall, and with Stonehenge and Avebury has the most important stone circles in England. In Devon there are several hundred Bronze Age monuments on Dartmoor. The climate of the area was warmer at the time of building these monuments, allowing a relatively high density of population where today few people live.

By the time of the Roman invasion, the West Country was occupied by Celtic tribal groupings. These were the Dumnonii in Cornwall, the Durotriges in Devon and central Somerset, and the Dobunii in the north of the region. The Romans under Vespasian took the area to the east of Exeter and the town became a frontier post at the southern end of the Fosse Way. There were forts on this route, probably at Bath, Shepton Mallet and Ilchester. The Durotriges territory became Roman land, and the chief town was established at Dorchester (Durnovaria), while Bath became an important Roman spa town with hot spring baths and a temple to Sulis Minerva. The Saxons began to invade the region from about 500, and by 700 the area to the east of Exeter had been converted to Christianity, although Cornwall remained unconquered until the early 800s. Christianity reached Cornwall not from the Saxons, but from other Celtic areas such as Wales, Brittany and Ireland, and the Celtic language, traditions and culture survived for a long time throughout the Roman period and early Saxon times. King Arthur may well have been a Roman-trained Celtic leader who successfully repelled the invading Saxons at a number of battles in the region.

By 900 Danes had pushed westwards into Somerset and Devon. Alfred the Great took refuge from the Danes on the Somerset Levels and it was from here that he led an army to victory at the Battle of Edington, in Wiltshire, in 992, although by 1016 the whole of the West Country was under the Danish King, Cnut (Canute).

During the medieval period a number of fine monasteries and churches were built, with houses being established at Glastonbury, Sherborne, Abbotsbury, Buckfastleigh and Tintagel, and cathedrals built at Wells and Exeter.

The region is closely linked with the Monmouth Rebellion of 1685. Monmouth was the eldest illegitimate son of Charles II and he believed he had the support to oust the Catholic King James II. Landing from France at Lyme Regis with a small band of supporters in the summer of 1685, he marched to Taunton. Here he was proclaimed king. They marched on, with an ever-growing band of followers, to Bridgwater. The intention was to take Bristol, then to march on London, but at the Battle of Sedgemoor, near Bridgwater, Monmouth and his supporters were defeated. There followed an unpleasant retribution at Judge Jeffries' 'Bloody Assizes' which were held at Exeter, Taunton and Wells. These were the trials of the unfortunate followers of Monmouth who were mostly poor farming people. Many were hanged and others transported to the West Indies.

The major town of the region is Bristol which, during the 1700s, was the country's second port after London. Bristol grew rich on the wine trade with France, and on the slave trade with the West Indies. Ships also sailed from the port to colonise many parts of the North American continent in the 1700s and 1800s. The name Brunel is associated with Bristol as it was this famous 19th-century engineer who designed the Clifton Suspension Bridge that spans the Avon Gorge. He also designed the Tamar Bridge that links Devon and Cornwall, the *Great Western*, the first iron steamship to cross the Atlantic and was chief engineer on the Great Western Railway that ran from Cornwall to Paddington. Brunel's ships, the *Great Western*, the *Great Eastern* and *Great Britain*, were all built in the shipyards of Bristol.

Plymouth is the other major port of the region and it was Sir Francis Drake's influence that led to its choice as a naval base, although nearby Devonport took over as the main port area during the 1800s. It was from Plymouth that the first groups of colonisers to North America set sail in the 1600s. Plymouth was heavily bombed during the Second World War and much of the city centre has been rebuilt in the last forty years.

Bath, once a Roman spa, developed its popularity initially in the 1600s when Charles II visited it, but particularly in the 1700s when Beau Nash encouraged members of the Royal Family to visit the town. By the latter part of the 18th century it had become the leading centre of fashionable society outside London and as a result of royal patronage the city contains many fine Georgian buildings. The region has therefore been an important tourist destination for a long time. The Romans took to the waters of Bath for their health and relaxation. Sea bathing developed in the late 1700s at places such as Exmouth and the arrival of the railways in the second half of the 1800s promoted the development of resorts like Torquay and Newquay. Today the region remains a major tourist destination, with the small villages, both coastal and inland, and the moors attracting increasing numbers of tourists.

In terms of recent economic developments there is evidence of mixed fortunes. Tourism is one of only a few activities showing economic growth. The traditional land use of dairy farming has been hit by EC milk quotas and several farms have had to merge, while others have gone out of business. On the drier, more fertile land, arable farming has expanded, partly as a result of EC grain subsidies. Fishing continues to decline, both in terms of catches and numbers employed, while china clay and tin mining have been reduced to the extent that parts of Cornwall have had unemployment reaching the levels of industrial cities of the North. The computing industry however, has selected the area as one in which to expand, with the M4 corridor, especially between Bristol and Swindon, as the axis of growth. Despite the varied economic conditions, the region remains a highly desirable place in which to live, with Exeter recently voted in a national survey as the most attractive urban environment in England.

Geography

The West Country is a peninsula, at its widest over 70 miles (130 km.) and at its narrowest less than 21.5 miles (25 km.). The influence of the sea is reflected in the landscape of the region and the livelihood of the people.

Few people today earn their living directly from the sea, but there are many old fishing villages, such as Brixham, Fowey, and Falmouth. Pilchards, sprats and mackerel are the main fish still caught, but the fishing industry has been in decline for at least 100 years, although indirectly many people still depend on the sea for their livelihood. Most of the main towns of the region are located on the coast and several of the old fishing ports have become tourist centres with many people employed in the tourist industry, particularly in hotel and catering. The beaches have traditionally attracted large numbers of tourists in the summer months. The mild climate of, particularly, southern Cornwall and the Torbay area (which is often referred to as the 'English Riviera'), enable some resorts to have a significant winter trade. The larger resorts are Torquay, and its neighbour Paignton, (together forming Torbay), with a population exceeding 120,000, although smaller resorts with populations of 10,000 to 20,000 are more typical.

Bristol has the greatest population, 430,000. It was once a major port, but is now an important manufacturing, marketing and servicing centre. Plymouth is the second largest town with almost a quarter of a million people and is the main service centre for Devon and Cornwall. The nearby Devonport is a major naval port. The only other towns exceeding 100,000 population are Exeter and Bath. Exeter is the administrative centre for Devon and Bath is one of the foremost tourist cities in Britain and attracts visitors in large numbers from all over the world.

The physical landscape of the region exhibits a great variety of forms. Most of the lowland areas of Devon and Cornwall are the eroded remains of red sandstone. This gives the soil – which is suitable for arable and pastoral farming – its distinctive red hue. This area is a low plateau that has been cut into by deep valleys and forms steep cliffs at the coast (the name Devon comes from a Celtic word meaning 'deep valley'). The valley sides in the lowland area tend to be densely wooded. On the south side of the region are some low-lying drier areas, such as Mounts Bay, the Fal valley, the Tamar valley and the Exe valley. These are market gardening regions with an emphasis on green vegetables, soft fruit, cider apples and cut flowers. The Isles of Scilly specialise in growing spring flowers, which are sold at markets in London and the Midlands. The Somerset Levels have a very different landscape from that of Devon or Cornwall, being like the Fens, although their land use is similar, being mostly pasture land. Most of the inland towns of the region, such as Taunton, are marketing centres for agricultural produce.

The upland areas consist of two general rock types: granite or sedimentary. Several highland areas are composed of granite and as this rock is formed underground from molten lava, it only appears at the surface when rocks above it are worn away. The exposed rock forms the distinctive tors on top of the granite uplands. The granite uplands are bleak moorlands – rising to over 2000 ft (610 m.) in the case of Dartmoor – although the other granite areas, Bodmin, Hensbarrow, Carmnellis, Land's End and the Isles of Scilly are lower, but also form distinctive landscapes. These areas are generally treeless with outcrops of bare rock and many boggy hollows, where the granite produces thin, sandy, infertile soils. On the granite uplands, too, the quarrying of china clay occurs, particularly in the St Austell area.

The other upland areas are made of sedimentary rocks. Exmoor is composed mostly of resistant sandstone and there are no tors, but like Dartmoor the higher parts are virtually treeless. The Mendips, south of Bristol, are composed of limestone, although the land here is generally lower than the Pennines, which are made of the same type of rock, and have similar features. Cheddar Gorge, on the Mendips, is the best known limestone feature in the country.

Climate

The western side of Britain has one advantage for the tourist in that it is generally milder than the east, but one disadvantage in that it is much wetter. The West Country is particularly influenced by the sea as it is from here that most of the weather that affects the region comes. The Gulf Stream reaches the South-West Peninsula, bringing with it water from the tropics. The predominant wind direction is parallel to the Gulf Stream (south-westerly), and the wind acquires considerable moisture as it travels over the sea. Thus it is that warm, damp air is most common in the region. When the air hits the land it either comes into contact with a surface which is generally colder in winter, or rises over the coast and moorland. Either way the result is rain, which is spread throughout the year, although the wettest times are during the autumn and winter. The amount of rainfall tends to decrease the further east one goes and the greater the distance from the sea. The moors have much more rain than lowland and coastal locations, so it can be raining heavily on Dartmoor when there is no rain in Exeter or Plymouth.

The great benefit of the area for the tourist is the amount of sunshine received, particularly between June and the end of September. High pressure areas in summer can last for up to three weeks, although a week to ten days is most common. Temperatures are on average in the low 20s°C (around 70°F) in the period June to August, although coasts and exposed uplands such as the moors will be several degrees cooler. The climate of the West Country is, therefore, one of the main attractions for the British holidaymaker.

Attractions

It is the variety of natural scenery that has attracted visitors to the region for a long period. The main natural attractions of the West Country are the coast and moorland, and the fact that these are in close proximity to each other enables visitors to combine both a seaside and moorland holiday in the traditional one or two week period.

Devon and Cornwall both have long coastlines with a great variety of features, although of particular interest to visitors are the long sandy beaches found at Paignton, Exmouth, Woolacombe, Bude,

Newquay and Weston-super-Mare. A major disadvantage is that these beaches tend to be very crowded during the main holiday period and are not necessarily clean. Not all were awarded the Blue Flag in 1990 nor are they all recommended in *The Good Beach Guide*, but there are many small coves and beaches, such as Croyde Bay, Harylyn Bay and Whitesand Bay in Cornwall, and Branscombe in Devon, which are maintained to a high standard and where few other visitors go, even in the peak season. Some of the best quality and least visited beaches are on the Isles of Scilly.

The moorlands are the closest to wilderness one can get in the region and both Dartmoor and Exmoor are recognised as National Parks and offer much of interest to the discerning tourist. Bodmin Moor is generally less well known than the other two Moors, and tends to be less visited, hence it is well worth seeking out. The Mendips also tend to be neglected by most visitors.

Villages in Devon, along with some in Somerset and Cornwall, have made frequent appearances on the lids of chocolate boxes. Those of note include Otterton and Broadhembury in Devon, St Mawes and Mevagissey in Cornwall and Selworthy and Allerford in Somerset. The larger settlements of the region have much to attract the tourist and Bristol, in particular, is beginning to emerge as one of the greenest cities in Britain. It has an integrated public transport system, a centre for urban appropriate technology and a city farms movement. Bath has probably the finest Georgian urban landscape of any city in Britain. Exeter, as the gateway to the South-West and because it serves such a large hinterland, offers much to the tourist. Glastonbury, which should also be on the discerning visitor's list of places, is worth visiting.

The region has a large number of ancient monuments, castles, churches and historic houses. In addition there are many gardens, museums and craft centres open to the public, as well as four steam railways and an electric tramway.

Cuisine

The region is probably best known for its cream teas and Cornish pasties. Dairy products are popular and there are several locally produced ice-creams, such as Salcombe and the organic Rocombe Farm, both of Devon, which come in a variety of flavours from the traditional Cornish to Christmas pudding!

Cheese is another local speciality and the most well known is Cheddar. Visitors can watch Cheddar being made at Chewton Cheese

Dairy, at Chewton Mendip in Somerset. Quickes of Newton St Cyres near Exeter produce a range of Cheddar cheeses, including a smoked variety, Cheddar with herbs and a vegetarian Cheddar. Bath is well known for a variety of biscuits and buns, including Bath buns, Bath Oliver biscuits and Sally Lunn cakes, all of which are available from a number of outlets in the town.

People of Cornwall and Devon include a large amount of seafood in their diet. When in season, fresh mackerel and sprats are cheap and delicious, as are crabs and other shellfish, available at certain times of the year.

The most famous drink of the region is cider and several farms in the area press and produce their own from local apples. Most of these farms advertise their products on roadside signs. Sheppy's of Bradford-on-Tone near Taunton provide a tour of their cider-making process and orchards and they also have a museum of cider-making, whilst Perry's Cider Mills at Dowlish Wake near Ilminster has a collection of equipment used in making cider. Mead is still produced in Cornwall and three long established breweries in the region are Devenish, St Austell and Wadworth. Since the late 1970s there has also been a revival of real ale brewing in the region. Three new breweries producing quality real ale are Smiles, based in Bristol and serving mainly the north-eastern part of the region; Butcombe of Blagdon near Bristol, again serving the north-eastern area, and Exmoor Ales of Wiveliscombe, serving the west of the region.

Level of Tourism

Although there are some wilderness areas, or at least semi-wild parts of the region, generally tourism has a very significant impact. There are many honeypots and these include not just the coastal locations of Torbay, Newquay and Land's End, but also the moorlands where there are heavily visited locations, including Haytor and Postbridge on Dartmoor and Tarr Steps on Exmoor. Just as tourism's impact is not spread evenly over the geographical area, neither is it spread evenly throughout the year. The summer season is longer than in many other areas of the country as it often begins at Easter and continues well into the autumn. The peak period is certainly the school holiday time of July and August, but most weekends from early April to mid-September are busy.

The West Country Tourist Board recognises the advantages and disadvantages of tourism in the region. In their publication *Tourism in the West Country: Towards a Strategy for the 1990s* they note that tourism is focused on particular areas of the region. The greatest concentration is in Devon and Cornwall and there is heavy dependence on the established resorts, particularly on the southern coast, where the industry is seen as relying fundamentally on the domestic holiday market. The advantages of the region for tourism are summarised as: good for family tourism, better weather than average, generally clean and unspoilt environment, particularly beautiful scenery, strong historic and cultural associations and continuing appeal to higher socio-economic groups. The disadvantages of tourism are perceived as: overcrowding, congestion, the distance of the region from population centres (making it difficult to reach), limited parking, too few all-weather, year-round attractions/activities, and too much reliance on main season domestic holidays.

The natural environment is noted as being a major reason for the existence of tourism in the area. The report discusses the meaning of conservation, indicating that it need not imply a negative 'preservationist' approach, nor a 'museumization' approach. It also states that tourism planning will necessitate better management techniques to ensure a balance between tourism (and other leisure) use of the environment and the conservation of the physical environment. The report, however, fails to indicate in any detail, relevant and appropriate strategies to meet these laudable aims. Much of the work of the West Country Tourist Board is in marketing and attracting tourists to the region, and although controls are placed on tourist developments, particularly in the National Park and Heritage Coast areas, the current tourism development strategies can be summarised as: encourage, via marketing, tourists to stay in the already heavily congested coastal resorts, and in relation to the moors and inland attractions, spread the load to the fringe areas of the moors and to other undeveloped attractions. There is an element of contradiction here, but the 'ghettoisation' of tourism in places such as Torquay and Newquay may help preserve the natural attractions of the region. It is questionable whether or not in the long term, spreading the load may contribute to damage and ultimate destruction of areas such as the moors.

Despite the omission of strategies from the Board's report, there are areas in the region already benefiting from well-structured projects which aim to promote tourism in a manner compatible with conservation policies. One such example is Kynance Cove. A popular beauty spot since Victorian days, attention was drawn to it in the 1970s when it became clear that it was suffering from considerable erosion. Owned by the National Trust, the cove offers a wide variety of fauna and flora (in addition to its natural beauty), including some very rare plants. The main problem of the area was that visitor capacity was being continually exceeded, with increasing pressure being placed on a relatively small area of coast. Since 1986 however, the National Trust has implemented a series of policies to regenerate the area. These have included a revegetation plan and a rerouting system to channel visitors along defined paths away from areas of severe erosion. In addition, the problem of visitor numbers has been brought under control by limiting access to the site (both vehicular and pedestrian) and by adhering to a cut-off point in the car park. When the car park is full no further vehicles are admitted and visitors are directed elsewhere. So successful have these policies been that the project received a Europa Nostra Diploma of Merit in 1989 for 'the outstanding management of a famous stretch of coastline, reconciling the interests of conservation and tourism'.

Land's End is a part of the country which has received considerable media coverage over recent years. Mainland Britain's most westerly point had been suffering from severe neglect and misuse until it was acquired and developed by a private company, and reopened to the public in 1988. The site now includes a visitor centre and hotel, shops and themed attractions, and, since its opening, has attracted roughly 600,000 visitors each year.

Like Kynance Cove, Land's End has suffered from a mixture of natural erosion due to its exposed location on the coast, and erosion caused by visitors. But also like Kynance Cove, the area is now benefiting from, amongst other things, the creation of established paths along which visitors are channelled. Other benefits have included conservation and restoration of the landscape, visitor education about the area, and the creation of a surface drainage system. According to Cairns Boston, the managing director of Land's End Limited, the introduction of an entrance fee has also 'reduced litter, created awareness, encouraged stewardship and, above all, protected the site from over-use and commercial prostitution.'

There is a major difference between the Land's End project and work at Kynance Cove however, in that Land's End is a commercial enterprise which depends on money from fee-paying visitors to finance further conservation work, while the National Trust is a charity and relies to a large extent on donations and grants (supplemented by entrance fees). Also, while the National Trust is eager to limit development (unsympathetic or otherwise), the success of the Land's End project has rested on the creation of new facilities and services needed to cater for large numbers of tourists.

Inevitably this has given rise to a certain amount of controversy, and the problem still exists of how best to deal with the volume of traffic, which continues to cause congestion and environmental damage. Parked cars and coaches at Land's End are an eyesore in themselves and alternative arrangements are becoming increasingly necessary. Ideally there should be no parking at all in this area, but finding somewhere else and providing alternative means of transport to the site itself are solutions to which practicalities do not lend themselves readily. For the time being the areas in question have been landscaped in order to hide parked vehicles.

Final mention should be given to proposals to develop Stonehenge. In May 1991 English Heritage, who are responsible for Stonehenge, in conjunction with the National Trust announced a £10 million scheme to transform the site into a 1400 acre (567 hectares) archaeological park, catering for a million visitors each year. The proposals include the construction of a visitor centre and better parking facilities on 27 acres (11 hectares) of Ministry of Defence land at Larkhill. It is also intended to close the A344 where it runs past Stonehenge, in order to create a quieter atmosphere more suited to viewing the 5000-year-old monument.

Plans to improve tourist facilities at Stonehenge have been discussed since the creation of English Heritage in 1984. At present the site is one of the organisation's greatest sources of revenue, raising around £500,000 each year from roughly 700,000 tourists. Under the new scheme, management of the park would be in the hands of an independent conservation trust, and visitors would have access to the 'Stones' down a half mile (0.8 km.) route. Immediate opposition to the proposals was voiced, notably over the intended closure of the A344, and also regarding the more stringent controls concerning entry to the site. English Heritage and the National Trust are submitting their plans to Salisbury District Council and, if accepted, it is estimated that the project could be completed by the mid-1990s.

Good Alternatives

Meeting People

There are a number of festivals that take place during the summer months in the West Country. One of the most significant is the Bath International Music Festival which takes place during the last week of May and the first week of June. Another music festival is the Sidmouth International Folk Festival, which is the major international folk festival in Britain and takes place during the first week in August. An international folk, jazz and blues festival, the WOMAD festival, takes place at Wadebridge in Cornwall, usually in the middle of August. Bicton Park, East Devon is the location for the International Clowns Festival, which occurs over a weekend in early July.

Discovering Places

Centres offering multi-activity holidays are scattered throughout the region. Holidays usually have an emphasis on sport, and both adult and children's courses are available. The West Country Tourist Board produces a brochure on activity holidays, available from them at Trinity Court, Southernay East, Exeter, EX1 1QS (Tel 0392 76351). Several centres for riding holidays are found on Dartmoor, Exmoor and The Mendips. The coast offers many opportunities for water sports and a variety of organisations provide a range of courses and facilities for sailing, sea canoeing, windsurfing and snorkelling (brochure from West Country Tourist Board). Cycling is another form of activity that is very suited to the West Country and most towns have shops that will hire out bicycles on a daily basis. **Avon Valley Cyclery** of Bath (Tel 0225 461880) provide a variety of cycles and equipment for longer periods of hire. The **Cyclists' Touring Club** offer a week's cycling tour of the hillier parts of Devon and Somerset during midsummer.

There are two field study centres in the region run by the Field Studies Council. **Nettlecombe Court**, near Williton, West Somerset is a beautiful Elizabethan mansion lying in secluded grounds with its own church. It offers a variety of courses, most of them concerned with the environment, including natural history, ecology, geology, flowers and birds, and there are also walking courses and painting and drawing weekends. For details of courses contact Nettlecombe Court, Williton, Taunton, Somerset TA4 4HT (Tel 0984 40320). The other centre is **Slapton Ley** in the village of Slapton in South Devon and it offers a limited range of courses during the summer, concerned with wildlife photography, coastal scenery and rural rambles through South Devon countryside. Contact Slapton Ley, Slapton, Kingsbridge, Devon (Tel 0548 580466).

Working Weekends on Organic Farms (WWOF) have a number of organic farms in the region that are involved with their work. Also, the **British Trust for Conservation Volunteers (BTCV)** are involved with a number of sites in the region, where work continues throughout the year: Aylesbeare and Woodbury Commons in East Devon, the Tarka Trail in North Devon and the Erme Valley Footpath in South Devon. Details from BTCV, 36 St Marys Street, Wallingford, Oxfordshire (Tel 0491 39766).

Specific attention should be drawn to the **Tarka Project**. Inspired by the book *Tarka the Otter* by Henry Williamson, and set up roughly three years ago, it covers an area of over 500 square miles (1280 sq. km.) of North Devon, from Ilfracombe on the coast to Oakhampton in the middle of Dartmoor National Park. The project combines tourism and recreation (and subsequent financial benefits) with conservation and environmental education. Although the landscape has changed since the book was published sixty years ago, it has retained its rural atmosphere and still constitutes an area of relatively unspoilt countryside.

The project's initial aim is to complete what is to be known as the 'Tarka Trail'. Covering much of the ground frequented by Williamson's famous otter, this is a 180-mile (290 km.) path which takes in both countryside and coast. The northern coastal route and the southern route from Bideford to Dartmoor were opened in 1991, and the whole trail is scheduled to be opened in May 1992. It is also hoped that a Tarka Visitor Information Centre will be created within the next five years. Access for walkers has been achieved by using existing paths and old railway routes (helped by Devon County Council's acquisition of the Bideford to Meeth railway line), along with the development of new permissive routes.

Administration of the project falls to a project officer and assistant. Both posts are funded jointly be Devon County Council, the Countryside Commission and the four relevant district councils. In addition there is also an Otter Conservation Officer, whose position is funded by private sponsorship. The Project is still in its early stages but already has been shortlisted for the Green Tourism category of the English Tourist Board's England for Excellence programme, and has won the Special Projects Category of Devon's Keep Devon Shipshape competition. It offers visitors the opportunity to enjoy the countryside and learn about otter habitats, but without causing irreparable environmental damage to their surroundings. By following a clearly marked robust path, visitors will only tread within a controlled area, yet still be able to benefit from popular attractions. Further information is available from the Project Officer, Eric Palmer Community Centre, Barley Grove, Torrington EX38 8EZ (Tel 0805 23355).

Communications

How to Get There

AIR: It is possible to fly to the region from London, the East Midlands, Manchester and Glasgow. There are airports at Bristol, Exeter and Plymouth, as well as smaller airfields at Newquay, Penzance and on the Isles of Scilly.

RAIL: Rail services to some parts of the region are reasonably good. London is linked via Paddington to Penzance (Tel 0872 76244), with the main en route stations of Taunton, Tiverton, Exeter (Tel 0392 433551) and Plymouth (Tel 0752 221300). Trains run approximately every half hour. Exeter is two and a half to three hours from the capital and Plymouth about four hours. There is also a slower route from London to Exeter from Waterloo Station. InterCity 125 trains serve the route from London to Bristol (Tel 0272 294255), Bath (Tel 0225 463075) and Weston-super-Mare, and there are also fairly good services from the Midlands, North-west England, North-east England and Scotland to Penzance via Bristol, Exeter and Plymouth. Services to London, Glasgow and Edinburgh have sleeper facilities and there is also a Motorail service to West Country locations from London, Birmingham and Glasgow.

COACH: Fast luxury coaches are a fairly recent addition to the routeways of the West Country and **National Express** (details in *London* chapter on page 515) operate services to Bristol, Exeter and Plymouth. These coaches have steward service with hot drinks and sandwiches. Travelling on the motorways, journey time from London to Exeter for example, is only slightly longer than the equivalent rail trip, but considerably cheaper.

CAR: On a map, road access to the region appears good. From the Midlands and the north the M6 joins the M5 at Birmingham and then continues to Exeter. The M4 from London joins the M5 just north of Bristol. Beyond Exeter however, there is no motorway and, although there is some dual carriageway, the road quality tends to deteriorate the further west one travels.

When You're There

RAIL: Rail connections around the region are good with branch lines connecting St Ives, Newquay, Falmouth and Barnstaple to the main line network. A number of reduced fare tickets are available for varying periods of time, and these can save a significant amount of money. Ask at any mainline station for details.

COACH: A comprehensive series of bus networks runs throughout the region, administered by the various bus companies: **Cornwall Busways, Western National, Southern National, Devon General** and **Badgerline** (Somerset and Avon). Reduced-fare tickets are available; enquire at bus stations.

CAR: The main Exeter to Plymouth route, the A38, is dual carriageway throughout its length and the A30 is now dual carriageway for 25 miles (40 km.) west of Exeter, bypassing Okehampton. The A30 into Cornwall also has several stretches of dual carriageway, but driving conditions on this road beyond Okehampton to the west can be very frustrating if not downright dangerous. After the dual carriageway sections traffic has to slow down and tends to bunch up. During the summer months the situation is aggravated not only by increased holiday traffic but also by agricultural vehicles. This road is busiest during the summer but is particularly bad on Saturdays from Easter until early September. The following route is an alternative for those heading for western Cornwall: A386 from Okehampton to Tavistock, then the A390 to Liskeard and A38 to Bodmin (this itself can be busy during July and August). It is possible to take the A38 Exeter to Plymouth road to reach Cornwall, but this involves crossing the Tamar Bridge in Plymouth, which is also a problem area.

North Devon and West Somerset have traditionally been difficult to reach quickly and, despite improvements to the A39 Bridgwater–Lynton (via Minehead) road, this remains a slow route.

A new link road has recently been opened from the M5 to the north coast. Called the North Devon Link it leaves the motorway at junction 27 and joins the A39 in North Devon, carrying on into Cornwall as the rather grandly titled Atlantic Highway.

The route to the south coast was once the scene of major hold-ups, particularly around Honiton, but this is now a thing of the past. Nevertheless, the A30/A303, despite improvements and notably at Sparkford and Ilchester, is still very congested during the summer and is not a good alternative route from London and the South-east unless travelling at night.

Many of the narrow lanes in Cornwall and Devon are extremely busy from Whitsun to early September and can barely cope with the amount of traffic. Drivers are advised to take extra care when travelling in this part of the region.

Roads are very congested during the peak season and the M5 can be a problem, particularly at its termination near Exeter. Here the main route divides, with traffic taking either the southerly route via the A38 or the northerly route along the A30. The A380 from just south of

Exeter to the Torbay area is a route which is busy throughout the year and in the holiday period is heavily congested with lengthy hold-ups, especially at weekends. The A39, the north coast route, is generally slow and there are likely to be delays at peak season weekends at Porlock, Lynmouth, Bude and along the A3059 to Newquay. The A30 from Bodmin to Penzance is also usually heavily congested on Saturdays during the holidays. Other places where traffic will be heavy during the peak season include, on the north coast, St Ives, Perranporth, Padstow, Tintagel, Clovelly and Minehead, and on the south coast, Mousehole, Falmouth, Polperro, Dawlish and Sidmouth. Parking is also difficult in these locations.

WALKING: This is one of the best ways of discovering the West Country and walking is excellent on both the coast and Moors. The **South-West Peninsula Coast Path** follows both the south and north coast of the region and gives a continuous opportunity to explore the edge of the sea. It is the longest official footpath in Britain, running for 560 miles (890 km.) from Minehead in Somerset around the south-west peninsula to South Haven Point on the south side of Poole Harbour in Dorset. The path was created at the same time as the National Parks in 1949 and is administered by various county and district councils, which explains the variations in the path's quality and maintenance. It passes through some of the finest coastal scenery in Britain and to walk the whole way would take about five to six weeks. Information and guidebooks are available from the **South-West Way Association**, Delamein, Bracken Rise, Paignton, Devon TQ4 6JU (Tel 0803 842844).

Both National Parks offer some quality walking, including guided walks and short and long circular walks, and guidebooks and leaflets are produced by each park authority. Contact **Dartmoor National Park**, Parke, Haytor Road, Bovey Tracey (Tel 0626 832 093), and **Exmoor National Park**, Exmoor House, Dulverton (Tel 0398 23665). The **Two Moors Way**, a walk of 102 miles (163 km.), links Dartmoor to Exmoor.

Bodmin Moor has guided walks sponsored by the **Ramblers' Association**, who publish *Walks with a Point*, a guide to circular walks in Devon. The **National Trust** also publishes a series of leaflet maps describing walking possibilities on 23 of its open space properties.

Useful Local Contacts

The following organisations represent a number of the main interests in the area. In AVON, the **Avon Wildlife Trust**, The Old Police

Station, 32 Jacob's Well Road, Bristol BS8 1DR and the **National Federation of City Farms**, The Old Vicarage, 66 Fraser Street, Windmill Hill, Bedminster, Bristol BS3 4LY (Tel 0272 660663). In WILTSHIRE, the **Wiltshire Trust for Nature Conservation**, 19 High Street, Devizes SN10 1AT (Tel 0380 5670) and the **National Trust Volunteer Unit**, PO Box 12, Westbury BA13 4NA (Tel 0373 826302). In DORSET, the **Dorset Countryside Volunteers**, 33 Putton Lane, Chickerell, Weymouth and the **Dorset Trust for Nature Conservation**, 39 Christchurch Road, Bournemouth BH1 3NS (Tel 0202 24241). In SOMERSET, the **Somerset Archaeological and Natural History Society**, Taunton Castle, Taunton TA1 4AD and the **Somerset Ornithological Society**, Barnfield, Tower Hill Road, Crewkerne. In DEVON, the **Devon Conservation Forum**, County Hall, Topsham Road, Exeter EX2 4QQ (Tel 0392 273327) and the **Devon Wildlife Trust**, 35 New Bridge Street, Exeter EX3 4AH (Tel 0392 79244). In CORNWALL, the **Cornwall Trust for Nature Conservation**, Five Acres, Allet, Truro TR4 9DJ (Tel 0872 73939) and the **Cornish Seal Sanctuary**, Gweek, near Helston (Tel 032 622 361).

Geographical Breakdown of Region
Avon

Bristol

Bristol has a wealth of fine houses, churches and theatres. The dock area has been restored over the past twenty years and has several attractions worth visiting. The world's first propeller driven steam ship, *Great Britain*, is in **Great Western Dock**, Cumberland Rd and further along this waterfront is Princes Wharf where the **Bristol Maritime Heritage Centre** is to be found. Also here is the **Bristol Industrial Museum**. Three other attractions in this area close to the water are within walking distance of each other. The **Arnolfini Arts Centre** is an art gallery with modern art in a variety of media, a bar and wholefood restaurant. Across the dock is **The Watershed**, which is a media and communications centre with film and video cinemas, shops, boutiques, galleries and waterside cafes, and behind this is the **Bristol Exhibition Centre**, with the **World Wine Fair** held here every July and an **International Beer Festival** in October or November.

Close to the docks in Princes Street is the **Theatre Royal**, home of the Bristol Old Vic. Behind the theatre is the university area, where the main road of **Park Street** is good for shopping and offering

George's Bookshop and numerous other bookshops. Broadmead, the area around **St Michael's** between the university area and the main pedestrianised shopping centre, has the city's alternative activities and the **Tourist Information Centre**, Colston House, Colston St. (Tel 0272 293891). North and west of the university area is **Clifton**, which was once a village but is now a wealthy suburb of Bristol. Here there are numerous pubs, restaurants and antique shops.

Clifton Down, an area of common land, is a playground for Bristolieans, but is also an important city wild area. There are open areas and scattered trees and dense scrub and, although the grass on the Downs is cut regularly, some cowslips and common orchids can be seen. Adjacent to the Downs is **Avon Gorge**, where a number of rare plants are found, although many are on inaccessible limestone ledges. It is possible however, to see some of these plants from the footpaths on the Downs. Spanning the Gorge is Brunel's famous **Suspension Bridge**, which provides the best vantage point for viewing the Gorge. There are numerous other semi-wild areas in and close to the city and information is available from **Bristol City Council Parks Dept,** Colston Street BS1 5AQ (Tel 0272 266031) and **Avon Wildlife Trust**, Jacob's Well Road BS8 1DR (Tel 0272 268018).

Close to the gorge is the **Riverside Garden Centre,** one of Britain's first organic nurseries, while in the southern part of the city at Philips St Bedminster is **Windmill Hill City Farm**. Bristol has a good public transport system and a free City Line Overground Bus map is available from bus stations and the Tourist Information Centre. Information on cycle hire and cycle routes in the city can be obtained from **Cyclebag** at 35 King Street.

Accommodation

First Class

Avon Gorge Hotel, Sion Hill, Bristol BS8 4LD (Tel 0272 738955). Eighty bedrooms in this Victorian building, some with fine views of the Gorge.

Rodney Hotel, Clifton, Bristol BS8 4HY (Tel 0272 735422). Refurbished Georgian building close to the centre of Clifton and the famous suspension bridge.

Middle Range

Dornden Guest House, Church Lane, Old Sodbury BS17 6NB (Tel 0454 313325). Bed and breakfast in a former vicarage built of

Cotswold stone standing in beautiful gardens. Grass tennis court available to guests.

Arches Hotel, 132 Cotham Brow, Cotham BS6 6AE (Tel 0272 247398). Bed and breakfast in a friendly, privately run hotel just off the A38. Traditional, vegetarian and vegan breakfasts available.

Economy

Eastcote Cottage, Crossways Knapp Road, Thornbury BS12 2HJ (Tel 0454 413106). Bed and breakfast in a 200-year-old stone house in a rural setting with magnificent views across the open countryside.

Hillside, Sutton Hill Road, Bishop Sutton BS18 4UN (Tel 0272 332208). Small bed and breakfast in a delightful converted stone cottage close to Bristol.

Eating Out

First Class

Edward's Restaurant, 24 Alma Vale Road, Clifton (Tel 0272 741533). Traditional English cuisine (with a few Continental touches) in this oak-panelled and candle-lit restaurant.

Harvey's, 12 Denmark Street (Tel 0272 277665). English and French cuisine in the wine cellar of this famous company of wine merchants.

Middle Range

Millward's, 40 Alfred Place, Kingsdown (Tel 0272 245026). Small, good-value vegetarian and vegan restaurant serving a wide range of dishes.

The Bridge, St Vincent Rocks Hotel, Sion Hill, Clifton (Tel 0272 738544). English and French dishes, and magnificent views of the Clifton Bridge.

Economy

Rainbow, 10 Waterloo Street, Clifton (Tel 0272 738937). Home-made meat, fish and vegetarian dishes in this popular restaurant. Second-hand books on sale and changing local art exhibitions.

McCreadies, 26 Broad Street (Tel 0272 265580). Vegetarian cooking. All the food is home-made and most of the fruit and vegetables are organic.

Bath

Bath is the most complete Georgian town in Britain and it also has a large number of medieval and Roman buildings. Unfortunately it is one of the most visited attractions in the country, and unless one enjoys crowds, it is best avoided from June to September and on most weekends throughout the year. Not only are there a large number of British visitors, but an increasing number of foreign tourists. Much of the pedestrianised city centre is heavily congested with people, and parking (a major headache in the town at the best of times) is particularly bad during the summer season.

The **Roman Bath Museum** is adjacent to the Great Bath Site of the Romans and tickets also include admission to the **Temple Precinct** which lies beneath the 18th-century **Pump Room** (which is now a restaurant). Close by is **Bath Abbey**, built at the end of the 15th century. Between the Roman Baths and the Abbey is an attractive **Square,** which is a good meeting place and offers pavement cafes such as **Binks** (excellent cream teas and ice-creams), where it is possible to sit and watch street entertainers. A short walk away is **Pulteney Bridge,** modelled on Florence's Ponte Vecchio. There is a cafe on the bridge and shops selling antiques, hand-made chocolates and flowers. The main shopping streets are **Milsom Street** and **Union Street** and there are several alleyways such as **Northumberland Passage**, running off these two streets. On Milsom Street is the Octagon which houses the **Royal Photographic Society National Centre of Photography**, and north of Milsom Street is **The Circus**, an elegant circle of three blocks of Georgian houses. Beyond the Circus is **Royal Crescent**, one of the most famous streets in Britain: No 1 has been authentically restored as an 18th-century house and is open to the public.

Bath is surrounded by hills and is fairly easy to get out of. **Brown's Folly Nature Reserve** is a couple of miles to the east of the city and offers excellent views over Bath. It is also close to the **University**, a concrete product of the 1960s but with attractive surroundings.

Accommodation

First Class

The Royal Crescent, 16 Royal Crescent, Bath BA1 2LS (Tel 0225 319090). The Royal Crescent Hotel occupies the prime position of Bath's most famous architectural showpiece. The hotel is gracious and elegant in every way and offers a large secluded walled garden to the rear.

The Priory Hotel, Weston Road, Bath BA1 2XT (Tel 0225 331922). Close to the town centre, this is a Georgian house built in Gothic style from Bath stone. The Priory offers guests the chance to experience an English country house hotel at its best.

Middle Range

Paradise House, 88 Holloway, Bath BA2 4PX (Tel 0225 317723). Bed and breakfast in a delightful 18th-century house, lovingly restored to its full charm. Set on the hillside with good views over Bath, it is within a ten minute walk of the town centre.

Somerset House, 35 Bathwick Hill, Bath BA2 6LD (Tel 0225 66451). More-than-comfortable accommodation at this Georgian mansion, including bed, breakfast, four-course dinners, lunch on Sundays and vegetarian/special diets if ordered in advance. Run by a former director of a regional tourist board – who arranges local themed weekends – and his wife, who is an expert in the kitchen.

Economy

Footman's Cottage, High Street, Wellow BA2 8QQ (Tel 0225 837024). Small bed and breakfast in a 250-year-old cottage, delightfully restored with antiques and sympathetic decoration.

Eagle House, Church Street, Bathford BA1 7RS (Tel 0225 859946). Spacious and bright bed and breakfast three miles (4.8 km.) north-east of Bath. Friendly and warm, and suitable for families.

Eating Out

First Class

Flowers, 27 Monmouth Street (Tel 0225 313774). Brightly decorated restaurant in an 18th-century courtesan's house, serving traditional English food.

Old Mill, Tollbridge Road, Batheaston (Tel 0225 858476). Lovely location on the river just outside Bath, serving traditional English fare.

Middle Range

Huckleberry's, 34 Broad Street (Tel 0225 464876). Excellent value vegetarian restaurant catering for virtually every type of diet imaginable.

Carriages Restaurant, Lord Nelson Inn, Marshfield, near Chippenham (Tel 0225 891820). Seventeenth-century inn situated on the High Street of this pretty Cotswold village a short drive from Bath. Seafood specialities served.

Economy

Pump Room, Stall Street (Tel 0225 444488). The Georgian architecture of the Pump Room is enough in itself to merit a visit to this good value coffee shop. Morning coffee, light lunches and afternoon teas.

Lovejoys Cafe, 7–10 Bartlett Street (Tel 0225 446322). Relaxed cafe offering traditional and vegetarian dishes in the same building as the Bartlett Street Antiques Centre.

Wiltshire

Salisbury

Old Sarum was the original site of the city but in the early 13th century this moved with the establishment of the **Cathedral**. Begun in 1220 the Cathedral was completed in 1258, and has a consistency of style found in few other cathedrals. It has the highest spire of any ecclesiastical structure in the country and the interior has tall columns and a large number of stained glass windows. **Cathedral Close** is a relatively quiet area, but is often very congested during the summer months. Salisbury is built at the confluence of four rivers: the Avon, Bourne, Nadder and Ebble, and there are attractive riverside walks in and around the city. **Tourist Information Centre** is at Fish Row (Tel 0722 334956).

Stonehenge and Avebury

Stonehenge and **Avebury** are the most famous early prehistoric monuments in Britain. Unfortunately this has made them very attractive to visitors and parts of them are now fenced off. Stonehenge is eight miles (12.8 km.) north of Salisbury and is regarded by some as a prehistoric cathedral. The 'Stones', as they have been known since the hippy invasions of the 1980s, can be easily seen from the A344. The site is managed by English Heritage (a small entrance fee is charged) but the Stones themselves are roped off permanently and it is only possible to walk around the perimeter. In the summer months, it is likely that this walk will be made with many other visitors, in procession.

Avebury, six miles (9.6 km.) west of **Marlborough**, is in many ways more impressive than Stonehenge. This is partly due to the site being larger, but also because it tends to be less visited. And this is despite the fact that the site is cut in two by the A361 and much of the present Avebury village is within the stone circle. There were probably about

100 stones in the original stone circle and the central area covers almost 24 acres (10 hectares). The circle of stones is enclosed by an enormous earthwork ditch and bank. It is possible to walk close to and even touch the standing stones that remain, although touching is to be discouraged, as this will lead to damage in the long term.

Salisbury Plain

This is one of the more important wild or semi-wild areas in central/southern Britain. Unfortunately much of the area is used for military training, so rare chalkland plants and animals share the plain with unexploded shells and burnt-out tanks. Access is, necessarily, severely restricted. On the north scarp of the plain at Bratton, near Westbury, is the **Westbury White Horse**, the largest and probably oldest of Wiltshire's white horses. Good views towards Bath, Bristol and the Marlborough Downs can be enjoyed from the summit of the scarp slope. **Tourist Information** is available from Westbury (Tel 0373 827158).

Other places in Wiltshire worth visiting include the **Avon Valley** between Bath and Bradford-on-Avon which cuts through a gorge in the jurassic limestone. The **Kennet and Avon Canal** runs parallel to the river and has a surfaced towpath. The towpath is part of the **Wiltshire Cycleway** but is good for walking, and there are also walks along the river side. The train journey through the valley, part of the Bristol to Portsmouth line, makes an interesting outing. The area between **Devizes** and **Marlborough** is relatively unknown to most tourists. The Kennet and Avon Canal links Devizes to Marlborough, via **Pewsey**, and to the south of the canal are the **Marlborough Downs** and to the west of Marlborough, **Savernake Forest**. **Tourist Information** is available from Devizes (Tel 0380 729408) and Marlborough (Tel 0672 53989).

Accommodation

First Class

White Hart Hotel, 1 St John Street, Salisbury SP1 2SD (Tel 0722 327476). Traditional hotel in the centre of Salisbury offering real comfort. The White Hart is part of Salisbury's stonework.

White Horse Hotel, 38 Castle Street, Salisbury SP1 1BN (Tel 0722 327844). Small hotel in the centre of town, close to the market and cathedral.

Middle Range

Red Lion, Lacock, near Chippenham SN15 2LB (Tel 024973 456). Bed and breakfast, dinner, packed lunches and snacks are offered at this historic building. The Red Lion was originally a 17th-century coaching inn and still retains some marvellous features. Today it is owned by the National Trust and run by a friendly family.

West House, 12 West Street, Warminster BA12 8JJ (Tel 0985 213936). Bed, breakfast, three-course dinner and packed lunches in an 18th-century stone house. Attractive rooms and delightful rose gardens.

Economy

Bradford Old Windmill, 4 Masons Lane, Bradford-on-Avon BA15 1QN (Tel 02216 6842). No-smoking bed and breakfast in a converted windmill. Guests are promised an intriguing visit in an establishment which has round beds, a minstrel's gallery and oval rooms.

Crookwood Watermill, Stert, near Devizes SN10 3JA (Tel 0380 2985). Only one bedroom is available at this charming converted watermill on four floors, situated in picturesque Wiltshire countryside. Dinner is cooked with organic produce by the lady of the house, who is also a wildlife expert.

Eating Out

First Class

Harper's, 7 Ox Row, Market Square, Salisbury (Tel 0722 333118). Home-cooked nouvelle English cuisine in a friendly restaurant.

Blunsdon House Hotel, Blunsdon, near Swindon (Tel 0793 721701). Family owned hotel with a very popular restaurant serving English and Continental cuisine.

Middle Range

Just Brahms, 68 Castle Street, Salisbury (Tel 0722 28402). Informal restaurant (and cheaper bistro) offering an à la carte menu with inventive cuisine.

Dove Inn, Warminster (Tel 0985 50378). Cosy inn set in peaceful countryside offering traditional and original cuisine.

Economy

Stones, Avebury (Tel 06723 514). Vegetarian restaurant in a converted stable with views of Avebury stone circle. Most ingredients are locally and organically grown.

Polly Tea-Rooms, 26 High Street, Marlborough (Tel 0672 512146). Delightful English tea-room, traditional in every sense and also offering some vegetarian dishes.

Dorset

For the most part, Dorset is one of England's least developed counties, boasting the type of scenery and unspoiled environment that originally inspired Thomas Hardy to set many of his novels here around a century ago. On reaching the south-east of the region however, the picture changes as the coastal towns of Bournemouth, Poole and Christchurch emerge, forming between them an extensive built-up area which has paid scant regard to both the expanse of heath which used to be here and to the shoreline. The contrast between here and the rest of the county is great, and is accentuated even further by the extremes of rural life and 20th-century commercialism.

In the west of the county chalk hills form the beginning of the downs which stretch southward from Cranborne Chase to Dorchester, before heading to West Lulworth in the south-east, where they become the Purbeck Hills. In the east much of the land is formed from sands, gravels and clays, which are bounded by a fringe of younger Lower Tertiary sediments. Dorset's main rivers are the Frome, which drains the eastern plain, and the Stour, which crosses the western downs before joining the River Avon near its mouth at Christchurch. Main towns include Dorchester, to the south-west on the River Frome; Bournemouth, Poole and Christchurch in the south-east; Lyme Regis and Bridport in the west, and Shaftesbury and Sherborne in the north. Like Hampshire and the Isle of Wight (see *South-East* chapter, page 533), Dorset comes under the jurisdiction of the **Southern Tourist Board**, 40 Chamberlayne Road, Eastleigh, Hampshire S05 5JH (Tel 0703 620006).

Dorchester

The county town, Dorchester was founded following the Roman conquest of the Celtic tribesmen of Maiden Castle, when a settlement was established at what is now the centre of the town. Remains of Roman Dorchester, which was known as Durnovaria, have been uncovered throughout the years. One of the most notable finds was a collection of 22,000 coins, most of them from the 3rd century, which was discovered in **South Street**.

Also found and dating from that time are the sections of the town wall, which was six feet (1.8 metres) thick and twelve feet (3.7 metres) high, and enclosed an area of around 80 acres (32 hectares). Other Roman remains include mosaics and ruined villas, while to the south of the town, an 'amphitheatre' at **Maumbury Rings** dates from pre-Roman times and **Maiden Castle** has revealed evidence of occupation between Neolithic times and the Iron Age.

In later days Dorchester acquired another name, when Thomas Hardy, who was born near here at **Upper Bockhampton** and spent much of his life in the area, based his descriptions of Casterbridge on the town. A statue of Hardy can be seen opposite the **Military Museum** at the Top o' Town, while another statue, that of William Barnes, Hardy's mentor, is down from the **Shire Hall** on the High Street. Also on the High Street is the house where **Judge Jeffreys** stayed in the 17th century. **Max Gate** was Hardy's former home, and the novelist's heart is buried in **Stinford Churchyard** to the east. **Dorset County Museum** on High West Street is worth a brief visit, offering insights into the area's history from prehistoric times to the present day. **Morris dancing** takes place between April and October (check with Tourist Information) in the town and the area in general offers perfect walking country for both the energetic and the amblers. **Tourist Information** is at 7 Acland Road (Tel 0305 267992).

The South-Eeast

Bournemouth, Poole and **Christchurch** are popular, all-year-round resorts offering the expected coastal town attractions. In **Bournemouth** it's worth taking time to visit the **Russell Cotes Art Gallery and Museum** and **St Peter's Churchyard**, where Mary, the second wife of the poet Shelley, is buried. Along in **Poole**, the town has an old **postern gate** and several **almshouses**. The **Old Town House** (or Scaplen's Court) dates from the 14th–15th centuries, while the fine **Guildhall** was built in 1761. The **Customs House** with the **Town Beam** is also 18th-century, and both the **Town Cellars** and **Wool House** are of interest. **Poole Pottery**, one of the town's most famous exports, can be bought and demonstrations are offered on the finer touches of this tricky art. **Poole Harbour** is popular with yachtsmen and **Brownsea Island**, lying within it, has a rebuilt **castle**. Further east, **Christchurch**, on the estuaries of the Avon and Stour rivers, has a fine **priory church**, which is a good example of Norman and Perpendicular styles and which is also known for its chantry chapels and a monument to Shelley.

Tourist Information centres in the area can be found on Pier Approach, Bournemouth (Tel 0202 789789); The Quay, Poole (Tel

0202 673322), and 30 Saxon Square, Christchurch (Tel 0202 471780; open summer months only).

Lyme Regis and the West

The quintessential seaside town, Lyme Regis is extremely popular during the summer, but quieter for the rest of the year. The town's most famous sight is arguably the **Cobb** which, as John Fowles, author of *The French Lieutenant's Woman* and a native of Lyme Regis, described it, is 'a long claw of old grey wall that flexes itself against the sea'. The Duke of Monmouth landed on the Cobb in 1685 to raise his rebellion. A collection of local fossils is on display at the **Lyme Regis Museum**, while if you prefer the do-it-yourself approach, fossil hunting is a popular pastime along the imposing cliffs near the town. Local architecture abounds and throughout Lyme Regis there are many attractive Georgian buildings, while the **Church of St Michael** is mainly Perpendicular in style. **Tourist Information** is at the Guildhall, Bridge Street (Tel 02974 2138).

Of Dorset's 38 nature reserves, several are located in this area. Just to the east of the town, **Black Ven and the Spittles** is an attractive site with meadows containing rich grassland flora, as well as roe deer, fox and badger. Unfortunately the site can be dangerous due to continual slipping, and visitors are advised to check with Tourist Information about the suitability of a visit. Slightly further east, **Alington Hill** reserve at **Bridport** offers lovely hedgerows and woodland, as well as magnificent views of the surrounding area and coastline. North-east of Bridport, **Loscombe** reserve offers a wide range of butterflies and the occasional glimpse of a buzzard, while **Lower Kingcombe**, once called 'a farm held in a rural time-warp', offers an excellent variety of fauna and flora, and is particularly loved for its lowland meadows.

Accommodation

First Class

Chedington Court, Chedington, Beaminster DT8 3HY (Tel 093589 265). Impressive mid-19th-century country house hotel built in Jacobean style and offering extremely comfortable accommodation in elegant surroundings. Lovely views and gardens and fine cuisine.

Summer Lodge, Evershot DT2 OJR (Tel 0935 83424). Highly recommended country house hotel in the lovely village of Evershot. Country living at its best, with charming bedrooms, good food and a super walled garden.

Maiden Newton House, Maiden Newton, near Dorchester DT2

OAA (Tel 0300 20336). Here on the edge of Maiden Newton guests are invited to relax with their hosts in opulent surroundings, situated in extensive grounds on the River Frome.

Middle Range

The Mansion House Hotel, Thames Street, Poole BH15 1JN (Tel 0202 685666). Georgian townhouse hotel in a quiet location in Poole offering luxury accommodation at the upper end of Middle Range prices.

Plumber Manor, Sturminster Newton DT10 2AF (Tel 0258 72507). A delightful manor which has been in the same family since the 17th century. Guests are warmly welcomed by their hosts and are at leisure to admire the many fascinating ornaments and furnishings which help to make this a country house hotel of real character.

Casterbridge Hotel, 49 High East Street, Dorchester DT1 1HU (Tel 0305 264043). Traditional old hotel in the centre of Dorchester offering bed and breakfast. Perfect for a real taste of Hardy country.

Economy

Lamperts Cottage, Sydling St Nicholas, Cerne Abbas, near Dorchester DT2 9NU (Tel 0300 341659). A wonderful bed and breakfast in a 16th-century thatched cottage surrounded by fields and streams on the edge of the village.

Red House, Sidmouth Road, Lyme Regis DT7 3ES (Tel 02974 2055). Turn-of-the-century house originally built for Aldis (as in Aldis lamps) and now offering bed and breakfast, with large bedrooms.

The Beehive, Osmington, near Weymouth DT3 6EL (Tel 0305 834095). This charming thatched stone cottage offers really great value for money accommodation. Unpretentious yet comfortable, friendly and cosy, it is situated in an area known for its scenic beauty. Bed and breakfast at good prices, and evening meals on occasions (worth making a point of being there for).

Eating Out

First Class

Norfolk Royale Hotel, Richmond Hill, Bournemouth (Tel 0202 21521). Edwardian country house hotel more notable for its restaurant than accommodation (though staying here would by no means be a hardship). Two restaurants offering excellent cuisine and making good use of local produce.

Haddon House Hotel, West Bay, Bridport (Tel 0308 23626). Regency-style country house hotel serving fine local cuisine and producing their own wines.

Middle Range

Riverside Restaurant, West Bay, Bridport (Tel 0308 22011). Friendly restaurant specialising in seafood but also offering meat dishes. A good family place.

Manor Hotel, Beach Road, West Bexington (Tel 0308 897616). Traditional manor house offering up-market bar meals in elegant surroundings.

Economy

The Fox, Ansty, near Dorchester (Tel 0258 880328). Traditional pub offering wholesome food and local ale.

The Sea Cow, 7 Custom House, Quay, Weymouth (Tel 0305 783524). Bistro-style restaurant serving light lunches and more expensive dinners, which are a mixture of British and Continental cuisine.

Somerset

The Mendips, carboniferous limestone hills reaching just over 1000 feet (325 m.), dominate much of the north of the county. Stretching from close to the Bristol Channel into Somerset, the hills are designated an Area of Outstanding Natural Beauty and are the closest semi-wildscape to Bristol and Bath. Being limestone there is little or no surface water on the Mendips, but there is a vast system of underground inter-connected caves. **Cheddar Caves** and **Wookey Hole** are probably the best known and the Cheddar area is the most visited limestone region of Britain. Much of the Gorge is overrun by souvenir shops, cafes and restaurants that do little to add to the scenic attractions. Higher up the Gorge, about a mile and a half (2.4 km.) from Cheddar is **Black Rock Nature Trail** which passes through woodland. The slopes of the hills have broadleaved woodlands and the surface of the limestone is a plateau with peat bogs. Excellent views across the Somerset Levels, over the Bristol Channel to Wales and towards Bristol and Bath are possible from **Black Down**, the highest point on the Mendips.

Nearby, **Wells**, England's smallest cathedral city, boasts its **Cathedral**, a masterpiece of Gothic architecture built in two stages between 1180 and 1340. In the vicinity, **Bishop's Palace** is open to the public, and **Vicar's Close** is a unique street of 14th-century terraced houses. The central part of the town can be very congested in the summer and parking is a problem.

Glastonbury

Glastonbury is associated with King Arthur and this and other legends have attracted visitors for many centuries. Most visitors are drawn to the **Tor**, a 500 ft (152 m.) hill which originally had an Iron Age fort on it and is thought by some to be the burial place for the Holy Grail. From here there are excellent views over the Somerset Levels and towards the Mendips. The **Abbey**, established in the 10th century and once the greatest Benedictine house in England, is now mainly in ruins: an abbey church was built in the 1100s and this still dominates the town. **Tourist Information Centre** is at 1 Marchant's Buildings, Northload Street (Tel 0458 32954).

Exmoor

Exmoor, unlike Dartmoor and Bodmin Moor, is made of sedimentary rocks, mainly sandstones, and is bordered on its northern side by the sea. The moor is shared by both Devon and Somerset, with Somerset having the higher parts. Much of the moor is between 1200 and 1500 ft (350–450m), and the highest point is **Dunkery Beacon** at 1706 ft (520 m). The higher parts of the moor are covered with heather, bracken and peat bogs, whilst lower down are grass moorland areas with beech-hedged pasture land. The wooded areas are mainly on the north coast, but also on the steep **sided valleys**, known as cleaves. There is heavy rainfall, often exceeding 70 inches (1778 mm.) per year, and the rivers **Exe**, **Lyn** and **Barle** rise on the moor.

The variety of landscape on the moor ensures a wide range of fauna and flora. In the wooded valleys are plants such as water mint and spearwort, insects like the mayfly, damselfly and dragonfly and birds like dipper, heron and kingfisher. The core of Exmoor is the old Royal Hunting Forest centred on **Simonsbath**, where it may be possible to see red deer, although most are found in the valley woods. The open uplands have adders, grass snakes and slow worms, as well as buzzards, kestrels and sparrowhawks and the shaggy Exmoor ponies. The coast, which forms the northern boundary of the moor, has some of the highest cliffs in the country and the most dramatic parts are between **Porlock** and **Lynmouth**, with a sheer cliff of 800 ft (250 m) at **Great Hangman**. Most of the beaches of this north coast failed to meet EC standards for clean bathing in 1990, but those that passed were **Porlock Weir, Blue Anchor, Woolacombe, Croyde Bay** and **Saunton Sands**.

It is relatively easy to explore some of the higher parts of Exmoor by car as there is a network of minor roads that allows a good deal of access (during the summer these roads are not as congested as those around Dartmoor). The Exmoor Park headquarters is at **Dulverton** (Tel 0398 23665) and a circular tour beginning here will take in a range of the human and physical landscapes of the moor. The B3223 from Dulverton towards Exford passes close to **Tarr Steps** (left at Spire Cross from the B3223). The steps are a medieval clapper bridge over the River Barle, and the site can be very busy on summer weekends. Rejoining the main road will lead on to **Winsford Hill**, which provides excellent views north towards the coast and Dunkery Beacon. The road then descends into **Exford**, a small and attractive moorland village. From Exford to **Simonsbath** the road runs between the Exe and Barle valleys and then rises from Simonsbath, crosses the Exe and passes through the rounded hills, sedge and heather of **Brendon Common**. It then descends via **Watersmeet**, the confluence of the East and West Lyn rivers, to **Lynmouth**. Parts of Lynmouth have been overdeveloped for tourism, but its neighbour on the hill, **Lynton**, accessible by the water-driven funicular railway, manages to maintain most of the charm of a Victorian resort.

The way out of Lynmouth is up the steep **Countisbury Hill**, along the A39 to **Oare**. Oare church is the setting for the marriage of Lorna Doone in R. D. Blackmoore's work, and nearby is **Doone Valley**, where the oulaws in *Lorna Doone* lived, with a picnic site and numerous walks. Following the A39 towards Minehead and turning right near Culbourne towards Lucott Cross leads over the high moorland to Exford again. An alternative is to carry on along the A39, down **Porlock Hill** to Porlock and then return to Exford. **Dunkery Beacon** can be visited by taking the B3224 from Exford and turning left before reaching Wheddon Cross, and there are several long and short walks around the Beacon with excellent views. Returning to the B3224 and following to Wheddon Cross, turn right and right again to **Winsford**, which has a packhorse bridge and thatched houses around a green. The A396 can then be followed back to Dulverton or a detour can be made to **Wimbleball Lake**. This is a reservoir, serving North Devon and West Somerset and there are several walks by the lake, a nature reserve and good views towards the Brendon Hills.

Walking on the moor is excellent with over 600 miles (965 km.) of marked paths. The Park Authority publishes a series of detailed guides *Waymarked Walks*, and also offer a number of guided walks, details of which are in *The Exmoor Visitor*, published by the Park Authority.

Accommodation

First Class

Simonsbath House, Simonsbath, near Minehead TA24 7SH (Tel 064383 259). Delightful, informal country house with views of the River Barle.

The Crown, Exford TA24 7PP (Tel 064383 554). Friendly hotel in a 17th-century building; a good place to meet the locals.

Middle Range

Carnarvon Arms Hotel, Dulverton TA22 9AE (Tel 0398 23302). Nineteenth-century hotel combining traditional service with modern facilities, including swimming pool, games room, tennis, fishing and shooting. Set in 50 acres (20.25 hectares) of grounds.

Old Manor Farmhouse, Norton Fitzwarren, near Taunton TA2 6RZ (Tel 0823 289801). Small, friendly hotel with comfortable rooms and excellent food, including a good range of vegetarian dishes.

Economy

Penscot Farmhouse Hotel, Shipham, near Cheddar BS25 1ZW (Tel 093484 2659). Cosy hotel in converted 15th-century farm cottages. Open fires, exposed beams, a conservatory and beautiful views complement the excellent cuisine (some vegetarian) served in the two dining-rooms.

Box Tree House, Westbury-sub-Mendip, Wells BA5 1HA (Tel 0749 870777). Bed and breakfast in a converted 17th-century farmhouse. The owners also have stained-glass and picture-framing workshops, with some items for sale.

Eating Out

First Class

Walnut Tree Inn, North Petherton, near Bridgwater (Tel 0278 662255). Nothing but the best of English fare made from local produce is offered at this pleasant inn, situated between Bridgwater and Taunton.

Almshouse, The Square, Axbridge, near Glastonbury (Tel 0934 732493). Immaculately restored 15th-century building now housing a new restaurant, serving English cuisine made from the best local produce.

Middle Range

Ye Old Punch Bowl Tavern, Henton, Wells (Tel 0749 72212). English and Italian cuisine in a 16th-century inn, set in beautiful grounds. Some vegetarian dishes available.

The Three Horse Shoes, Shepton Mallet (Tel 074985 359). Fish and meat dishes, as well as chef's specials served in a friendly 16th-century inn.

Economy

Rainbow's End, 17a High Street, Glastonbury (Tel 0458 533896). Wholefood cafe and buffet with some seating outdoors.

Settle Inn, Cheap Street, Frome (Tel 0373 65975). Home-made, traditional, local cooking and a vast selection of home-made wines.

Devon

Exeter

Exeter is the county town of Devon and, although the city has a history stretching back 2000 years, its appearance is mainly modern as many of the older parts, particularly the medieval streets and buildings, were destroyed by bombing raids in World War II. The **Cathedral** is not that impressive from the outside compared with other English cathedrals, but the interior is well worth looking at, with a minstrels' gallery, a rood screen, 13th-century misericords and a carved wooden bishop's throne. **Cathedral Close** has several attractive houses, including **Mol's Coffee Shop** which has connections with Sir Francis Drake. Nearby in Castle Street, **Rougemont House Museum** is a fine Georgian house with displays of archaeology, folk history and the Royal Devon Yeomanry. In the High Street is the 14th-century **Guildhall** which has displays of local paintings and the civic silver. The **Tourist Information Office** is at the Civic Centre in Paris Street (Tel 0392 72434).

About ten minutes' walk from the Cathedral is **Exeter Quay**. This is on a 16th-century canalised part of the Exe, and is the oldest ship canal in England. There are several 17th- and 19th-century warehouses that have been restored and now house a number of pubs, clubs and discos. Across the Exe, via a suspension bridge or hand pulled ferry, is **Exeter Maritime Museum**, housing a number of boats from around the world, as well as a cafe and a shop. In the area of the town known as **Pennsylvania** is the **University**; the campus is landscaped and well worth a visit and includes the **Northcott Theatre**. The city is easy to get out of, being surrounded by low hills to the north and west and the **Exe Estuary** to the south. The Estuary is the most important marine wetland area in the South-west, yet it has no official status. Access is possible on both sides of the estuary, particularly at **Powderham** on the right side and **Lympstone** and **Exmouth** on the left. Many wildfowl and waders visit here in winter, including avocet, sandpiper, greenshank and whimbrel. Exeter is a well located centre for exploring East Devon, Dartmoor and the North Devon coast.

Plymouth

The largest town in Devon. The fleet that was to save England from the invasion of the Spanish Armada forces set sail from here under the command of Drake in 1588 and Plymouth was the last port of call of the Pilgrim Fathers before they headed for the New World in 1620. Explorers such as Cook and Sir Humphrey Gilbert, the first Englishman in Newfoundland, also sailed from here, as did Drake on his round the world voyage. Unfortunately the city was very badly bombed in World War II and has a mainly modern appearance today.

Attractions worth visiting include the remains of the church of **St James**; the **Barbican**, with its memorial to the Pilgrim Fathers; the **Mayflower Stone**; **New Street**, which paradoxically has many old buildings; the **Citadel**, and the **Hoe**, where Drake reputedly insisted on finishing his game of bowls before setting out to sea against the Armada. **Devonport** is the site of the naval dockyard and has several interesting 19th-century buildings.

There are a wide range of animal habitats in a relatively small area around Plymouth and the local council makes reference to the setting up of nature reserves within the city. City wildscapes include **Ford Park Valley, Southway Valley, Whiteleigh Wood** and **Woodland Wood Valley**. Further information from Plymouth City Council, Civic Centre (Tel 0752 668000) and Plymouth Urban Wildlife Group (Tel 0752 264878). Cycles can be hired from **Battery Cycle Works**, 125 Embankment (Tel 0752 665553).

Plymouth is in an excellent location for visits to Dartmoor, the South Devon coast and the Cornish coast.

Dartmoor

Dartmoor, covering over 350 square miles (906 sq. m.) is the most southerly National Park in Britain and parts of it are wild and desolate. The average height of Dartmoor is over 1200 ft (366 m.) making it the highest area of southern Britain; the highest points, **Yes Tor** and **High Willhays**, rise to over 2000 ft (610 m.). Tors are the most distinctive natural features of the moor; there are more than 150 of them and almost all are made of granite. This fairly resistant igneous rock was formed about 300 million years ago and was injected into underlying rocks, swelling the area to a dome that once approached Alpine heights. In the succeeding years the effects of rain, water and frost have removed the upper covering layers to expose the granite. The release of pressure caused by the removal of this covering material has allowed the vertical cracks or joints that formed in the granite, as it cooled, to be opened up. This has enabled water and frost action to form the fabulous shapes now known as tors. This is the theory, but nobody is quite sure of the processes that contributed to these distinctive features.

The best known tors are **Hay Tor, Hound Tor, Great Mis Tor** and **Yes Tor** and many of them appear to be human structures with distinctive forms: **Shape Tor**, near Merrivale, looks like a series of steeples; **Hound Tor** like a castle with battlements, and **Blackingstone Rock**, near Moretonhampstead, like a dome.

The moor, being close to the sea and fairly high, receives heavy annual rainfall, most of which occurs in winter, although summer rain is common and there is much more of it here than on the coast. The rain has contributed to the formation of blanket bog; this is peat as much as 3–4 metres thick which acts like a giant sponge. Most of the peat bogs are not as dangerous as **Fox Tor Mire**, which is the setting for Arthur Conan Doyle's *The Hound of the Baskervilles* (under the fictitious name of Grimpen Moor). The only prisoner never to have been recaptured after escaping from Dartmoor Prison was last seen heading for Fox Tor Mire. The water that is soaked up by the peat eventually flows as rivers and some of the more important rivers, such as the **Dart, Taw, Erme, Plym, Teign** and **Tavy** rise on the moor. There is little vegetation or wildlife on the higher parts of the moor, but the open vistas can be very rewarding.

Although much of the moor appears natural there are many relics of past human occupation, particularly remains of Stone Age and Bronze Age settlements. It appears that the sites of settlement on the higher part of the moor were abandoned during the Iron Age as the climate became cooler and iron was mined in the valleys. One of the best places to see a number of Bronze Age hut circles and also a long double row of standing stones is **Merrivale**. Access is from the A384 Tavistock to Ashburton road with parking on the right side of the road 800 ft (250 m) after a pub on the left hand side – there is a map on display here. At **Grimspound**, which is one and a half miles (2.4 km.) south of Challacombe Cross, there is a Bronze Age village settlement where some of the village huts have been restored.

The lower slopes of the moor and the river valleys are often densely wooded and at **Wistman's Wood**, an English Nature Reserve north of Two Bridges there is a unique dwarf oak wood. Fast flowing rivers in steep-sided wooded valleys are a common feature of these lower slopes and **Lydford Gorge** at Lydford is an example. The **White Lady** waterfall, where water drops over 100 ft (30 m.), can be reached on a path along the Gorge from Lydford. **Yarner Wood**, a National Nature Reserve near Lustleigh, is an oak woodland with a variety of bird and animal life and well laid out nature trails. Nearby, on the other side of the B3344, is the River Bovey valley which has attractive walks to **Lustleigh** and **Becky Falls**.

The following locations are honeypots during the summer and they are likely to be crowded, but worth visiting out of season: **Hay Tor**, near Bovey Tracey, which is the nearest sizeable tor to Exeter and Torquay; **Dartmeet** on the A384, at the point where the East and West Dart join; **Postbridge** on the B3212 north of Princetown, which has a medieval clapper bridge; and **Widecombe**, the village made famous in the song 'Widecombe Fair'. The well-known prison on the moor is at **Princetown**.

Guidebooks to the moor can be obtained from **Dartmoor National Park Dept**, Parke, Bovey Tracey (Tel 0626 832093).

Rest of Devon

The south Devon coast away from Torbay has several places worth visiting, such as the **Dart Estuary** and **Dartmouth**, **Totnes**, the **Kingsbridge Estuary** and **Salcombe**, **Slapton Sands** and **Prawle Point**. In North Devon the area between the **Taw** and **Torridge** valleys has been recently designated by the West Country Tourist Board as **Tarka Country** after Henry Williamson's creation, *Tarka the Otter*, and there are some excellent walks – details from the Tourist Board Offices (see address page 583). The east Devon coast from **Beer** to **Budleigh Salterton** has impressive cliffs. An excellent cliff top walk is from Beer over dramatic chalk headlands, via a collapsed cliff section to **Branscombe**. Budleigh Salterton has red sandstone cliffs and a fine shingle spit across the **River Otter** estuary, which is an excellent site for observing autumn and winter migrant birds.

Accommodation

First Class

Gidleigh Park, near Chagford TQ13 8HH (Tel 0647 432367). Elegant, turn-of-the-century country house in Tudor style offering all comforts and fine cuisine. Set in 50 acres (20.25 hectares) of beautiful grounds.

Bel Alp House, Haytor, Newton Abbott TQ13 9XX (Tel 0634 661217). Small, Edwardian country house hotel with good views of Dartmoor.

Middle Range

Wigham, Morchard Bishop EX17 6RJ (Tel 03637 350). Sixteenth-century Devon longhouse with five bedrooms. Part of a dairy farm, much use is made of home-grown produce. Snooker room, outdoor heated swimming pool and riding available. No children.

Woolston House, Loddiswell, Kingsbridge TQ7 4DU (Tel 0548 550341). Georgian mansion offering family run bed, breakfast and evening meal. Delightful gardens, outdoor heated swimming pool, and particularly suitable for families with children.

Economy

The Wood, De Courcy Road, Moult Hill, Salcombe, near Plymouth TQ8 8LQ (Tel 054884 2778). Exceptionally positioned turn-of-the-century house, perched on the edge of a cliff with magnificent views of Salcombe estuary and the English Channel. Bed, breakfast and dinner available.

Waldon Cottage, The Square, Sheepwash, Beaworthy, near Okehampton EX21 5NE (Tel 040923 382). Bed, breakfast and dinner in a charming thatched house in the conservation village of Sheepwash.

Eating Out

First Class

Angel Diner, 23 Church Street, Ilfracombe (Tel 0271 866833). Fish and vegetarian restaurant in a converted butcher's shop. Good choice of organic wines.

Knightshayes Court, Knightshayes (Tel 0884 259416). Traditional restaurant situated in a National Trust property. Local produce and recipes, all in the old-fashioned way.

Middle Range

Sloops, Bridge Street, Bideford (Tel 0237 471796). Good value cooking in a friendly restaurant. The cuisine is English but with some intriguing imaginative touches.

The Angler's Rest, Drewsteignton (Tel 064721 287). Situated on the River Teign next to Fingle Bridge in Fingle Gorge, and serving traditional wholesome food. Good cream teas.

Economy

Reapers, 23 Gold Street, Tiverton (Tel 0884 255310). Wholefood cafe and shop making good use of organically-grown ingredients.

Cherub, 11 Higher Street, Dartmouth (Tel 0803 832571). Straightforward cooking and good bar meals in one of Dartmouth's oldest buildings.

Cornwall

Bodmin Moor

This tends to be less visited than Dartmoor and Exmoor although it has the status of an Area of Outstanding Natural Beauty. It covers about 80 square miles (207 sq. km.) and, like Dartmoor, is composed of granite and has a similar landscape with craggy tors, peat bogs and rolling moorland. There is a very large number of prehistoric remains and other historic stone relics in a relatively small area on the moor. Some of the most interesting include **The Hurlers**, a stone circle, probably early Bronze Age, near Minions; **Trethevy Quoit**, a prehistoric burial chamber near St Cleer; the **King Doniert Stone**, a 9th-century wayside monument at Common Moor, and **Dozmary Pool**, where hundreds of artefacts, including prehistoric, have been found. The **Cheesewring**, near Minions appears to be a prehistoric monument, but is a naturally weathered granite tor. **Roughtor**, reaching over 1300 ft (400 m.) and located about three miles (5 km.) south-east of Camelford is probably the most popular tor on the moor and can be very busy in the summer season.

The highest point on the moor, and in Cornwall, is **Brown Willy** at 1375 ft (419 m.). Excellent views can be obtained from the higher points of the moor; on clear days it is possible to see both the north and south coasts of Cornwall. The moor has a variety of bogland plants and rare orchids. The Ramblers' Association sponsor guided walks of the Moor. Local tourist offices are at **Camelford** (Tel 0840 212954) and **Launceston** (Tel 0566 2321).

The North Cornish Coast

The north Cornish coast has a number of excellent beaches, such as **Whitesand Bay, Portheras Cove, St Ives, Holywell Bay, Constantine Bay, Hayle Bay** and **Daymer Bay**, all of which are considered by many to be among the best beaches in Britain. **Cape Cornwall** is much more impressive than the overdeveloped Land's End, the **Camel Estuary** at **Padstow** is particularly attractive and the coast from **Boscastle** to **Crackington Haven** is good for walking.

The Lizard

Much of this peninsula is an Area of Outstanding Natural Beauty. Unlike much of Cornwall, the rock here is not granite, but a mixture of shales, slates, micas and serpentine. The coast from **Mullion**, an old fishing cove, to **Lizard Point** offers some of the most spectacular coastal scenery in the South-West. **Poldhu Cove, Polurrian Cove** and **Gunwalloe Cove** have sandy beaches which are safe for swimming in calm weather.

Lizard Point is the most southerly point on mainland Britain and the lighthouse, which is open to the public, has an impressive light and foghorn. To the east are a number of fine beaches, including **Kennack Sands, Coverack** and **Porthoustock**. **Cadgwith** was once a picturesque fishing village in a secluded cove, but is suffering increasingly from too many visitors. On the eastern side of the Peninsula is the **Helford River**. This is the setting for several Daphne du Maurier novels, including *Frenchman's Creek*, named after a small haven on the **Helford Estuary**. At **Gweek** there is a seal sanctuary, devoted to the rescue and care of seals, while other places on the estuary worth visiting include **Helford, Manaccan** and **Gillan**.

Inland are **Goonhilly Downs**, a predominantly granite-based area, something like a plateau. Here there are rare plants such as Cornish heather and there is a National Nature Reserve. The Downs are dominated by the futuristic dishes of British Telecom's **Goonhilly Earth Station**, the relay point for trans-Atlantic messages. A visitor centre was opened here in 1988 and bus tours of the station are offered. Nearby, **Helston**, the largest town of the area offers the impressive **Floral Day** with dancing on 8 May. Also here is the famous home brew pub, The Blue Anchor.

Accommodation

First Class

Talland Bay Hotel, Talland-by-Looe PL13 2JB (Tel 0503 72667). Charming 16th-century country house hotel with views of the coast, set in pleasant gardens and offering croquet, games room, sauna, heated outdoor swimming pool and special interest breaks.

The Abbey, Abbey Street, Penzance TR18 4AR (Tel 0736 66906). An informal country house within Penzance itself overlooking the harbour.

Middle Range

Crackington Manor, Crackington Haven, near Bude EX23 OJG (Tel 08403 397536). Peaceful country manor set in an attractive cove, offering outdoor heated swimming pool, gym, sauna and games room. A good base for walking and outdoor pursuits. No smoking throughout the hotel.

Nanscawen House, Prideaux Road, St Blazey, Par PL24 2SR (Tel 0726 814488). Welcoming Georgian mansion in five acres (2 hectares) of grounds, located in a conservation area. Heated swimming pool available and pony trekking within easy distance.

Economy

Manor Farm, Crackington Haven, near Bude EX23 OJW (Tel 08403 304). Historic 11th-century manor house which once belonged to the half brother of William the Conqueror and is mentioned in the 1086 Domesday Book. Bed, breakfast and excellent dinners with fresh fruit and vegetables from the garden.

Trewerry Mill, Trerice, near Newquay TR8 5HS (Tel 0872 510345). Seventeenth-century watermill owned by the National Trust and run as a bed and breakfast.

Eating Out

First Class

Allhays Country House, Talland Bay, Looe (Tel 0503 72434). English nouvelle cuisine in a delightful period country house set in beautiful grounds.

Stanton's Restaurant, 11 Esplanade, Fowey (Tel 072683 2631). High quality local seafood and home-raised poultry dishes are served at this family run restaurant.

Middle Range

The Feast, 15 Kenwyn Street, Truro (Tel 0872 72546). Vegetarian and vegan restaurant in a relaxed, plant-filled environment.

Pelynt Dagger Restaurant, Barton Meadow, Pelynt, near Looe (Tel 0503 20386). Popular restaurant in an attractive setting serving English and Continental cuisine.

Economy

Sail Loft, St Michael's Mount, Marazion (Tel 0736 710748). Local, home-made cuisine in a converted carpenter's shop owned by the National Trust.

Mr Bistro, East Quay, The Harbour, Mevagissey (Tel 0726 842432). Good value fish restaurant in a converted pilchard shop.

The Isles of Scilly

Located at the southernmost part of Britain, these islands (there are almost 200 of them) are granite outliers of the Cornish landmass, lying 22 miles (35 km.) south-west of Land's End. Only five of the islands are inhabited and the total resident population is less than 2000. The largest island, with the capital of **Hugh Town**, is **St Mary's**. The islands have one of the cleanest, least polluted environments in southern Britain and both the sea and air can be remarkably clear in comparison with mainland locations. The islands also have several excellent white sand beaches, unusual plants and numerous native and migratory birds. May and June are the best times to see breeding birds and the uninhabited island of **Annet**, a bird sanctuary, offers some of the best viewing. The climate is the mildest in the British Isles, with sub-tropical plants growing on **Tresco**, and it is possible to take an outdoor holiday between early March and November. It is worth noting that storms, particularly from the south-west, can whip up massive Atlantic waves at any time of the year and the islands can remain fog-bound for several days at a time. A major attraction for visitors is the virtual absence of cars and only **St Mary's** has significant amounts of paved road. Most visitors leave their vehicles on the mainland and travel around the islands on foot, although minibus and taxi services operate on St Mary's. Small open boats operate from **Hugh Town Quay**, weather permitting, throughout the year and island-hopping is another attraction.

All the islands have good beaches, but particularly fine ones are found on **St Martin's**. **St Agnes** is the wildest island, being most exposed to south-westerly gales, whilst **Bryher** is the smallest inhabited island with rough terrain and few people. Holidays on the islands are enhanced by the pace of life, much slower than on the mainland, and by the fact that visitor numbers tend to be low, partly due to the cost of travel, but also because of the limited amount of accommodation available. Access by air is from Bristol, Exeter, Plymouth and Heathrow with **Brymon Airways** (Tel 0752 707023), and by helicopter from Penzance with **British Airways Helicopters** (Tel 0736 63871). By sea the *Scillonia* takes two and a half hours from Penzance (Tel 0736 62009). **Tourist Information** and details of accommodation are available from **Town Hall**, Hugh Town, St Mary's (Tel. 0720 22536).

Accommodation & Eating Out

First Class

Star Castle Hotel, Garrison, St Mary's (Tel 0720 22317). Elizabethan castle offering traditional comfort (some rooms have four-posters) and cuisine. Set in lovely grounds and also offering a heated swimming pool and tennis.

Tregarthen's Hotel, Hugh Town, St Mary's (Tel 0720 22540). Nineteenth-century hotel in a pleasant harbour position.

Middle Range

Atlantic Hotel, Hugh Town, St Mary's (Tel 0720 22417). Friendly and welcoming hotel offering good value for money, overlooking the harbour.

Brantwood Hotel, Rocky Hill, St Mary's (Tel 0720 22531). Small, intimate and traditional hotel offering high standards of service and cuisine.

Economy

Carn Vean Guest House, Pelistry, St Mary's (Tel 0720 22462). Small, family run guest house set in its own grounds close to Pelistry Bay, and offering bed and breakfast.

Blue Carn Cottage, Old Town, St Mary's (Tel 0720 22309). Two cottages joined together offering friendly bed and breakfast accommodation.

WALES

17 Wales

One of the world's smallest countries (roughly half the size of Switzerland), Wales lies to the west of England. Since local government reorganisation in 1974 it has had 37 districts but just eight counties: Gwent, South, West and Mid Glamorgan, Dyfed, Powys, Gwynedd and Clwyd. The Wales Tourist Board further divides the country into South, North and Mid Wales in recognition of its geographical diversity.

Of Great Britain's regions, Wales is one of the most distinctive. It is a bilingual country with roughly 500,000 people out of close on 3 million speaking Welsh as their native language. This is akin to Gaelic, Galician and other Celtic tongues but with Latin, Norman-French and English elements. When William Morgan translated the Bible into Welsh in 1588, he gave it a respectability previously denied it by the 1536 Act of Union with England, which had prohibited Welsh-speakers from holding official posts. A copy of his Bible is displayed in St Asaph's cathedral. In 1821 around 80 per cent of the population spoke Welsh, but the Industrial Revolution brought an influx of English-speaking factory and mine owners, and gradually the proportion of Welsh speakers declined, to just 19 per cent in 1981. Today the Welsh language television channel S4C is avidly watched in the western counties of Gwynedd (63 per cent Welsh-speaking) and Dyfed (47 per cent). The Welsh Language Society has been in the forefront of efforts to get full recognition of Welsh. All road signs are now bilingual, civil service jobs must be advertised in Welsh as well as English, and some primary schooling is conducted in Welsh.

The late 20th century has seen a revival of Welsh nationalism, notably with the creation of a political party in 1925 devoted to winning the country's independence. Plaid Cymru's first MP, Gwynfor Evans, was elected in 1925. In a 1979 referendum however, the idea of independence was rejected.

About 70 per cent of the Welsh population lives either in and around Cardiff, the capital, in South Glamorgan, South Wales with its coal and iron resources, or in the slate-quarrying district of Blaenau Ffestiniog in Gwynedd. Both were, and still are, the most heavily industrialised areas in the country.

King Arthur crops up in Welsh mythology, much of it enshrined in the *Mabinogion*. The harp-playing and male voice choirs so typical of Welsh culture date back at least as far as the 12th century, when they were recorded by the writer-monk, Giraldus Cambrensis or Gerald of Wales. The annual *eisteddfodau* are music, drama and poetry competitions traditionally linked with the Druids. The Royal National Eisteddfod moves between north and south Wales in alternate years, while the International Musical Eisteddfod is held in Llangollen every July. Eisteddfodau are some of the few occasions where women in Welsh national dress, including tall black hats, can still be seen.

Typical of Welsh crafts are lovespoons, traditionally carved out of single pieces of wood and given to women at the start of courtship since the 17th century. Nowadays they're mainly a tourist souvenir, but you can watch them being carved at St Fagan's Museum, at Castle Welsh Crafts (1 Castle St, Cardiff. Tel 0222 343038) and at the Lovespoon Centre (The Druid Inn, Goginan, Aberystwyth. Tel 0970 84368).

Welsh place names, immortalised by the world's longest – Llanfairpwllgwyngyllgogerychwyrndrobwllllantysiliogogogoch ('the church of St Mary by the hollow of white aspen over the whirlpool and St Tysilio's Church close to the red cave') – can seem tongue-twistingly impossible until you realise that they consist of common elements with specific meanings, including the following:

aber	estuary	*mynydd*	mountain
afon	river	*ogof*	cave
bach	small	*pen*	headland
caer	fort	*pistyll*	waterfall
capel	chapel	*pwll*	pit/pool
coed	wood	*rhiw*	slope
cwm	valley	*rhos*	moor/marsh
glan	shore	*tre*	town
gwyn	white	*ty*	house
Llan	church	*ystwyth*	winding
Llyn	lake		

The Welsh flag is green and white with a distinctive red dragon. Wales also has its own stamps although not its own coinage. On 1 March, feast day of Welsh patron saint, St David, daffodils and leeks are worn.

History

Prehistoric remains like the impressive burial mound at Pentre Ifan are scattered throughout north and south Wales, and provide evidence of occupation before the Celtic invasion left the Silures the dominant tribe in the south and the Ordovices in the north. From AD 50 the Romans struggled to assert their authority, fighting off resistance led by Caractacus from bases in Caerleon and Chester. Although they established towns at Carmarthen and Caerwent, Roman influence was mainly restricted to lowland Wales; in the highlands the Celts were left to pursue their age-old lifestyle virtually unchanged.

Christianity had already reached Wales by the time the Romans withdrew in 381, and Llantwit Major became an important base for Celtic missionaries. After the Roman retreat, as many as eighteen separate princedoms were established in Wales, eventually consolidating into Gwynedd in the north, Powys in the East, and Deheubarth and Morgannwg in the south. After constant demarcation disputes between the English and Welsh, King Offa of Mercia eventually created an earthwork barrier indicating the borders of the two territories; parts of Offa's Dyke still survive today. In the meantime west coast Wales was subjected to sporadic Viking raids.

In the 11th century the Normans invaded Wales, establishing their authority in the south and east and along the border area which came to be known as the Marches and which was controlled by powerful semi-independent barons. Castle strongholds were established in towns like Caerphilly and Pembroke, but the Normans, like the Romans before them, were happy to leave the highlands to the Welsh.

In the 13th century the native Prince Llywelyn ap Gruffudd united many of the tribes in resistance to Edward I. After the Prince's defeat and death at Cilmuri in 1282 however, Edward I imposed English law on Wales and ringed Snowdonia, the heart of the rebellion, with impregnable castles to prevent any recurrence. His son, later Edward II, was invested as the first Prince of Wales in Caernarfon Castle in 1301.

Owain Glyndwr made a last attempt to be rid of the English at the start of the 15th century, setting up his own parliament in Machynlleth in mid Wales. His rebellion also led to defeat, but in 1485 Henry Tudor, a descendant of the 7th century Welsh prince Cadwaladr, defeated Richard III at the Battle of Bosworth to become King of England. In 1536 his son Henry VIII formally joined the two countries with his Act of Union.

Wales still retained a separate identity, becoming a stronghold of Methodism and Non-Conformist Christianity. The Industrial Revolution made Welsh coal, iron and steel vital to the English economy, and a work force from England and Ireland was drafted in to supplement the native Welsh. Post-World War I competition from European imports led to a decline in the industries which had brought the boom, and the local population fell as many Welsh emigrated in search of a better life. In the 20th century trade unionism and the Labour Party became increasingly important to Welsh politics; in the 1970s the Prime Minister, the Speaker of the House of Commons and several cabinet ministers were Welsh or represented Welsh constituencies. Wales now has thirty-eight MPs and a Secretary of State responsible solely for Welsh affairs.

In the 1980s heavy industry declined even further. Following the 1984–5 miners' strike the coal mines of the South Wales valleys steadily closed. In 1990, Mardy, the last mine in the Rhondda Valley where fifty pits once employed 40,000 men, closed down. Now only 'super-pits' like Margam survive.

Geography

Roughly 160 miles (257 km.) long by 60 miles (96 km.) wide, Wales is a mountainous country, much of it lying at more than 600 ft (183 m.). In all there are 225 peaks, with Mount Snowdon (Yr Wyddfa) at 3560 ft (1085 m.), the highest mountain in England and Wales. Wales is surrounded by the Severn Estuary and Bristol Channel to the south, St George's Channel and Cardigan Bay to the west, and the Irish Sea to the north.

Behind the low-lying, arable coastal areas of the south-east the famous Valleys cut north to the 521 square mile (1350 sq. km.) **Brecon Beacons National Park**, with the Black Mountains extending to east and west. The Brecon Beacons, once used as signal stations, have softer, smoother outlines than Snowdonia and are littered with lakes, reservoirs, waterfalls, *cwms* or semicircular valleys and forests, including the Crynant, Glasfynydd, Talybont, Rheola, Margam and Mynydd Du Forests. Within the National Park are the Craig Cerrig Gleishiad, Craig y Cilau and Cwm Cydach nature reserves, with beechwoods and rare trees, including the Ley's white beam. Great crested grebes, little grebes, coots, goosanders and red-breasted mergansers nest around Llangorse Lake. Grouse and merlin can be seen on the Brecon moors, while ravens and buzzards soar overhead.

To the east the Wye Valley Area of Outstanding Natural Beauty follows the English/Welsh border for much of its route with the Offa's Dyke Path retracing the route of the 7th-century earthwork from Sedbury Cliffs near Chepstow to Prestatyn in the north (more information from Offa's Dyke Association, West Street, Knighton, Tel 0547 528753). Knighton is also the starting point for the 121-mile (194 km.) Glyndwr Way (details from Powys County Council Tel 0597 826581). To the west of the central mountain area the Vale of Neath has more picturesque waterfalls, including the Aberdulais Falls.

South-west Wales is dominated by its coastline. The Gower Peninsula Area of Outstanding Natural Beauty juts out from Swansea and has limestone cliffs and fine beaches to the south and east (at The Mumbles, Caswell Bay, Three Cliffs Bay, Slade, Rhosilli Bay and Broughton Bay). Its proximity to the large southern towns robs it of remoteness which can, however, be found west of the fine beach at Pendine Sands where the 225 square mile (583 sq. km.) Pembrokeshire Coast National Park starts. The Pembrokeshire Coast area makes up the southern claw of Wales, with Milford Haven cutting in to Pembroke Dock, and St Bride's Bay sheltering inside it. Fine headlands and 400 ft (122 m.) sandstone cliffs, many of them owned by the National Trust, ring the National Park coast from Stackpole Head in the east. Sea campions, thrift, vernal squill and kidney vetch grow on the clifftops. Offshore island nature reserves include Ramsey, Stokholm, Grassholme (one of the world's largest gannetries with more than 30,000 breeding pairs), and Skomer, with a unique species of vole and colonies of Manx shearwaters, storm petrels and grey seals. Dolphins and porpoises can sometimes be spotted from the 178 mile (286 km.) Pembrokeshire Coastal Path.

Inland the scenery is gentler than elsewhere in Wales. Tenby is a major seaside resort (with its own species of daffodil), while Pembroke and Fishguard are ferry ports for Eire. Sheep graze on the Preseli Hills where curlews, skylarks and buzzards may be spotted. Salmon breed in the Rivers Taf and Tywi.

Mid Wales stretches from Porthmadog in the north-west to Llansantffraid ym Mechain in the north-east, and from Cardigan in the south-west to Painscastle in the south-east. Much of this area is also mountainous, with Snowdonia National Park, including Cader Idris (the Seat of Arthur) extending as far south as the Dovey Valley in the west. The River Dee, flowing south from near Chester, finally reaches Lake Bala which contains the gwyniad, a unique species of white fish. Sandy beaches extend from the bay of Portmeirion in the north, through Barmouth and Aberdovey to Aberystwyth, with traditional seaside resorts at Barmouth and Aberystwyth. The salmon-carrying River Teifi flows north from Cardigan. Forest areas of Mid Wales include Coed y Brenin, Penllyn Forest, Dyfnant Forest and Dyfi Forest in Snowdonia, and Rhedol, Hafren, Ystwyth, Tywi, Irfon, Ceri and Radnor Forests to the south. Scattered through these forest and mountains are attractive lakes, reservoirs and smaller rivers. The waterfalls at Devil's Bridge are especially attractive.

North Wales is the most mountainous area, much of it inside the 837 square mile (2170 sq. km.) Snowdonia National Park. Scenery within Snowdonia is dramatic, with towering, craggy peaks and vast lakes, like Llyns Llydaw and Padarn created by past volcanic activity; a landscape reminiscent of the Lake District and parts of Scotland. The Swallow Falls, near Betws-y-Coed, are especially attractive. The Coed Ganllweded Dolgarrog and Coed Camlyn nature reserves contain beautiful sessile oakwoods, while the Cwm Idwal nature reserve has unique Snowdon lilies. In the Gwydyr Forest along the River Conwy to the east live rare pine martens. Feral goats can also be seen in Snowdonia.

To the west of Snowdonia the claw-shaped Llyn Peninsula Area of Outstanding Natural Beauty juts out to Bardsey Island, with Caernarfon Bay to the north and Tremadog Bay to the south. Two major rivers, the Conwy and Clwyd, drain out to the north coast with a network of smaller rivers in between. East of Snowdonia the land is slightly lower, but there are more dramatic mountains north of Llangollen, which is reached by road over the spectacular Horseshoe Pass between the Llantysilio and Ruabon Mountains. The Vale of Ceiriog, south of Llangollen, also offers impressive mountain scenery. Along the coast of North Wales in particular a string of beach resorts including Llandudno, Colwyn Bay, Rhyl and Prestatyn grew up in the 19th century. Great Orme's Head, near Llandudno, is a breeding ground for rare dwarf grayling butterflies.

Anglesey (Ynys Mon), a large island separated from north-west Wales by the Menai Straits, is linked to Bangor by the Menai Bridge and offers fine views of Snowdonia. Anglesey is mainly low-lying and its coastline is an Area of Outstanding Natural Beauty. Holyhead in the north-west is the main southern port for Dun Laoghaire (and Dublin). Newborough Warren, to the south-west, is a national nature reserve with tern colonies and migratory wading birds including curlews, whimbrels, godwits, stints, sandpipers and oystercatchers.

Lucky visitors may spot endangered red kites near Gwenffrwd and rare polecats in Tregaron Bog, a 'raised bog' of marshland plants. Choughs can sometimes be seen in old slate quarries.

Climate

Wales' position ensures it bears the brunt of westerly and south-westerly winds, often bringing rain and howling gales; rain can fall for 175-200 days a year on the coast, and for up to 225 days in the mountains. Upland areas can also experience severe winter snowstorms, sometimes closing the mountain passes. The hills, however, protect the north coast in particular from extremes of temperature; winter temperatures in Llandudno average 6°C (44°F), rising to an average 22°C (70°F) in summer, comparable with southern England. South coast temperatures are also moderated by the warm Gulf Stream.

Attractions

Most tourists in Wales arrive in search of mountains, lakes, unspoilt countryside and beautiful coastline. Climbers and walkers of all abilities from beginners to experts frequent Snowdonia and the Brecon Beacons even in the depths of winter. Canoeing, pony trekking and birdwatching are also popular, especially in the national parks. The villages and towns of Beddgelert, Betws-y-Coed, Llanberis, Llangollen and Crickhowell are particularly well-equipped to deal with the needs of walkers, mountaineers and other outdoor sport-lovers. The most popular long-distance footpaths, the Pembrokeshire Coastal Path, Offa's Dyke Path and Glyndwr Way, receive almost too many visitors in peak periods. Recently a Bluestone Heritage Trail from the Preseli Hills to Salisbury Plain was developed to help spread the load. The Forestry Commission owns much of Snowdonia and has laid out forest walks and drives. In contrast the Ministry of Defence owns much of Pembrokeshire, and walkers are restricted in where they can go. The most visited natural attractions are the Pembrey, Padarn and Margam Country Parks, Swallow Falls and the Dan-yr-Ogof Showcaves.

Wales is also famous for its magnificent, mainly ruined castles, especially those built by the Normans in the south and by Edward I in the north. Caernarfon, Beaumaris, Conwy and Harlech Castles appear on UNESCO's list of World Heritage sites. In the south Pembroke and Caerphilly Castles are particularly striking. Nine out of the ten most visited historic properties are castles. There are also many picturesque ruined abbeys, often visited and described in the 12th century by Gerald of Wales. Particularly popular are Tintern which is within easy reach of Bristol, Cardiff and Newport, and Valle Crucis Abbey, near Llangollen.

Of Wales' cathedrals, the most beautiful and remote is St David's. Llandaff Cathedral in a picturesque Cardiff suburb, and St Asaph's, the smallest in the UK, are also popular. Few Welsh churches have the beautiful exteriors of those in England, although many in Dyfed have attractive stone-built square towers. But external drabness can be deceptive and two of the UK's most spectacular surviving rood screens and lofts can be found in tiny remote churches at Llananno and Llanegryn. (Welsh churches are more rarely locked than English ones.)

Wales' industrial heritage has provided a wealth of attractions, ranging from the Dolaucothi Gold Mine in South Wales to the Big Pit Mining Museum at Blaenafon and various slate-quarrying museums near Blaenau Ffestiniog. Many flour-mills, dairies, potteries and craft workshops also admit the public. The Pembroke, Ffestiniog, Trandsfyndd, Wylfa and Dinorwy power stations also welcome visitors. A unique working attraction is the Centre for Alternative Technology near Machynlleth.

Railway enthusiasts can choose from fourteen preserved narrow and standard gauge railways, including the Talyllyn Railway at Tywyn, which was the first to be rescued, and the Snowdon Mountain Railway which takes visitors to the summit from Llanberis.

Important museums include the first of the open air models, the Welsh Folk Museum at St Fagan's outside Cardiff, and the Museum of the North at Llanberis. Maritime and industrial museums have recently opened in Cardiff and Swansea Docks. Rhyl's new heritage centre, the Knights' Cavern, draws on Celtic mythology for its subject matter.

Cuisine

Famed for its lamb, leeks and laverbread, Welsh cuisine mixes familiar English dishes with something more indigenous. Traditional dishes include cawl, a vegetable broth often with meat; stwns, a stew with meat and mixed vegetables; oatmeal pancakes, and Welsh rarebit (seasoned cheese, butter, milk and a dash of beer browned on toast). Laverbread is actually seaweed, and is often eaten, thickened with oatmeal, on toast; Swansea and Cardiff markets are good places to buy it. The most famous Welsh cheese, Caerphilly, is made on only a very few farms now. Other local cheeses include Llangloffan, Caws

Fferm Teifi and Llanboidy. Non-meat Glamorgan sausages are made from cheese, breadcrumbs, herbs and chopped onion or leek. Soft fruits are grown in Gwent and Glamorgan, and early potatoes come from Pembrokeshire.

Cockles gathered from Gower, and North Welsh peaches are frequently made into pies. Oysters and mussels are also collected in the Menai Straits, while lobsters are once again being caught in Cardigan Bay. In general however, the Welsh fishing industry is declining.

Welsh oatcakes are like thinner versions of Scottish ones. Crempog are buttermilk pancakes which are buttered, piled up and sliced into layers, sometimes with sweet or savoury fillings between them. Bara brith is spicy fruit bread, often served with a coating of salty Welsh butter. Welsh cakes are fruit cakes baked on a griddle and sprinkled with sugar and a knob of butter.

The strong Methodist and temperance traditions of Wales mean there are few local alcohols. Cardiff, however, does have the Brains brewery, and the Welsh Whisky Company of Brecon produces herb-flavoured whisky and a honey-flavoured cream liqueur. At Parva Farm, Tintern, guided tours and tastings of locally-produced wine are available. Bottled waters are produced by Brecon Beacons Natural Water, Carmarthen Water and Decantae.

Taste of Wales (Blas ar Gymru) was set up in 1988 to promote high catering standards and the use of indigenous ingredients. Restaurants apply for inclusion in the *Taste of Wales Food Guide* (a combined recipe and travel book) but are also inspected to ensure they meet required standards. They can then display a circular slate plaque bearing a place setting laid with a red dragon. Taste of Wales also sponsors a Restaurant of the Year award. The scheme currently has most members in Gwynedd, Powys and Dyfed.

Level of Tourism

In 1989 UK residents made approximately 9.5 million visits to Wales (71 per cent of them for holiday purposes) lasting 43 million nights and costing £985 million. In addition 640,000 overseas visitors, who make up 6 per cent of all visitors to Wales, spent a further £117 million on tourism. Day trippers spent another £375 million, making the total tourism expenditure for 1989 £1477 million. Of all holiday visits to Wales in 1989, 45 per cent were to South Wales, 40 per cent to North Wales and only 16 per cent to Mid Wales. Of the Welsh population 95,000 people, or 9 per cent are directly employed in tourism and many others, including local shopkeepers, indirectly depend on it, especially during the summer.

Honeypot destinations in Wales include Mount Snowdon, the Welsh Folk Museum, Penscynor Wildlife Park, Pembrey Country Park, Barry Island Pleasure Beach and Swallow Falls. Of these only Pembrey Country Park and Barry Island Pleasure Beach attract over 400,000 people, in contrast with a London attraction like Madame Tussaud's which receives more than 2,700,000. While more than 285,000 people a year visit Caernarfon Castle, only 19,000 visit Denbigh Castle. In 1989 Bodelwyddan Castle won the National Heritage Museum of the Year award.

Traditionally tourism has been concentrated along the coasts and in the National Parks. As industry has declined, however, tourism has often taken its place as the main source of potential employment. Big Pit Museum was created by a co-operative of ex-miners who now act as tour guides. The Rhondda Heritage Park is also being developed in an area where thousands of coal-mining jobs disappeared in the late 1980s; work on the site will take until 1995–6 to complete. The 1992 Ebbw Vale Garden Festival is expected to generate further interest in the Valleys.

A similar situation exists in North Wales, where old slate quarries have been adapted for tourism, as around Blaenau Ffestiniog. The Centre for Alternative Technology was also developed in an old quarry and increasingly markets itself as a tourist attraction; in 1990 it attracted 70,000 visitors, but numbers are expected to rise to nearer 150,000 once development of the site makes it more easily accessible.

Cardiff and Swansea Docks have also been refurbished to make them appealing to tourists. The Wales Tourist Board (WTB) is currently participating in a Marina Review Group to decide where else marinas should be developed. Cardiff and Swansea are both participants in the Great British Cities Marketing Group, which aims to increase short-break business to cities which were not traditionally tourist destinations.

The paraphernalia of mass tourism litters much of Wales; double yellow lines mar narrow Gower roads, and many panoramas, especially in Meirionnydd, Dwyfor, Rhuddlan and Conwy, are scarred by ugly caravan sites. In contrast, carefully screened Saundersfoot Bay Caravan Park in Pembrokeshire shows that it is possible to design less intrusive sites. So many people climb Snowdon each year that paths are wearing away and litter is mounting up. Portmeirion Italian village, which attracts around 350,000 visitors annually, was originally created by Sir William Clough-Ellis to prove that a beauty spot could be developed without spoiling its surroundings.

Tourist development in Wales has often proved controversial. Plans for a self-catering complex in Llanberis village at the foot of Snowdon were crushed after vociferous protests at their scale. An 'Animation Now' exhibition, proposed as the centre-piece of a shopping development in Cardiff's Old Library, was also rejected as inappropriate to local needs. Welsh nationalists often object to non-Welsh speaking incomers snapping up village housing, sometimes for second homes, and pushing prices beyond local people's reach. Nevertheless, many small tourism businesses, including bed and breakfast accommodation, are owned and run by settlers, especially from the Midlands.

Dr Geraint Jenkins, curator of the Welsh Folk Museum, has also criticised a spate of what he calls 'copycat' heritage attractions, arguing that too many corn-mills, quarry railways and winnowing machines are being preserved, frequently with Tourist Board aid.

Aware of the potential problems, the Wales Tourist Board has had a 'green' policy for tourism in its national parks, agreed with the Countryside Commission, since 1978. This reinforces the conclusion of the 1974 Sandford Report which states that where the preservation and enhancement of natural beauty and the promotion of public enjoyment through tourism are in irreconcilable conflict, then it is the former which must prevail. In 1986 the Tourist Board also commissioned the European Centre for Traditional and Regional Cultures (in Llangollen) to undertake research into the socio-cultural and linguistic impact of tourism in Wales. Its findings were published in 1988. In 1990 the WTB also added a 'green award' to its annual tourism prizes.

Except in the climbing areas, Welsh tourism is a summer-only business. Most attractions, Youth Hostels, tourist information centres and even restaurants close from October to March. Always phone in advance to avoid disappointment.

Good Alternatives

Meeting People

With the survival of Welsh being such an important and potentially divisive issue, taking a language course ensures you can talk to as many people as possible. **Iaith ar Daith** offer two to ten-day courses in the Aberystwyth area, as well as coach tours which let you study Welsh simultaneously; contact Jaci Taylor, Minffordd, Rhydypennau, Bow Street, Dyfed (Tel 0970 828080) for more details.

The expanding **Nant Gwytheyren National Language Centre** in an old Llyn Peninsula quarrying village also offers courses; the Office, Llithfaen, Pwllheli, Gwynedd (Tel 075885 334) can supply information.

EC milk quotas and other economic pressures (including the effects of the Chernobyl fallout which stopped some farmers selling their sheep) are making farming increasingly difficult, and many Welsh farmers have diversified into tourism, offering bed and breakfast accommodation, pony trekking, craft workshops and other attractions. Staying on a farm, especially in the quieter low season, offers a chance to learn about rural life at first hand. The free brochure, *Holiday Wales Farm Holidays*, has details.

Working holidays are available on Skomer Island, helping with conservation, wildlife surveys and summer visitors; more details from the Islands Booking Officer, Dyfed Wildlife Trust, 7 Market Street, Haverfordwest (Tel 0437 765462). Courses on photography, art, and bird and island ecology are also available. The **Centre for Alternative Technology** offers residential courses on all aspects of 'alternative' living and welcomes volunteers for one or two weeks; more details from the Volunteer Co-Ordinator, Centre for Alternative Technology, Machynlleth, Powys.

Wales also has many festivals, most notably the various *eisteddfodau*. Festival-goers should obtain a copy of the free Wales Tourist Board booklet listing each year's events. The **Royal National Eisteddfod** is devoted to celebrating the Welsh language (Tel 0443 821677 for programme), while the **International Music Eisteddfod** at Llangollen brings together folk singers, dancers and musicians from around the world (Tel 0978 860236 for programme). Music-lovers may also want to hear a male voice choir (*cor meibion*) performing; the events booklet includes a list of rehearsal nights offering visitors a look behind the scenes.

Since 1985 Cynefin (a Welsh Conservation Foundation), the Development Board for Rural Wales, the Countryside Commission, the Nature Conservancy Council and local tourist organisations have worked together to organise the **Mid Wales Festival of the Countryside**, which aims to bring socio-economic benefits to local people while also helping visitors enjoy the countryside and learn about the environment. Festival themes are nature and wildlife, the working landscape, rural rides, arts and crafts and history and tradition. Each year around 250,000 people take part in Festival activities. For a free programme contact Festival of the Countryside, Frolic Street, Newtown, Powys (Tel 0686 625384).

Discovering Places

Many of Wales' most important historic monuments are in the care of **Cadw: Welsh Historic Monuments** (Brunel House, 2 Fitzalan Road, Cardiff. Tel 0222 46511). An annual subscription offers free admission to all sites.

National Museum of Wales staff offer a programme of guided walks of between two and ten miles (3 and 16 km.) to explore the flora and fauna, rocks, fossils and minerals, industrial remains and local history of Mid and South Wales; details from Public Services Dept, National Museum of Wales, Cardiff (Tel 0222 397951). Ask at tourist offices for the *Great Nature Trails of Wales* map produced by the WTB with the RSPB and listing thirty-six of the country's best wildlife spots. Tourist offices also keep details of guided walks in areas like the Wye Valley. Walkers can explore the border areas by following the 168-mile (270 km.) **Offa's Dyke Path** from Sedbury Cliffs, near Chepstow in the south, to Prestatyn in the north. Independent travellers can also follow in the footsteps of Gerald of Wales whose writings are readily available in local bookshops, or retrace the route of the medieval pilgrimage to Bardsey Island.

Safaris along the Severn and Wye rivers in four-wheel drive vehicles can be booked at Chepstow Leather, Cromwell House, 10 Bridge Street, Chepstow (Tel 0600 6655). Organised **mountain-bike** holidays are on offer from **Clive Powell Mountain-Bikes**, The Mount, East Street, Rhayader, Powys (Tel 0597 810585). **Sea fishing trips** are offered by Stan Zalot, Little Bryn, Beaumaris, Anglesey (Tel 0248 810251), and Beaumaris Marine Services, The Anchorage, Rosemary Lane, Beaumaris (Tel 0248 810746). Pleasure cruises to Puffin Island, Menai Bridge and Bangor Pier are also available.

Llangollen is a good base for activity holidays, and tandems, canoes and mountain-bikes can be hired from Llangollen Wharf (Tel 0978 860702). The **Twr-y-Felin Outdoor Centre** in St David's (Tel 0437 720391) offers climbing, surfing and sea canoeing holidays. **Bicycle Beano** operates cycle tours of the Black Mountains, Wye Valley and Pembrokeshire Coast (Tel 0981 251087 for details), while **Roman Road Cycle Tours** offers individually-tailored bicycle tours of rural Wales; details from Ddol-Las, Ffarmers, Llanwrda (Tel 05585 336).

Communications

How to Get There

CAR: South Wales is easily accessible from England via the Severn

Bridge (a toll road) just beyond Bristol, and the M4 motorway which terminates west of Swansea. A second Severn crossing will eventually take some of the strain off the ageing original bridge which needs constant maintenance work.

From Chester the dual carriageway A55 'Expressway' runs via Colwyn Bay, Llandudno and Conwy to Bangor where it links with the A5 across the Menai Bridge to Holyhead. Slower roads connect Mid Wales to Shrewsbury and the Midlands. The A465, or 'Heads of the Valleys Road', runs from Abergavenny, through Ebbw Vale to Methryr Tydfil and then along the Vale of Neath to Swansea.

Within Wales **roads** are often narrow and mountainous, and drivers must depend on passing places. High roads like the **Horseshoe Pass** may also be closed after snow, and flooding is common.

BUS: Tourist Information Centres stock local bus timetables, with information about bus rovers and ticketholder discounts at tourist attractions. A novel way of getting around and meeting knowledgeable drivers and local travellers is to travel by Royal Mail Postbus; enquire at post offices for details.

CYCLING: Mountain-bikes can be hired from **Tan Lan**, Betws-y-Coed (Tel 06902 766); **Red Kite Mountain-Bike Centre**, Neuadd Arms, Llanwrtyd Wells (Tel 05913 236) and **Greenstiles Cycles**, High Street, Llandrindod Wells (Tel 0597 4594).

RAIL: Links with Wales are good, with regular fast services to Swansea via Cardiff and to Llandudno, Bangor and Holyhead. Attractive British Rail routes within Wales include the **Cambrian Coast Service** between Aberystwyth and Pwllheli, with connections through Welshpool to Shrewsbury, and the **Conwy Valley** line from Llandudno to Blaenau Ffestiniog. In summer seven day **Coast and Peaks, Freedom of Wales**, and **North and Mid Wales** rover tickets as well as various circular, and day and evening ranger tickets are available; ask at British Rail stations for details.

Train-lovers will want to explore North and Mid Wales (and the Brecon area) on the **Great Little Trains** narrow gauge steam services. Most operate summer and Christmas only timetables. Four and eight day rover tickets, valid on all services, are available. Details can be obtained from the following:

Railway	*Tel*
Ffestiniog Railway (Porthmadog to Blaenau Ffestiniog)	0766 512340
Llanberis Lake Railway (Padarn Park to Penllyn)	0286 870549
Brecon Mountain Railway (Merthyr Tydfil to Pontsticill)	0685 4854

Talyllyn Railway, (Tywyn to Nant Gwernol)	0654 710472
Vale of Rheidol Railway (Aberystwyth to Devil's Bridge)	0685 4854
Bala Lake Railway (Llanuwchllyn to Bala)	06784 666
Welshpool and Llanfair Light Railway (Llanfair Caereinion to Welshpool)	0938 810441
Welsh Highland Railway (Porthmadog to Pen-y-Mount)	0766 513402

Shorter preserved routes include:

Snowdon Mountain Railway, Llanberis	0286 870223
Llangollen Steam Railway	0978 860979
Fairbourne and Barmouth Railway	0341 250362
Gwili Railway	0267 371077
Pontypool and Blaenavon Railway	0495 772200
Teifi Valley Railway	0559 371077

BOAT: Canal trips are available on the Montgomery Canal at Welshpool (Tel 0938 552043), the Llangollen Canal (Tel 0978 860702) and the Monmouthshire and Brecon Canal. Boats to the island nature reserves operate summer only services.

RIDING: Many areas can be explored on horse-back; ask at tourist information centres for farms which offer pony trekking. **Welsh Horse-Drawn Holidays** also offers horse-drawn caravan tours; contact Greystones, Talgarth (Tel 0874 711346).

Useful Local Contacts

Good contacts in Wales include the **Wales Council for Voluntary Action**, Llys Ifor, Crescent Road, Caerphilly, Mid Glamorgan CF8 1XL (Tel 0222 869224), always keen to hear from volunteers looking to improve the environment; the **Welsh Plant Breeding Station**, Plas Gogerddan, Aberystwyth, Dyfed SY23 3EB (Tel 0970 828255), and the **Welsh Railways Action Group**, 6 Mill Park, Cowbridge, Cardiff CF7 7BG (Tel 04463 2910). Also of note is **CADW – Welsh Historic Monuments**, Brunel House, 2 Fitzalan Road, Cardiff CF2 1UY (Tel 0222 465511).

Geographical Breakdown of Region

Vale of Usk and Wye Valley

The wooded Wye Valley which joins the River Severn at Chepstow forms a natural border between England and Wales, with gentle pastoral scenery surrounding it. The Usk flows from north of Abergavenny to join the sea at Newport.

Attractively sited on limestone cliffs overlooking the Wye, **Chepstow** is marred by a busy road running through it, but has an impressive ruined Norman castle and an excellent local museum in an 18th-century house. It also offers a busy market on Sundays. Racing takes place at nearby Piercefield Park. Further up the valley, the ruins of the 12th-century Cistercian **Tintern Abbey**, surrounded by steep wooded hills, can become crowded on sunny days because of their proximity to Bristol and Newport. The Victorian Old Station contains a railway exhibition and audio-visual displays. **Monmouth**, with Tudor and Georgian houses lining its High Street, has a bridge with a unique 13th-century gatehouse and portcullis, and a combined Nelson Museum and Local History Centre. The **Lantern Theatre** here (Church Street, Tel 0600 3146) offers a variety of entertainment. **Kymin Hill** to the south-east offers views of the Wye and Monnow valleys.

Along the Monnow River there are ruined Norman castles at **Skenfrith** and **Grosmont**, with a third to the south-west at **White Castle**. West of Monmouth, **Raglan** has a ruined 15th-century fortified house. Nearby **Cefntilla Court** contains Crimean War memorabilia.

West of Chepstow there are Bronze Age remains in the grounds of partially ruined medieval **Caldicot Castle**. Rubble walls of the Roman town of Venta Silurum survive at **Caerwent** and the church porch houses finds from local Roman sites (more in Newport Museum). Ruins of Roman baths, barracks and an amphitheatre can be seen at **Caerleon**, which also has an excellent Roman Legionary Museum (inclusive tickets available for all Caerleon sites). **Penhow Castle** is Wales' oldest lived-in castle, with a 15th-century Great Hall and minstrels' gallery. An industrial town, **Newport/Casnewydd** has few attractions other than **St Woolos Cathedral**, with magnificent Norman arches and fine views from the churchyard. There are craft workshops in the grounds of nearby 17th-century **Tredegar House**. At **Usk**, a market town with ruined Norman castle, 13th-century church and priory gatehouse, the **Gwent Rural Life Museum** is housed in a barn. There is a **Tourist Information Centre** at Newport Museum and Art Gallery, John Frost Square (Tel 0633 842962).

Accommodation

First Class

Cwrt Bledyyn Hotel, Tredunnock, near Usk (Tel 063349 521). Period bedrooms.

Middle Range

Glen-y-Afr House, Pontypool Rd, Usk (Tel 02913 2302).
Pentwyn Farm, Little Mill, Pontypool (Tel 049528 249). Sixteenth-century house with swimming pool.
Wye Valley Hotel, Tintern (Tel 0291 689441).

Economy

Church Farm Guest House, Mitchel Troy, Monmouth (Tel 0600 2176). Sixteenth-century former farmhouse.
The Smithy, Trellech Grange, Llanishen, Chepstow (Tel 0600 860027). Recently renovated blacksmith's/carpenter's workshop.
The Grange, Penrhos, Raglan (Tel 0600 85202). Mixed farm near Offa's Dyke Path.
Youth Hostel, Mounton Rd, Chepstow (Tel 02912 2685).

Eating Out

First Class

Caldicot Castle (Tel 0291 421425). Medieval banquets.

Middle Range

Castle View Hotel, 16 Bridge St, Chepstow (Tel 02912 70349).
The Huntsman Hotel, Shirenewton near Chepstow (Tel 02917 521).
The Crown, Whitebrook (Tel 0600 860254).

Economy

Bush House Bistro, Usk (Tel 02913 2929).

Cardiff

Cardiff/Caerdydd used to be an important coal-exporting port. By the end of the 1980s however, the Tiger Bay area was run-down, with a reputation for violence. The Cardiff Bay Development Corporation is mid-way through redevelopment plans which include a controversial barrage scheme which opponents believe will damage birdlife on the local mudflats.

Cardiff Castle encapsulates Welsh history, with a stretch of Roman wall, a Norman keep and ornate Victorian additions by architect William Burges. The **National Museum of Wales** in Cathays Park has a superb Impressionist art collection. The **Old Library**, opposite Cardiff Market, temporarily houses art and craft exhibitions and the unique **Museum of Magical Machines**. There are Victorian shopping arcades opposite the castle. The most exciting part of the **Welsh Industrial and Maritime Museum** in the developing docks area is the simulated dockside environment at 126 Bute Street. **Techniquest** in the same area is a hands-on science exhibition. The development of the Docks is explained in a curious tube-shaped **Visitor Centre**. Twin-towered **Llandaff Cathedral**, with Epstein's 'Majestas' alongside Norman architecture, sits in a hollow in a pretty northern suburb. **St Fagan's**, the Welsh Folk Museum to the north-east, shows building styles from all around Wales and has a lively events programme. Cardiff **Tourist Information** is at 8–14 Bridge Street (Tel 0222 227281).

Around Cardiff

Castell Coch, the fairy-tale Rhine castle built by William Burges, stands on wooded slopes north-west of Cardiff, while magnificent 13th-century **Caerphilly Castle** occupies a 60-acre (24-hectare) site directly to the north. **Dinas Powys** is a pretty village on the way to **Barry**, an unattractive dock town but with the popular Pleasure Beach on Barry Island. The Bristol paddle-steamer, the *Waverley*, operates to Penarth pier in summer (Tel 0446 720656 for timetable details).

Entertainments

Concerts take place in **St David's Hall** (Box Office enquiries Tel 0222 342611), **New Theatre** (Box Office enquiries Tel 0222 394844) and **Sherman Theatre** (Box Office Tel 0222 230451). **Barry Arts Centre** is at Winston Rd (Tel 0446 739702) and there is rugby football at **Cardiff Arms Park** (Tel 0222 390111).

Accommodation

First Class

Egerton Grey Country House, Porthkerry, Barry (Tel 0446 711666).

Economy

Plas-y-Bryn, 93 Fairwater Rd, Llandaff (Tel 0222 561717).
White Barn House, Rhyladfar, St Fagan's (Tel 0222 843152).
Ty Gwyn, 7 Dyfig St, Pontcanna, Cardiff (Tel 0222 239785).

Cardiff YMCA Hostel, The Walk, Roath, Cardiff (Tel 0222 489101).
Youth Hostel, 1 Lake Rd West, Roath Park (Tel 0222 462303).

Eating Out

First Class

De Courcy's, Tyla Morris House, Church Rd, Pentyrch (Tel 0222 892232).

Middle Range

Armless Dragon, 97 Wyvern Rd, Cathays Park (Tel 0222 382357).

Economy

Swallows Coffee House, 8 Royal Arcade (Tel 0222 373816).
New Harvesters, 5 Pontcanna St. (Tel 0222 232616).
Celtic Cauldron, Castle Arcade (Tel 0222 387185).
Lloyds Cafe Bar, Castle Arcade (Tel 0222 239746).

The South Wales Coast

West of Cardiff the flat, pastoral Vale of Glamorgan spreads towards Port Talbot which is entirely dominated by the steelworks.

Cowbridge, an attractive market town (market on Tuesday) full of gift shops, has a semi-fortified church, an old grammar school and a small museum in the Town Hall. **Llantwit Major**, a pretty village, has a marvellous medieval church with Norman arches. The ruins of Norman **Ogmore Castle** stand on the River Ewenny flood-plain with picturesque black and white cottages for company. Nearby **Ewenny Priory** retains impressive fortification-like 12th-century walls. Other ruined castles are at **Coity** and **Bridgend**. At Llantrisant, home of the Royal Mint, the **Model House** contains an exhibition and craft workshops.

The **Glamorgan Heritage Coast** runs from **Ogmore-by-Sea** to **Margam Sands**. A typical British seaside resort, **Porthcawl** is marred by amusement arcades but has Victorian guest houses and fine beaches too. There is a **Tourist Information** office here at The Old Police Station on John Street (Tel 065691 6639). Towards Port Talbot, 800-acre (324-hectare) **Margam Country Park** contains an 18th-century Orangery, medieval abbey ruins and a huge fallow deer herd.

Accommodation
First Class
Coed-y-Mwstwr Hotel, Coychurch, Bridgend (Tel 0656 860621).

Middle Range
Court Colman, Pen-y-Fai, Bridgend (Tel 0656 720212).
Bear Hotel, High St, Cowbridge (Tel 04463 4814).

Economy
Ye Olde Mason's Arms, 66 High St, Cowbridge (Tel 04463 2633).
Treguff Farm, Llantrithyd, Cowbridge (Tel 04463 750210).
Mary Street, **Porthcawl** is lined with virtually identical bed and breakfast hotels.
Youth Hostel, West Aberthaw, near Barry (Tel 0446 750233).

Eating Out
First Class
Mulligan's, Stallingdon, near Cowbridge (Tel 04463 2221). Fish restaurant.

Middle Range
Basil's Brasserie, 2 Eastgate, Cowbridge (Tel 04463 3738).
Off the Beeton Track, Town Hall Square, Cowbridge (Tel 04463 3599).
Quaintways Restaurant, Colhugh St, Llantwit Major (Tel 04465 2321).
Old Swan Inn, Church St, Llantwit Major (Tel 04465 2230).

South Wales Valleys
Although the Rhondda, Taff, Cynon and Rhymney Valleys were amongst the most heavily industrialised parts of Wales, the confined terrain prevented huge towns developing. Instead, close-knit village communities living in long rows of terraced, back-to-back houses grew up in the shadow of the coal pits. In 1966 disaster overtook Aberfan, near Merthyr Tydfil, when a slag heap engulfed a school, killing over 130 people, tragically mainly children. More recently the valleys have been irrevocably

changed by the contraction of UK coal mining and the ensuing job losses.

North of the Valleys Inheritance Centre at **Pontypool** is **Blaenafon**, site of an 18th-century ironworks and the Big Pit Mining Museum, in a mine which closed down in 1980. The five-month 1992 Garden Festival, with horticultural, craft and entertainment displays, is taking place in **Ebbw Vale** (Tel 0495 350198 for programme details). In **Merthyr Tydfil**, Cyfartha Castle, a castellated mansion built by a 19th-century ironmaster, houses a museum and art gallery. **Tourist Information** is at 14A Glebeland Street (Tel 0685 79884) and the town has a market on Tuesday and Saturday. The nearby **Rhondda Heritage Park** is a gradually-evolving celebration of life in the Valleys, centred on the redundant Lewis Merthyr colliery. There is already a Visitor Centre and art gallery but by 1995 the one and a half mile (2.4 km.) site will include 'Black Coal', an exhibition about coal's history, a reconstructed 1920s mining village with actor-interpreters, forest and riverside walks, a country park and a resource centre.

West of the other valleys, the **Vale of Neath** runs from Swansea to Glyn Neath, passing the 12th-century ruins of Neath Abbey, the Aberdulais Falls and tinplate works, and Penscynor Wildlife Park. There are pleasant towpath walks along the restored Neath and Tennant Canal, especially from **Resolven** (Tel 0639 641121 for details). From **Glyn Neath** paths lead to nine waterfalls on four different rivers (details from Pontneddfechan Tourist Information Centre, Tel 0639 721795). Near **Crynant** the Cefn Coed Colliery Museum is next to an operational mine. From the **Pelenna Mountain Centre** walkers can follow the Roman Coed Morgannwg Way across the valley tops. Another Roman road, Sarn Helen, takes walkers across the Brecon Beacons from Resolven Forest to Brecon.

Accommodation

First Class

Heritage Park Hotel, Merthyr Tydfil.
Castle Hotel, The Parade, Neath (Tel 0639 643591). Seventeenth-century coaching inn.

Economy

Briony, Ystradfellte Rd, Pontneddfechan (Tel 0639 720679).
Gelli Farm Country House and Restaurant, Crynant, Neath (Tel 0639 750209).

638 The Good Tourist in the UK

Hillside House, 1 Sunnybank, Tirphil, New Tredegar (Tel 0443 834460).

Youth Hostel at Glyncornel House, once a mine owner's house, now an environmental education centre (Tel 0443 430859).

Eating Out

Economy

Rhondda Heritage Park for teas and light lunches.
Gelli Farm (as above).

Brecon Beacons

The 520-acre (210 hectares) Brecon Beacon National Park extends from Abergavenny in the east to Llandovery in the west. The Beacons themselves reach heights of more than 2900 ft (884 m.) in places and are riddled with caves.

Abergavenny/Y-Fenni, a market town and good base for exploring the Beacons, has a ruined Norman castle housing an agricultural machinery museum. It is surrounded by the Sugar Loaf, Ysgyrd Fawr and Blorenge Mountains and has a Tourist Information Centre at Swan Meadow (Tel 0873 77588). Four miles (6.5 km.) north-east, **Llanfihangel Court** is an Elizabethan manor house with lovely gardens. **Crickhowell** on the River Usk has a 13-arch medieval bridge, attractive Georgian houses and a 14th-century church. At **Tretower** to the north-west are a ruined Norman castle and Tretower Court, a 14th-century fortified manor house. Two miles (3.2 km.) south-west is one of Britain's longest caves, the fourteen mile (22 km.) **Agen Allwedd**. **Patricio** church to the north-east has a fine rood screen, while **Llanthony** has the ruins of a 12th-century priory. Over the 1778 ft (542 m.) **Gospel Pass** is Hay-on-Wye, the UK's secondhand book capital, with tracks leading to the Black Mountains and to **Pen-y-Beacon** and the **Tumpa**.

At **Bronllys** on the Brecon road the church has a detached tower where women, children and cattle could take refuge during times of attack. **Brecon/Aberhonddu** itself is an attractive town full of craft shops, its partly 13th-century fortified cathedral containing a large cresset stone once used for lighting the building. From **Storey Arms** a path leads to **Pen-y-Fan**, at 2906 ft (886 m.) the Beacons' highest point. On a clear day there are views of the Bristol Channel, industrial South Wales and mountainous North Wales. In the surrounding **Fforest Fawr** there are caves and waterfalls.

The River Mellte eventually vanishes underground in the **Porth-yr-Ogof** Cave.

From **Trecastle**, a village with a 12th-century ruined castle, a mountain road passes the 2632 ft (802 m.) **Bannau Brycheiniog**, before cutting south to **Dan-yr-Ogof** and **Ogof Fynnon Ddu** caves, with stalactites, stalagmites and underground lakes. **Llandovery/ Llanymddyfri** is a market town, one mile (1.6 km.) west of the **Dolaucothi Gold Mines**, opened up by the Romans and worked until 1938; the National Trust runs a Visitor Centre and Miners Way there, and there are summer-only underground tours.

Accommodation

First Class

Llansantffraed Court Hotel, Llanvihangel Gobion, near Abergavenny (Tel 0873 840678).

Middle Range

Bear Hotel, Crickhowell (Tel 0873 810408). Old coaching inn.

Old Gwernyfed Country Manor, Felindre, Three Cocks, Brecon (Tel 04974 376). Sixteenth-century hotel with priest's hole. In Black Mountain foothills.

Lansdowne Hotel and Restaurant, 39 The Watton, Brecon (Tel 0874 3321). Town-centre Georgian hotel.

Economy

The Cloisters, Llanvihangel Crucorney, Abergavenny (Tel 0873 890738). Former coachman's house near Wales' oldest pub, the Skirrid Inn.

Dragon House Hotel, High St, Crickhowell (Tel 0873 810362).

Scethrog Tower, Scethrog, Brecon (Tel 087487 672). Medieval house with steep stone staircase. In Usk valley.

Trehenry Farm, Felingfach, Brecon (Tel 0874 754312). 200-acre (81 hectares) farm with inglenook fireplaces.

Youth Hostels at Capel-y-Ffin (Tel 0873 890650), Llanddeusant (Tel 05504 634), Llwyny Celyn (Tel 0874 4261), Ty'n-y-caeau (Tel 087486 270) and Ystradfellte (Tel 0639 720301).

Eating Out

First Class

Walnut Tree Inn, Llandewi Skirrid, Gwent (Tel 0873 2797).

Llangoed Hall, Llyswen (Tel 0874 754525).

Middle Range

Duke's, Wellington Hotel, the Bulwark, Brecon (Tel 0874 5225).

Economy

Bridge End Inn, Crickhowell (Tel 0873 810338).
Granary, Broad St, Hay-on-Wye (Tel 0497 820790).

Swansea, The Mumbles and the Gower Peninsula

Swansea/Abertawe, Wales' second largest town, bestrides the River Tawe where it flows into Swansea Bay. As in Cardiff the decaying dock area has been redeveloped to create a marina. The Mumbles is a flourishing seaside resort where the Gower Peninsula, Britain's first Area of Outstanding Natural Beauty, joins the mainland.

Swansea's **Industrial and Maritime Museum** is in the marina, a picturesque area for exploring. The brand-new **Plantasia** is an indoor botanical garden, with arid, tropical and humid zones and an aviary. The market is a good place for local delicacies like laverbread. Nearby **Oystermouth** has a ruined Norman castle, while **The Mumbles** has a fine pier. **Tourist Information** is at Singleton Street, Swansea (Tel 0792 468321).

The southern Gower Peninsula is criss-crossed with footpaths and feels less remote than the north because of its proximity to Swansea. There are fine beaches at **Langland, Caswell, Oxwich, Port Eynon** and **Rhosili**, and a dramatic headland at westerly **Worms Head**.

Entertainment

Recently refurbished **Grand Theatre**, Swansea (Box Office Tel 0792 474715). **Dylan Thomas Theatre**, 7 Gloucester Place, Swansea (Tel 0792 473238). **Swansea Arts Workshop Gallery** in St Nicholas, a redundant seaman's church in the docks. Fishing trips and boat excursions round Gower available from **Swansea Sports Fishermen** (Tel 0792 654705).

Accommodation

First Class

Fairyhill Country Hotel, Reynoldston, Gower (Tel 0792 390139).

Langland Court Hotel, Langland Court Rd, Langland Bay, Swansea (Tel 0792 361545).
Oxwich Bay Hotel, Oxwich, Gower (Tel 0792 390329).

Middle Range

North Gower Hotel, Llanrhidian, Gower (Tel 0792 390042).
Langrove Lodge and Country Club, Parkmill, Gower (Tel 044128 2410).

Economy

Broad Park Guest House, Rhosili, Gower (Tel 0792 390515).
Parc Le Breos, Parkmill, Gower (Tel 0792 371636).
Malbork Guest House, 2 Bonville Terrace, Uplands, Swansea (Tel 0792 473420).
Solid streets of identikit bed and breakfast establishments in **The Mumbles**.
Youth Hostel in Port Eynon (Tel 0792 390706).

Eating Out

Middle Range

The Pump House, Swansea (Tel 0792 651080). Steak restaurant in converted dock building.
Woodside Restaurant, Oxwich, Gower (Tel 0792 390791).
Roots, 2 Woodville Rd, Mumbles (Tel 0792 366006).

Coastline and Vales of Dyfed

The rivers Teifi and Towy flow south through **Dylan Thomas Country** into Carmarthen Bay which is lined with the sweeping beaches of Pendine Sands. To the north-east, Brechfa Forest offers country trails and picnic spots.

Llanelli, an industrial town, has the Parc Howard Museum and Art Gallery in Bryncaerau Castle, and a fine beach. **Pembrey Forest**, with the Towyn prehistoric burrows, stands on extensive sand dunes. **Kidwelly** has a marvellous moated medieval castle and an industrial museum. Despite its ruined Norman castle, **Carmarthen/Caerfyrddin** is disappointingly redeveloped. **Tourist Information** here is at Lammas Street (Tel 0267 231557).

To the east, the magnificent ruined **Carreg-Cennen Castle** offers fine views of the Black Mountains. South of Carmarthen, picturesque **Llansteffan** village is squeezed in between the two rivers with an impressive medieval church and castle ruins. Fine Georgian houses line the High Street and surround the market square and clock tower of **Laugharne**, where Dylan Thomas lived in a boathouse and worked in a garden shed overlooking the Taf estuary (both open to the public in summer). **Marros Beach** between Pendine and Amroth, a pretty coastal village, is difficult to get to but quiet and unspoilt.

The **Cenarth Falls**, near **Newcastle Emlyn**, are on a stretch of the Teifi where coracle fishermen can still occasionally be seen. **Felin Geri** is a working watermill in the wooded valley of the Ceri river. At **Drefach Felindre** the Museum of the Woollen Industry commemorates a vital local industry. On the last Thursday of each month a huge horse sale takes place at **Llanbydder**.

Accommodation

Middle Range

Ty Maur Country Hotel, Brechfa (Tel 0267 202332).

Economy

Ystrad Farmhouse, Llansteffan Rd, Johnstown, Carmarthen (Tel 0267 235073).

Pen-y-Bac Farm, Mynddgarreg, Kidwelly (Tel 0554 891200).

Delacorse Farm Guest House, Taf Estuary, Ants Hill, Laugharne (Tel 0994 427647).

Eating Out

First Class

Felin Geri Japanese Restaurant, near Newcastle Emlyn (Tel 0239 710810).
The Old Rectory, Llanddowror, St Clears (Tel 0994 230030).

Middle Range

Hamilton's Wine Bar and Brasserie, Queen St, Carmarthen (Tel 0831 341136).
Waverley, 23 Lammas St, Carmarthen (Tel 0267 236521).
Langtrey's, Jackson's Lane, Carmarthen (Tel 0267 230507).

Economy

Welsh Tea Shop in Dylan Thomas Boathouse Museum (Tel 0994 427420).

Pembrokeshire

To the south-west of Wales, Pembrokeshire contains the country's most spectacular coastal scenery. Pembroke itself is a major ferry port for Eire, while the Pembrokeshire long-distance coast path stretches from Amroth in the south to St Dogmael's in the north.

Tenby is an attractive resort of pastel-coloured houses inside 13th-century walls. Boats go to **Caldy Island** which has caves with prehistoric remains and where monks still produce and sell perfumes. Choughs can sometimes be seen here. **Manorbier** to the west has a fine, moated Norman castle. Half a mile (0.8 km.) south-west the **King's Quoit** is a group of prehistoric standing stones. Dominated by the ruins of a Norman castle with a circular keep, **Pembroke** has an attractive High Street of old buildings; Castle Hill **Museum of the Home** displays toys and bygones. Down a country lane to the east are the impressive ruins of a medieval bishop's palace at **Lamphey**. **Carew** has a ruined castle and the fine 11th-century Celtic Cross, now used as a symbol by CADW (meaning "care"), the Welsh Historic Monuments Organisation responsible for funding the restoration of the site. To the south **Bosherston** has a huge, water-lily-covered lake. A path leads to the sandy beach at Barafundle Bay. One and a half miles (2 km.) further south across Ministry of Defence land, steep steps lead down the cliff to the 13th-century chapel of St Govan.

Milford Haven/Milffwrd, a large port originally founded by

Sir William Hamilton, was visited by Nelson. At **Haverfordwest/ Hwlffordd** the county museum can be found inside the ruined 12th-century castle. Five miles (8 km.) east, Picton Castle houses the Graham Sutherland picture collection. The road west leads to a shingle beach at **Dale**, and **St Ann's Head** where Henry Tudor landed in 1485 before assuming the throne after defeating Richard III at Bosworth. Nearby **Marloes** also has a beautiful beach, reached by a tricky climb down the cliff behind the church. One hundred Iron Age huts stand on **Gateholm Island**, connected to the mainland by a spit. Boats to the nature reserves on Grassholme, Skomer and Skokholm Islands leave from Martin's Haven near Marloes. **Dale Sailing Company** also organises cruises round the bay (Tel 0646 636349 for details).

To the north-west of Haverfordwest, the medieval cathedral of **St David's**, a purple, greeney-blue and yellow building concealed in the River Alun valley, has one of the finest settings in Wales, surrounded by rolling agricultural land, with the sea on the horizon. Next to it the jackdaw-infested ruins of **Bishop's Palace** complete the picture. Inside, the cathedral has magnificent Norman pillars, an impressive timber roof, fine misericords and the shrine of St David. St David's also has a Marine Life Centre and a **Tourist Information Office** at the City Hall (Tel 0437 720392). Coastal roads lead to fine beaches at **St Non's** (which also has a medieval chapel), **Caerbwdi** and **Caerfai Bays**. Boats to the nature reserve on **Ramsey Island**, where grey seals can sometimes be seen, go from nearby Porthstinian.

Despite being a major ferry port, **Fishguard/Abergwaun** remains an attractive town overlooking steep cliffs. Slightly inland from **Newport** the prehistoric burial chamber of **Pentre Ifan** offers fine views of the countryside. **Nevern** church has well-preserved Celtic crosses and Ogham inscriptions. The 'Bleeding Yew' in the churchyard drips sap constantly. **Cilgerran** on the River Teifi has a fine ruined 13th-century castle. At **St Dogmael's** there are ruins of a 12th-century Tironian priory and a working flourmill (Y Felin) with a large duck pond. Between Fishguard and St Dogmael's stretch the **Preseli Hills**, where pretty villages like Felindre Farchog and Mynacholg-Ddu are interspersed with Iron Age hill forts and prehistoric cromlechs. At **Cwm-yr-Eglwys** a small church stands right on the beach.

Accommodation

First Class

Penally Abbey Hotel, Penally, near Tenby (Tel 0834 3033).

St Non's Hotel, St David's (Tel 0437 720239).
Wolfscastle Country Hotel, Wolfscastle, near Haverfordwest (Tel 043787 225).

Middle range

Glanmoy Country House Hotel, Goodwick, Fishguard (Tel 0348 872844). Edwardian country house hotel.
Milton Manor Hotel, Milton, near Tenby (Tel 0646 651398).

Economy

Rigsby's, Royal Terrace, 49 Nun Street, St David's (Tel 0437 720632). Excellent disabled facilities.
The Foxes, Marloes, Haverfordwest (Tel 0646 527).
Youth Hostels at Pentlepoir, near Saundersfoot (Tel 0834 812333); Marloes (Tel 06465 257); Broad Haven (Tel 043783 688); St David's (Tel 0437 720345); Trevine (Tel 03483 414); Pwll Deri (Tel 03485 233); and Poppit Sands (Tel 0239 612936).
Accommodation details for Skomer and Skokholm from Dyfed Wildlife Trust, Haverfordwest (Tel 0437 765462).

Eating Out

First Class

Gelli Fawr Country House, Newport, near Fishguard (Tel 0239 820343).
George's Restaurant, Nun Street, St David's (Tel 0437 720508).

Middle Range

Digby's Restaurant, Cross Square, St David's (Tel 0437 720488).
Woodlands Restaurant, 40 Main St, Pembroke (Tel 0646 687140).

Economy

Sunnyside Tearooms, Nevern (Tel 0239 820864).
Cnapan, East St, Newport (Tel 0239 820575).

Ceredigion

Stretching from Cardigan in the south to Borth, south of the Dovey Valley, in the north, Ceredigion in Mid Wales has two university towns: **Lampeter** and **Aberystwyth**.

Cardigan/Aberteifi is an attractive town on the Teifi which continues east to **Lampeter/Llanbedr Pont Steffan**, focus of an annual horse fair each May. On National Trust land at **Mwnt** stands a tiny medieval church, once a stopping point on the pilgrimage route to Bardsey Island. **New Quay** is a particularly attractive terraced town which may have inspired Dylan Thomas's 'Llareggub' in *Under Milk Wood*. **Aberaeron** on the coast offers easy access to riverside walks. Halfway to the market town of **Tregaron** it is also possible to climb the 1127 ft (343 m.) Trichrug Mountain. The four mile-long (6 km.) **Tregaron Bog** is a nature reserve with plants like sundews, bog rosemary, bladderworts and sedges. Lakeside **Brimstone Wildlife Park**, at Penuwch, Tregaron, has tropical birds and butterflies, shire horses and a host of other attractions. Remote **Strata Florida**, to the north-east, has the ruins of a 12th-century abbey visited by Gerald of Wales.

At **Devil's Bridge** in **Coed Rheidol** the River Mynach gorge has three bridges over attractive waterfalls and a half-hour nature trail past sessile oaks, ferns and Welsh poppies. Vale of Rheidol steam trains run to **Aberystwyth**, a typical seaside resort with pier and Victorian terraced hotels. The Ceredigion Museum is housed, like the **Tourist Information Centre** (Tel 0970 612125), in the converted Colisseum music hall, and there are ruins of one of Edward I's castles on a headland. A Victorian **camera obscura** has recently been recreated and opened to the public; access is via Britain's longest electric cliff railway. The National Library of Wales is also in Aberystwyth. A mile (1.6 km.) long nature trail leads north to **Clarach Bay**. At **Ystumtuen** prehistoric standing stones ring the churchyard. There are good beaches at picturesque **Borth** near **Borth Bog**, a nature reserve with rare plants. At **Trer-ddol** an old chapel houses a museum of Welsh religious life.

Entertainment

Aberystwyth Arts Centre, University of Wales campus, mixed arts programme (Tel 0970 623232). **Theatr y Castell**, Aberystwyth (Tel 0970 624606). **Theatr Mwldan**, Cardigan (Tel 0239 612687).

Accommodation

First Class

Conrah Country Hotel, Chancery, Aberystwyth (Tel 0970 62456).

Middle Range

Gwesty Fferm Hotel, Glynarthen, near Cardigan (Tel 0239 810248).

Brynafor Hotel, New Road, New Quay (Tel 0545 560358).

Economy

Glan-y-Mar, Poppit Sands, St Dogmael's (Tel 0239 612329).
Helmsman, 43 Marine Terrace, Aberystwyth (Tel 0970 624132).
Caerllyn, Gilfachreda, New Quay (Tel 0545 580121).
Youth Hostels at New Quay (Tel 0545 560337); Ystumtuen (particularly remote. Tel 097085 693); and Borth (Tel 0097081 498).

Eating Out

Middle Range

Rhoshill, near Bancath, Cardigan (Tel 0239 841378).
Pavilion, The Royal Pier, Aberystwyth (Tel 0970 624888).

Economy

Principaliteas, opposite Cardigan market.
Granary Restaurant, Teifi Wharf, Cardigan (Tel 0239 614932).
Y-Craig, 34 Pier St, Aberystwyth (Tel 0970 611606).

Heart of Wales

In a part of Wales distinguished by its gentler countryside, towns have 'wells' added to their name as a reminder of the mineral-bearing waters that gave rise to popular Victorian spas.

Llanwrtyd Wells no longer has a functioning spa, but offers pony-trekking into the **Irfon** and **Crychan Forests** and **Mynydd Eppynt hills**. At the Cambrian Factory visitors can watch woollen textile production. The Lake Hotel at **Llangammarch Wells** on the River Crammach still contains a spring with barium chloride, once a popular cure for heart disease. The Crammach offers opportunities for trout and salmon fishing. The saline and sulphur springs at **Builth Wells/Llanfair-yn-Muallt** are no longer used for cures, but the *Welcome to Builth Wells* brochure describes walks, drives, mountain bike rides and church crawls in the area. Three miles (4.8 km.) west is **Cilmuri** where Prince Llewelyn was killed in 1282. **Llandrindod Wells** has the same sort of airy Victorian gentility as Harrogate, with impressive 19th-century architecture in the High Street; the waters can still be taken at the spa in Rock Park Gardens, a wooded valley housing the Spas of Wales Visitor Centre. **Tourist Information** is at the Town Hall (Tel 0597 2600). A Victorian Festival takes place every September. The tiny church of **Llananno** by the River Ithon to the north contains a spectacular rood screen and loft. Bikes can be hired from the **Bike Shed** (Tel 0597 3240).

From the small market town of **Rhayader/Rhaeadr** to the north-west there is easy access to Elan and several reservoirs, including the **Pen-y-garreg**, in attractive Cambrian Mountain scenery; the road continues to **Claerwn Reservoir** which has Britain's highest gravity dam. **New Radnor** has a ruined Norman castle, and **Old Radnor** an impressive medieval church, its font incorporating a Bronze Age slab. In Radnor Forest to the north, **Bach Hill** reaches a height of 2002 ft (610 m.); **The Smatcher** to the south reaches 1396 ft (425 m.). **Presteigne** on the River Lugg has fine black and white half-timbered buildings and Georgian houses, while at **Knighton** to the north, the Offa's Dyke Centre is close to a remaining 30 ft (9 m.) high stretch of the earthwork barrier. **Clyro**, to the south, was home to Kilvert, the 19th-century diarist.

Entertainment

Wyeside Arts Centre, Builth Wells (Tel 0982 552555).

Accommodation

First Class

Cae'r Beris Manor, Builth Wells (Tel 0982 552601).

Middle Range

Milebrook House Hotel, Milebrook, Knighton (Tel 0547 528632).
Greenway Manor Hotel, Cross Gates (Tel 059787 230).

Economy

Stredders Vegetarian Guest House, Park Crescent, Llandrindod Wells (Tel 0597 2186).
Beili Neuadd Farmhouse, Rhayader (Tel 0597 810211).
New Hall Farm Guest House, Llandew Ir Cwm, Builth Wells (Tel 0982 552483).
Youth Hostels at Glascwm, near Llandrindod Wells (Tel 09824 367) and Knighton (Tel 0547 528807).
The **Rock Park Hotel**, Llandrindod Wells, houses an activities centre (Tel 0597 2021).

Eating Out

Middle Range

Rock Park Hotel, Llandrindod Wells.

Economy

Spa Tea-Rooms, Rock Park Gardens, Llandrindod Wells.
Cosy Corner, 55 High St, Builth Wells (Tel 0982 553585).

Meirionnydd Area

From the Dovey Valley in the south to Maentwrog in the north, Meirionnydd is an area of magnificent scenery, most of it within Snowdonia National Park.

Aberdovey/Aberdyfi is an attractive small resort where the Dovey meets the sea. A track leads east to the **Bearded Lake** and **Carn March Arthur**. **Cader Idris**, a national nature reserve with alpine and arctic flora, rises to 2927 ft (892 m.) to the north. **Machynlleth** is an attractive town, one of the centres for 'alternative' Wales, with the Owain Glyndwr Institute in what is said to have been his parliament building. **Tourist Information** here is at Canolfan Owain Glyndwr (Tel 0654 702401). To the north the **Centre for Alternative Technology** in an old slate quarry lets visitors see wind and water power in action and examine organic farming principles. Further along the river the pretty village of **Dinas Mawddwy** is a good base for climbing Aran Fawddwy (2970 ft; 905 m.) and Aran Benllyn (2901 ft; 884 m.); there are also attractive waterfalls in the area. At **Tywyn**, a resort to the north of Aberdovey, the church contains the oldest example of written Welsh, **St Cadfan's Stone**. The **Tallyllyn Railway** from Tywyn to Abergynolwyn stops at the impressive **Dolgoch Falls**. North-east of Tywyn in the Dysynni valley, wild goats and choughs can sometimes be seen on **Craig-yr-Aderyn** (Bird Rock), while tiny Llanegryn church has a spectacular medieval rood screen and loft, and there are 13th-century castle ruins at **Castell-y-Bere**.

Dolgellau, a very Welsh town at the head of the Mawddach estuary where the church has pillars made from uncut tree trunks, is a good base for ramblers; the **Precipice Walk** starts from **Nannau**, two miles (3 km.) north-east, and offers views of Cader Idris and the Cambrian Mountains, while the **Torrent Walk** follows the River Cywedog, two miles (3 km.) east. **Barmouth/Abermaw** at the sea end of the Mawddach estuary is a typical seaside resort, overlooked by the **Dinas Oleu** cliffs, the first property bought by the National Trust. **Harlech** to the north has one of the most beautiful of all Welsh castles, built by Edward I and overlooking Tremadog Bay.

Ffestiniog is an attractive village south of **Blaenau Ffestiniog**, a slate-quarrying town which can look menacingly grey in bad weather.

The Llechwedd Slate Caverns offer summer visitors the opportunity to descend into caverns created by mining activity and view an underground lake. The Ffestiniog Railway runs to **Porthmadog**, a sleepy harbour town built, like neighbouring **Tremadog**, in the 19th century. Just before Porthmadog, **Portmeirion** is an artificial village designed in Italian style with pastel-coloured shops and houses set round a central garden, surrounded by woods and leading down to a beautiful beach. East of Ffestiniog, **Bala**, on Wales' largest lake, is surrounded by some of the highest peaks.

Accommodation

First Class

Hotel Plas Penhelig, Aberdovey (Tel 065472 676).
Hotel Portmeirion, Portmeirion (Tel 0766 770228).
Hotel Maes-y-Neuadd, Talsarnau, Harlech (Tel 0766 780211).

Middle Range

Plas Coch, High St, Bala (Tel 0678 520309).
Ystumgwern Hall Farm, Dyffryn, Ardudwy (Tel 03417 249).
Rum Hole Hotel, Harlech (Tel 0766 780477).

Economy

Penybryn Farm Guest House, Sarnau, Bala (Tel 06783 297).
Llwyn Talcen, Vrithdir, Dolgellau (Tel 034141 276).
Novelty **self-catering cottages** available in **Portmeirion** village (Tel 0766 771331).
Youth Hostels at Corris (Tel 065473); Kings (Tel 0341 422392); Bala (Tel 0678 520215); Llanbedr (Tel 034123 287); Ffestiniog (Tel 076676 265); and Harlech (Tel 0766 780285).

Eating Out

First Class

Abregwynant Hall, Penmaenpool, Dolgellau (Tel 0341 422238).
Portmeirion Hotel (see above).

Middle Range

Fronoleu Farm Restaurant, Tabor, Dolgellau (Tel 0341 422361).
Brittania Arms, Aberdovey (Tel 0654 767426).
Hotel Plas Penhelig, Aberdovey (Tel 0654 767676).
Ivy House Restaurant, Dolgellau (Tel 0341 422538).

Economy

  Llew Glas, High St, Harlech (Tel 0766 780700)
  Felin Crewi, Penegoes (Tel 0654 3113).
  Quarry Shop, 13 Maengwyn St, Machynlleth (Tel 0654 702624).
  Quarry, Centre for Alternative Technology (Tel 0654 702400).

Llyn Peninsula

An Area of Outstanding Natural Beauty, the Llyn Peninsula which juts out from Porthmadog is ringed with sandy beaches and rocky headlands.

Ruined 13th-century **Criccieth** castle offers fine views along the southern coast. At nearby **Llanstumdwy**, where Lloyd George is buried, there is a commemorative museum. **Pwllheli** is an overdeveloped typical seaside resort; **Tourist information** here on Y Maes LL53 6HE (Tel 075861 3000). More attractive is the harbour village of **Abersoch**, where boats can be found running to the privately-owned **St Tudwal's Islands**. Around the bay, the beaches of **Porth Neigwl** (Hell's Mouth) can be reached via steep cliff paths. Medieval pilgrims used to cross from **Aberdaron** village to **Bardsey Island** (now a national nature reserve) where so many holy men were buried that it became known as the 'Island of 20,000 Saints'.

At north coast **Porth-oer**, sand on the fine beach seems to whistle below the feet. Four miles (6 km.) north of **Porth Dinllaen** stand **Yr Eifl** (The Forks) and the 100 Iron Age hut circles of **Tre'r Ceiri** (Town of the Giants), both offering magnificent coastal views.

Accommodation

First Class

  Plas Bodegroes, Pwllheli (Tel 0758 612363).
  Bron Eifion Country House Hotel, Criccieth (Tel 0766 522385).

Middle Range

  Abereistedd Hotel, West Parade, Criccieth (Tel 0766 522710).

Economy

  Preswylfa Guest House, 4 Castle Terrace, Criccieth (Tel 0766 522829).
  Carreg Plas Guest House, Aberdaron (Tel 075886 308).
  Self-catering accommodation is available on Bardsey; contact the

Bookings Secretary, Stabal Hen, Tyddyn Du, Criccieth (Tel 0766 522239) one month in advance.

Eating Out

First Class

Plas Bodegroes (as above).

Middle Range.

Three Herrings, Well St, Nefyn (Tel 0758 720864).

The Snowdonia Mountains and Coastal Resorts

This part of Wales is completely dominated by its mountains, with spectacular roads across the passes. Important towns like Caernarfon and Bangor cling to the thin strip of lowland near the coast, overlooking the Menai Straits and Anglesey.

Beddgelert, a pretty village called 'Grave of Gelert' after a supposedly medieval legend, is an excellent centre for walking and climbing. Local shops sell all necessary equipment and guest houses and restaurants are geared to the hearty appetites of outdoor aficionados. Visitors to the **Sygun Copper Mine** can explore its 19th-century workings on foot. To the south is the **Abreglaslyn Pass** and to the west **Beddgelert Forest**, both offering fine walks. The dramatic **Nant Gwynant** road leads east to **Pen-y-Gwyrd**, while the A4085 cuts north in the shadow of Mount Snowdon to **Caernarfon**. Halfway is **Betws Garmon**, a base for climbing **Moel Eilio** (2382ft; 726 m.) and **Myndd Mawr** (2290 ft; 698 m.). Nearby Hafodty has a rock and water garden with marvellous spring azaleas and rhododendrons. **Snowdonia Riding Stables** can be found at Waunfawr (Tel 028685 342).

Despite depressing suburbs, central **Caernarfon** is dominated by the magnificent preserved castle built by Edward I, where Prince Charles was invested as Prince of Wales in 1969. Flights around **Mount Snowdon** are available from Caernarfon Airport (Tel 0286 830800). **Tourist Information** is at Oriel Pendeitsh (Tel 0286 672232). **Segontium**, half a mile (0.8 km.) east, is the site of a Roman military camp with an on-site museum. From Caernarfon the A4086 tracks inland to **Llanberis**, a large village on a huge lake, the base for climbing Mount Snowdon or taking a train to the summit. The Museum of the North and the Welsh Slate Museum are also in Llanberis. The road continues past **Glyder Fawr** (3279 ft; 1000 m.) and over the Llanberis Pass to Pen-y-Gwyrd.

To the east **Capel Curig** is another good base for climbers and walkers and has a mountaineering centre, the Plas y Brenin. The A5 heads north past **Carnedd Dafydd** (3427 ft; 1045 m.) and over Nant Ffrancon to the slate-quarrying town of **Betheseda**. From **Llyn Ogwen** a path leads to **Llyn Idwal** and the **Devil's Kitchen** rock formation. The road emerges at **Bangor**, a university town with a 19th-century cathedral designed by Sir George Gilbert Scott, and a restored Victorian pier. To the east, neo-Norman Penrhyn Castle has a pottery in its grounds. Typical seaside resorts can be found clinging to the coast at **Llanfairfechan** and **Penmaenmawr**, and there are good walks inland to the **Aber Falls** and across the **Sychnant Pass** to Conwy.

Conwy, home to one of the most impressive of Edward I's castles and with intact medieval city walls, has been plagued by summer traffic jams which should vanish when the new bypass opens in 1992. The ramparts offer fine views of Telford's suspension bridge over the River Conwy, built in 1826 and replaced in importance by the 1958 road bridge. Half-timbered **Aberconway House** is owned by the National Trust, while 16th-century stone **Plas Mawr** is the finest Elizabethan building in Wales. Four miles (6 km.) south-east are Bodnant Gardens in a wonderful setting overlooking Snowdon. South of Conwy, the **Trefiw** woollen mills offer demonstrations of weaving and hand-spinning (open all year round). Trefiw Wells spa generates iron-rich water, first discovered by the Romans; visitors can visit a cyclopean bath house made from Welsh slate and see how the Victorians bottled the water. Inigo Jones is said to have designed the bridge at **Llanrwst**, near Gwydir Forest Visitor Centre and 17th-century Gwydir Uchaf private chapel. **Betws-y-Coed**, on the Conwy, Llugwy and Lledr rivers, is famous for the pretty **Swallow Falls**, one mile to the north opposite the Swallow Falls Hotel Visitor Centre. Mountain-bikes can be hired to explore the area (Tel 06902 766 for details). **Snowdonia Guides** (Tel 06902 766) also offer rock-climbing, scrambling, abseiling and walking tours.

Entertainment

Theatr Gwynedd, Bangor (Tel 0248 351707).

Accommodation

First Class

Ty'n Rhos Farm, Llanddeiniolen, Caernarfon (Tel 0248 670489).
The Old Rectory, Llansantffraid Glan Conwy, near Conwy (Tel 0492 580611).

Middle Range

Sygun Fawr Country House Hotel, Beddgelert (Tel 076686 258).
Royal Victoria Hotel, Llanberis (Tel 0286 870253).

Economy

Ael-y-Bryn, Caernarfon Road, Beddgelert (Tel 076686 310).
Alpine Lodge Hotel, 1 High St, Llanberis (Tel 0286 870294).
Chatham Farmhouse, Llandwrog, Caernarfon (Tel 0286 831257).
Youth Hostels at Bryn Gwynant (Tel 076686 251); Capel Curig (Tel 06904 225); Idwal Cottage (Tel 0248 600225); Lledr Valley (Tel 06906 202); Bangor (Tel 0248 353516); Penmaenmawr (Tel 0492 623476); and Snowdon Ranger (Tel 0492 531406).

Eating Out

First Class

Meadowstreet Hotel, Llanrwst (Tel 0492 640732).

Middle Range

Bangor Pier Restaurant (Tel 0248 362807).
Tanronen Hotel, Beddgelert (Tel 076686 347).
Prince Llewelyn Hotel, Beddgelert (Tel 076686 242).
Bubbling Kitchen, Holyhead Road, Betws-y-Coed (Tel 06902 667).
Herbs, 30 Mount St, Bangor (Tel 0248 351249).

Economy

Castle Gallery Restaurant, Car Park, Rose Hill St, Conwy (Tel 0492 596159).
Trefiw Wells Spa Tea-Room (Tel 0492 640057).

Anglesey

The 125-mile (201 km.) coastline of Anglesey, a large, flat island connected to the mainland by the Menai Bridge, is lined with attractive beaches.

To the east, attractive **Beaumaris** has one of Edward I's castles with a romantic moat and a Museum of Childhood. The road contines to **Penmon**, with a pebble beach, passing a ruined 12th-century priory and a wishing well. **Puffin Island (Priestholm)**, one mile (1.5 km.)

offshore, has a bird sanctuary. To the north-east there are bathing beaches at **Moelfre**, **Cemaes Bay** and **Cemlyn Bay**. A medieval church stands at **Llaneilian**, on the way to Point Lynas which used to be a signalling station. Wylfa Nuclear Power Station at **Cemaes Bay** is open to visitors.

The road west passes **Llanfair PG** (the name-plate for the station with the world's longest name (see page 616) is now in Penrhyn Castle) and arrives at **Newborough**, where a national nature reserve protects tern colonies and migrant waders. En route it also passes Anglesey Sea Zoo at **Brysiencyn** and Bird World at **Dwyran**. The Anglesey Coastal Heritage Centre (Llys Llywelyn) is at **Aberffraw**.

From Llanfair a road heads straight to the port at **Holyhead/Caergybi** on Holy Island which is connected to Anglesey by a causeway. **Holyhead Mountain** (700 ft; 213 m.) offers views of the Isle of Man, Cumbria and Ireland. A bridge leads to **South Stack**, a rocky promontory with a lighthouse where seals can sometimes be seen. Razorbills, cormorants and guillemots nest on **North Stack**. On the way to Holyhead are Plas Newydd, an 18th-century house containing Whister's largest wall painting, Hen Blas Country Park and 'Farm Life' where visitors can watch farm crafts like sheep-shearing. Holyhead **Tourist Information** is at Marine Square, Salt Island Approach (Tel 0407 762622).

Accommodation

First Class

Olde Bull's Head, Castle St, Beaumaris (Tel 0248 810329).

Middle Range

Bishopsgate House Hotel, Castle St, Beaumaris (Tel 0248 810302).

Llwydiarth Fawr, Llanerchymedd (Tel 0248 470321)

Economy

Plas Cichle, Beaumaris (Tel 0248 810488).
Drws y Coed, Llanerchymedd (Tel: 0248 470473).
Tre'rddol Farm, Llanerchymedd (Tel 0248 470278).

Eating Out

First Class

Olde Bull's Head (as above).

Middle Range

Jodie's Wine Bar and Bistro, Telford Road, Menai Bridge (Tel 0248 714864).
The Honey Pot, Rhosneigr (Tel 0407 810302).

Economy

The Sidings, Victorian tea-room in Llanfair PG station.

North Wales Coastal Resorts

Hemmed in between the A55 and the sea are a string of seaside resorts, easily reached from Chester and Liverpool. In general these towns are overdeveloped and unappealing.

To the west, **Llandudno** is the largest resort, with North Shore beach enclosed by Great and Little Orme's Head. A Victorian cable tramway runs to the top of Great Orme's Head which can also be reached on foot through the Happy Valley rock garden. On the beach at **Rhos-on-Sea** St Trillo's chapel stands over a holy well. Britain's first permanent puppet theatre is also in Rhos (Tel 0492 48166 for programme). Fishing trips are available from Rhos Point (Tel 0492 44829 for details). The new Alice in Wonderland 'Rabbit Hole' Visitor Centre is in Trinity Square.

Just outside **Colwyn Bay** is the Welsh Mountain Zoo, a conservation centre for endangered species and free-flying eagles. Nearby are two important churches: **Bryn-y-Maen**, 'the cathedral on the hill' with fine views from its tower, and **Llanelian-yn-Rhos** with a rare rood loft. **Rhyl** has two vast funfairs and the new Knights' Cavern, a mythological heritage centre. There is a **Tourist Information Centre** here at the Central Promenade (Tel 0745 355068).

Rhuddlan to the south has another of Edward I's impressive castles. At the northern end of Offa's Dyke, modern **Prestatyn** is a huge holiday resort, backed by attractive walking country around **Gwaensysgor** and **Trelawnyd**.

Accommodation

First Class

Bodysgallen Hall, Llandudno (Tel 0492 584466).
St Tudno Hotel, North Parade, Llandudno (Tel 0492 874411).

Middle Range

Ambassador Hotel, Grand Promenade, Llandudno (Tel 0492 76886).

Economy

Croma, 50A Rhos Road, Rhos-on-Sea (Tel 0492 49423).
Bryn Car Farm, Betws-yn-Rhos, Abergele (Tel 049260 605).

Eating Out

First Class

Bodysgallen Hall (as above).
St Tudno Hotel, (as above).

Middle Range

Good Taste Bistro, 18 Seaview Rd, Colwyn Bay (Tel 0492 534786).
Bells of St Mary's, Mostyn Road, Cronant, Prestatyn (Tel 07456 3770).

North Clwyd Area

The gentle lowlands of northern Clwyd rapidly give way to more mountainous scenery, especially round Llangollen, a popular centre for canoeists in particular.

A steep hill leads to **St Asaph's** cathedral, restored by Sir George Gilbert Scott in 1870. To the north-west at **Bodelwyddan**, Williams Hall has been refurbished as a setting for the National Portrait Gallery's Victorian collections. The 'Marble Church' of St Margaret is an unaltered Victorian church with a pleasingly ornate interior. To the east **Pantasaph** monastery has a reproduction of the Lourdes Grotto, while St Winifred's Well at **Holywell** has been called the 'Lourdes of Wales'.

Another of Edward I's castles stands on the Dee estuary at **Flint**. The castle at **Hawarden** dates only from 1752 and was home to Gladstone. Inland, at the edge of the **Clwydian Hills**, is the picturesque market town of **Mold**, where the 15th-century church contains animal frescos. To the south is the large town of **Wrexham**, where Elihu Yale is buried in St Giles' churchyard. Nearby Erddig House dates from the 17th century and has formal 18th-century gardens. To the north the church bells at **Gresford** are one of the Seven Wonders of Wales, as are the yew trees in the churchyard at **Overton** to the south. Two miles (3 km.) south-west, **Bersham** industrial heritage centre focuses on the site of the Wilkinsons' ironworks, where cannons for the American War

of Independence were made. **Erbistock** is a beauty spot on the River
Dee, while **Rhosllanerchrugog** has a surprising number of chapels
and two renowned choirs.

South of the spectacular **Horseshoe Pass** and the ruins of 13th-
century **Valle Crucis Abbey**, **Llangollen** on the River Dee has
the Horseshoe Falls, a Canal Museum, horse-drawn barge trips
and a steam railway. The European Centre for Traditional and
Regional Culture (ECTARC) hosts a regular programme of temporary
exhibitions. Plas Newydd, a half-timbered building in attractive
gardens, was home to the late-18th-century 'Ladies of Llangollen',
Lady Eleanor Butler and Sarah Ponsonby, who wore men's clothes
and entertained everyone from the Duke of Wellington to William
Wordsworth. A path also leads to the 8th-century ruins of Castell
Dinas Bran and the limestone cliffs of Egywlseg Mountain. Every
July the International Musical Eisteddfod is held at Llangollen. To the
east, Telford built **Pont-Cysyllte Aqueduct** to carry the Shropshire
Union Canal. On the road to Ruabon is Ty Mawr Country Park, with
riverside walks and fine views. Llangollen **Tourist Information** is at
the Town Hall (Tel 0978 860828).

To the west **Corwen** is a market town offering walks into the
Berwyn Mountains. The River Dee flows south through the **Vale
of Edeyrmon** to Bala.

North of Llangollen, **Ruthin** has a 19th-century Gothic-style castle
built within the ruins of a 13th-century one. Curfew is still sounded
every night, and on summer Wednesdays locals don medieval costume
for the fair. The tourist office has a leaflet listing all the town's older
buildings and their histories. Craftsmen can be watched at work at the
Ruthin Craft Centre on the outskirts. **Loggerheads Country Park**,
with woodland walks, a restored water mill and industrial trails, is
on the road to Mold.

North of Ruthin, **Denbigh's** ruined 13th-century castle stands in a
prominent position and contains a museum. There are also old town
walls and the ruins of a church built in an attempt to usurp St Asaph's
authority.

Accommodation

First Class

Bodidris Hall, Llandegla, Wrexham (Tel 097888 434).

Llwyn Onn Hall, Cefn Road, Wrexham (Tel 0978 261225).

Tyddyn Llan Country House, Llandrillo, near Corwen (Tel
049084 264).

Middle Range

Owain Glyndwr Hotel, The Square, Corwen (Tel 0490 2115).
Abbey Grange Hotel, Abbey Road, Llangollen (Tel 0978 860753).
The Four Poster Hotel, Mill Street Square, Llangollen (Tel 0978 861062).

Economy

Glanafon, Abbey Road, Llangollen (Tel 0978 860725).
Eyarth Station, Llanfair D.C, Ruthin (Tel 08242 3643).
College Farm, Peniel, Denbigh (Tel 0754570 276).
Youth Hostels at Llangollen (Tel 0978 860330) and Maeshafn (Tel 0492 531406).

Eating Out

Medieval banquets in **Ruthin Castle** (Tel 08242 2664).

First Class

Tyddyn Llan (as above).

Middle Range

Gales, 18 Bridge St, Llangollen (Tel 0978 860089). Prize-winning wine list.
Good Taste, Market St, Llangollen (Tel 0978 861425).
Boat Inn, Erbistock (Tel 0978 780143).

South Clwyd and Montgomeryshire

A varied region, with mountains to the north and fertile farmland and black and white half-timbered houses to the east, southern Montgomeryshire is very popular with 'alternative' lifestylers who have made Llanidloes their capital.

Chirk castle, east of Llangollen, has been continuously inhabited since the 14th century. From Chirk, the **Vale of Ceiriog** to the south offers remote, winding mountain roads and fine views. Attractive villages in the vale include **Llanarmon Dyffryn Ceiriog** and **Llanhaedar-ym-Mochnant**, with access to the beautiful **Pistyll Rhaeadr Falls**. From **Llanfyllin** there are walks to **Lake Vrynwy**, with a Severn Trent Interpretive Centre, in the Dyfnant Forest.

Powis Castle at **Welshpool/Trallwng** has been continuously inhabited since the 13th century and has gardens by Capability Brown.

Tourist Information here is at Vicarage Gardens Car Park (Tel 0938 552043). To the south-east, **Montgomery** is a gem of a town bypassed by history, with much Georgian architecture, a ruined 13th-century castle and a church with two screens, one of them probably stolen from neighbouring Chirbury. East of **Newtown/Drenewydd** there are gentle walks into the hills around Kerry.

Caersws has Maes-Mawr, an impressive half-timbered house. **Llanidloes** has a thoroughly attractive, open, airy centre, focused on a half-timbered Market House (1609). There are pleasant walks in the **Hafren Forest** and **Plynlimon Hills** to the sources of the Rivers Severn and Wye. A long-distance footpath passes **Llyn Clwedog**, a huge reservoir built in 1967, on its way to Machynlleth.

Accommodation

First Class

  Lake Vyrnwy Hotel, Llanwyddyn, Via Oswestry (Tel 069173 692).

Middle Range

  Cain Valley Hotel, High St, Llanfyllin (Tel 069184 366).
  Cyfie Farm, Llanfihangel-Yng-Ngwynfa, Llanfyllin (Tel 069184 451).

Economy

  Little Brompton Farm, Montgomery (Tel 068681 371).
  Peniarth, 10 Cefn Hawys, Red Bank, Welshpool (Tel 0938 552324).
  Tynmaes Farm, Llanwyddyn (Tel 069173 216).

Eating Out

Middle Range

  Dragon Hotel, Market Square, Montgomery.

Economy

  Granary, 42 High St, Welshpool (Tel 0938 3198).
  Great Oak Cafe, 12 Great Oak St, Llanidloes (Tel 05512 3211).
  Castle Kitchen, 15 Broad St, Montgomery.

NORTHERN IRELAND

18 Northern Ireland

Very few people give Northern Ireland a chance. Most visitors to the province tend to be there either on business trips, or visiting friends and relations. The official statistics are depressing: only 13 per cent of those visiting Northern Ireland do so as holiday tourists. Europe and North America represent the largest source of pure holiday visitors, in contrast to the British market which accounts for only 3 per cent.

For over twenty years, continuous media coverage of the violence and civil unrest has painted the negative and very bleak picture of a community torn apart by religious differences and appalling acts of terrorism. Hardly a week goes by without some reminder of what seems to be an ongoing, unsolvable and ultimately tragic situation. From a tourism point of view, this is hardly good news, and the inevitable result is that Northern Ireland is totally dismissed as a credible – or even potential – holiday option.

So why feature it in the *Good Tourist* guide? Well, firstly it may come as a complete surprise to discover that Northern Ireland is possibly the most scenically varied region in the United Kingdom, and exploring it can be a genuine delight. Admittedly, there may not be the same sense of product identity as there is with, say, Scotland, but the province has a considerable number of excellent attractions and unique places to visit, and because it is so compact (about the size of Yorkshire) nearly everywhere is within a two-hour drive. Areas of Outstanding Natural Beauty stand comparison with the most popular scenic areas of the British Isles and there is a wide range of amenities and facilities.

Secondly, the obvious worry about security and how much 'the troubles' will impinge on a holiday turns out to be much less of a problem in most areas than you might think. You will have to look very hard to see evidence of a military presence. It is unlikely that you will notice anything unusual except for fortress style police stations and manned checkpoints in control zones. This can come as something of a visual shock to the uninitiated, but once you overcome this first impression, you will be glad that you made the effort to visit the country and meet the people. Belfast is unfairly 'twinned' with Beirut. Berlin – before the reunification – would be a more appropriate comparison. There are areas of the city where travel is restricted, and you can almost eliminate the possibility of trouble by avoiding these pockets. Much of the violence is focused on the west side of Belfast and parts of the border area with the Irish Republic. Attacks are usually directed at the security forces rather than civilians and, as in most other parts of the UK, life tends to go on as normal. The average visitor to the province will see little evidence of 'the troubles'.

Many experienced travellers rate the success of their trip on the contact and interaction they have with the local population. Irish people are generally noted for their friendliness and hospitality, and the Northern Irish are no exception. Everyone has time for a chat and an overseas accent of any kind is guaranteed to involve the visitor in countless conversations, or a bit of 'crack', as the Irish term it.

Having said all this though, the province has a severe image problem, which must at some point be addressed. Those who have reason to visit Ulster realise how distorted the image really is, but it is unlikely that global perceptions will change enough to cause tourists to flock there *en masse*. In a bizarre way, the violence has protected this environment from the outside world, and for the good tourist, exploring it is well worth the rewards.

History

In Ulster, history and politics go hand-in-hand and it is almost impossible to discuss one without the other. Much of the present unrest relates to perceived historical injustices and events of the past are part of the fabric of everyday life. Whilst it is obviously not the intention of this book to involve the reader in political dispute, it is important to have a basic overview of the history of the province.

The Celts arrived in Ireland around 300 BC. The Romans and the Saxons never got this far, and the Celts were able to settle down and develop in their own way. Their social system was based on the extended family, and gave rise to the tradition of hospitality and story-telling which still survives today. There were no landowners – the cultivated land belonged to the tribe and was periodically redistributed so that everybody got a share of the good and the bad – and the chiefs were elected from certain families, so they had no rights in the land except while they were chief. All this guaranteed trouble when Celtic tribes clashed later with a land-owning, hereditary-based aristocracy from across the Irish Channel.

Saint Patrick was a Romanised Welsh Christian who learned the faith of his time in a French monastery. He returned to Ireland in AD 432 to organise the Christians there into dioceses, and to do this he had to convert the pagan kings. Since there were no towns as such, his structure gradually broke down and was replaced by a Christianity based on monasteries. In the centuries which followed, there was a great blossoming of monastic fervour, with hundreds of Irish men and women devoting themselves to God as monks and nuns.

In 795 the Vikings invaded Ireland, pillaging the monasteries and then founding trade settlements which later became towns. The Normans conquered England in the ten years from 1066, and 100 years later they began the conquest of Ireland. They built castles, introduced new farming techniques, and became Celtic chiefs, combining with or replacing the Celtic aristocracy. The Gaelic order was born and lasted until after 1600.

A significant turning-point for Ireland was Henry VIII's break with Rome. He proclaimed himself King of Ireland by right of conquest, and faced the task of effectively conquering Ireland. He did this by smashing down all opposition and then driving the rebel lords and landowners from their estates and granting these to his own loyal followers.

The Reformation continued to make progress in England, and under Elizabeth I all effective opposition to it was snuffed out. In Ireland however, things were vastly different and the Irish remained steadfast in their allegiance to Rome. Elizabeth's death in 1603 coincided with the conquest of Ireland, and the Irish, with their land destroyed by war and racked by famine, were left to the mercy of the conquerors. In 1607, the few remaining princes and lords of Ulster became fearful for their lives and fled the country. Their lands, or rather the lands of their people, were confiscated and parcelled out amongst English and Scottish settlers who were loyal to the crown. This was the beginning of the Ulster problem which has continued ever since.

After the execution of Charles I, Oliver Cromwell invaded Ireland. To show that a new order had arrived, he ordered the massacre of the garrison of the first town to oppose him (Drogheda), and went on to crush the rest.

In 1690, the Battle of the Boyne was fought when the troops of the Protestant Dutch King William of Orange defeated armies of the Catholic King James II. This battle is commemorated on 12 July each year, when 'Orangemen' march with pipe bands and drums throughout the province.

The great famine took place in the years 1845–49, due to a failure in the potato crop. It is estimated that almost 800,000 people died of starvation and disease; about 700,000 emigrated to Britain and one million to North America. By 1851 the population had dropped to 6.5 million, and emigration from Ireland continued for another hundred years.

The Anglo-Irish War was fought from 1919–21. It ended with a treaty by which twenty-six counties became the Irish Free State, while the remaining six counties in the north-east remained as part of the UK. Until 1972, the province of Northern Ireland (informally, Ulster) was governed by its own parliament, but a rising tide of civil rights protests resulted in waves of violence, which caused the British government to dissolve the local parliament and impose direct rule from London. Army battalions were dispatched to help contain the rioting and impose order. Initially, the Roman Catholic community welcomed the military with open arms, but the republican movement saw this as a further restrictive control from a 'foreign' power. The results of what followed were flashed around the world and, some twenty years on, the solution seems as far away as ever.

The Northern Irish Protestants are fiercely patriotic, loyal to Queen and Country. The North is financially linked with the UK and its citizens enjoy the same benefits as the rest of the mainland. This majority have no desire to lose the association with the mother country, and to be governed from Dublin is for them unthinkable.

And so it goes on. For each solution there are twenty problems. Some of the best political minds in the land have not been able to find a way through this never-ending crisis. Visitors to the province may gain a sense of the inbred suspicions and convictions which have set communities against each other, and perhaps leave with the realisation that some questions have no logical answers, and some problems are sadly, without solution.

Geography

Northern Ireland is made up of six small counties: Antrim, Armagh, Down, Fermanagh, Londonderry (or Derry) and Tyrone. Unlike the rest of Britain, local people tend to use the prefix 'county' when they refer to a particular area.

Although the province is small – almost 85 miles (136 km.) from top to bottom and 110 miles (177 km.) wide – it is geographically varied. Lough Neagh, the largest lake in the British Isles, is right in the centre and surrounded by predominantly low-lying land mostly given over to agriculture. The Mournes in the south-east and the Sperrins in the north-west are the two main mountain ranges. For the most part they are bare hills, open walking country, too high to be farmed. Most of the small lakes and rivers of the forested south-west drain into Lough Erne, a 50-mile-long (80 km.) waterway that is popular for boating and fishing. The lowlands of Armagh and south Down are covered with hillocks called drumlins. These are oval masses of boulder clay deposited during the Ice Age, and richly farmed now. The two cathedrals of Armagh are built on drumlins.

Bogs once covered almost 15 per cent of the surface of Ireland, though cutting and land restoration has reduced this in recent years to about 6 per cent. A bog is a bed of peat up to 32 feet (10 m.) deep, with a thin layer of soil that supports acid-loving plants like sphagnum, sedges and bog cotton.

In the distant past nearly all Ireland was covered in forest, but by the start of this century hunger for fuel and land had made this the most treeless country in Europe. Almost the only trees were on the estates of the great landowners. Since then, there has been a great revival of forestry and over 5 per cent of the total land area is now covered by trees. Northern Ireland has over sixty forests and many have been opened to the public as forest parks, with car parking, toilets, adequate but unobtrusive signposting and often a cafe or small restaurant.

One of the most famous areas of the North Antrim Coast is the Giant's Causeway, a geological freak which is the result of volcanic action. Over 40,000 hexagonal basalt columns extend from the cliff foot to the sea. It is a most spectacular sight. The tallest columns are about 40 feet (12 m.) high, and the solidified lava in the cliffs is 90 feet (27 m.) thick in places. Much of the coastline here is more reminiscent of Iceland than Ireland. South of the Causeway, the Antrim coast is cut into the chalk cliffs to form one of the most striking coastal landscapes in Ireland. Many of the beaches along here are double-layered – a smooth, tidal stretch of land rising slowly to a rim of sand dunes, and then another flat stretch beyond – the result of a drop in the sea level a few thousand years ago. The sea is warmed by the Gulf Stream and in sheltered areas, particularly around Strangford Lough where it has created a micro-climate, the result has been dramatic plant and foliage growth.

Dozens of rounded drumlins extend into Strangford Lough giving the appearance of small islands in a large freshwater lake. Although the lough is relatively calm, 400 million tons of water rush through the gap between Portaferry and Strangford twice a day. The Vikings named it 'violent fjord' (Strangford) after the fierce currents in these tidal narrows.

The lough is a great bird sanctuary and wildlife reserve. A large flock of brent geese winters here and greylag and white-fronted geese often visit from the Downpatrick marshes. Waders – oyster catchers, redshanks and curlews – love the mudflats, and many species of tern and gulls take up summer residence. Over a hundred different species of fish live in the lough, and sea hares, sun stars and octopus sometimes appear on the shore.

Climate

England is often referred to as a 'green and pleasant land', but Ireland is even greener. It rains a lot here. The air is always moist – even during the summer – and it would be foolish to visit without a raincoat. Being such a small island, clouds are constantly blowing in from the Atlantic, and a morning that starts out warm and sunny can change dramatically by lunchtime. The climate is temperate; it never gets too hot in summer or extremely cold in winter. There is little or no snow and the average temperature in January is 4°C (40°F), and in July and August 14–17°C (57–60°F). The sunniest months are May and June.

Ireland is smog-free and virtually fog-free, but sea mists are common along the north coast and can cause the temperature to drop quickly. This area is also prone to strong winds which can occur at any time throughout the year.

Attractions

One of the real pleasures of holidaying in Northern Ireland is the quality of the travel experience. The country and the people are genuinely interesting; the variety of the landscape is impressive; many of the attractions are planned and maintained with great care, and they reflect an understanding and concern for the surrounding environment. Ulster people spend much of their leisure time outdoors and, as a result, they tend to be highly critical of shoddy or inadequate amenities, so facilities on the whole are good.

The province has its fair share of historic monuments ranging from castles and ancestral homes to Stone Age antiquities. Neolithic tombs (known as dolmens) are scattered all over the province. They usually consist of three irregular slabs of stone standing upright in the earth and capped with a large flat stone. Stone circles or rings are common;

stone crosses, round towers, churches and ruined castles are accepted as part of the countryside. Most of these monuments are protected as historic sites, and unusually, many have been left as they were found – as unrestored ruins. The sites are well signposted and factual information boards are provided.

Extensive areas of countryside are designated as Areas of Outstanding Natural Beauty (AONB), and include most of the coast, much of which is protected by the National Trust, as well as Mourne and Sperrin mountain ranges, and areas of parkland and towpaths along stretches of the river Lagan in south Belfast. For walkers and ramblers, there is the Ulster Way, a long-distance footpath which encircles Northern Ireland. Much of it is waymarked but some sections require close attention to a detailed map. Accommodation is available in hotels, farmhouses, guesthouses and hostels en route.

A number of lakeside resorts, principally on Lough Erne and Lough Neagh, not content to let the coastal areas get the lion's share of holidaymakers, have developed first-class marinas with boating, sailing and other recreations. Sea angling is excellent all around the coast and freshwater angling is likewise of a high standard. Tyrone and Fermanagh tend to be the favourite areas.

Sailing is another popular activity with Strangford Lough one of the most favoured centres; another is at Ballyhome and Groomsport, near Bangor. Inland, Lough Erne and Lough Neagh are very popular.

Away from the tourist attractions, the countryside has a lot to offer. The land is cultivated with a blend of care and efficiency and an eye for neatness and landscape. The small towns and villages are trim and well looked after. Many of these smaller places have not only retained the peace of a past age, but have somehow allowed political troubles to pass them by.

Cuisine

Traditional Irish cuisine is plain local produce, simply cooked. Hotel food is usually adequate but often unadventurous. In the larger towns, you can find a fair range of restaurants catering for all tastes and pockets. American-style fast food outlets and pizza parlours are spreading fast, and are well patronised.

Fresh seafood is available all round the coast, from Kilkeel up to Portaferry and along to Lough Foyle. Pubs serve reasonably-priced shellfish at lunchtime, and some go in for smoked fish pâtés. Ardglass herrings, Portavogie prawns and smoked trout and eel on toast are specialities, and you might try Guinness soup with oysters from Strangford Lough.

Breakfast is a substantial meal and usually consists of bacon, sausage, egg, tomato and a variety of fried breads, and is known as an 'Ulster Fry'.

The midday meal is called 'dinner' in many areas, but 'lunch' where the habit of a cooked evening meal is taking hold. High tea, served between 5.00 p.m–7.30 p.m., is a substantial meal of tea and cakes following a cooked meat or fish dish.

Breadmaking is something the Northern Irish excel at. Every little town has its home bakery with delicious baked breads or 'farls' – soda farls, wheaten farls and potato farls, sweet round brannocks, barmbracks filled with fruit and spices, apple soda and currant bread, and all sorts of scones. The word 'farl' is from fardel, meaning 'fourth part' or quarter of a round cake. Farls are baked on a griddle and shaped like triangles with one rounded side. Soda and buttermilk, instead of yeast, provides the leavening, and wheaten flour is often used.

Northern Ireland boasts the world's oldest (licit) whisky distillery at Bushmills. Irish whisky is often drunk along with a bottle of stout. Guinness is Ireland's most famous drink. It is a dark heavy beer (referred to as 'stout'), and its particular taste and texture depend on how it's stored (and poured). Real ale drinkers can try Hilden, an interesting ale produced at Lisburn, with an unusual crisp bitter taste. Pubs are open from 11.30 a.m.–11.00 p.m, Monday to Saturday; 12.30 p.m.–2.30 p.m. and 7.00 p.m.–10.00 p.m. on Sunday.

Level of Tourism

Although Northern Ireland has a few honeypots that the visitor may wish to avoid during the July and August peak holiday period, in general the region has a low level of tourism. This is perhaps the greatest charm of the province, not just for the British but for any other visitor. The country has modern amenities but retains the simplicity of the rural countryside, something which has vanished from many other parts of the world.

The busiest areas tend to be on the coastal resorts such as Newcastle in the south-east, Portrush in the north and Bangor in north Down. Traffic on the coast road from the Giant's Causeway to Portstewart can be slow at weekends (particularly when the weather is good), but it is worth pointing out that volume is extremely low in comparison with Britain and the style of driving is unaggressive and relaxed.

There is a traditional two-week works holiday around the 12 July commemoration of the Battle of the Boyne, and those wishing to avoid the anniversary processions tend to head for the seaside resorts on the coast. The largest procession is in Belfast and there are smaller regional parades throughout the province. Both 12 and 13 July are busy days, and most towns are likely to be congested.

Although tourism is a growth industry worldwide, it is clear that it is not making the scale of contribution to the Northern Ireland economy which it might. Since 1970, the annual volume of tourist traffic into Great Britain has almost doubled, and in the Republic of Ireland it has shown a 50 per cent increase. In Northern Ireland however, it is only in recent years that the volume has recovered from its dramatic slump in the early 1970s and returned towards even the 1970 level. As a result, it has the weakest tourism sector in the British Isles.

Despite the fact that tourism levels may be twenty years behind the rest of the country, development has not come to a standstill. On the contrary, both the Northern Ireland Tourist Board and the Department of the Environment have set up an agenda for action to develop a more attractive product for the incoming tourist. It is accepted that the question of Northern Ireland's image needs to be addressed, but that the basic tourist framework is already there; it will be necessary to build on the strengths of the 'product' and eliminate (or minimise) the weaknesses.

There is also a lack of international awareness of the sheer range and quality of the holiday experience in Northern Ireland. Again, this is a direct result of the media image. Those who live in, and have had reason to visit the province know the reality, and are very much aware of the enormity of the gap between perception and the actuality. Possibly only a major investment in marketing strategy can redress this problem, but then the switch from low impact to mass scale tourism development could itself severely damage the 'real' attractions of the province.

In October 1988 the Tourism Review Group was commissioned to carry out a fundamental survey of Northern Ireland's tourist industry. Working from first principles, it reviewed the government's entire involvement in tourism as well as assessing the existing and potential contribution that tourism could make to the local economy. One of the criticisms made in the report (published June 1989), was that tourism generally is too poorly integrated and packaged to make it accessible to the modern market. It is impossible, for example, for the tourist to book a series of stays in hotels and guest houses by one enquiry. If a group wants to tour scenic and historic sites, there is no organisation to plan the itinerary. If a fisherman wishes to come, there is no easily accessible channel for him to find out what holiday opportunities exist for the rest of his family. As a result, tourists who are unaccustomed to the formalities of booking a holiday are not that well catered for, but for the individual who knows how the system works, the rewards can be great. Although the UK is suffering from the effects of congestion, as a result of the increased population, unplanned housing schemes and far too many cars for the existing space – Northern Ireland is still relatively untouched by all of this and remains a comparatively peaceful place to visit. Some of the issues perceived as negative factors by the tourist board, are in fact positive reasons to visit the province. The simple, natural and uncommercial pleasures of this kind of holiday appeal to many people, and although wet weather facilities, theme parks and other moneymaking family entertainment complexes may be viewed as desirable ways to draw in more tourists and lengthen the season, they will require careful commercial judgement or they may destroy the very environment that draws visitors to the destination in the first place.

Good Alternatives

Meeting People

The Northern Irish on the whole tend to be rather shy; people are polite but informal, attentive but not pressing. Any sign of friendliness is almost guaranteed to be returned and visitors to the province are made to feel welcome. It is relatively easy to strike up a conversation almost anywhere, and you will find the locals genuinely interested in why you have come to visit the province and what your perceptions of it are. Many Ulster people are embarrassed by 'the troubles'; the problems of making a living are more important to almost all of them, and they display a refreshing 'life must go on' attitude.

A great many festivals are held throughout the year and provide opportunities to meet people on a social basis. Any of the Tourist Board's offices will supply up-to-date information – some of the main events include Belfast Music Festival, which is held annually in March; Northern Ireland Games and Country Fair, the premier field sports event, held in June; Fiddle Stone Festival, part of the ten-day Belleek Festival, and the Lurghnasa Medieval Fair and Crafts Market at Carrickfergus Castle, held in July; Oul' Lammas Fair, Ballycastle, oldest of Ireland's traditional fairs, held every August; Belfast Folk

Festival, in September, and the Belfast Festival at Queen's – the UK's biggest arts festival after Edinburgh, held annually in November.

Discovering Places

For simple country **walking** along footpaths, through forests and over mountains, meeting people and finding somewhere to stay as you go, Northern Ireland is very well organised. The Ulster Way is a 481 mile (775 km.) walk around the borders of the province, along country lanes and across moorland, beaches and parkland. A series of leaflets published by the Sports Council detailing different sections of the walk are available from the Northern Ireland Tourist Board.

There are nine major Forest Parks in the region; three in Tyrone, one in Antrim, two in Armagh, two in Down and one in Fermanagh. All are open from 10.00 a.m. to dusk. Campers and caravanners can enjoy short or extended holidays in most parks. Details can be obtained from: Forest Service, Department of Agriculture, Dundonald House, Upper Newtownards Road, Belfast BT4 3SF.

The province's seven Country Parks never close. Some have visitor centres (open till dusk), and entrance is free. For further details contact the tourist office.

Cycling is a popular activity in Ulster and a bike is great for exploring the countryside. There are a number of cycle hire outlets including Bike-It, 4 Belmont Road, Belfast; Centers at the Cycle Shop, 8 Railway Street, Lisburn; P. McNulty & Son, 24–26 Belmore Street, Enniskillen; and W. Nutt, 20 Circular Road, Coleraine. Daily and weekly rates are offered and a deposit is usually required.

Those who enjoy **riding** will find Northern Ireland a good place for trekking over farmlands and along mountain and forest trails. Most schools offer private tuition and many farm and country houses can arrange riding on an informal basis. For further details try the **Mount Pleasant Trekking Centre** or the **Newcastle Riding Centre**, Castlewellan, County Down.

Rathlin Island and Strangford Lough are extremely popular with ornithologists. Facilities are excellent and there are a number of open-air 'classrooms' where you can get very close to wild birds. For information contact the **RSPB**, Belvoir Forest Park, Belfast BT8 4QT.

The National Trust have a significant involvement in the province. In addition to the fine houses and gardens under their care, they own vast stretches of unspoiled coastline and are at the forefront of conservation and countryside preservation issues. You are certain to be able to visit all National Trust houses from Easter to September from 2.00 p.m. until 6.00 p.m. Many are open at other times, but you should check before setting out. The Trust's headquarters is at Rowallane, minutes from Belfast city centre. Contact: National Trust, Rowallane, Saintfield, County Down BT24 7LH.

James Watson Painting Courses are based in two attractive County Antrim villages – **Portballintrae** with its sandy beaches, and the Glens village of **Cushendall** – and two County Down centres, **Newcastle** and **Portaferry**, the picturesque harbour village at the mouth of Strangford Lough. Contact the Secretary, 340 Belmont Road, Belfast BT4 2LA.

A **residential craft centre** based in a Georgian house in Fermanagh offers courses in traditional weaving and spinning all year round. In addition, classes in patchwork, tapestry, painting and other crafts are available during the summer (day, weekend or longer sessions). For further information contact **Ardess Craft Centre**, Ardess House, Kesh, County Fermanagh.

Visitors with Ulster roots may wish to trace where their ancestors lived. Heritage holidays (groups or individuals) are arranged by the **Ulster Historical Foundation**, 68 Balmoral Avenue, Belfast BT9 6NY, and by the **Irish Heritage Association**, 162a Kingsway, Dunmurry, Belfast BT17 9AD.

Communications

How to Get There

AIR: There are direct scheduled flights to Belfast from all major UK Airports. International carriers offer scheduled services from the USA and Canada to Belfast International Airport via London (Heathrow & Gatwick), and to Shannon Airport in the Irish Republic. There are also direct charter services from New York and Toronto. Most carriers offer advance purchase discounts which are ideal for the holiday traveller and provide a substantial saving on the standard air fare.

FERRY: **Sealink Ferries** (Tel 0776 2662) sail from Stranraer in Scotland to Larne in County Antrim. There are several daily sailings and the crossing takes approximately $2^{1}/2$ hours. **P&O Ferries** (Tel 05812 276), sail between Cairnryan (five miles, 8 km., north of Stranraer), and Larne. The fare structure is similar for both companies and excursion fares are available for passengers and vehicles.

RAIL: **British Rail** offers a through service to Belfast (Tel 0232 230310) connecting with Sealink and Northern Ireland Railways.

Railcard holders are entitled to the usual discounts on this route. For further information, check with any British Rail office.

COACH: There is a direct bus service from London and other major centres to Belfast. This is often much cheaper than rail travel although it can involve an overnight journey. **Ulsterbus** central enquiries (Tel 0232 320011) will provide up-to-date information and fares.

When You're There

Using public transport alone is not the easiest way to tour Ulster – services between main centres are adequate, but reliance on buses or trains for out-of-the-way places demands planning, patience and careful study of timetables. The advantages of public transport however are not only that it is cheaper, but that it brings you into contact with other passengers and fellow travellers.

BUS: Northern Ireland has a good network of regular bus services. **Ulsterbus**, who operate the most extensive network, also run day and half-day tours to the main sights. Unlimited travel tickets may be purchased from the company. Contact Ulsterbus (Tel 0232 320011).

RAIL: There are three main rail routes from Belfast Central Station (Tel 0232 230310): north to Londonderry, via Ballymena and Coleraine; east to Bangor along the shores of Belfast Lough, and south to Dublin, via Lisburn, Portadown and Newry. The Belfast–Dublin non-stop express takes just two hours. There are six trains daily in both directions (three on Sundays). Rail Runabout tickets, valid for seven days, are available from main Northern Ireland railway stations. York Road Station is the terminal for the Larne boat train which connects with the ferries to Scotland.

CAR: Visitors from Great Britain will find that the rules of the road – speed limits, seat belt wearing, drink/driving laws, etc. – are the same as at home. The big differences you will notice is the low volume of traffic and the uncompetitive style of driving. You will also notice that some drivers have 'R' plates on their cars, meaning Restricted: when an Ulster learner-driver passes his test, he can take off his L plates but he must show R plates for the next 12 months, and keep to low speeds. This sensible rule helps to identify inexperienced drivers and lets other road users make allowances.

Important Note

Control Zones, which are usually found in town centres are indicated by yellow signs, 'Control Zone: No Unattended Parking'. An unattended car in a Control Zone is treated as a security risk and dealt with accordingly.

WALKING: Northern Ireland is an excellent region for walking.

For serious walkers who wish to explore the North Antrim area, contact Joseph McKernan (Chairman), **Ulster Rambling Federation**, 27 Market Road, Ballymena, County Antrim (Tel 0266 44685/653203). If walking in the Mournes, contact **Heart of Down Accommodation Association**, Down District Council, Strangford Road, Downpatrick, County Down. (Tel 0396 614331).

The **Youth Hostels Association of Northern Ireland** organises walking and rambling tours throughout the year. Contact the association at 56 Bradbury Place, Belfast BT7 1RU (Tel 0232 324733).

The old granite milestones that still exist throughout the six counties are marked in Irish miles. Take no notice of them if you are walking: an Irish mile, at 2240 yards (2047 m.), is 480 yards (438 m.) longer than an English mile!

Geographical Breakdown of Region
Belfast

A metropolis of some 400,000 people – almost a third of the whole population of Northern Ireland – Belfast has much in common with Liverpool and Manchester. The development of industries such as linen, rope-making, ship building and tobacco caused the city to grow at a phenomenal rate. Belfast, in its prime at the turn of the century, was more of a thriving industrial centre than a cultural city, as it remains today. The world's largest dry dock is here, and you can see the shipyard's giant cranes from the foot of the Albert Memorial Clock Tower – Belfast's equivalent of Big Ben – at the end of the High Street.

The city is currently being redeveloped and much of the centre is pedestrianised. Despite two decades of bombing, it still has many attractive Victorian and Edwardian buildings with elaborate sculptures over doors and windows. A walk around the compact city centre and a visit to the **university area** will provide a good introduction for the first-time visitor. The **City Hall** in Donegall Square dominates the main shopping area. Constructed of white Portland stone, it bears close resemblance to an American state capital building, except for the large statue of Queen Victoria in front of it. She came to the city in 1849, and was obviously held in high esteem by the citizens since a hospital, the university, a park, a man-made island and a few dozen streets were named after her.

Just under a mile (1.6 km.) away is the **Queen's University**. It is a mid-19th century building, modelled on Magdalen College, Oxford. The university area is full of attractive little Victorian terraces. The

Botanic Gardens and **Ulster Museum** are here too and well worth a visit. Try and keep a look out for Belfast's street architecture. There is a whole stone population of mythological figures perching on the ledges of shops, banks and warehouses. Some of the city's best buildings are banks, so look around if you go in to change money.

Approximately 7 miles (11 km.) east of the city centre is the **Ulster Folk Museum**. This offers one of the best opportunities to capture the essence of the heritage, life and folk art of Northern Ireland. It has been developed over the past thirty years on the **Cultra Estate** and deserves an extended visit. This is an outdoor museum, set in 180 acres (73 hectares) of farmland and totally in harmony with the surrounding countryside. The museum has a unique collection of historical buildings that were dismantled at their original locations and carefully reconstructed piece by piece in the museum park. The collection includes a village which will grow eventually into a small town, and various rural industry buildings, including a blacksmith's forge, a flax mill, a school, a row of terraced houses, a court house, rectory and a church. All the buildings are appropriately furnished to the last period detail, including chickens in the yard and peat in the fireplace. Visitors are encouraged to wander freely through the houses and guides are on hand to provide further information. Demonstrations of traditional farming methods continue on a year-round basis and you may picnic anywhere in the grounds. Contact **Ulster Folk and Transport Museum**, Cultra, (Tel 0232 428428) for further details. Open 11 a.m-6 p.m. (Sunday 2 p.m–6 p.m). In winter the museum closes at 5 p.m.

Accommodation

Belfast hotels are more expensive than you might expect, but it is possible to get better value for money if you stay just out of town.

First Class

Conway Hotel, 300 Kingsway, Dunmurry, Belfast (Tel 0232 612101). Distinctive country house hotel a few miles south-west of the city centre. Fishing and pony trekking can be arranged.

Culloden Hotel, 142 Bangor Road, Holywood (Tel 02317 5223). Seven miles (11 km.) east of Belfast. Historic property in superb setting with views across Belfast Lough.

Middle Range

Wellington Park Hotel, 21 Malone Road, Belfast (Tel 0232 38111).

Set in exclusive residential area a few minutes from the city centre. Family run property with high standard of cuisine. (First Class/Middle range.)

Beechlawn House Hotel, 4 Dunmurry Lane, Belfast (Tel 0232 612974). Attractive family run hotel in country setting.

Park Avenue Hotel, 158 Holywood Road, Belfast (Tel 0232 656271). Four miles (6 km.) east of city centre. Very pleasant area and good access to sights.

Economy

East Sheen House, 81 Eglantine Avenue, Belfast (Tel 0232 667149). Two miles (3 km.) from city centre. Seven bedrooms, family run and very comfortable.

Helga Lodge Hotel, 7 Cromwell Road, Belfast (Tel 0232 324820). Fifteen bedrooms in a family run bed and breakfast near the university. Convenient and comfortable. Look out for the paintings in the dining-room.

Queen's Elms, Queen's University, 78 Malone Road, Belfast (Tel 0232 668525). Rooms in residence halls available March–April and July–September.

The Cottage, 377 Comber Road, Dundonald (Tel 0247 878189). Attractive family cottage offering bed and breakfast seven miles (11 km.) east of city near Comber.

Eating Out

First Class

Restaurant 44, 44 Bedford Street (Tel 0232 244844).

The Carlton, 11 Wellington Place (Tel 0232 329814). Popular restaurant, traditional and dignified.

Middle Range

La Belle Epoque, 103 Great Victoria Street (Tel 0232 323244). French and Irish cuisine, game in season, fish, steak.

Skandia, 12 Callender Street (Tel 0232 245385) & 50 Howard Street (0232 320357).

Economy

Spice of Life, 82 Donegall Place (Tel 0232 332744). Vegetarian/Wholefood.

Chalet d'or, 48 Fountain Street (Tel 0232 324810). 'Ulster fry' and set lunches.

Front Page, 106 Donegall Street (Tel 0232 324924). Seafood and live traditional music.

Crown Liquor Saloon, 46 Great Victoria Street (Tel 0232 249476). Historic pub serving traditional food. National Trust-owned.

Entertainments

The best sources of information on Belfast's entertainment are the tourist office's guide *What's On*, the Arts Council's *Artslink*, and the evening newspaper, the *Belfast Telegraph*. The **Grand Opera House** (Tel 0232 324936), is the city's main venue for ballet, opera and theatre, while the **Lyric Players Theatre** (Tel 0232 660081) and the **Arts Theatre** present Irish and International plays.

Useful addresses

Tourist Office: River House, 52 High Street, Belfast (Tel 0232 246609). Information, accommodation booking service, city maps, etc. Extremely helpful staff.

Post Office: 25 Castle Place, Belfast (Tel 0232 323740).

Hospital: Royal Victoria Hospital: Grosvenor Road (Tel 0232 240503).

Transport Options

Belfast is best explored on foot and it is very easy to walk around the main sights. For a quick orientation, you can try **Belfast City Tours** by bus, with multilingual commentary on history, architecture, etc; duration 3$^{1}/_{2}$ hours. Leaves Castle Place 2 p.m Tues, Wed and Thur. (Tel 0232 246485). **Citybus** (red), and **Ulsterbus** (blue), provide efficient transportation within the city. Most Citybuses leave from and return to Donegall Square.

Bike Rental: Bike–It, 4 Belmont Road, Belfast (Tel 0232 471141). Daily and weekly rates. Deposit required.

County Antrim

Some of the most dramatic scenery to be found on the Irish coast is in the Glens of Antrim and along the Antrim Coast Road: Glenarm, Glencloy, Glenariff, Glenballyeamon, Glenann, Glencorp, Glendun, Glenshesk and Glentaisie. Each of these nine green valleys has a character of its own. This is a very rural and unspoiled area. For the most part, the people are the descendants of both the ancient Irish and their cousins the Hebridean Scots, across the sea. It is interesting to note that the glens were one of the last places in Northern Ireland where Gaelic was spoken.

Moving out from Belfast along the Antrim Coast Road and passing through **Carrickfergus** (the castle is worth a visit and there is a **Tourist Information** centre here, Tel 09603 51604) and **Larne**, the scenic road twists and turns along 50 miles (80 km.) of truly breathtaking coastline. The picturesque fishing village of **Cushendun** (population 50), famous for its Cornish-style cottages, beach and fabulous views is well worth a stop. The unusual architecture was commissioned from the famous Clough Williams-Ellis, who designed the unique Portmerion village in North Wales. If you enjoy dramatic scenery and stunning views, take the steep road to **Torr Head** and continue toward **Murlough Bay** in a beautiful inlet down a long and steep road from Crockanore. Watch out for hairpin bends and cattle blocking the narrow road down to the beach. Ample picnic facilities are provided by the National Trust. Further along is **Fairhead**, where the cliffs plunge over 600 ft (183 m.) into the sea and the rocks below. Birds of prey frequent these heights, and on a clear day it is possible to see Donegal and Scotland from here. The scree of great rocks at the foot of the cliffs is home to a herd of wild goats. Other attractions in the area include **Glenariff Forest Park**, for spectacular glen walks, waterfalls, mountain trails and views. There is a visitor centre within the restaurant.

A 50-minute boat trip from the holiday resort town of Ballycastle is **Rathlin Island**. This unspoiled island (population 100) has a large bird sanctuary, popular with ornithologists. Robert the Bruce hid in a cave on the island in 1306 after his defeat by the English at Perth. Look out for the Neolithic axe factory. There are daily crossings from Ballycastle (Easter–Sept) and a mailboat leaves all year round at about 10.30 a.m on Mon, Wed and Fri (Tel 02657 62024).

Accommodation

Economy

The Bay Hotel, Cushendun (Tel 026674 267). Lovely little family hotel in National Trust village.

Rathlin Guesthouse, The Quay, Rathlin Island (Tel 02657 63917). Offers B&B or just a home-cooked meal.

Eating Out

Middle Range

Dieskirt, 104 Glen Road, Martinstown, Nr Glenariff (Tel 026673 71308). À la carte in converted farmhouse.

Economy

National Trust Tea-Room, Cushendun (Tel 026674 266).

Beyond Ballycastle is **Whitepark Bay**, a National Trust protected area, popular with swimmers and naturalists. A walk along the beach to the west end of the bay will bring you to St Gobhan's church, the smallest church in Ireland, measuring only 11ft × 6ft (3.4 m. × 1.8 m.). Just 2½ miles (4 km.) east of Whitepark Bay along the cliff path – which is part of the Ulster Way – is the Carrick-a-rede rope bridge (National Trust), connecting the mainland to a small rocky island, famous for its 350-year-old salmon fishery. The plank and rope bridge (with two handrails but no safety netting), swings 80 feet (24 metres) above the sea and spans a 60 feet (18 metres) wide chasm. The bridge is open only during the fishing season (May–Sept), and the warning sign makes it quite clear that you cross the suspended structure at your own risk!

A few miles on is **Port Ballintoy**, a tiny fishing cove with dramatic volcanic rock formations that you might perhaps expect to find in Iceland. For £1, the local fishing boats will take you out to view the rope bridge from another perspective. The trip takes about thirty minutes and is well worth the effort.

Five miles (8 km.) west, the lunar landscape of the **Giant's Causeway** is now classified by UNESCO as a World Heritage Site. The Causeway is a mass of basalt columns packed tightly together, forming stepping stones from the cliff foot and disappearing under the sea. There are over 40,000 of these hexagonal stone columns. The formation is a geological freak resulting from volcanic action, and a spectacular sight. A splendid circular walk from the National Trust information centre will take you through the Causeway and some superb scenery. The cliff paths are well tended, but children should be supervised at all times. Before leaving the area, make a point of visiting the Giant's Causeway Centre. A permanent exhibition (including film) on the history, geology, flora and fauna of the Causeway is on show. There is also a **Tourist Information** office here (Tel 02657 31855).

Portballintrae is another tiny port well worth exploring. From here a team of Belgian divers brought up the greatest Spanish Armada treasure ever recovered. The gold and silver jewellery is on show at the Ulster Museum, Belfast.

The romantic ruin of **Dunluce Castle** is worth visiting. Perched on the edge of an isolated rocky crag, it offers spectacular views. It was the main fort of the Irish MacDonnells, chiefs of Antrim, and fell into ruin after the kitchen fell into the sea during a storm. Guided tours are available and the sea caves can be visited by boat in calm weather. Nearby is **Bushmills Distillery**, the oldest legal whisky distillery in the world (charter 1608). There is a Visitor Centre and inspection tours can be arranged.

A few miles along the coast is **Portrush**. This popular resort has the usual seaside attractions. Although the town has a beautiful position, it is now a shadow of its own past. Run-down hotels and boarding houses; endless amusement arcades and souvenir shops. Avoid it if you can.

A better choice is to stop in **Portstewart** (County Derry), three miles (5 km.) further on at the western end of the Causeway Coast. Although the resort is surrounded by golf courses and caravan sites, it is quite attractive. The whole town forms an Atlantic promenade leading to a beach of two miles (3 km.) where cars are permitted to park on the firm sand. Portstewart claims to have the best surfing in Northern Ireland. Judging by the number of people who go there with boards, it is probably true.

Accommodation

Middle Range

Causeway Hotel, 40 Causeway Road, Giant's Causeway (Tel 02657 312226). Fine country setting for this family run hotel. À la carte restaurant and carvery.

Bushmills Inn, Main Street, Bushmills (Tel 02657 32339). Eleven-bedroom character inn in famous distillery town. Good food in small bistro.

Economy

White Gables, 83 Dunluce Road, Portballintrae (Tel 02657 31611). Country house, home cooking, coastal location and bed and breakfast.

Loguestown Farm, 59 Magherboy Road, Nr. Portrush (Tel 0265 822742). Non-smoking family farm. Huge breakfasts.

Maddybenny Farm, 18 Maddeybenny Park, Loguestown Road, Nr. Portrush (Tel 0265 823394). Four-bedroom family farmhouse, non-smoking.

Eating Out

Middle Range

Hillcrest House, 306 Whitepark Road, Giant's Causeway (Tel 02657 312226). Quality traditional food.

Economy

National Trust Tea-Room, Causeway Centre (Tel 02657 31582). Soup, snacks, home baking.

Ballintrae Inn, Portballintrae (Tel 02657 31483). Good food at reasonable prices.

Stairway, 25 Main Street, Portrush (Tel 0265 822348). Set lunch, home baked cakes.

Useful addresses

Tourist Information Offices: 7 Mary Street, Ballycastle (Tel 02657 62024); Town Hall, Carrickfergus (Tel 09603 51604); 1 Main Street, Cushendun, (Tel 026674 506); Giant's Causeway, (Tel 02657 31855); Town Hall, Portrush, (Tel 0265 823333).

Transport Options

The Bushmills Bus. An open topped bus travels the scenic route between Coleraine and Bushmills stopping at Portstewart, Portrush and the Causeway. Details from Ulsterbus (Tel 0265 43334). Public transportation can be erratic. A car or bike is best. Ulsterbus do offer special trips to the area but these are usually limited to day or half-day tours. **Northern Ireland Railways** operate a service to Portrush.

County Armagh

This has been the spiritual capital of Ireland for 1500 years and the seat of both Protestant and Roman Catholic archbishops. It is a quite delightful rural county on the southern shores of Lough Neagh.

Armagh (population 12,500) is an elegant small city best explored on foot. Many of the public buildings and Georgian townhouses are the work of Francis Johnston, a native of the city, who also left his mark on much of Georgian Dublin. Quite a number of these buildings are built from local limestone, which gives the city an attractive warm glow even on the dullest day. Take a stroll along the Mall (once the city's racecourse), a very pleasant promenade where cricket is played during summer. Look out for the **Armagh County Museum**. Based in an old schoolhouse, the museum has an art gallery, library and interesting folk collection.

The **Anglican Cathedral of St Patrick** is one of the most visible sights in the city. In AD 447 St Patrick ordained that his church should have pre-eminence over all others and since then approximately seventeen churches have occupied the site. The **Cathedral Library** (1771) was the first public library outside Dublin. It houses a copy of *Gulliver's Travels* with annotations by Swift. The **Roman Catholic Cathedral** on the opposite hill is also dedicated to St Patrick. The building was completed in 1873. Much of the funding to complete the cathedral was raised from collections, donations and raffles. The cathedral still contains a grandfather clock dating from 1865 – a raffle prize that was never collected by the winner.

Other places of interest within the city include the **Planetarium** (weather station, museum and star shows), and **Armagh Friary**, founded in 1263 in the grounds of the archbishop's palace. **Tourist Information** is at 40 English Street (Tel 0861 527808).

Six miles (9 km.) south-east of the city is **Gosford Forest Park**. The park surrounds a large mock Norman castle. Jonathan Swift spent many months here and several of the nature walks were designed by him. In addition to the walks there is an aboretum, a walled garden and camping facilities.

Accommodation

Middle Range

Drumsill House Hotel, 35 Moy Road, Armagh (Tel 0861 522009). Ten beds. Country hotel in rural setting. Specialises in fish dishes.

Economy

Clonhugh House, College Hill, Armagh (Tel 0861 522693). Five beds. Family run, B&B.

Altavallen House, 99 Cathedral Road, Armagh (Tel 0861 522387). Six bedrooms. Attractive family run B&B.

Eating Out

Middle Range

Swallows, 17 Lower English Street, Armagh (Tel 0861 524956). Good traditional food.

Banisters, 147 Railway Street, Armagh (Tel 0861 522103). Steak, grills.

Economy

Loudan's Cellars, 49 English Street, Armagh (Tel 0861 525873). Open sandwiches, quiche, salads.

Lurgan (population 20,000) is a small town that owes much to linen-damask weaving and textile manufacture. Many of the old weavers' cottages have extended front parlours built to accommodate the looms. **Portadown** (population 21,000) also developed with the linen industry. Today it weaves carpets, and produces industrial ceramics and jam.

If possible, do not miss the **Oxford Island Nature Reserve** and **Kinnego Marina** on Lough Neagh. The shores and little islands in this area have extensive bird populations, including herons and nesting grebe. Oxford Island is in reality a peninsula that was created in 1846 when the lough level was lowered. The nature reserve is extremely well planned and tours leave from the information centre. Boats may be hired if you wish to explore the inlets, and hides are provided for the serious birdwatcher.

The area north-east of Armagh is apple-growing country. In the 17th century, settlers from Worcester planted the orchards and the region has a striking resemblance to the Vale of Evesham. There are two National Trust properties worth visiting. **The Argory**, a neo-Classical house set on the Blackwater river, has a lovely lived-in feeling. A fully operational gas plant located in the yard supplies both heat and light. Look out for the rare-breed cattle on the estate. Less than three miles (5 km.) away is **Ardress House**. Originally a 17th-century farm house, it has been cleverly extended and enlarged. At the rear of the house is a functional 18th-century farm yard complete with a smithy, chicken houses and piggery. Both properties can be comfortably seen in an afternoon.

Accommodation

Economy

Cedarbrook Farm, 84 Brackagh Road, Portadown (Tel 0762 840347). Three beds. Well positioned family run farmhouse. B&B.

Oak Cottage, 23 Springhill Road, Magheralin (Tel 0762 322865). Two bedrooms. Attractive cottage in country setting. B&B.

Eating Out

Middle Range

Waterside House, Oxford Island (Tel 0762 327573). Lough Neagh trout and seafood. Excellent food. Advance booking essential.

Economy

Huntsman, 65 Market Street, Tandragee (Tel 0762 841115). À la carte restaurant. Quality food.

Gallery Tea Shop, 16 Church Street, Portadown (Tel 0762 331796). Lunches, teas and dietary meals.

The Pie Man, 74 Woodhouse Street, Portadown (Tel 0762 330743). Vegetarian, preservative and additive-free food.

Useful addresses

Tourist & Information Centre: 40 English Street, Armagh (Tel 0861 527808).

County Down

This is an attractive and extremely varied county that provides numerous opportunities for interesting and worthwhile visits to beauty spots and ecological sites.

The Ards Peninsula

Ten miles (16 km.) south-east of Belfast will bring you to the Ards Peninsula and Strangford Lough. The lough is a great bird sanctuary and wildlife reserve. Large flocks of brent geese winter here, along with migratory birds such as golden plovers, godwits and red-shanks. The Ards Peninsula is 25 miles (40 km.) of low, gently undulating sandy land that separates the lough from the Irish Sea. Much of the coastline is protected by local conservation groups and the National Trust. The whole area is exceptionally beautiful and should be explored at a leisurely pace.

Around the shores of the lough are many interesting and historic places. Four miles (6 km.) east of Newtownards is **Mount Stewart,** the childhood home of Lord Castlereagh, Foreign Secretary of England during the Napoleonic wars. The gardens, rather than the house, are the main attraction here. Created by the 7th Marchioness of Londonderry, an avid traveller and collector of exotic plants, they contain many unique species not found elsewhere. The influence of the Gulf Stream has helped create a micro-climate which has resulted in spectacular growth. The estate has delightful pools and terraces, topiary art, stone griffens, dodos, duck-billed platypi and a lake. It is a truly magical place, under the care of the National Trust.

The ruins of **Greyabbey** are two miles (3 km.) further along the lough road. Founded in 1193 by the Normans, who imported monks from England in an attempt to Anglicise the Irish church, the gardens here are also worth a visit.

There is much bird and wildlife to observe in and around the lough. **Castle Espie** (near Comber) has a large collection of ducks, geese and swans. Viewing from the hides and refuges can be easily arranged. The **Quoile Centre,** next to the old castle on the south side of the lough, offers guided walks of the conservation area. This 450 acre (182 hectare) national nature reserve was once a saltwater basin. It is now freshwater, rich in plant life and a haven for wild birds. There is good rudd fishing in the river, plenty of picnic places and marked walks.

The sea coast of the peninsula is almost one continuous beach from Donaghadee to Kearney Point. Some of the little seaside towns have seen better days, but there is still plenty for the visitor to see and do. **Holywood, Crawfordsburn** and **Helen's Bay** are all good coastal walking areas. The beach at Helen's Bay is part of the **Crawfordsburn Country Park,** which also has a Visitors Centre, slide show and cafe. Popular seaside towns include **Bangor, Groomsport** and **Donaghadee.** Look out for the **Ballycopeland windmill** near Millisle. This is the only working windmill left in the whole of Ireland. Try to visit the picturesque 19th-century fishing village at **Kearny** (National Trust).

Portaferry (population 21,000) is situated on the entrance to Strangford Lough. The town is a centre for sailing and sea angling. The Queen's University of Belfast has had a marine biology station here for the last 40 years.

Accommodation

First Class

The Old Inn, 15 Main Street, Crawfordsburn (Tel 0247 853255). Thirty-two bedrooms. One of Ulster's most historic inns. Pretty village location. Good food.

Middle Range

Portaferry Hotel, 10 The Strand, Portaferry (Tel 02477 28231). Five bedrooms. Popular family run hotel. Seafood a speciality.

Economy

Ballycastle House, 20 Mountstewart Road, Near Newtownards (Tel 024774 357). Four bedrooms. Family run bed and breakfast in beautiful setting on Strangford Lough.

Bridge House, 93 Windmill Road, Donaghadee (Tel 0247 883348). Two bedrooms in a bed and breakfast country house in a delightful area.

Eating Out

First Class

The Old Inn (see *Accommodation*) Superb cuisine. Eighteenth-century minstrels gallery. Atmospheric pub serves good value, less expensive meals.

Schooner, 30 High Street, Holywood (Tel 0232 428880). Sesame prawn fingers, apple and stilton flan, nutty duckling, orange and hazelnut cottage cheese. Wonderful food.

Middle Range

Portaferry Hotel (see *Accommodation*) Stuffed mussels, fried oysters, turbot.

Red Pepper, 28 Main Street, Groomsport (Tel 0266 270097). Excellent food ranging from rack of lamb to cheese fondue.

Economy

Humble Pie, 28 Dufferin Avenue, Bangor (Tel 0247 466572). Home baking and savoury food.

Wildfowler, 1 Main Street, Greyabbey (Tel 024774 260). Good range of meals. Lunch, high tea and à la carte.

Across Strangford Lough from Portaferry lies **Castle Ward**. Take the car ferry across (only ten minutes), and continue just a mile (1.6 km.) beyond the small town of Strangford. Built by the first Lord Bangor in 1765, the house has two opposing façades. He favoured the classical style, while his wife preferred 'Strawberry Hill' Gothic. As you will see, they both got their way. The stable yard contains a Victorian laundry and a converted barn, which is used for musical events and theatrical productions. There are lovely walks to the lough shore from here. On the way, make a point of viewing the sunken garden, classical temple, lake and wildfowl collection (National Trust).

St Patrick's Country and the Mournes

Eight miles (13 km.) west of Strangford is **Downpatrick**, the county capital. If you look in the churchyard of **Down Cathedral**, you will find the stone marking the place where St Patrick is believed to have been buried. The Cathedral closes at 6 p.m. every day. For guided tours, contact the Rev Kingston (Tel 0396 841311). The Old County Down Gaol is now the headquarters for the new **Down Museum** and the **St Patrick Heritage Centre**. Beyond the town lies rich agricultural country, with many historical and cultural associations. The best view is from **Slieve Patrick**. From here you can see the surrounding countryside and the lough. Look out for the healing wells (reputed to cure eye ailments), and bath houses in Struell Wells, 1¹/2 miles (2.5 km.) east of Downpatrick. Further south, on the slopes of Cratlieve mountain, stands **Legananny Dolmen**, one of Ireland's finest neolithic tombs, while just south of Dromore, is the cottage where Patrick Brontë, father of the famous novelist sisters, was born.

Accommodation

Middle Range

Abbey Lodge Hotel, Belfast Road, Downpatrick (Tel 0396 614511). Attractive family run hotel. Excellent local cuisine.

Economy

Havine Farm, 51 Ballydonnell Road (Tel 039685 242). Pleasantly situated farmhouse. Tea & dinner.

Eating Out

Middle Range

Lobster Pot, 11 The Square, Strangford (Tel 039686 288). Lobster, clams, fresh salmon. Book in advance.

Economy

Countryside Inn & Restaurant, Saul (Tel 0396 615750). Traditional food.

Oakley Fayre, Market Street, Downpatrick (Tel 0396 612500). Simple good value cooking and baking.

The Mourne Mountains

Tucked away in the south-east corner of the county, and covering an area 15 miles (24 km.) long and 8 miles (12 km.) wide, are the Mourne Mountains. The resort of **Newcastle** – 1991 UK winner of the environmental 'Tourism for Tomorrow' award – is the best place from which to explore the region. This clean, attractive town, in a dramatic setting at the foot of Slieve Donard, has benefited from recent government investment in its tourism facilities. **The Mourne Countryside Centre** serves as a conservation office and a centre for hikers, ramblers and walkers. For campers and caravanners, **Tollymore Forest Park** is 2 miles (3 km.) down the road and has excellent facilities, including a resident mountain rescue team. The park has over 1432 acres (580 hectares) of marked walks and gardens. Newcastle **Tourist Information** is at the Central Promenade (Tel 03967 22222).

A worthwhile excursion is to the **Silent Valley** in the centre of the Mournes. The two huge artificial lakes that supply Belfast's water are surrounded by a drystone wall over 6 feet (1.8 metres) high and 22 miles (35 km.) long. The Mourne Wall Walk each June attracts walkers from all over the world. The scenery here is glorious and the Department of the Environment has opened a visitor centre, a small restaurant and provided a regular shuttle bus up the mountain to see the dam.

Castlewellan Forest Park is approximately 4 miles (6 km.) from Newcastle. The park began life as an aboretum in 1740. Inside, a castle overlooks a lake surrounded by Castlewellan gold conifers. This is a quite outstanding park with spectacular gardens, wooded areas and miles of marked walks. Trout fishing is permitted in the lake and pony trekking is available from the stables. Like Tollymore Forest, it is a popular area with ramblers and walkers. There are full facilities for camping and caravans.

For something completely different, try and visit the pretty fishing village of **Annalong** and head for the marine park and harbour. Here you can see the 1830 working cornmill and the mills and milling exhibition. **Rostrevor** is the most sheltered place in Northern Ireland, with Mediterranean plants growing by the seashore in the lee of the Mourne Mountains. There are good walks and views in Rostrevor Forest.

Also worth a visit is **Greencastle**, a ruined fortress with views across Carlingford Lough; **Dundrum Castle** with a lovely panorama across the bay; and **Rowallane Gardens** in Saintfield, noted for azaleas, rhododendrons and herbaceous plants (National Trust).

Accommodation

First Class

Slieve Donard Hotel, Downs Road, Newcastle (Tel 03967 23681). An established character hotel (120 bedrooms) set on broad sweep of Newcastle bay.

Middle Range

Brook Cottage Hotel, 58 Bryansford Road (Tel 03967 23681). Nine bedrooms in a lovely family hotel. Attractive gardens.

Chestnut Inn, 28 Lower Square, Castlewellan (Tel 03967 78247). Seven bedrooms. Family run, excellent food.

Economy

Mayburn Lodge, 10 Ballyhafry Road, Newcastle (Tel 03967 24201). Three bedrooms in a good location near Tollymore forest. Family run bed and breakfast.

Eating Out

Middle Range

Brook Cottage Hotel (see above). Traditional food.
Fisherman Restaurant, Benmore House, Kilkeel Road, Newcastle (Tel 03967 68733). Local prawns, lobster, salmon, clams, turbot.

Economy

Chestnut Inn (see above). Good value traditional food.
Mario's, 65 South Promenade, Newcastle. Simple Italian cooking.

County Fermanagh

Beautiful lakes and rolling forest land are typical of this area. As a border county with the Irish Republic, Fermanagh is frequently in the news, but away from the trouble spots it is surprisingly quiet and peaceful. Upper and lower Lough Erne form a lake district that is several times larger – and much less trampled – than England's.

Stretching 50 miles (80 km.) from end to end, **Lough Erne** is divided in the middle by the county town of Enniskillen. The lakeside is high and rocky and, in addition to the 154 islands, there are dozens of coves and inlets to explore. Lower Lough Erne is 5 miles (8 km.) wide in places, and in windy weather has waves of open-sea proportions. Upper Lough Erne is a shallow maze of islands and a chart is almost a necessity to find your way out. The majority of visitors (many from Germany) come to this area for the sailing. Hire craft ranging from canoes to cabin cruisers are available and well-equipped. There are plenty of public marinas and jettys with lakeside shops to stock up on provisions.

If you want to fish, you will require a permit which may be purchased locally. For non-sailors, **Erne Tours**, 16 Meadow Lane, Enniskillen (Tel 0365 25783), offer 2–3 hour boat tours. The tours stop at **Devinish Island** where St Molaise's ancient monastery and Ireland's best-preserved round tower stand.

Other islands on the Lower Lough worth a visit for their Celtic and early Christian antiquities are **Galloon**, **Boa Island**, **Inishmacsaint**, **White Island** and **Lustybeg**. The latter has a bird sanctuary and a small private ferry to take visitors across. Most of the islands on the Upper Lough are uninhabited and are visited for their natural beauty.

Keen birdwatchers should make a point of visiting the **Castle Caldwell Estate** (Lower Lough). Although the castle is now a ruin, the estate is an excellent nature reserve with first-rate facilities. This is the main breeding site in the British Isles of the common scoter, a species of duck. There are plenty of marked nature trails and hides.

Accommodation

Middle Range

Jamestown House, Magheracross (Tel 0365 81209). Historic country house (*c.* 1760). Excellent accommodation and good food.

Lough Erne Hotel, Kesh (Tel 0365 631275). Sixteen bedrooms. Family run small hotel.

Economy

Teach a Ceili, Inniscorkish Island (Tel 03657 21360). Two bedrooms. Lovely little family house. Island location. B&B.

Eating Out

Middle Range

Lakeview Farmhouse, Drumcrow, Blaney (Tel 03654 263). Home cooking in country house. Advance booking essential.

Lough Erne House, Blaney (Tel 0365 216). Quality food. Traditional. Advance booking.

Economy

Hunting Lodge, Lusty Beg, Boa Island (Tel 03656 31342). Traditional home cooking. Good value.

Enniskillen (population 10,500) is built on an island between Upper and Lower Lough Erne. The **Lakeland Visitor Centre** on Shore Road can provide specific information on the area and book accommodation free of charge. The **Fermanagh County Museum** is somewhat disappointing. Look instead for the **Royal School**, once attended by Oscar Wilde and Samuel Beckett. For panoramic views of the lake, head for Forthill Park.

One mile (1.6 km.) south of Enniskillen is **Castle Coole**, an 18th-century neo-classical plantation mansion, renovated and reopened in 1988. The garden overlooks a lake where a colony of greylag geese have lived since 1700 (National Trust). Another Trust property worth visiting is **Florence Court**. Set in a Forest Park, the house has a dramatic position surrounded by mountains. Look out for the walled garden and extensive nature walks. Just past Florence Court are the **Marble Arch underground caves**. As a result of extensive engineering work, the caves are now open to the public. In addition to the stalagmites, there are underground lakes, and the highlight for visitors is a boat trip across the lower lake.

Belleek, directly on the border, is famous for its distinctive lattice-style pottery and china which is exported all over the world. Factory tours can be arranged from the Beleek Pottery and Visitor Centre. Nearby is **Lough Navar Forest Park**. The viewpoint here offers spectacular views of the Lough. Also worth visiting is **Castle Archdale Country Park**. It has an extensive wildlife reserve, a Youth Hostel, camping and caravanning facilities and a small marina with regular ferry crossings to White Island.

Serious walkers should consider tackling the Fermanagh section of the Ulster Way. With over 23 miles (37 km.) of mostly forested paths climbing to 1000 feet (305 m.), it offers some good views of the county.

Accommodation

Economy

Tullyhona House, Marble Arch Road, Florencecourt (Tel 0365 82452). Seven bedrooms. Country house in rural but convenient location. Family run. B&B.

The Crest, Rossa (Tel 0365 82317). Three bedrooms. Country house. Home cooking. B&B.

Eating Out

Middle Range

The Horseshoe, Belmore Street, Enniskillen (Tel 0365 26223). Bistro style. Wide range of food.

Economy

Blake's of the Hollow, 6 Church Street, Enniskillen (Tel 0365 22143). Good value meals in Victorian atmosphere.

Florence Court House, in the grounds of the National Trust property, Florence Court (see previous page), south-west of Enniskillen via A4 and A32 Swanlinbar road. (036582 249). Traditional home cooked meals.

Useful addresses

Tourist Information: Lakeland Visitor Centre, Shore Road, Enniskillen (Tel 0365 23110/25050).

Hire cruiser companies: Aghinver Boat Company, Lisnarick (Tel 03656 31400); Lakeland Marina, Kesh (Tel 03656 31414); Lochside Cruisers, Enniskillen (Tel 0365 24368). For Lough Erne cruises contact MV *Kestral*, Enniskillen (Tel 0365 22882).

Transport options

You can hire **bicycles** from Connor Folley, 146 Windmill Heights, Enniskillen (Tel 0365 27583).

County Londonderry

The county capital, with a population of 65,000, is the province's second largest city. Set on a hill on the banks of the Foyle estuary, the city came under siege and attack for over 1000 years. St Columb founded the first monastery here in AD 546, and Derry (the full name Londonderry is not widely used), has seen more than its fair share of strife and trouble. James II held a siege on the city for 105 days in 1689, and twenty years of modern-day terrorism has left its scars on both the city and its people. Unemployment here is reckoned to be the worst in western Europe, but despite this, the area holds many pleasant surprises.

The layout of **Derry city** preserves its medieval plan with the four main streets leading out from the Diamond, or square, to the four old gateways – Bishop's Gate, Butcher's Gate, Ferryquay Gate and Shipquay Gate. Three more gates were opened into the walls later. The **city walls** are a striking feature. Completed in 1618, they are still intact, complete with cannon pointing over the ramparts. It is possible to make a circuit along the top of the walls, except for the security look-out perched on top of Bishop's Gate. The views of the surrounding countryside are quite magnificent and it is well worth the effort. The **Guildhall** is a convenient place for gaining access to the walls and you should make a point of going inside to view the dozens of stained glass windows which portray the city's history. The building was badly bombed in 1972 and a major restoration project was undertaken to restore the glass (completed in 1984).

Within the walls are some very historic buildings in varying states of repair. Look out for the **Irish Society House**, the **Courthouse** and **St Columb's Cathedral**, built in 1633. The main thoroughfare, Shipquay Street, is exceptionally steep, with many narrow streets running off it. The **Chapterhouse** contains the ancient locks and keys of the city gates. Traditional Irish music is an important feature of life here and No. 71 Carslile Road has a large range of quality hand-made Irish fiddles. The **Tourist Office** on Doyle Street (Tel 0504 267284) will provide details of the different venues where you can hear Irish music played.

Accommodation

Middle Range

The White Horse Inn, 68 Clooney Road, Derry (Tel 0504 860606). Forty-four bedrooms. Large country hotel in rural setting. B&B.

Economy

Killarney Cottage, 12 Limavady Road, Derry (Tel 0504 45855). Four bedrooms. Character cottage. Good home cooking. B&B.

Elagh Hall, Buncrana Road, Derry (Tel 0504 263116). Three bedrooms. Family run country house. B&B.

Cherry Tree Cottage, 49 Kilnappy Road, Derry (Tel 0504 860325). Two bedrooms. Attractive family home. B&B.

Eating Out

Middle Range

Bells, 59 Victoria Road, Derry (Tel 0504 41078). Grills and traditional roasts.

White Horse Inn (see Accommodation). Grilled seafood dishes.

Economy

Browns, 1 Victoria Road, Derry (Tel 0504 45180). Rack of ribs, Caesar salad, vegetarian dishes.

Dorrian's Buttery, 12a Shipquay Street, Derry (Tel 0504 264286). Chilli, lasagne, daily specials.

For an unusual visit, try the **Amelia Earhart Centre** at Ballyarnet Field (3 miles [5 km.] north of Derry), a cottage exhibition commemorating the first transatlantic flight by a woman in 1932.

Limavady (population 8000) is a very pleasant market town on the river Roe. Continue a mile (1.6 km.) south to the **Roe Valley Country Park**. This is an interesting and unusual attraction which contains a vast collection of restored industrial heritage buildings, which include water mills, a hydroelectric plant, tannery, beetling mill and a weaving shed. The park is popular for game fishing, canoeing and camping.

Springhill House near Moneymore is a 17th-century property with 18th-and 19th-century additions, which has been the home of an Ayrshire family for ten generations. There are extensive outbuildings housing a costume collection, walled gardens and woodland walks (National Trust).

Also worth visiting is the small linen museum at **Upperlands**, north-east of Draperstown, with its collection of original weaving machinery.

North of Limavady is the scenic **Bishop's Road**. The road was built by the Earl Bishop giving access to Limavady from his palace situated at Downhill. Stop at **Bishop's View** for one of the most visually stunning panoramas in Ireland. From here you can see across the plain to Magilligan Point, where a curious tower sits perched on a cliff edge. A fabulous seven-mile (11 km.) stretch of golden sandy beach at the cliff foot is popular with tourists and day-trippers. Nearby is **Bellarena** with its fish smokery and home of the Ulster Gliding Club. **Downhill Palace** was destroyed by fire in 1851 and only a shell remains today, but the **Mussenden Temple** (National Trust), a domed rotunda used by the bishop as a library, is maintained in perfect order. The views here are quite breathtaking and there are miles of marked walks along the cliffs and surrounding countryside.

Coleraine (population 16,000) is a quiet market town situated on the river Bann. Although there is an active university campus, the town is unexceptional. The main attraction is the extensive fishing available on the river Bann.

Accommodation

Middle Range

The Golf Hotel, 17 Main Street, Castlerock (Nr. Downhill) (Tel 0265 848204). Sixteen bedrooms. Pleasant resort hotel. Excellent location.

Blackheath House, 112 Killeague Road, Blackhill (Tel 0265 868433). Six bedrooms. Eighteenth-century rectory run with the aims of promoting the best of Ulster food and hospitality. Beautiful setting.

Economy

Carnmeety House, 120 Mussenden Road, Castlerock (Tel 0265 848640). Three bedrooms. Country house, home cooking.

Eating Out

Middle Range

MacDuff's, Blackheath House, 112 Killeague Road, Blackhill (Tel 0265 868433). Game in season, local country produce. Very high standard.

Ballymaclary House, 573 Seacost Road, Magillian (Tel 05047 50283). Fresh seafood and steaks. Eighteenth-century house.

Useful addresses

Tourist Information: Swimming Pool, Castlerock (Tel 0265 848258).

Council Offices: 7 Connell Street, Limavady (Tel 05047 62226); Foyle Street, Derry (Tel 0504 267284).

County Tyrone

The Sperrin Mountains are bounded by the towns of Strabane, Dungiven, Magherafelt and Newtownstewart. This is splendid walking country frequented by red grouse, golden plover and sheep. Sawel – at 2240 feet (683 m.) the highest mountain in the range – is in the centre of the province and very accessible.

Dungannon (population 8000) is a busy market town where the main interest is the **Tyrone Crystal factory** which is open all year round. The crystal is made by traditional methods (mouth-blown and hand-cut) and exported worldwide. **Parkanour**, to the west of Dungannon, is a picturesque forest park with an arboretum and a herd of white deer.

An interesting sight is the 10th-century cross at **Ardboe**. Standing over 18 feet (5.5 metres) tall it has 22 carved stone panels. The small farms around Ardboe are mostly owned by eel fishermen. Eels are a major income earner for this area, generating several million pounds a year.

West of **Cookstown**, past Drum Manor Forest Park, is the **Wellbrook Beetling Mill**. Beetling is the final process in linen manufacture. The cloth is pounded with heavy wooden hammers or beetled to give it an even finish and a sheen. The mill has been fully restored by the National Trust and there is an exhibition on linen-making.

Try to see the prehistoric stone circles at **Beaghmore**. This is a striking sight: seven stone circles and an assortment of cairns all dating from the Bronze Age. The stones were discovered in the 1930s by local turf cutters and many more sets of circles have been discovered throughout the Sperrins, including Moneymore, near Lough Bracken.

Tyrone has many historical connections with North America. You can discover more at the **Ulster-American Folk Park** at Camphill, Omagh. First opened in 1976 and attracting over 70,000 visitors a year, the park has been developed around the Mellon family, who were responsible for the building of Pittsburgh, the Waldorf Hotel and the Golden Gate Bridge. Like the Ulster Folk Museum near Belfast, the park is open-air with traditional cottages and farm buildings, log houses, craft demonstrations and audio-visual presentations. There is also a re-creation of conditions on an emigrant voyage to the New World at the ship and dockside gallery. Before leaving the Omagh area, try and visit the **Gortin Glen Forest Park**. A historical park is in the process of being developed at the site.

Baronscourt, set in a landscaped park with three lakes and Italian-style gardens, is a worthwhile visit. Although the estate is in private hands, there is a visitor centre, cafe and craft shop.

Sion Mills (population 1800) is a mixture of brick, black and white timbered buildings and millworkers' cottages. The village was designed for the manufacture of linen and the old factory is still in working order. **Tourist Information** is at Melmount Road (Tel 06626 58027). Nearby is the border town of **Strabane** (population 10,500), an important printing and publishing centre in the 18th-century. Look out for Gray's Printing Shop in the Main Street (National Trust). **Tourist Information** is at Abercorn Square (Tel 0504 883735).

Accommodation

First Class

Bessingbourne, Fivemiletown (Tel 03655 21221). Beautiful Victorian Gothic Mansion on a lake. Original fixtures and fittings including four-poster beds. Excellent food and good location for exploring the county.

Middle Range

Grange Lodge, Grange Road, Dungannon (Tel 08687 84212). Gracious Georgian residence. Elegant decor and superb local cuisine.

Economy

Parkside Country House, 140 Blackisland Road, Annaghmore (Tel 0762 852250). Family run house offering bed and breakfast in a country setting.

Knock-na-Moe Castle, 59 Old Mountfield Road, Nr. Omagh (Tel 0662 3131). Eleven bedrooms in a family run castle. Good food.

Eating Out

First Class

Grange Lodge (see above). Roast duckling in plum sauce, brandy snap baskets. Advance booking.

Middle Range

Lough Neagh Lodge, Annaghmore (Tel 0762 851901). Traditional home cooking. À la carte.

Cohannon Inn, Tamnamore (Tel 08687 24488). Grills, potted eel, sole. À la carte.

Economy

Knock-na-Moe Castle (See above). Good food in historic setting.

Useful addresses

Tourist Information: 48 Molesworth Street, Cookstown (Tel 06487 66727); **The Library**, Main Street, Fivemiletown (Tel 03655 21409); Main Street, Newtownstewart (Tel 06626 61560); Melmount Road, Sion Mills (Tel 06626 58027); **Sperrin Heritage Centre**, 274 Glenally Road, Cranagh, (Tel 06626 41842); Abercorn Square, Strabane (Tel 0504 883735).

Also by Katie Wood and available in Mandarin

The Good Tourist in France

The number one destination for British holidaymakers, France is a country of extraordinary diversity. And as most people make their own way to France rather than taking a package, a good guidebook is an essential companion.

Following the success of *The Good Tourist* (which Jonathon Porritt called 'the definitive guide to the art of seeing the world without destroying it'), *The Good Tourist in France* is packed with completely new information and ideas to help you really enjoy France – without damaging it. By applying simple green principles you can radically reduce the impact that you, as a tourist, have on the places you visit.

We've asked the people who *really* know – the locals – for their inside information on holidaying in the UK:
- Where to go and where to avoid
- Ways to experience the local lifestyle
- Where to eat and stay in the best locally owned restaurants and hotels

Here is absolutely everything you need to be a 'good tourist', from Katie Wood, bestselling author and leading travel journalist, and Syd House, an experienced conservationist.

The Good Tourist

KATIE WOOD & SYD HOUSE

The environmental and social impact of tourism, the world's largest industry, is increasingly hard to ignore: the concrete Costas, the eroding Alps, crumbling Sphinx and cordoned-off Lake District all bear testament to the damage we do as holiday-makers.

Yet there are many ways to see and experience the world in a less intrusive way. The second edition of Katie Wood and Syd House's definitive guide to being a 'good tourist' explores and analyses the impact of tourism and is packed with practical and imaginative ideas for holidays to enjoy – without damaging the environment.

'A must for both the seasoned and fledgling traveller . . . I strongly recommend it'
Dick Sisman, The Countryside Commission, & President, Green Flag International

'A timely handbook for the sensitive tourist'
Magnus Magnusson

'An excellent guide'
Royal Geographical Society

A Selected List of Non-Fiction Available from Mandarin

While every effort is made to keep prices low, it is sometimes necessary to increase prices at short notice. Mandarin Paperbacks reserves the right to show new retail prices on covers which may differ from those previously advertised in the text or elsewhere.

The prices shown below were correct at the time of going to press.

☐	7493 0109 0	**The Warrior Queens**	Antonia Fraser £4.99
☐	7493 0108 2	**Mary Queen of Scots**	Antonia Fraser £5.99
☐	7493 0010 8	**Cromwell**	Antonia Fraser £7.50
☐	7493 0106 6	**The Weaker Vessel**	Antonia Fraser £5.99
☐	7493 0014 0	**The Demon Drink**	Jancis Robinson £4.99
☐	7493 0016 7	**Vietnam – The 10,000 Day War**	Michael Maclear £3.99
☐	7493 0061 2	**Voyager**	Yeager/Rutan £3.99
☐	7493 0113 9	**Peggy Ashcroft**	Michael Billington £3.99
☐	7493 0177 5	**The Troubles**	Mick O'Connor £4.99
☐	7493 0004 3	**South Africa**	Graham Leach £3.99
☐	7493 0254 2	**Families and How to Survive Them**	Creese/Skynner £5.99
☐	7493 0060 4	**The Fashion Conspiracy**	Nicolas Coleridge £3.99
☐	7493 0179 1	**The Tao of Pooh**	Benjamin Hoff £2.99
☐	7493 0000 0	**Moonwalk**	Michael Jackson £2.99

All these books are available at your bookshop or newsagent, or can be ordered direct from the publisher. Just tick the titles you want and fill in the form below.

Mandarin Paperbacks, Cash Sales Department, PO Box 11, Falmouth, Cornwall TR10 9EN.

Please send cheque or postal order, no currency, for purchase price quoted and allow the following for postage and packing:

UK   80p for the first book, 20p for each additional book ordered to a maximum charge of £2.00.

BFPO   80p for the first book, 20p for each additional book.

Overseas   £1.50 for the first book, £1.00 for the second and 30p for each additional book
including Eire thereafter.

NAME (Block letters) ....

ADDRESS ....

....

....